Audi TT

Owners Workshop Manual

Peter T Gill

Models covered *(6369 - 320)*

Coupe & Roadster (convertible) 'Mk 1' with 1.8 litre (1781cc) 4-cylinder turbo engines and 2WD or 4WD (Quattro) transmissions

Does NOT cover models with 3.2 litre V6 engines, DSG transmission or 'Quattro Sport' models
Does NOT cover 'Mk 2' TT range introduced September/December 2006

ABCDE
FGHIJ
KLMN

A book in the **Haynes Owners Workshop Manual Series**

ISBN **978 1 78521 369 4**

British Library Cataloguing in Publication Data
A catalogue record for this book is available from the British Library.

Printed in India

Haynes Group Limited
Sparkford, Yeovil, Somerset BA22 7JJ, England

Haynes North America, Inc
2801 Townsgate Road, Suite 340, Thousand Oaks, CA 91361

The manufacturer's authorised representative in the EU for product safety is:
HaynesPro BV
Stationsstraat 79 F, 3811MH Amersfoort, The Netherlands
gpsr@haynes.co.uk

Disclaimer

There are risks associated with automotive repairs. The ability to make repairs depends on the individual's skill, experience and proper tools. Individuals should act with due care and acknowledge and assume the risk of performing automotive repairs.

The purpose of this manual is to provide comprehensive, useful and accessible automotive repair information, to help you get the best value from your vehicle. However, this manual is not a substitute for a professional certified technician or mechanic.

This repair manual is produced by a third party and is not associated with an individual vehicle manufacturer. If there is any doubt or discrepancy between this manual and the owner's manual or the factory service manual, please refer to the factory service manual or seek assistance from a professional certified technician or mechanic.

Even though we have prepared this manual with extreme care and every attempt is made to ensure that the information in this manual is correct, neither the publisher nor the author can accept responsibility for loss, damage or injury caused by any errors in, or omissions from, the information given.

Contents

LIVING WITH YOUR AUDI TT

Roadside repairs

Weekly checks

MAINTENANCE

Routine maintenance and servicing

Contents

REPAIRS AND OVERHAUL

The Audi TT models covered by this manual date from late 1998 to June 2006 and have the 1.8 litre turbo-charged petrol engine.

Models where produced with a 1.8 litre (1781 cc), 20-valve turbo petrol engine, with either a 180 bhp or 225 bhp power output. In 2003 a 3.2 litre (3183 cc) VR6 engine was added (NOT covered in this manual), which has a power output of 250 bhp. These engines use fuel injection, and are fitted with a wide range of emission control systems. The engines are of a well-proven design and, provided regular maintenance is carried out, are unlikely to give trouble.

Models are available as either a Coupe or Roadster "Convertible" bodystyle, with a 2-wheel drive or 4-wheel drive " Quattro" layout. The Audi TT is based on the Volkswagen group platform as used on the Golf Mk4, Audi A3, Skoda Octavia etc... models.

On all models a fully-independent front suspension using MacPherson struts is fitted, with the components attached to the subframe assembly. The rear suspension fitted to the 2-wheel drive models is semi-independent, with a torsion beam, trailing arms and anti-roll bar. The rear suspension on the 4-wheel drive "Quattro" models has a dual link trailing arm axle (DLTA) with Haldex viscous coupling and an anti-roll bar fitted to the axle subframe.

Audi TT Roadster

Audi TT Coupe

A five-speed manual transmission is fitted to the 180 bhp models as standard, with an option of a six-speed transmission. Models with the 225 bhp engine, are fitted with the six-speed transmission.

The 4-wheel drive "Quattro" model has a transfer box "bevel box" fitted to the rear of the transmission, which takes the drive via a propshaft to the Haldex viscous coupling fitted to the rear axle final drive unit.

A wide range of standard and optional equipment is available within the model range to suit most tastes, including an anti-lock braking system and air conditioning.

For the home mechanic, Audi TT models are straightforward vehicles to maintain, and most of the items requiring frequent attention are easily accessible.

Your Audi TT Manual

The aim of this manual is to help you get the best value from your vehicle. It can do so in several ways. It can help you decide what work must be done (even should you choose to get it done by a garage). It will also provide information on routine maintenance and servicing, and give a logical course of action and diagnosis when random faults occur. However, it is hoped that you will use the manual by tackling the work yourself. On simpler jobs it may even be quicker than booking the car into a garage and going there twice, to leave and collect it. Perhaps most important, a lot of money can be saved by avoiding the costs a garage must charge to cover its labour and overheads.

The manual has drawings and descriptions to show the function of the various components so that their layout can be understood. Tasks are described and photographed in a clear step-by-step sequence.

References to the 'left' and 'right' of the vehicle are in the sense of a person in the driver's seat facing forward.

Acknowledgements

Thanks are due to Draper Tools Limited, who provided some of the workshop tools, and to all those people at Sparkford who helped in the production of this manual.

This manual is not a direct reproduction of the vehicle manufacturer's data, and its publication should not be taken as implying any technical approval by the vehicle manufacturers or importers.

We take great pride in the accuracy of information given in this manual, but vehicle manufacturers make alterations and design changes during the production run of a particular vehicle of which they do not inform us. No liability can be accepted by the authors or publishers for loss, damage or injury caused by any errors in, or omissions from, the information given.

Working on your car can be dangerous. This page shows just some of the potential risks and hazards, with the aim of creating a safety-conscious attitude.

General hazards

Scalding

• Don't remove the radiator or expansion tank cap while the engine is hot.
• Engine oil, transmission fluid or power steering fluid may also be dangerously hot if the engine has recently been running.

Burning

• Beware of burns from the exhaust system and from any part of the engine. Brake discs and drums can also be extremely hot immediately after use.

Crushing

• When working under or near a raised vehicle, always supplement the jack with axle stands, or use drive-on ramps.
Never venture under a car which is only supported by a jack.
• Take care if loosening or tightening high-torque nuts when the vehicle is on stands. Initial loosening and final tightening should be done with the wheels on the ground.

Fire

• Fuel is highly flammable; fuel vapour is explosive.
• Don't let fuel spill onto a hot engine.
• Do not smoke or allow naked lights (including pilot lights) anywhere near a vehicle being worked on. Also beware of creating sparks (electrically or by use of tools).
• Fuel vapour is heavier than air, so don't work on the fuel system with the vehicle over an inspection pit.
• Another cause of fire is an electrical overload or short-circuit. Take care when repairing or modifying the vehicle wiring.
• Keep a fire extinguisher handy, of a type suitable for use on fuel and electrical fires.

Electric shock

• Ignition HT and Xenon headlight voltages can be dangerous, especially to people with heart problems or a pacemaker. Don't work on or near these systems with the engine running or the ignition switched on.

• Mains voltage is also dangerous. Make sure that any mains-operated equipment is correctly earthed. Mains power points should be protected by a residual current device (RCD) circuit breaker.

Fume or gas intoxication

• Exhaust fumes are poisonous; they can contain carbon monoxide, which is rapidly fatal if inhaled. Never run the engine in a confined space such as a garage with the doors shut.
• Fuel vapour is also poisonous, as are the vapours from some cleaning solvents and paint thinners.

Poisonous or irritant substances

• Avoid skin contact with battery acid and with any fuel, fluid or lubricant, especially antifreeze, brake hydraulic fluid and Diesel fuel. Don't syphon them by mouth. If such a substance is swallowed or gets into the eyes, seek medical advice.
• Prolonged contact with used engine oil can cause skin cancer. Wear gloves or use a barrier cream if necessary. Change out of oil-soaked clothes and do not keep oily rags in your pocket.
• Air conditioning refrigerant forms a poisonous gas if exposed to a naked flame (including a cigarette). It can also cause skin burns on contact.

Asbestos

• Asbestos dust can cause cancer if inhaled or swallowed. Asbestos may be found in gaskets and in brake and clutch linings. When dealing with such components it is safest to assume that they contain asbestos.

Special hazards

Hydrofluoric acid

• This extremely corrosive acid is formed when certain types of synthetic rubber, found in some O-rings, oil seals, fuel hoses etc, are exposed to temperatures above 4000C. The rubber changes into a charred or sticky substance containing the acid. *Once formed, the acid remains dangerous for years. If it gets onto the skin, it may be necessary to amputate the limb concerned.*
• When dealing with a vehicle which has suffered a fire, or with components salvaged from such a vehicle, wear protective gloves and discard them after use.

The battery

• Batteries contain sulphuric acid, which attacks clothing, eyes and skin. Take care when topping-up or carrying the battery.
• The hydrogen gas given off by the battery is highly explosive. Never cause a spark or allow a naked light nearby. Be careful when connecting and disconnecting battery chargers or jump leads.

Air bags

• Air bags can cause injury if they go off accidentally. Take care when removing the steering wheel and trim panels. Special storage instructions may apply.

Diesel injection equipment

• Diesel injection pumps supply fuel at very high pressure. Take care when working on the fuel injectors and fuel pipes.

Warning: Never expose the hands, face or any other part of the body to injector spray; the fuel can penetrate the skin with potentially fatal results.

Remember...

DO

• Do use eye protection when using power tools, and when working under the vehicle.

• Do wear gloves or use barrier cream to protect your hands when necessary.

• Do get someone to check periodically that all is well when working alone on the vehicle.

• Do keep loose clothing and long hair well out of the way of moving mechanical parts.

• Do remove rings, wristwatch etc, before working on the vehicle – especially the electrical system.

• Do ensure that any lifting or jacking equipment has a safe working load rating adequate for the job.

DON'T

• Don't attempt to lift a heavy component which may be beyond your capability – get assistance.

• Don't rush to finish a job, or take unverified short cuts.

• Don't use ill-fitting tools which may slip and cause injury.

• Don't leave tools or parts lying around where someone can trip over them. Mop up oil and fuel spills at once.

• Don't allow children or pets to play in or near a vehicle being worked on.

The following pages are intended to help in dealing with common roadside emergencies and breakdowns. You will find more detailed fault finding information at the back of the manual, and repair information in the main chapters.

If your car won't start and the starter motor doesn't turn

- ☐ Open the bonnet and make sure that the battery terminals are clean and tight.
- ☐ Switch on the headlights and try to start the engine. If the headlights go very dim when you're trying to start, the battery is probably flat. Get out of trouble by jump starting using a friend's car.

If your car won't start even though the starter motor turns as normal

- ☐ Is there fuel in the tank?
- ☐ Is there any moisture on electrical components under the bonnet? Switch off the ignition, then wipe off any obvious dampness with a dry cloth. Spray a water-repellent aerosol product (WD-40 or equivalent) on ignition and fuel system electrical connectors.

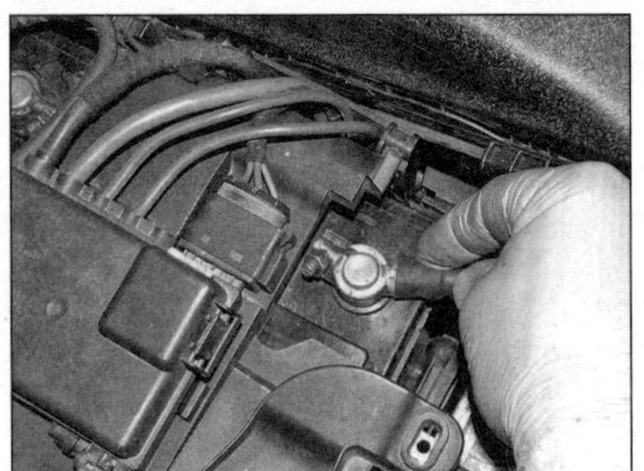

A Check the condition and security of the battery connections.

B Check the fuses and fusible links in the fusebox located on top of the battery.

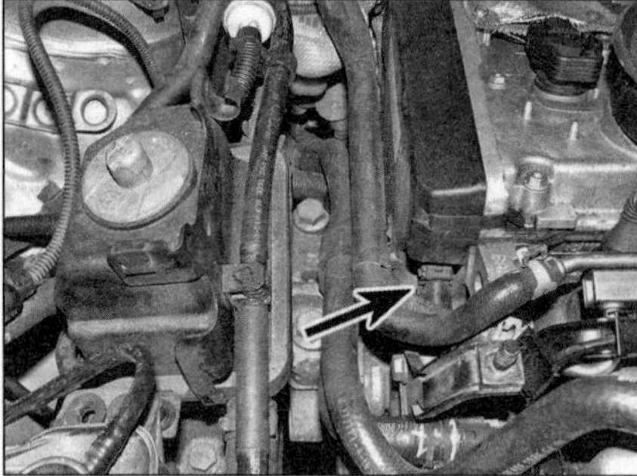

C Check the wiring to the camshaft sensor beneath the timing belt upper cover

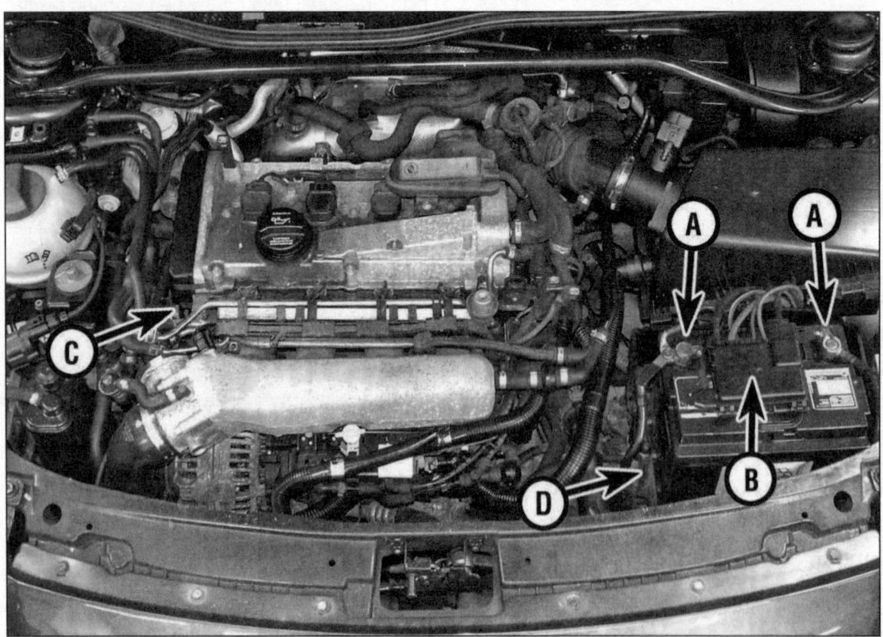

Check that electrical connections are secure (with the ignition switched off) and spray them with a water-dispersant spraylike WD-40 if you suspect a problem due to damp

D Check that the starter motor wiring is secure (viewed from under the n/s/f wheel arch – inner liner removed)

Jump starting

HAYNES HiNT

Jump starting will get you out of trouble, but you must correct whatever made the battery go flat in the first place. There are three possibilities:

***1** The battery has been drained by repeated attempts to start, or by leaving the lights on.*

***2** The charging system is not working properly (alternator drivebelt slack or broken, alternator wiring fault or alternator itself faulty).*

***3** The battery itself is at fault (electrolyte low, or battery worn out).*

When jump-starting a car, observe the following precautions:

Note: *Remove the key in case the central locking engages when the jump leads are connected*

- ✓ Before connecting the booster battery, make sure that the ignition is switched off.
- ✓ Ensure that all electrical equipment (lights, heater, wipers, etc) is switched off.
- ✓ Take note of any special precautions printed on the battery case.
- ✓ Make sure that the booster battery is the same voltage as the discharged one in the vehicle.
- ✓ If the battery is being jump-started from the battery in another vehicle, the two vehicles MUST NOT TOUCH each other.
- ✓ Make sure that the transmission is in neutral.

Budget jump leads can be a false economy, as they often do not pass enough current to start large capacity or diesel engines. They can also get hot.

1 Connect one end of the red jump lead to the positive (+) terminal of the flat battery

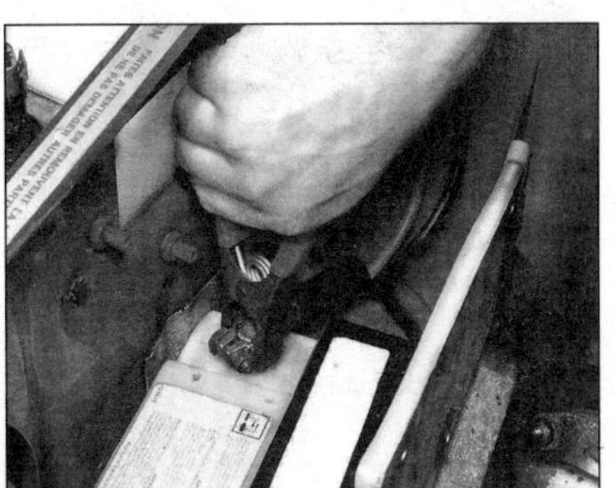

2 Connect the other end of the red lead to the positive (+) terminal of the booster battery.

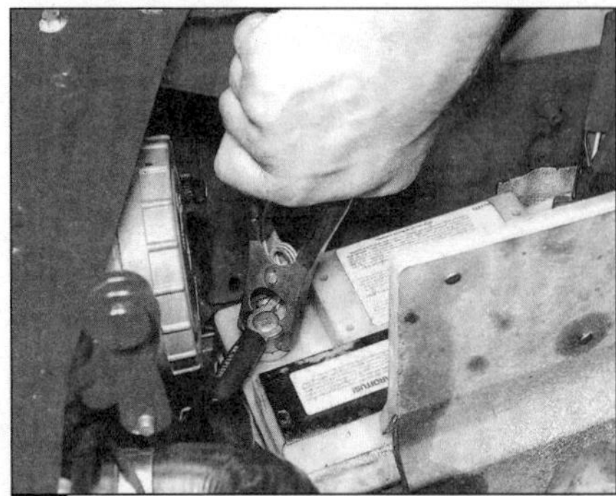

3 Connect one end of the black jump lead to the negative (-) terminal of the booster battery

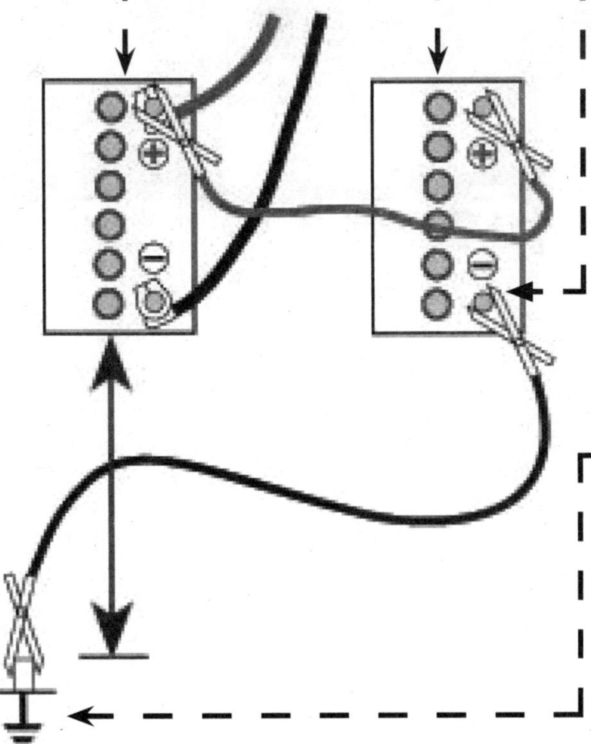

4 Connect the other end of the black jump lead to a suitable metal part of the engine on the vehicle to bestarted.

5 Make sure that the jump leads will not come into contact with the fan, drive-belts or other moving parts of the engine.

6 Start the engine using the booster battery and run it at idle speed. Switch on the lights, rear window demister and heater blower motor, then disconnect the jump leads in the reverse order of connection. Turn off the lights etc.

Identifying leaks

Puddles on the garage floor or drive, or obvious wetness under the bonnet or underneath the car, suggest a leak that needs investigating. It can sometimes be difficult to decide where the leak is coming from, especially if an engine undershield is fitted. Leaking oil or fluid can also be blown rearwards by the passage of air under the car, giving a false impression of where the problem lies.

Warning: Most automotive oils and fluids are poisonous. Wash them off skin, and change out of contaminated clothing, without delay.

HAYNES HiNT *The smell of a fluid leaking from the car may provide a clue to what's leaking. Some fluids are distinctively coloured. It may help to clean the car carefully and to park it over some clean paper overnight as an aid to locating the source of the leak. Remember that some leaks may only occur while the engine is running.*

Sump oil

Engine oil may leak from the drain plug...

Oil from filter

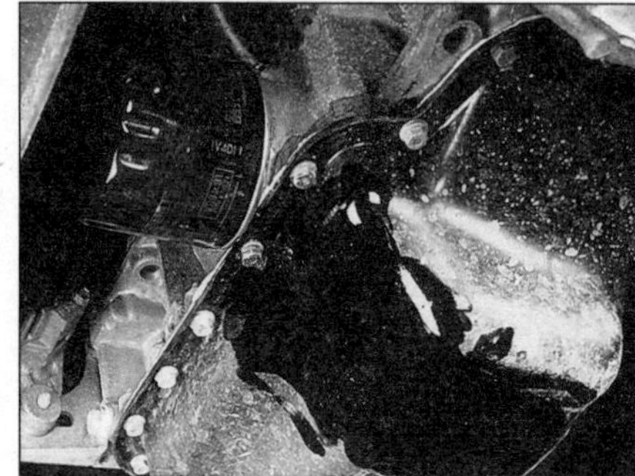

...or from the base of the oil filter.

Gearbox oil

Gearbox oil can leak from the seals at the inboard ends of the driveshafts.

Antifreeze

Leaking antifreeze often leaves a crystalline deposit like this.

Brake fluid

A leak occurring at a wheel is almost certainly brake fluid.

Power steering fluid

Power steering fluid may leak from the pipe connectors on the steering rack.

Wheel changing

Some of the details shown here will vary according to model

Preparation

- ☐ When a puncture occurs, stop as soon as it is safe to do so.
- ☐ Park on firm level ground, if possible, and well out of the way of other traffic.
- ☐ If you have one, use a warning triangle to alert other drivers of your presence.
- ☐ Apply the handbrake and engage first or reverse gear, or P on automatic transmission models.
- ☐ Use hazard warning lights if necessary.
- ☐ If the ground is soft, use a flat piece of wood to spread the load under the jack.

Warning: Do not change a wheel in a situation where you risk being hit by another vehicle. On busy roads, try to stop in a lay-by or a gateway. Be wary of passing traffic while changing the wheel – it is easy to become distracted by the job in hand.

1 The spare wheel and tools are stored in the luggage compartment under the floor carpet panel.

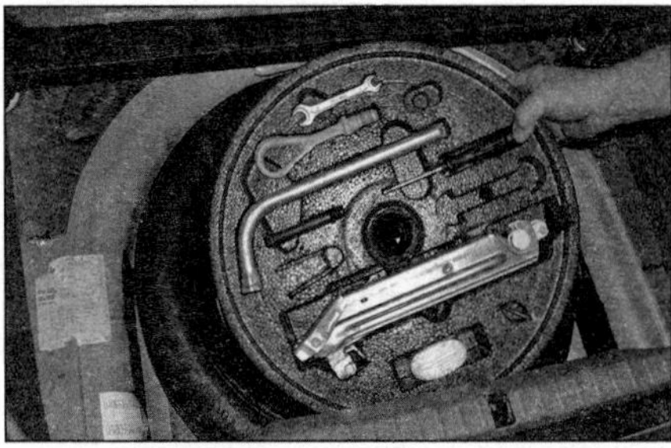

2 Unscrew the retaining bolt, remove the plastic cover and lift out the jack and wheel changing tools from the centre of the spare wheel.

3 Remove the spare wheel from the rear luggage compartment.

4 For safety, chock the diagonally opposite wheel – a couple of large stones will do for this.

5 Use the wire hook from the tool kit to remove the small central trim from over the wheel bolts.

6 Slacken each wheel bolt by half a turn.

7 Use the special adapter when slackening the locking wheel bolt.

8 Locate the jack below the reinforced point on the sill (don't jack the vehicle at any other point of the sill) and onfirm ground, then turn the jack handle clockwise until the wheel is raised clear of the ground.

9 Unscrew the wheel bolts (using the spanner provided) and remove the wheel. Fit the spare wheel, and screw in the bolts. Lightly tighten the bolts with the wheelbrace then lower the vehicle to the ground.

10 Securely tighten the wheel bolts in the sequence shown, then stow the punctured wheel back in the luggage compartment. Note that the wheel bolts should be tightened to the specified torque at the earliest possible opportunity.

Finally . . .

- ☐ Remove the wheel chocks.
- ☐ Stow the jack and tools in the luggage compartment.
- ☐ Check the tyre pressure on the wheel just fitted. If it is low, or if you don't have a pressure gauge with you, drive slowly to the next garage and inflate the tyre to the correct pressure.
- ☐ Have the damaged tyre or wheel repaired as soon as possible.

Towing

When all else fails, you may find yourself having to get a tow home – or of course you may be helping somebody else. Long-distance recovery should only be done by a garage or breakdown service. For shorter distances, DIY towing using another car is easy enough, but observe the following points:

☐ Use a proper tow-rope – they are not expensive. The vehicle being towed must display an ON TOW sign in its rear window.
☐ Always turn the ignition key to the 'on' position when the vehicle is being towed, so that the steering lock is released, and that the direction indicator and brake lights will work.
☐ On models with automatic transmission, do not exceed 30 mph (50 kph) and do not tow for more than 30 miles (50 km). If in doubt, do not tow, or transmission damage may result.
☐ Before being towed, release the handbrake and select neutral on the transmission.
☐ Only attach the tow-rope to the towing eyes provided.
☐ Note that greater-than-usual pedal pressure will be required to operate the brakes, since the vacuum servo unit is only operational with the engine running.
☐ Because the power steering will not be operational, greater-than-usual steering effort will be required.
☐ The driver of the car being towed must keep the tow-rope taut to avoid snatching.
☐ Make sure that both drivers know the route before setting off.
☐ Only drive at moderate speeds and keep the distance towed to a minimum. Drive smoothly and allow plenty of time for slowing down at junctions.

The towing eye is supplied as part of the tool kit stored in the luggage compartment. The front towing eye position is located behind the right-hand vent panel at the lower part of the front bumper.

The rear towing eye is located beneath the right-hand side of the rear bumper.

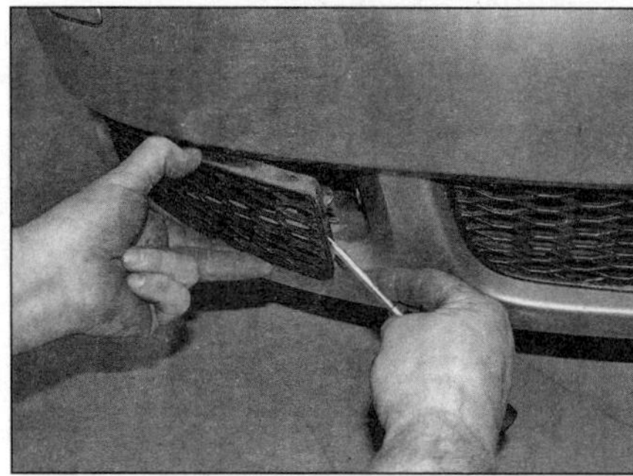

Unclip the vent panel from the lower part of the front bumper

Screw the towing eye into position, and tighten with wheel brace handle

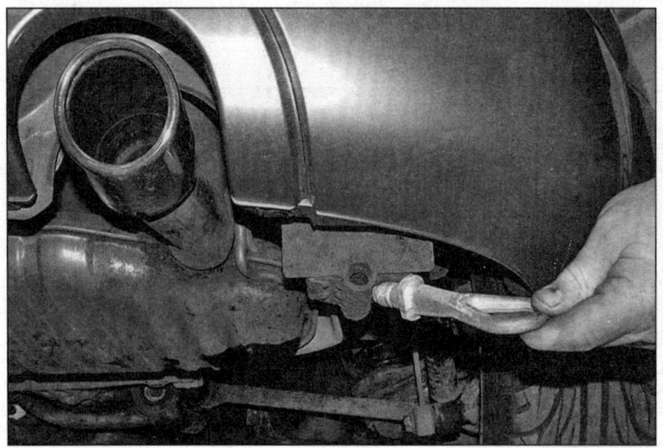

Screw the eye into position...

...and tighten using the wheelbrace handle.

Introduction

There are some very simple checks which need only take a few minutes to carry out, but which could save you a lot of inconvenience and expense.

These checks require no great skill or special tools, and the small amount of time they take to perform could prove to be very well spent, for example:

☐ Keeping an eye on tyre condition and pressures, will not only help to stop them wearing out prematurely, but could also save your life.

☐ Many breakdowns are caused by electrical problems. Battery-related faults are particularly common, and a quick check on a regular basis will often prevent the majority of these.

☐ If your car develops a brake fluid leak, the first time you might know about it is when your brakes don't work properly. Checking the level regularly will give advance warning of this kind of problem.

☐ If your car develops a brake fluid leak, the first time you might know about it is when your brakes don't work properly. Checking the level regularly will give advance warning of this kind of problem.

☐ If the oil or coolant levels run low, the cost of repairing any engine damage will be far greater than fixing the leak, for example.

Underbonnet check points

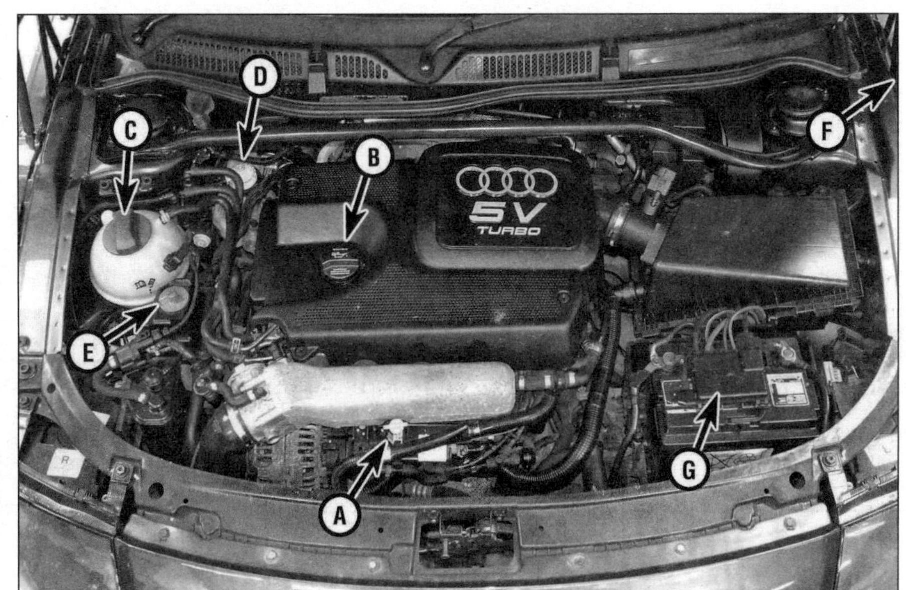

◀ **1.8 litre 150-180bhp engine**

A *Engine oil level dipstick*
B *Engine oil filler cap*
C *Coolant expansion tank*
D *Brake (and clutch) fluid reservoir*
E *Power steering fluid reservoir*
F *Screen washer fluid reservoir*
G *Battery*

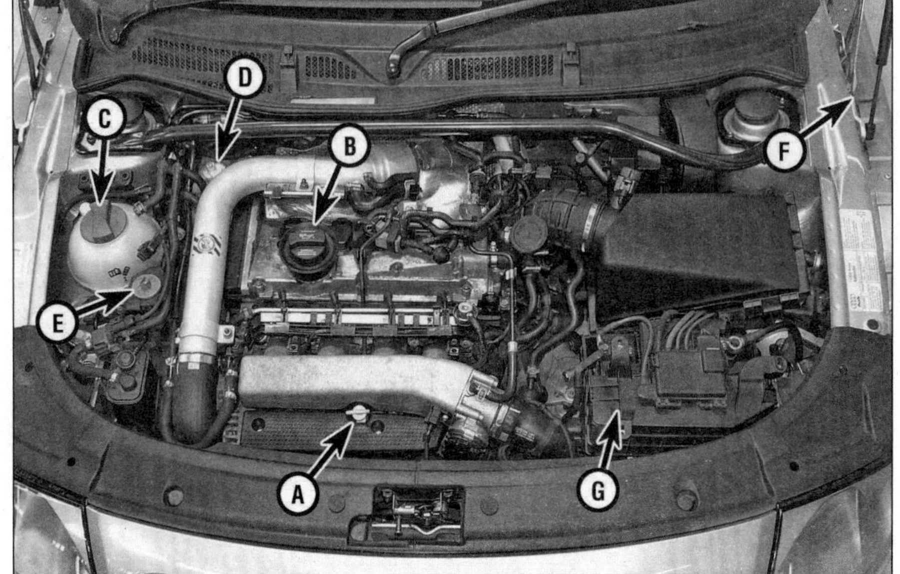

◀ **1.8 litre 225bhp engine**

A *Engine oil level dipstick*
B *Engine oil filler cap*
C *Coolant expansion tank*
D *Brake (and clutch) fluid reservoir*
E *Power steering fluid reservoir*
F *Screen washer fluid reservoir*
G *Battery*

Engine oil level

Before you start

✔ Make sure that your car is on level ground.
✔ Check the oil level before the car is driven, or at least 5 minutes after the engine has been switched off.

If the oil is checked immediately after driving the car, some of the oil will remain in the upper engine components, resulting in an inaccurate reading on the dipstick.

The correct oil

Modern engines place great demands on their oil. It is very important that the correct oil for your car is used (see *Lubricants and fluids*).

Car care

● If you have to add oil frequently, you should check whether you have any oil leaks. Place some clean paper under the car overnight, and check for stains in the morning. If there are no leaks, the engine may be burning oil.

● Always maintain the level between the upper and lower dipstick marks. If the level is too low severe engine damage may occur. Oil seal failure may result if the engine is overfilled by adding too much oil.

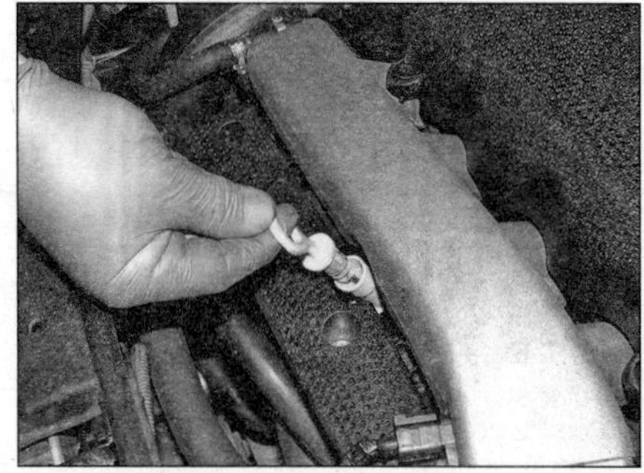

1 The dipstick is often brightly coloured for easy identification (see Underbonnet check points for exact location).Withdraw the dipstick, then use a clean rag or paper towel to wipe the oil from it. Insert the clean dipstick into the tube asfar as it will go, then withdraw it again.

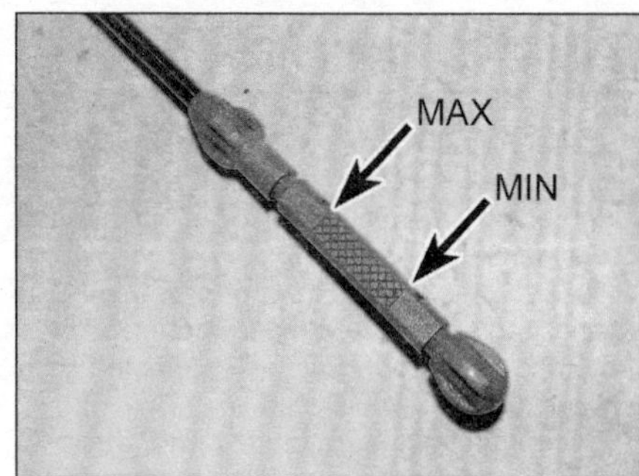

2 Note the level on the end of the dipstick, which should be between the upper (MAX) and lower (MIN) mark.

3 Oil is added through the filler cap aperture. Unscrew the cap.

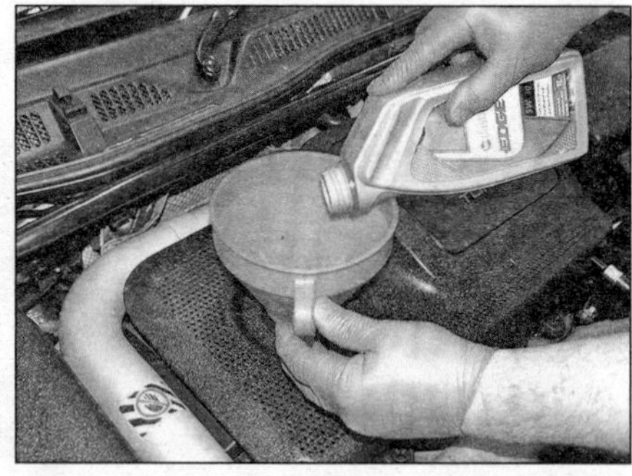

4 Place some cloth rags around the filler cap aperture, then top-up the level. A funnel may help to reduce spillage.Add the oil slowly, checking the level on the dipstick frequently. Avoid overfilling (see *Car care*)

Coolant level

Warning: DO NOT attempt to remove the expansion tank pressure cap when the engine is hot, as there is a very great risk of scalding. Do not leave open containers of coolant about, as it is poisonous.

Car care

● With a sealed-type cooling system, adding coolant should not be necessary on a regular basis. If frequent topping-up is required, it is likely there is a leak. Check the radiator, all hoses and joint faces for signs of staining or wetness, and rectify as necessary.

● It is important that antifreeze is used in the cooling system all year round, not just during the winter months. Don't top-up with water alone, as the antifreeze will become too diluted.

1 The coolant level varies with the temperature of the engine. When the engine is cold, the coolant level should bebetween the MIN and MAX marks.

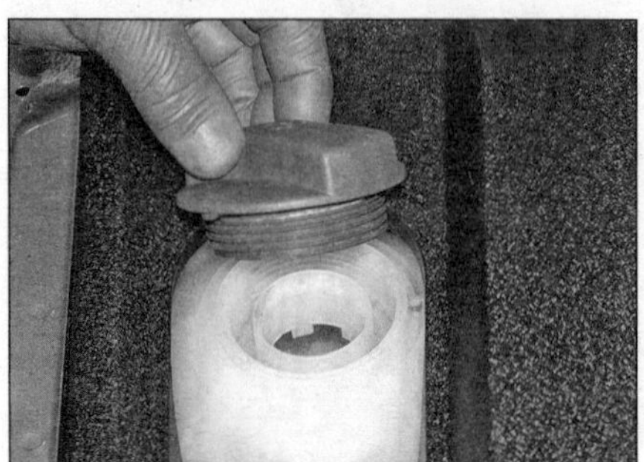

2 If topping-up is necessary, wait until the engine is cold. Slowly unscrew the cap to release any pressure present inthe cooling system, and remove the cap.

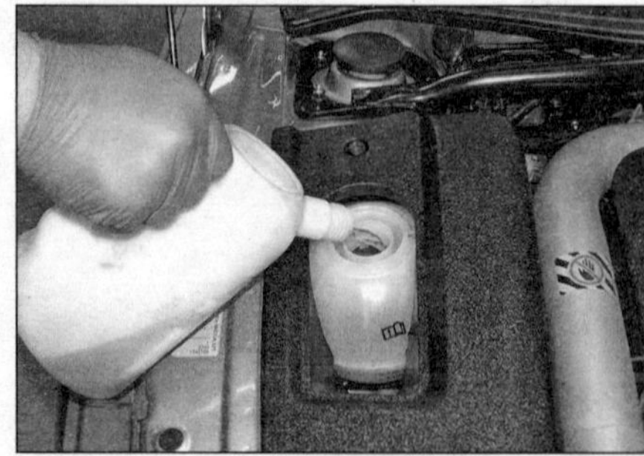

3 Add a mixture of water and the specified antifreeze (see Lubricants and fluids) to the expansion tank until the coolant level is halfway between the level marks. Refit the cap and tighten it securely.

Brake (and clutch*) fluid level

* On manual transmission models, the fluid reservoir also supplies the clutch master cylinder with fluid.

Warning: Brake fluid can harm your eyes and damage painted surfaces, so use extreme caution when handling and pouring it.

Warning: Do not use fluid that has been standing open for some time, as it absorbs moisture from the air, which can cause a dangerous loss of braking effectiveness.

Before you start

✔ Make sure that your car is on level ground.

✔ Cleanliness is of great importance when dealing with the braking system, so take care to clean around the reservoir cap before topping-up. Use only clean brake fluid.

Safety first!

● If the reservoir requires repeated topping-up this is an indication of a fluid leak somewhere in the system, which should be investigated immediately.

● If a leak is suspected, the car should not be driven until the braking system has been checked. Never take any risks where brakes are concerned.

1 The MIN and MAX marks are indicated on the reservoir. The fluid level must be kept between the marks at all times. Note that the level will drop naturally as the brake pad linings wear, but must never be allowed to fall below the MIN mark. If topping-up is necessary, first wipe clean the area around the filler cap to prevent dirt entering the hydraulic system.

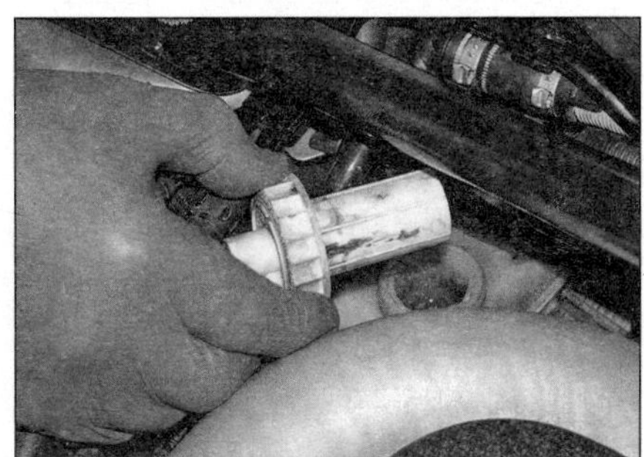

2 Unscrew and remove the reservoir cap.

3 Carefully add fluid, taking care not to spill it onto the surrounding components. Use only the specified fluid (see *Lubricants and fluids*); mixing different types can cause damage to the system. Use a funnel and length of tube to prevent any spillage. On completion, securely refit the cap and wipe away any spilt fluid.

Electrical systems

✔ Check all external lights and the horn. Refer to the appropriate Sections of Chapter 12 for details if any of the circuits are found to be inoperative, and renew the fuse if necessary.

✔ Visually check all accessible wiring connectors, harnesses and retaining clips for security, and for signs of chafing or damage.

If you need to check your brake lights and indicators unaided, back up to a wall or garage door and operate the lights. The reflected light should show if they are working properly.

1 If a single indicator light, brake light or headlight has failed, it is likely that a bulb has blown and will need to be renewed. Refer to Chapter 12 for details. If both brake lights have failed, it is possible that the brake light switch operated by the brake pedal has failed. Refer to Chapter 9 for details.

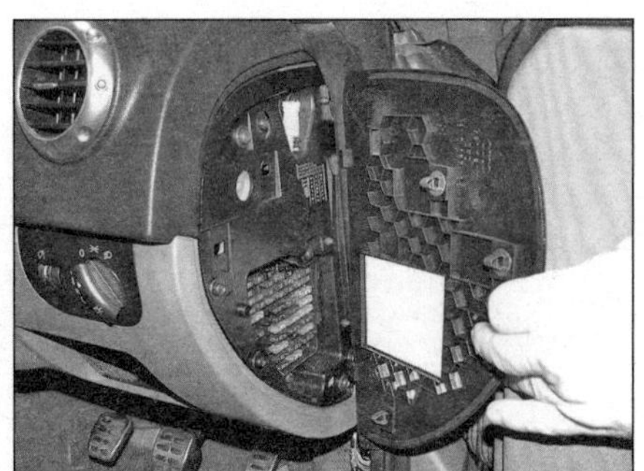

2 If more than one indicator light or headlight has failed, it is likely that either a fuse has blown or that there is a fault in the circuit (see Electrical fault finding in Chapter 12). The main fuses are in the fusebox behind a cover on the right-hand end of the facia panel. Use a small screwdriver to carefully prise off the cover. The circuits protected by the fuses are shown on the inside of the cover. Additional fuses and fusible links are in the fusebox located on the top of the battery in the engine compartment.

3 To renew a blown fuse, pull it from its location in the fusebox, using the plastic pliers provided. Fit a new fuse of the same rating, available from car accessory shops. It is important that you find the reason that the fuse blew (see Electrical fault finding in Chapter 12).

Battery

Caution: Before carrying out any work on the vehicle battery, read the precautions given in,2 ! at the start of this manual.

✔ Make sure that the battery tray is in good condition, and that the clamp is tight. Corrosion on the tray, retaining clamp and the battery itself can be removed with a solution of water and baking soda. Thoroughly rinse all cleaned areas with water. Any metal parts damaged by corrosion should be covered with a zinc-based primer, then painted.

✔ Periodically (approximately every three months), check the charge condition of the battery as described in Chapter 5A. A 'magic eye' charge indicator is fitted to the standard battery – if the indicator is green in colour, the battery is fully charged, however, if it is colourless, it should be recharged. If it is yellow in colour, the battery should be renewed.

✔ If the battery is flat, and you need to jump start your vehicle, see *Jump starting*.

1 The battery is located in the front left – hand corner of the engine compartment. Undo the fasteners and remove the plastic trim cover from the top of the battery.

2 Check the security and condition of the battery terminals, including the fuses and connections inside the fusebox on top of the battery. The exterior of the battery should be inspected periodically for damage such as a cracked case or cover.

3 If corrosion (white, fluffy deposits) is evident, remove the cables from the battery terminals (refer to *Disconnecting the battery* in the Reference chapter at the end of this manual), clean them with a small wire brush,then refit them. Automotive stores sell a tool for cleaning the battery post …

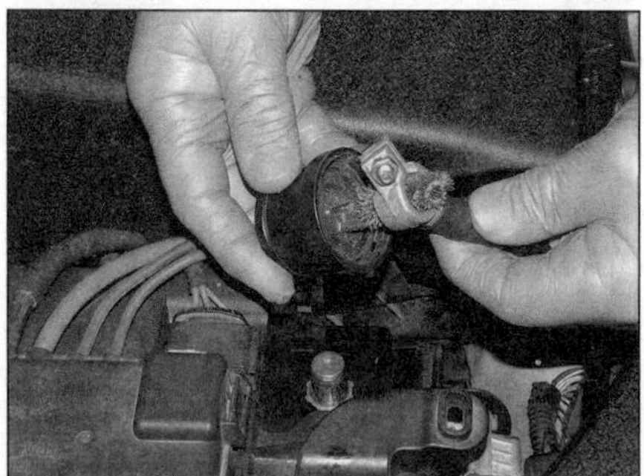

4 … as well as the battery cable clamps. Note: *Manufacturer specifically prohibits the use of grease on the battery terminals.*

Washer fluid level

● Screenwash additives not only keep the windscreen clean during bad weather, they also prevent the washer system freezing in cold weather – which is when you are likely to need it most. Don't top up using plain water, as the screenwash will become diluted and will freeze in cold weather.

Warning: On no account use coolant antifreeze in the washer system – this could discolour or damage paintwork.

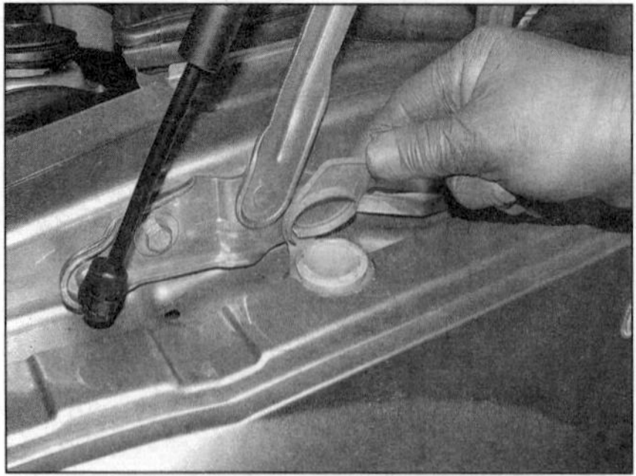

1 The screenwash fluid reservoir is located on the left-hand side of the engine compartment, in the top of the near side front wing. Pull up the filler cap to release it from the reservoir.

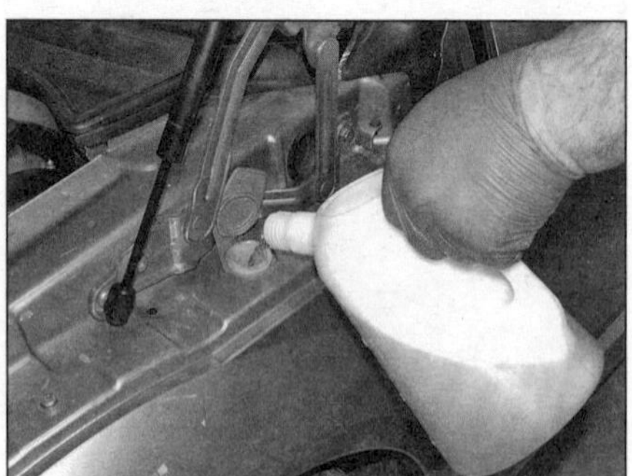

2 When topping-up the reservoir, a screen-wash additive should be added in the quantities recommended on thebottle.

Tyre condition and pressure

It is very important that tyres are in good condition, and at the correct pressure – having a tyre failure at any speed is highly dangerous.

Tyre wear is influenced by driving style – harsh braking and acceleration, or fast cornering, will all produce more rapid tyre wear. As a general rule, the front tyres wear out faster than the rears. Interchanging the tyres from front to rear ("rotating" the tyres) may result in more even wear. However, if this is completely effective, you may have the expense of replacing all four tyres at once!

Remove any nails or stones embedded in the tread before they penetrate the tyre to cause deflation. If removal of a nail does reveal that the tyre has been punctured, refit the nail so that its point of penetration is marked. Then immediately change the wheel, and have the tyre repaired by a tyre dealer.

Regularly check the tyres for damage in the form of cuts or bulges, especially in the sidewalls. Periodically remove the wheels, and clean any dirt or mud from the inside and outside surfaces. Examine the wheel rims for signs of rusting, corrosion or other damage. Light alloy wheels are easily damaged by "kerbing" whilst parking; steel wheels may also become dented or buckled. A new wheel is very often the only way to overcome severe damage.

New tyres should be balanced when they are fitted, but it may become necessary to re-balance them as they wear, or if the balance weights fitted to the wheel rim should fall off. Unbalanced tyres will wear more quickly, as will the steering and suspension components. Wheel imbalance is normally signified by vibration, particularly at a certain speed (typically around 50 mph). If this vibration is felt only through the steering, then it is likely that just the front wheels need balancing. If, however, the vibration is felt through the whole car, the rear wheels could be out of balance. Wheel balancing should be carried out by a tyre dealer or garage.

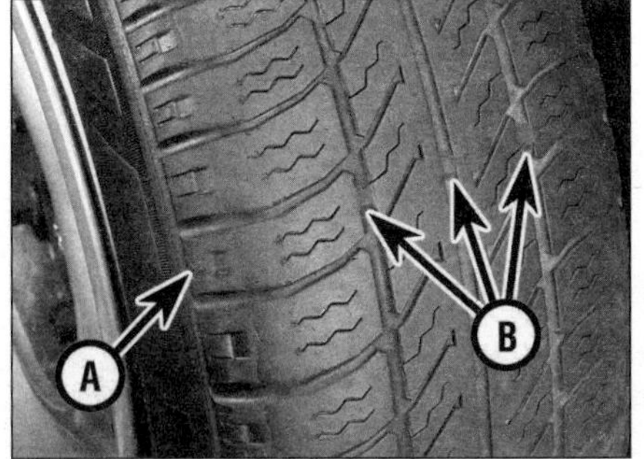

1 ***Tread Depth - visual check***
The original tyres have tread wear safety bands (B), which will appear when the tread depth reaches approximately 1.6 mm. The band positions are indicated by a triangular mark on the tyre sidewall (A).

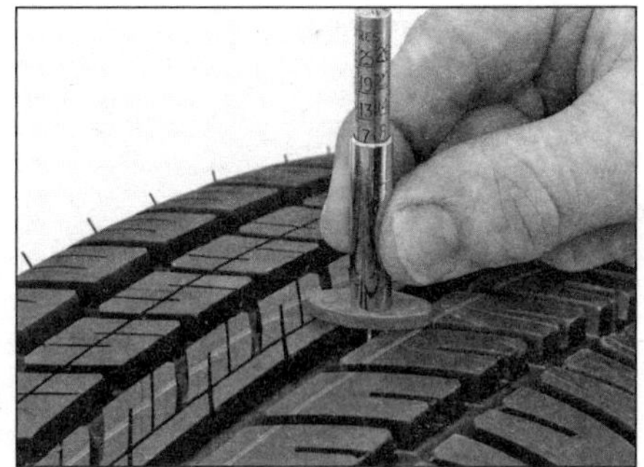

2 ***Tread Depth - manual check***
Alternatively, tread wear can be monitored with a simple, inexpensive device known as a tread depth indicator gauge.

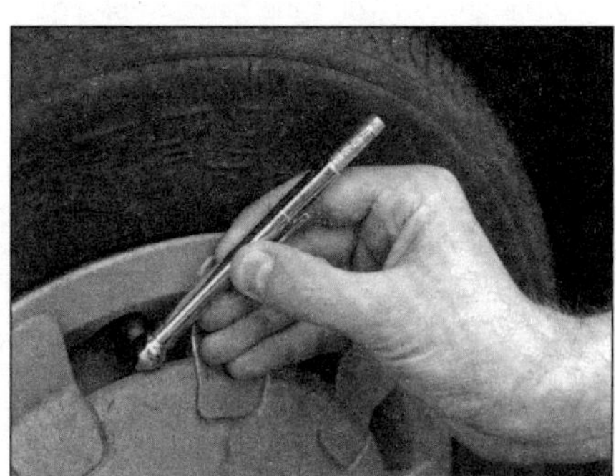

3 ***Tyre Pressure Check***
Check the tyre pressures regularly with the tyres cold. Do not adjust the tyre pressures immediately after the vehicle has been used, or an inaccurate setting will result.

Tyre tread wear patterns

Shoulder Wear

Underinflation (wear on both sides)
Under-inflation will cause overheating of the tyre, because the tyre will flex too much, and the tread will not sit correctly on the road surface. This will cause a loss of grip and excessive wear, not to mention the danger of sudden tyre failure due to heat build-up.
Check and adjust pressures
Incorrect wheel camber (wear on one side)
Repair or renew suspension parts
Hard cornering
Reduce speed!

Centre Wear

Overinflation
Over-inflation will cause rapid wear of the centre part of the tyre tread, coupled with reduced grip, harsher ride, and the danger of shock damage occurring in the tyre casing.
Check and adjust pressures

If you sometimes have to inflate your car's tyres to the higher pressures specified for maximum load or sustained high speed, don't forget to reduce the pressures to normal afterwards.

Uneven Wear

Front tyres may wear unevenly as a result of wheel misalignment. Most tyre dealers and garages can check and adjust the wheel alignment (or "tracking") for a modest charge.
Incorrect camber or castor
Repair or renew suspension parts
Malfunctioning suspension
Repair or renew suspension parts
Unbalanced wheel
Balance tyres
Incorrect toe setting
Adjust front wheel alignment
Note: *The feathered edge of the tread which typifies toe wear is best checked by feel.*

Wiper blades

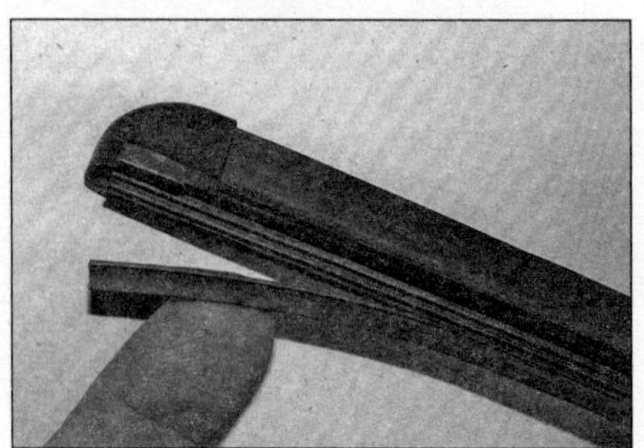

1 Check the condition of the wiper blades; if they are cracked or show any signs of deterioration, or if the glasssswept area is smeared, renew them. For maximum clarity of vision, wiper blades should be renewed annually, as a matter ofcourse.

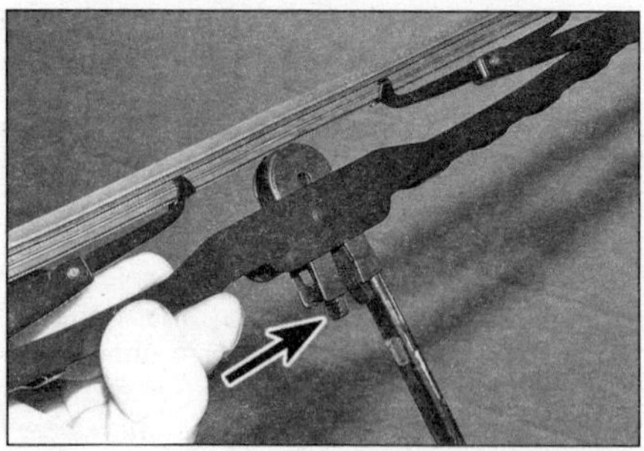

2 To remove a windscreen wiper blade, pull the arm fully away from the screen until it locks. Swivel the blade through 90°, press the locking tab (arrowed).

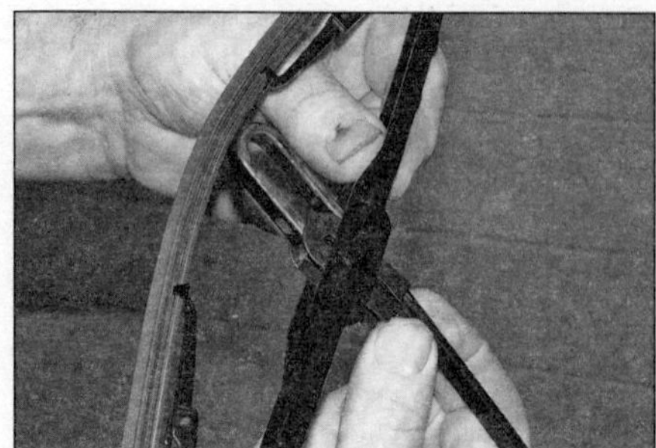

3 ... slide the wiper blade downwards and out of the hooked end of the wiper arm.

Lubricants and fluids

Note: *Using lubricants and fluids which do not meet the Audi standard may invalidate the warranty*

Engine (petrol)	
Standard (distance/time) service interval	Multigrade engine oil, viscosity SAE 5W/40 to 20W/50 VW 504 00 or better
LongLife (variable) service interval	VW LongLife engine oil VW 504 00 or better*
Cooling system	VW/Audi additive G12 plus (antifreeze and corrosion protection) – comforming to TL VW 774 F
Manual transmission	VWG50 gear oil, viscosity SAE 75W/90 (synthetic)
Automatic transmission:	
Main transmission (01M)	VW ATF
Final drive (01M)	VWG50 gear oil, viscosity SAE 75W/90 (synthetic)
Main transmission and final drive (09A)	VW ATF
Braking system	Hydraulic fluid to SAE J1703F or DOT 4
Power steering reservoir	VW/Audi hydraulic oil G 002 000

** A maximum of 0.5 litres of standard engine oil may be used for topping-up when LongLife oil is unobtainable*

Tyre pressures

Note: *The recommended tyre pressures for each vehicle are given on a sticker attached to the rear of the fuel filler flap. The pressures given are for the original equipment tyres – the recommended pressures may vary if any other make or type of tyre is fitted; check with the tyre manufacturer or supplier for latest recommendations.*

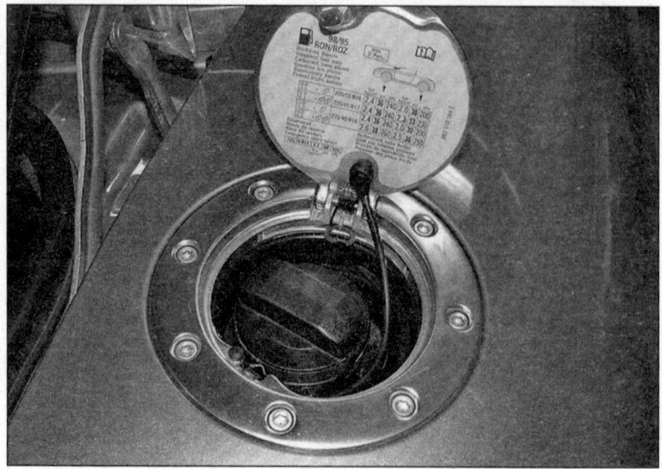

Chapter 1
Routine maintenance and servicing

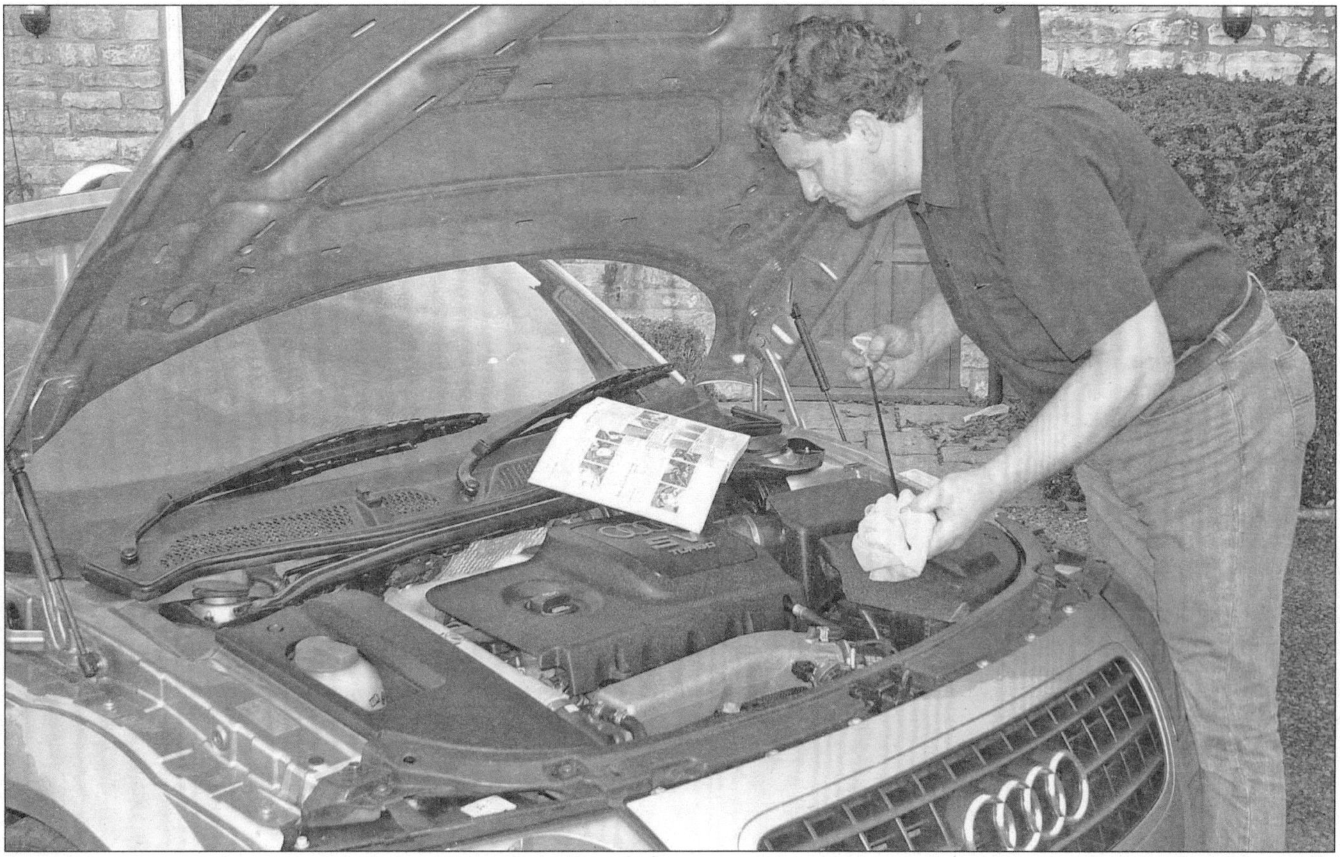

Contents

Degrees of difficulty

Easy, suitable for novice with little experience	**Fairly easy,** suitable for beginner with some experience 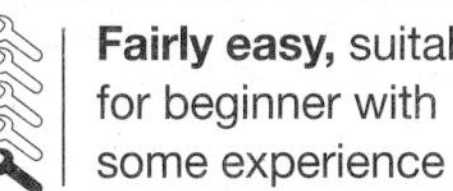	**Fairly difficult,** suitable for competent DIY mechanic	**Difficult,** suitable for experienced DIY mechanic 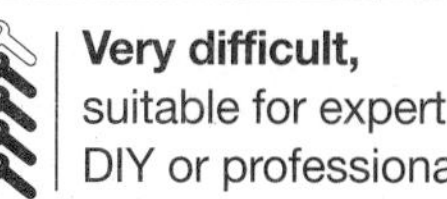	**Very difficult,** suitable for expert DIY or professional 

Lubricants and fluids

Refer to Lubricants and Fluids

Capacities (approximate)

Engine oil – including filter	4.5 litres
Cooling system	5.0 litres
Power assisted steering (PAS)	0.7 to 0.9 litres

Transmission

Manual transmission:	
Type 02M and 02Y:	
Front wheel drive (FWD)	2.3 litres
Four wheel drive (4WD)	2.6 litres
Type 02J (FWD)	2.0 litres
Automatic transmission (Type 09G):	
Main transmission unit incl final drive	5.9 litres

Fuel tank (approximate)

All models	55 litres

Washer reservoirs

Models with headlight washers	5.5 litres
Models without headlight washers	3.0 litres

Cooling system

Antifreeze mixture:	
40% antifreeze	Protection down to -25°C
50% antifreeze	Protection down to -35°C

Note: *Refer to antifreeze manufacturer for latest recommendations.*

Ignition system

Spark plugs:	Type	Electrode gap
1.8 litre engine	Bosch FR-7-KPP-33+	0.8 mm
NGK PFR6Q	0.8 mm	
VAG 101000063AA	0.8 mm	
Champion RC9YC	0.8 mm	

Brakes

Brake pad minimum thickness:	
Front and rear	2.0 mm (without backing plate)
Front and rear	7.0 mm (including backing plate)

Torque wrench settings

	Nm	lbf ft
Automatic transmission:		
Level inspection tube plug	27	20
Drain plug	39	30
Filler plug	39	30
Manual gearbox filler/level plug:		
Haxagon socket	30	22
Multi-point socket	45	33
Roadwheel bolts	120	89
Spark plugs	30	22
Ignition coils	10	7
Sump drain plug	30	22

1 The maintenance intervals in this manual are provided with the assumption that you, not the dealer, will be carrying out the work. These are the minimum intervals recommended by us for vehicles driven daily. If you wish to keep your vehicle in peak condition at all times, you may wish to perform some of these procedures more often. We encourage frequent maintenance, since it enhances the efficiency, performance and resale value of your vehicle.

2 When the vehicle is new, it should be serviced by a dealer service department, in order to preserve the factory warranty.

3 All Audi models are equipped with a service interval display indicator in the instrument panel. Every time the engine is started the panel will illuminate for approximately 20 seconds with service information. With the standard non-variable display, the service intervals are in accordance with specific distances and time periods. With the LongLife display, the service interval is variable according to the number of starts, length of journeys, vehicle speeds, brake pad wear, bonnet opening frequency, fuel consumption, oil level and oil temperature, however the vehicle must be serviced at least every two years. At a distance of 2000 miles (3000 km) before the next service is due, 'Service in 2000 miles' (or '3000 km') will appear at the bottom of the speedometer, and this figure will reduce in steps of 100 units as the vehicle is used. Once the service interval has been reached, the display will flash 'Service' or 'Service Now'. Note that if the variable (LongLife) service interval is being used, the engine must only be filled with the recommended long-life engine oil (see Recommended lubricants and fluids).

4 After completing a service, Audi technicians use a special instrument to reset the service display to the next service interval, and a print-out is put in the vehicle service record. The display can be reset by the owner as described in Section 10, but note that for models using the 'LongLife' interval, the procedure will automatically reset the display to the 10 000 miles/15 000 km 'distance' interval. To have the display reset to the 'variable' (LongLife) interval, it is necessary to take the vehicle to an Audi dealer who will use a special instrument to encode the on-board computer.

Models using distance and time intervals

Every 250 miles (400 km) or weekly

- ☐ Refer to *Weekly checks*

Every 5000 miles (7500 km) or 6 months

- ☐ Renew the engine oil and filter (Section 3)

Note: *Frequent oil and filter changes are good for the engine. We recommend changing the oil at the mileage specified here, or at least twice a year if the mileage covered is a less.*

Every 10 000 miles (15 000 km) or 12 months, whichever comes first – 'Oil' on display

In addition to the items listed above, carry out the following:

- ☐ Check the front and rear brake pad thickness (Section 4)
- ☐ Reset the service interval display (Section 5)

Every 20 000 miles (30 000 km) or 2 years, whichever comes first – '01' on display

In addition to the items listed above, carry out the following:

- ☐ Check the condition of the exhaust system and its mountings (Section 6)
- ☐ Check all underbonnet components and hoses for fluid and oil leaks (Section 7)
- ☐ Check the condition of the auxiliary drivebelt (Section 8)
- ☐ Check the coolant antifreeze concentration (Section 9)
- ☐ Check the brake hydraulic circuit for leaks and damage (Section 10)
- ☐ Check the headlight beam adjustment (Section 11)
- ☐ Renew the pollen filter element (Section 12)
- ☐ Check the manual transmission oil level (Section 13)
- ☐ Check the underbody protection for damage (Section 14)
- ☐ Check the condition of the driveshaft gaiters (Section 15)
- ☐ Check the steering and suspension components for condition and security (Section 16)
- ☐ Check the battery condition, security and electrolyte level (Section 17)
- ☐ Lubricate all hinges and locks (Section 18)
- ☐ Check the condition of the airbag unit(s) (Section 19)
- ☐ Check the operation of the windscreen/tailgate/ headlight washer system(s) (as applicable) (Section 20)
- ☐ Check the engine management self-diagnosis memory for faults (Section 21)
- ☐ Carry out a road test and check exhaust emissions (Section 22)

Every 40 000 miles (60 000 km) or 4 years, whichever comes first

- ☐ Renew the air filter element (Section 23)
- ☐ Renew the spark plugs (Section 24)
- ☐ Check the condition of the auxiliary drivebelt (Section 25)
- ☐ Check the power steering hydraulic fluid level (Section 26)
- ☐ Check the automatic transmission fluid level (Section 27)
- ☐ Check the automatic transmission final drive oil level (Section 27)

Every 60 000 miles (90 000 km) or 4 years, whichever comes first

- ☐ Renew the timing belt (Section 28)

Note: *Audi specify timing belt inspection after the first 60 000 miles (90 000 km) and then every 20 000 mile (30 000 km) until the renewal interval of 120 000 miles (180 000 km), however, if the vehicle is used mainly for short journeys, we recommend that this shorter renewal interval is adhered to. The belt renewal interval is very much up to the individual owner but, bearing in mind that severe engine damage will result if the belt breaks in use, we recommend the shorter interval.*

Every 2 years

- ☐ Renew the brake (and clutch) fluid (Section 29)
- ☐ Renew the coolant (Section 30)*

* **Note:** *This work is not included in the Audi schedule and should not be required if the recommended G12 LongLife coolant antifreeze/inhibitor is used.*

Models using 'LongLife' variable intervals

38 The LongLife variable service intervals are only applicable to models with a PR number of QG1 (shown in the vehicle Service Schedule booklet or on the Next Service sticker located on the driver's door pillar). The occurrence of the service on the display unit will depend on how the vehicle is being used (number of starts, length of journeys, vehicle speeds, brake pad wear, bonnet opening frequency, fuel consumption, oil level and oil temperature). For example, if a vehicle is being used under extreme driving conditions, the 'oil' service may occur at 10 000 miles, whereas, if the vehicle is being used under moderate driving conditions, it may occur at 20 000 miles. It is important to realise that this system is completely variable according to how the vehicle is being used, and therefore the service should be carried out when indicated on the display. When an OIL CHANGE SERVICE ('Oil') or INSPECTION SERVICE ('01') is due, follow the relevant procedure described for the normal 'distance and time' intervals.

Every 250 miles (400 km) or weekly

☐ Refer to *Weekly checks*

Every 5000 miles (7500 km) or 6 months

☐ Renew the engine oil and filter (Section 3)

Note: *Frequent oil and filter changes are good for the engine. We recommend changing the oil at the mileage specified here, or at least twice a year if the mileage covered is a less.*

'Oil' on display

In addition to the items listed above, carry out the following:

☐ Check the front and rear brake pad thickness (Section 4)
☐ Reset the service interval display (Section 5)

'01' on display or every 2 years, whichever comes first

In addition to the items listed above, carry out the following:

☐ Check the condition of the exhaust system and its mountings (Section 6)
☐ Check all underbonnet components and hoses for fluid and oil leaks (Section 7)
☐ Check the condition of the auxiliary drivebelt (Section 8)
☐ Check the coolant antifreeze concentration (Section 9)
☐ Check the brake hydraulic circuit for leaks and damage (Section 10)
☐ Check the headlight beam adjustment (Section 11)
☐ Renew the pollen filter element (Section 12)
☐ Check the manual transmission oil level (Section 13)
☐ Check the underbody protection for damage (Section 14)
☐ Check the condition of the driveshaft gaiters (Section 15)
☐ Check the steering and suspension components for condition and security (Section 16)
☐ Check the battery condition, security and electrolyte level (Section 17)
☐ Lubricate all hinges and locks (Section 18)
☐ Check the condition of the airbag unit(s) (Section 19)
☐ Check the operation of the windscreen/tailgate/headlight washer system(s) (as applicable) (Section 20)
☐ Check the engine management self-diagnosis memory for faults (Section 21)
☐ Carry out a road test and check exhaust emissions (Section 22)

Every 40 000 miles (60 000 km) or 4 years, whichever comes first

☐ Renew the air filter element (Section 23)
☐ Renew the spark plugs (Section 24)
☐ Check the condition of the auxiliary drivebelt (Section 25)
☐ Check the power steering hydraulic fluid level (Section 26)
☐ Check the automatic transmission fluid level (Section 27)
☐ Check the automatic transmission final drive oil level (Section 27)

Every 60 000 miles (90 000 km) or 4 years, whichever comes first

☐ Renew the timing belt (Section 28)

Note: *Audi specify timing belt inspection after the first 60 000 miles (90 000 km) and then every 20 000 mile (30 000 km) until the renewal interval of 120 000 miles (180 000 km), however, if the vehicle is used mainly for short journeys, we recommend that this shorter renewal interval is adhered to. The belt renewal interval is very much up to the individual owner but, bearing in mind that severe engine damage will result if the belt breaks in use, we recommend the shorter interval.*

Every 2 years

☐ Renew the brake (and clutch) fluid (Section 29)
☐ Renew the coolant (Section 30)*

* **Note:** *This work is not included in the Audi schedule and should not be required if the recommended G12 LongLife coolant antifreeze/inhibitor is used.*

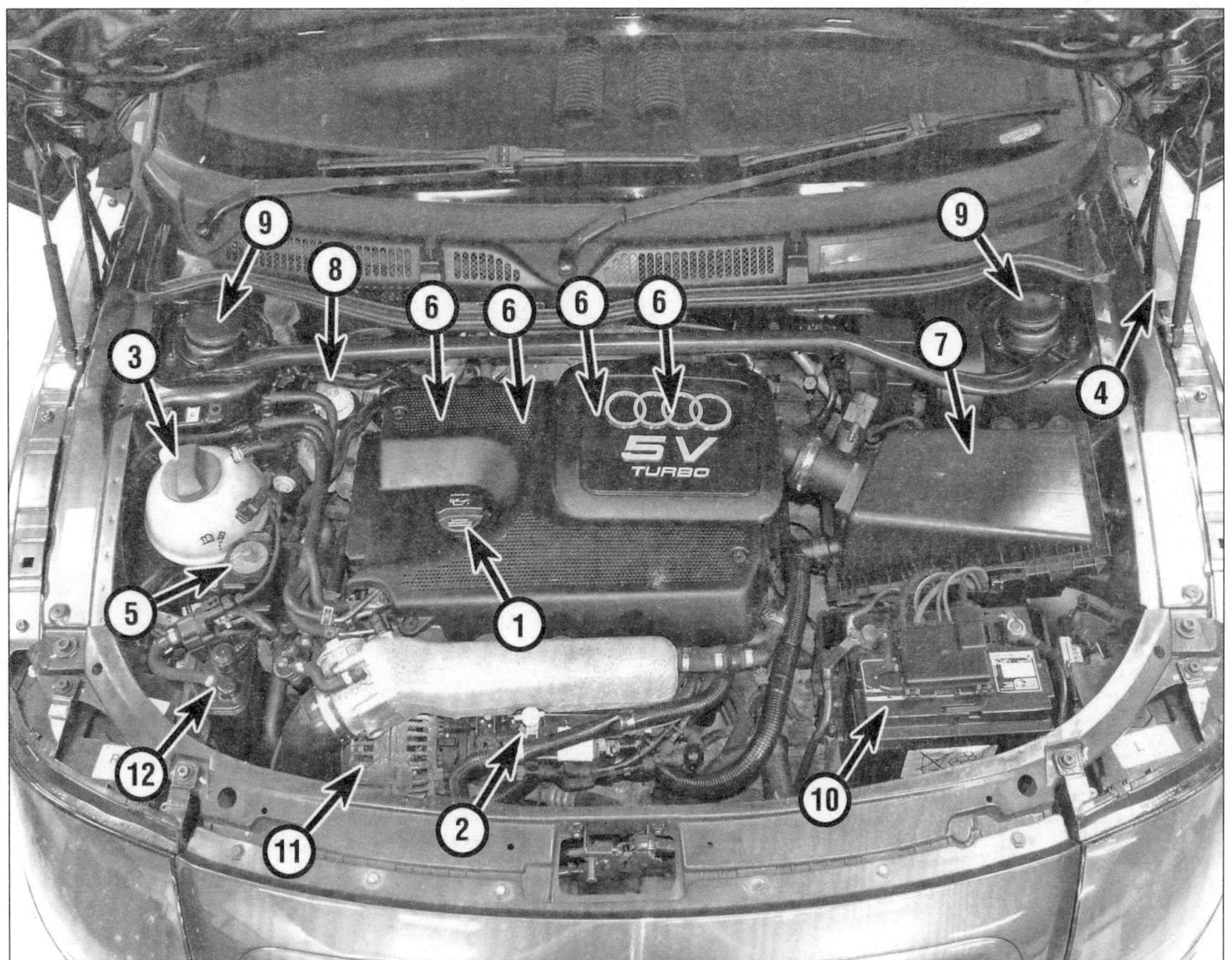

Underbonnet view of a 150bhp 1.8 turbo model

1 Engine oil filler cap
2 Engine oil dipstick
3 Coolant expansion tank
4 Windscreen / headlight washer fluid reservoir
5 Power steering fluid reservoir
6 Ignition coils and spark plugs (beneath top cover)
7 Air cleaner
8 Brake master cylinder fluid reservoir
9 Front suspension strut upper mountings
10 Battery
11 Alternator
12 Evaporative emission charcoal canister

Front underbody view – 2-wheel drive

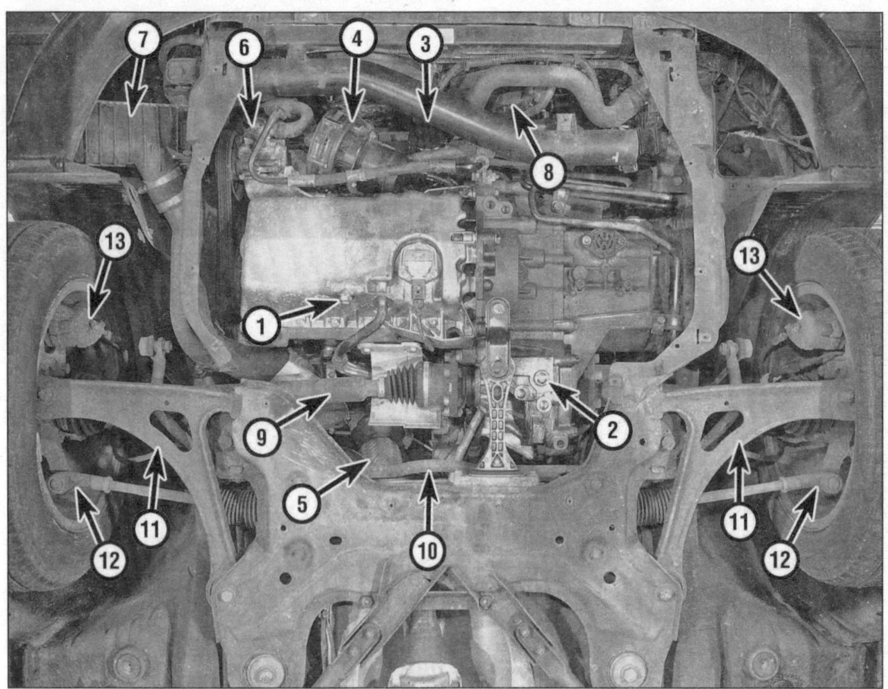

1 Engine oil drain plug
2 Manual transmission oil drain plug
3 Oil filter location
4 Secondary air injection pump
5 Exhaust front flexible pipe
6 Power steering pump
7 Charge air intercooler
8 Radiator and cooling fan
9 Right-hand side driveshaft
10 Anti-roll bar
11 Lower suspension arms
12 Track rod ends
13 Front brake calipers

Rear underbody view – 2-wheel drive

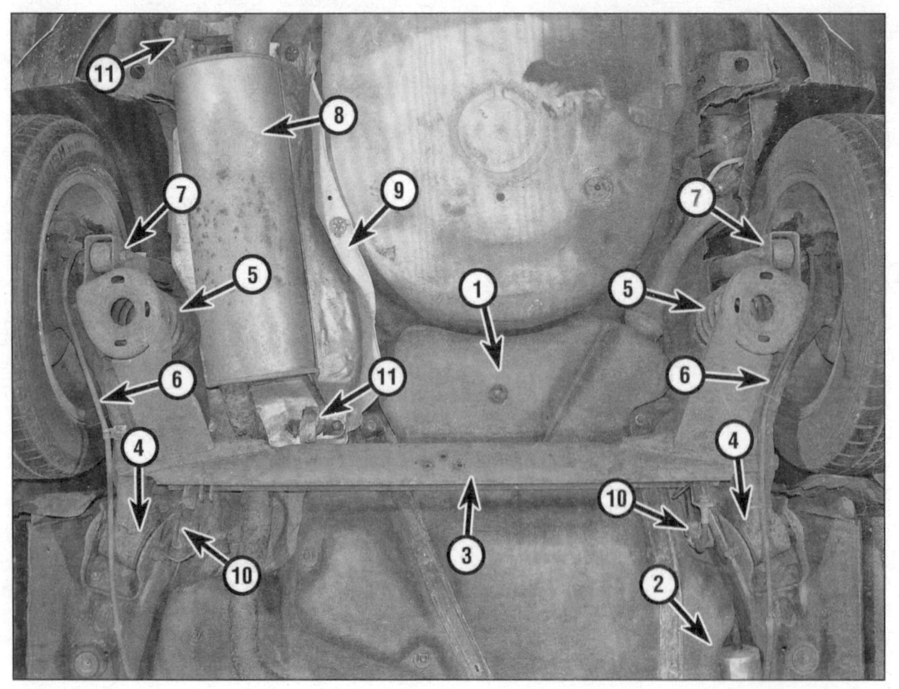

1 Fuel tank
2 Fuel filter
3 Rear axle assembly
4 Rear axle front mountings
5 Rear suspension coil springs
6 Handbrake cables
7 Rear suspension shock absorbers
8 Exhaust rear silencer and tailpipe
9 Exhaust heat shield
10 Brake flexible hoses
11 Exhaust rubber mountings

1 Introduction

1 This Chapter is designed to help the home mechanic maintain his/her vehicle for safety, economy, long life and peak performance.

2 The Chapter contains a master maintenance schedule, followed by Sections dealing specifically with each task in the schedule. Visual checks, adjustments, component renewal and other helpful items are included. Refer to the accompanying illustrations of the engine compartment and the underside of the vehicle for the locations of the various components.

3 Servicing your vehicle will provide a planned maintenance programme, which should result in a long and reliable service life. This is a comprehensive plan, so maintaining some items but not others will not produce the same results.

4 As you service your vehicle, you will discover that many of the procedures can – and should – be grouped together, because of the particular procedure being performed, or because of the proximity of two otherwise unrelated components to one another. For example, if the vehicle is raised for any reason, the exhaust can be inspected at the same time as the suspension and steering components.

5 The first step in this maintenance programme is to prepare yourself before the actual work begins. Read through all the Sections relevant to the work to be carried out, then make a list and gather all the parts and tools required. If a problem is encountered, seek advice from a parts specialist, or a dealer service department.

2 Regular maintenance

1 If, from the time the vehicle is new, the routine maintenance schedule is followed closely, and frequent checks are made of fluid levels and high-wear items, as suggested throughout this manual, the engine will be kept in relatively good running condition, and the need for additional work will be minimised.

2 It is possible that there will be times when the engine is running poorly due to the lack of regular maintenance. This is even more likely if a used vehicle, which has not received regular and frequent maintenance checks, is purchased. In such cases, additional work may need to be carried out, outside of the regular maintenance intervals.

3 If engine wear is suspected, a compression test (refer to Chapter 2A Section 2) will provide valuable information regarding the overall performance of the main internal components. Such a test can be used as a basis to decide on the extent of the work to be carried out. If, for example, a compression test indicates serious internal engine wear, conventional maintenance as described in this Chapter will not greatly improve the performance of the engine, and may prove a waste of time and money, unless extensive overhaul work is carried out first.

4 The following series of operations are those most often required to improve the performance of a generally poor-running engine:

Primary operations

a) Clean, inspect and test the battery (See Weekly checks).
b) Check all the engine-related fluids (See Weekly checks).
c) Check the condition and tension of the auxiliary drivebelt (Section 14).
d) Renew the spark plugs (Section 31).
e) Check the condition of the air filter, and renew if necessary (Section 30).
f) Check the condition of all hoses, and check for fluid leaks (Section 13).

5 If the above operations do not prove fully effective, carry out the following secondary operations:

Secondary operations

6 All items listed under Primary operations, plus the following:

a) Check the charging system (see Chapter 5A).
b) Check the ignition system (see Chapter 5B).
c) Check the fuel system (see Chapter 4A).
d) Renew the ignition HT leads (where applicable).

3 Engine oil and filter renewal

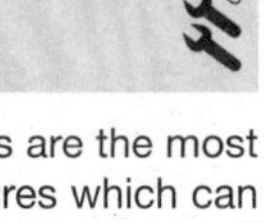

1 Frequent oil and filter changes are the most important maintenance procedures which can be undertaken by the DIY owner. As engine oil ages, it becomes diluted and contaminated, which leads to premature engine wear.

2 Before starting this procedure, gather all the necessary tools and materials. Also make sure that you have plenty of clean rags and newspapers handy, to mop-up any spills. Ideally, the engine oil should be warm, as it will drain better, and more built-up sludge will be removed with it. Take care, however, not to touch the exhaust or any other hot parts of the engine when working under the vehicle. To avoid any possibility of scalding, and to protect yourself from possible skin irritants and other harmful contaminants in used engine oils, it is advisable to wear gloves when carrying out this work. Access to the underside of the vehicle will be greatly improved if it can be raised on a lift, driven onto ramps, or jacked up and supported on axle stands (see *Jacking and vehicle support*). Whichever method is chosen, make sure that the vehicle remains level, or if it is at an angle, that the drain plug is at the lowest point. Undo the retaining screws and remove the engine undershield(s), then also remove the engine top cover where applicable.

3.3 The engine oil drain plug location on the sump

3 Using a socket and wrench or a ring spanner, slacken the drain plug about half a turn **(see illustration)**. Position the draining container under the drain plug, at the rear of the sump, and then remove the plug completely (see Haynes Hint). Recover the sealing ring from the drain plug.

4 Allow some time for the old oil to drain, noting that it may be necessary to reposition the container as the oil flow slows to a trickle.

5 After all the oil has drained, wipe off the drain plug with a clean rag, and fit a new sealing washer. Clean the area around the drain plug opening, and refit the plug. Tighten the plug to the specified torque.

6 If the filter is also to be renewed, move the container into position under the oil filter, which is located on the left-hand side of the cylinder block.

7 Using an oil filter removal tool if necessary, slacken the filter initially, then unscrew it by hand the rest of the way. Empty the oil in the filter into the container.

8 Use a clean rag to remove all oil, dirt and sludge from the filter sealing area on the engine. Check the old filter to make sure that the rubber sealing ring has not stuck to the engine. If it has, carefully remove it.

Keep the drain plug pressed into the sump while unscrewing it by hand the last couple of turns. As the plug releases, move it away sharply so the stream of oil issuing from the sump runs into the container, not up your sleeve.

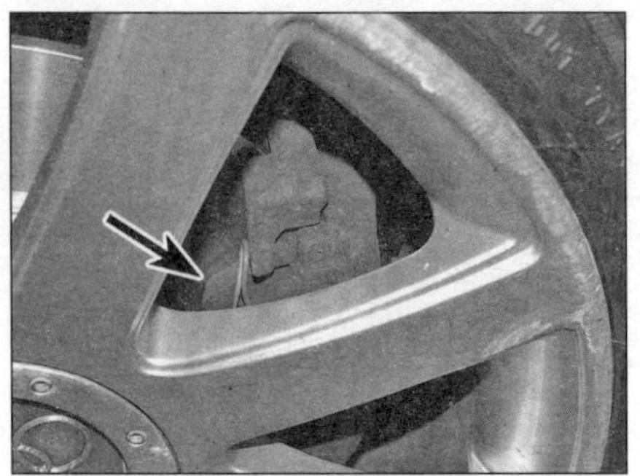

4.1 The outer brake pads can be observed through the spaces in the alloy wheels

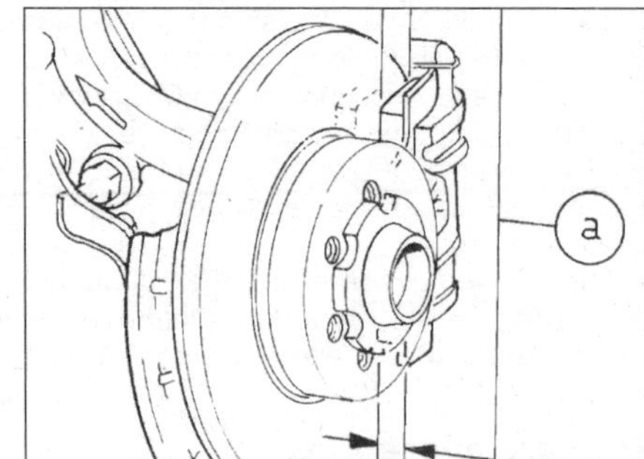

4.3 The thickness (a) of the brake pads must not be less than the specified amount

9 Apply a light coating of clean engine oil to the sealing ring on the new filter, then screw it into position on the engine. Tighten the filter firmly by hand only – do not use any tools.

10 Remove the old oil and all tools from under the car. Refit the engine undershield(s), tighten the retaining screws securely, then lower the car to the ground. Also refit the engine top cover where applicable.

11 Remove the dipstick, then unscrew the oil filler cap from the cylinder head cover. Fill the engine, using the correct grade and type of oil (see Lubricants and fluids). An oil can spout or funnel may help to reduce spillage. Pour in half the specified quantity of oil first, then wait a few minutes for the oil to run to the sump. Continue adding oil a small quantity at a time until the level is up to the maximum mark on the dipstick. Refit the filler cap.

12 Start the engine and run it for a few minutes; check for leaks around the oil filter seal and the sump drain plug. Note that there may be a few seconds delay before the oil pressure warning light goes out when the engine is started, as the oil circulates through the engine oil galleries and the new oil filter (where fitted) before the pressure builds-up.

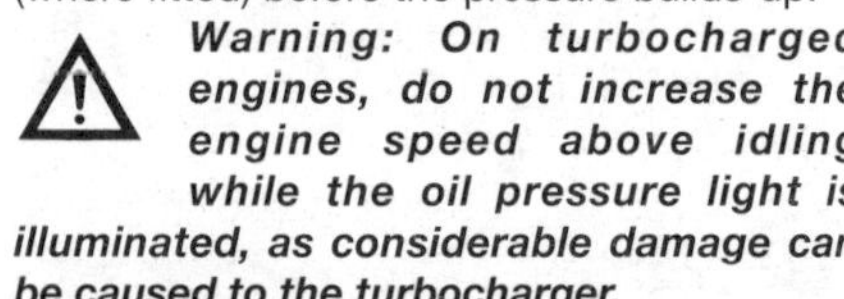

Warning: On turbocharged engines, do not increase the engine speed above idling while the oil pressure light is illuminated, as considerable damage can be caused to the turbocharger.

13 Switch off the engine, and wait a few minutes for the oil to settle in the sump once more. With the new oil circulated and the filter completely full, recheck the level on the dipstick, and add more oil as necessary.

14 Dispose of the used engine oil safely, with reference to General repair procedures in the Reference section of this manual.

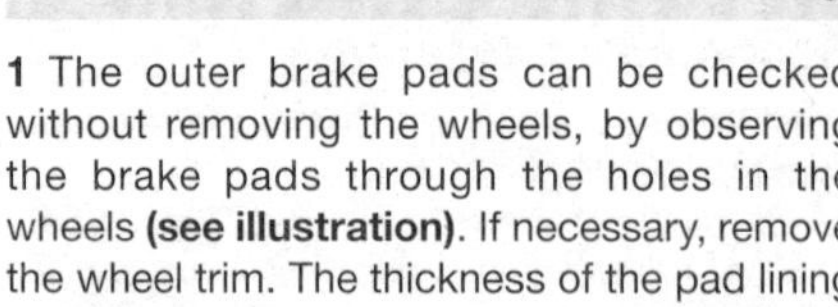

4 Brake pad check

1 The outer brake pads can be checked without removing the wheels, by observing the brake pads through the holes in the wheels **(see illustration)**. If necessary, remove the wheel trim. The thickness of the pad lining and backing plate must not be less than the dimension given in the Specifications.

2 If the outer pads are worn near their limits, it is worthwhile checking the inner pads as well. Apply the handbrake then jack up vehicle and support it on axle stands (see *Jacking and vehicle support*). Remove the roadwheels.

3 Use a steel rule to check the thickness of the brake pads (including the backing plate), and compare with the minimum thickness given in the Specifications **(see illustration)**.

4 For a comprehensive check, the brake pads should be removed and cleaned. The operation of the caliper can then also be checked, and the condition of the brake disc itself can be fully examined on both sides. Refer to Chapter 9 Section 4.

5 If any pad's friction material is worn to the specified minimum thickness or less, all four pads at the front or rear, as applicable, must be renewed as a set.

6 On completion of the check, refit the road-wheels and lower the vehicle to the ground.

5 Resetting the service interval display

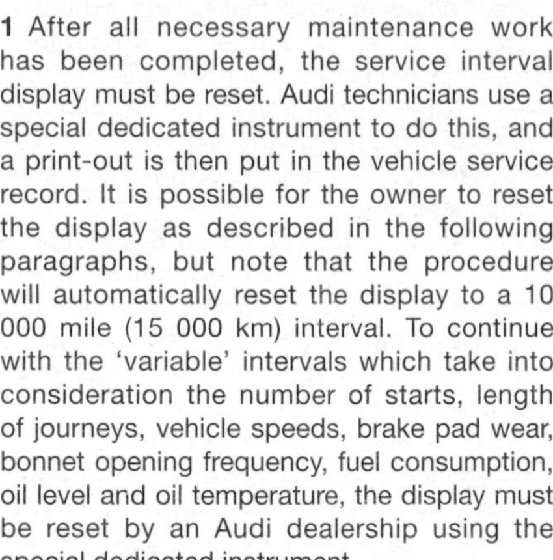

1 After all necessary maintenance work has been completed, the service interval display must be reset. Audi technicians use a special dedicated instrument to do this, and a print-out is then put in the vehicle service record. It is possible for the owner to reset the display as described in the following paragraphs, but note that the procedure will automatically reset the display to a 10 000 mile (15 000 km) interval. To continue with the 'variable' intervals which take into consideration the number of starts, length of journeys, vehicle speeds, brake pad wear, bonnet opening frequency, fuel consumption, oil level and oil temperature, the display must be reset by an Audi dealership using the special dedicated instrument.

2 To reset the service display manually, switch off the ignition, then press and hold down the trip reset button beneath the speedometer **(see illustration)**. Turn the ignition back on, whilst still holding down the reset button and the service light will appear in the display in the centre of the instrument panel. Release the trip reset button on the right of the instrument panel and press and hold down the digital clock reset button on the left-hand side, the relevant service interval will show in the display. Release the digital clock reset button and 'OK' will appear in the display. Switch off the ignition to complete the resetting procedure.

6 Exhaust system check

1 With the engine cold (at least an hour after the vehicle has been driven), check the complete exhaust system from the engine to the end of the tailpipe. The exhaust system is most easily checked with the vehicle raised on a hoist, or supported on axle stands, so that the exhaust components are readily visible and accessible (see *Jacking and vehicle support*).

2 Check the exhaust pipes and connections for evidence of leaks, severe corrosion and damage. Make sure that all brackets and mountings are in good condition, and that all relevant nuts and bolts are tight. Leakage at any of the joints or in other parts of the system will usually show up as a black sooty stain in the vicinity of the leak.

3 Rattles and other noises can often be traced to the exhaust system, especially the brackets and mountings **(see illustration)**. Try to move

5.2 (A) Trip reset button (B) Digital clock reset button

6.3 Check the rubber mountings

the pipes and silencers. If the components are able to come into contact with the body or suspension parts, secure the system with new mountings. Otherwise separate the joints (if possible) and twist the pipes as necessary to provide additional clearance.

7 Hose and fluid leak check

1 Visually inspect the engine joint faces, gaskets and seals for any signs of water or oil leaks. Pay particular attention to the areas around the camshaft cover, cylinder head, oil filter and sump joint faces. Bear in mind that, over a period of time, some very slight seepage from these areas is to be expected – what you are really looking for is any indication of a serious leak. Should a leak be found, renew the offending gasket or oil seal by referring to the appropriate Chapters in this manual.

2 Also check the security and condition of all the engine-related pipes and hoses. Ensure that all cable-ties or securing clips are in place and in good condition. Clips which are broken or missing can lead to chafing of the hoses, pipes or wiring, which could cause more serious problems in the future.

3 Carefully check the radiator hoses and heater hoses along their entire length. Renew any hose which is cracked, swollen or deteriorated. Cracks will show up better if the hose is squeezed. Pay close attention to the hose clips that secure the hoses to the cooling system components. Hose clips can pinch and puncture hoses, resulting in cooling system leaks.

4 Inspect all the cooling system components (hoses, joint faces, etc) for leaks (see Haynes Hint). Where any problems of this nature are found on system components, renew the component or gasket with reference to Chapter 3.

5 Where applicable, inspect the automatic transmission fluid cooler hoses for leaks or deterioration.

6 With the vehicle raised, inspect the petrol tank and filler neck for punctures, cracks and other damage. The connection between the filler neck and tank is especially critical. Sometimes a rubber filler neck or connecting hose will leak due to loose retaining clamps or deteriorated rubber.

7 Carefully check all rubber hoses and metal fuel lines leading away from the petrol tank. Check for loose connections, deteriorated hoses, crimped lines, and other damage. Pay particular attention to the vent pipes and hoses, which often loop up around the filler neck and can become blocked or crimped. Follow the lines to the front of the vehicle, carefully inspecting them all the way. Renew damaged sections as necessary.

8 From within the engine compartment, check the security of all fuel hose attachments and pipe unions, and inspect the fuel hoses and vacuum hoses for kinks, chafing and deterioration.

9 Where applicable, check the condition of the power steering fluid hoses and pipes.

A leak in the cooling system will usually show up as white- or rust-coloured deposits on the area adjoining the leak.

8 Auxiliary drivebelt check

1 Apply the handbrake, then jack up the front of the vehicle and support it on axle stands (see *Jacking and vehicle support*).

2 Using a socket on the crankshaft pulley bolt, turn the engine slowly clockwise so that the full length of the auxiliary drivebelt can be examined. Look for cracks, splitting and fraying on the surface of the belt; check also for signs of glazing (shiny patches) and separation of the belt plies. Use a mirror to check the underside of the drivebelt **(see illustration)**. If damage or wear is visible, or if there are traces of oil or grease on it, the belt should be renewed (see Section 32).

8.2 Checking the underside of the auxiliary drivebelt with a mirror

9 Antifreeze check

1 The cooling system should be filled with the recommended G12 plus antifreeze and corrosion protection fluid – do not mix this antifreeze with any other type. Over a period of time, the concentration of fluid may be reduced due to topping-up (this can be avoided by topping-up with the correct antifreeze mixture – see Specifications) or fluid loss. If loss of coolant has been evident, it is important to make the necessary repair before adding fresh fluid.

2 With the engine cold, carefully remove the cap from the expansion tank. If the engine is not completely cold, place a cloth rag over the cap before removing it, and remove it slowly to allow any pressure to escape.

3 Antifreeze checkers are available from car accessory shops. Draw some coolant from the expansion tank and observe how many plastic balls are floating in the checker. Usually, 2 or 3 balls must be floating for the correct concentration of antifreeze, but follow the manufacturer's instructions.

4 If the concentration is incorrect, it will be necessary to either withdraw some coolant and add antifreeze, or alternatively drain the old coolant and add fresh coolant of the correct concentration (see Section 37).

10 Brake hydraulic circuit check

1 Check the entire brake hydraulic circuit for leaks and damage. Start by checking the master cylinder in the engine compartment. At the same time, check the vacuum servo unit and ABS units for signs of fluid leakage.

2 Raise the front and rear of the vehicle and support it on axle stands (see *Jacking and vehicle support*). Working your way from the front of the vehicle to the rear, check the metal rigid hydraulic brake lines for corrosion and damage.

3 At the front of the vehicle, check that the flexible hydraulic hoses to the calipers are not twisted or chafing on any of the surrounding suspension components. Turn the steering on full lock to make this check. Also check that the hoses are not brittle or cracked.

4 At the rear of the vehicle, check the flexible hoses to the rear axle/hub for damage or chafing against surrounding components (suspension, handbrake cables.....etc.). Also check that the hoses are not brittle or cracked.

5 Lower the vehicle to the ground after making the checks.

11 Headlight beam adjustment

1 Accurate adjustment of the headlight beam is only possible using optical beam-setting equipment, and this work should therefore be carried out by a Audi dealer or service station with the necessary facilities.

2 Basic adjustments can be carried out in an emergency, and further details are given in Chapter 12 Section 9.

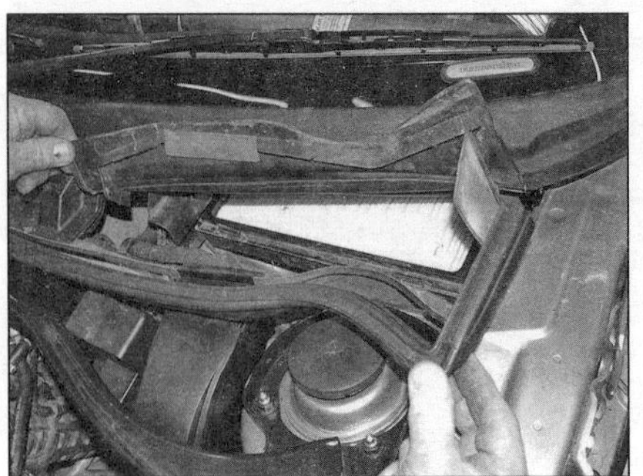
12.2 Ease off the rubber seal and lift up the cowling...

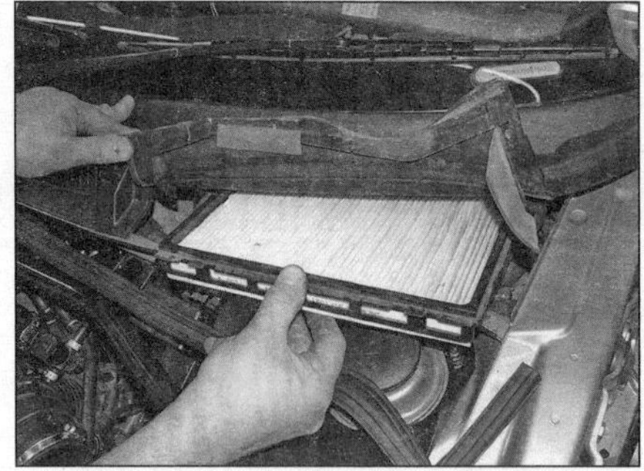
12.3 ... and remove the pollen filter

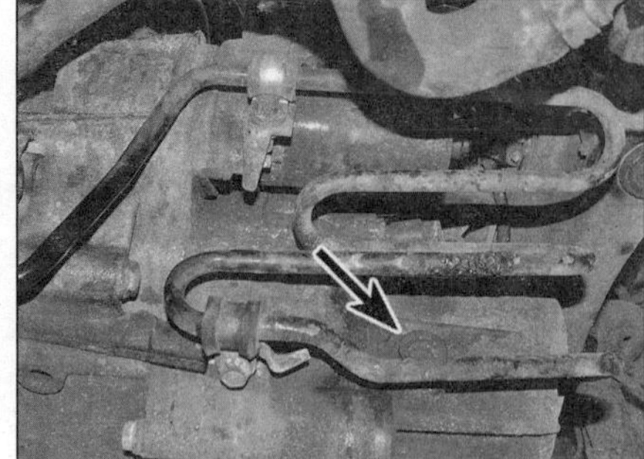
13.2 Filler/level plug location – 02M/02Y transmission shown

12 Pollen filter element renewal

1 The pollen filter is located on the bulkhead, in front of the windscreen – on RHD models it is on the left-hand side, and on LHD models it is on the right-hand side.

2 Ease off the rubber seal from along the front edge of the bulkhead plastic trim panel, then pull up and release the plastic trim from above the pollen filter housing **(see illustration)**.

3 Release the clips and withdraw the filter element complete with frame, then remove the element from the frame, noting its fitted position **(see illustration)**.

4 Locate the new filter element back into the frame, as noted on removal, then fit back in place in the top of the housing, making sure that the lugs engage in the recess correctly.

5 Refit the plastic trim cover, and then press down the rubber seal into position along the front edge of the bulkhead panel.

13 Manual transmission oil level check

1 Park the car on a level surface. For improved access to the filler/level plug, apply the hand-brake, then jack up the front of the vehicle and support it on axle stands (see *Jacking and vehicle support*), but note that the rear of the vehicle should also be raised to ensure an accurate level check. The oil level must be checked before the car is driven, or at least 5 minutes after the engine has been switched off. If the oil is checked immediately after driving the car, some of the oil will remain distributed around the transmission components, resulting in an inaccurate level reading.

2 Undo the retaining screws and remove the engine undershield. Wipe clean the area around the transmission filler/level plug, which is situated on the front of the transmission housing **(see illustration)**.

3 The oil level should reach the lower edge of the filler/level hole. A certain amount of oil will have gathered behind the filler/level plug, and will trickle out when it is removed; this does not necessarily indicate that the level is correct. To ensure that a true level is established, wait until the initial trickle has stopped, then add oil as necessary until a trickle of new oil can be seen emerging. The level will be correct when the flow ceases; use only good-quality oil of the specified type.

4 If the transmission has been overfilled so that oil flows out when the filler/level plug is removed, check that the car is completely level (front-to-rear and side-to-side), and allow the surplus to drain off into a suitable container.

5 When the oil level is correct, refit the filler/level plug and tighten it to the specified torque. Wipe off any spilt oil then refit the engine undershield(s), tighten the retaining screws securely, and lower the car to the ground.

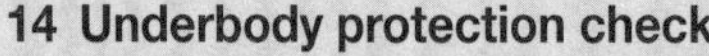

14 Underbody protection check

1 Raise and support the vehicle on axle stands (see *Jacking and vehicle support*). Inspect the entire underside of the vehicle, paying particular attention to the wheel arches. Look for any damage to the flexible underbody sealant coating, which may crack or flake off with age, leading to corrosion. Also check that the wheel arch liners are securely attached with any clips provided – if they come loose, dirt may get in behind the liners and defeat their purpose. If there is any damage to the under-seal, or any corrosion, it should be repaired before the damage gets too serious.

15 Driveshaft gaiter check

1 With the vehicle raised and securely supported on stands, slowly rotate the roadwheel. Inspect the condition of the outer constant velocity (CV) joint rubber gaiters, squeezing the gaiters to open out the folds. Check for signs of cracking, splits or deterioration of the rubber, which may allow the grease to escape, and lead to water and grit entry into the joint. Also check the security and condition of the retaining clips. Repeat these checks on the inner joints **(see illustrations)**. If any damage or deterioration is found, the gaiters should be renewed (see Chapter 8A).

2 At the same time, check the general condition of the CV joints themselves by first holding the driveshaft and attempting to rotate the wheel. Repeat this check by holding the inner joint and attempting to rotate the driveshaft. Any appreciable movement indicates wear in the joints, wear in the driveshaft splines, or a loose driveshaft retaining nut.

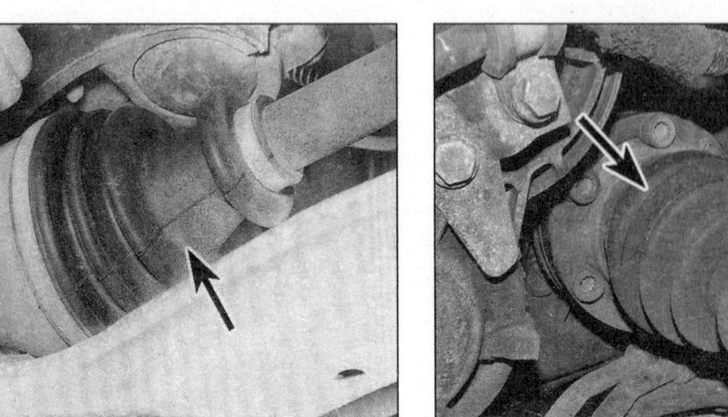
15.1a Check the condition of the outer...

15.1b...and inner driveshaft gaiters (arrowed)

16.4 Check for wear in the hub bearings by grasping the wheel and trying to rock it

17.1 Removing the battery cover

17.3 Battery retaining clamp bolt (arrowed)

16 Steering and suspension check

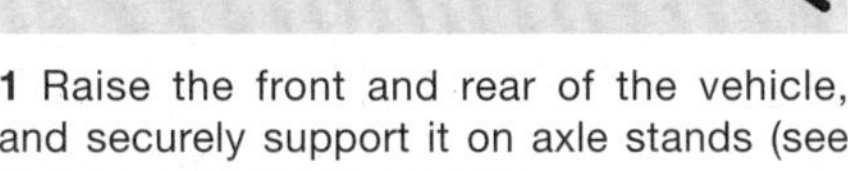

1 Raise the front and rear of the vehicle, and securely support it on axle stands (see *Jacking and vehicle support*).

2 Visually inspect the track rod end balljoint dust cover, the lower front suspension balljoint dust cover, and the steering rack-and-pinion gaiters for splits, chafing or deterioration. Any wear of these components will cause loss of lubricant, together with dirt and water entry, resulting in rapid deterioration of the balljoints or steering gear.

3 Check the power steering fluid hoses for chafing or deterioration, and the pipe and hose unions for fluid leaks. Also check for signs of fluid leakage under pressure from the steering gear rubber gaiters, which would indicate failed fluid seals within the steering gear.

4 Grasp the roadwheel at the 12 o'clock and 6 o'clock positions, and try to rock it **(see illustration)**. Very slight free play may be felt, but if the movement is appreciable, further investigation is necessary to determine the source. Continue rocking the wheel while an assistant depresses the footbrake. If the movement is now eliminated or significantly reduced, it is likely that the hub bearings are at fault. If the free play is still evident with the footbrake depressed, then there is wear in the suspension joints or mountings.

5 Now grasp the wheel at the 9 o'clock and 3 o'clock positions, and try to rock it as before. Any movement felt now may again be caused by wear in the hub bearings or the steering track rod balljoints. If the inner or outer balljoint is worn, the visual movement will be obvious.

6 Using a large screwdriver or flat bar, check for wear in the suspension mounting bushes by levering between the relevant suspension component and its attachment point. Some movement is to be expected as the mountings are made of rubber, but excessive wear should be obvious. Also check the condition of any visible rubber bushes, looking for splits, cracks or contamination of the rubber.

7 With the car standing on its wheels, have an assistant turn the steering wheel back-and-forth about an eighth of a turn each way. There should be very little, if any, lost movement between the steering wheel and roadwheels. If this is not the case, closely observe the joints and mountings previously described, but in addition, check the steering column universal joints for wear, and the rack-and-pinion steering gear itself.

8 Check for any signs of fluid leakage around the front suspension struts and rear shock absorber. Should any fluid be noticed, the suspension strut or shock absorber is defective internally, and should be renewed. **Note:** *Suspension struts/shock absorbers should always be renewed in pairs on the same axle to ensure correct vehicle handling.*

9 The efficiency of the suspension strut/shock absorber may be checked by bouncing the vehicle at each corner. Generally speaking, the body will return to its normal position and stop after being depressed. If it rises and returns on a rebound, the suspension strut/shock absorber is probably suspect. Examine also the suspension strut/shock absorber upper and lower mountings for any signs of wear.

17 Battery check

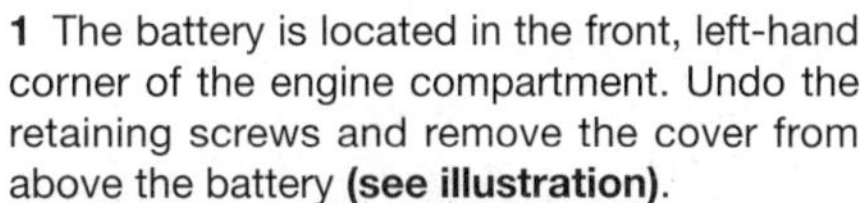

1 The battery is located in the front, left-hand corner of the engine compartment. Undo the retaining screws and remove the cover from above the battery **(see illustration)**.

2 Check that both battery terminals and all the fuse holder connections are securely attached and are free from corrosion. **Note:** *Before disconnecting the terminals from the battery, refer to* Disconnecting the battery *in the Reference chapter at the end of this manual.*

3 Check the battery casing for signs of damage or cracking and check the battery retaining clamp bolt is securely tightened **(see illustration)**. If the battery casing is damaged in any way the battery must be renewed (see Chapter 5A).

4 If the vehicle is not fitted with a sealed-for-life maintenance-free battery, check the electrolyte level is between the MAX and MIN level markings on the battery casing. If topping-up is necessary, remove the battery (see Chapter 5A) from the vehicle then remove the cell caps/cover (as applicable). Using distilled water, top the electrolyte level of each cell up to the MAX level mark then securely refit the cell caps/cover. Ensure the battery has not been overfilled then refit the battery to the vehicle (see Chapter 5A).

5 On completion of the check, refit the plastic trim cover over the battery.

18 Hinge and lock lubrication

1 Lubricate the hinges of the bonnet, doors and tailgate with a light general-purpose oil. Similarly, lubricate all latches, locks and lock strikers. At the same time, check the security and operation of all the locks, adjusting them if necessary (see Chapter 11).

2 Lightly lubricate the bonnet release mechanism and cable with a suitable grease.

19 Airbag unit check

1 Inspect the exterior condition of the airbag(s) for signs of damage or deterioration. If an airbag shows signs of damage, it must be renewed (see Chapter 12 Section 25). Note that it is not permissible to attach any stickers to the surface of the airbag, as this may affect the deployment of the unit.

20 Windscreen/headlight washer system check

1 Check that each of the washer jet nozzles are clear and that each nozzle provides a strong jet of washer fluid.

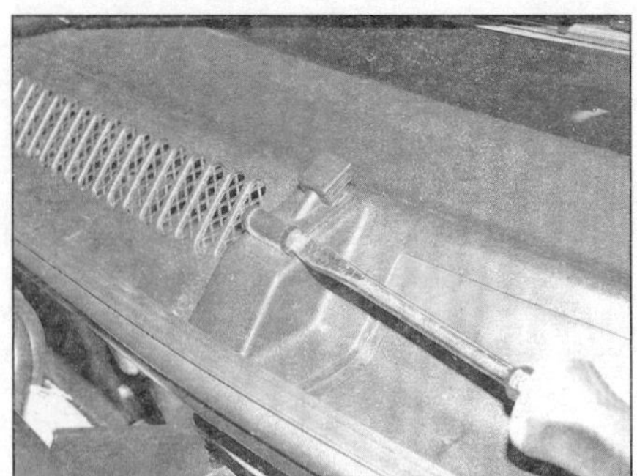

20.2 Adjusting the washer jet

2 The windscreen washer nozzles should be aimed slightly above the centre of the screen using a small screwdriver to turn the jet eccentric **(see illustration)**.

3 The headlight inner jet should be aimed slightly above the horizontal centreline of the headlight, and the outer jet should be aimed slightly below the centreline. Audi technicians use a special tool to adjust the headlight jet after pulling the jet out onto its stop.

4 Especially during the winter months, make sure that the washer fluid frost concentration is sufficient. DO NOT use antifreeze in the washer reservoir, as this will damage the paintwork.

21 Engine management self-diagnosis memory fault check

1 This work should be carried out by an Audi dealer or diagnostic specialist using special equipment. The diagnostic socket is located below the right-hand side of the facia, next to the bonnet release lever **(see illustration)**.

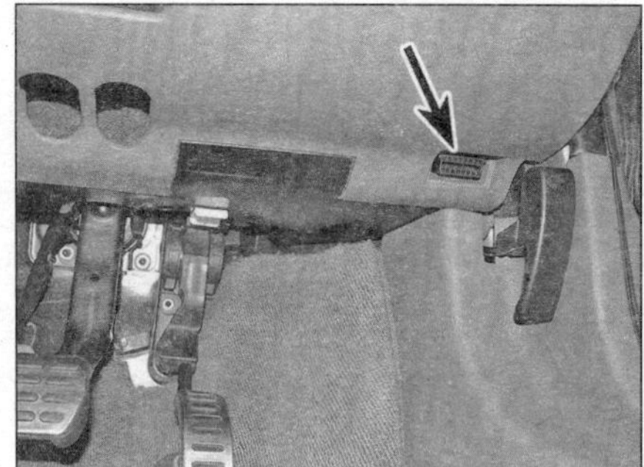

21.1 Diagnostic socket location (arrowed)

22 Road test and exhaust emissions check

Instruments and electrical equipment

1 Check the operation of all instruments and electrical equipment including the air conditioning system.

2 Make sure that all instruments read correctly, and switch on all electrical equip-ment in turn, to check that it functions properly.

Steering and suspension

3 Check for any abnormalities in the steering, suspension, handling or road 'feel'.

4 Drive the vehicle, and check that there are no unusual vibrations or noises which may indicate wear in the driveshafts, wheel bearings, etc.

5 Check that the steering feels positive, with no excessive 'sloppiness', or roughness, and check for any suspension noises when cornering and driving over bumps.

Drivetrain

6 Check the performance of the engine, clutch (where applicable), gearbox/transmission and driveshafts.

7 Listen for any unusual noises from the engine, clutch and gearbox/transmission.

8 Make sure the engine runs smoothly at idle, and there is no hesitation on accelerating.

9 Check that, where applicable, the clutch action is smooth and progressive, that the drive is taken up smoothly, and that the pedal travel is not excessive. Also listen for any noises when the clutch pedal is depressed.

10 On manual gearbox models, check that all gears can be engaged smoothly without noise, and that the gear lever action is smooth and not abnormally vague or 'notchy'.

11 On automatic transmission models, make sure that all gearchanges occur smoothly, without snatching, and without an increase in engine speed between changes. Check that all the gear positions can be selected with the vehicle at rest. If any problems are found, they should be referred to an Audi dealer.

12 Listen for a metallic clicking sound from the front of the vehicle, as the vehicle is driven slowly in a circle with the steering on full-lock. Carry out this check in both directions. If a clicking noise is heard, this indicates wear in a driveshaft joint, in which case renew the joint if necessary.

Braking system

13 Make sure that the vehicle does not pull to one side when braking, and that the wheels do not lock when braking hard.

14 Check that there is no vibration through the steering when braking.

15 Check that the handbrake operates correctly without excessive movement of the lever, and that it holds the vehicle stationary on a slope.

16 Test the operation of the brake servo unit as follows. With the engine off, depress the footbrake four or five times to exhaust the vacuum. Hold the brake pedal depressed, then start the engine. As the engine starts, there should be a noticeable 'give' in the brake pedal as vacuum builds-up. Allow the engine to run for at least two minutes, and then switch it off. If the brake pedal is depressed now, it should be possible to detect a hiss from the servo as the pedal is depressed. After about four or five applications, no further hissing should be heard, and the pedal should feel considerably harder.

17 Under controlled emergency braking, the pulsing of the ABS unit must be felt at the footbrake pedal.

Exhaust emissions check

18 Although not part of the manufacturer's maintenance schedule, this check will normally be carried out on a regular basis according to the country the vehicle is operated in. Currently in the UK, exhaust emissions testing is included as part of the annual MOT test after the vehicle is 3 years old.

23 Air filter element renewal

1 Undo the retaining screws at the rear of the filter cover, then lift the cover up and release the locating pegs at the front of the cover **(see illustrations)**. If preferred, the cover may be completely removed from the inlet duct, by slackening the retaining clip and disconnecting the wiring connector from the air mass/flow meter.

2 Note how the filter element is fitted, then

23.1a Undo the retaining screws (arrowed)...

23.1b...and release the locating pegs

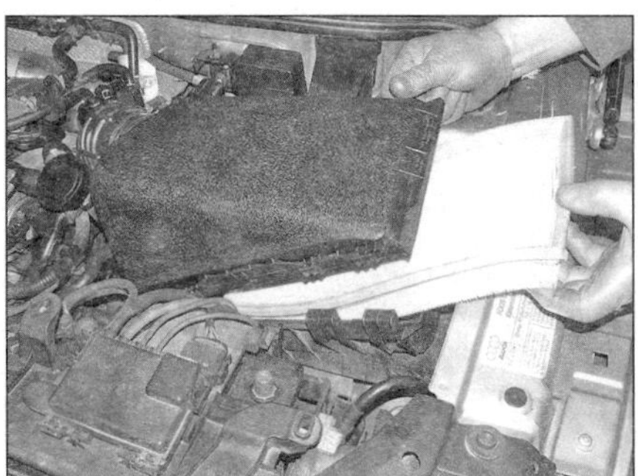

23.2 Withdraw the filter element

withdraw it from the lower part of the air filter housing **(see illustration)**.

3 Remove any debris and wipe clean the interior of the housing, before refitting the filter element.

4 Fit the new air filter element in position, ensuring that the edges are securely seated.

5 Refit the cover and secure with the retaining screws, making sure the locating pegs at the front of the cover are positioned correctly.

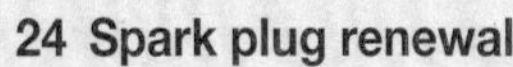

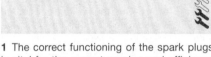

24 Spark plug renewal

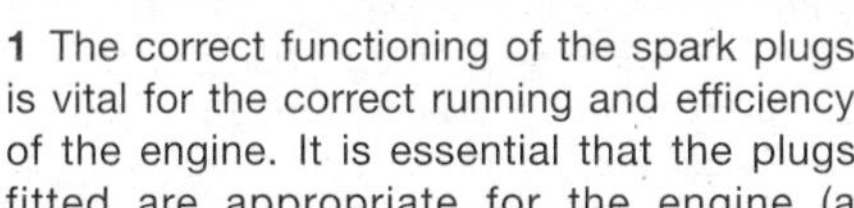

1 The correct functioning of the spark plugs is vital for the correct running and efficiency of the engine. It is essential that the plugs fitted are appropriate for the engine (a suitable type is specified at the beginning of this Chapter). If this type is used and the engine is in good condition, the spark plugs should not need attention between scheduled renewal intervals. Spark plug cleaning is rarely necessary, and should not be attempted unless specialised equipment is available, as damage can easily be caused to the firing ends.

24.2 Engine top cover retaining screws (arrowed)

All models (except engine codes AMU, APX and BAM)

2 Undo the securing screws and lift the cover from the top of the engine, releasing it from the locating pegs at the rear **(see illustration)**.

3 Undo the retaining nut and move the vacuum reservoir to one side **(see illustration)**, then undo the retaining bolts and remove the mounting bracket.

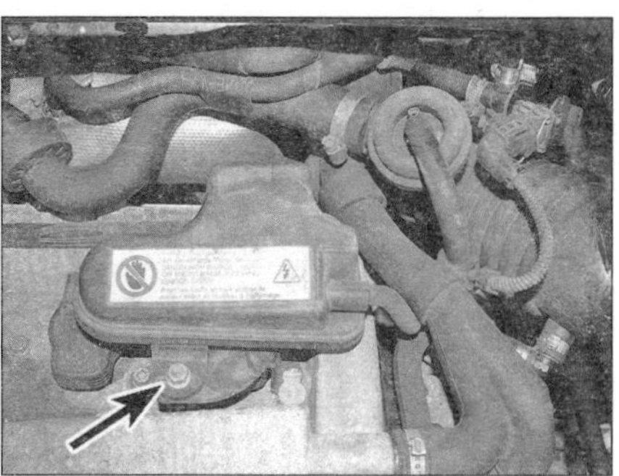

24.3 Undo the reservoir retaining nut (arrowed)

Engine codes AMU, APX and BAM

4 Undo the securing screws and lift the cover from the top of the engine, releasing it from the locating pegs at the rear **(see illustration)**.

5 Unclip and remove the heat protective covers from around the turbocharger divert valve and vacuum reservoir **(see illustration)**.

6 Disconnect the wiring connector from the turbocharger divert air valve, release the valve from the mounting bracket and then move it to one side **(see illustrations)**. Note you will need to unclip the hoses from the securing clips as it is moved to one side.

7 Undo the retaining nut and move the vacuum reservoir to one side **(see illustration)**.

8 Unbolt and remove the reservoir bracket from over number 3 and 4 coils **(see illustration)**.

24.4 Engine top cover retaining screws (arrowed)

24.5 Unclip the heat protective covers (arrowed)

24.6a Disconnect the wiring connector...

24.6b...and unclip the valve from the mounting bracket

24.7 Remove the reservoir from the bracket

24.8 Remove the mounting bracket from over the coils

24.9 Disconnect the wiring connectors

24.10 Remove the ignition coils from the spark plugs

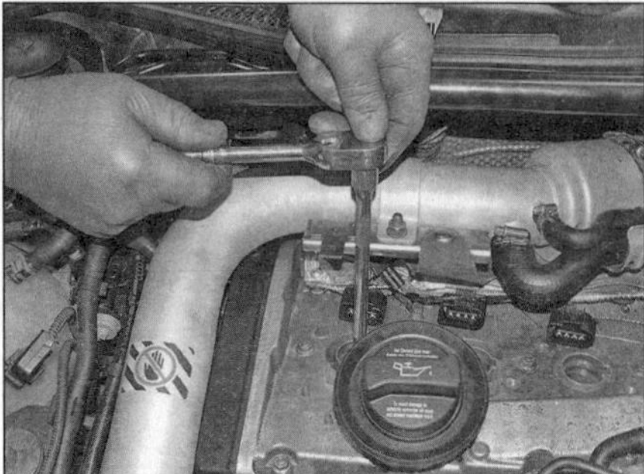
24.12 Using a deep socket and extension bar to remove spark plugs

All models

9 Release the securing clips and disconnect the wiring connectors from the four ignition coils **(see illustration)**.

10 With all the wiring connectors disconnected pull the ignition coils straight upwards to release them from the top of the spark plugs **(see illustration)**.

11 It is advisable to remove the dirt from the spark plug recesses using a vacuum cleaner or compressed air before removing the plugs, to prevent dirt dropping into the cylinders, once the spark plugs have been removed.

12 Unscrew the plugs using a spark plug spanner, or a deep socket and extension bar **(see illustration)**. Keep the socket aligned with the spark plug – if it is forcibly moved to one side, the ceramic insulator may be broken off.

13 If required, use a magnet or rubber hose to remove the spark plugs from inside the plug hole **(see illustrations)**. Also the ignition coil could be used, by pushing it back down onto the top of the spark plug.

14 As each plug is removed, examine it as follows, as it will give a good indication of the condition of the engine. If the insulator nose of the spark plug is clean and white, with no deposits, this is indicative of a weak mixture or too hot a plug (a hot plug transfers heat away from the electrode slowly, a cold plug transfers heat away quickly).

15 If the tip and insulator nose are covered with hard black-looking deposits, then this is indicative that the mixture is too rich. Should the plug be black and oily, then it is likely that the engine is fairly worn, as well as the mixture being too rich.

16 If the insulator nose is covered with light tan to greyish-brown deposits, then the mixture is correct and it is likely that the engine is in good condition.

17 The spark plug electrode gap is of considerable importance as, if it is too large or too small, the size of the spark and its efficiency will be seriously impaired. On engines fitted with multi-electrode spark plugs, it is recommended that the plugs are renewed rather than attempting to adjust the gaps. On other spark plugs, the gap should be set to the value given by the manufacturer.

18 To set the gap on single electrode plugs, measure it with a feeler blade and then bend open, or closed, the outer plug electrode until the correct gap is achieved. The centre electrode should never be bent, as this may crack the insulator and cause plug failure, if nothing worse. If using feeler blades, the gap is correct when the appropriate-size blade is a firm sliding fit **(see illustrations)**.

19 Special spark plug electrode gap adjusting tools are available from most motor accessory shops, or from some spark plug manufacturers **(see illustration)**.

20 Before fitting the spark plugs, check that the threaded connector sleeves are tight, and that the plug exterior surfaces and threads are

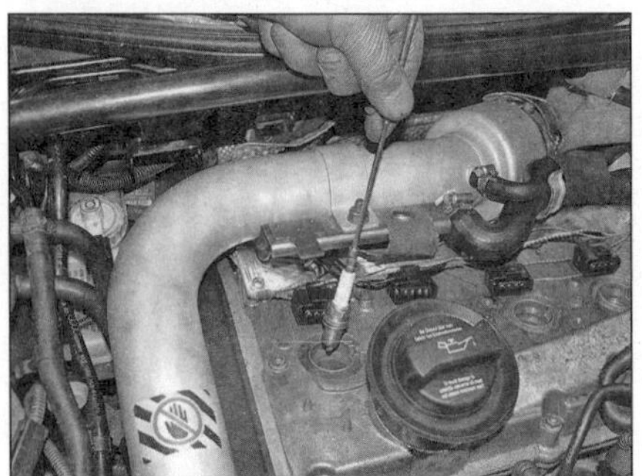
24.13a Using a magnet...

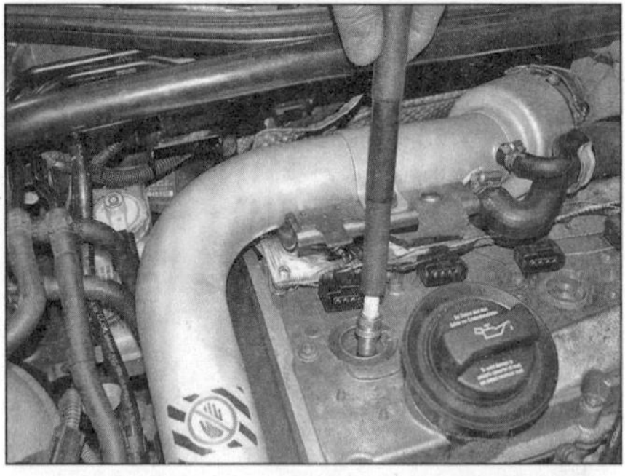
24.13b...or rubber hose to remove plugs

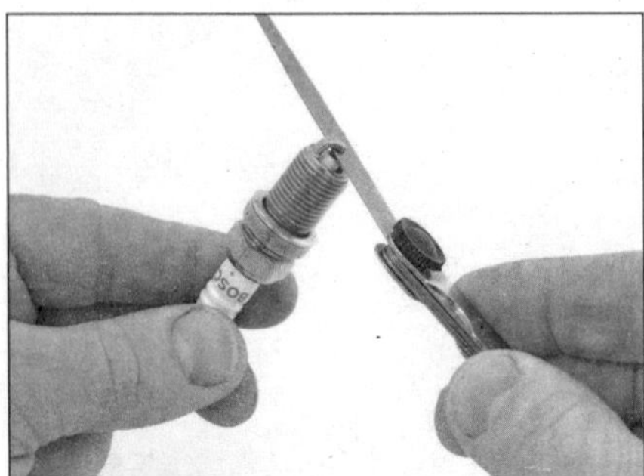
24.18a If single electrode plugs are being fitted, check the electrode gap using a feeler gauge ...

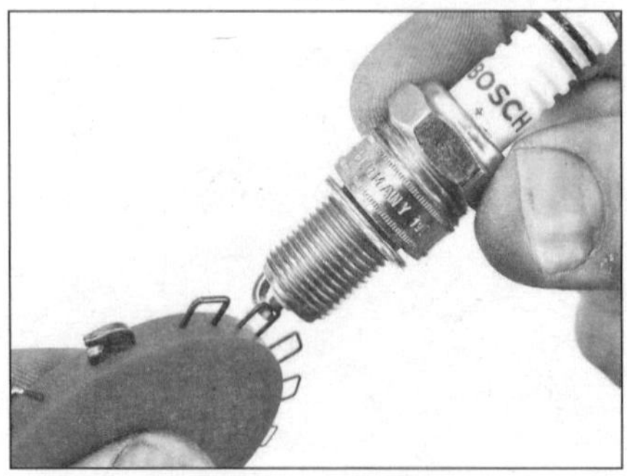

24.18b ... or a wire gauge ...

24.19 ... and if necessary adjust the gap by bending the electrode

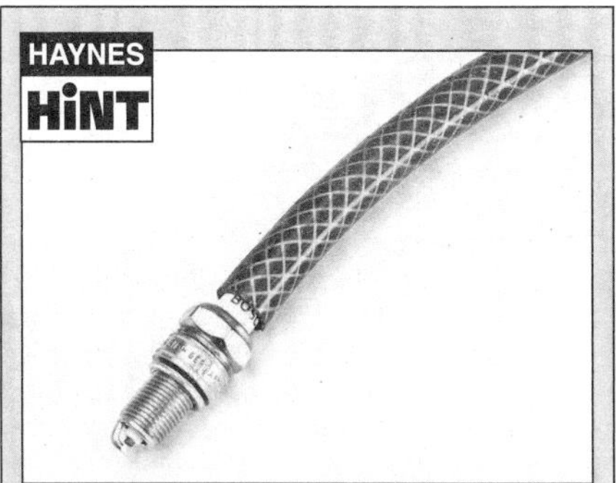

It is very often difficult to insert spark plugs into their holes without cross-threading them. To avoid this possibility, fit a short length of rubber hose over the end of the spark plug. The flexible hose acts as a universal joint to help align the plug with the plug thread, the hose will slip on the spark plug, preventing thread damage to the aluminium cylinder head.

clean. It's often difficult to screw in new spark plugs without cross-threading them – this can be avoided using a piece of rubber hose (see **Haynes Hint**).

21 Remove the rubber hose (if used), and tighten the plug to the specified torque using the spark plug socket and a torque wrench **(see illustration)**. Refit the remaining spark plugs in the same manner.

22 Refit the ignition coils back to the top of the spark plugs, making sure they are firmly pressed into position and the locating lug is aligned correctly **(see illustration)**. When in position, reconnect the wiring connectors to the ignition coils, making sure they secured by the retaining clip.

23 Refit the vacuum reservoir and mounting bracket using a reversal of the removal procedure.

24 On engine codes AMU, APX and BAM models, refit the turbocharger divert air valve, using a reversal of the removal procedure.

25 When complete refit the engine plastic trim cover back to the top of the engine.

24.21 Using a torque wrench to tighten spark plugs

24.22 Align locating lug arrowed

25 Auxiliary drivebelt check and renewal

Checking

1 See Section 14.

Renewal

Note: *Some of the illustrations in this section where taken with the engine out of the vehicle to give better clarity.*

2 Open the bonnet and remove the trim panels from the top of the engine and from over the coolant reservoir.

3 Undo the retaining bolts and move the charcoal canister and power steering reservoir to one side **(see illustrations)**. There is no need to disconnect any pipes/hoses, just release them from any retaining clips.

4 On models with engine codes AMU, APX and BAM, remove the charge air pipe from around the top, right-hand side of the engine **(see illustration)**, as described in Chapter 4B Section 7.

5 Use a spanner on the lug provided and turn the tensioner clockwise. Lock the tensioner in its released position by inserting an Allen key through the lug into the hole in the rear of the tensioner body **(see illustrations)**.

6 Remove the drivebelt from around the power steering pump pulley, crankshaft

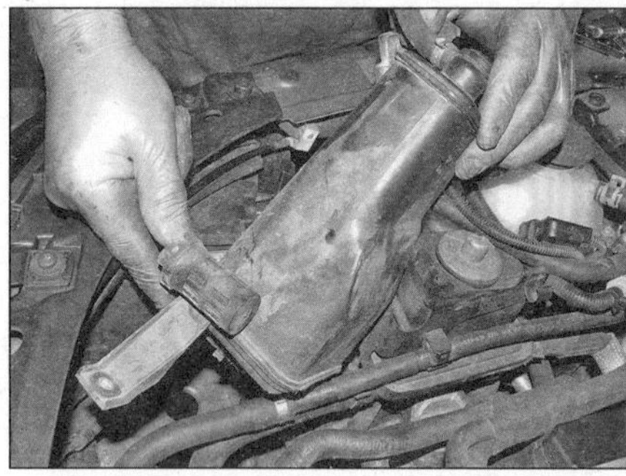

25.3a Move the charcoal canister to one side

25.3b Undo bolt (arrowed) and move PAS reservoir to one side

25.4 Remove charge air pipe

25.5a Release the tensioner clockwise...

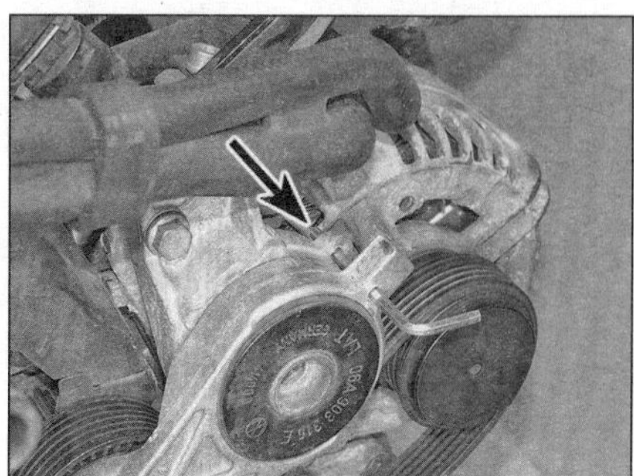

25.5b...and insert the Allen key through the tensioner body

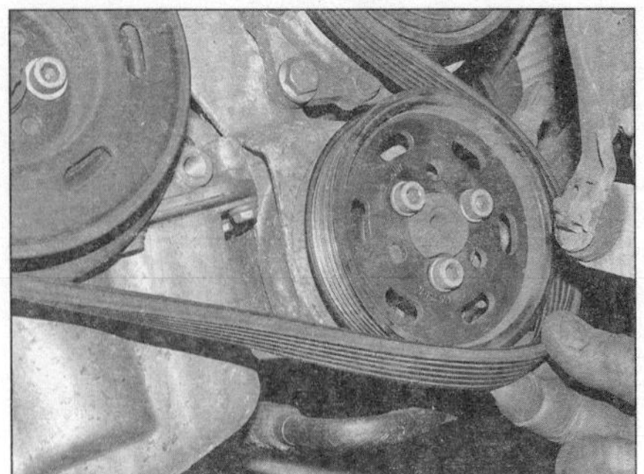

25.6a Remove the belt from around the pulleys

25.6b Auxiliary drivebelt configuration – AMU, APX and BAM engine with air-con shown

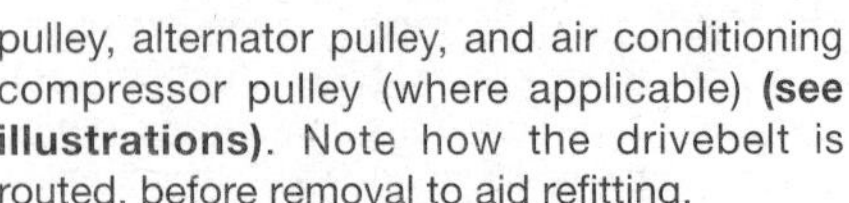

pulley, alternator pulley, and air conditioning compressor pulley (where applicable) **(see illustrations)**. Note how the drivebelt is routed, before removal to aid refitting.

7 When refitting the new drivebelt around the pulleys, make sure that it is located correctly in the multi-grooves in all of the pulleys. When in position, hold the tensioner in position with the spanner and remove the Allen Key. Carefully release the tensioner anti-clockwise so that it takes up the tension on the new belt. Note that depending on model, there may be five or six ribs along the length of the belt, make sure the correct belt is fitted.

8 Refit the trim panel back under the wheel arch and refit the roadwheel, and lower the vehicle to the ground and tighten the wheel bolts to the specified torque setting..

26 Power steering hydraulic fluid level check

1 Turn the front roadwheels to the straight-ahead position without starting the engine. If the vehicle has been left standing for an hour or more, the power steering fluid will be cold (below 50°C), and the 'cold' level markings must be used. If, however, the engine is at normal temperature (above 50°C), the fluid will be hot, so use the 'hot' level markings.

2 The reservoir is located on the right-hand side of the engine compartment, next to the coolant expansion tank. The fluid level is checked with a dipstick attached to the reservoir filler cap. Using a screwdriver, unscrew the cap from the hydraulic fluid reservoir, and wipe clean the integral dipstick with a clean cloth **(see illustration)**.

3 Screw on the cap hand tight then unscrew it again and check the fluid level on the dipstick. If the fluid is cold (below 50°C), it must be in the 'hashed' cold area indicated on the dipstick. If the fluid is hot (above 50°C), it must be between the hot MAX and MIN marks indicated on the dipstick **(see illustration)**.

4 If the level is above the maximum level mark, syphon off the excess amount. If it is below the minimum level mark, add the specified fluid as necessary (see Lubricants and fluids0,6), but in this case also check the system for leaks. On completion, screw on the cap and tighten with the screwdriver.

27 Automatic transmission fluid level check

Note: *An accurate fluid level check can only be made with the transmission fluid at a temperature of between 35 and 45°C, and if it is not possible to ascertain this temperature, it is strongly recommended that the check be made by an Audi dealer who will have the instrumentation to check the temperature and to check the transmission electronics for fault codes. Overfilling or underfilling adversely affects the function of the transmission.*

1 Take the vehicle on a short journey to warm the transmission slightly (see Note at the start of this Section), then park the vehicle on level ground and engage P with the selector lever. Raise the front and rear of the vehicle and support it on axle stands (see *Jacking and vehicle support*), ensuring the vehicle is kept level. Undo the retaining screws and remove the engine undertray to gain access to the base of the transmission unit.

2 Start the engine and run it at idle speed until the transmission fluid temperature reaches 35°C.

3 Unscrew the fluid level plug from the bottom of the transmission sump **(see illustration)**.

4 If fluid continually drips from the level tube as the fluid temperature increases, the fluid level is correct and does not need to be topped-up. Note that there will be some fluid already present in the level tube, and it will be necessary to observe when this amount has drained before making the level check. Make sure that the check is made before the fluid temperature reaches 45°C.

5 If no fluid drips from the level tube, even when the fluid temperature has reached 45°C, it will be necessary to add fluid. Audi technicians use an adapter which screws into the bottom of the transmission sump, however, a tube inserted up through the drain plug (into the space above the fluid), will allow fluid to be added. Ideally, the fluid should be allowed to cool before adding the fluid.

6 Check the condition of the seal on the level plug and renew it if necessary by cutting off the old seal and fitting a new one. Refit the plug and tighten to the specified torque.

7 Refit the engine undertray, tighten the retaining screws securely, and lower the vehicle to the ground.

8 Frequent need for topping-up indicates that there is a leak, which should be corrected as soon as possible.

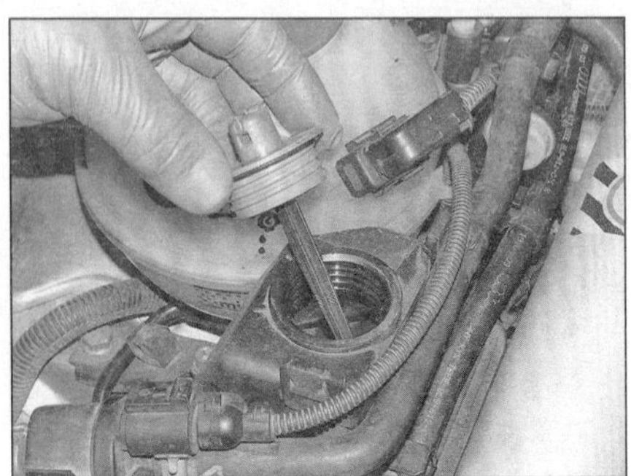

26.2 Unscrew the cap from the hydraulic fluid reservoir, and wipe clean the integral dipstick with a clean cloth

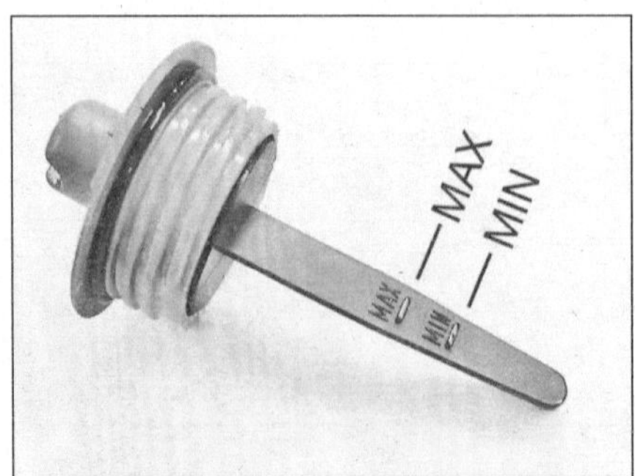

26.3 Screw on the cap hand tight then unscrew it again and check the fluid level on the dipstick

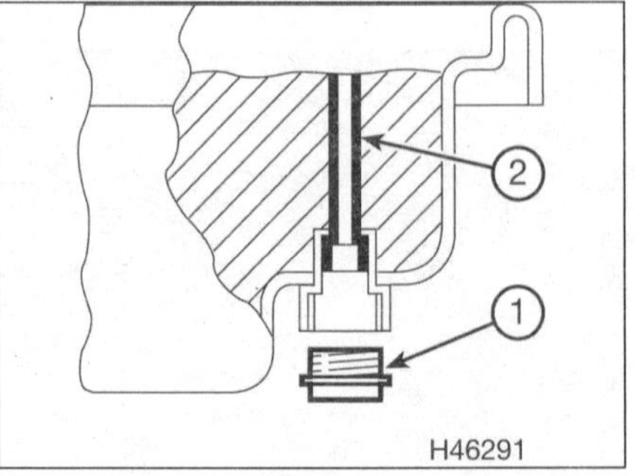

27.3 Automatic transmission fluid level check

(1) Level plug (2) Level tube

28 Timing belt renewal

Note: *Audi specify that the timing belt tensioner roller is also renewed.*

Inspection

1 Release the clips and remove the upper timing belt cover (refer to Chapter 2A Section 6).

2 Using a spanner or socket on the crankshaft pulley bolt, turn the engine slowly in a clockwise direction. Do not turn the engine on the camshaft bolt.

3 Check the complete length of the timing belt for signs of cracking, tooth separation, fraying, side glazing, and oil or grease contamination. Use a torch and mirror to check the underside of the belt.

4 If there is any evidence of wear or damage as described in the last paragraph, the timing belt must be renewed. A broken belt will cause major damage to the engine.

5 After making the check, refit the upper timing belt cover and remove the spanner/socket from the crankshaft pulley bolt.

Renewal

6 Refer to Chapter 2A Section 7, for details.

29 Brake (and clutch) fluid renewal

Warning: Brake hydraulic fluid can harm your eyes and damage painted surfaces, so use extreme caution when handling and pouring it. Do not use fluid that has been standing open for some time, as it absorbs moisture from the air. Excess moisture can cause a dangerous loss of braking effectiveness.

1 The procedure is similar to that for the bleeding of the hydraulic system as described in Chapter 9 Section 2, except that the brake fluid reservoir should be emptied by syphoning, using a clean poultry baster or similar before starting, and allowance should be made for the old fluid to be expelled when bleeding a section of the circuit. Since the clutch hydraulic system also uses fluid from the brake system reservoir, it should also be bled at the same time by referring to Chapter 6 Section 2.

2 Working as described in, open the first bleed screw in the sequence, and pump the brake pedal gently until nearly all the old fluid has been emptied from the master cylinder reservoir.

Old hydraulic fluid is often much darker in colour than the new, making it easy to distinguish the two.

3 Top-up to the MAX level with new fluid, and continue pumping until only the new fluid remains in the reservoir, and new fluid can be seen emerging from the bleed screw. Tighten the screw, and top the reservoir level up to the MAX level line.

4 Work through all the remaining bleed screws in the sequence until new fluid can be seen at all of them. Be careful to keep the master cylinder reservoir topped-up to above the MIN level at all times, or air may enter the system and greatly increase the length of the task.

5 When the operation is complete, check that all bleed screws are securely tightened, and that their dust caps are refitted. Wash off all traces of spilt fluid, and recheck the master cylinder reservoir fluid level.

6 On models with a manual transmission unit, once the brake fluid has been changed the clutch fluid should also be renewed. Referring to Chapter 6 Section 2, bleed the clutch until new fluid is seen to be emerging from the slave cylinder bleed screw, keeping the master cylinder fluid level above the MIN level line at all times to prevent air entering the system. Once the new fluid emerges, securely tighten the bleed screw then disconnect and remove the bleeding equipment. Securely refit the dust cap then wash off all traces of spilt fluid.

7 On all models, ensure the master cylinder fluid level is correct (see *Weekly checks*) and thoroughly check the operation of the brakes and (where necessary) clutch before taking the car on the road.

30 Coolant renewal

Note: *This work is not included in the Audi schedule and should not be required if the recommended G12 LongLife coolant antifreeze/inhibitor is used. However, if standard antifreeze/inhibitor is used, the work should be carried out at the recommended interval.*

Warning: Wait until the engine is cold before starting this procedure. Do not allow antifreeze to come in contact with your skin, or with the painted surfaces of the vehicle. Rinse off spills immediately with plenty of water. Never leave antifreeze lying around in an open container, or in a puddle in the driveway or on the garage floor. Children and pets are attracted by its sweet smell, but antifreeze can be fatal if ingested.

Cooling system draining

1 With the engine completely cold, unscrew the expansion tank cap.

2 Firmly apply the handbrake then jack up the front of the vehicle and support it on axle stands (see *Jacking and vehicle support*). Undo the retaining screws and remove the engine undershield(s) to gain access to the base of the radiator.

3 Position a suitable container beneath the coolant drain outlet **(see illustration)**, which is fitted to the coolant bottom hose end fitting. Loosen the drain plug (there is no need to remove it completely) and allow the coolant to drain into the container. If desired, a length of tubing can be fitted to the drain outlet to direct the flow of coolant during draining. Where no drain outlet is fitted to the hose end fitting, remove the retaining clip and disconnect the bottom hose from the radiator to drain the coolant (see Chapter 3 Section 2).

4 To help fully drain the cooling system also disconnect the lower coolant hose from the oil cooler, which is located at the front of the cylinder block, above the oil filter **(see illustration)**.

5 If the coolant has been drained for a reason other than renewal, then provided it is clean, it can be re-used, though this is not recommended.

6 Once all the coolant has drained, securely tighten the radiator drain plug or reconnect the bottom hose to the radiator (as applicable). Where necessary, also reconnect the coolant hose to the oil cooler and secure it in position with the retaining clip. Refit the undershield(s), tighten the retaining screws securely.

Cooling system flushing

7 If the recommended coolant has not been used and coolant renewal has been neglected, or if the antifreeze mixture has become diluted, the cooling system may gradually lose efficiency, as the coolant passages become

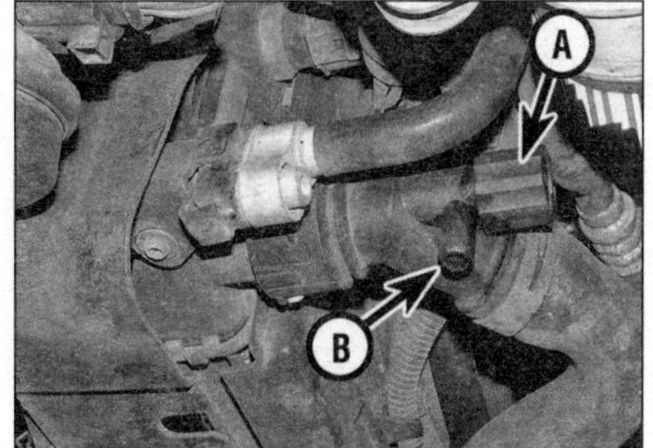

30.3 Drain plug (A) and drain outlet (B)

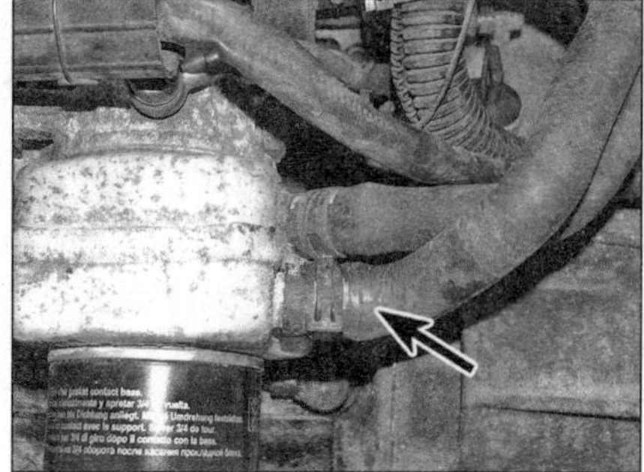

30.4 Disconnect the hose (arrowed) from the oil cooler

restricted due to rust, scale deposits, and other sediment. The cooling system efficiency can be restored by flushing the system clean.

8 The radiator should be flushed separately from the engine, to avoid excess contamination.

Radiator flushing

9 To flush the radiator, first tighten the radiator drain plug.

10 Disconnect the top and bottom hoses and any other relevant hoses from the radiator (see Chapter 3).

11 Insert a garden hose into the radiator top inlet. Direct a flow of clean water through the radiator, and continue flushing until clean water emerges from the radiator bottom outlet.

12 If after a reasonable period, the water still does not run clear, the radiator can be flushed with a good proprietary cleaning agent. It is important that their manufacturer's instructions are followed carefully. If the contamination is particularly bad, insert the hose in the radiator bottom outlet, and reverse-flush the radiator.

Engine flushing

13 To flush the engine, remove the thermostat (see Chapter 3 Section 4).

14 With the bottom hose disconnected from the radiator, insert a garden hose into the coolant housing. Direct a clean flow of water through the engine, and continue flushing until clean water emerges from the radiator bottom hose.

15 When flushing is complete, refit the thermostat and reconnect the hoses (see Chapter 3 Section 4).

Cooling system filling

16 Before attempting to fill the cooling system, ensure the drain plug is securely closed and make sure that all hoses are securely connected and their retaining clips are in good condition. If the recommended Audi/VW coolant is not being used, ensure that a suitable antifreeze mixture is used all year round, to prevent corrosion of the engine components (see following sub-Section).

17 Remove the expansion tank filler cap and slowly fill the system with the coolant. Continue to fill the cooling system until bubbles stop appearing in the expansion tank. Help to bleed the air from the system by repeatedly squeezing the radiator bottom hose.

18 When no more bubbles appear, top the coolant level up to the MAX level mark then securely refit the cap to the expansion tank.

19 Run the engine at a fast idle speed until the cooling fan cuts in. Wait for the fan to stop then switch the engine off and allow the engine to cool.

20 When the engine has cooled, check the coolant level with reference to *Weekly checks*. Top-up the level if necessary, and refit the expansion tank cap.

Antifreeze mixture

21 If the recommended coolant is not being used, the antifreeze should always be renewed at the specified intervals. This is necessary not only to maintain the antifreeze properties, but also to prevent corrosion which would otherwise occur as the corrosion inhibitors become progressively less effective.

22 Always use an ethylene-glycol based antifreeze which is suitable for use in mixed-metal cooling systems. The quantity of antifreeze and levels of protection are indicated in the Specifications.

23 Before adding antifreeze, the cooling system should be completely drained, preferably flushed, and all hoses checked for condition and security.

24 After filling with antifreeze, a label should be attached to the expansion tank, stating the type and concentration of antifreeze used, and the date installed. Any subsequent topping-up should be made with the same type and concentration of antifreeze.

25 Do not use engine antifreeze in the windscreen/tailgate washer system, as it will damage the vehicle paintwork. A screenwash additive should be added to the washer system in the quantities stated on the bottle.

Chapter 2 Part A
Engine in-car repair procedures

Contents

Degrees of difficulty

Easy, suitable for novice with little experience	**Fairly easy,** suitable for beginner with some experience	**Fairly difficult,** suitable for competent DIY mechanic	**Difficult,** suitable for experienced DIY mechanic	**Very difficult,** suitable for expert DIY or professional

Specifications

General

Manufacturer's engine codes*:	
1781 cc	APX, AJQ, APP, ATC, AMU, BAM, ARY, AUQ, AWP, AUM, BVR and BVP
Maximum power output:	
AUM	110 kW/148 bhp @ 5500-6000 rpm
BVP	120 kW/160 bhp @ 5700 rpm
AJQ, APP, ATC, ARY, AUQ and AWP	132 kW/180 bhp @ 5500-6000 rpm
BVR	140 kW/188 bhp @ 5700 rpm
APX, AMU and BAM	165 kW/225 bhp @ 5500-6000 rpm
Maximum torque output:	
AUM	210 Nm @ 1750 to 4600 rpm
BVP	225 Nm @ 1950 to 4700 rpm
AJQ, APP and ATC	235 Nm @ 1950 to 4700 rpm
ARY, AUQ and AWP	235 Nm @ 1950 to 5000 rpm
BVR	240 Nm @ 1980 to 5400 rpm
APX, AMU and BAM	280 Nm @ 2200 to 5500 rpm

* **Note:** *See 'Vehicle identification' at the end of this manual for the location of engine code markings.*

Bore	81.0 mm
Stroke	86.4 mm
Compression ratio:	
AJQ, APP, ARY, ATC, AUM, AUQ, AWP, BVP and BVR engine codes	9.5 : 1
AMU, APX and BAM engine codes	9.0 : 1
Compression pressures:	
Minimum compression pressure	Approximately 7.0 bar
Maximum difference between cylinders	Approximately 3.0 bar
Firing order	1 – 3 – 4 – 2
No 1 cylinder location	Timing belt end

Camshafts

Camshaft endfloat (maximum)	0.20 mm
Camshaft bearing running clearance (maximum)	0.10 mm
Camshaft run-out (maximum)	0.01 mm

Lubrication system

Oil pump type	Gear type, chain-driven from crankshaft
Oil pressure (oil temperature 80°C):	
At idling	2.0 bar
At 2000 rpm:	3.0 to 4.5 bar

Torque wrench settings

	Nm	lbf ft
Ancillary (alternator, etc) bracket mounting bolts:	45	33
Auxiliary drivebelt tensioning pulley bolts:	25	18
Big-end bearing caps bolt/nuts*:		
Stage 1	30	22
Stage 2	Angle-tighten a further 90°	
Camshaft bearing cap bolts	10	7
Camshaft cover nuts	10	7
Camshaft exhaust sprocket bolt	65	48
Camshaft timing chain tensioner/camshaft adjuster mechanism bolts	10	7
Coolant pump bolts	15	11
Crankcase breather/oil separator bolts	10	7
Crankshaft left-hand oil seal housing bolts	15	11
Crankshaft right-hand oil seal housing bolts	15	11
Crankshaft pulley bolts	25	18
Crankshaft speed/position sensor wheel-to-crankshaft bolts*:		
Stage 1	10	7
Stage 2	Angle-tighten a further 90°	
Crankshaft sprocket bolt*:		
Stage 1	90	66
Stage 2	Angle-tighten a further 90°	
Cylinder head bolts*:		
Stage 1	40	30
Stage 2	Angle-tighten a further 90°	
Stage 3	Angle-tighten a further 90°	
Engine-to-automatic transmission bolts:		
M12 bolts	80	59
M10 cylinder block-to-transmission bolts	60	44
M10 sump-to-transmission bolts	25	18
Engine-to-manual transmission bolts:		
Cylinder block-to-transmission (M12 bolts)	80	59
Alloy sump-to-transmission bolts (M10 bolts):		
02J transmission	45	33
02M transmission	40	30
Engine-to-manual transmission cover plate bolts	10	7
Engine mountings:		
Left-hand mounting-to-body bolts:		
Large bolts*:		
Stage 1	40	30
Stage 2	Angle-tighten a further 90°	
Small bolts	25	18
Left-hand mounting-to-engine bracket bolts	100	74
Right-hand mounting-to-body bolts*:		
Stage 1	40	30
Stage 2	Angle-tighten a further 90°	
Right-hand mounting plate bolts (small bolts)	25	18
Right-hand mounting-to-engine bracket bolts	100	74
Right-hand mounting bracket-to-engine bolts	45	33
Rear engine/transmission mounting:		
Bracket-to-subframe bolts*:		
Stage 1	20	15
Stage 2	Angle-tighten a further 90°	
Bracket-to-transmission bolts*:		
Stage 1	40	30
Stage 2	Angle-tighten a further 90°	
Exhaust camshaft timing belt sprocket bolt	65	48
Exhaust manifold nuts	25	18
Exhaust pipe-to-manifold nuts	40	30

Torque wrench settings (continued)

	Nm	lbf ft
Inlet camshaft adjuster valve bolts	3	2
Inlet camshaft position sensor bolts	10	7
Inlet camshaft position sensor rotor bolt	25	18
Main bearing cap bolts:		
Stage 1	65	48
Stage 2	Angle-tighten a further 90°	
Oil cooler securing nut	25	18
Oil drain plug	30	22
Oil filter housing-to-cylinder block bolts*:		
Stage 1	15	11
Stage 2	Angle-tighten a further 90°	
Oil level/temperature sender-to-sump bolts	10	7
Oil pressure relief valve plug	40	30
Oil pressure warning light switch	25	18
Oil pump chain tensioner bolt	15	11
Oil pump securing bolts	15	11
Piston oil spray jet/oil pressure relief valve bolt	27	20
Sump-to-cylinder block bolts	15	11
Sump baffle plate bolts	15	11
Thermostat cover bolts	15	11
Timing belt idler pulley bolt	20	15
Timing belt outer cover bolts	10	7
Timing belt tensioner:		
Tensioner roller securing bolt	27	20
Timing belt tensioner housing bolts:		
Small bolt	15	11
Large bolt	20	15
Turbocharger oil supply pipe-to-oil filter housing banjo bolt	30	22

* **Note:** *Use new bolts*

1 General Information

Using this Chapter

1 Chapter 2 is divided into two Parts; A and B. Repair operations that can be carried out with the engine in the vehicle are described in Part A. Part B covers the removal of the engine/transmission as a unit, and describes the engine dismantling and overhaul procedures.

2 In Part A, the assumption is made that the engine is installed in the vehicle, with all ancillaries connected. If the engine has been removed for overhaul, the preliminary dismantling information that precedes each operation may be ignored.

Engine description

3 Throughout this Chapter, engines are identified and referred to, where necessary, by the manufacturer's code letters. A listing of all engine codes covered, are given in the Specifications at the beginning of this Chapter.

4 The engines are water-cooled, double overhead camshaft, in-line four-cylinder units with cast-iron cylinder blocks and aluminium-alloy cylinder heads. The engine is mounted transversely at the front of the vehicle, with the transmission bolted to the left-hand end of the engine.

5 The crankshaft is of five-bearing type, and thrustwashers are fitted to the centre main bearing to control crankshaft endfloat.

6 The exhaust camshaft is driven via a toothed timing belt from the crankshaft sprocket, and the inlet camshaft is driven from the left-hand end of the exhaust camshaft via a chain.

7 These engines, have variable inlet valve timing, and the valve timing is varied by altering the tension on the drive chain using an electronically-actuated mechanical tensioner.

8 The valves are closed by coil springs, and run in guides pressed into the cylinder head. The camshafts are located inside the cylinder head and actuate the valves directly via hydraulic tappets. There are five valves per cylinder; three inlet valves and two exhaust valves.

9 The gear-type oil pump is driven via a chain from a sprocket on the crankshaft. Oil is drawn from the sump through a strainer, and then forced through an externally-mounted, renewable filter. From there, it is distributed to the cylinder head, where it lubricates the camshaft journals and hydraulic tappets, and also to the crankcase, where it lubricates the main bearings, connecting rod big-ends, gudgeon pins and cylinder bores. A coolant-fed oil cooler is fitted to most engines.

10 On all engines, engine coolant is circulated by a pump, driven by the timing belt. For details of the cooling system, refer to Chapter 3.

Operations with engine in car

11 The following operations can be performed without removing the engine:

a) Compression pressure – testing.
b) Camshaft cover – removal and refitting.
c) Crankshaft pulley – removal and refitting.
d) Timing belt covers – removal and refitting.
e) Timing belt – removal, refitting and adjustment.
f) Timing belt tensioner and sprockets – removal and refitting.
g) Inlet camshaft timing chain, sprockets and adjuster mechanism – removal and refitting.
h) Inlet camshaft adjuster mechanism – removal and refitting.
i) Camshaft oil seal(s) – renewal.
j) Camshaft(s) and hydraulic tappets – removal, inspection and refitting.
k) Cylinder head – removal and refitting.
l) Cylinder head and pistons – decarbonising.
m) Sump – removal and refitting.
n) Oil pump – removal, overhaul and refitting.
o) Crankshaft oil seals – renewal.
p) Engine/transmission mountings – inspection and renewal.
q) Flywheel – removal, inspection and refitting.

Note: *It is possible to remove the pistons and connecting rods (after removing the cylinder head and sump) without removing the engine. However, this is not recommended. Work of this nature is more easily and thoroughly completed with the engine on the bench, as described in Chapter 2B.*

2 Compression test – description and interpretation

Note: *A suitable compression tester will be required for this test.*

1 When engine performance is down, or if misfiring occurs which cannot be attributed to the ignition or fuel systems, a compression test can provide diagnostic clues as to the engine's condition. If the test is performed regularly, it can give warning of trouble before any other symptoms become apparent.

2 The engine must be fully warmed-up to normal operating temperature, the battery must be fully-charged and the spark plugs must be removed. The aid of an assistant will be required.

3 Disconnect the wiring connectors, remove the ignition coils and remove the spark plugs, with reference to Chapter 1 Section 31.

4 Fit a compression tester to the No 1 cylinder spark plug hole. The type of tester that screws into the plug thread is preferred.

5 Have the assistant hold the throttle wide open and crank the engine for several seconds on the starter motor. **Note:** *These models are fitted with a throttle position sensor instead of a cable, the throttle will not operate until the ignition is switched on.* After one or two revolutions, the compression pressure should build-up to a maximum figure and then stabilise. Record the highest reading obtained.

6 Repeat the test on the remaining cylinders, recording the pressure in each.

7 All cylinders should produce very similar pressures. Any difference greater than that specified indicates the existence of a fault. Note that the compression should build-up quickly in a healthy engine. Low compression on the first stroke, followed by gradually increasing pressure on successive strokes, indicates worn piston rings. A low compression reading on the first stroke, which does not build-up during successive strokes, indicates leaking valves or a blown head gasket (a cracked head could also be the cause). Deposits on the undersides of the valve heads can also cause low compression.

8 If the pressure in any cylinder is reduced to the specified minimum or less, carry out the following test to isolate the cause. Introduce a teaspoonful of clean oil into that cylinder through its spark plug hole and repeat the test.

9 If the addition of oil temporarily improves the compression pressure, this indicates that bore or piston wear is responsible for the pressure loss. No improvement suggests that leaking or burnt valves, or a blown head gasket, may be to blame.

10 A low reading from two adjacent cylinders is almost certainly due to the head gasket having blown between them and the presence of coolant in the engine oil will confirm this.

11 If one cylinder is about 20 percent lower than the others and the engine has a slightly rough idle, a worn camshaft lobe could be the cause.

12 If the compression reading is unusually high, the combustion chambers are probably coated with carbon deposits. If this is the case, the cylinder head should be removed and decarbonised.

13 On completion of the test, refit the spark plugs, with reference to Chapter 1 Section 31.

3 Engine assembly and valve timing marks – general information and usage

General information

1 TDC is the highest point in the cylinder that each piston reaches as it travels up-and-down when the crankshaft turns. Each piston reaches TDC at the end of the compression stroke and again at the end of the exhaust stroke, but TDC generally refers to piston position on the compression stroke. No 1 piston is at the timing belt end of the engine.

2 Positioning No 1 piston at TDC is an essential part of many procedures, such as timing belt removal and camshaft removal.

3 The design of the engines covered in this Chapter is such that piston-to-valve contact may occur if the camshaft or crankshaft is turned with the timing belt removed. For this reason, it is important to ensure that the camshaft and crankshaft do not move in relation to each other once the timing belt has been removed from the engine.

4 The crankshaft pulley has a marking which, when aligned with a corresponding reference marking on the timing belt cover, indicates that No 1 piston (and hence also No 4 piston) is at TDC. Note that on some models, the crankshaft pulley timing mark is located on the outer flange of the pulley **(see illustration)**.

5 The exhaust camshaft sprocket is equipped with a timing mark. When this mark is aligned with a mark on the camshaft cover, No 1 piston is at TDC on the compression stroke **(see illustration)**.

6 Additionally, on some models (depending on transmission), the flywheel/driveplate has a TDC marking, which can be observed by removing a protective plastic plug from the front of the transmission bell-housing **(see illustrations)**. Note that it is not possible to use these marks on all models due to the limited access available to view the marks.

Setting No 1 cylinder to TDC

7 Before starting work, make sure that the ignition is switched off (ideally, the battery negative lead should be disconnected – see *Disconnecting the battery*).

8 To make the engine easier to turn, remove all of the spark plugs as described in Chapter 1 Section 31.

9 Apply the handbrake, then jack up the front of the vehicle and support on axle stands

3.4 Crankshaft pulley timing mark aligned with TDC mark on timing belt cover

3.5 Camshaft sprocket timing mark (arrowed) aligned with mark on camshaft cover (No 1 piston at TDC)

3.6a Remove the plastic plug (arrowed)...

3.6b...to view the timing marks (arrowed)

3.9 Remove cover from over crankshaft pulley

4.2 Remove mounting bracket (arrowed)

4.3a Wiring heat shield/cover (arrowed) – where applicable

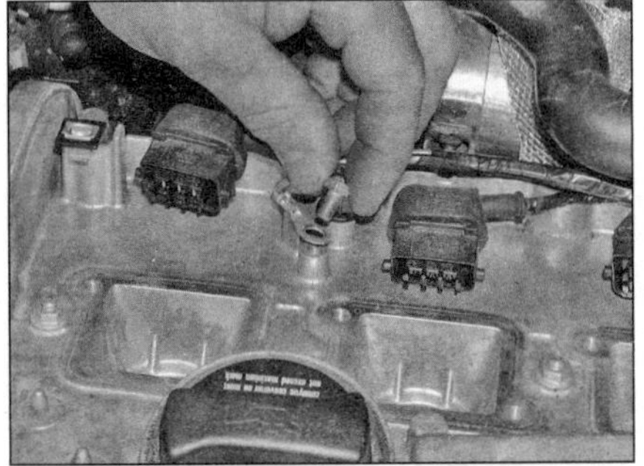
4.3b Unbolt the coil earth wiring lead ...

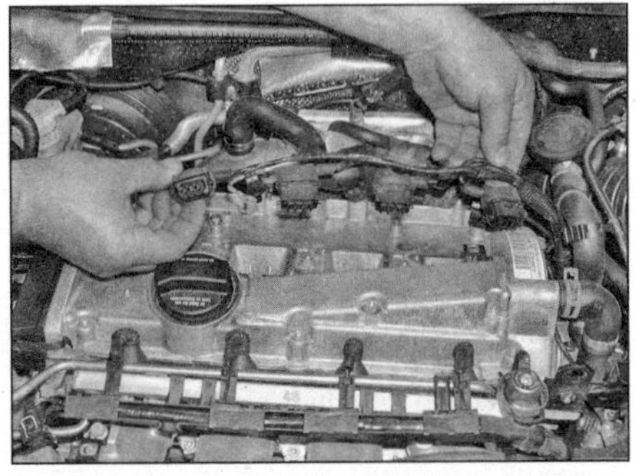
4.3c ... then release the coil wiring from the clips on the camshaft cover

4.4 Camshaft sensor wiring connector (arrowed)

(see *Jacking and vehicle support*). Remove the right-hand front roadwheel, then remove the securing screws and/or clips, and remove the appropriate engine undershields to enable access to the crankshaft pulley **(see illustration)**.

Note: *It may be necessary to use a small engineer's mirror to view the timing marks from under the wheel arch.*

10 Remove the upper timing belt cover as described in Section 6.

11 Turn the engine clockwise, using a spanner on the crankshaft sprocket bolt, until the TDC mark on the crankshaft pulley or flywheel/driveplate is aligned with the corresponding mark on the timing belt cover or transmission casing, and the mark on the exhaust camshaft sprocket is aligned with the corresponding mark on the camshaft cover **(see illustrations 3.4 and 3.5)**.

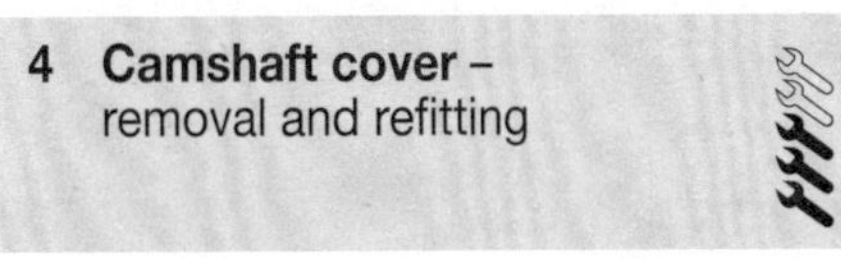

4 Camshaft cover – removal and refitting

Note: *Suitable sealant (D 454 300 A2 or equivalent) will be required on refitting.*

Removal

1 Remove the ignition coils as described in Chapter 5B Section 3.

2 On models with engine codes AMU, APX and BAM, remove the charge air pipe from around the right-hand side of the engine as described in Chapter 4B Section 7. Also remove the charge air pipe mounting bracket **(see illustration)**, from the rear of the camshaft cover.

3 Unbolt the coil wiring earth lead from the top of the camshaft cover, then release the coil wiring from the clips on the camshaft cover, and move the wiring clear of the camshaft cover **(see illustrations)**. **Note:** *on models with engine codes AMU, APX and BAM it will be necessary to undo the four retaining screws and remove the heat shield/cover from around the wiring loom.*

4 Disconnect the wiring connector from the camshaft sensor at the front edge of the timing belt cover **(see illustration)**.

5 Release the clips securing the upper timing belt cover to the camshaft cover **(see illustration)**.

6 Where applicable, unscrew the bolt securing the metal pipe to the rear left-hand corner of the camshaft cover **(see illustration)**.

7 On all models (except engine codes AMU, APX and BAM), release the three clips, and remove the plastic cover from the front of the engine, above the inlet manifold **(see illustration)**.

4.5 Release the clips securing the upper timing belt cover to the camshaft cover

4.6 Unscrew the bolt (arrowed)

4.7 Remove the plastic cover from the front of the engine

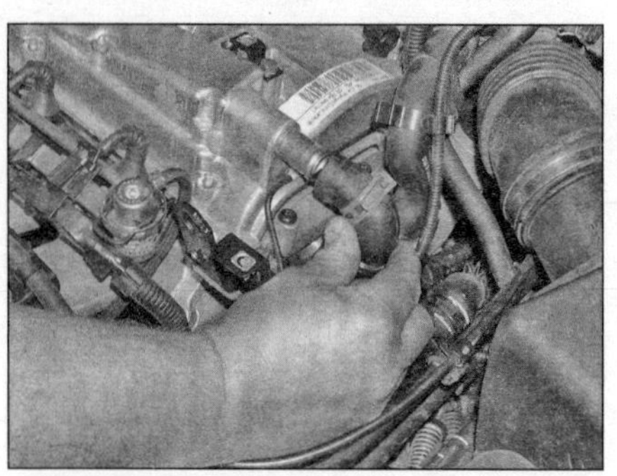

4.8 Disconnect the breather hose from camshaft cover

8 Slacken the hose clip and disconnect the breather hose from the left-hand end of the camshaft cover **(see illustration)**.

9 Make a final check to ensure that all relevant pipes, hoses and wires have been disconnected and moved clear of the working area.

10 Unscrew the securing nuts, and carefully lift the camshaft cover from the cylinder head. Note the locations of any brackets or spacers under the securing nuts. Recover the gaskets, noting that a separate gasket is used to seal the spark plug holes in the centre of the cover.

Refitting

11 Inspect the camshaft cover gaskets, and renew if worn or damaged.

12 Thoroughly clean the mating surfaces of the camshaft cover and the cylinder head, then (if removed) lay the oil deflectors back in position over the camshaft bearing caps.

13 Working at the timing belt end of the cylinder head, apply sealant (D 454 300 A2 or equivalent) to the four points where the combined camshaft bearing cap contacts the edge of the cylinder head **(see illustration)**.

14 Similarly, working at the transmission end of the cylinder head, apply sealant to the four points where the camshaft drive chain tensioner/camshaft adjustment mechanism contacts the edge of the cylinder head **(see illustration)**.

15 Carefully fit the camshaft cover gaskets to the cylinder head, then carefully slide the camshaft cover over the studs on the cylinder head. If removed, place any spacer(s) and/or bracket(s) in position, then refit the securing nuts. Tighten the nuts starting from the inner ones, and then in a diagonal sequence working outwards. Tighten to the specified torque.

16 Refit the ignition coils with reference to Chapter 5B Section 3.

17 On models with engine codes AMU, APX and BAM, refit the charge air pipe, with reference to Chapter 4B Section 7

18 Further refitting is a reversal of removal.

5 Crankshaft pulley – removal and refitting

Removal

1 Disconnect the battery negative lead. **Note:** *Before disconnecting the battery, refer to* Disconnecting the battery *at the rear of this manual.*

2 For improved access, jack up the front of the vehicle, and support securely on axle stands (see *Jacking and vehicle support*). Remove the right-hand front roadwheel.

3 Remove the securing screws and/or release the clips, and withdraw the relevant engine undershield(s) to enable access to the crankshaft pulley.

4 On all models (except engine codes AMU, APX and BAM), it will be necessary to remove the charge air duct-to-intercooler

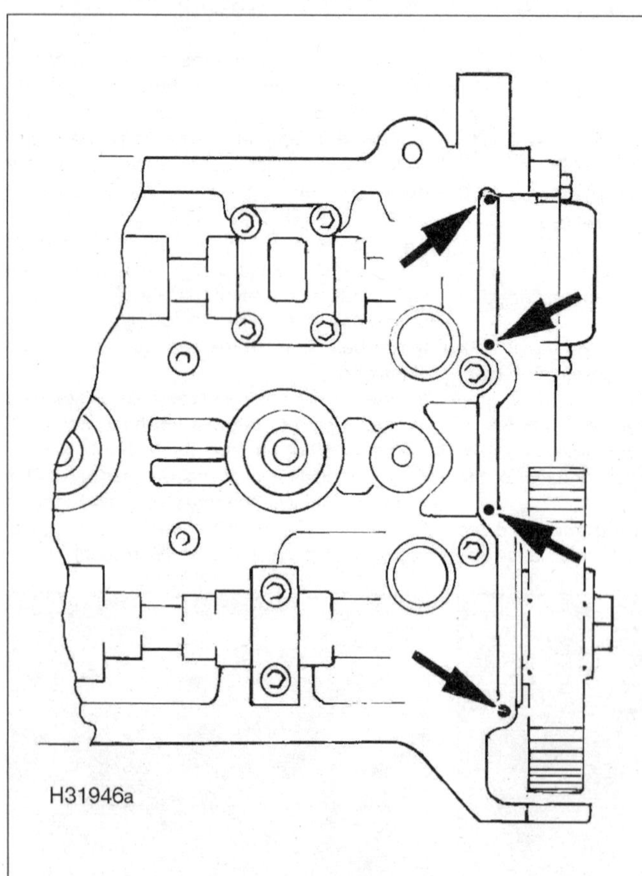

4.13 Apply sealant to the points shown (arrowed) where the combined bearing cap contacts the cylinder head

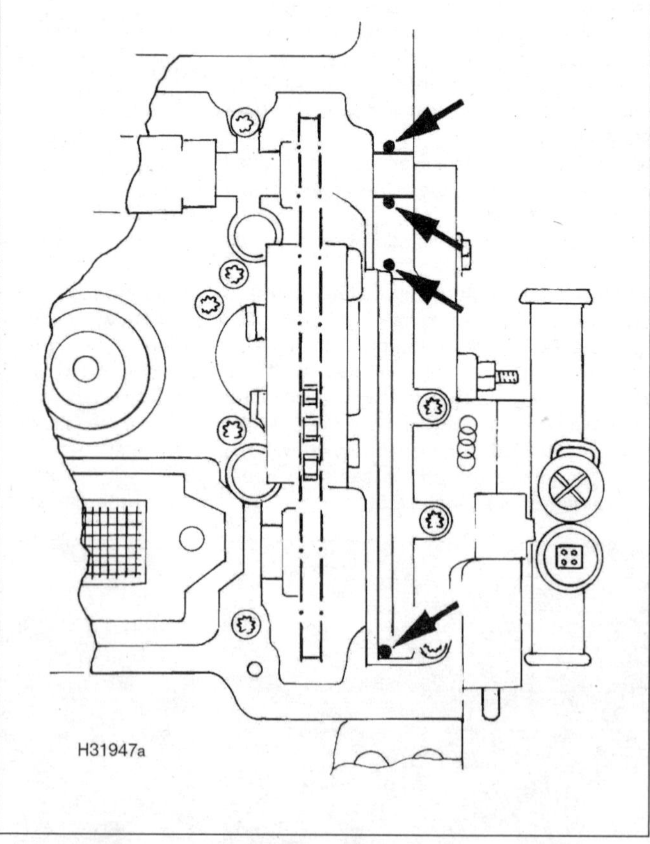

4.14 Apply sealant to the points shown (arrowed) where the camshaft drive chain tensioner/camshaft adjustment mechanism contacts the cylinder head

5.4 Remove charge air pipe/duct (arrowed)

5.6 Slacken crankshaft pulley bolts (arrowed)

5.9 Alignment holes in the pulley (arrowed)

pipe to access the crankshaft pulley **(see illustration)**. If required, refer to Chapter 4B Section 7, for information on the removal and refitting procedure.

5 If necessary (for any later work to be carried out), turn the crankshaft using a socket or spanner on the crankshaft sprocket bolt until the relevant timing marks align (see Section 3).

6 Slacken the bolts securing the crankshaft pulley **(see illustration)**, using an Allen key or a hexagon bit. If necessary, the pulley can be prevented from turning by counter-holding with a spanner or socket on the centre crankshaft sprocket bolt.

7 Remove the auxiliary drivebelt, as described in Chapter 1 Section 32.

8 The bolts can now be fully removed, and the crankshaft pulley withdrawn from the end of the crankshaft.

Refitting

9 Refit the pulley to the end of the crankshaft, and refit the securing bolts. Note the locating lugs align with the holes in the pulley **(see illustration)**, so can only be fitted in one position.

10 Refit and tension the auxiliary drivebelt as described in Chapter 1 Section 32.

11 Prevent the crankshaft from turning as during removal, then tighten the pulley securing bolts to the specified torque.

12 Where applicable, refit the charge air-to-intercooler air pipe/duct, and then refit the engine undershield(s).

13 Refit the roadwheel, lower the vehicle to the ground, and reconnect the battery negative lead. Tighten the roadwheel bolts to the specified torque.

6 Timing belt covers – removal and refitting

Upper cover

1 On models with engine codes AMU, APX and BAM, remove the charge air pipe from around the top, right-hand side of the engine, as described in Chapter 4B Section 7.

2 Release the fasteners, and remove the plastic trim covers from the top of the engine and the coolant reservoir.

3 Release the two securing clips, and manipulate the timing belt cover from the engine **(see illustrations)**.

4 Refitting is a reversal of removal. Making sure that the lower part of the cover engages correctly with the centre cover **(see illustration)**, and the securing clips are securely engaged.

Centre cover

5 Remove the upper timing belt cover as described previously in this Section.

6 Remove the auxiliary drivebelt as described in Chapter 1 Section 32.

7 Unscrew the three securing bolts, and withdraw the centre cover downwards from the engine **(see illustration)**. Note that the lower two securing bolts also secure the lower timing belt cover.

8 Refitting is a reversal of removal.

Lower cover

9 Remove the crankshaft pulley as described in Section 5.

10 If the centre timing belt cover has not been removed, unscrew the two lower bolts from the centre cover **(see illustration 6.7)**, as these also secure the top of the lower cover.

11 Unscrew the two lower timing belt cover lower securing bolts, and withdraw

6.3a Release the securing clips (arrowed)...

6.3b ... and remove the upper timing belt cover

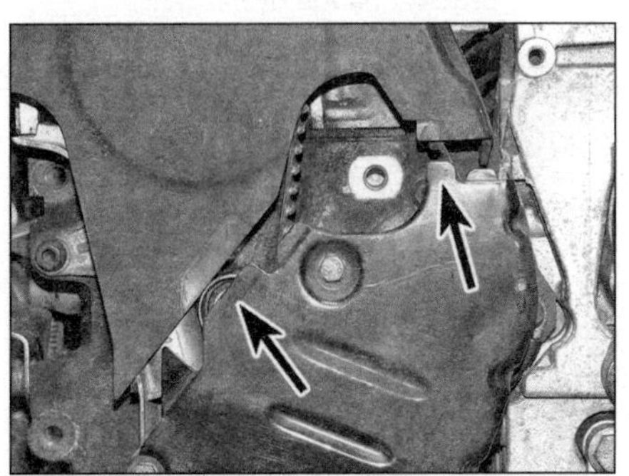
6.4 Align the upper cover with the lower cover (arrowed)

6.7 Centre timing belt cover securing bolts (arrowed) viewed with right-hand engine mounting removed

6.11a Unscrew the lower securing bolts (arrowed) ...

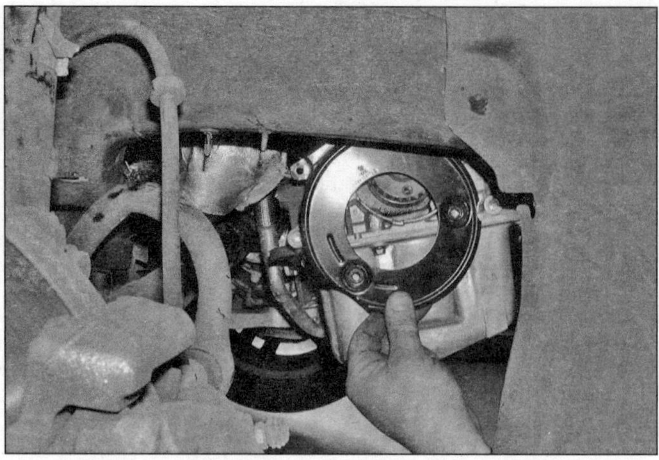
6.11b ... and withdraw the lower timing belt cover

the cover downwards from the engine **(see illustrations)**.

12 Refitting is a reversal of removal, but refit the crankshaft pulley with reference to Section 5.

7 Timing belt – removal and refitting

Note: *An M5 bolt (length of approximately 55 mm) or threaded rod with nut and washer, will be required to depress the timing belt tensioner piston during this procedure.*

Removal

1 The exhaust camshaft is driven via a toothed belt from the crankshaft sprocket, and the inlet camshaft is driven from the left-hand end of the exhaust camshaft via a chain. Refer to Section 9 for details of inlet camshaft timing chain removal, inspection and refitting.

2 Disconnect the battery negative lead. **Note:** *Before disconnecting the battery, refer to* Disconnecting the battery *at the rear of this manual.*

3 For improved access, raise the front right-hand side of the vehicle, and support securely on axle stands (see *Jacking and vehicle support*). Remove the roadwheel.

4 Remove the securing screws and withdraw the front engine undershield.

5 On all models (except engine codes AMU, APX and BAM), it will be necessary to remove the charge air duct-to-intercooler pipe to access the crankshaft pulley **(see illustration 5.5)**. If required, refer to Chapter 4B Section 7, for information on the removal and refitting procedure.

6 Remove the auxiliary drivebelt as described in Chapter 1 Section 32.

Note: *Some of the illustrations in this section where taken with the engine out of the vehicle to give better clarity.*

7 Unscrew the three securing bolts, and remove the auxiliary drivebelt tensioner **(see illustrations)**. Note that the top two securing bolts may also secure a wiring/pipe support bracket.

8 Turn the crankshaft to position No 1 piston at TDC on the firing stroke, as described in Section 3.

9 Unscrew the securing screw, and move the power steering fluid reservoir clear of the working area, leaving the fluid hoses connected **(see illustrations)**. Unclip any hoses from the side of the reservoir to allow the reservoir to be moved.

10 Similarly, unscrew the two securing screws, and move the coolant expansion tank clear of the working area **(see illustration)**.

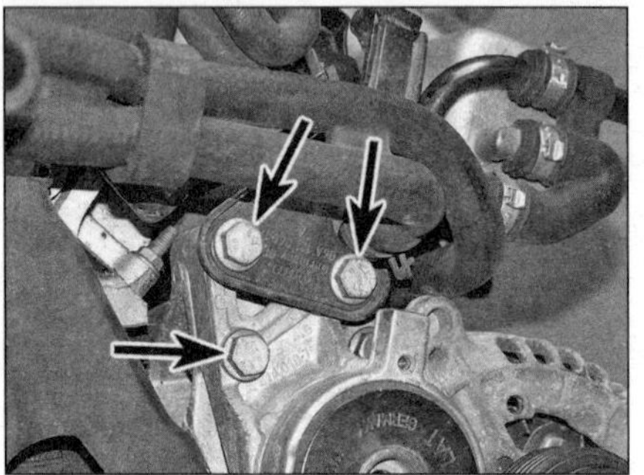
7.7a Undo the three mounting bolts (arrowed)...

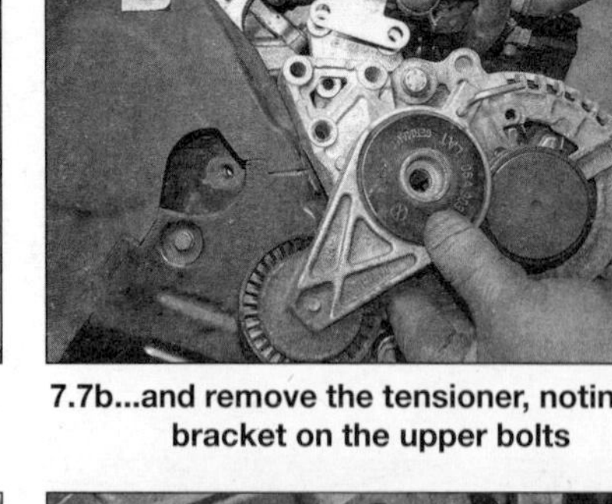
7.7b...and remove the tensioner, noting the bracket on the upper bolts

7.9a Undo the securing screw (arrowed)...

7.9b...and remove the reservoir clear of the working area

7.10 Undo the securing screws (arrowed)

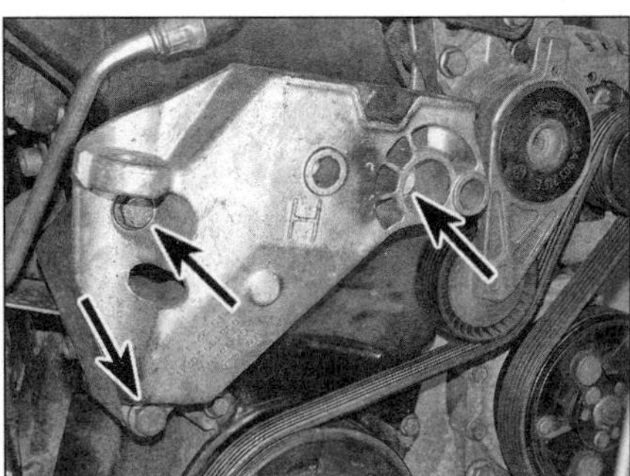
7.13 Mounting bracket bolts (arrowed)

7.17 Screw an M5 threaded bolt into the timing belt tensioner (arrowed)

Unclip any hoses from the side of the reservoir to allow the reservoir to be moved.

11 Attach a hoist and lifting tackle to the right-hand (timing belt end) engine lifting bracket, and raise the hoist to just take the weight of the engine.

12 Remove the complete right-hand engine mounting assembly, as described in Section 17.

13 Unscrew the three securing bolts, and remove the right-hand engine mounting bracket from the engine. One bolt is accessible from above the engine, and two from below. It may be necessary to raise or lower the engine slightly, using the hoist, to enable the bracket to be manipulated out of position from below the vehicle **(see illustration)**.

14 Remove the crankshaft pulley as described in Section 5.

15 Remove the centre and lower timing belt covers, with reference to Section 6 if necessary.

16 If for any reason the original timing belt is to be refitted, mark the running direction to ensure correct refitting. **Note:** *we would advise that a new timing belt should always be used on refitting.*

17 Screw an M5 bolt (length of approximately 55 mm) or threaded rod and nut into the threaded hole in the timing belt tensioner. Fit a large washer/nut to the bolt/rod **(see illustration)**.

18 The next stage in the procedure is to lock the tensioner piston in position, using a piece of wire, or a twist drill. If necessary, turn the tensioner piston using pointed pliers or a length of wire, until the hole in the piston aligns with the hole in the housing **(see illustration)**.

19 Turn the bolt (or nut on the threaded rod) to depress the tensioner piston, until the piston can be locked in position using a metal pin/rod inserted through the hole in the housing **(see illustration)**.

20 With the tension on the belt released, slide the timing belt from the sprockets, and remove it from the engine.

21 If desired, as a safety precaution, turn the crankshaft a quarter-turn (90°) anti-clockwise to position Nos 1 and 4 pistons slightly down their bores from the TDC position. This will eliminate any risk of piston-to-valve contact if a camshaft is turned whilst the timing belt is removed.

Refitting

22 Check that the timing marks on the camshaft sprocket and camshaft cover are still aligned, as described in Section 3.

23 If the crankshaft has been turned anti-clockwise to avoid piston-to-valve contact, turn the crankshaft clockwise back to the TDC position. If desired, the lower timing belt cover and the crankshaft pulley can be temporarily refitted to check that the timing mark on the pulley aligns with the mark on the cover – once the timing marks are aligned, remove the crankshaft pulley and the lower timing belt cover.

24 Engage the timing belt with the crankshaft sprocket, observing the running direction markings if the original belt is being refitted. **Note:** *we would advise that a new timing belt should always be used on refitting.*

25 Ensure that the timing belt is securely engaged with the crankshaft sprocket, then fit the belt around the coolant pump, tensioner roller and camshaft sprocket.

26 Pull out the metal pin/rod used to lock the tensioner piston in position, and unscrew the M5 bolt (nut and threaded rod) from the timing belt tensioner. This will allow the tensioner to automatically tension the belt. Always remove the locking pin/rod from the piston before unscrewing the M5 bolt from the tensioner arm.

27 Turn the crankshaft clockwise through two complete revolutions, and check that the crankshaft and camshaft timing markings are still aligned as described in Section 3. If the marks do not align, the timing belt has been incorrectly fitted (again, temporarily refit the lower timing belt cover and the crankshaft pulley to view the marks).

28 Fit the lower timing belt cover, and tighten the securing bolts.

29 Refit the centre timing belt cover, and tighten the securing bolts.

30 Refit the crankshaft pulley, and tighten the securing bolts to the specified torque.

31 Refit the right-hand engine mounting bracket, noting that the two lower securing bolts must be in position in the bracket as it is fitted, then tighten the bolts to the specified torque. If necessary, raise or lower the engine slightly, using the hoist, to enable the bracket to be manipulated into position.

32 Refit the right-hand engine mounting assembly, as described in Section 17.

33 Disconnect the hoist and lifting tackle from the engine.

34 Refit the upper timing belt cover.

35 Refit the auxiliary drivebelt tensioner, then refit the auxiliary drivebelt, with reference to Chapter 1 Section 32.

36 Refit the power steering fluid reservoir and the coolant expansion tank, ensuring that the fixings are secure. Secure any hoses/cables back in their retaining clips.

37 Refit the engine undershields and, where applicable, refit the charge air-to-intercooler air pipe/duct.

38 Refit the roadwheel, and lower the vehicle to the ground.

7.18 Align the holes (arrowed)

7.19 lock in position using a metal pin (arrowed)

8 Timing belt tensioner and sprockets – removal and refitting

Timing belt tensioner

1 Remove the timing belt as described in Section 7.

2 With the locking pin/rod still left in position in the tensioner piston, remove the M5 bolt (nut and threaded rod) from the tensioner roller arm. Unscrew the securing bolt, and remove the tensioner roller from the cylinder head **(see illustrations)**. Recover the washer that fits between the tensioner roller and the cylinder head.

3 To remove the tensioner piston assembly from the cylinder block, first undo the retaining bolt and remove the idler roller, then undo the two retaining bolts and remove the tensioner piston assembly from the cylinder block **(see illustrations)**. Do not remove the locking pin/rod.

4 Refitting is a reversal of removal, but ensure that the washer is in place between the tensioner roller and the cylinder head **(see illustration 8.2b)**. Refit the M5 bolt (nut and threaded rod) to the tensioner arm and take up the slack to the tensioner piston before the locking pin/rod is removed. Refit the timing belt as described in Section 7.

Crankshaft sprocket

Note: *A new crankshaft sprocket bolt must be used on refitting.*

5 For improved access, jack up the front of the vehicle, and support securely on axle stands (see *Jacking and vehicle support*). Remove the right-hand front roadwheel, and the inner trim panel for access to the crankshaft pulley.

6 The centre sprocket securing bolt must now be slackened, and the crankshaft must be prevented from turning as the sprocket centre bolt is slackened. To hold the pulley/sprocket, make up a suitable tool to counterhold the pulley **(see illustration)**. Take care, as the bolt is very tight. Only slacken the centre sprocket securing bolt at this time.

7 Remove the timing belt as described in Section 7.

8 The sprocket centre securing bolt can now be completely removed, unscrew the bolt, and slide the sprocket from the end of the crankshaft, noting its orientation.

9 Commence refitting by positioning the sprocket on the end of the crankshaft, with the raised boss outermost **(see illustration)**.

10 Fit a new sprocket securing bolt, then counterhold the sprocket using the method employed on removal, and tighten the bolt to the specified torque in the two stages given in the Specifications.

11 Refit the timing belt as described in Section 7.

8.2a Remove the retaining bolt (arrowed)...

8.2b...then removing the timing belt tensioner and washer

8.3a Remove the idler roller...

8.3b...and remove the tensioner piston assembly

Exhaust camshaft sprocket

12 Remove the timing belt as described in Section 7. Ensure that the crankshaft has been turned a quarter-turn (90°) anti-clockwise to position Nos 1 and 4 pistons slightly down their bores from the TDC position. This will eliminate any risk of piston-to-valve contact if a camshaft is turned whilst the timing belt is removed.

13 The camshaft sprocket bolt must now be slackened, and the camshaft must be prevented from turning as the sprocket bolt is unscrewed. Make up a tool and use it to hold the sprocket stationary by means of the holes in the sprocket **(see illustration 8.6)**.

14 Unscrew the camshaft sprocket bolt and withdraw the sprocket from the front of the camshaft, noting which way round it is fitted. Where applicable, recover the Woodruff key from the end of the camshaft.

15 Commence refitting by refitting the Woodruff key to the end of the camshaft (where applicable), then offer the sprocket up to the camshaft, ensuring that it is fitted the correct way round **(see illustration 8.13)**.

16 Refit the sprocket bolt, then counterhold the sprocket using the tool employed on removal, and tighten the bolt to the specified torque.

17 Refit the timing belt as described in Section 7.

Coolant pump sprocket

18 The coolant pump sprocket is integral with the coolant pump. Refer to Chapter 3 Section 7 for details of coolant pump removal.

Idler pulley

19 Remove the timing belt as described in Section 7.

8.6 Using tool to prevent the crankshaft pulley from turning

8.9 Crankshaft sprocket fitted position

8.13 Exhaust camshaft sprocket fitted position

10.7 Inlet camshaft position sensor securing bolts (arrowed)

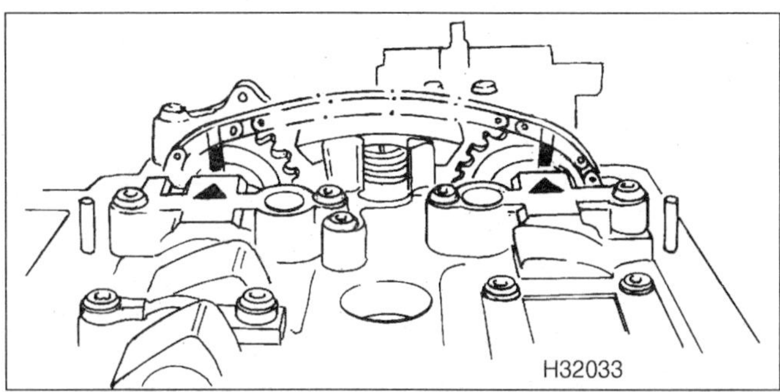

10.9 Mark the inlet camshaft drive chain and the sprockets in relation to each other (see text)

20 The idler pulley is secured in position with a bolt that also holds the tensioner piston assembly in position. Refer to tensioner removal, as described in Section 8, **(see illustration 8.3a)**.

21 Refitting is a reversal of removal, but tighten the idler pulley bolt to the specified torque, and refit the timing belt as described in Section 7.

9 Inlet camshaft timing components/camshaft adjuster

1 Removal and refitting of the timing chain and chain tensioner/camshaft adjuster mechanism is described as part of the camshaft removal and refitting procedure in Section 10. The sprockets are integral with the camshafts.

10 Camshafts and tappets – removal, inspection and refitting

Note: *A suitable tool will be required to lock the camshaft adjuster, or chain tensioner, in position during this procedure – see text. Sealant (D 454 300 A2 sealant, or equivalent) will be required on refitting.*

Removal

1 Disconnect the battery negative lead, then remove the engine top cover. **Note:** *Before disconnecting the battery, refer to* Disconnecting the battery *at the rear of this manual.*

2 Remove the upper timing belt cover, with reference to Section 6.

3 Turn the crankshaft to position No 1 piston at TDC on the firing stroke, as described in Section 3.

4 Remove the camshaft cover as described in Section 4.

5 Remove the timing belt, as described in Section 7. Note that there is no need to remove the timing belt completely – the belt can simply be released from the exhaust camshaft sprocket. Ensure that the crankshaft has been turned a quarter-turn (90°) anti-clockwise to position Nos 1 and 4 pistons slightly down their bores from the TDC position; this will eliminate any risk of piston-to-valve contact if a camshaft is turned whilst the timing belt is removed.

6 Remove the exhaust camshaft sprocket, with reference to Section 8.

7 Disconnect the wiring plug from the inlet camshaft position sensor (if not already disconnected), then unscrew the securing bolts, and remove the sensor from the front of the cylinder head **(see illustration)**.

8 With the camshaft sensor removed, unscrew the centre securing bolt and remove the tapered washer and sensor rotor from the end of the inlet camshaft.

9 Clean the inlet camshaft drive chain, and the camshaft sprockets, in line with the arrows on the tops of the camshaft rear bearing caps, then mark the chain and sprockets in relation to each other **(see illustration)**. Mark the chain with paint or a scriber – do not mark the chain using a punch. Note that the distance between the two marks must be 16 chain rollers, but also note that the mark on the exhaust camshaft side will be slightly offset towards the centre of the cylinder head.

10 The camshaft adjuster or chain tensioner, as applicable, must now be locked in position. Special tool 3366 is available for this purpose; alternatively, it is possible to make up a similar tool using a threaded rod, nuts, and a small metal plate to keep the adjuster compressed. As a safety precaution, use a plastic cable-tie to keep the home-made tool in position **(see illustrations)**.

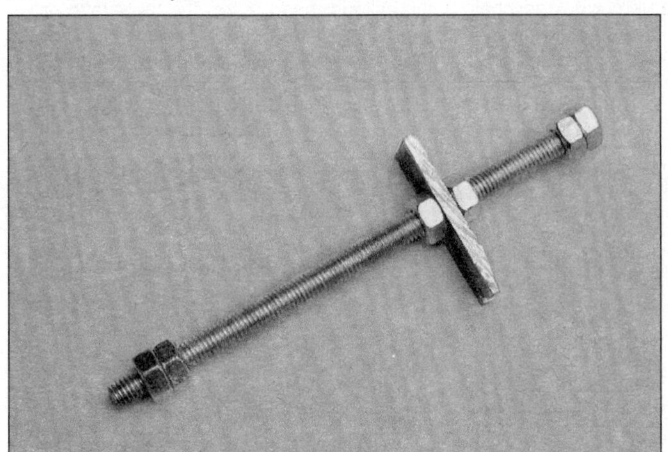
10.10a Home-made tool for locking camshaft adjuster, or chain tensioner, in position

10.10b Home-made tool in position, locking camshaft adjuster in its compressed condition (shown with camshaft adjuster removed for clarity)

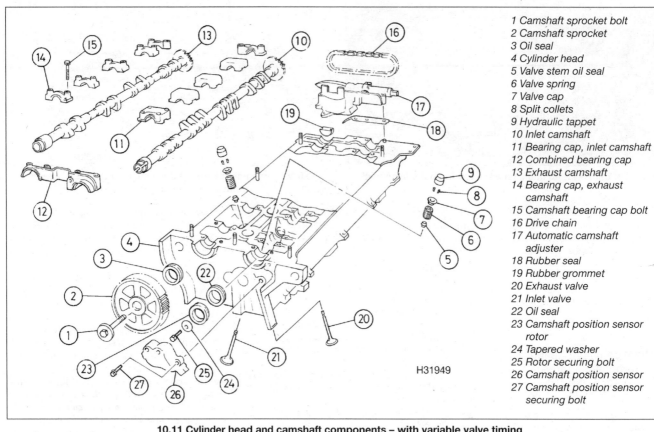

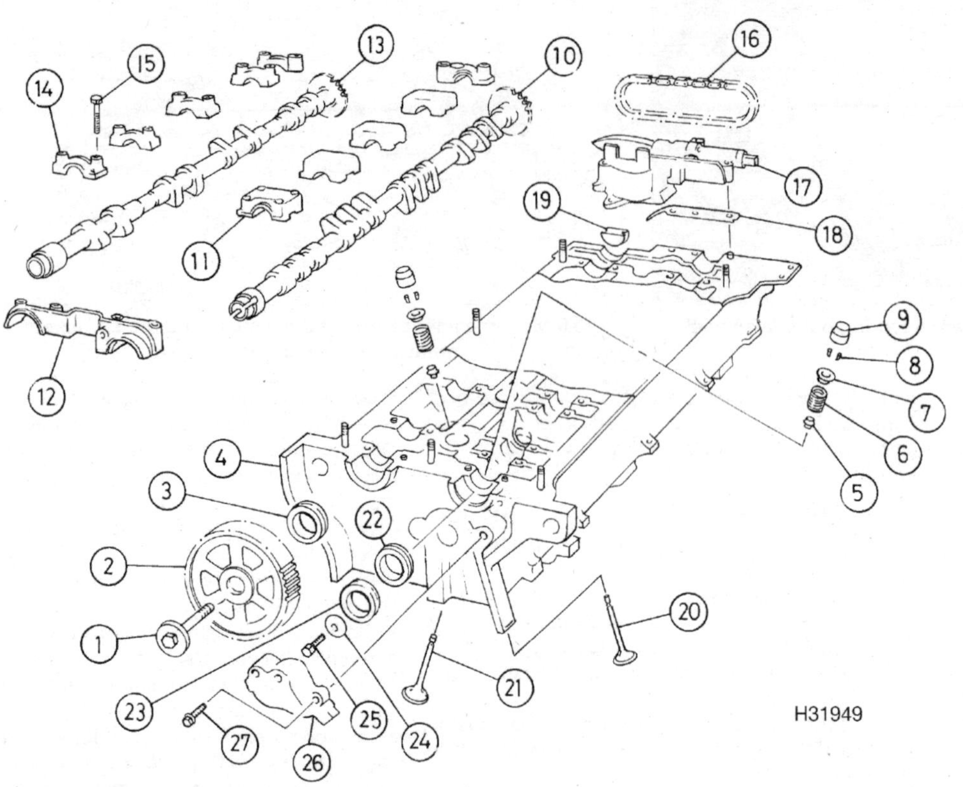

H31949

1 Camshaft sprocket bolt
2 Camshaft sprocket
3 Oil seal
4 Cylinder head
5 Valve stem oil seal
6 Valve spring
7 Valve cap
8 Split collets
9 Hydraulic tappet
10 Inlet camshaft
11 Bearing cap, inlet camshaft
12 Combined bearing cap
13 Exhaust camshaft
14 Bearing cap, exhaust camshaft
15 Camshaft bearing cap bolt
16 Drive chain
17 Automatic camshaft adjuster
18 Rubber seal
19 Rubber grommet
20 Exhaust valve
21 Inlet valve
22 Oil seal
23 Camshaft position sensor rotor
24 Tapered washer
25 Rotor securing bolt
26 Camshaft position sensor
27 Camshaft position sensor securing bolt

10.11 Cylinder head and camshaft components – with variable valve timing

Warning: Compressing the chain tensioner too far can result in damage to the camshaft adjuster mechanism.

11 Check the camshaft bearing caps for identification markings, and make suitable marks if necessary. The bearing caps should be numbered 1 to 6 from the chain end of the cylinder head, number 6 being the combined cap which straddles both camshafts. Note on which side of the bearing caps the marks are made, to ensure correct refitting **(see illustration)**.

12 Progressively slacken Nos 3 and 5 bearing cap bolts for both the inlet and exhaust camshafts, then repeat the process for the double No 6 bearing cap, then the No 1 bearing caps.

13 Slacken and remove the chain adjuster/tensioner securing bolts. Also disconnect the wiring connector from the adjuster/tensioner solenoid valve.

14 Progressively slacken Nos 2 and 4 bearing cap bolts for both the inlet and exhaust camshafts, then lift both camshafts from the cylinder head, complete with the chain tensioner/camshaft adjuster mechanism **(see illustrations)**.

15 Release the chain tensioner/camshaft adjuster mechanism from the chain, and remove the chain from the camshaft sprockets. Remove the oil seal from each camshaft.

16 Lift the hydraulic tappets from their bores, and store them with the valve contact surface facing downwards, to prevent the oil from draining out **(see illustration)**. It is recommended that the tappets are kept immersed in oil whilst they are removed from the cylinder head. Keep the tappets in order, as they must be refitted to their original valves – accelerated wear, leading to early failure may result if they are interchanged.

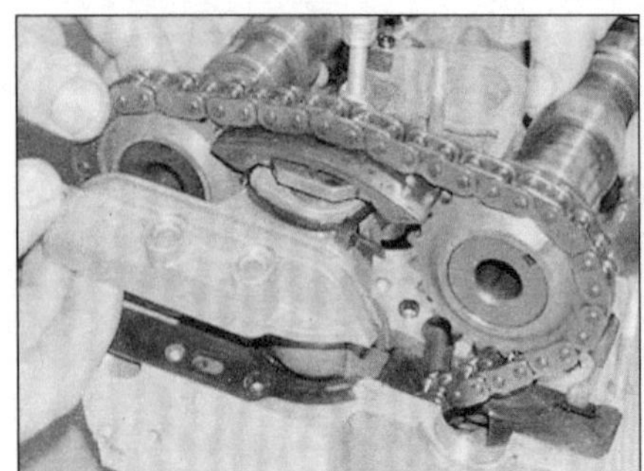

10.14a Removing the camshaft adjuster mechanism

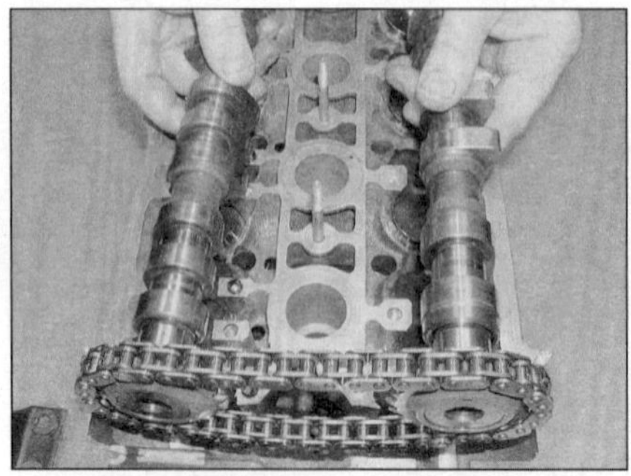

10.14b Lifting the camshafts and drive chain from the cylinder head

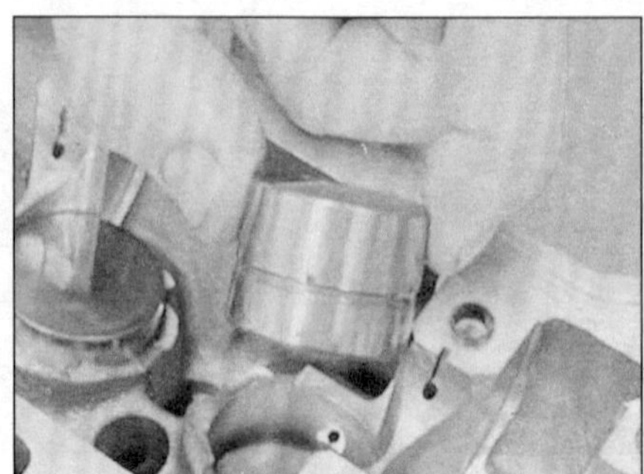

10.16 Lift the hydraulic tappets from their bores

10.19 Checking camshaft endfloat using a DTI gauge

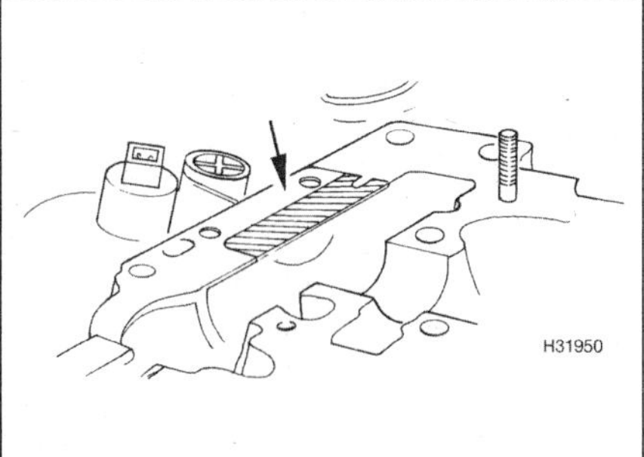

10.23 Apply sealant to the area of the chain tensioner/camshaft adjuster gasket shown

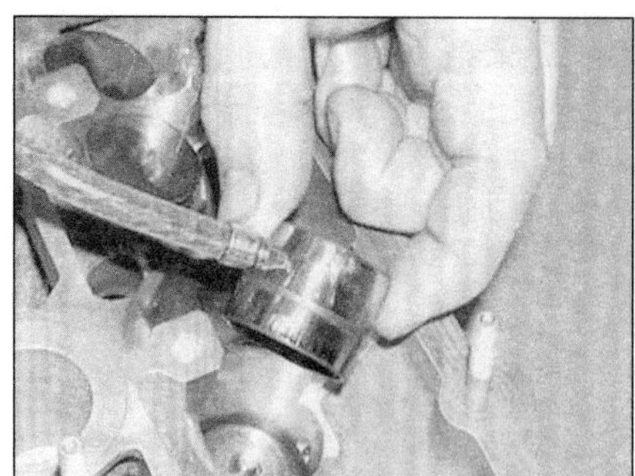
10.24 Oil the tappets before fitting

Inspection

17 Visually inspect each camshaft for evidence of wear on the surfaces of the lobes and journals. Normally their surfaces should be smooth and have a dull shine; look for scoring, erosion or pitting and areas that appear highly polished, indicating excessive wear. Accelerated wear will occur once the hardened exterior of the camshaft has been damaged, so always renew worn items. **Note:** *If these symptoms are visible on the tips of the camshaft lobes, check the corresponding tappet, as it will probably be worn as well.*

18 If the machined surfaces of the camshaft appear discoloured or blued, it is likely that it has been overheated at some point, probably due to inadequate lubrication. This may have distorted the shaft, so check the run-out as follows: place the camshaft between two V-blocks and using a DTI gauge, measure the run-out at the centre journal. If it exceeds the figure quoted in the Specifications at the start of this Chapter, renew the camshaft.

19 To measure the camshaft endfloat, temporarily refit the camshafts to the cylinder head, then Nos 2 and 4 bearing caps for both camshafts, and tighten the retaining bolts to the specified torque. Anchor a DTI gauge to the timing belt end of the cylinder head and align the gauge probe with the relevant camshaft axis. Push the camshaft to one end of the cylinder head as far as it will travel, then rest the DTI gauge probe on the end of the camshaft, and zero the gauge display. Push the camshaft as far as it will go to the other end of the cylinder head, and record the gauge reading. Verify the reading by pushing the camshaft back to its original position and checking that the gauge indicates zero again **(see illustration)**. Repeat the checking procedure for the remaining camshaft. **Note:** *The hydraulic tappets mustnotbe fitted whilst this measurement is being taken.*

20 Check that the camshaft endfloat measurement for each camshaft is within the limit given in the Specifications. Wear outside of this limit is unlikely to be confined to any one component, so renewal of the camshafts, cylinder head and bearing caps must be considered.

21 Inspect the hydraulic tappets for obvious signs of wear or damage, and renew if necessary. Check that the oil holes in the tappets are free from obstructions.

Refitting

22 Commence refitting by thoroughly cleaning all traces of old gasket and sealant from the chain tensioner/camshaft adjuster mating faces on the cylinder head.

23 Fit a new chain tensioner/camshaft adjuster gasket to the cylinder head, then coat the area shown with D 454 300 A2 sealant, or a suitable equivalent **(see illustration)**.

24 Smear the hydraulic tappets with clean engine oil, then fit them to their original positions in the cylinder head. Push the tappets down until they contact the valves, then lubricate the camshaft contact surfaces **(see illustration)**.

25 Lubricate the camshafts and the cylinder head bearing journals with clean engine oil.

26 Engage the chain with the camshaft sprockets, making sure that the marks made on the chain and sprockets before removal are aligned. Make sure that the distance between the marks is 16 chain rollers **(see illustration 10.9)**. Locate the chain tensioner/camshaft adjuster between the chain runs, then carefully lower the camshafts, chain and chain tensioner/camshaft adjuster into position in the cylinder head. Support the ends of the camshafts as they are fitted, to avoid damaging the lobes and journals.

27 The camshaft oil seals may be fitted at this stage, or alternatively fitted later. Dip the new seals in engine oil, then locate them on each camshaft. Make sure that the closed ends of the seals face outwards from the camshafts, and take care not todamage the seal lips. Locate the seals against the seats in the cylinder head.

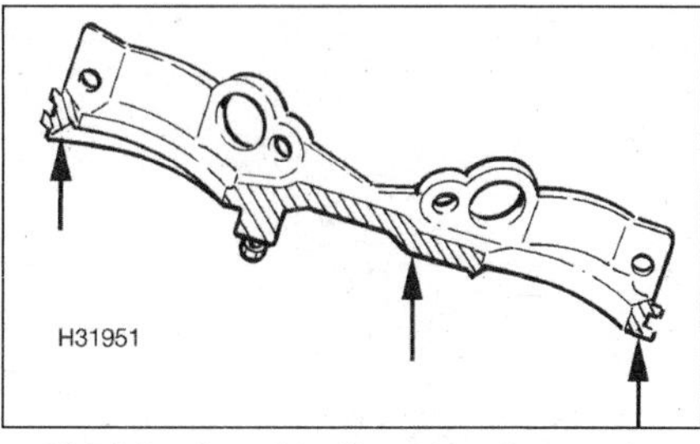

10.32 Apply a thin film of sealant to the contact face of the combined bearing cap in the areas shown

28 Refit the chain adjuster/tensioner bolts and tighten them to the specified torque. Reconnect the wiring connector to the adjuster/tensioner solenoid valve.

29 Refit Nos 2 and 4 bearing caps for both camshafts. Ensure that the bearing caps are fitted the correct way round, as noted before removal. Refit the bearing cap securing bolts, and working progressively in a diagonal sequence, tighten the bolts to the specified torque.

30 Refit the No 1 bearing caps for both camshafts (again, ensure that the bearing caps are fitted the correct way round), then refit the bearing cap bolts and tighten progressively to the specified torque.

31 Remove the tool used to lock the camshaft adjuster or chain tensioner (as applicable) in position.

32 Apply a thin film of sealant to the cylinder head contact faces of the combined bearing cap (No 6 bearing cap), then fit the cap, making sure that the oil seals (where fitted) locate against their seatings **(see illustration)**. Progressively tighten the bearing cap securing bolts to the specified torque.

33 Fit Nos 3 and 5 bearing caps for both camshafts (again, ensure that the bearing caps are fitted the correct way round), then refit the bearing cap bolts and tighten progressively to the specified torque.

34 Check that the marks made on the chain and sprockets before removal are still aligned. If not, the components have been incorrectly refitted.

35 Refit the inlet camshaft sensor rotor, and refit the washer and securing bolt. Tighten the securing bolt to the specified torque.

36 Refit the inlet camshaft position sensor to the cylinder head, then refit the securing bolts and tighten to the specified torque.

37 Refit the exhaust camshaft sprocket with reference to Section 8, then refit the timing belt as described in Section 7.

38 Refit the camshaft cover as described in Section 4.

39 If not already done, refit the upper outer timing belt cover as described in Section 6.

40 Refit the engine top cover, and reconnect the battery negative lead.

11 Camshaft oil seals - renewal

Exhaust camshaft oil seal

1 Remove the timing belt as described in Section 7.

2 Remove the camshaft sprocket as described in Section 8.

3 Drill two small holes into the existing oil seal, diagonally opposite each other. Take great care to avoid drilling through into the seal housing or camshaft sealing surface. Thread two self-tapping screws into the holes and, using a pair of pliers, pull on the heads of the screws to extract the oil seal.

4 Clean out the seal housing and the sealing surface of the camshaft by wiping it with a lint-free cloth. Remove any swarf or burrs that may cause the seal to leak.

5 Lubricate the lip and outer edge of the new oil seal with clean engine oil, and push it over the camshaft until it is positioned above its housing. To prevent damage to the sealing lips, wrap some adhesive tape around the end of the camshaft.

6 Using a hammer and a socket of suitable diameter, drive the seal squarely into its housing. **Note:** *Select a socket that bears only on the hard outer surface of the seal, not the inner lip which can easily be damaged.*

7 Refit the camshaft sprocket as described in Section 8.

8 Refit and tension the timing belt as described in Section 7.

Inlet camshaft oil seal

9 Remove the upper timing belt cover, with reference to Section 6.

10 Disconnect the wiring plug from the inlet camshaft position sensor, then unscrew the securing bolts, and remove the sensor from the front of the cylinder head **(see illustration 10.7)**. With the sensor removed, unscrew the securing bolt and remove the tapered washer and sensor rotor from the end of the inlet camshaft.

11 Proceed as described in paragraphs 3 to 6.

12 Refit the inlet camshaft sensor rotor, refit the tapered washer and securing bolt. Tighten the securing bolt to the specified torque.

13 Refit the inlet camshaft position sensor to the cylinder head, then refit the securing bolts and tighten to the specified torque.

14 Refit the upper timing belt cover, with reference to Section 6.

12 Cylinder head - removal, inspection and refitting

Note: *The cylinder head must be removed with the engine cold. New cylinder head bolts and a new cylinder head gasket will be required on refitting. Suitable studs (see text) will be required to guide the cylinder head into position on refitting.*

Removal

1 Disconnect the battery negative lead, then remove the engine top cover. **Note:** *Before disconnecting the battery, refer to* Disconnecting the battery *at the rear of this manual.*

2 Drain the cooling system as described in Chapter 1.

3 If the cylinder head is to be removed leaving the inlet manifold in the engine compartment, unscrew the securing bolts and lift the inlet manifold back from the engine. Ensure that the inlet manifold is adequately supported in the engine compartment, and take care not to strain any wires, cables or hoses. Recover the gaskets it they are loose.

4 Alternatively, if the cylinder head is to be removed complete with the inlet manifold, work around the manifold and disconnect all relevant pipes, hoses and wires. When disconnecting the fuel supply and return hoses at the connections on the fuel rail, take care, because the fuel supply hose will be pressurised. Wrap a clean cloth around each connection to absorb escaping fuel, then slacken the hose clip and pull the relevant hose from the connection. Clamp or plug the open ends of the hoses and connections to prevent dirt entry and further fuel spillage.

5 Release the hose clips, and disconnect the coolant hoses from the coolant housing at the transmission end of the cylinder head.

6 Disconnect the wiring plug from the inlet camshaft position sensor.

7 Disconnect the wiring plug from the coolant temperature sensor, located in the coolant housing at the transmission end of the cylinder head.

8 Disconnect the exhaust front section from the manifold or turbocharger, as applicable, as described in Chapter 4B.

9 Remove the timing belt as described in Section 7 then remove the tensioner as described in Section 8.

10 As the engine is currently supported using a hoist attached to the engine lifting brackets bolted to the cylinder head, it is now necessary to attach a suitable bracket to the cylinder block, so that the engine can still be supported as the cylinder head is removed.

11 A suitable bracket can be bolted to the cylinder block using spacers, and a long bolt screwed into the hole located next to the coolant pump. Ideally, attach a second set of lifting tackle to the hoist, adjust the lifting tackle to support the engine using the bracket attached to the cylinder block, then disconnect the lifting tackle attached to the bracket on the cylinder head. Alternatively, temporarily support the engine under the sump using a jack and a block of wood, then transfer the lifting tackle from the bracket on the cylinder head to the bracket bolted to the cylinder block.

12 Remove the camshaft cover as described in Section 4.

13 Work around the cylinder head (and manifolds, where applicable), and disconnect all remaining pipes, wires and hoses to facilitate cylinder head removal. Note the location and routing of all pipes, wires and hoses to aid refitting.

14 Progressively slacken the cylinder head bolts in order, then unscrew and remove the bolts **(see illustration)**.

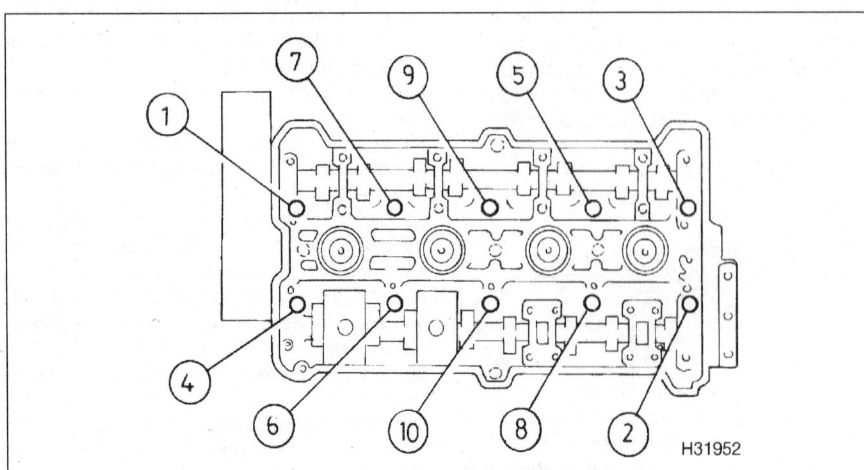

12.14 Cylinder head bolt slackening sequence

15 With all the bolts removed, lift the cylinder head from the block. If the cylinder head is stuck, tap it with a soft-faced mallet to break the joint. Do not insert a lever into the gasket joint, as the cylinder head is lifted off.

16 Carefully lift the cylinder head gasket from the block.

Inspection

17 Dismantling and inspection of the cylinder head is covered in Part B of this Chapter.

Refitting

18 The mating faces of the cylinder head and block must be perfectly clean before refitting the head. Use a scraper to remove all traces of gasket and carbon, also clean the

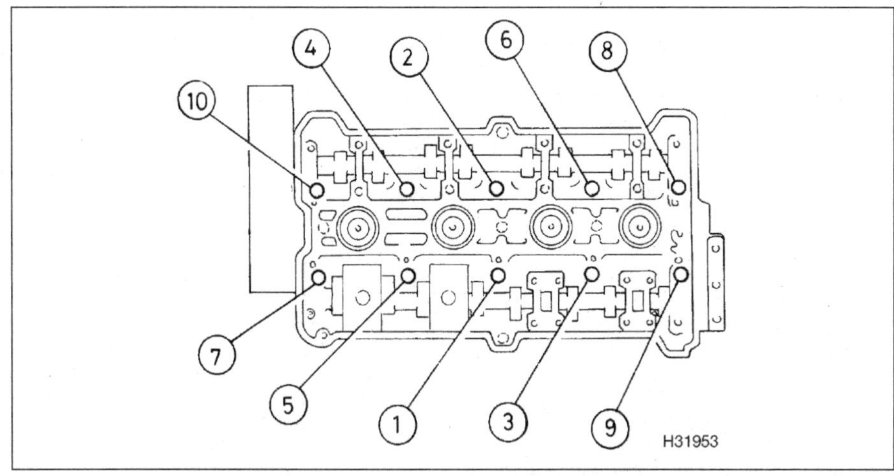

12.28 Cylinder head bolt tightening sequence

tops of the pistons. Take particular care with the aluminium surfaces, as the soft metal is easily damaged. Make sure that debris is not allowed to enter the oil and water passages – this is particularly important for the oil circuit, as carbon could block the oil supply to the camshaft and crankshaft bearings. Using adhesive tape and paper, seal the water, oil and bolt holes in the cylinder block. To prevent carbon entering the gap between the pistons and bores, smear a little grease in the gap. After cleaning a piston, rotate the crankshaft to that the piston moves down the bore, then wipe out the grease and carbon with a cloth rag. Clean the other piston crowns in the same way.

19 Check the head and block for nicks, deep scratches and other damage. If slight, they may be removed carefully with a file. More serious damage may be repaired by machining, but this is a specialist job.

20 If warpage of the cylinder head is suspected, use a straight-edge to check it for distortion, as described in Part B of this Chapter.

21 Ensure that the cylinder head bolt holes in the crankcase are clean and free of oil. Syringe or soak up any oil left in the bolt holes. This is most important in order that the correct bolt tightening torque can be applied, and to prevent the possibility of the block being cracked by hydraulic pressure when the bolts are tightened.

22 Ensure that the crankshaft has been turned to position Nos 1 and 4 pistons slightly down their bores from the TDC position. This will eliminate any risk of piston-to-valve contact as the cylinder head is refitted. Also ensure that the camshaft sprockets are locked in the TDC position using the locking tool. Refer to Section 3.

23 To guide the cylinder head into position, screw two long studs (or old cylinder head bolts with the heads cut off, and slots cut in the ends to enable the bolts to be unscrewed) into the end cylinder head bolt locations on the exhaust side of the cylinder block.

24 Ensure that the cylinder head locating dowels are in place in the cylinder block, then fit a new cylinder head gasket over the dowels, ensuring that the part number is uppermost. Where applicable, the OBEN/TOP marking should also be uppermost. Note that it is recommended that the gasket is only removed from its packaging immediately prior to fitting.

25 Lower the cylinder head into position on the gasket, ensuring that it engages correctly over the guide studs and dowels.

26 Fit the new cylinder head bolts to the eight remaining bolt locations, and screw them in as far as possible by hand.

27 Unscrew the two guide studs from the exhaust side of the cylinder block, then screw in the two remaining cylinder head bolts as far as possible by hand.

28 Working progressively, in sequence, tighten all the cylinder head bolts to the specified Stage 1 torque **(see illustration)**.

29 Again working progressively, in sequence, tighten all the cylinder head bolts through the specified Stage 2 angle.

30 Finally, tighten all the cylinder head bolts, in sequence, to the specified Stage 3 angle.

31 Reconnect the lifting tackle to the right-hand engine lifting bracket on the cylinder head, then adjust the lifting tackle to support the engine. Once the engine is adequately supported using the cylinder head bracket, disconnect the lifting tackle from the bracket bolted to the cylinder block, and unbolt the improvised engine lifting bracket from the cylinder block. Alternatively, remove the trolley jack and block of wood from under the sump.

32 Further refitting is a reversal of removal, bearing in mind the following points.

a) *Ensure that all pipes, wires and hoses are correctly reconnected and routed as noted before removal.*
b) *Refit the camshaft cover as described in Section 4.*
c) *Install the tensioner as described in Section 8 then fit the timing belt as described in Section 7.*
d) *Reconnect the exhaust front section to the manifold or turbocharger, as applicable, as described in Chapter 4B.*
e) *Where applicable, refit the inlet manifold using new gaskets.*
f) *Tighten all fixings to the specified torque, where applicable.*
g) *On completion, refill the cooling system as described in Chapter 1.*

13 Sump – removal and refitting

Note: *Sealant (D 176404 A2 or equivalent) will be required to seal the sump on refitting.*

Removal

1 Apply the handbrake, then jack up the front of the vehicle and support securely on axle stands (see *Jacking and vehicle support*).

2 Remove the securing screws and withdraw the engine undershield(s).

3 Drain the engine oil as described in Chapter 1 Section 7.

4 Unscrew the two bolts and disconnect the turbocharger oil return pipe from the rear of the sump. Also disconnect the wiring connector from the oil level/temperature sender in the base of the sump **(see illustration)**.

5 Undo the three bolts securing the sump to the lower edge of the transmission casing **(see illustration)**. Discard these bolts, as new ones are required for refitting.

13.4 Oil return pipe (A) and oil level/temp sensor (B)

13.5 Sump to transmission bolts (arrowed)

13.6 Four bolts (arrowed) inside end of sump housing casting

6 Slacken and remove the bolts securing the sump to the cylinder block (20 in total), making sure that the four at the transmission end of the sump are removed from inside the four slots in the end of the sump **(see illustration)**, then withdraw the sump. If necessary, release the sump by tapping with a soft-faced hammer. Note that it will be necessary to use a ratchet and long extension to reach some of the sump securing bolts.

7 Where applicable, unbolt the oil baffle plate from the cylinder block.

Refitting

8 Begin refitting by thoroughly cleaning the mating faces of the sump and cylinder block. Ensure that all traces of old sealant are removed.

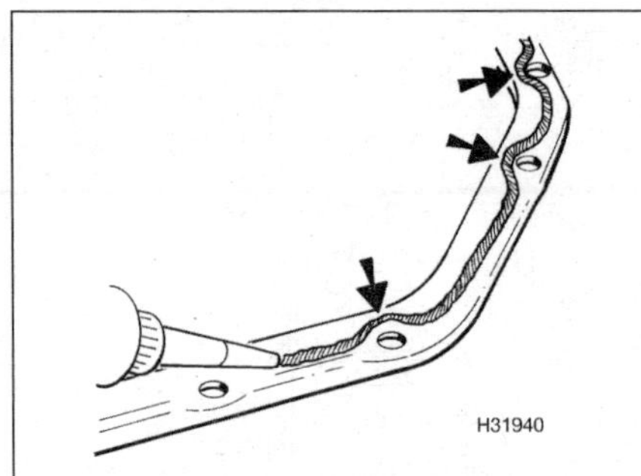

13.10 Apply the sealant around the inside of the bolt holes

9 Where applicable, refit the oil baffle plate, and tighten the securing bolts.

10 Ensure that the cylinder block mating face of the sump is free from all traces of old sealant, oil and grease, and then apply a 2.0 to 3.0 mm thick bead of silicone sealant (D 176404 A2 or equivalent) to the sump **(see illustration)**. Note that the sealant should be run around the inside of the bolt holes in the sump. The sump must be fitted within 5 minutes of applying the sealant.

11 Offer the sump up to the cylinder block, then refit the sump-to-cylinder block bolts, and lightly tighten them by hand, working progressively in a diagonal sequence. **Note:** *If the sump is being refitted with the engine and transmission separated, make sure that the sump is flush with the flywheel/driveplate end of the cylinder block, using a straight edge.*

12 Working in a diagonal sequence, lightly tighten the sump-to-cylinder block bolts to 5Nm.

13 Tighten the three sump-to-transmission casing bolts to the specified torque, using new bolts.

14 Working in a diagonal sequence, progressively tighten the sump-to-cylinder block bolts to the specified torque.

15 Refit the turbocharger oil return pipe back to the rear of the sump, using a new gasket and tighten the retaining bolts to the specified torque (10Nm).

16 Refit the wiring connector to the oil level/ temperature sender, then refit the engine undershield(s), and lower the vehicle to the ground.

17 Allow at least 30 minutes from the time of refitting the sump for the sealant to dry, then refill the engine with oil, with reference to Chapter 1 Section 7.

14 Oil pump, drive chain and sprockets – removal, inspection and refitting

Oil pump removal

1 Remove the sump as described in Section 13.

2 Where applicable unscrew the securing bolts, and remove the oil baffle from the cylinder block.

3 Unscrew and remove the three mounting bolts, and release the oil pump from the dowels in the crankcase **(see illustration)**. Unhook the oil pump drive sprocket from the chain and withdraw the oil pump and oil pick-up pipe from the engine. Note that the tensioner will attempt to tighten the chain, and it may be necessary to use a screwdriver to hold it in its released position before releasing the oil pump sprocket from the chain.

4 If desired, unscrew the flange bolts and remove the suction pipe from the oil pump. Recover the O-ring seal. Unscrew the bolts and remove the cover from the oil pump. **Note:** *If the oil pick-up pipe is removed from the oil pump, a new O-ring will be required on refitting.*

Oil pump inspection

5 Clean the pump thoroughly, and inspect the gear teeth/rotors for signs of damage or wear. If evident, renew the oil pump.

6 To remove the sprocket from the oil pump, unscrew the retaining bolt and slide off the sprocket (note that the sprocket can only be fitted in one position).

Oil pump refitting

7 Prime the pump with oil by pouring oil into the pick-up pipe aperture while turning the driveshaft.

8 Refit the cover to the oil pump and tighten

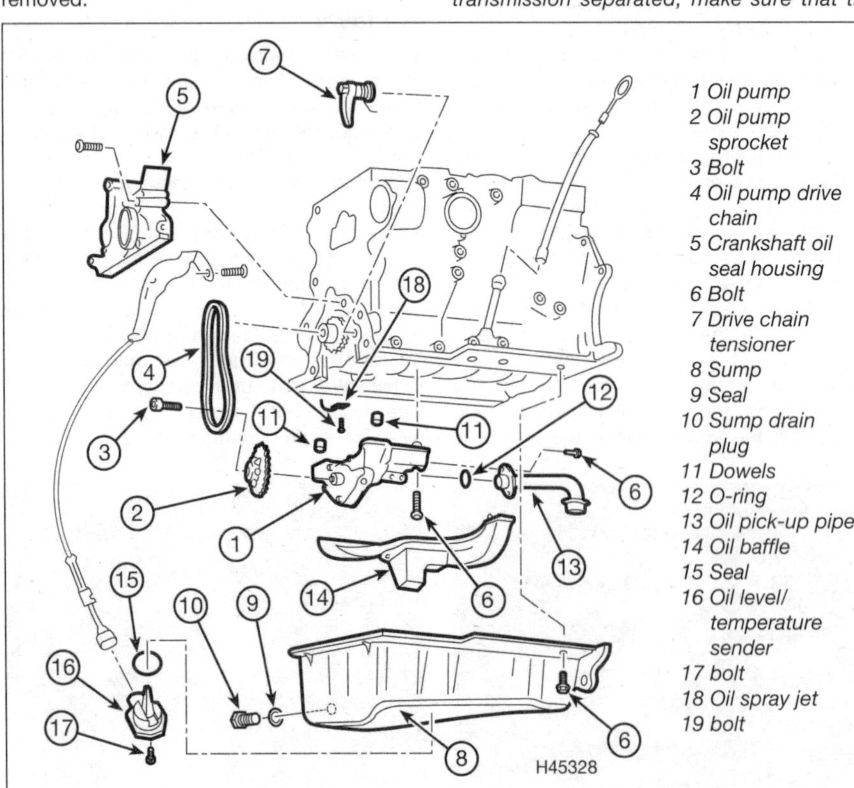

14.3 Sump and oil pump components

the bolts securely. Where applicable, refit the pick-up pipe to the oil pump, using a new O-ring seal, and tighten the securing bolts.
9 If the drive chain, crankshaft sprocket and tensioner have been removed, delay refitting them until after the oil pump has been mounted on the cylinder block. If they have not been removed, use a screwdriver to press the tensioner against its spring to provide sufficient slack in the chain to refit the oil pump.
10 Engage the oil pump sprocket with the drive chain, then locate the oil pump on the dowels. Refit and tighten the three mounting bolts to the specified torque.
11 Where applicable, refit the drive chain, tensioner and crankshaft sprocket using a reversal of the removal procedure.
12 Refit the oil baffle, and tighten the securing bolts.
13 Refit the sump as described in Section 13.

Drive chain and sprockets

Note: *Sealant (D 176404 A2 or equivalent) will be required to seal the crankshaft oil seal housing on refitting, and it is advisable to fit a new crankshaft oil seal.*

Removal

14 Proceed as described in paragraphs 1 and 2.
15 To remove the oil pump sprocket, unscrew the securing bolt, then pull the sprocket from the pump shaft, and unhook it from the drive chain.
16 To remove the chain, remove the timing belt as described in Section 7, then unbolt the crankshaft oil seal housing from the cylinder block. Unbolt the chain tensioner from the cylinder block, then unhook the chain from the sprocket on the end of the crankshaft.
17 The oil pump drive sprocket is a press-fit on the crankshaft, and cannot easily be removed. Consult an Audi dealer or specialist for advice if the sprocket is worn or damaged.

Inspection

18 Examine the chain for wear and damage. Wear is usually indicated by excessive lateral play between the links, and excessive noise in operation. It is wise to renew the chain in any case if the engine is to be overhauled. Note that the rollers on a very badly worn chain may be slightly grooved. If there is any doubt as to the condition of the chain, renew it.
19 Examine the teeth on the sprockets for wear. Each tooth forms an inverted V. If worn, the side of each tooth under tension will be slightly concave in shape when compared with the other side of the tooth (ie, the teeth will have a hooked appearance). If the teeth appear worn, the sprocket should be renewed (consult an Audi dealer or specialist for advice if the crankshaft sprocket is worn or damaged).

Refitting

20 If the oil pump has been removed, refit the oil pump as described previously in this Section before refitting the chain and sprocket.
21 Refit the chain tensioner to the cylinder block, and tighten the securing bolt to the specified torque. Make sure that the tensioner spring is correctly positioned to pretension the tensioner arm.
22 Engage the oil pump sprocket with the chain, then engage the chain with the crankshaft sprocket. Use a screwdriver to press the tensioner against its spring to provide sufficient slack in the chain to engage the sprocket with the oil pump. Note that the sprocket will only fit in one position.
23 Refit the oil pump sprocket bolt, and tighten to the specified torque.
24 Fit a new crankshaft oil seal to the housing, and refit the housing as described in Section 16.
25 Where applicable, refit the oil baffle, and tighten the securing bolts.
26 Refit the sump as described in Section 13.
27 Refit the timing belt as described in Section 7.

15 Flywheel/driveplate – removal, inspection and refitting

Note: *New flywheel/driveplate securing bolts will be required on refitting.*

Removal

1 On manual transmission models, remove the gearbox (see Chapter 7A Section 3) and clutch assembly (see Chapter 6 Section 6).
2 On automatic transmission models, remove the automatic transmission (see Chapter 7B Section 2).
3 The flywheel/driveplate bolts are offset to ensure correct fitment. Unscrew the bolts while holding the flywheel/driveplate stationary. Temporarily insert a bolt in the cylinder block, and use a screwdriver to hold the flywheel/ driveplate, or make up a holding tool **(see illustration)**.
4 Lift the flywheel/driveplate from the crankshaft taking care, as this is heavy. If removing a driveplate, note the location of the shim (where applicable – between the driveplate and the crankshaft), and the spacer under the securing bolts. Recover the engine-to-transmission plate if it is loose.

15.3 Tool used to hold the flywheel/ driveplate stationary

Inspection

5 Check the flywheel/driveplate for wear and damage. Examine the starter ring gear for excessive wear to the teeth. If the driveplate or its ring gear are damaged, the complete driveplate must be renewed. The flywheel ring gear, however, may be renewed separately from the flywheel, but the work should be entrusted to a specialist. If the clutch friction face is discoloured or scored excessively, it may be possible to regrind it, but this work should also be entrusted to a specialist.

Refitting

6 Refitting is a reversal of removal, bearing in mind the following points.
a) *Ensure that the engine-to-transmission plate is in place before fitting the flywheel/ driveplate.*
b) *On automatic transmission models temporarily refit the driveplate using the old bolts tightened to 30 Nm, and check that the distance from the rear machined face of the cylinder block to the torque converter mounting face on the driveplate is between 19.5 and 21.1 mm. The measurement is most easily made through one of the holes in the driveplate, using vernier calipers. If necessary, remove the driveplate, and fit a shim between the driveplate and the crankshaft to achieve the correct dimension.*
c) *On automatic transmission models, the raised pip on the spacer under the securing bolts must face the torque converter.*
d) *Use new bolts when refitting the flywheel or driveplate, and coat the threads of the bolts with locking fluid before inserting them. Tighten the securing bolts to the specified torque.*

16 Crankshaft oil seals – renewal

Timing belt end oil seal

Note: *If the oil seal housing is removed, suitable sealant (D 176 404 A2, or equivalent) will be required on refitting.*
1 Remove the timing belt as described in Section 7, and the crankshaft sprocket with reference to Section 8.
2 To remove the seal without removing the oil seal housing, drill two small holes diagonally opposite each other, insert self-tapping screws, and pull on the heads of the screws with pliers.
3 Alternatively, to remove the oil seal complete with its housing, proceed as follows.
a) *Remove the sump as described in Section 13. This is necessary to ensure a*

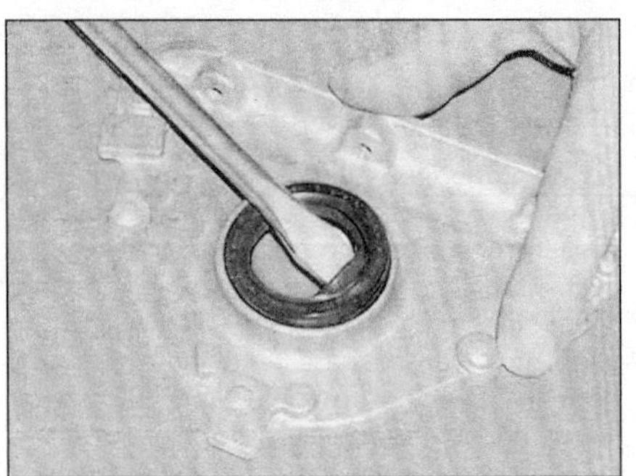
16.3 Using a screwdriver to lever the crankshaft oil seal from its housing

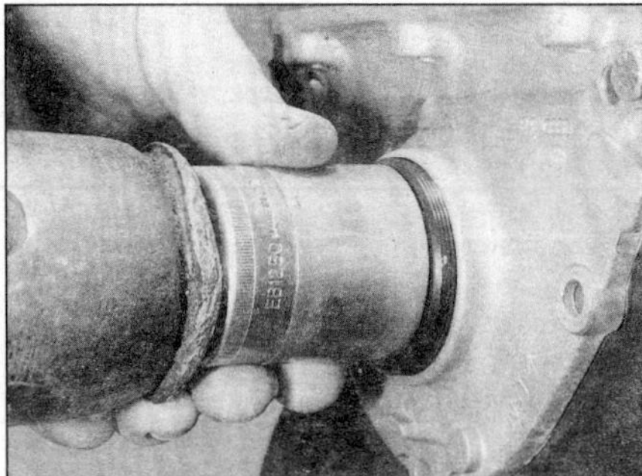
16.6 Driving a new crankshaft oil seal into position using a socket

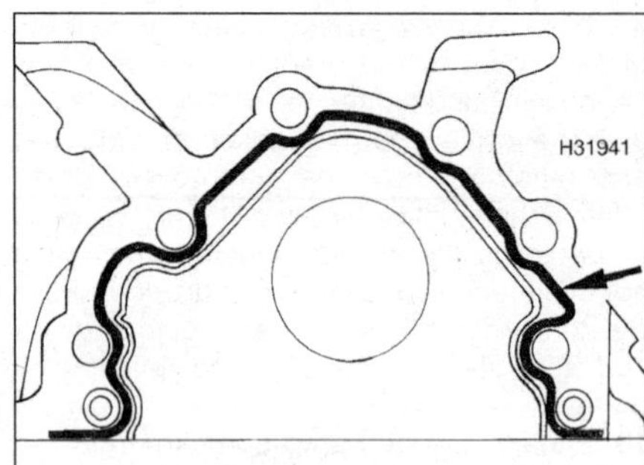

16.8 Apply sealant as shown to the crankshaft oil seal housing

satisfactory seal between the sump and oil seal housing on refitting.

b) Unbolt and remove the oil seal housing.

c) Working on the bench, lever the oil seal from the housing using a suitable screwdriver **(see illustration)***.*

d) Take care not to damage the seal seating in the housing.

4 Thoroughly clean the oil seal seating in the housing.

5 Wind a length of tape around the end of the crankshaft to protect the oil seal lips as the seal (and housing, where applicable) is fitted.

6 Fit a new oil seal to the housing, pressing or driving it into position using a socket or tube of suitable diameter **(see illustration)**. Ensure that the socket or tube bears only on the hard outer ring of the seal, and take care not to damage the seal lips. Press or drive the seal into position until it is seated on the shoulder in the housing. Make sure that the closed end of the seal is facing outwards.

7 If the oil seal housing has been removed, proceed as follows, otherwise proceed to paragraph 11.

8 Clean all traces of old sealant from the crankshaft oil seal housing and the cylinder block, then coat the cylinder block mating faces of the oil seal housing with a 2.0 to 3.0 mm thick bead of sealant (D 176 404 A2, or equivalent). Note that the seal housing must be refitted within 5 minutes of applying the sealant **(see illustration)**.

9 Refit the oil seal housing, and tighten the bolts progressively to the specified torque.

10 Refit the sump as described in Section 13.

11 Refit the crankshaft sprocket with reference to Section 8, and the timing belt as described in Section 7.

Flywheel/driveplate end oil seal

Note: *If the original oil seal housing was fitted using sealant, suitable sealant (D 176 404 A2, or equivalent) will be required to seal the housing on refitting.*

12 Remove the flywheel/driveplate as described in Section 15.

13 Remove the sump as described in Section 13. This is necessary to ensure a satisfactory seal between the sump and oil seal housing on refitting.

14 Unbolt and remove the oil seal housing, complete with the oil seal.

15 The new oil seal will be supplied ready-fitted to a new oil seal housing.

16 Thoroughly clean the oil seal housing mating face on the cylinder block.

17 If the original oil seal housing was fitted using sealant, apply a thin bead of suitable sealant (D 176 404 A2, or equivalent) to the cylinder block mating face of the oil seal housing. Note that the seal housing must be refitted within 5 minutes of applying the sealant.

18 New oil seal/housing assemblies are supplied with a fitting tools to prevent damage to the oil seal as it is being fitted. Locate the tool over the end of the crankshaft **(see illustration)**.

19 Carefully fit the oil seal/housing assembly over the end of the crankshaft, and tighten the bolts progressively, in a diagonal sequence, to the specified torque **(see illustration)**.

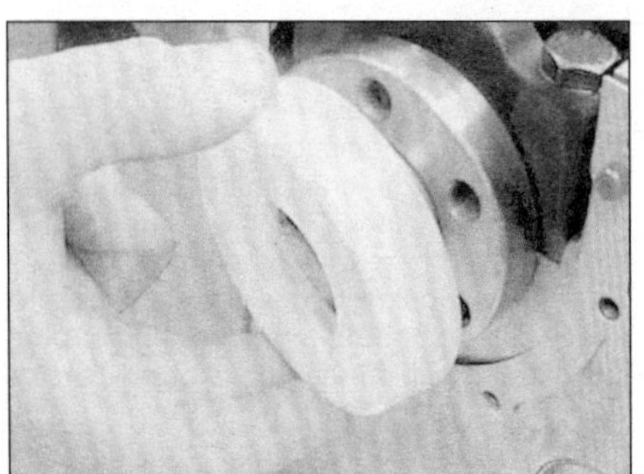
16.18 Locate the oil seal fitting tool over the end of the crankshaft

16.19 Fit the oil seal/housing assembly over the end of the crankshaft

20 Remove the oil seal protector tool from the end of the crankshaft.

21 Refit the sump as described in Section 13.

22 Refit the flywheel/driveplate as described in Section 15.

17 Engine/transmission mountings – inspection and renewal

Inspection

1 If improved access is required, jack up the front of the vehicle, and support it securely on axle stands (see *Jacking and vehicle support*). Remove the securing screws and remove the engine undershield(s).

2 Check the mounting rubbers to see if they are cracked, hardened or separated from the metal at any point; renew the mounting if any such damage or deterioration is evident.

3 Check that all the mounting fasteners are securely tightened; use a torque wrench to check if possible.

4 Using a large screwdriver or a crowbar, check for wear in the mounting by carefully levering against it to check for free play. Where this is not possible, enlist the aid of an assistant to move the engine/transmission back-and-forth, or from side-to-side, whilst you observe the mounting. While some free play is to be expected, even from new components, excessive wear should be obvious. If excessive free play is found, check first that the fasteners are correctly secured, then renew any worn components as described in the following paragraphs.

Renewal

Right-hand mounting

Note: *New mounting securing bolts will be required on refitting.*

5 Attach a hoist and lifting tackle to the engine lifting brackets on the cylinder head, and raise the hoist to just take the weight of the engine. Alternatively the engine can be supported on a trolley jack under the engine. Use a block of wood between the sump and the head of the jack, to prevent any damage to the sump.

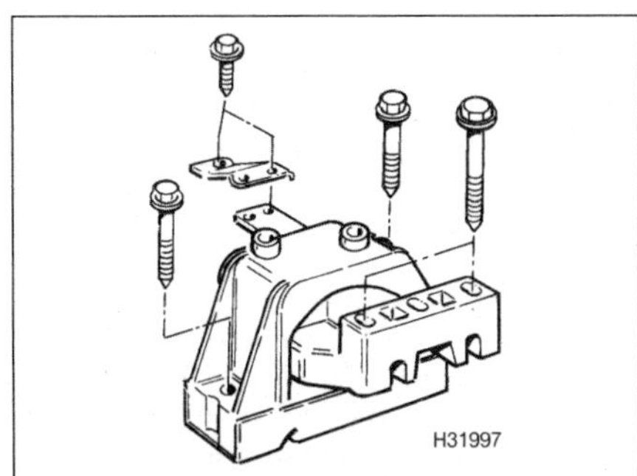

17.9 Engine right-hand mounting components

17.10 View of the engine right-hand mounting – three of the main mounting bolts visible

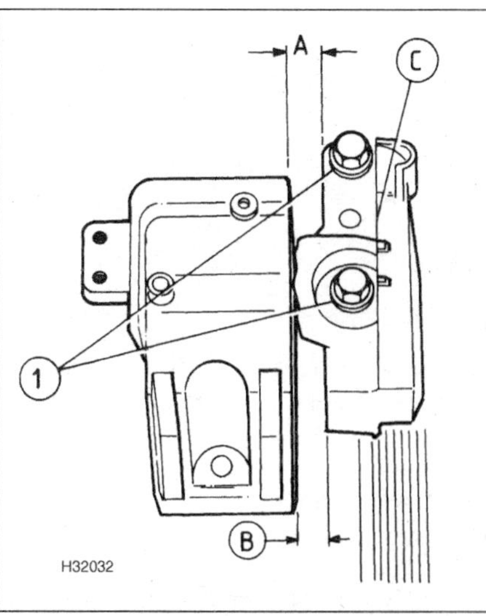

17.11 Engine right-hand mounting alignment details – both bolt heads (1) must be flush with edge (C)

A = 13.0 mm B = at least 10.0 mm

6 Unbolt the power steering fluid reservoir, and move it to one side, leaving the fluid hoses connected.

7 Similarly, unbolt the coolant reservoir and move it to one side, leaving the coolant hoses connected.

8 Where applicable, move any wiring harnesses, pipes or hoses to one side to enable removal of the engine mounting. Note that it may be necessary to disconnect certain hoses.

9 Unscrew the two securing bolts, and remove the small bracket from the top of the mounting **(see illustration)**.

10 Unscrew the two bolts securing the mounting to the bracket on the engine, and the two bolts securing the mounting to the body, then lift the mounting from the engine compartment **(see illustration)**.

11 Refitting is a reversal of removal, bearing in mind the following points:

a) *Use new bolts when refitting the main mounting assembly.*

b) *Before fully tightening the mounting securing bolts, ensure that the distance between the mounting and the engine mounting bracket is as shown, and also check the mounting-to-engine mounting bracket bolt heads are flush with the edge of the mounting **(see illustration)**.*

c) *Tighten all fixings to the specified torque.*

Left-hand mounting

Note: *New mounting bolts will be required on refitting (there is no need to renew the smaller mounting-to-body bolts).*

12 Proceed as described in paragraph 5.

13 Remove the air cleaner assembly as described in Chapter 4A Section 2.

14 Remove the battery, as described in Chapter 5A Section 3, then disconnect the main starter motor feed cable from the positive battery terminal box.

15 Release any relevant wiring or hoses from the clips on the battery tray, then unscrew the securing bolts and remove the battery tray **(see illustration)**.

16 On some models, it may be necessary to unclip wiring harnesses and/or hoses from brackets close to the engine/transmission mounting to enable the mounting to be removed.

17 Carefully lift the wiring harness housing from the wing panel to improve access to the mounting-to-body bolts. Note that access to the smaller mounting-to-body bolt can be gained by unclipping the cover from the wiring harness housing, and moving the harnesses to one side to expose the bolt.

18 Unscrew the two bolts securing the mounting to the transmission, and the three bolts securing the mounting to the body, then lift the mounting from the engine compartment, noting that it may be necessary to manipulate the mounting out from under the wiring harness housing **(see illustrations)**.

19 Refitting is a reversal of removal, bearing in mind the following points:

a) *The edge of the engine/transmission mounting must be parallel with the body **(see illustration)**.*

b) *Use new mounting bolts (there is no need to renew the smaller mounting-to-body bolt).*

c) *Tighten all fixings to the specified torque.*

17.15 Removing the battery tray

17.18a View of the engine/transmission left-hand mounting

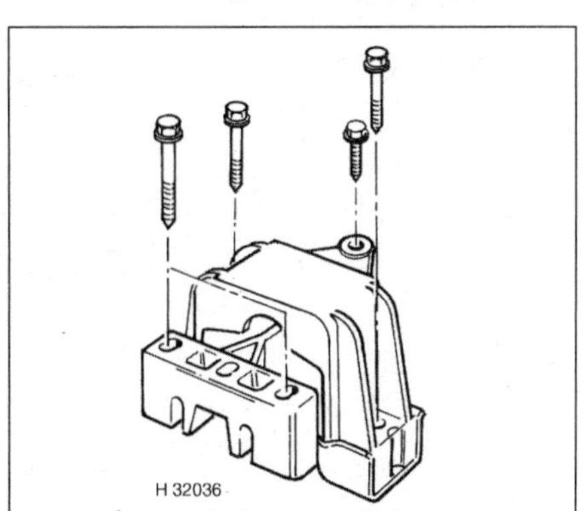

17.18b Engine/transmission left-hand mounting components

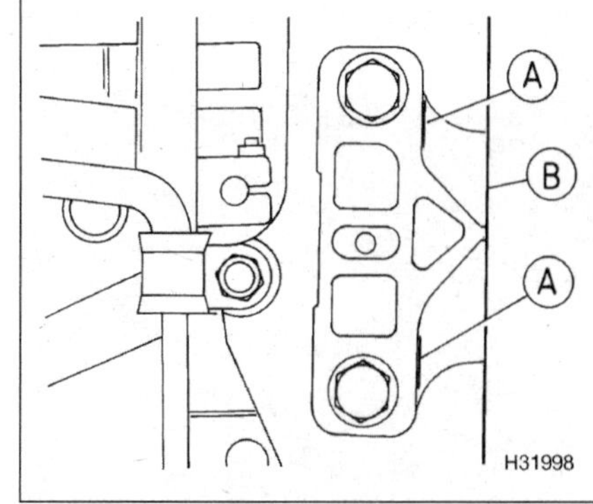

17.19 Engine/transmission left-hand mounting alignment details – edges (A) and (B) must be parallel

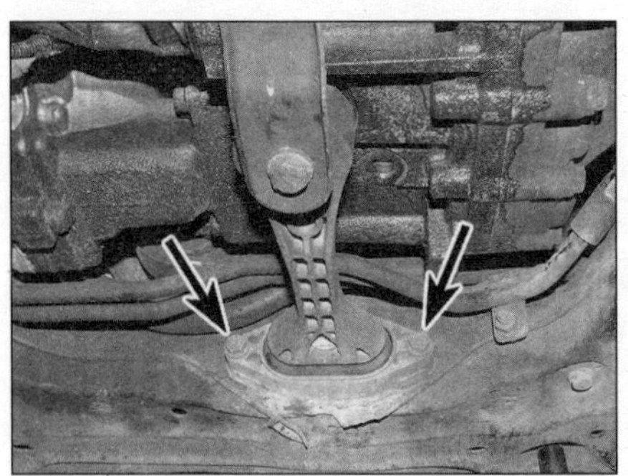

17.22 Mounting bracket-to-subframe bolts (arrowed)

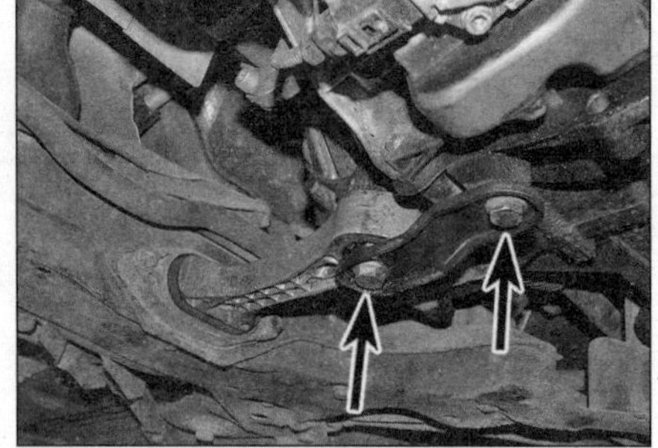

17.23 Mounting bracket-to-transmission bolts (arrowed)

Rear mounting

Note: *New mounting bolts will be required on refitting.*

20 Apply the handbrake, then jack up the front of the vehicle and support securely on axle stands (see *Jacking and vehicle support*). Remove the engine undershield(s) for access to the rear engine/transmission mounting.

21 Proceed as described in paragraph 5.

22 Working under the vehicle, unscrew and remove the two bolts securing the mounting assembly to the subframe **(see illustration)**.

23 Unscrew the two bolts securing the mounting to the transmission **(see illustration)**, then withdraw the mounting from under the vehicle.

24 Refitting is a reversal of removal, but use new mounting securing bolts, and tighten all fixings to the specified torque.

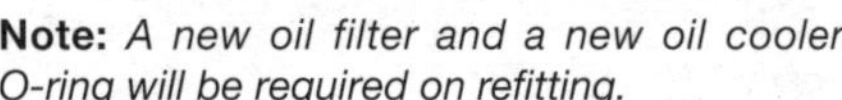

18 Engine oil cooler – removal and refitting

Note: *A new oil filter and a new oil cooler O-ring will be required on refitting.*

Removal

1 The oil cooler is mounted above the oil filter, at the front of the cylinder block **(see illustrations)**.

2 Position a container beneath the oil filter to catch escaping oil and coolant, then remove the oil filter, with reference to Chapter 1 Section 7 if necessary.

3 Clamp the oil cooler coolant hoses to minimise coolant spillage, then remove the clips, and disconnect the hoses from the oil cooler. Be prepared for coolant spillage.

4 Where applicable, release the oil cooler pipes from any retaining brackets or clips.

5 Unscrew the oil cooler securing nut from the oil filter mounting threads, then slide off the oil cooler. Recover the O-ring from the top of the oil cooler.

Refitting

6 Refitting is a reversal of removal, bearing in mind the following points.

a) Use a new oil cooler O-ring.

b) Fit a new oil filter.

c) On completion, check and if necessary top up the oil and coolant levels.

18.1a Oil cooler (arrowed)

19 Oil pressure relief valve – removal, inspection and refitting

Removal

1 The oil pressure relief valve is fitted to the right-hand side of the oil filter housing **(see illustration 18.1b)**.

2 Wipe clean the area around the relief valve plug then slacken and remove the plug and sealing ring from the filter housing. Withdraw the valve spring and piston, noting their correct fitted positions. If the valve is to be left removed from the engine for any length of time, plug the hole in the oil filter housing.

Inspection

3 Examine the relief valve piston and spring for signs of wear or damage. At the time of writing it appears that the relief valve spring and piston were not available separately; check with your Audi dealer for the latest parts availability. If the spring and piston are worn it will be necessary to renew the complete oil filter housing assembly. The valve plug and sealing ring are listed as separate components.

Refitting

4 Fit the piston to the inner end of the spring then insert the assembly into the oil filter housing. Ensure the sealing ring is correctly fitted to the valve plug then fit the plug to the housing, tightening it to the specified torque.

1 Sealing plug
2 Seal
3 Oil pressure relief valve spring
4 Oil pressure relief valve piston
5 Gasket
6 Non-return valve
7 Seal
8 Sealing cap (not fitted to this engine)
9 Retaining clip
10 Sealing plug
11 Seal
12 Oil pressure warning light switch
13 Seal
14 Oil filter housing
15 Bolt
16 Seal
17 Oil cooler
18 Nut
19 Oil filter
20 Connecting pipe

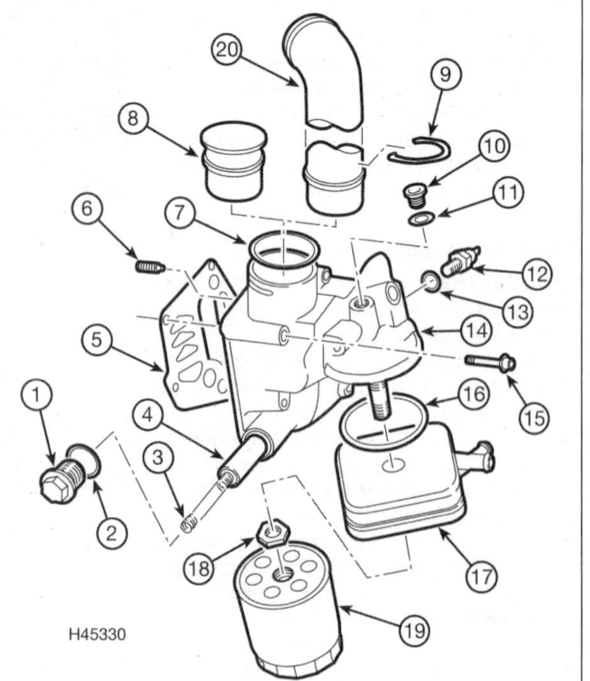

18.1b Oil cooler details

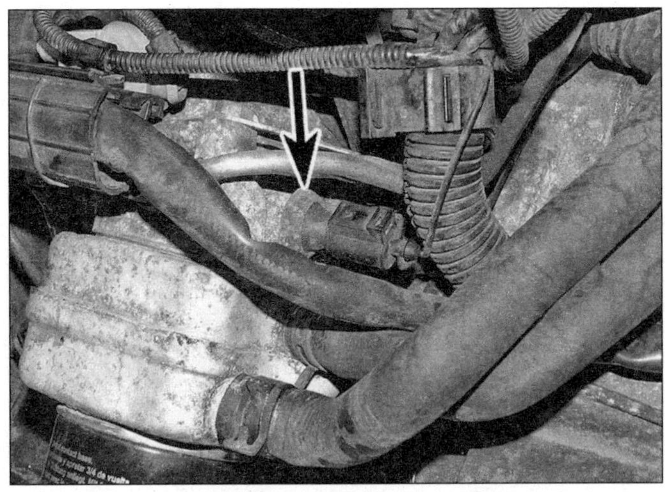

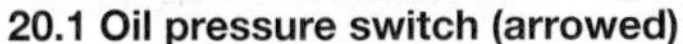

20.1 Oil pressure switch (arrowed)

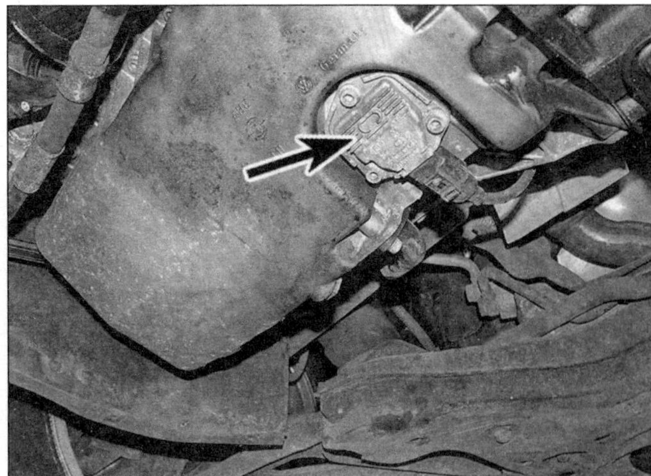

21.1 Oil level/temperature sender (arrowed)

5 On completion, check and, if necessary, top-up the engine oil as described in *Weekly checks*.

20 Oil pressure warning light switch - removal and refitting

Removal

1 The oil pressure warning light switch is fitted to the left-hand side of the oil filter housing **(see illustration)**, also the oil pressure warning light switch can be seen in diagram 18.1b.

2 Disconnect the wiring connector and wipe clean the area around the switch.

3 Unscrew the switch from the filter housing and remove it, along with its sealing washer. If the switch is to be left removed from the engine for any length of time, plug the oil filter housing aperture.

Refitting

4 Examine the sealing washer for signs of damage or deterioration and if necessary renew.

5 Refit the switch, complete with washer, and tighten it to the specified torque.

6 Securely reconnect the wiring connector then check and, if necessary, top-up the engine oil as described in *Weekly checks*.

21 Oil level/temperature sender - removal and refitting

Removal

1 The oil level/temperature sender is fitted to bottom of the sump **(see illustration)**.

2 Drain the engine oil as described in Chapter 1 Section 7.

3 Disconnect the wiring connector and wipe clean the area around the sender.

4 Undo the three retaining bolts and remove the sender.

Refitting

5 Examine the sealing washer for signs of damage or deterioration and if necessary renew.

6 Refit the switch and tighten the retaining bolts to the specified torque.

7 Securely reconnect the wiring connector then refill the engine with oil, with reference to Chapter 1 Section 7.

8 On completion, check and, if necessary, top-up the engine oil as described in *Weekly checks*.

Notes

Chapter 2 Part B
Engine removal and overhaul procedures

Contents

Degrees of difficulty

Easy, suitable for novice with little experience 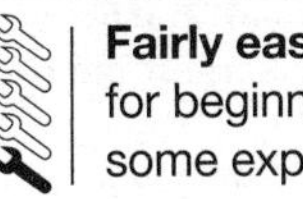	**Fairly easy,** suitable for beginner with some experience	**Fairly difficult,** suitable for competent DIY mechanic	**Difficult,** suitable for experienced DIY mechanic	**Very difficult,** suitable for expert DIY or professional 

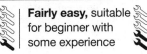

Specifications

Cylinder head

Minimum permissible dimension between top of valve stem and top surface of cylinder head:

Outer inlet valves	31.0 mm
Centre inlet valves	32.2 mm
Exhaust valve	31.9 mm
Minimum cylinder head height	139.2 mm
Maximum cylinder head gasket face distortion	0.1 mm

Valves

	Inlet valves	Exhaust valves
Valve stem diameter	5.963 mm	5.943 mm
Valve head diameter	26.9 mm	29.9 mm
Valve length	104.84 to 105.34 mm	103.64 to 104.14 mm
Valve seat angle (all engines)	45°	

Crankshaft

Main journal diameter (basic dimension)	54.00 mm (Nominal)
Big-end journal diameter (basic dimension)	47.80 mm (Nominal)
Endfloat:	
New	0.07 to 0.23 mm
Wear limit	0.30 mm

Bearing running clearances

Main bearings	0.01 to 0.04 mm	0.07 mm
Big-end bearings	0.01 to 0.05 mm	0.09 mm

Pistons/connecting rods	**New**	**Wear limit**
Connecting rod side-play on crankshaft journal	0.10 to 0.31 mm	0.40 mm
Piston rings		
End gaps:	New	Wear limit
Compression rings	0.20 to 0.40 mm	0.8 mm
Oil scraper ring	0.25 to 0.50 mm	0.8 mm
Ring-to-groove clearance:		
Common conrods:		
Compression rings	0.02 to 0.07 mm	0.12 mm
Oil scraper ring	0.02 to 0.06 mm	0.12 mm
Cracked conrods:		
Compression rings	0.06 to 0.09 mm	0.20 mm
Oil scraper ring	0.03 to 0.06 mm	0.15 mm
Piston and cylinder bore diameters	**Piston**	**Cylinder bore**
Standard	80.965 mm	81.010 mm
1st oversize	81.465 mm	81.510 mm

Torque wrench settings

Refer to Chapter 2A.

1 General Information

1 Included in this Part of Chapter 2 are details of removing the engine from the car and general overhaul procedures for the cylinder head, cylinder block and all other engine internal components.

2 The information given ranges from advice concerning preparation for an overhaul and the purchase of new parts, to detailed step-by-step procedures covering removal, inspection, renovation and refitting of engine internal components.

3 After Section 5, all instructions are based on the assumption that the engine has been removed from the car. For information concerning in-car engine repair, as well as the removal and refitting of those external components necessary for full overhaul, refer to the in-car repair procedure section (Chapter 2A) and to Section 5 of this Chapter. Ignore any preliminary dismantling operations described in the in-car repair sections that are no longer relevant once the engine has been removed from the car.

4 Apart from torque wrench settings, which are given at the beginning of the in-car repair procedure in Chapter 2A, all specifications relating to engine overhaul are given at the beginning of this Part of Chapter.

2 Engine overhaul – general information

1 It is not always easy to determine when, or if, an engine should be completely overhauled, as a number of factors must be considered.

2 High mileage is not necessarily an indication that an overhaul is needed, while low mileage does not preclude the need for an overhaul. Frequency of servicing is probably the most important consideration. An engine which has had regular and frequent oil and filter changes, as well as other required maintenance, should give many thousands of miles of reliable service. Conversely, a neglected engine may require an overhaul very early in its life.

3 Excessive oil consumption is an indication that piston rings, valve seals and/or valve guides are in need of attention. Make sure that oil leaks are not responsible before deciding that the rings and/or guides are worn. Perform a compression (or leakdown) test, as described in Chapter 2A, to determine the likely cause of the problem.

4 Check the oil pressure with a gauge fitted in place of the oil pressure switch, and compare it with that specified (see Specifications in Chapter 2A). If it is extremely low, the main and big-end bearings, and/or the oil pump, are probably worn.

5 Loss of power, rough running, knocking or metallic engine noises, excessive valve gear noise, and high fuel consumption may also point to the need for an overhaul, especially if they are all present at the same time. If a complete service does not remedy the situation, major mechanical work is the only solution.

6 An engine overhaul involves restoring all internal parts to the specification of a new engine. During an overhaul, the pistons and the piston rings are renewed. New main and big-end bearings are generally fitted (where possible); if necessary, the crankshaft may be renewed to restore the journals. The valves are also serviced as well, since they are usually in less-than-perfect condition at this point. While the engine is being overhauled, other components, such as the starter and alternator, can be overhauled as well. The end result should be an as-new engine that will give many trouble-free miles. **Note:** *Critical cooling system components such as the hoses, thermostat and coolant pump should be renewed when an engine is overhauled. The radiator should be checked carefully, to ensure that it is not clogged or leaking. Also, it is a good idea to renew the oil pump whenever the engine is overhauled.*

7 Before beginning the engine overhaul, read through the entire procedure, to familiarise yourself with the scope and requirements of the job. Overhauling an engine is not difficult if you follow carefully all of the instructions, have the necessary tools and equipment, and pay close attention to all specifications. It can, however, be time-consuming. Plan on the car being off the road for a minimum of two weeks, especially if parts must be taken to an engineering works for repair or reconditioning. Check on the availability of parts and make sure that any necessary special tools and equipment are obtained in advance. Most work can be done with typical hand tools, although a number of precision measuring tools are required for inspecting parts to determine if they must be renewed. Often the engineering works will handle the inspection of parts and offer advice concerning reconditioning and renewal. **Note:** *Always wait until the engine has been completely dismantled, and until all components (especially the cylinder block and the crankshaft) have been inspected, before deciding what service and repair operations must be performed by an engineering works. The condition of these components will be the major factor to consider when determining whether to overhaul the original engine, or to buy a reconditioned unit. Do not, therefore, purchase parts or have overhaul work done on other components until they have been thoroughly inspected. As a general rule, time is the primary cost of an overhaul, so it does not pay to fit worn or sub-standard parts.*

8 As a final note, to ensure maximum life and minimum trouble from a reconditioned engine, everything must be assembled with care, in a spotlessly-clean environment.

3 Engine/transmission removal – preparation and precautions

1 If you have decided that the engine must be removed for overhaul or major repair work, several preliminary steps should be taken.

2 Locating a suitable place to work is extremely important. Adequate work space, along with storage space for the vehicle, will be needed. If a workshop or garage is not available, at the very least a solid, level, clean work surface is required.

3 If possible, clear some shelving close to the work area and use it to store the engine components and ancillaries as they are removed and dismantled. In this manner, the compo-nents stand a better chance of staying clean and undamaged during the overhaul. Laying out components in groups together with their fixings bolts, screws, etc, will save time and avoid confusion when the engine is refitted.

4 Clean the engine compartment and engine before beginning the removal procedure; this will help visibility and help to keep tools clean.

5 The help of an assistant is essential; there are certain instances when one person cannot safely perform all of the operations required to remove the engine from the vehicle. Safety is of primary importance, considering the potential hazards involved in this kind of operation. A second person should always be in attendance to offer help in an emergency. If this is the first time you have removed an engine, advice and aid from someone more experienced would also be beneficial.

6 Plan the operation ahead of time. Before starting work, obtain (or arrange for the hire of) all of the tools and equipment you will need. Access to the following items will allow the task of removing and refitting the engine to be completed safely and with relative ease: a hoist and lifting tackle – rated in excess of the weight of the engine, complete sets of spanners and sockets as described at the rear of this manual, wooden blocks, and plenty of rags and cleaning solvent for mopping up spilled oil, coolant and fuel. A selection of different-sized plastic storage bins will also prove useful for keeping dismantled components grouped together. If any of the equipment must be hired, make sure that you arrange for it in advance, and perform all of the operations possible without it beforehand; this may save you time and money.

7 Plan on the vehicle being out of use for quite a while, especially if you intend to carry out an engine overhaul. Read through the whole of this Section and work out a strategy based on your own experience, and the tools, time and workspace available to you. Some of the overhaul processes may have to be carried out by an Audi dealer or an engineering works – these establishments often have busy schedules, so it would be prudent to consult them before removing or dismantling the engine, to get an idea of the amount of time required to carry out the work.

8 When removing the engine from the vehicle, be methodical about the disconnection of external components. Labelling cables and hoses as they are removed will greatly assist the refitting process.

9 Always be extremely careful when lifting the engine from the engine compartment. Serious injury can result from careless actions. If help is required, it is better to wait until it is available rather than risk personal injury and/or damage to components by continuing alone. By planning ahead and taking your time, a job of this nature, although major, can be accomplished successfully and without incident.

4 Engine/transmission – removal and refitting

1 The engine and transmission are removed by lowering them out as a unit from underneath the engine compartment.

2 Disconnect the battery negative lead. Note: Before disconnecting the battery, refer to *Disconnecting the battery* at the rear of this manual.

3 To allow improved access and clearance for removal of the engine/transmission, it is useful to unbolt and remove the body front panel as follows:

a) Remove the front bumper as described in Chapter 11 Section 6.

b) Disconnect the bonnet release cable from the bonnet lock, with reference to Chapter 11 Section 9.

c) Unscrew the four bolts (two on each side) securing the front bumper carrier to the brackets on the body.

d) Disconnect the cooling fan switch wiring plug.

e) Release the cooling fan wiring connector from the clips on the rear of the cooling fan shroud, then separate the two halves of the connector.

f) Disconnect the headlight wiring connectors (one connector for each headlight).

g) Unscrew the two upper bolts securing the body front panel to the front wing panels.

h) Make a final check to ensure that all relevant wiring, hoses and pipes have been disconnected, then pull the front body panel forwards, and withdraw it from the vehicle.

4 Remove the engine top cover(s). Release the plastic screws/fasteners and lift the cover(s) from the engine **(see illustrations).** Also release the fasteners are remove the plastic trim covers from over the battery, coolant reservoir and front crossmember.

5 Remove the air cleaner assembly as described in Chapter 4A Section 2.

6 Work around the engine and transmission, and disconnect all relevant vacuum and breather hoses to facilitate engine removal. Note the location and routing of the hoses to aid refitting.

7 Depressurise the fuel system as described in Chapter 4A Section 7. Place a wad of clean cloth around the fuel supply and return hose connections on the right-hand side of the engine compartment, then depress the quick release connector locking tabs, and disconnect the fuel line connectors **(see illustration)**. Be prepared for fuel spillage, and take adequate fire precautions.

8 Disconnect the vacuum hose from the valve on the charcoal canister at the right-hand side of the engine compartment.

9 Remove the air intake trunking connecting the air mass meter to the throttle housing on non-turbo models, or the air intake trunking connecting the air mass meter to the turbocharger on turbocharged engines.

4.4a Engine cover fasteners (arrowed) – all engine codes (except AMU, APX and BAM)

4.4b Engine cover fasteners (arrowed) – engine codes AMU, APX and BAM

4.7 Fuel supply and return hose connections (arrowed)

10 On turbocharged models, remove the air intake trunking which connects the intercooler to the throttle housing.

11 On models with manual transmission, remove the clutch slave cylinder as described in Chapter 6 Section 5. **Note:** *Do not depress the clutch pedal once the slave cylinder has been removed.*

12 On models with manual transmission, disconnect the gear selector mechanism from the transmission, with reference to Chapter 7A Section 2

13 Apply the handbrake, then jack up the front of the vehicle and support securely on axle stands (see *Jacking and vehicle support*). Note that the vehicle must be raised to give sufficient clearance to allow removal of the engine/transmission assembly from underneath the vehicle. Remove both front roadwheels.

14 Remove the securing screws and/or clips, and remove the engine undershield(s).

15 On models with automatic transmission, disconnect the gear selector cable from the transmission (see Chapter 7B Section 4).

16 Drain the cooling system as described in Chapter 1 Section 39.

17 Slacken the hose clips and disconnect the radiator top and bottom hoses from the engine.

18 Remove the charge air pipe from across the front of the engine compartment, as described in Chapter 4B Section 7

19 Remove the engine rear mounting with reference to Chapter 2A Section 17.

20 Disconnect all relevant wiring from the transmission, alternator and starter motor, noting the location and routing of the wiring to aid refitting.

21 Remove the exhaust front section as described in Chapter 4B Section 9.

22 Remove the auxiliary drivebelt as described in Chapter 1 Section 32.

23 Remove the clamps securing the power steering fluid pressure pipe. This will allow the power steering pump to be removed from the engine without disconnecting the fluid lines.

24 Unbolt the power steering pump from the engine, with reference to Chapter 10 Section 24, but leave the fluid lines connected, and support the pump clear of the working area.

25 Work around the engine and transmission, and disconnect any remaining hoses, pipes and wires to allow removal of the engine/transmission assembly, noting their location and routing to aid refitting.

26 Remove the right-hand driveshaft as described in Chapter 8A Section 3, and disconnect the left-hand driveshaft from the transmission.

27 On models with air conditioning, remove the air conditioning compressor as described in Chapter 3 Section 12.

Warning: Have the air conditioning system discharged by a suitably-qualified specialist before attempting to remove the compressor.

28 If not already done, connect a hoist and lifting tackle to the engine lifting brackets on the cylinder head, and raise the hoist to just take the weight of the engine.

29 Remove the right-hand and left-hand engine/transmission mountings, with reference to Chapter 2A Section 17.

30 Carefully lower the engine/transmission assembly out from under the vehicle. Support the assembly on a trolley, or on wooden blocks. Manipulate the assembly out from underneath the vehicle.

Engine and manual transmission separation

31 Unscrew the two securing bolts, and remove the starter motor.

32 Where applicable, unscrew the bolt securing the small engine-to-transmission plate to the transmission.

33 Ensure that both engine and transmission are adequately supported, then unscrew the remaining engine-to-transmission bolts, noting the location of each bolt, and the locations of any brackets secured by the bolts.

34 Carefully withdraw the transmission from the engine, ensuring that the weight of the transmission is not allowed to hang on the input shaft while it is engaged with the clutch friction disc. Recover the engine-to-transmission plate.

Engine and automatic transmission separation

35 Unscrew the two securing bolts, and remove the starter motor.

36 Prise out the torque converter nuts cover from the transmission casing. The cover is located behind the left-hand driveshaft flange. Turn the crankshaft to position one of the torque converter-to-driveplate nuts in the access aperture. Unscrew and remove the nut whilst preventing the engine from turning using a wide-bladed screwdriver engaged with the ring gear teeth on the driveplate.

37 Using the same method described in the previous paragraph, unscrew the remaining two torque converter-to-driveplate nuts, turning the crankshaft a third-of-a-turn at a time to locate them.

38 Ensure that both engine and transmission are adequately supported, then unscrew the engine-to-transmission bolts, noting the location of each bolt, and the locations of any brackets secured by the bolts.

39 Carefully withdraw the transmission from the engine (take care – the transmission is heavy), making sure that the torque converter remains fully engaged with the transmission input shaft. If necessary, use a lever to release the torque converter from the driveplate. Recover the engine-to-transmission plate.

40 Once the transmission has been separated from the engine, strap a restraining bar across the front of the bellhousing to keep the torque converter in position.

Engine reconnection and refitting

Engine and manual transmission

41 Reconnection and refitting are a reversal of removal, bearing in mind the following points:

a) *Smear the splines of the transmission input shaft with a little high-melting-point grease.*
b) *Ensure that any brackets noted before removal are in place on the engine-to-transmission bolts.*
c) *Tighten all fixings to the specified torque, where given.*
d) *Refit the engine mountings with reference to Chapter 2A.*
e) *Reconnect the driveshafts to the transmission with reference to Chapter 8A.*
f) *Where applicable, refit the air conditioning compressor, with reference to Chapter 3, and have the system recharged with refrigerant by a suitably-qualified professional.*
g) *Refit the auxiliary drivebelt with reference to Chapter 1.*
h) *Refit the exhaust front section as described in Chapter 4B.*
i) *Ensure that all wiring, hoses and pipes are correctly reconnected and routed as noted before removal.*
j) *Ensure that the fuel lines are correctly reconnected. The lines are colour-coded, white for supply, and blue for return.*
k) *On completion, refill the cooling system as described in Chapter 1.*

Engine and automatic transmission

42 Proceed as described in paragraph 41, but note the following additional points:

a) *When fitting the torque converter, make sure that both the drive pins engage with the transmission fluid pump.*
b) *Reconnect and if necessary adjust the gear selector cable, as described in Chapter 7B Section 4.*
c) *On completion, check and if necessary top-up the automatic transmission fluid level as described in Chapter 1.*

5 Engine overhaul – preliminary information

1 It is much easier to dismantle and work on the engine if it is mounted on a portable engine stand. These stands can often be hired from a tool hire shop. Before the engine is mounted on a stand, the flywheel should be removed, so that the stand bolts can be tightened into the end of the cylinder block/crankcase. **Note:** *Do not measure cylinder bore dimensions with the engine mounted on this type of stand.*

2 If a stand is not available, it is possible to dismantle the engine with it blocked up on a sturdy workbench, or on the floor. Be very

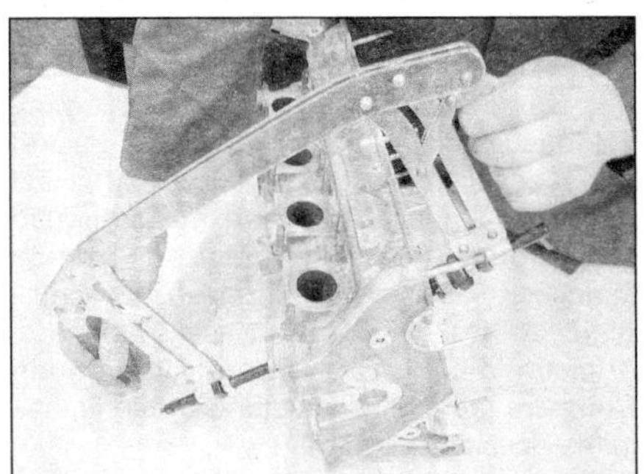

6.6a Compressing a valve spring with a compressor tool

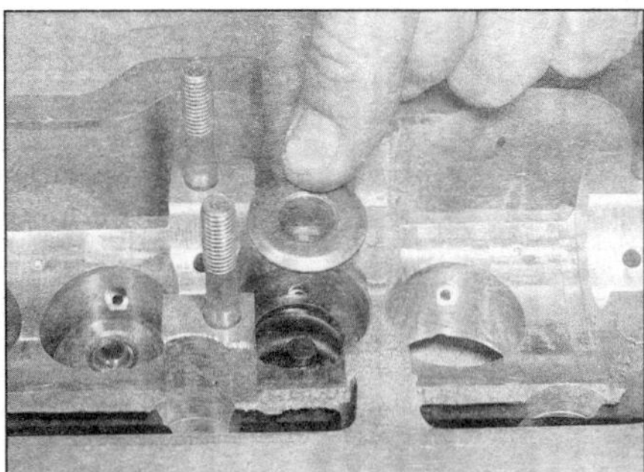

6.6b Removing the spring cap ...

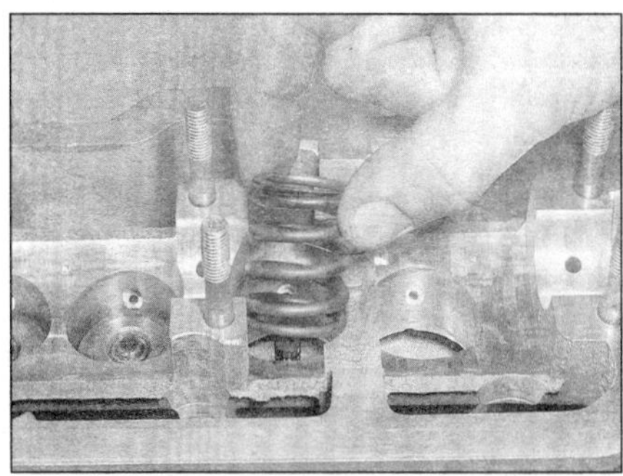

6.6c ... and valve spring

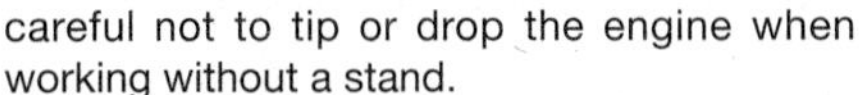

careful not to tip or drop the engine when working without a stand.

3 If you intend to obtain a reconditioned engine, all ancillaries must be removed first, to be transferred to the new engine (just as they will if you are doing a complete engine overhaul yourself). These components include the following (it may be necessary to transfer additional components, such as the oil level dipstick/tube assembly, oil filter housing, etc, depending on which components are supplied with the reconditioned engine:

a) *Alternator (including mounting brackets) and starter motor (Chapter 5A).*
b) *The ignition system components including all sensors, ignition coils and spark plugs (Chapter 1 and Chapter 5B).*
c) *The fuel injection system components (Chapter 4A).*
d) *All electrical switches, actuators and sensors, and the engine wiring harness (Chapters 3, 4A and 5B).*
e) *Inlet and exhaust manifolds, and turbo-charger (where applicable) (Chapter 4B).*
f) *Engine mountings (Chapter 2A Section 17).*
g) *Clutch components (Chapter 6).*
h) *Oil separator (where applicable).*

Note: *When removing the external components from the engine, pay close attention to details that may be helpful or important during refitting. Note the fitted position of gaskets, seals, spacers, pins, washers, bolts, and other small components.*

4 If you are obtaining a short engine (the engine cylinder block/crankcase, crankshaft, pistons and connecting rods, all fully assembled), then the cylinder head, sump, oil pump, timing belt(s) and chain (as applicable – together with tensioner(s) and covers), auxiliary drivebelt (together with its tensioner), coolant pump, thermostat housing, coolant outlet elbows, oil filter housing and where applicable oil cooler will also have to be removed.

5 If you are planning a full overhaul, the engine can be dismantled in the order given below:

a) *Inlet and exhaust manifolds (see the relevant part of Chapter 4A).*
b) *Timing belt, sprockets and tensioner(s) (see Chapter 2A Section 7, 8).*
c) *Inlet camshaft timing chain and tensioner/ camshaft adjuster mechanism (see Chapter 2A Section 9).*
d) *Cylinder head (see Chapter 2A Section 12).*
e) *Flywheel/driveplate (see Chapter 2A Section 15).*
f) *Sump (see Chapter 2A Section 13).*
g) *Oil pump (see Chapter 2A Section 14).*
h) *Piston/connecting rod assemblies (see Section 12).*
i) *Crankshaft (see Section 10).*

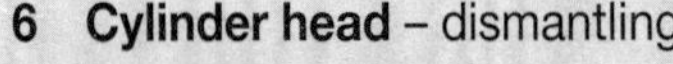

6 Cylinder head – dismantling

Note: *A valve spring compressor tool will be required for this operation.*

1 With the cylinder head removed as described in Chapter 2A Section 12, proceed as follows.

2 Remove the inlet and exhaust manifolds (and turbocharger, where applicable) as described in Chapters 4A and 4B.

3 Remove the camshafts and hydraulic tappets as described in Chapter 2A Section 10.

4 Unbolt any remaining auxiliary brackets and/or engine lifting brackets from the cylinder head as necessary, noting their locations to aid refitting.

5 Turn the cylinder head over, and rest it on one side.

6 Using a valve spring compressor, compress each valve spring in turn, until the split collets can be removed. Release the compressor, and lift off the spring cap and spring. If, when the valve spring compressor is screwed down, the spring cap refuses to free and expose the split collets, gently tap the top of the tool, directly over the spring cap, with a light hammer. This will free the retainer **(see illustrations)**.

Note: *The following sequence is from a single over head (SOHC) camshaft engine, double overhead camshaft (DOHC) procedure is similar.*

7 Using a pair of pliers, or a removal tool, carefully extract the valve stem oil seal from the top of the valve guide **(see illustration)**.

8 Withdraw the valve from the gasket side of the cylinder head **(see illustration)**.

9 It is essential that each valve is stored together with its collets, cap, spring and spring seat. The valves should be kept in

6.7a Using a removal tool ...

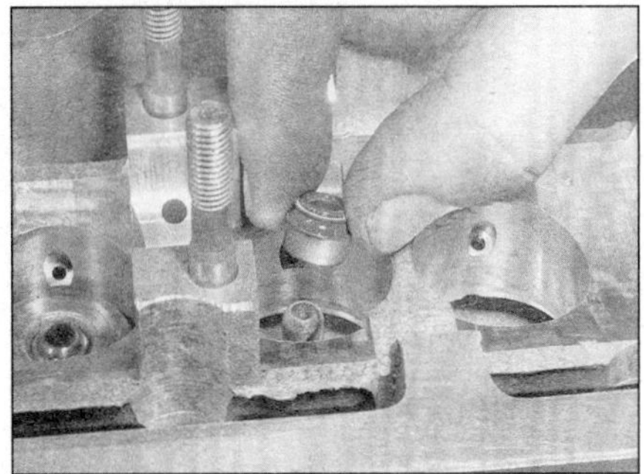

6.7b ... to remove the valve stem oil seals

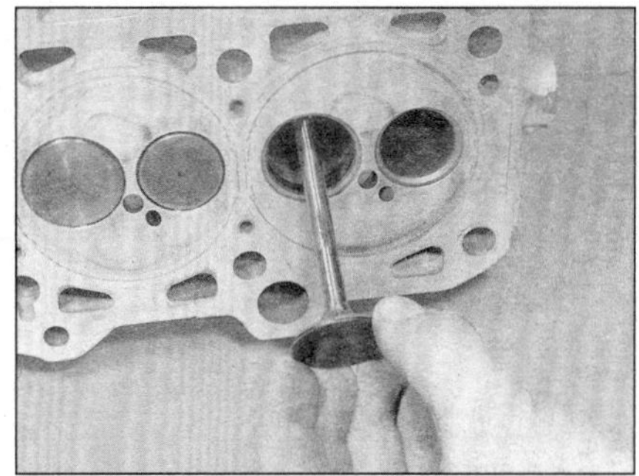

6.8 Removing a valve

their correct sequences, unless they are so badly worn that they are to be renewed. When labelling the valve components, make sure that the valves are identified as inlet and exhaust, as well as numbered.

If they are going to be kept and used again, place each valve assembly in a labelled polythene bag or similar small container.

7 Cylinder head and valves – cleaning and inspection

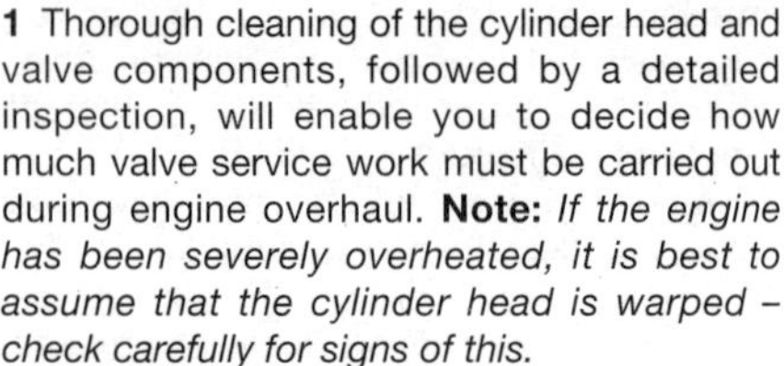

1 Thorough cleaning of the cylinder head and valve components, followed by a detailed inspection, will enable you to decide how much valve service work must be carried out during engine overhaul. **Note:** *If the engine has been severely overheated, it is best to assume that the cylinder head is warped – check carefully for signs of this.*

Cleaning

2 Using a suitable degreasing agent, remove all traces of oil deposits from the cylinder head, paying particular attention to the camshaft bearing surfaces, hydraulic tappet bores, valve guides and oilways. Scrape off any traces of old gasket from the mating surfaces, taking care not to score or gouge them. Turn the head over and, using a blunt blade, scrape any carbon deposits from the combustion chambers and ports. Finally, wash the entire head casting with a suitable solvent to remove the remaining debris.

3 Clean the valve heads and stems using a fine wire brush (or a power-operated wire brush). If the valve is covered with heavy carbon deposits, scrape off the majority of the deposits with a blunt blade first, then use the wire brush.

4 Thoroughly clean the remainder of the components using solvent and allow them to dry completely. Discard the oil seals, as new ones must be fitted when the cylinder head is reassembled.

Inspection

Cylinder head

Note: *If the valve seats are to be recut, ensure that the maximum permissible reworking dimension is not exceeded (the maximum dimension will only allow minimal reworking to produce a perfect seal between valve and seat). If the maximum dimension is exceeded, the function of the hydraulic tappets cannot be guaranteed, and the cylinder head must be renewed. Refer to paragraph 6 for details of how to calculate the maximum permissible reworking dimension.*

5 Examine the head casting closely to identify any damage or cracks that may have developed. Cracks can often be identified from evidence of coolant or oil leakage. Pay particular attention to the areas around the valve seats and spark plug/fuel injector holes.

6 Moderately pitted and scorched valve seats can be repaired by lapping the valves in during reassembly, as described later in this Chapter. Badly worn or damaged valve seats may be restored by recutting, however the maximum permissible reworking dimension must not be exceeded, which will only allow minimal reworking (see note at beginning of paragraph 5). To calculate the maximum permissible reworking dimension, proceed as follows **(see illustration)** :

a) *If a new valve is to be fitted, use the new valve for the following calculation.*
b) *Insert the valve into its guide in the cylinder head, and push the valve firmly on to its seat.*
c) *Using a flat edge placed across the top surface of the cylinder head, measure the distance between the top face of the valve stem, and the top surface of the cylinder head. Record the measurement obtained.*
d) *Consult the Specifications, and look up the value for the minimum permissible dimension between the top face of the valve stem and the top surface of the cylinder head.*
e) *Now take the measured distance and subtract the minimum permissible dimension, to give the maximum permissible reworking dimension; e.g. Measured distance (31.4 mm) minus Minimum permissible dimension (outer inlet valves – 31.0 mm) = Maximum permissible reworking dimension (0.4 mm).*

7 Measure any distortion of the gasket surfaces using a straight-edge and a set of feeler blades. Take one measurement longitudinally on the manifold mating surface(s). Take several measurements across the head gasket surface, to assess the level of distortion in all planes **(see illustration)**. Compare the measurements with the figures in the Specifications.

8 If the head is distorted beyond the specified limit, it may be possible to have it machined by an engineering works, provided that the minimum permissible cylinder head height is maintained.

Camshaft

9 Inspection of the camshaft is covered in Chapter 2A Section 10.

Valves and associated components

Note: *The valve heads cannot be re-cut, although they may be lapped in. If new valves are to be fitted, the old valves must be disposed of carefully (do not dispose of them as normal scrap), as the valve stems are filled with sodium. Consult your local scrap or recycling centre for advice.*

10 Examine each valve closely for signs of wear. Inspect the valve stems for wear ridges, scoring or variations in diameter; measure their diameters at several points along their lengths with a micrometer, and compare with the figures given in the Specifications **(see illustration)**.

11 The valve heads should not be cracked, badly pitted or charred. Note that light pitting of the valve head can be rectified by lapping-in the valves during reassembly, as described in Section 8.

12 Check that the valve stem end face is free from excessive pitting or indentation; this could be caused by defective hydraulic tappets.

13 Using vernier calipers, measure the free length of each of the valve springs. As a manufacturer's figure is not quoted, the only way to check the length of the springs is by comparison with a new component. Note that

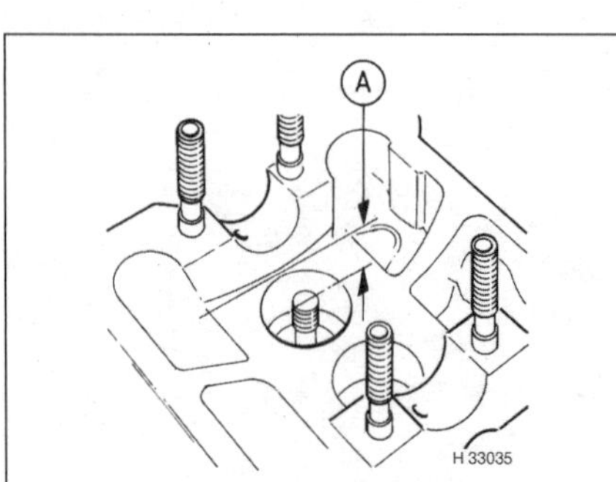

7.6 Measure the distance (A) between the top face of the valve stem and the top surface of the cylinder head

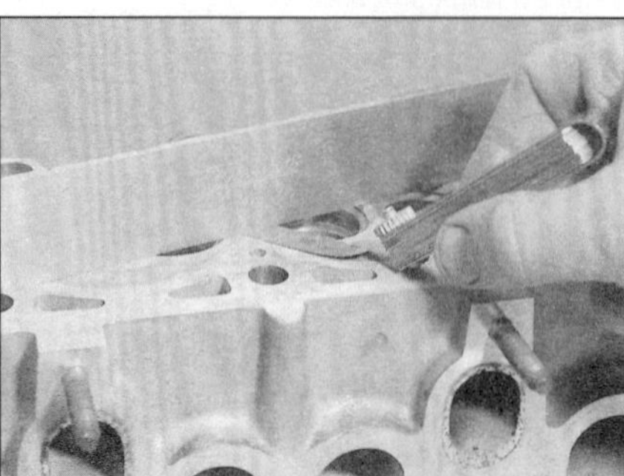

7.7 Measuring the distortion of the cylinder head gasket surface

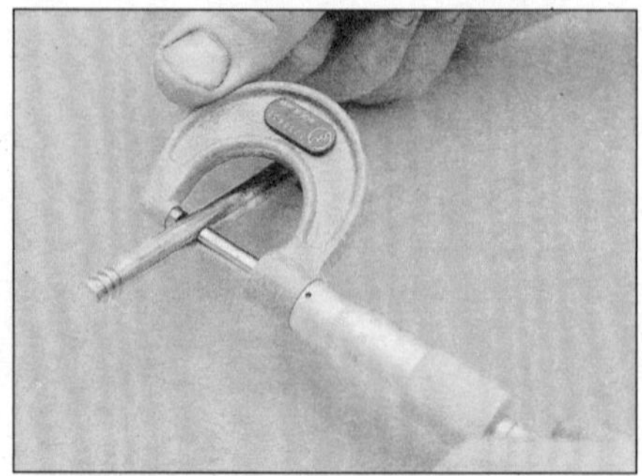

7.10 Measure the diameter of the valve stems using a micrometer

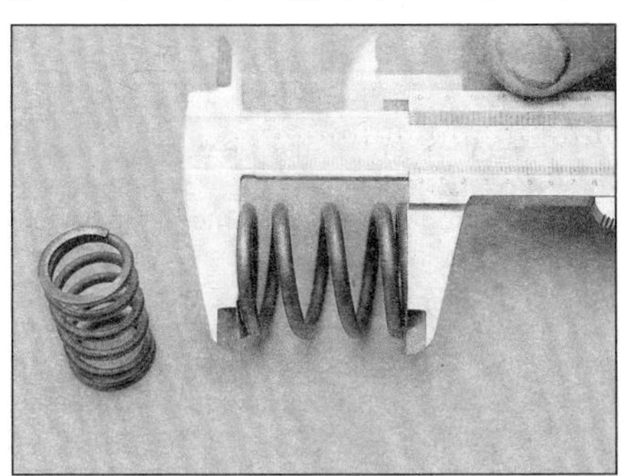
7.13 Measure the free length of each valve spring

7.14 Checking the squareness of a valve spring

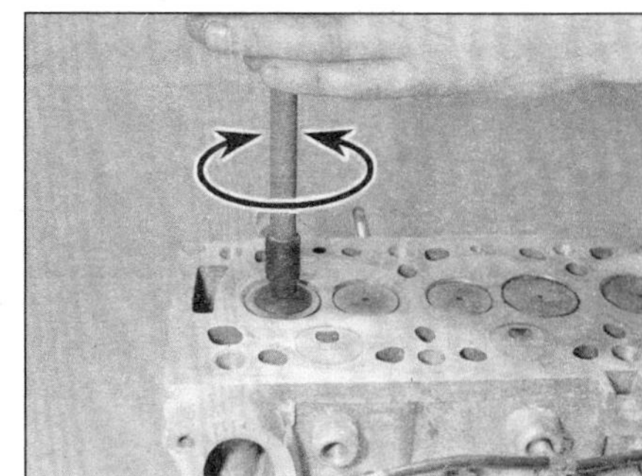
8.2 Grinding-in a valve

valve springs are usually renewed during a major engine overhaul **(see illustration)**.

14 Stand each spring on its end on a flat surface, against an engineer's square **(see illustration)**.Check the squareness of the spring visually, and renew it if it appears distorted.

15 Renew the valve stem oil seals regardless of their apparent condition.

8 Cylinder head – reassembly

Note: *A valve spring compressor tool will be required for this operation.*

Note: *The following sequence is from a single over head (SOHC) camshaft engine, double overhead camshaft (DOHC) procedure is similar.*

1 To achieve a gas-tight seal between the valves and their seats, it will be necessary to lap-in (or grind-in) the valves. To complete this process you will need a quantity of fine/ coarse grinding paste and a grinding tool – this can either be of the rubber sucker type, or the automatic type which is driven by a rotary power tool.

2 Smear a small quantity of fine grinding paste on the sealing face of the valve head. Turn the cylinder head over so that the combustion chambers are facing upwards and insert the valve into the correct guide. Attach the grinding tool to the valve head and using a backward/forward rotary action, grind the valve head into its seat. Periodically lift the valve and rotate it to redistribute the grinding paste **(see illustration)**.

3 Continue this process until the contact between valve and seat produces an unbroken, matt grey ring of uniform width, on both faces. Repeat the operation on the remaining valves.

4 If the valves and seats are so badly pitted that coarse grinding paste must be used, bear in that there is a maximum permissible reworking dimension for the valves and seats. Refer to the Specifications at the beginning of this Chapter for the minimum dimension from the end of the valve stem to the top face of the cylinder head (see Section 7, paragraph 6). If this minimum dimension is exceeded due to excessive lapping-in, the hydraulic tappets may not operate correctly, and the cylinder head must be renewed.

5 Assuming the repair is feasible, work as described previously, but use coarse grinding paste initially, to achieve a dull finish on the valve face and seat. Wash off the coarse paste with solvent and repeat the process using fine grinding paste to obtain the correct finish.

6 When all the valves have been ground in, remove all traces of grinding paste from the cylinder head and valves using solvent, and allow the head and valves to dry completely.

7 Turn the cylinder head on its side.

8 Working on one valve at a time, lubricate the valve stem with clean engine oil, and insert the valve into its guide. Fit one of the protective plastic sleeves supplied with the new valve stem oil seals over the end of the valve stem – this will protect the oil seal as it is being fitted **(see illustrations)**.

9 Dip a new valve stem seal in clean engine oil, and carefully push it over the valve stem and onto the top of the valve guide – take care not to damage the stem seal as it is fitted. Use a suitable long-reach socket or a suitable valve stem seal fitting tool to press the seal firmly into position **(see illustration)**. Remove the protective sleeve from the valve stem.

10 Locate the valve spring over the valve stem, ensuring that the lower end of the spring seats correctly on the cylinder head **(see illustration)**.

11 Fit the upper spring seat over the top of the spring, then using a valve spring com-pressor, compress the spring until the upper seat is pushed beyond the collet grooves in the valve stem. Refit the split collets. Gradually release the spring compressor, checking that the

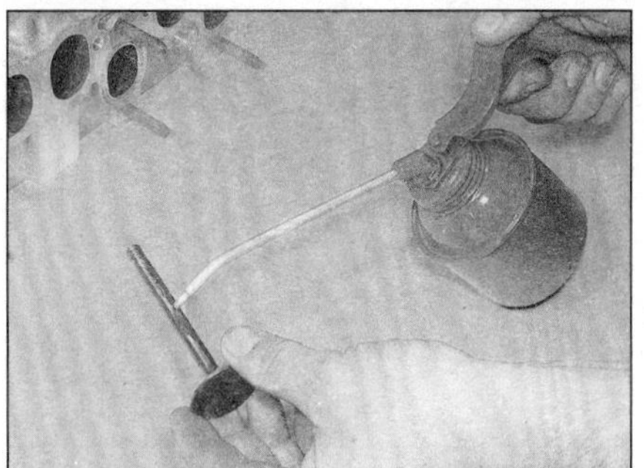
8.8a Lubricate the valve stem with clean engine oil

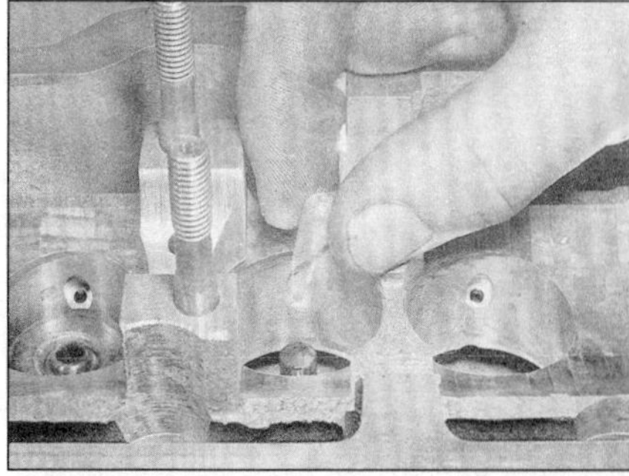
8.8b Fitting a protective sleeve over the valve stem before fitting the stem seal

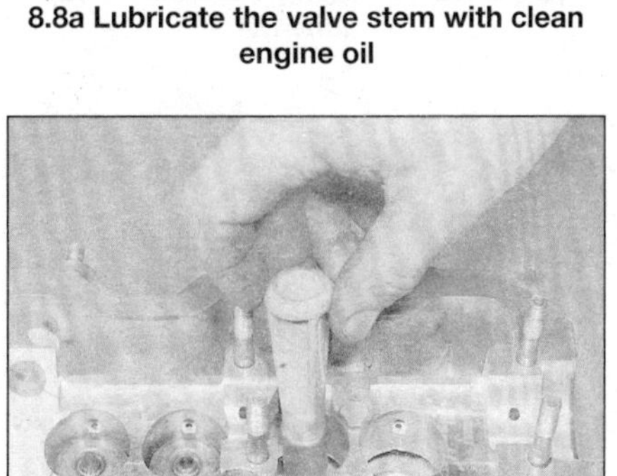
8.9 Using a special installer to fit a valve stem oil seal

8.10 Fitting a valve spring

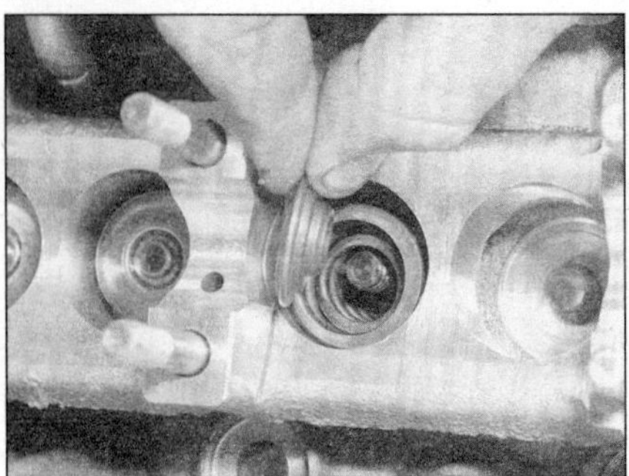
8.11a Fitting the upper spring seat

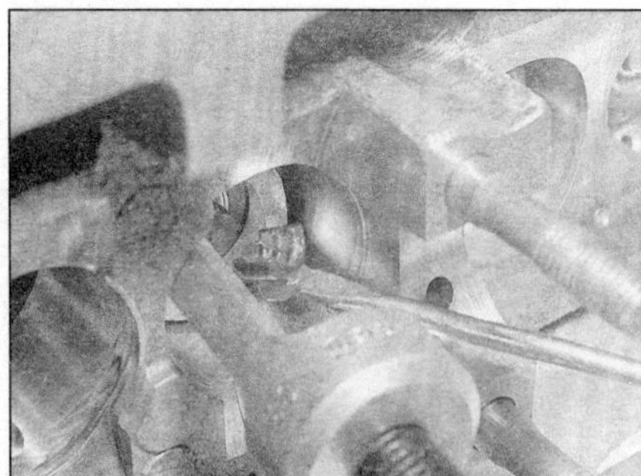
8.11b Use grease to hold the split collets in the groove

collets remain correctly seated as the spring extends. When correctly seated, the upper spring seat should force the collets securely into the grooves in the end of the valve stem **(see illustrations)**.

Use a little dab of grease to holdthe collets in position on the valvestem while the spring compressoris released.

12 Repeat this process for the remaining sets of valve components, ensuring that all components are refitted to their original locations. To settle the components after installation, strike the end of each valve stem with a mallet, using a block of wood to protect the stem from damage. Check before progressing any further that the split collets remain firmly seated in the grooves in the end of the valve stem.

13 Refit any auxiliary brackets and/or engine lifting brackets to their original locations, as noted before removal.

14 Refit the hydraulic tappets and camshafts as described in Chapter 2A Section 10.

15 Refit the inlet and exhaust manifolds as described in Chapter 4A and 4B.

9 Piston/connecting rod assemblies – removal

1 Remove the cylinder head, sump and oil baffle plate, and oil pump and pick-up pipe, as described in Chapter 2A Section 12

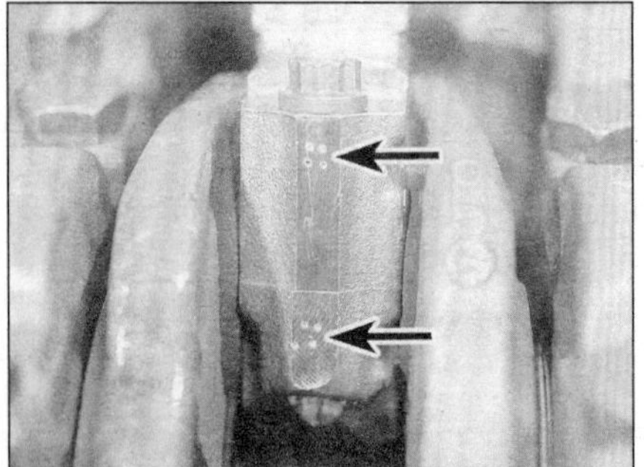
9.3 Mark the big-end caps and connecting rods with their cylinder numbers (arrowed)

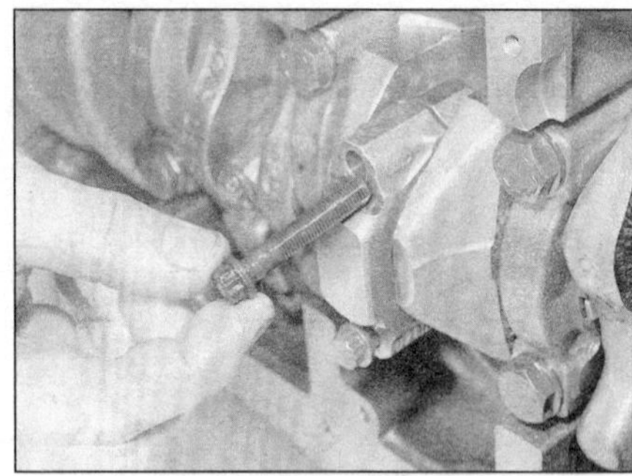
9.6a Unscrew the big-end bearing cap bolts ...

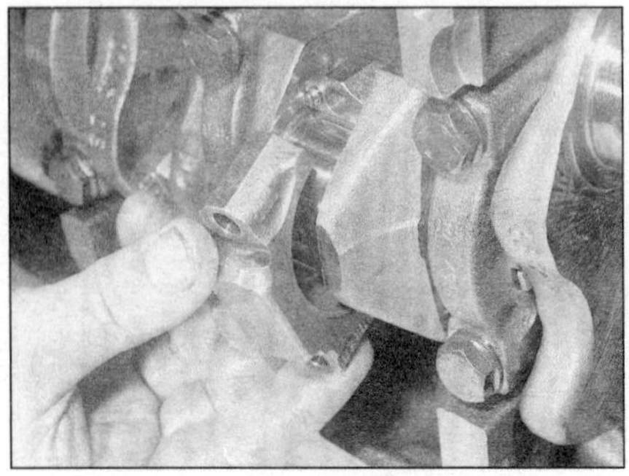
9.6b ... and remove the cap

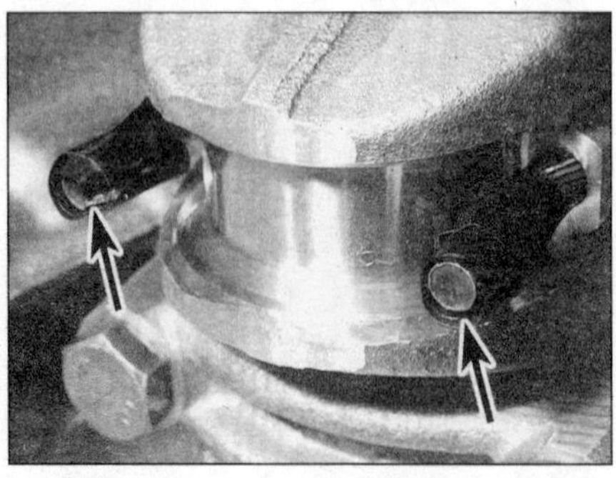
9.7 Wrap the threaded ends of the bolts with tape

2 Inspect the tops of the cylinder bores for ridges at the point where the pistons reach top dead centre. These must be removed otherwise the pistons may be damaged when they are pushed out of their bores. Use a scraper or ridge reamer to remove the ridges. Such a ridge indicates excessive wear of the cylinder bore.

3 Check the connecting rods and big-end caps for identification markings. Both connecting rods and caps should be marked with the cylinder number on one side of each assembly. Note that No 1 cylinder is at the timing belt end of the engine. If no marks are present, using a hammer and centre-punch, paint or similar, mark each connecting rod and big-end bearing cap with its respective cylinder number – note on which side of the connecting rods and caps the marks are made **(see illustration)**.

4 Similarly, check the piston crowns for direction markings. An arrow on each piston crown should point towards the timing belt end of the engine. On some engines, this mark may be obscured by carbon build-up, in which case the piston crown should be cleaned to check for a mark. In some cases, the direction arrow may have worn off, in which case a suitable mark should be made on the piston crown using a scriber – do not deeply score the piston crown, but ensure that the mark is easily visible.

5 Turn the crankshaft to bring Nos 1 and 4 pistons to bottom dead centre.

6 Unscrew the bolts or nuts, as applicable, from No 1 piston big-end bearing cap. Lift off the cap, and recover the bottom half bearing shell. If the bearing shells are to be re-used, tape the cap and bearing shell together. Note that if the bearing shells are to be re-used, they must be fitted to the original connecting rod and cap **(see illustrations)**.

7 Where the bearing caps are secured with nuts, wrap the threaded ends of the bolts with insulating tape to prevent them scratching the crankpins and bores when the pistons are removed **(see illustration)**.

8 Using a hammer handle, push the piston up through the bore, and remove it from the top of the cylinder block. Where applicable, take care not to damage the piston cooling oil spray jets in the cylinder block as the piston/connecting rod assembly is removed. Recover the upper bearing shell, and tape it to the connecting rod for safe-keeping.

9 Loosely refit the big-end cap to the connecting rod, and secure with the bolts or nuts, as applicable – this will help to keep the components in their correct order.

10 Remove No 4 piston assembly in the same way.

11 Turn the crankshaft as necessary to bring Nos 2 and 3 pistons to bottom dead centre, and remove them in the same way.

12 Remove the securing bolts, and

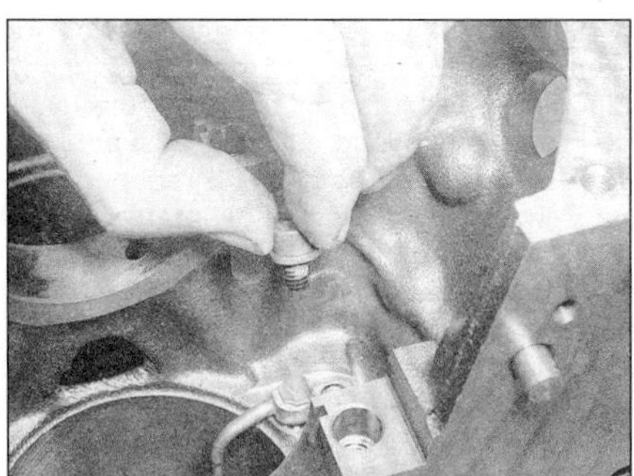
9.12a Remove the securing bolts ...

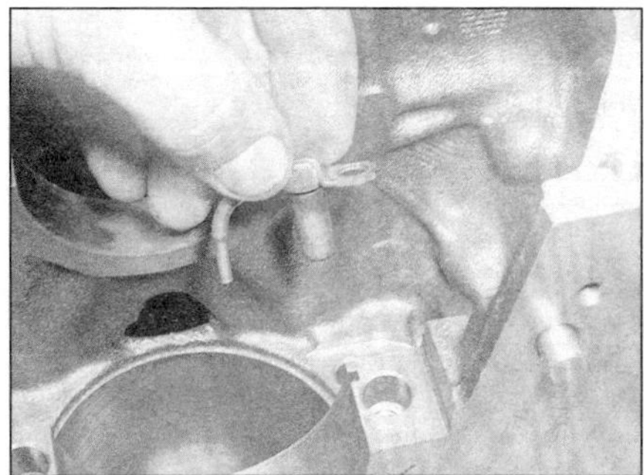
9.12b ... and withdraw the piston cooling oil spray jets

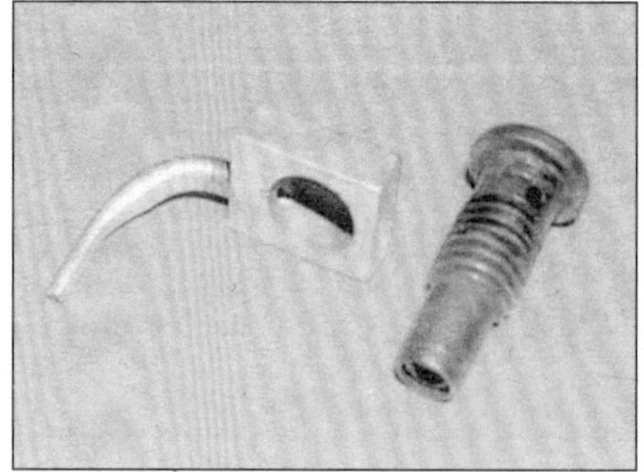
9.12c Piston cooling spray jet and retainer

withdraw the piston cooling oil spray jets from the bottom of the cylinder block **(see illustrations)**.

10 Crankshaft - removal

Note: *If no work is to be done on the pistons and connecting rods, there is no need to push the pistons out of the cylinder bores. The pistons should just be pushed far enough up the bores so that they are positioned clear of the crankshaft journals.*

1 Remove the timing belt and crankshaft sprocket, sump and oil baffle plate, oil pump and pick-up pipe, flywheel/driveplate, and the crankshaft oil seal housings, as described in Chapter 2A

2 Remove the pistons and connecting rods, or disconnect them from the crankshaft, as described in Section 9 (see Note at the beginning of this Section).

3 Check the crankshaft endfloat as described in Section 13, then proceed as follows.

4 The main bearing caps should be numbered 1 to 5 from the timing belt end of the engine. If the bearing caps are not marked, mark them accordingly using a centre-punch. Note the orientation of the markings to ensure correct refitting.

5 Slacken and remove the main bearing cap bolts, and lift off each cap. If the caps appear to be stuck, tap them with a soft-faced mallet to free them from the cylinder block **(see illustration)**. Recover the lower bearing shells, and tape them to their caps for safe-keeping.

6 Recover the lower crankshaft endfloat control thrustwasher halves from either side of the No 3 main bearing cap, noting their orientation.

7 Lift the crankshaft from the cylinder block. Take care, as the crankshaft is heavy. The crankshaft is fitted with a speed/position sender wheel fitted to the flywheel end of the crankshaft, lay the crankshaft on wooden blocks - do not rest the crankshaft on the sender wheel.

8 Recover the upper bearing shells from the cylinder block, and tape them to their respective caps for safe-keeping. Similarly, recover the upper crankshaft endfloat control thrustwasher halves, noting their orientation.

9 Unscrew the securing bolts, and remove the sender wheel from the flywheel end of the crankshaft, noting which way round it is fitted. Discard bolts as new ones will be required for refitting.

11 Cylinder block/crankcase - cleaning and inspection

Cleaning

1 Remove all external components and electrical switches/sensors from the block, including mounting brackets, the coolant pump, the oil filter/cooler housing, etc. For complete cleaning, the core plugs should ideally be removed. Drill a small hole in the plugs, then insert a self-tapping screw into the hole. Extract the plugs by pulling on the screw with a pair of grips, or by using a slide hammer.

2 Scrape all traces of gasket and sealant from the cylinder block/crankcase, taking care not to damage the sealing surfaces.

3 Remove all oil gallery plugs (where fitted). The plugs are usually very tight - they may have to be drilled out, and the holes re tapped. Use new plugs when the engine is reassembled.

4 If the casting is extremely dirty, it should be steam-cleaned. After this, clean all oil holes and galleries one more time. Flush all internal passages with warm water until the water runs clear. Dry thoroughly, and apply a light film of oil to all mating surfaces and cylinder bores, to prevent rusting. If you have access to compressed air, use it to speed up the drying process, and to blow out all the oil holes and galleries.

Warning: Wear eye protection when using compressed air.

5 If the castings are not very dirty, you can do an adequate cleaning job with hot, soapy water and a stiff brush. Take plenty of time, and do a thorough job. Regardless of the cleaning method used, be sure to clean all oil holes and galleries very thoroughly, and to dry all components well. Protect the cylinder bores as described above, to prevent rusting.

6 Check the piston cooling oil spray jets **(see illustrations 9.12a and 9.12b)** for damage, and renew if necessary. Check the oil spray hole and the oil passages for blockage.

7 All threaded holes must be clean, to ensure accurate torque readings during reassembly. To clean the threads, run the correct-size tap into each of the holes to remove rust, corrosion, thread sealant or sludge, and to restore damaged threads **(see illustration)**. If possible, use compressed air to clear

10.5 Slacken and remove the main bearing cap bolts

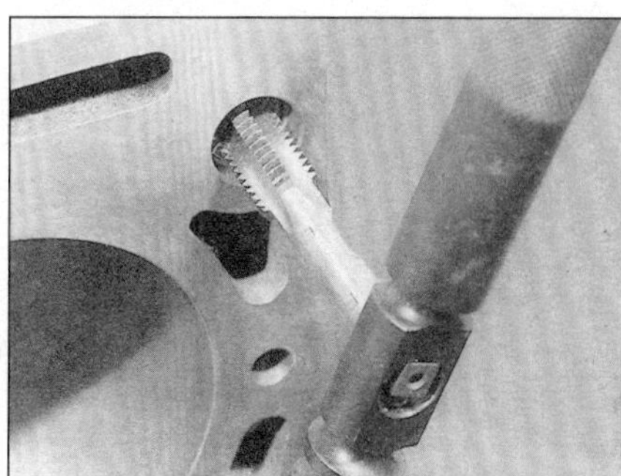
11.7 To clean the cylinder block threads, run a correct-size tap into the holes

the holes free of debris produced by this operation. **Note:** *Take extra care to exclude all cleaning liquid from blind tapped holes, as the casting may be cracked by hydraulic action if a bolt is threaded into a hole containing liquid.*

A good alternative is to inject aerosol – applied water dispersant lubricant into each hole, using the long spout usually supplied.

8 After coating the mating surfaces of the new core plugs with suitable sealant, fit them to the cylinder block. Make sure that they are driven in straight and seated correctly, or leakage could result.

A large socket with an outside diameter which will just fit into the core plug can be used to the drive core plug into position.

9 Apply suitable sealant to the new oil gallery plugs, and insert them into the holes in the block. Tighten them securely.

10 If the engine is not going to be reassembled immediately, cover it with a large plastic bag to keep it clean; protect all mating surfaces and the cylinder bores, to prevent rusting.

Inspection

11 Visually check the castings for cracks and corrosion. Look for stripped threads in the threaded holes. If there has been any history of internal coolant leakage, it may be worthwhile having an engine overhaul specialist check the cylinder block/crankcase for cracks with special equipment. If defects are found, have them repaired, if possible, or renew the assembly.

12 Check each cylinder bore for scuffing and scoring.

13 If in any doubt as the condition of the cylinder block have the block/bores inspected and measured by an engine reconditioning specialist. They will be able to advise on whether the block is serviceable, whether a rebore is necessary, and supply the appropriate pistons and rings.

14 If the bores are in reasonably good condition and not excessively worn, then it may only be necessary to renew the piston rings.

15 If this is the case, the bores should be honed, to allow the new rings to bed-in correctly and provide the best possible seal. Consult an engine reconditioning specialist

16 The cylinder block/crankcase should now be completely clean and dry, with all components checked for wear or damage, and repaired or overhauled as necessary.

17 Apply a light coating of engine oil to the mating surfaces and cylinder bores to prevent rust forming.

18 Refit as many ancillary components as possible, for safe-keeping. If reassembly is not to start immediately, cover the block with a large plastic bag to keep it clean, and protect the machined surfaces as described above to prevent rusting.

12 Piston/connecting rod assemblies – cleaning and inspection

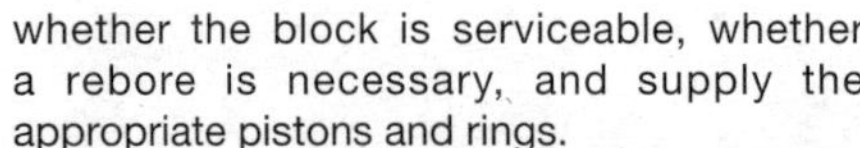

Cleaning

1 Before the inspection process can begin, the piston/connecting rod assemblies must be cleaned, and the original piston rings removed from the pistons.

2 The rings should have smooth, polished working surfaces, with no dull or carbon-coated sections (showing that the ring is not sealing correctly against the bore wall, so allowing combustion gases to blow by) and no traces of wear on their top and bottom surfaces. The end gaps should be clear of carbon, but not polished (indicating a too-small end gap), and all the rings (including the elements of the oil control ring) should be free to rotate in their grooves, but without excessive up-and-down movement. If the rings appear to be in good condition, they are probably fit for further use; check the end gaps (in an unworn part of the bore) as described in Section 16.

3 If any of the rings appears to be worn or damaged, or has an end gap significantly different from the specified value, the usual course of action is to renew all of them as a set. **Note:** *While it is usual to renew piston rings when an engine is overhauled, they may be re-used if in acceptable condition. If re-using the rings, make sure that each ring is marked during removal to ensure that it is refitted correctly.*

4 Carefully expand the old rings over the top of the pistons. The use of two or three old feeler blades will be helpful in preventing the rings dropping into empty grooves **(see illustration)**. Be careful not to scratch the piston with the ends of the ring. The rings are brittle, and will snap if they are spread too far. They are also very sharp – protect your hands and fingers. Note that the third ring incorporates an expander.

5 Scrape away all traces of carbon from the top of the piston. A hand-held wire brush (or a piece of fine emery cloth) can be used, once the majority of the deposits have been scraped away.

6 Remove the carbon from the ring grooves in the piston, using an old ring. Break the ring in half to do this (be careful not to cut your fingers – piston rings are sharp). Be careful to remove only the carbon deposits – do not remove any metal, and do not nick or scratch the sides of the ring grooves.

7 Once the deposits have been removed, clean the piston/connecting rod assembly with paraffin or a suitable solvent, and dry thoroughly. Make sure that the oil return holes in the ring grooves are clear.

Inspection

8 If the pistons and cylinder bores are not damaged or worn excessively, and if the cylinder block does not need to be rebored, the original pistons can be refitted.

9 Using a micrometer, measure the diameter of all four pistons at a point 10 mm from the bottom of the skirt, at right-angles to the gudgeon pin axis **(see illustration)**. Compare the measurements with those listed in the Specifications. Note that the piston size grades are stamped on the piston crowns.

10 If the piston diameter is incorrect for its particular size, then it must be renewed. **Note:** *If the cylinder block was rebored during a previous overhaul, oversize pistons may already have been fitted.* Record all of the measurements and use them to check the piston clearances against the cylinder bore measurements made in Section 11.

11 Normal piston wear shows up as even vertical wear on the piston thrust surfaces, and slight looseness of the top ring in its groove. New piston rings should always be used when the engine is reassembled.

12 Carefully inspect each piston for cracks around the skirt, around the gudgeon pin holes, and at the piston ring 'lands' (between the ring grooves).

13 Look for scoring and scuffing on the

12.4 Old feeler blades can be used to prevent piston rings from dropping into empty grooves

12.9 Using a micrometer to measure the diameter of a piston

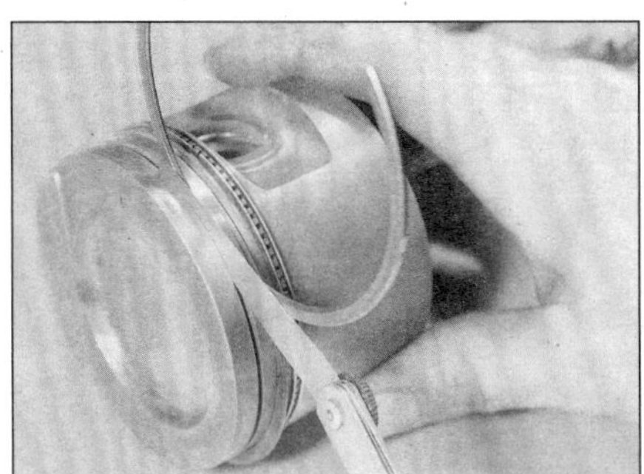
12.18 Measuring the piston ring-to-groove clearance using a feeler blade

12.22a Use a small flat-bladed screwdriver to prise out the circlip ...

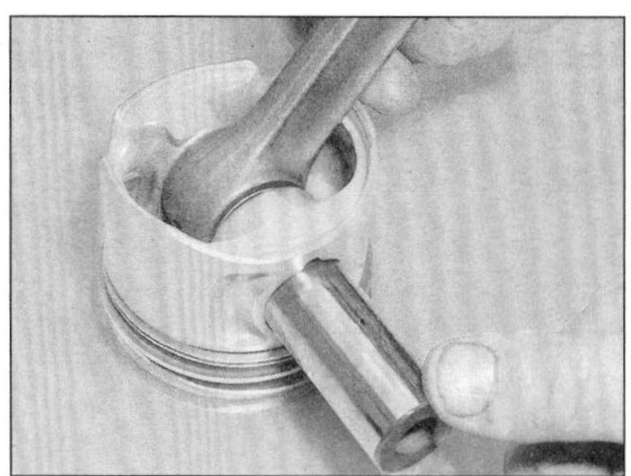
12.22b ... then push out the gudgeon pin and separate the piston and connecting rod

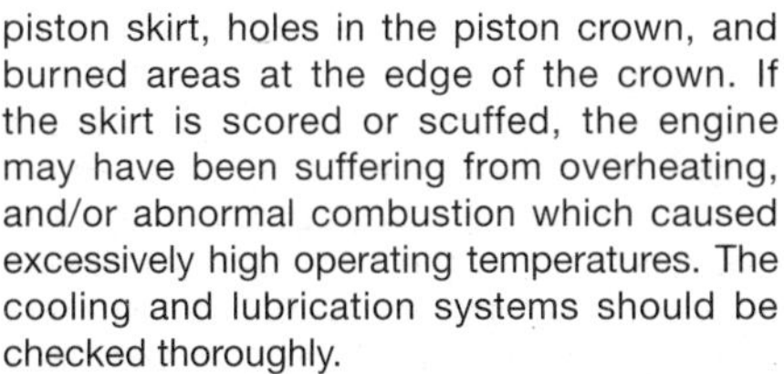

piston skirt, holes in the piston crown, and burned areas at the edge of the crown. If the skirt is scored or scuffed, the engine may have been suffering from overheating, and/or abnormal combustion which caused excessively high operating temperatures. The cooling and lubrication systems should be checked thoroughly.

14 Scorch marks on the sides of the pistons show that blow-by has occurred.

15 A hole in the piston crown, or burned areas at the edge of the piston crown, indicates that abnormal combustion (pre-ignition, knocking, or detonation) has been occurring.

16 If any of the above problems exist, the causes must be investigated and corrected, or the damage will occur again. The causes may include incorrect ignition/injection pump timing, inlet air leaks or incorrect air/fuel mixture.

17 Corrosion of the piston, in the form of pitting, indicates that coolant has been leaking into the combustion chamber and/or the crankcase. Again, the cause must be corrected, or the problem may persist in the rebuilt engine.

18 Locate a new piston ring in the appropriate groove and measure the ring-to-groove clearance using a feeler blade **(see illustration)**. Note that the rings are of different widths, so use the correct ring for the groove. Compare the measurements with those listed; if the clearances are outside of the tolerance band, then the piston must be renewed. Confirm this by checking the width of the piston ring with a micrometer.

19 New pistons can be purchased from an Audi dealer or an engine repair specialist.

20 Examine each connecting rod carefully for signs of damage, such as cracks around the big-end and small-end bearings. Check that the rod is not bent or distorted. Damage is highly unlikely, unless the engine has been seized or badly overheated. Detailed checking of the connecting rod assembly can only be carried out by an Audi dealer or engine repair specialist with the necessary equipment.

21 The gudgeon pins are of the floating type, secured in position by two circlips. The pistons and connecting rods can be separated as follows.

22 Using a small flat-bladed screwdriver, prise out the circlips, and push out the gudgeon pin **(see illustrations)**. Hand pressure should be sufficient to remove the pin. Identify the piston and rod to ensure correct reassembly. Discard the circlips – new ones must be used on refitting. If the gudgeon pin proves difficult to remove, heat the piston to 60°C with hot water – the resulting expansion will then allow the two components to be separated.

23 Examine the gudgeon pin and connecting rod small-end bearing for signs of wear or damage. It should be possible to push the gudgeon pin through the connecting rod bush by hand, without noticeable play. Wear can be cured by renewing both the pin and bush. Bush renewal, however, is a specialist job – press facilities are required, and the new bush must be reamed accurately.

24 Examine all components, and obtain any new parts from your Audi dealer. If new pistons are purchased, they will be supplied complete with gudgeon pins and circlips. Circlips can also be purchased individually.

25 The orientation of the piston with respect to the connecting rod must be correct when the two are reassembled. The piston crown is marked with an arrow (which may be obscured by carbon deposits); this must point towards the timing belt end of the engine when the piston is installed. The connecting rod and its bearing cap both have recesses machined into them on one side, close to their mating surfaces – these recesses must both face the same way as the arrow on the piston crown (ie, towards the timing belt end of the engine) when correctly installed. Reassemble the two components to satisfy this requirement **(see illustrations)**.

26 Apply a smear of clean engine oil to the gudgeon pin. Slide it into the piston and through the connecting rod small-end. Check that the piston pivots freely on the rod, then secure the gudgeon pin in position with two new circlips. Ensure that each circlip is correctly located in its groove in the piston.

27 Repeat the cleaning and inspection process for the remaining pistons and connecting rods.

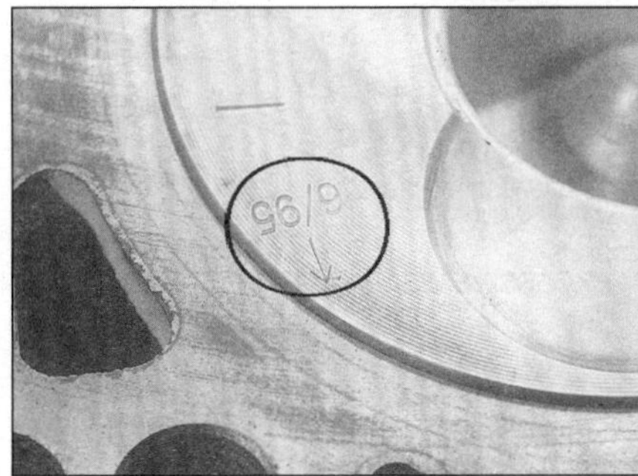
12.25a The piston crown is marked with an arrow which must point towards the timing belt end of the engine

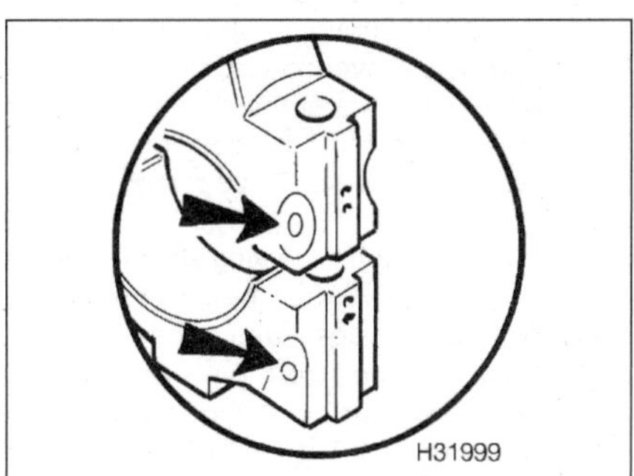

12.25b The recesses (arrowed) in the connecting rod and bearing cap must face towards the timing belt end of the engine

13 Crankshaft – checking endfloat and inspection

Checking endfloat

1 If the crankshaft endfloat is to be checked, this must be done when the crankshaft is still installed in the cylinder block/crankcase, but is free to move (see Section 10).

2 Check the endfloat using a dial gauge in contact with the end of the crankshaft. Push the crankshaft fully one way, and then zero the gauge. Push the crankshaft fully the other way, and check the endfloat. The result can be compared with the specified amount,

13.2 Measuring crankshaft endfloat using a dial gauge

13.3 Measuring crankshaft endfloat using feeler blades

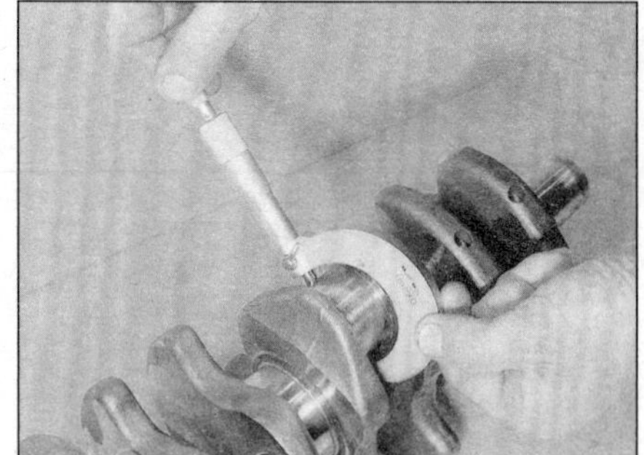
13.10 Use a micrometer to measure the diameter of each crankshaft bearing journal

and will give an indication as to whether new thrustwasher halves are required **(see illustration)**. Note that all thrustwashers must be of the same thickness.

3 If a dial gauge is not available, feeler blades can be used. First push the crankshaft fully towards the flywheel end of the engine, then use feeler blades to measure the gap between the web of No 3 crankpin and the thrust-washer halves **(see illustration)**.

Inspection

4 Clean the crankshaft using paraffin or a suitable solvent, and dry it, preferably with compressed air if available. Be sure to clean the oil holes with a pipe cleaner or similar probe, to ensure that they are not obstructed.

Warning: Wear eye protection when using compressed air.

5 Check the main and big-end bearing journals for uneven wear, scoring, pitting and cracking.

6 Big-end bearing wear is accompanied by distinct metallic knocking when the engine is running (particularly noticeable when the engine is pulling from low speed) and some loss of oil pressure.

7 Main bearing wear is accompanied by severe engine vibration and rumble – getting progressively worse as engine speed increases – and again by loss of oil pressure.

8 Check the bearing journal for roughness by running a finger lightly over the bearing surface. Any roughness (which will be accompanied by obvious bearing wear) indicates that the crankshaft requires regrinding (where possible) or renewal.

9 If the crankshaft has been reground, check for burrs around the crankshaft oil holes (the holes are usually chamfered, so burrs should not be a problem unless regrinding has been carried out carelessly). Remove any burrs with a fine file or scraper, and thoroughly clean the oil holes as described previously.

10 Using a micrometer, measure the diameter of the main and big-end bearing journals, and compare the results with the Specifications **(see illustration)**. By measuring the diameter at a number of points around each journal's circumference, you will be able to determine whether or not the journal is out-of-round. Take the measurement at each end of the journal, near the webs, to determine if the journal is tapered.

11 Check the oil seal contact surfaces at each end of the crankshaft for wear and damage. If the seal has worn a deep groove in the surface of the crankshaft, consult an engine overhaul specialist; repair may be possible, but otherwise a new crankshaft will be required.

12 If the crankshaft journals have not already been reground, it may be possible to have the crankshaft reconditioned, and to fit oversize shells (see Section 17). If no oversize shells are available and the crankshaft has worn beyond the specified limits, it will have to be renewed. Consult your Audi dealer or engine specialist for further information on parts availability.

14 Main and big-end bearings - inspection

Inspection

1 Even though the main and big-end bearings should be renewed during the engine overhaul, the old bearings should be retained for close examination, as they may reveal valuable information about the condition of the engine **(see illustration)**.

2 Bearing failure can occur due to lack of lubrication, the presence of dirt or other foreign particles, overloading the engine, or corrosion. Regardless of the cause of bearing failure, the cause must be corrected before the engine is reassembled, to prevent it from happening again.

3 When examining the bearing shells, remove them from the cylinder block/crankcase, the main bearing caps, the connecting rods and the connecting rod big-end bearing caps. Lay them out on a clean surface in the same general position as their location in the engine. This will enable you to match any bearing problems with the corresponding crankshaft journal. Do not touch any shell's internal bearing surface with your fingers while checking it, or the delicate surface may be scratched.

4 Dirt and other foreign matter gets into the engine in a variety of ways. It may be left in the engine during assembly, or it may pass through filters or the crankcase ventilation system. It may get into the oil, and from there into the bearings. Metal chips from machining operations and normal engine wear are often present. Abrasives are sometimes left in engine components after reconditioning, especially when parts are not thoroughly cleaned using the proper cleaning methods. Whatever the source, these foreign objects often end up embedded in the soft bearing material, and are easily recognised. Large particles will not embed in the bearing, but will score or gouge the bearing and journal. The best prevention for this cause of bearing failure is to clean all parts thoroughly, and keep everything spotlessly-clean during engine assembly. Frequent and regular engine oil and filter changes are also recommended.

5 Lack of lubrication (or lubrication breakdown) has a number of interrelated

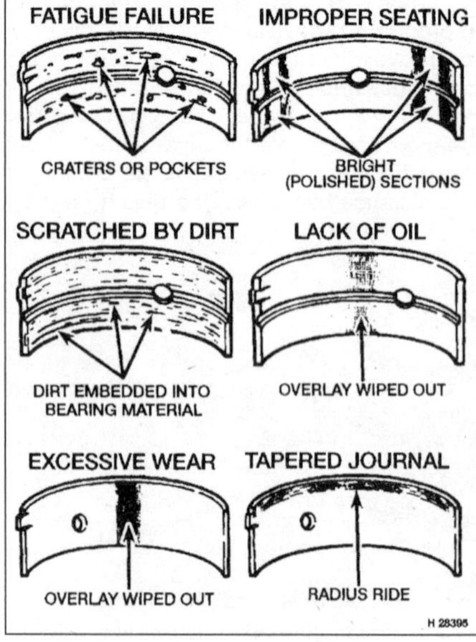

14.1 Typical bearing failures

causes. Excessive heat (which thins the oil), overloading (which squeezes the oil from the bearing face) and oil leakage (from excessive bearing clearances, worn oil pump or high engine speeds) all contribute to lubrication breakdown. Blocked oil passages, which usually are the result of misaligned oil holes in a bearing shell, will also oil-starve a bearing, and destroy it. When lack of lubrication is the cause of bearing failure, the bearing material is wiped or extruded from the steel backing of the bearing. Temperatures may increase to the point where the steel backing turns blue from overheating.

6 Driving habits can have a definite effect on bearing life. Full-throttle, low-speed operation (labouring the engine) puts very high loads on bearings, tending to squeeze out the oil film. These loads cause the bearings to flex, which produces fine cracks in the bearing face (fatigue failure). Eventually, the bearing material will loosen in pieces, and tear away from the steel backing.

7 Short-distance driving leads to corrosion of bearings, because insufficient engine heat is produced to drive off the condensed water and corrosive gases. These products collect in the engine oil, forming acid and sludge. As the oil is carried to the engine bearings, the acid attacks and corrodes the bearing material.

8 Incorrect bearing installation during engine assembly will lead to bearing failure as well. Tight-fitting bearings leave insufficient bearing running clearance, and will result in oil starvation. Dirt or foreign particles trapped behind a bearing shell result in high spots on the bearing, which lead to failure.

9 Do not touch any shell's internal bearing surface with your fingers during reassembly as there is a risk of scratching the delicate surface, or of depositing particles of dirt on it.

10 As mentioned at the beginning of this Section, the bearing shells should be renewed as a matter of course during engine overhaul. To do otherwise is false economy.

Main and big-end bearings selection

11 Main and big-end bearings for the engines described in this Chapter are available in standard sizes and a range of undersizes to suit reground crankshafts.

12 The running clearances will need to be checked when the crankshaft is refitted with its new bearings (see Sections 19 and 20).

15 Engine overhaul – reassembly sequence

1 Before reassembly begins, ensure that all new parts have been obtained, and that all necessary tools are available. Read through the entire procedure to familiarise yourself with the work involved, and to ensure that all items necessary for reassembly of the engine are at hand. In addition to all normal tools and materials, thread-locking compound will be needed. A suitable tube of liquid sealant will also be required for the joint faces that are fitted without gaskets.

2 In order to save time and avoid problems, engine reassembly can be carried out in the following order, referring to Chapter 2A, unless otherwise stated. Where applicable, use new gaskets and seals when refitting the various components.

a) Crankshaft (Section 17).
b) Piston/connecting rod assemblies (Section 18).
c) Oil pump.
d) Sump.
e) Flywheel/driveplate.
f) Cylinder head.
g) Timing belt(s), tensioner and sprockets.
h) Engine external components.

3 At this stage, all engine components should be absolutely clean and dry, with all faults repaired. The components should be laid out (or in individual containers) on a completely clean work surface.

16 Piston rings – refitting

1 Before fitting new piston rings, the ring end gaps must be checked as follows.

2 Lay out the piston/connecting rod assemblies and the new piston ring sets, so that the ring sets will be matched with the same piston and cylinder during the end gap measurement and subsequent engine reassembly.

3 Insert the top ring into the first cylinder, and push it down the bore using the top of the piston. This will ensure that the ring remains square with the cylinder walls. Position the ring approximately 15.0 mm the bottom of the cylinder bore, at the lower limit of ring travel. Note that the top and second compression rings are different.

4 Measure the end gap using feeler blades, and compare the measurements with the figures given in the Specifications **(see illustration)**.

5 If the gap is too small (unlikely if genuine Audi parts are used), it must be enlarged, or the ring ends may contact each other during engine operation, causing serious damage. Ideally, new piston rings providing the correct end gap should be fitted. As a last resort, the end gap can be increased by filing the ring ends very carefully with a fine file. Mount the file in a vice equipped with soft jaws, slip the ring over the file with the ends contacting the file face, and slowly move the ring to remove material from the ends. Take care, as piston rings are sharp, and are easily broken.

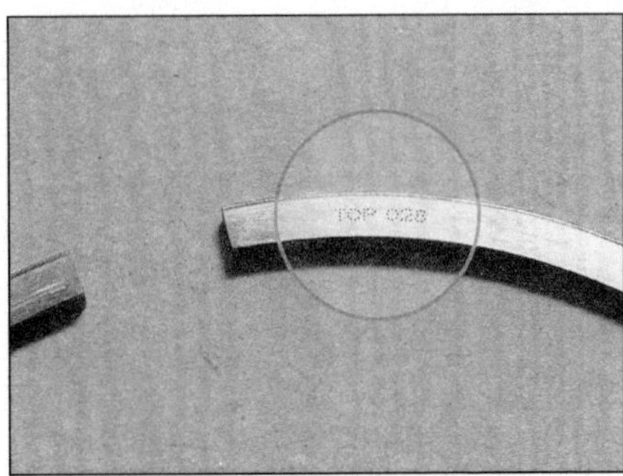

16.9 Piston ring TOP marking

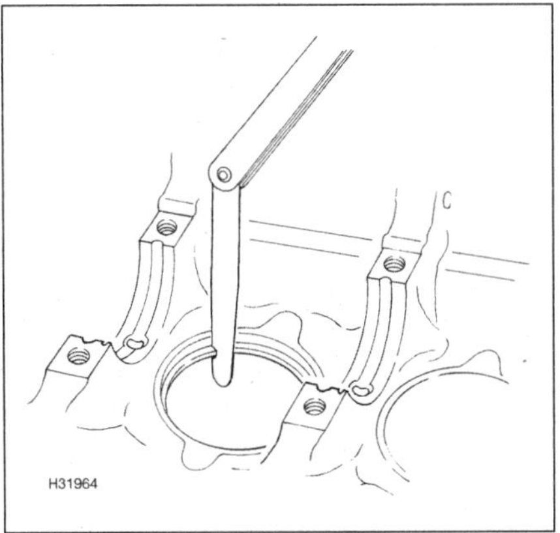

16.4 Checking a piston ring end gap using a feeler blade

6 With new piston rings, it is unlikely that the end gap will be too large. If the gaps are too large, check that you have the correct rings for your engine and for the particular cylinder bore size.

7 Repeat the checking procedure for each ring in the first cylinder, and then for the rings in the remaining cylinders. Remember to keep rings, pistons and cylinders matched up.

8 Once the ring end gaps have been checked and if necessary corrected, the rings can be fitted to the pistons.

9 Fit the piston rings using the same technique as for removal. Fit the bottom (oil control) ring first, and work up. Note that a two- or three-section oil control ring may be fitted; where a two-section ring is fitted, first insert the wire expander, then fit the ring. Ensure that the rings are fitted the correct way up – the top surface of the rings is normally marked TOP **(see illustration)**. Offset the piston ring gaps by 120° from each other. **Note:** *Always follow any instructions supplied with the new piston ring sets – different manufacturers may specify different procedures. Do not mix up the top and second compression rings, as they have different cross-sections.*

17 Crankshaft – refitting and main bearing clearance check

Main bearing clearance check

1 The running clearance check can be carried out using the original bearing shells. However, it is preferable to use a new set, since the

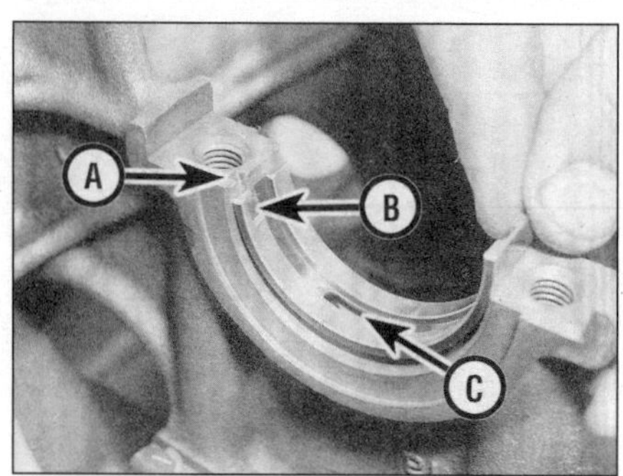

17.3 Bearing shell correctly refitted

A Recess in cylinder block
B Lug on bearing shell
C Oil hole

results obtained will be more conclusive. If new shells are being fitted, ensure that all traces of the protective grease are cleaned off using paraffin.

2 Clean the backs of the bearing shells, and the bearing locations in both the cylinder block/crankcase and the main bearing caps.

3 With the cylinder block positioned on a clean work surface, with the crankcase uppermost, press the bearing shells into their locations, ensuring that the tab on each shell engages in the notch in the cylinder block or bearing cap, and that the oil holes in the cylinder block and bearing shell are aligned **(see illustration)**. Take care not to touch any shell's bearing surface with your fingers. If the original bearing shells are being used for the check, ensure that they are refitted in their original locations.

4 Fit the crankshaft endfloat control thrustwasher halves either side of the No 3 bearing location. Use a small quantity of grease to hold them in place. Ensure that the thrustwashers are seated correctly in the machined recesses, with the oil grooves facing outwards.

5 The running clearance can be checked, although this will be difficult to achieve without a range of internal micrometers or internal/external expanding calipers. Refit the main bearing caps to the cylinder block/crankcase, with bearing shells in place. With the original cap retaining bolts tightened to the specified torque, measure the internal diameter of each assembled pair of bearing shells. If the diameter of each corresponding crankshaft journal is measured and then subtracted from the bearing internal diameter, the result will be the main bearing running clearance.

Final crankshaft refitting

6 Carefully lift the crankshaft out of the cylinder block once more, and wipe off the surfaces of the bearing shells in the crankcase and bearing caps.

7 Where applicable, refit the crankshaft speed/position sensor wheel, and tighten the securing bolts to the specified torque. Make sure that the sensor wheel is correctly orientated as noted before removal.

8 Liberally coat the bearing shells in the crankcase with clean engine oil of the appropriate grade **(see illustration)**. Make sure that the bearing shells are still correctly seated in their locations.

9 Lower the crankshaft into position so that No 1 cylinder crankpin is at BDC, ready for fitting No 1 piston. Ensure that the crankshaft endfloat control thrustwasher halves, either side of the No 3 main bearing location, remain in position. Where applicable, take care not to damage the crankshaft speed/position sensor wheel as the crankshaft is lowered into position.

10 Lubricate the lower bearing shells in the main bearing caps with clean engine oil. Make sure that the crankshaft endfloat control thrustwasher halves are still correctly seated either side of No 3 bearing cap **(see illustrations)**.

11 Fit the main bearing caps in the correct order and orientation – No 1 bearing cap must be at the timing belt end of the engine and the bearing shell tab locating recesses in the crankcase and bearing caps must be adjacent to each other **(see illustration)**. Insert the bearing cap bolts (using new bolts where necessary – see Torque wrench settings in the Specifications), and hand-tighten them only.

12 Working from the centre bearing cap outwards, tighten the bearing cap bolts to their specified torque. On engines where two Stages are given for the torque, tighten all bolts to the Stage 1 torque, then go round again, and tighten all bolts through the Stage 2 angle **(see illustrations)**.

13 Check that the crankshaft rotates freely by

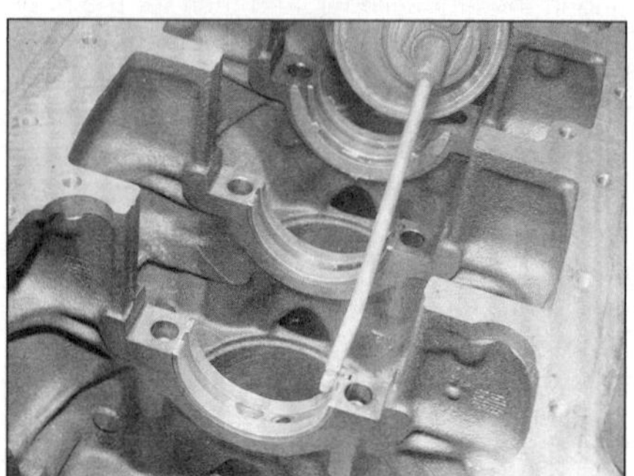

17.8 Lubricate the upper bearing shells

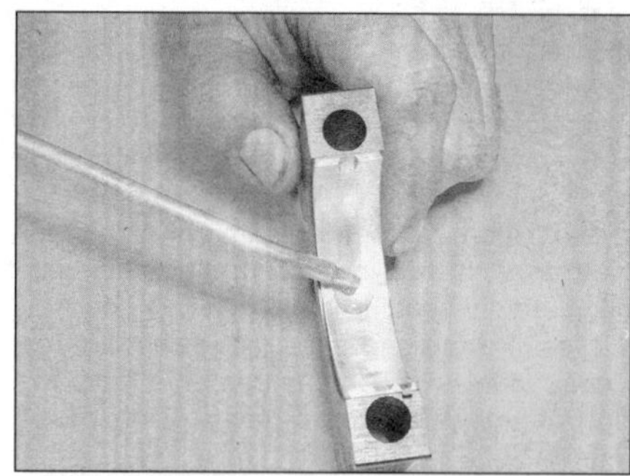

17.10a Lubricate the lower bearing shells ...

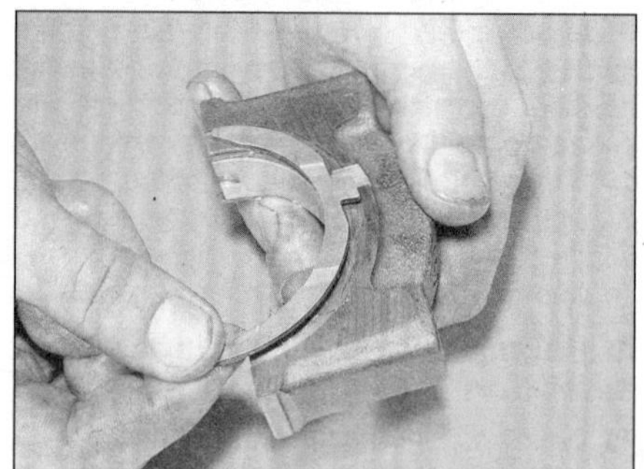

17.10b ... and make sure that the thrustwashers are correctly seated

17.11 Fitting No 1 main bearing cap

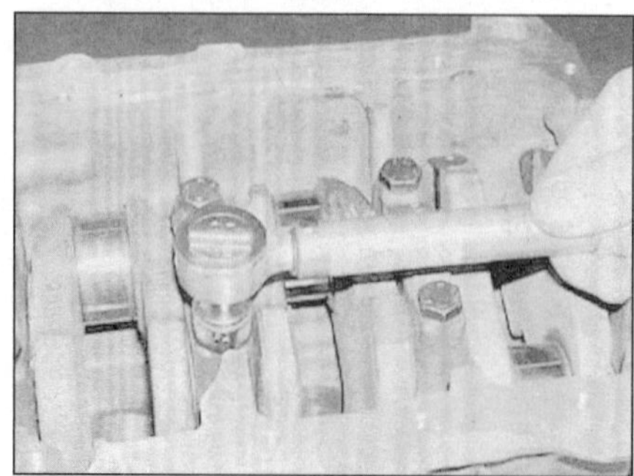

17.12a Tighten the main bearing cap bolts to the specified torque ...

17.12b ... then through the specified angle

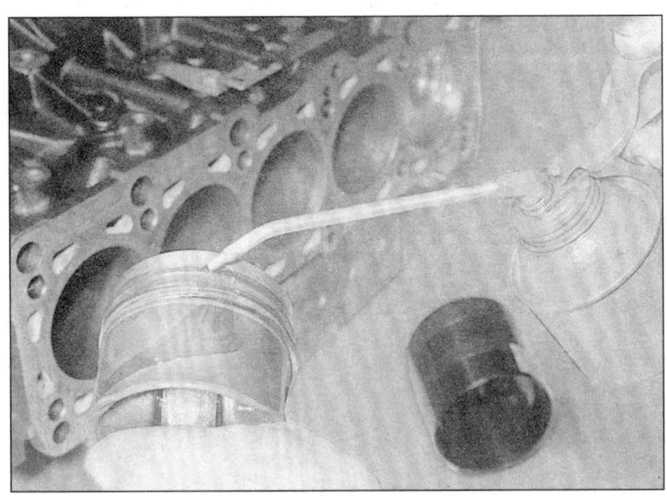
18.9a Lubricate the pistons ...

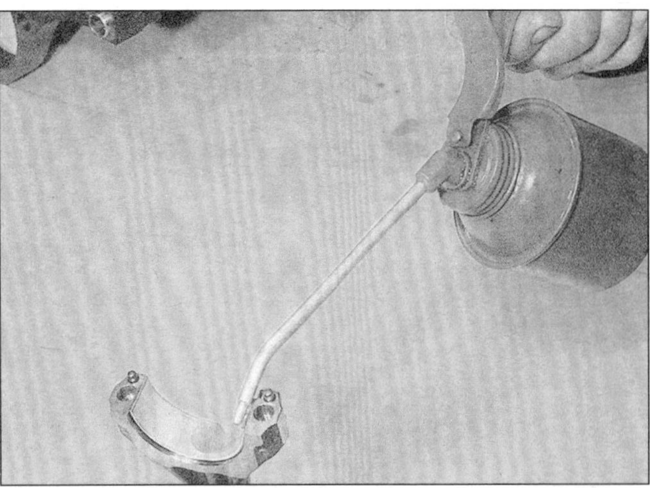
18.9b ... and big-end upper bearing shells with clean engine oil

turning it by hand. If resistance is felt, recheck the bearing running clearances, as described previously.

14 Check the crankshaft endfloat as described at the beginning of Section 13. If the thrust surfaces of the crankshaft have been checked and new thrustwashers have been fitted, then the endfloat should be within specification.

15 Refit the pistons and connecting rods or reconnect them to the crankshaft as described in Section 18.

16 Refit the crankshaft oil seal housings, flywheel/driveplate, oil pump and pick-up pipe, sump and oil baffle plate, and the crankshaft sprocket and timing belt, as described in Chapter 2A

18 Piston/connecting rod assemblies – refitting and big-end bearing clearance check

Note: *A piston ring compressor tool will be required for this operation.*

Big-end bearing clearance check

1 The running clearance check can be carried out using the original bearing shells. However, it is preferable to use a new set, since the results obtained will be more conclusive.

2 Clean the backs of the bearing shells, and the bearing locations in both the connecting rods and the big-end bearing caps.

3 Press the bearing shells into their locations, ensuring that the tab on each shell engages in the notch in the connecting rod or cap. Take care not to touch any shell's bearing surface with your fingers. If the original bearing shells are being used for the check, ensure that they are refitted in their original locations.

4 The running clearance can be checked, although this will be difficult to achieve without a range of internal micrometers or internal/ external expanding calipers. Refit the big-end bearing cap to the connecting rod, using the marks made or noted on removal to ensure that they are fitted the correct way around, with the bearing shells in place. With the original cap retaining bolts or nuts (as applicable) correctly tightened, use an internal micrometer or vernier caliper to measure the internal diameter of each assembled pair of bearing shells. If the diameter of each corresponding crankshaft journal is measured, and then subtracted from the bearing internal diameter, the result will be the big-end bearing running clearance.

Piston/connecting rods refitting

5 Note that the following procedure assumes that the crankshaft main bearing caps are in place.

6 Where applicable, refit the piston cooling oil spray jets to the bottom of the cylinder block, and tighten the securing bolts to the specified torque.

7 On engines where the big-end bearing caps are secured by nuts, fit new bolts to the connecting rods. Tap the old bolts out of the connecting rods using a soft-faced mallet, and tap the new bolts into position.

8 Ensure that the bearing shells are correctly fitted, as described at the beginning of this Section. If new shells are being fitted, ensure that all traces of the protective grease are cleaned off using paraffin. Wipe dry the shells and connecting rods with a lint-free cloth.

9 Lubricate the cylinder bores, the pistons, piston rings and upper bearing shells with clean engine oil **(see illustrations)**. Lay out each piston/connecting rod assembly in order on a clean work surface. Where the bearing caps are secured with nuts, pad the threaded ends of the bolts with insulating tape to prevent them scratching the crankpins and bores when the pistons are refitted.

10 Start with piston/connecting rod assembly No 1. Make sure that the piston rings are still spaced as described in Section 16, then clamp them in position with a piston ring compressor tool.

11 Insert the piston/connecting rod assembly into the top of cylinder No 1. Lower the big-end in first, guiding it to protect the cylinder bores. Where oil jets are located at the bottoms of the bores, take particular care not to damage them when guiding the connecting rods onto the crankpins.

12 Ensure that the orientation of the piston in its cylinder is correct – the piston crown, connecting rod and big-end bearing cap have markings, which must point towards the timing belt end of the engine when the piston is installed in the bore – refer to Section 12 for details.

13 Using a block of wood or hammer handle against the piston crown, tap the assembly into the cylinder until the piston crown is flush with the top of the cylinder **(see illustration)**.

14 Ensure that the bearing shell is still correctly installed in the connecting rod, then liberally lubricate the crankpin and both bearing shells with clean engine oil.

15 Taking care not to mark the cylinder bores, tap the piston/connecting rod assembly down the bore and onto the crankpin. On engines where the big-end caps are secured by nuts, remove the insulating tape from the threaded ends of the connecting rod bolts. Oil the bolt threads, and on engines where the big-end caps are secured by bolts, oil the undersides of the bolt heads.

18.13 Using a hammer handle to tap the piston into its bore

18.17a Tighten the big-end bearing cap bolts/nuts to the specified torque ...

18.17b ... then through the specified angle

16 Fit the big-end bearing cap, tightening its retaining nuts or bolts (as applicable) finger-tight at first. The connecting rod and its bearing cap both have recesses machined into them on one side, close to their mating surfaces – these recesses must both face the same way as the arrow on the piston crown (ie, towards the timing belt end of the engine) when correctly installed **(see illustration 12.25b)**. Reassemble the two components to satisfy this requirement.

17 Tighten the retaining bolts or nuts (as applicable) to the specified torque and angle, in the two stages given in the Specifications **(see illustrations)**.

18 Refit the remaining three piston/ connecting rod assemblies in the same way.

19 Rotate the crankshaft by hand. Check that it turns freely; some stiffness is to be expected if new parts have been fitted, but there should be no binding or tight spots.

20 Refit the oil pump and pick-up pipe, sump and oil baffle plate, and cylinder head, as described in Chapter 2A

19 Engine – initial start-up after overhaul and reassembly

1 Refit the remainder of the engine components in the order listed in Section 5 of this Chapter. Refit the engine to the vehicle as described in the relevant Section of this Chapter. Double-check the engine oil and coolant levels, and make a final check that everything has been reconnected. Make sure that there are no tools or rags left in the engine compartment.

2 Reconnect the battery leads, with reference to *Disconnecting the battery*, at the rear of this manual.

3 Remove the spark plugs, referring to Chapter 1 Section 31 for details.

4 The engine must be immobilised such that it can be turned over using the starter motor, without starting – disable the fuel pump by unplugging the fuel pump power relay from the relay board with reference to Chapter 12, and also disable the ignition system by disconnecting the wiring from the DIS module or coils, as applicable.

Caution: To prevent damage to the catalytic converter, it is important to disable the fuel system.

5 Turn the engine using the starter motor until the oil pressure warning lamp goes out. If the lamp fails to extinguish after several seconds of cranking, check the engine oil level and oil filter security. Assuming these are correct, check the security of the oil pressure switch wiring – do not progress any further until you are satisfied that oil is being pumped around the engine at sufficient pressure.

6 Refit the spark plugs, and reconnect the wiring to the fuel pump relay and ignition coils.

7 Start the engine, but be aware that as fuel system components have been disturbed, the cranking time may be a little longer than usual.

8 While the engine is idling, check for fuel, water and oil leaks. Don't be alarmed if there are some odd smells and the occasional plume of smoke as components heat up and burn off oil deposits.

9 Assuming all is well, keep the engine idling until hot water is felt circulating through the top hose.

10 After a few minutes, recheck the oil and coolant levels, and top-up as necessary.

11 There is no need to retighten the cylinder head bolts once the engine has been run following reassembly.

12 If new pistons, rings or crankshaft bearings have been fitted, the engine must be treated as new, and run-in for the first 600 miles (1000 km). Do not operate the engine at full-throttle, or allow it to labour at low engine speeds in any gear. It is recommended that the engine oil and filter are changed at the end of this period.

Chapter 3
Cooling, heating and air conditioning systems

Contents

Degrees of difficulty

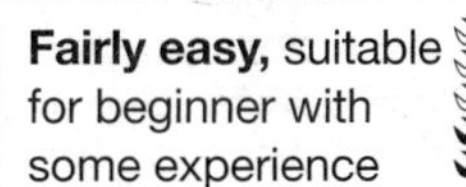

Easy, suitable for novice with little experience	**Fairly easy,** suitable for beginner with some experience	**Fairly difficult,** suitable for competent DIY mechanic	**Difficult,** suitable for experienced DIY mechanic	**Very difficult,** suitable for expert DIY or professional

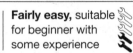

Specifications

Cooling system pressure cap

Opening pressure	1.4 to 1.6 bar

Thermostat

Begins to open	87°C
Fully open	102°C
Opening travel (minimum)	8 mm

Cooling fan

Fan speeds:	
1st speed cut-in	92 to 97°C
1st speed cut-out	84 to 91°C
2nd speed cut-in	99 to 105°C
2nd speed cut-out	91 to 98°C

Torque wrench settings

	Nm	lbf ft
Coolant pump housing/coolant pump-to-engine bolts	15	11
Facia crossmember retaining bolts	25	18
Radiator cooling fan shroud bolts	10	7
Radiator mounting bolts	10	7
Thermostat cover bolts	10	7

1 General information and precautions

1 A pressurised cooling system is used, comprising a pump, an aluminium crossflow radiator, an electric cooling fan, a thermostat and a heater matrix, as well as the interconnecting hoses. The system functions as follows. Cold coolant from the radiator passes through the hose to the coolant pump where it is pumped around the cylinder block and head passages. After cooling the cylinder bores, combustion surfaces and valve seats, the coolant reaches the underside of the thermostat, which is initially closed. The coolant passes through the heater and is returned through the cylinder block to the timing belt driven coolant pump.

2 When the engine is cold the coolant circulates only through the cylinder block, cylinder head, expansion tank and heater. When the coolant reaches a predetermined temperature, the thermostat opens and the coolant passes through to the radiator. As the coolant circulates through the radiator it is cooled by the inrush of air when the car is in forward motion. Airflow is supplemented by the action of the electric cooling fan(s) when necessary. Upon leaving the radiator, the coolant has been cooled and the cycle is repeated.

3 A thermostatic switch controls the electric cooling fan(s), this is located at the lower left-hand side on the rear of the radiator, above the bottom coolant hose. At a pre-set coolant temperature, the switch actuates the fan(s).

4 Refer to Section 11 for information on the air conditioning system, which is fitted to most models.

5 Coolant temperature information for the gauge mounted in the instrument panel, and for the fuel system, is provided by a single temperature sensor, mounted in the coolant hose connector on the left-hand end of the cylinder head.

Precautions

Warning: Do not attempt to remove the expansion tank filler cap or disturb any part of the cooling system while the engine is hot, as there is a high risk of scalding. If the expansion tank filler cap must be removed before the engine and radiator have fully cooled (even though this is not recommended) the pressure in the cooling system must first be relieved. Cover the cap with a thick layer of cloth, to avoid scalding, and slowly unscrew the filler cap until a hissing sound can be heard. When the hissing has stopped, indicating that the pressure has reduced, slowly unscrew the filler cap until it can be removed; if more hissing sounds are heard, wait until they have stopped before unscrewing the cap completely. At all times keep well away from the filler cap opening.

- ***Do not allow antifreeze to come into contact with skin or painted surfaces of the vehicle. Rinse off spills immediately with plenty of water. Never leave antifreeze lying around in an open container or in a puddle in the driveway or on the garage floor. Children and pets are attracted by its sweet smell. Antifreeze can be fatal if ingested.***
- ***If the engine is hot, the electric cooling fan may start rotating even if the engine is not running, so be careful to keep hands, hair and loose clothing well clear when working in the engine compartment.***
- ***Refer to Section 11 for additional precautions to be observed when working on models with air conditioning.***

2 Cooling system hoses – disconnection and renewal

Note: *Refer to the warnings given in Section 1 of this Chapter before proceeding.*

1 If the checks described in the relevant part of Chapter 1 Section 13 reveal a faulty hose, it must be renewed as follows.

2 First drain the cooling system as described in Chapter 1 Section 39. If the coolant is not due for renewal, it may be re-used if it is collected in a clean container.

3 To disconnect a hose, release its retaining clips, then move them along the hose, clear of the relevant inlet/outlet union. Carefully work the hose free.

4 In order to disconnect the radiator inlet and outlet hoses, apply pressure to hold the hose on to the relevant union, pull out the spring clip and pull the hose from the union **(see illustrations)**. Note that the radiator inlet and outlet unions are fragile; do not use excessive force when attempting to remove the hoses. If a hose proves to be difficult to remove, try to release it by rotating the hose ends before attempting to free it.

5 When fitting a hose, first slide the clips onto the hose, then work the hose into position. If clamp type clips were originally fitted, it is a good idea to use screw type clips when refitting the hose. If the hose is stiff, use a little soapy water as a lubricant, or soften the hose by soaking it in hot water.

6 Work the hose into position, checking that it is correctly routed, then slide each clip along the hose until it passes over the flared end of the relevant union, before securing it in position with the retaining clip.

7 Prior to refitting a radiator inlet or outlet hose, check the condition of the connection O-ring seals, renew if damaged. The connections are a push-fit over the radiator unions.

8 Refill the cooling system as described in Chapter 1 Section 39.

9 Check thoroughly for leaks as soon as possible after disturbing any part of the cooling system.

3 Radiator – removal, inspection and refitting

Warning: On air-conditioning models, DO NOT attempt to disconnect the refrigerant lines – refer to the warnings given in Section 11

Removal

1 Open the bonnet, release the fasteners and remove the plastic trim panels from over the battery, coolant reservoir and the two trim panels from along the front cross panel.

2 Disconnect the battery negative lead. **Note:** *Before disconnecting the battery, refer to* Disconnecting the battery *in the reference section at the rear of this manual.*

3 Remove the radiator cooling fan assembly, as described in Section 5. During this procedure the cooling system will need to be drained (Chapter 1 Section 39), before the cooling fan assembly can be removed.

4 Remove the front bumper cover as described in Chapter 11 Section 6.

2.4a Retaining clip lifted up in the released position

2.4b Retaining clip pressed down in the secured position

3.5 Cooling fan thermal switch wiring connector (arrowed)

3.6 Air-conditioning pipe securing screw (arrowed)

3.7 Release the securing clip (arrowed)

5 Disconnect the wiring plug from the cooling fan thermal switch mounted in the radiator **(see illustration)**.

6 On models with air-conditioning, undo the retaining screw and disconnect the air-conditioning pipe from the left-hand lower part of the radiator **(see illustration)**.

7 Release the securing clip and disconnect the top hose from the left-hand side of the radiator **(see illustration)**.

8 On models with air-conditioning, undo the four screws securing the condenser in position **(see illustration)**. Then using cable ties secure the condenser to the front crossmember, to prevent it from getting damaged.

9 Undo the four screws securing the radiator in position in the front panel, then withdraw the radiator downwards and out from below the front of the vehicle **(see illustrations)**. Take care not to damage the fins on the radiator, as it is removed. On air-conditioning models, make sure the condenser and pressure pipes are moved to one side to allow for the radiator to be removed.

10 Note the location of the four radiator mounting rubbers (two each side), fitted to the sides of the radiator. Remove the mounting rubbers from the radiator and check for any damage **(see illustrations)**.

Inspection

11 If the radiator has been removed due to suspected blockage, reverse flush it as described in Chapter 1 Section 39.

12 Clean dirt and debris from the radiator fins, using an air line (in which case, wear eye protection) or a soft brush. Be careful, as the fins are sharp and easily damaged.

13 If necessary, a radiator specialist can perform a 'flow test' on the radiator, to establish whether an internal blockage exists.

14 A leaking radiator must be referred to a specialist for permanent repair. Do not attempt to weld or solder a leaking radiator, as damage may result.

15 If the radiator is to be sent for repair or renewed, remove the cooling fan switch.

Refitting

16 Refitting is a reversal of the removal procedure; ensure all the hose and wiring are correctly and securely reconnected. On completion, refill the cooling system with the correct type of coolant as described in Chapter 1 Section 39.

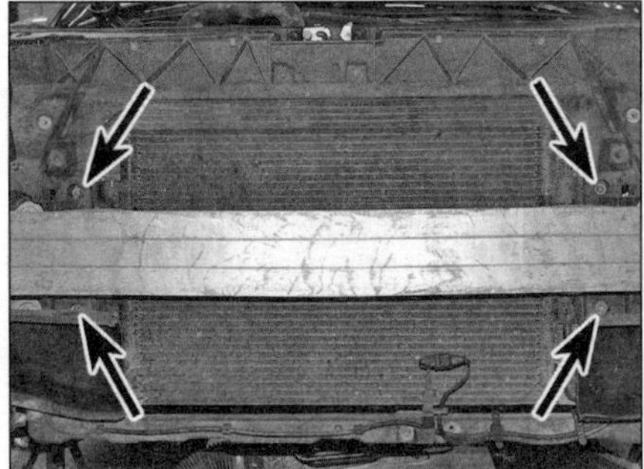
3.8 Condenser securing screws (arrowed)

3.9a Upper right mounting screw (arrowed)...

3.9b...and lower right mounting screw (arrowed) – one side shown

3.9c Withdraw the radiator carefully downwards to remove

3.10a Mounting rubbers located on side of radiator

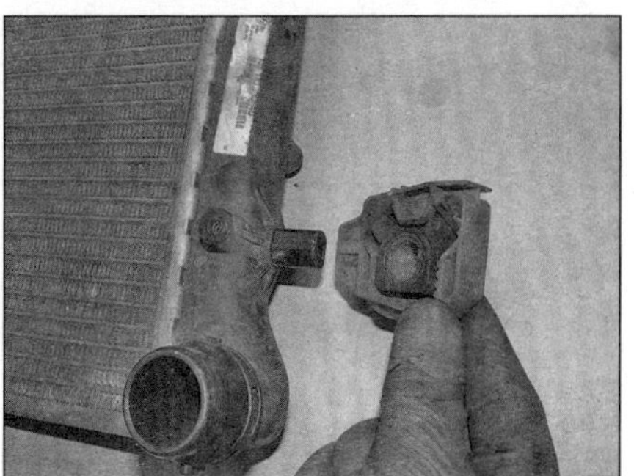
3.10b Check for any damage

4.3a Remove trim panel – engine codes AMU, APX and BAM

4.3b Remove trim panel – all models except engine codes AMU, APX and BAM

4.4 Disconnect wiring connector – engine codes AMU, APX and BAM

4 Thermostat – removal, testing and refitting

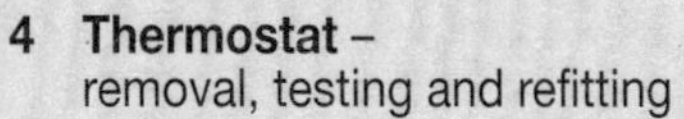

Removal

1 The thermostat is located behind a connection flange in the front of the engine block, to the rear of the alternator.

2 Disconnect the battery negative lead. **Note:** *Before disconnecting the battery, refer to* Disconnecting the battery *in the reference section at the rear of this manual.*

3 Open the bonnet, release the fasteners and remove the plastic trim panels from over the battery, coolant reservoir and the two trim panels from along the front cross panel. Also undo the fasteners and remove the plastic trim panel from along the front edge of the intake manifold **(see illustrations)**.

4 On models with engine codes AMU, APX and BAM disconnect the wiring connector from the exhaust gas temperature sender **(see illustration)**.

5 On models with secondary air injection, undo the retaining nuts from the two mounting brackets and disconnect the pipe from across the front of the intake manifold, and move it to one side **(see illustration)**.

6 Undo the two retaining bolts and remove the mounting bracket from the front of the intake manifold **(see illustration)**. As the mounting bracket is withdrawn, unclip the top of the dipstick tube from the bracket. As the mounting bracket is withdrawn, also disconnect the wiring connectors from the turbocharger air recirculation valve and secondary air inlet valve (where fitted), which may be bolted to the underside of the mounting bracket.

7 Remove the auxiliary drive belt, as described in Chapter 1 Section 32

8 Remove the alternator mounting bolts and move the alternator to the front of the engine compartment, to access the thermostat housing. The wiring connectors can be left connected to the rear of the alternator. Secure the alternator in place to prevent any damage to the cables or surrounding components. Refer to Chapter 5A Section 5, for further information on the alternator.

9 Drain the cooling system as described in Chapter 1 Section 39.

10 Release the retaining clip and disconnect the hose from the thermostat housing **(see illustration)**.

11 Undo the two securing bolts, and remove the thermostat housing from the cylinder block, then remove the thermostat and O-ring from the cylinder block, noting its fitted position **(see illustrations)**.

Testing

12 A rough test of the thermostat may be made by suspending it with a piece of string in a container full of water, but not touching the container. Heat the water to bring it to the boil – the thermostat must open by the time the water boils. If not, renew it.

13 If a thermometer is available, the precise opening temperature of the thermostat may be determined, and compared with the figures given in the Specifications. The opening temperature is also usually marked on the thermostat.

14 A thermostat which fails to close as the water cools must also be renewed.

4.5 Undo the two bracket (arrowed) securing nuts

4.6 Remove the mounting bracket – engine codes AMU, APX and BAM shown

4.10 Hose to thermostat housing (arrowed)

4.11a Undo the two bolts (arrowed)...

4.11b...and remove the thermostat and O-ring seal

4.15 Fit a new O-ring seal to the thermostat

5.5 Radiator fan control unit location (arrowed)

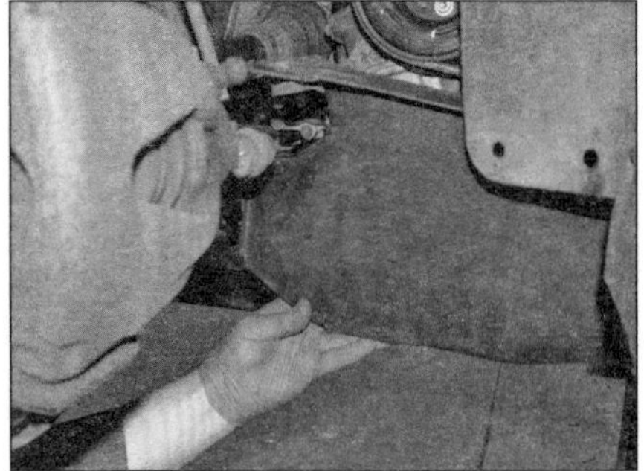

5.9a Remove the right-hand inner trim panel

Refitting

15 Refitting is a reversal of removal, bearing in mind the following points.

*a) Refit the thermostat using a new O-ring **(see illustration).***

b) The thermostat should be fitted with the brace almost vertical.

c) Ensure that any brackets are in place on the thermostat cover bolts as noted before removal.

d) Refill the cooling system with the correct type and quantity of coolant as described in Chapter 1 Section 39.

5 Radiator cooling fan assembly – testing, removal and refitting

Testing

1 Vehicles may be fitted with one or two cooling fans, depending on model. The cooling fan is supplied with current through the ignition switch, cooling fan control unit, relay(s) and fuses/fusible link (see Chapter 12). The circuit is completed by the cooling fan thermostatic switch, which is mounted in the left-hand lower end of the radiator. The cooling fan has two speed settings, one for the stage 1 fan speed setting and another for the stage 2 fan speed setting. Testing of the cooling fan circuit is as follows, noting that the following check should be carried out on both the stage 1 speed circuit and speed 2 circuit (see wiring diagrams at the end of Chapter 12).

2 If a fan does not appear to work, first check the fuses/fusible links (Chapter 12). If they are good, run the engine until normal operating temperature is reached, then allow it to idle. If the fan does not cut in within a few minutes, switch off the ignition and disconnect the wiring plug from the cooling fan switch. Bridge the relevant two contacts in the wiring plug using a length of spare wire, and switch on the ignition. If the fan now operates, the switch is probably faulty and should be renewed.

3 If the switch appears to work, the motor can be checked by disconnecting the motor wiring connector and connecting a 12 volt supply directly to the motor terminals. If the motor is faulty, it must be renewed, as no spares are available.

4 If the fan still fails to operate, check the cooling fan circuit wiring (Chapter 12). Check each wire for continuity and ensure that all connections are clean and free of corrosion.

5 If no fault can be found with the fuses/ fusible links, wiring, fan switch, or fan motor, then it is likely that the cooling fan control unit is faulty **(see illustration)**. Testing of the unit should be entrusted to an Audi dealer or specialist; if the unit is faulty it must be renewed.

6 On models equipped with air conditioning, there is also a second switch (fitted into the coolant outlet housings/hoses on the left-hand side of the cylinder head). This switch controls the cooling fan stage 3 speed setting.

Removal

7 Open the bonnet, release the fasteners and remove the plastic trim panels from over the battery, coolant reservoir and the two trim panels from along the front cross panel.

8 Disconnect the battery negative lead. **Note:** *Before disconnecting the battery refer to* Disconnecting the battery *in the reference section at the rear of this manual.*

9 Apply the handbrake, then jack up the front of the vehicle and support on axle stands (see *Jacking and vehicle support*). Remove the front roadwheels, then remove the securing screws and/or clips, and remove the engine undershield and both inner wheel arch trim panels **(see illustrations)**. To remove the left-hand inner trim panel, first remove the headlight range control sensor mounting bracket and move it to one side.

10 Remove the charge air pipe from across the front lower part of the engine compartment as described in Chapter 4B Section 7. **Note:** *On all engine codes (except AMU, APX and BAM), the charge air pipe only acts as a brace between the two chassis legs and also a support for the PAS cooler pipe, so does not have any charge air hoses fitted to each end.*

11 Drain the cooling system as described in Chapter 1 Section 39.

12 With the cooling system drained, release the securing clip and disconnect the bottom hose/drain connector from the radiator **(see illustration)**, with reference to Section 2 if necessary.

5.9b Remove the headlight range control sender (arrowed)...

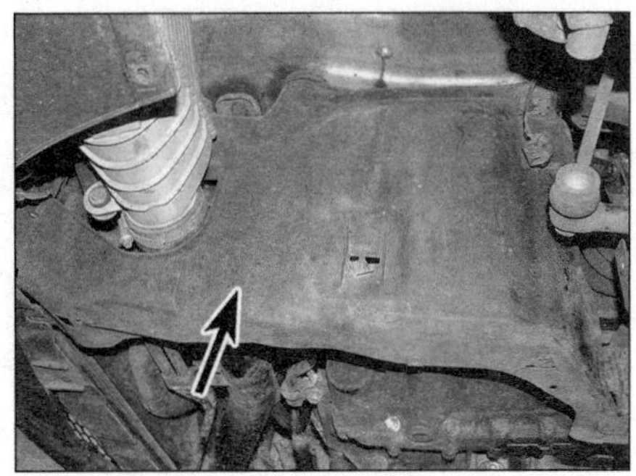

5.9c...and the left-hand inner trim panel

5.12 Disconnect the bottom hose connection

5.13 Radiator fan wiring connectors (arrowed)

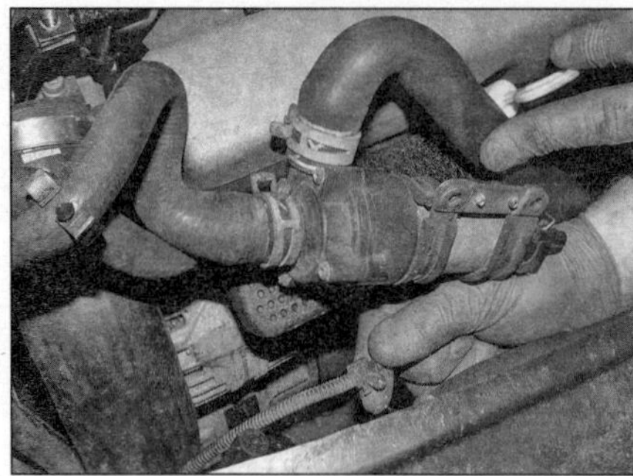
5.14 Remove the coolant circulation pump

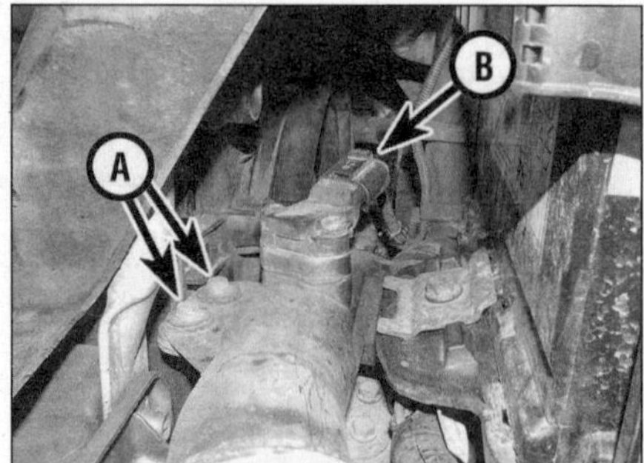

5.15a Undo bolts (A) and disconnect wiring connector (B)

5.15b Withdraw charge air pipe from in front of the battery

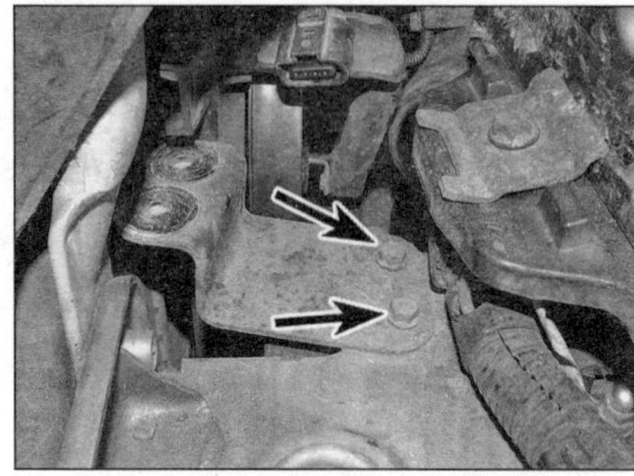
5.16a Undo the two retaining bolts (arrowed)...

5.16b...and remove the fan control unit

13 Disconnect the electric cooling fan wiring connectors **(see illustration)**, and release the wiring from the cooling fan shroud.

14 On models with engine codes AMU, APX and BAM, there is an electric coolant circulation pump fitted to the right-hand side upper part of the fan cowling. Disconnect the wiring connector, undo the mounting bolts and move the electric coolant circulation pump to one side **(see illustration)**. Note the coolant hoses do not need to be removed.

15 On models with engine codes AMU, APX and BAM, remove the left-hand headlight unit, as described in Chapter 12 Section 7. Then undo the retaining clips, undo the two retaining bolts and disconnect the wiring connector from the air pressure sensor. Withdraw the charge air pipe, releasing it from the top of the left-hand intercooler and the inlet manifold air intake hose **(see illustrations)**.

16 Undo the two retaining bolts and remove the mounting bracket from the left-hand side chassis leg in front of the battery. Remove the radiator fan control unit and move it to one side **(see illustrations)**. **Note:** *the same to bolts that hold the mounting bracket in place also secures the fan control unit.*

17 Undo the four Torx screws (two at each side) securing the cooling fan shroud to the radiator, then manoeuvre the cooling fan assembly, down and out from the engine compartment. Take care not to damage the radiator as the fan assembly is withdrawn **(see illustration)**.

18 If required the fan motor(s) can be removed from the shroud by removing the retaining screws and then uncliping the wiring loom from the shroud **(see illustration)**.

Refitting

19 Refitting is a reversal of removal, refill the cooling system with the correct type of coolant as described in Chapter 1 Section 39. On completion, check the operation of the cooling fan(s).

6 Cooling system electrical switches and sensors – testing, removal and refitting

Cooling fan thermostatic switch

Testing

1 Testing of the switch is described in Section 5, as part of the electric cooling fan test procedure.

Removal and refitting

2 The switch is located in the left-hand side lower part of the radiator, above the bottom hose **(see illustration)**. Make sure that the engine and radiator are cold and there is no

5.17 Withdraw the fan assembly downwards

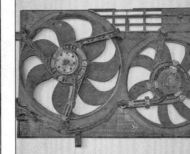

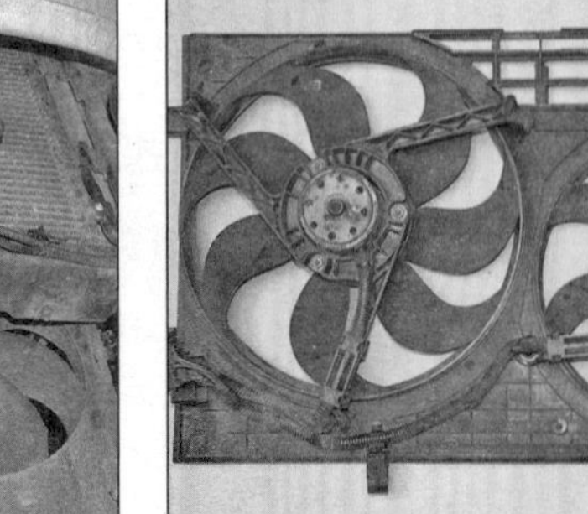
5.18 Cooling fan assembly

6.2 Radiator cooling fan switch location (arrowed)

6.5 Release the wiring plug securing clip (arrowed)

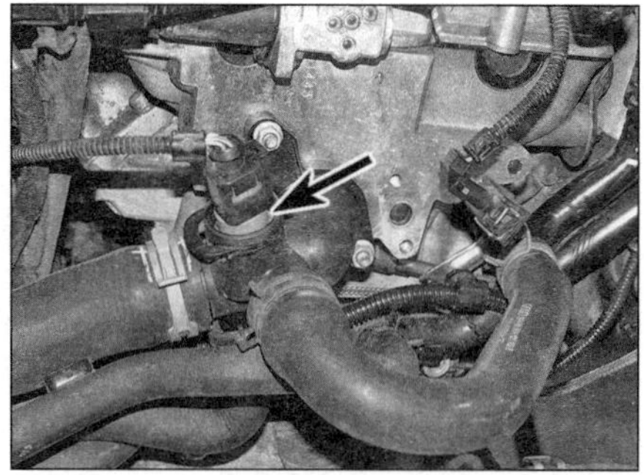
6.9 Coolant temperature sensor location (arrowed)

6.15 Withdraw the retaining clip (arrowed)

pressure in the system, before removing the switch from the radiator.

3 Disconnect the battery negative lead. **Note:** *Before disconnecting the battery, refer to* Disconnecting the battery *in the reference section at the rear of this manual. Where necessary, prise out the sealing caps, undo the retaining screws/ nuts and remove the engine cover(s).*

4 Either drain the radiator to below the level of the switch (as described in Chapter 1 Section 39), or have ready a suitable plug which can be used to plug the switch aperture in the radiator whilst the switch is removed. If a plug is used, take great care not to damage the radiator, and do not use anything which will allow foreign matter to enter the radiator.

5 Release the wiring plug securing clip and disconnect the wiring plug connector from the radiator fan switch **(see illustration)**.

6 Carefully unscrew the radiator cooling fan switch from the radiator, taking care not to damage the radiator.

7 Refitting is a reversal of removal, applying a smear of suitable grease to the threads of the switch and tightening it securely. On completion, refill the cooling system with the correct type and quantity of coolant as described in Chapter 1 Section 39, or top up as described in *Weekly checks*.

8 Start the engine and run it until it reaches normal operating temperature, then continue to run the engine and check that the cooling fan cuts in and functions correctly.

Coolant temperature sensor

Testing

9 The coolant temperature sensor is clipped into the top of the hose connector, bolted to the left-hand end of the cylinder head **(see illustration)**.

10 The sensor contains a thermistor, which consists of an electronic component whose electrical resistance decreases at a predetermined rate as its temperature rises. When the coolant is cold, the sensor resistance is high, current flow through the gauge is reduced, and the gauge needle points towards the 'cold' end of the scale. No resistance-to-temperature values are available. Therefore the only method of accurately checking the sensor is with dedicated diagnostic equipment, and should be entrusted to an Audi dealer or specialist. If the sensor is faulty, it must be renewed.

Removal and refitting

11 Open the bonnet, then release the fasteners and remove the plastic trim panels from the top of the engine and from over the battery.

12 Disconnect the battery negative lead. **Note:** *Before disconnecting the battery, refer to* Disconnecting the battery *in the reference section at the rear of this manual.*

13 Disconnect the wiring plug from the coolant temperature sensor.

14 Drain the cooling system as described in Chapter 1 Section 39. **Note:** *the cooling system only needs to be drained until the level is lower than the height of the sensor.*

15 Carefully withdraw the retaining clip and pull the sensor from the housing **(see illustration)**. Recover the O-ring and discard, as a new one will be required for refitting.

16 Refitting is a reversal of removal. Bearing in mind the following points.

a) Refit the sensor with a new O-ring.
b) Refill the cooling system as described in Chapter 1 Section 39, or top-up as described in ' Weekly checks '.

7 Coolant pump – removal and refitting

Removal

1 Drain the cooling system as described in Chapter 1 Section 39.

2 Remove the camshaft timing belt as described in Chapter 2A Section 7, noting the following points.

a) The lower part of the timing belt guard need not be removed.
b) The timing belt can be left in position on the crankshaft sprocket.
c) Cover the timing belt with a cloth to protect it from coolant.

Note: *Although in this procedure the timing belt is not completely removed, to replace the coolant pump. It is advisable to renew the timing belt as a matter of cause, due to the work required to change the coolant pump.*

3 Remove the retaining bolts, and withdraw the coolant pump from the engine block, noting its fitted position **(see illustration)**. If the pump is faulty, it must be renewed.

Refitting

4 Refitting is a reversal of removal, bearing in mind the following points.

a) Fit the coolant pump with a new O-ring.
b) Lubricate the O-ring with coolant.
c) Install the pump in the correct position, as noted on removal (see illustration).
d) Refill the cooling system as described in Chapter 1 Section 39.

7.3 Coolant pump securing bolts (arrowed)

7.4 Fitting new coolant pump

8 Heating and ventilation system – general information

1 The heating/ventilation system consists of a four-speed blower motor (housed in the passenger compartment), face-level vents in the centre and at each end of the facia, and air ducts to the front and rear footwells.

2 The control unit is located in the facia, and the controls operate flap valves to deflect and mix the air flowing through the various parts of the heating/ventilation system. The flap valves are contained in the air distribution housing, which acts as a central distribution unit, passing air to the various ducts and vents.
3 Cold air enters the system through the grille at the rear of the engine compartment. A pollen filter is fitted to the ventilation inlet to filter out dust, soot, pollen and spores from the air entering the vehicle.
4 The airflow, which can be boosted by the blower, then flows through the various ducts, according to the settings of the controls. Stale air is expelled through ducts below the rear window. If warm air is required, the cold air is passed through the heater matrix, which is heated by the engine coolant.
5 If necessary, the outside air supply can be closed off, allowing the air inside the vehicle to be recirculated. This can be useful to prevent unpleasant odours entering from outside the vehicle, but should only be used briefly, as the recirculated air inside the vehicle will soon deteriorate.

9 Heating/ventilation system components – removal and refitting

Heater/ventilation control unit

1 Switch off the ignition and all electrical consumers.
2 Open the ashtray and undo the retaining screw, then withdraw the ashtray from the facia and disconnect the wiring connectors as it is removed **(see illustrations)**.
3 Undo the retaining bolts and remove the support bars, one each side of the centre console, at the front **(see illustrations)**. As the support bars are removed, note the position of the spacers at the upper mounting bolts.
4 Undo the lower retaining screw, and then remove the heater control panel trim from the facia panel **(see illustrations)**.
5 Undo the four Torx screws and withdraw the control unit from the facia, disconnect the wiring connectors, as it is removed **(see illustrations)**. On some models, it will be necessary to release the retaining clips and disconnect the heater control cables from the rear of the heater control unit.
6 Where applicable, unclip the control cables and release each cable from the control unit, noting each cable's correct fitted location and routing; to avoid confusion on refitting, label each cable as it is disconnected. The outer cables are released by simply pressing the locking tab and lifting the retaining clips **(see illustration)**.

9.2a Undo the retaining screw...

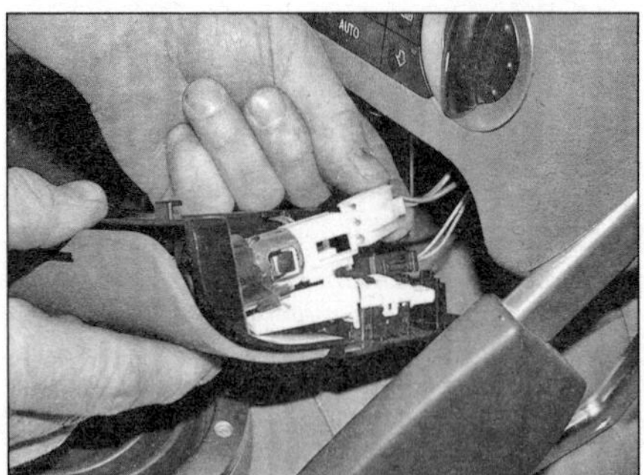

9.2b...and remove the ashtray, disconnecting the wiring

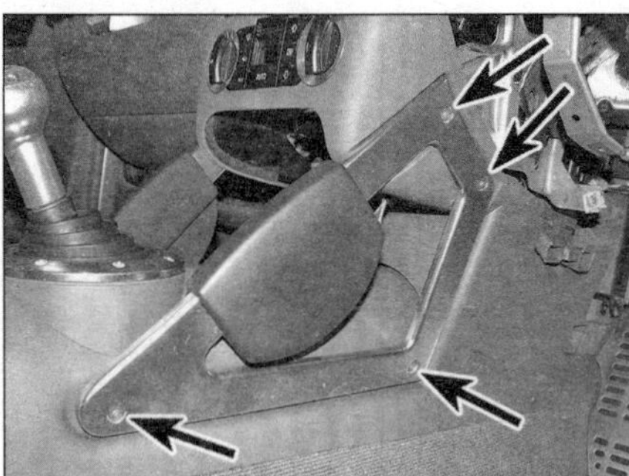

9.3a Undo the support bar retaining bolts (arrowed)

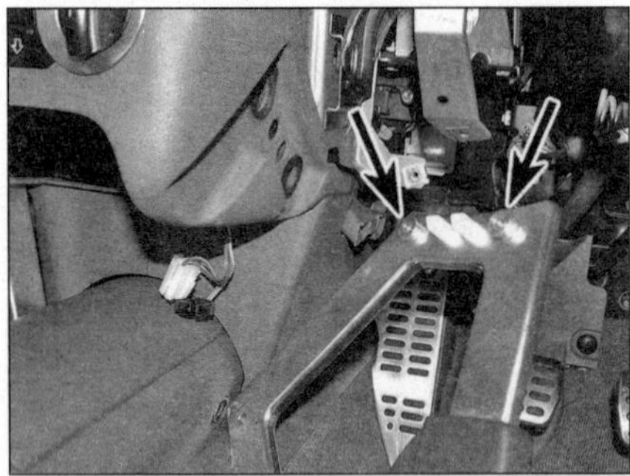

9.3b Check the spacers (arrowed)

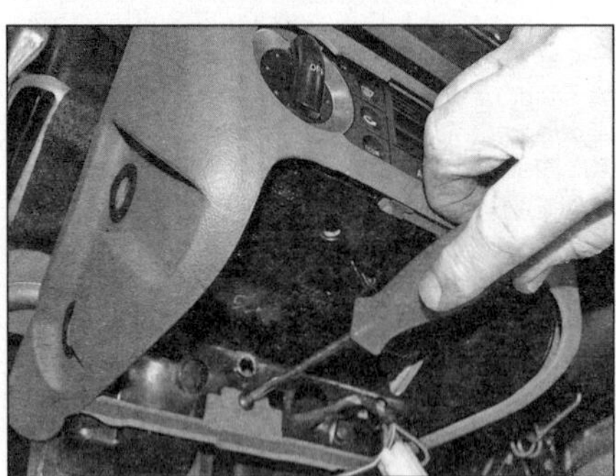

9.4a Undo the retaining screw...

9.4b...and remove the trim panel

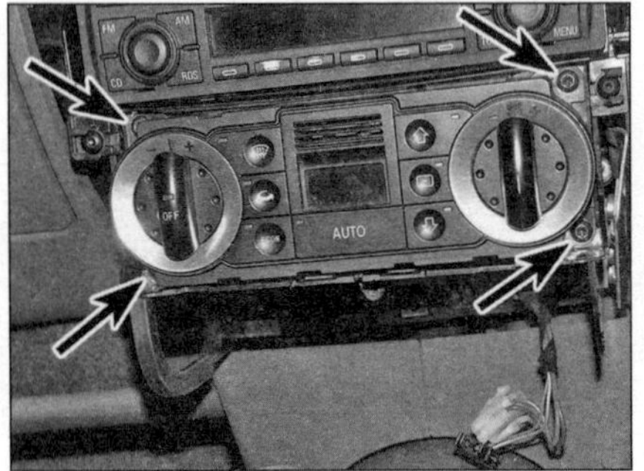

9.5a Undo the retaining screws (arrowed)...

9.5b...and remove the control panel, disconnecting the wiring

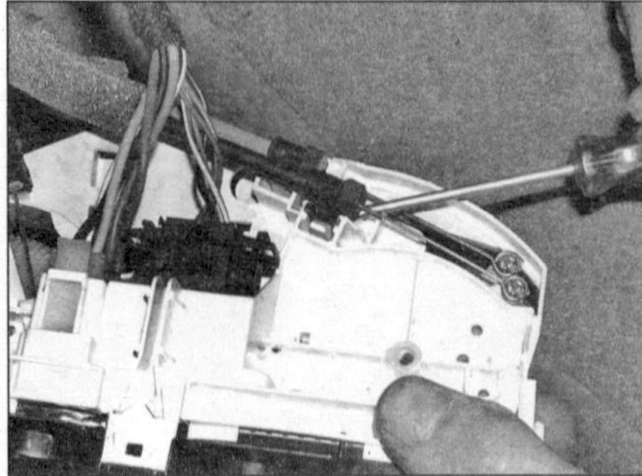

9.6 Press the lock tab, and lift the retaining clip

9.15 Location of heater hoses (arrowed) on bulkhead

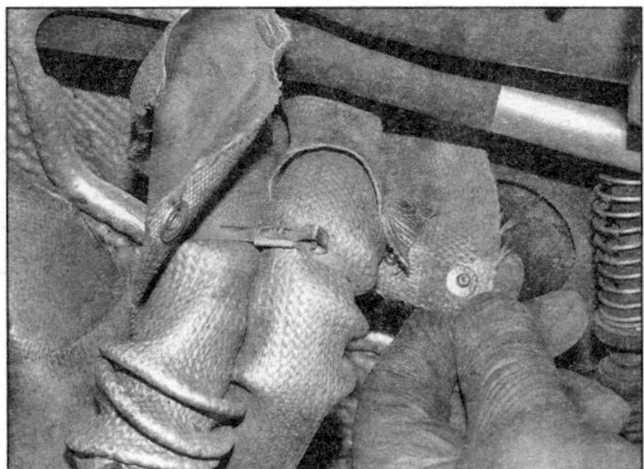
9.16a Unclip the heat cover from the hoses

9.16b Securing clips (arrowed) in the released position

7 Refitting is reversal of removal. Where applicable, ensure that the control cables are correctly routed and reconnected to the control panel, as noted before removal. Clip the outer cables in position and check the operation of each control knob/lever before refitting the switch mounting plate and the trim plate.

Heater/ventilation control cables

8 Remove the heater/ventilation control unit from the facia as described previously, detaching the relevant cable from the control unit.

9 Remove the right-hand lower facia trim panel for access to the heater control cable connections on the heater/ventilation distribution unit.

10 Follow the run of the cable behind the facia, taking note of its routing, and disconnect the cable from the lever on the air distribution/blower motor housing. Note that the method of fastening is the same as that used at the control unit.

11 Fit the new cable, ensuring that it is correctly routed and free from kinks and obstructions. The outer cable sleeves are colour-coded to assist correct reassembly.

a) *Central flap to rotary control: Grey (right-hand drive), Yellow (left-hand drive).*
b) *Footwell/Defrost flap to rotary control: Black (right-hand drive), Green (left-hand drive).*
c) *Temperature flap to rotary control: White (right-hand drive), Brown (left-hand drive).*

12 Connect the cable to the control unit and air distribution/blower motor housing making sure the outer cable is clipped securely in position.

13 Check the operation of the control knob then refit the control unit as described previously in this Section. Finally refit the facia trim panel.

Heater matrix

14 Unscrew the expansion tank cap (referring to the Warning note in Section 1) to release any pressure present in the cooling system, then securely refit the cap.

15 Remove the engine cover(s). Drain the cooling system, as described in Chapter 1 Section 39. Alternatively, clamp both heater hoses **(see illustration)**, as close to the bulkhead as possible to minimise coolant loss.

16 Unclip the heat cover from around the heater hoses, then release the securing clips and disconnect both hoses from the heater matrix unions. Prise out the retaining clips until they lock in the open position, and then pull the hoses from the connections **(see illustrations)**. Make a note of the position of the hoses, so that they are fitted the correct way around on refitting.

17 Pull back the heater hoses, and undo the two retaining nuts securing the heater unit to the bulkhead. To access the nuts, lift up the 'U' shaped cut-away in the heatshield across the back of the bulkhead **(see illustrations)**.

18 On models with air-conditioning, the expansion valve on the rear of the bulkhead will need to be removed as described in Section 12. Refer to the precautions given in Section 11, before attempting any work on the air-conditioning system. Do not attempt to open the refrigerant circuit yourself, until the refrigerant has been removed from the system by a qualified person.

19 Remove the facia assembly as described in Chapter 11 Section 28.

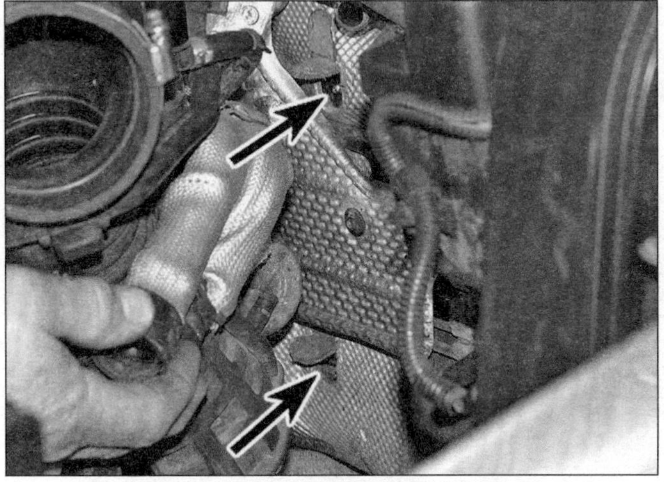
9.17a Undo the two retaining nuts (arrowed)

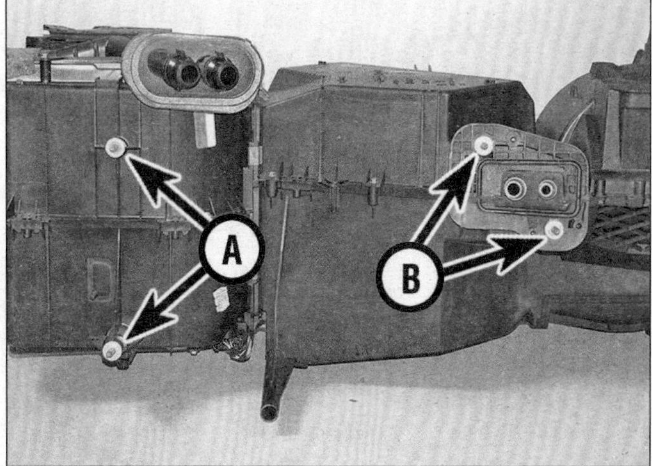

9.17b Location of heater securing points to bulkhead (arrowed)
A Heater unit securing studs
B Expansion valve securing studs – models with Air-con

9.20 Undo the earth wire securing nut (arrowed)

9.21a Unclip the ducting from the top...

9.21b...and right-hand side of the heater assembly

20 Undo the retaining nut and disconnect the earth wire from the earth point on the left-hand lower A-pillar **(see illustration)**.

21 Unclip the heater air ducting from the top of the heater housing and undo the retaining screw and remove the heater duct from the drivers side footwell **(see illustrations)**.

22 Release the cable tie from around the heater unit and then undo the fasteners and remove the soundproofing cover from under the heater unit assembly **(see illustrations)**.

23 Open the wiring loom retaining guide, and release the loom from the top of the heater assembly **(see illustrations)**.

24 Working at the left-hand end of the heater unit, release the wiring loom from the cable ties **(see illustration)**.

25 Check around the heater assembly to make sure there is nothing preventing it from being removed. Carefully pull the heater assembly from the bulkhead, disengaging the drain tube at the lower part of the housing **(see illustration)**. Be prepared for coolant spillage as the assembly is removed from the passenger compartment.

26 With the heater unit assembly on the bench, undo the two retaining screws, and carefully lift the heater matrix from the housing **(see illustrations)**.

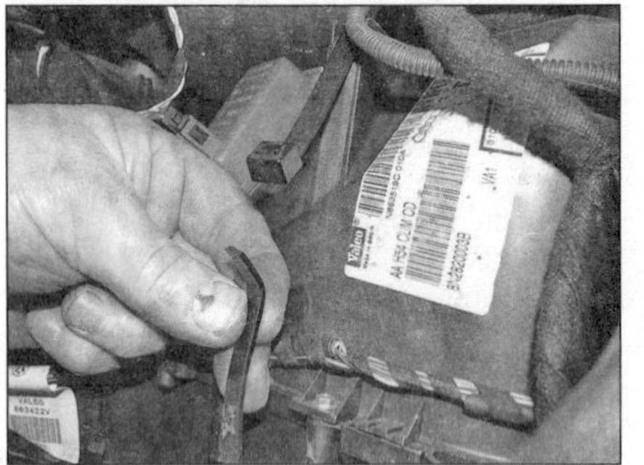
9.22a Release the cable tie...

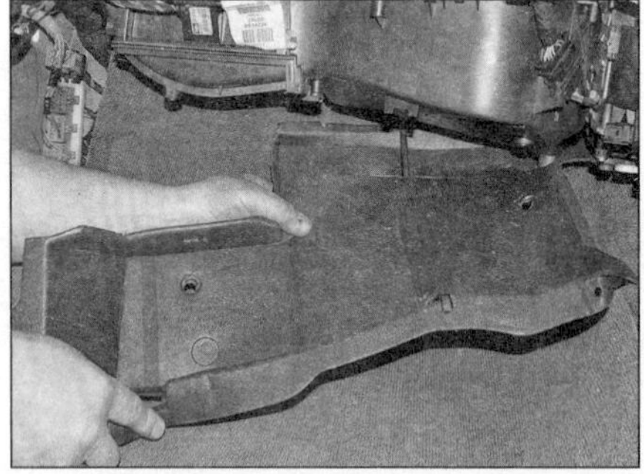
9.22b...and the fasteners to remove cover

9.23a Release the wiring looms...

9.23b...from the top of the heater unit

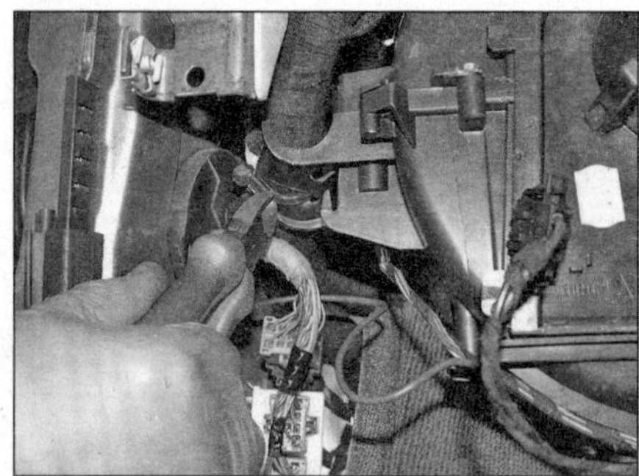
9.24 Using snips to cut cable ties

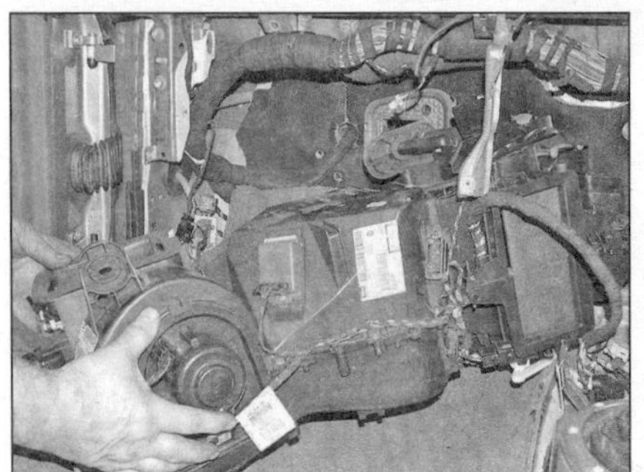
9.25 Removing the heater unit assembly

9.26a Undo the screws (arrowed)...

9.26b ... and lift out the matrix

9.31a Unclip the wiring loom...

9.31b ... and disconnect the wiring connector

9.32a Remove the retaining screws (arrowed)...

9.32b...and remove the lower cover

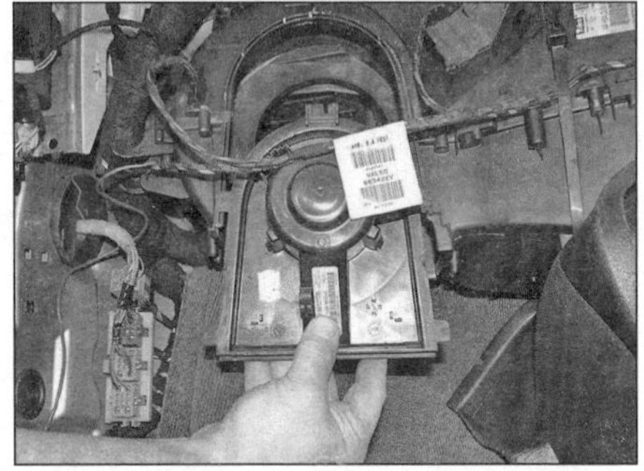
9.33 Remove the heater blower motor

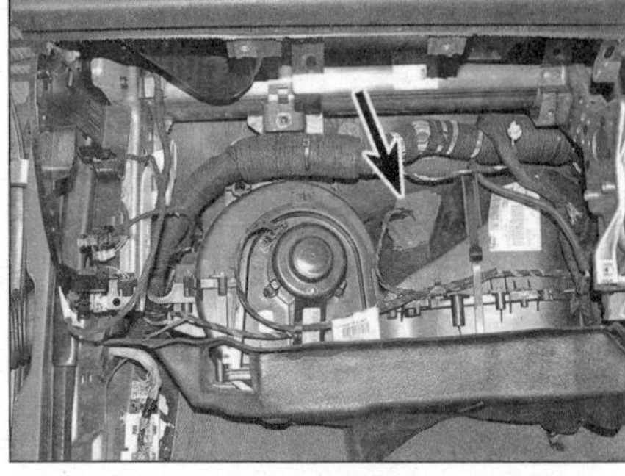
9.37 Location of heater blower resistor (arrowed)

27 Refitting is reversal of removal, noting the following points:

a) *Check the condition of the foam gasket which fits between the matrix pipes and the bulkhead, and renew if necessary.*
b) *Take care to avoid damage to the matrix fins when sliding the matrix into its housing.*
c) *Ensure that the wiring loom is refitted into the retainer on the top of the heater as the assembly is refitted.*
d) *Make sure that all wiring is correctly reconnected and routed.*
e) *Make sure that the air ducts are securely clipped into position.*
f) *Make sure the drain tube on the lower part of the housing is reconnected (air-conditioning models)*
g) *Refit the facia assembly as described in Chapter 11 Section 28.*
h) *On completion, refill the cooling system and check the coolant level and top-up if necessary as described in* Weekly checks.
i) *On air-conditioning models, have the system re-gassed by an Audi dealer or specialist.*

Heater blower motor

28 Switch off the ignition and all electrical consumers.

29 Remove the passenger side glovebox as described in Chapter 11 Section 26.

30 Release the cable tie from around the heater unit and then undo the fasteners and remove the soundproofing cover from under the heater unit assembly **(see illustrations 9.22a and 9.22b)**.

31 Release the wiring loom from the retaining clips on the housing, and then disconnect the blower motor wiring plug connector **(see illustrations)**.

32 Undo the two retaining screws, and remove the plastic cover from the below the heater blower motor **(see illustrations)**.

33 Slide the blower motor downwards and out from the heater housing **(see illustration)**.

34 Refitting is a reversal of removal.

Heater blower motor resistor

35 Switch off the ignition and all electrical consumers.

36 Remove the passenger side glovebox as described in Chapter 11 Section 26.

37 The heater motor blower resistor is located in the upper part of the heater housing to the right of the heater blower motor **(see illustration)**.

38 Disconnect the wiring connector, undo the retaining screw, and withdraw the resistor from the heater housing **(see illustrations)**.

39 Refitting is the reverse of removal.

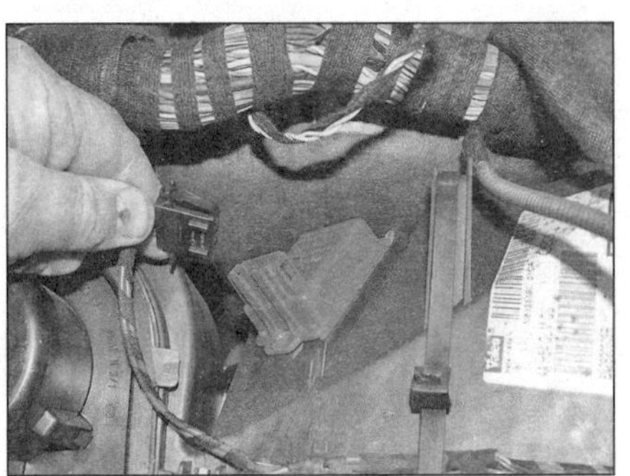
9.38a Disconnect the wiring connector...

9.38b...undo the retaining screw...

9.38c...and withdraw the resistor

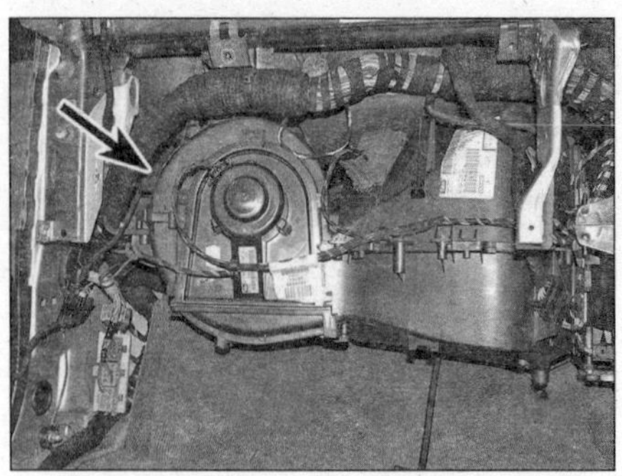
9.42 Location of motor (arrowed) – to the rear of the housing

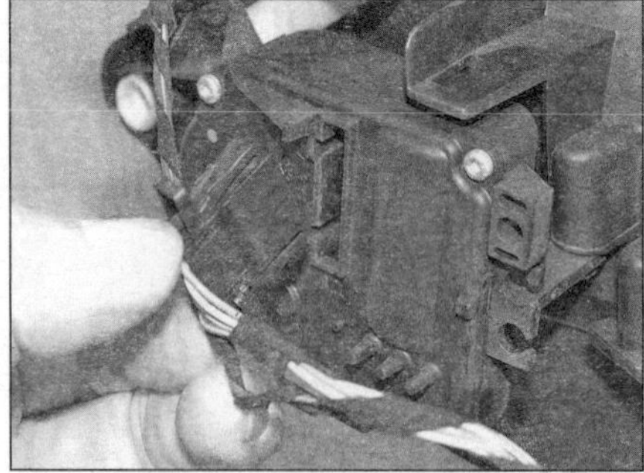
9.43a Disconnect the wiring connector...

9.43b..and release the actuating lever (arrowed)

Air flap positioning electric motors (models without heater control cables)

40 Where fitted, there are four air flap positioning motors fitted the heater housing assembly:

a) Air flow flap positioning motor
b) Footwell/defrost flap positioning motor
c) Temperature flap positioning motor
d) Central flap positioning motor
e) Air flow flap positioning motor

41 To access the air flow flap positioning motor it will be necessary to remove the passenger side glovebox as described in Chapter 11 Section 26.

42 The motor is located to the left-hand side of the heater unit assembly, to the rear of the heater blower motor **(see illustration)**.

43 Unclip the wiring loom and move it to one side to access the motor. Disconnect the wiring plug connector, carefully release the actuating arm from the flap lever **(see illustrations)**.

44 Undo the retaining bolt from the lower part of the motor, then rotate the motor downwards to release it from the air flap **(see illustration)**.

45 Refitting is a reversal of removal, making sure that any wiring is secured away from any moving parts and the actuating lever is connected securely.

Footwell/defrost flap positioning motor

46 To access the footwell/defrost flap positioning motor it will be necessary to remove the trim panel from the facia, below the steering wheel, as described in Chapter 11 Section 28.

47 The motor is located to the right-hand side of the heater unit assembly, to the left of the clutch pedal **(see illustration)**.

48 Disconnect the wiring plug connector, undo the retaining bolts, then disengage the actuating arm and remove the motor from the housing **(see illustrations)**.

49 Refitting is a reversal of removal, making sure that any wiring is secured away from any moving parts and the actuating lever is connected securely.

Temperature/Central flap positioning motors

50 To access the temperature and central flap motors it will be necessary to remove the trim panel from the left-hand side footwell at the front of the centre console, as described in Chapter 11 Section 27.

51 The motors are located under the heater unit assembly, at the centre of the vehicle, above the central tunnel **(see illustration)**.

52 The temperature flap and central flap motors are secured to the heater housing the same way as the footwell/defrost flap

9.44 Undo the retaining bolt (arrowed)

9.47 Location of motor (arrowed)

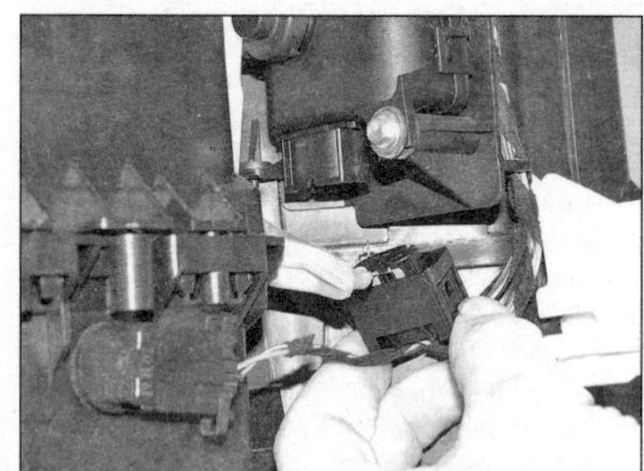
9.48a Disconnect wiring connector...

9.48b...undo the retaining bolts (arrowed)...

9.48c...disconnect the actuating arm (arrowed)

9.51 Temperature flap motor (A) and Central flap motor (B)

9.52 Note position of wiring bracket (arrowed)

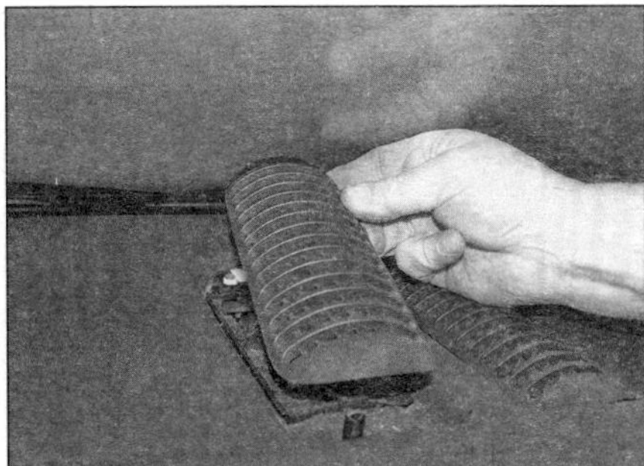

10.4a Unclip the vent from the facia

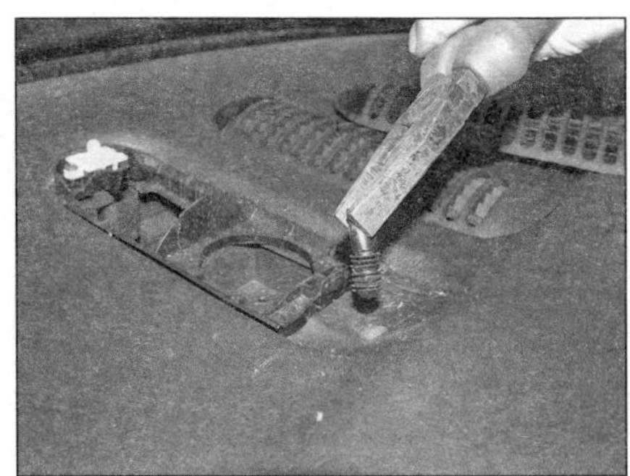

10.4b Using pliers to pull out the broken locating peg

motor. Disconnect the wiring plug connector, undo the retaining bolts, then disengage the actuating arm and remove the motor from the housing. Note the temperature flap motor has wiring support bracket fitted to two of the mounting bolts **(see illustration)**.

53 Refitting is a reversal of removal, making sure that any wiring is secured away from any moving parts and the actuating lever is connected securely.

10 Heating/ventilation system vents – removal and refitting

Circular side/central air vents

1 The circular air vents to the centre and outer ends of the facia panel can be removed from the facia, but may be damaged on removal. To remove them without any damage the complete facia panel will need to be removed, as described in Chapter 11 Section 28.

2 If the vent is already damaged and is being replaced with a new one, then carry out the following procedure. Using two lengths of 3mm metal rod, bend a hook of approx 6mm on one end of each rod, then insert the rods into the inside of the air vent, at opposite sides. When the hooked end is positioned around the inner edge of the air vent ducting, carefully pull it out from the facia. **Note:** *the vents may get damaged as they are removed, so a new one will be required for refitting.*

3 To refit, position the vent in the facia and carefully push the vent into position until the locating clips engage.

Upper central facia vents

4 There are two types of vent trim panels fitted to the top of the facia:

a) *The first type of vent can be removed without any damage, these are held in place by retaining clips, and using a small screwdriver can be carefully prised up from the facia panel.*

b) *The second type of vent that was fitted to our model, has a locating peg at the rear of the vent trim panel, as the trim is prised upwards the locating peg breaks off* ***(see illustrations)****. Carefully prise the air vent trim from the top of the facia panel, if the locating peg breaks, then a new vent trim panel will be required. Use a pair of pliers to remove the broken locating peg from the top of the facia.*

5 To refit, position the vent in the top of the facia, then carefully push down until the locating clips engage.

11 Air conditioning system – general information and precautions

General information

1 An air conditioning system is available on all models. It enables the temperature of incoming air to be lowered, and dehumidifies the air, which makes for rapid demisting and increased comfort.

2 The cooling side of the system works in the same way as a domestic refrigerator. Refrigerant gas is drawn into a belt-driven compressor and passes into a condenser mounted in front of the radiator, where it loses heat and becomes liquid. The liquid passes through an expansion valve to an evaporator, where it changes from liquid under high pressure to gas under low pressure. This change is accompanied by a drop in temperature, which cools the evaporator. The refrigerant returns to the compressor and the cycle begins again.

3 Air blown through the evaporator passes to the air distribution unit, where it is mixed with hot air blown through the heater matrix to achieve the desired temperature in the passenger compartment.

4 The heating side of the system works in the same way as on models without air conditioning.

5 The operation of the system is controlled electronically by coolant temperature switches, and pressure switches which are screwed into the compressor high-pressure line. Any problems with the system should be referred to an Audi dealer or an air conditioning specialist.

Precautions

• When an air conditioning system is fitted, it is necessary to observe special precautions whenever dealing with any part of the system, its associated components and any items which require disconnection of the system. If for any reason the system must be disconnected, entrust this task to your Audi dealer or an air conditioning specialist.

Warning: The refrigeration circuit contains a refrigerant and it is therefore dangerous to disconnect any part of the system without specialised knowledge and equipment. The refrigerant is potentially dangerous and should only be handled by qualified persons. If it is splashed onto the skin it can cause frostbite. It is not itself poisonous, but in the presence of a naked flame (including a cigarette) it forms a poisonous gas. Uncontrolled discharging of the refrigerant is dangerous and potentially damaging to the environment.

• Do not operate the air conditioning system if it is known to be short of refrigerant, as this may damage the compressor.

12 Air conditioning system components – removal and refitting

Warning: Refer to the precautions given in Section 11, before working on the air-conditioning system.

Caution: Before working on any components in the air-conditioning system, have the refrigerant evacuated from the air conditioning system by an Audi dealer or refrigeration specialist.

Caution: It is not recommended that the engine be started without refrigerant being present in the system, as the compressor may overheat causing internal damage. Note also that if the refrigerant circuit is not opened within 10 minutes of evacuation, slight pressure may develop due to re-evaporation.

Expansion valve

1 The expansion valve is positioned at the left-hand rear of the engine compartment

12.1 Location of expansion valve (arrowed)

12.3a Undo the bolt (arrowed)...

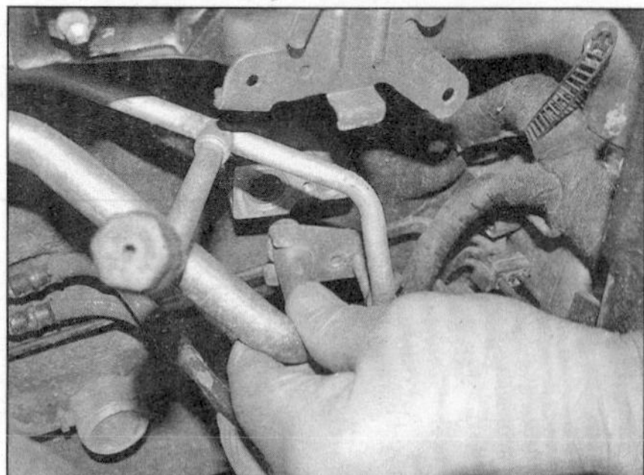

12.3b...and disconnect the refrigerant pipes

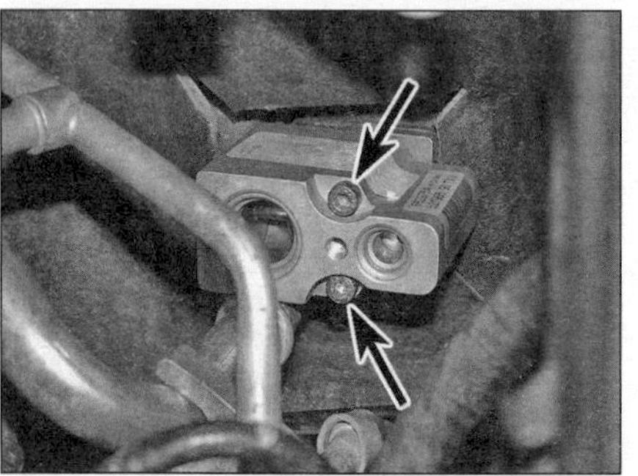

12.4a Undo the two retaining bolts...

12.4b...withdraw the expansion valve...

12.4c...and recover the spacer/plate (arrowed)

(see illustration), where the two (high and low pressure) air conditioning pipes go through the bulkhead to the evaporator in the heater housing.

2 Remove the heat insulation cover from around the expansion valve. **Note:** *If this insulation cover is not fitted around the expansion valve (or not fitted correctly), then it can have an adverse effect on the air-conditioning system.*

3 Undo the retaining bolt and disconnect the refrigerant lines from the expansion valve **(see illustrations)**. Recover the seals and plug the lines to prevent entry of foreign matter and water vapour.

4 Undo the two retaining bolts, remove the expansion valve, then remove the spacer/ plate from around the refrigerant pipes **(see illustrations)**. Recover the seals and plug the lines to prevent entry of foreign matter and water vapour.

5 If the expansion valve has been removed so that the heater housing can be removed, then pull back the soundproofing from around the outside of the valve and undo the two retaining nuts. With the nuts removed, withdraw the mounting plate from the bulkhead **(see illustrations)**.

6 Refitting is a reversal of the removal procedure, ensure that all the fixings are tightened to the specified torque settings, where given. On completion, have new O-rings fitted to the refrigerant lines, and then have the system recharged by an Audi dealer or refrigeration specialist.

Evaporator

7 Remove the heater housing, as described earlier in Section 9.

8 The heater housing is in two sections, one side houses the heater matrix and the other side houses the evaporator, blower motor and resistor.

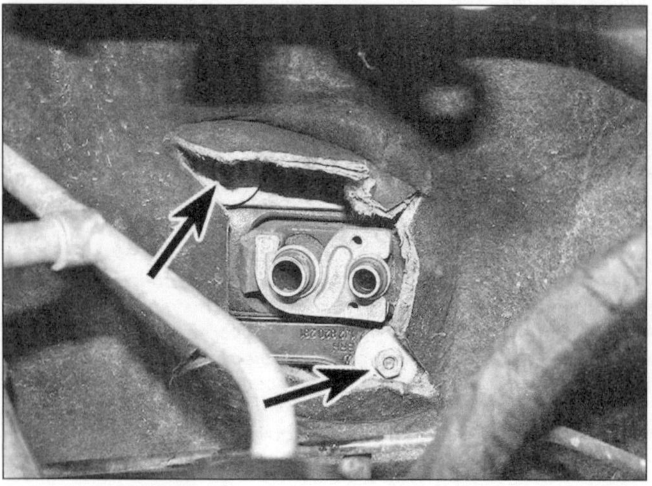

12.5a Undo the retaining nuts (arrowed)...

12.5b...and remove the mounting plate

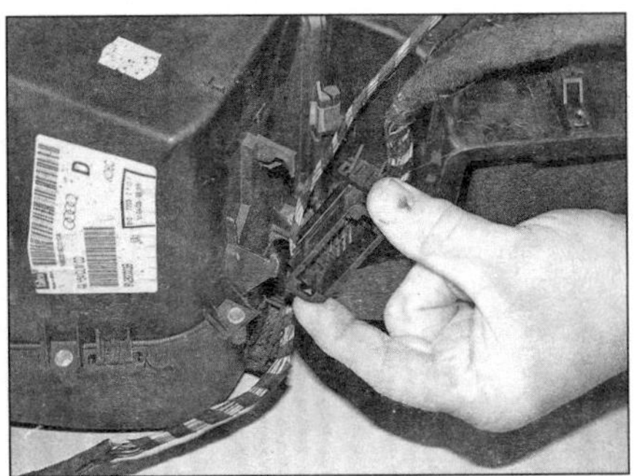
12.9a Unclip the wiring loom...

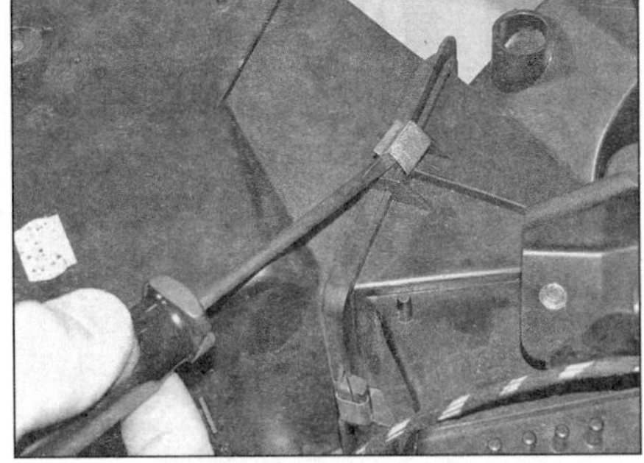
12.9b...release the six securing clips...

12.9c...and separate the two halves of the housing

9 First unclip the wiring loom from the heater housing, and then release the six securing clips from around the housing, so the two halves can be separated **(see illustrations)**.

10 With the two parts of the housing separated, remove the rubber seal from the end of the housing **(see illustration)**. Renew the seal if damaged.

11 Working your way around the housing, undo the eleven retaining bolts and split the upper housing from the lower housing **(see illustrations)**.

12 The evaporator can now be withdrawn from the housing together with the refrigerant pipes **(see illustration)**.

13 Refitting is a reversal of the removal procedure, ensure that all the fixings are tightened to the specified torque settings, where given. On completion, have new O-rings fitted to the refrigerant lines, and then have the system recharged by an Audi dealer or refrigeration specialist.

Condenser

14 Have the refrigerant evacuated from the air conditioning system by an Audi dealer or refrigeration specialist.

15 Remove the radiator as described in Section 3 of this Chapter. The condenser is attached to the front of the radiator.

16 Disconnect the refrigerant lines from the top and bottom of the receiver drier/filter, then undo the retaining bolt and remove it from the right-hand side front of the engine compartment **(see illustration)**. **Note:** *It is recommended that this filter/dryer be*

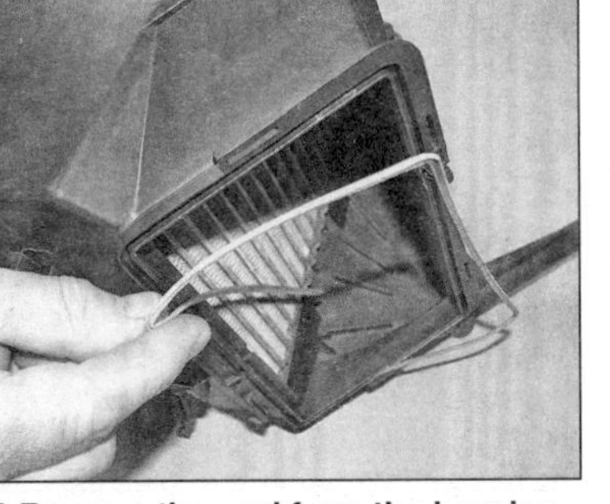
12.10 Remove the seal from the housing

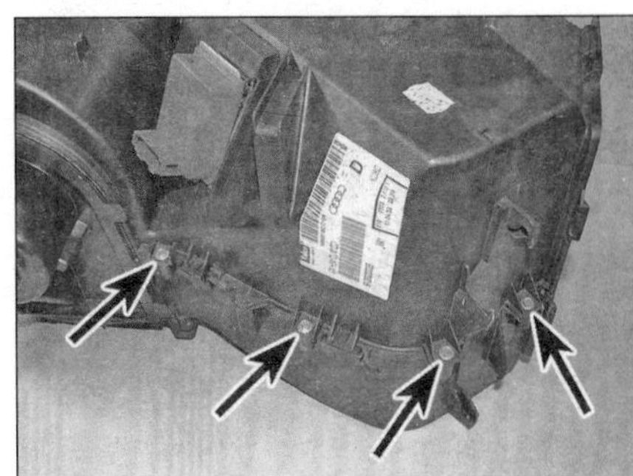
12.11a Undo the retaining bolts (four shown)...

12.11b...and separate the housing

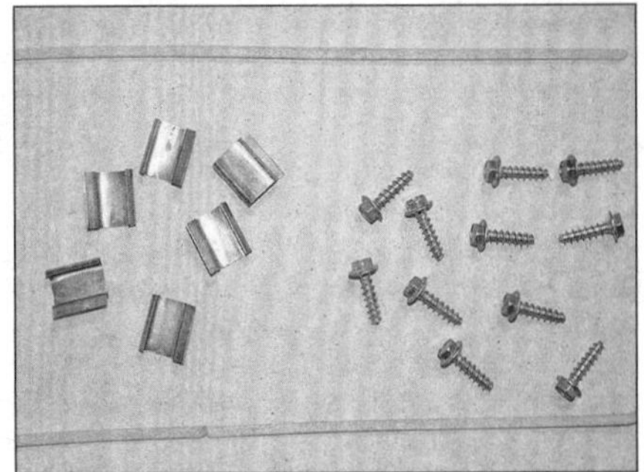
12.11c Clips, seal and bolts removed from the heater housing

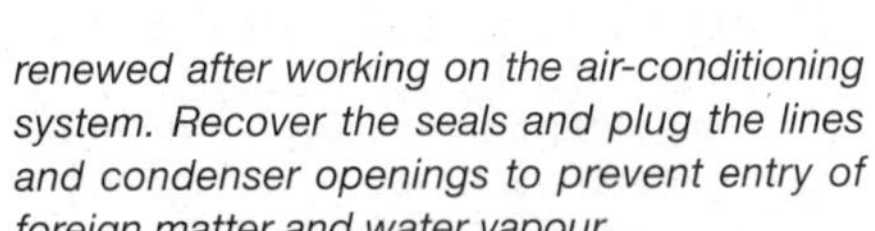
renewed after working on the air-conditioning system. Recover the seals and plug the lines and condenser openings to prevent entry of foreign matter and water vapour.

17 Undo the securing bolt and disconnect the refrigerant line from the lower left-hand corner of the condenser **(see illustration)**. Recover the seals and plug the lines and condenser

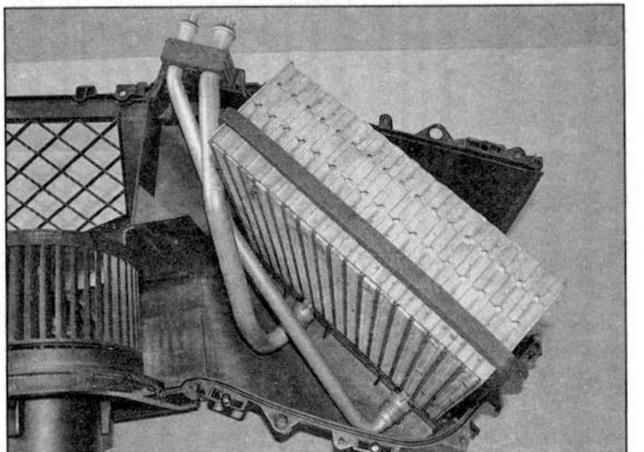
12.12 Remove the evaporator from the housing

12.16 Remove receiver drier/filter (arrowed)

12.17 Disconnect the refrigerant lines from the condenser

12.23 Undo the retaining bolts (arrowed)

12.24 Disconnect wiring connector (arrowed)

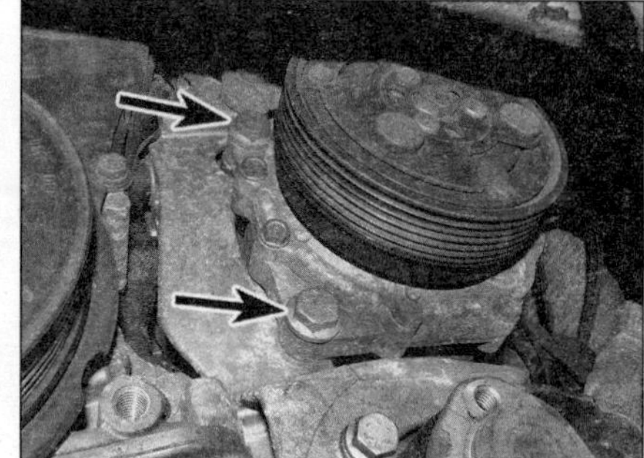
12.25 Air conditioning compressor securing bolts (arrowed)

openings to prevent entry of foreign matter and water vapour.

18 Carefully remove the condenser from the front of the engine compartment, taking care not to damage its fins.

19 Refitting is a reversal of the removal procedure, ensure that all the fixings are tightened to the specified torque settings, where given. On completion, have new O-rings fitted to the refrigerant lines, and then have the system recharged by an Audi dealer or refrigeration specialist.

Compressor

Note: *If necessary, when working on engine related components, the compressor can be unbolted and moved aside, without disconnecting its pipes/hoses. Part of the air-conditioning pipes have a section of flexible hose, so the compressor can be moved to one side, after removing the auxiliary drivebelt. Always take care not to damage or kink the air-conditioning pipes, if the compressor is moved.*

20 Have the refrigerant evacuated from the air conditioning system by an Audi dealer or refrigeration specialist.

21 Remove the auxiliary drivebelt as described in Chapter 1 Section 32.

22 Remove the charge air pipe from across the front lower part of the engine compartment, as described in Chapter 4B Section 7. **Note:** *On all engine codes (except AMU, APX and BAM), the charge air pipe only acts as a brace between the two chassis legs and also a support for the PAS cooler pipe, so does not have any charge air hoses fitted to each end.*

23 Undo the retaining bolts and disconnect the refrigerant lines from the rear of the compressor **(see illustration)**. Remove the O-ring seals and renew them if necessary. Plug the open pipes and ports to prevent the ingress of moisture.

24 Disconnect the wiring plug connector from the rear of the compressor **(see illustration)**.

25 Undo the two retaining bolts **(see illustration)**, and withdraw the compressor from the mounting bracket.

26 Refitting is a reversal of the removal procedure, ensure that all the fixings are tightened to the specified torque settings, where given. On completion, have new O-rings fitted to the refrigerant lines, and then have the system recharged by an Audi dealer or refrigeration specialist.

Receiver drier/filter

27 Have the refrigerant evacuated from the air conditioning system by an Audi dealer or refrigeration specialist.

28 The receiver drier/filter is attached to inner chassis leg on the right-hand side front, of the engine compartment **(see illustration)**.

29 Disconnect the refrigerant lines from the top and bottom of the receiver drier/filter, then undo the retaining bolt from the securing clamp and remove it from the engine compartment. **Note:** *It is recommended that this filter/dryer be renewed after working on the air-conditioning system. Recover the seals and plug the lines and condenser openings to prevent entry of foreign matter and water vapour.*

30 Refitting is a reversal of the removal procedure, ensure that all the fixings are tightened to the specified torque settings, where given. On completion, fit new O-rings and then have the system recharged by an Audi dealer or refrigeration specialist.

13 Climatronic system components – removal and refitting

General information

1 The Climatronic system, fitted to some models, works in conjunction with the heating and air conditioning systems to maintain a selected vehicle interior temperature fully automatically. The only components which can be removed easily without discharging the refrigerant, are as follows:

Sunlight penetration sensor

2 Switch off the ignition and all electrical consumers.

3 Remove the left-hand vent trim from the top of the facia panel, as described in Section 10

4 Undo the retaining screw and withdraw the sensor from the top of the facia **(see illustration)**. Disconnect the wiring plug and remove the sensor. **Note:** *Tape the end of the wiring once removed, to prevent it dropping down inside the top of the facia.*

5 Refitting is a reversal of removal.

Footwell vent temperature sender

6 Switch off the ignition and all electrical consumers.

7 To access the footwell vent temperature sender it will be necessary to remove the trim panel from the facia, below the steering wheel, as described in Chapter 11 Section 26.

8 The sensor is located to left of the clutch pedal in the right-hand end of the heater housing. Disconnect the wiring plug from the

12.28 Location of receiver drier/filter (arrowed)

13.4 Remove the sensor from the top of the facia

13.8a Location of temp sender (arrowed)

13.8b Disconnect the wiring connector...

13.8c...and remove the sender from the housing

sender, then turn it through 90° clockwise, and withdraw it from the housing **(see illustrations)**.

9 Refitting is a reversal of removal.

Fresh air intake duct temperature sensor

10 Switch off the ignition and all electrical consumers.

11 To access the fresh air intake duct temperature sensor it will be necessary to remove the glovebox, as described in Chapter 11 Section 26.

12 The sensor is located at the left-hand end of the heater housing above the air flow flap positioning motor, see Section 9. Disconnect the wiring plug from the sensor, then turn it through 90°, and withdraw it from the housing **(see illustrations)**.

13 Access to the air intake sensor is limited, if required, remove the pollen filter, as described in Chapter 1 Section 18. Reach inside the top of the air intake ducting, then turn the sensor from inside of the air ducting to remove it. It may be helpful to have someone inside the vehicle to catch the sensor, to prevent it falling down the back of the heater housing.

14 Refitting is a reversal of removal.

Temperature sensor blower and high pressure sensor

15 The temperature sensor blower and high pressure sensor are built into the heater control unit in the centre of the facia panel **(see illustration)**. These sensors cannot be replaced separately and are part of the heater control unit. Do not cover or obstruct this vent/grille panel. Remove the heater ventilation control unit, as described in Section 9.

13.12a Disconnect the wiring connector...

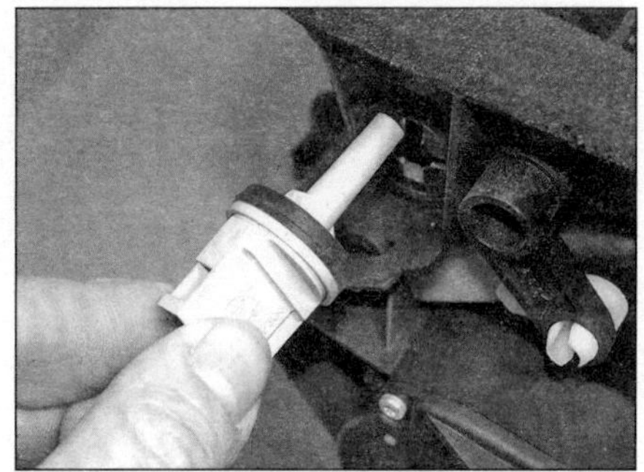
13.12b...and remove the sensor from the housing

13.15 Sensors (arrowed) built into heater control unit

Chapter 4 Part A
Engine fuel systems

Contents

Degrees of difficulty

Easy, suitable for novice with little experience	**Fairly easy,** suitable for beginner with some experience	**Fairly difficult,** suitable for competent DIY mechanic	**Difficult,** suitable for experienced DIY mechanic	**Very difficult,** suitable for expert DIY or professional

Specifications

System type*

All engines	Bosch Motronic ME7.5

Recommended fuel

Minimum octane rating:	
Engine codes AUM and BVP	95 RON unleaded (91 RON unleaded may be used, but with reduced performance)
All engines except engine codes AUM and BVP	98 RON unleaded (95 RON unleaded may be used, but with reduced performance)

Fuel system data

Fuel pump type	Electric, immersed in fuel tank
Fuel pump delivery rate	400 cc/min (battery voltage of 12.5 V)
Regulated fuel pressure	2.5 bar
Engine idle speed (non-adjustable, electronically controlled):	
FWD – Manual transmission	800 to 920 rpm
4WD – Manual transmission	700 to 850 rpm
Automatic transmission	640 to 760 rpm
Idle CO content (non-adjustable, electronically controlled)	0.5 % max
Injectors:	
Electrical resistance (typical)	12 to 13 ohms
Spray pattern	Two-hole nozzle
Injection quantity (30 seconds):	
132kW (180bhp)	145 ± 12 ml
165kW (225bhp)	179 ± 14 ml

Torque wrench settings

	Nm	lbf ft
Fuel tank strap retaining bolts	25	18
Knock sensor(s)	20	15
Oxygen sensor(s)	50	37
Air cleaner mounting 'bolts'	10	7
Camshaft position sensor inner element mounting bolt	25	18
Fuel rail mounting bolts	10	7
Inlet air temperature sensor mounting bolt	10	7
Inlet manifold support bracket:		
To cylinder block	45	33
To inlet manifold	20	15
Inlet manifold-to-cylinder head nuts/bolts	10	7
Throttle housing mounting bolts	10	7

1 General information and precautions

General information

1 The systems described in this Chapter are all self-contained engine management systems, which control both the fuel injection and ignition. This Chapter deals with the fuel system components only – see Chapter 4B for information on the turbocharger, exhaust and emission control systems, and to Chapter 5B for details of the ignition system.

2 The fuel injection system comprises a fuel tank, an electric fuel pump/level sender unit, a fuel filter, fuel supply and return lines, a throttle housing, a fuel rail, a fuel pressure regulator, four electronic fuel injectors, and an Electronic Control Unit (ECU) together with its associated sensors, actuators and wiring. The fuel systems used are essentially very similar, but there are significant detail differences, particularly in the sensors used and in the inlet manifold arrangements.

3 The fuel pump is immersed in the fuel inside the tank, and delivers a constant supply of fuel through a cartridge filter to the fuel rail, at a slightly higher pressure than required – the fuel pressure regulator maintains a constant fuel pressure to the fuel injectors, and returns excess fuel to the tank via the return line. This constant flow system also helps to reduce fuel temperature, and prevents vaporisation. On 4-wheel drive (Quattro) versions the fuel tank has a raised part down the centre to accept the propeller shaft. On this type, a second sender unit is fitted to the left-hand side of the fuel tank, so that it can feed the fuel across to the right-hand side of the fuel tank, to the main fuel pump/sender unit.

4 The fuel injectors are opened and closed by an Electronic Control Unit (ECU), which calculates the injection timing and duration according to engine speed, crankshaft/ camshaft position, throttle position and rate of opening, inlet manifold depression, inlet air temperature, coolant temperature, road speed and exhaust gas oxygen content information, received from sensors mounted on and around the engine.

5 Some models are equipped with a secondary air injection system, which feeds air into the exhaust gases, to promote combustion of any unburnt fuel during engine warm-up; this process also helps to heat the catalytic converter more quickly to its effective operating temperature. Refer to Chapter 4B for more information.

6 Inlet air is drawn into the engine through the air cleaner, which contains a renewable paper filter element. On some non-turbo models, the inlet air temperature is regulated by a valve mounted in the air cleaner inlet trunking, which blends air at ambient temperature with hot air, drawn from over the exhaust manifold.

7 The temperature and pressure of the air entering the throttle housing is measured either by a sensor mounted on the inlet manifold, or by the air mass meter attached to the air cleaner. This information is used by the ECU to fine-tune the fuelling requirements for different operating conditions. Turbocharged engines have an additional air temperature sensor mounted downstream of the throttle housing, which monitors the (compressed) air temperature after it has been through the turbocharger and intercooler.

8 Idle speed control is achieved partly by an electronic throttle valve positioning module, which is part of the throttle housing, and partly by the ignition system, which gives fine control of the idle speed by altering the ignition timing. As a result, manual adjustment of the engine idle speed is not necessary or possible.

9 The exhaust gas oxygen content is constantly monitored by the ECU via an oxygen sensor (also known as a lambda sensor), which is mounted in the front section of the exhaust pipe. On most engines (except AJQ, AMU and APX engine codes), two oxygen sensors are fitted, one before the catalytic converter, and one after – this improves sensor response time and accuracy, and the ECU compares the signals from each sensor to confirm that the converter is working correctly. The ECU uses the information from the sensor(s) to modify the injection timing and duration to maintain the optimum air/ fuel ratio – a result of this is that manual adjustment of the idle exhaust CO content is not necessary or possible. All models are fitted with a catalytic converter – see Chapter 4B Section 9.

10 Where fitted, the ECU controls the operation of the activated charcoal filter evaporative loss system – refer to Chapter 4B for further details.

11 It should be noted that fault diagnosis of all the engine management systems described in this Chapter is only possible with dedicated electronic test equipment. Problems with the systems operation should therefore be referred to a VW/Audi dealer for assessment. Once the fault has been identified, the removal/ refitting sequences detailed in the following Sections will then allow the appropriate component(s) to be renewed as required.

Precautions

Warning: Petrol is extremely flammable – great care must be taken when working on any part of the fuel system.

• Do not smoke, or allow any naked flames or uncovered light bulbs near the work area. Note that gas-powered domestic appliances with pilot flames, such as heaters boilers and tumble-dryers, also present a fire hazard – bear this in mind if you are working in an area where such appliances are present. Always keep a suitable fire extinguisher close to the work area, and familiarise yourself with its operation before starting work. Wear eye protection when working on fuel systems, and wash off any fuel spilt on bare skin immediately with soap and water. Note that fuel vapour is just as dangerous as liquid fuel – possibly more so; a vessel that has been emptied of liquid fuel will still contain vapour, and can be potentially explosive.

• Many of the operations described in this Chapter involve the disconnection of fuel lines, which may cause an amount of fuel spillage. Before commencing work, refer to the above 'Warning' and the information in 'Safety first!' at the beginning of this manual.

• Residual fuel pressure always remains in the fuel system, long after the engine has been switched off. This pressure must be relieved in a controlled manner before

work can commence on any component in the fuel system – refer to Section 7 for details.

- ***When working with fuel system components, pay particular attention to cleanliness – dirt entering the fuel system may cause blockages, which will lead to poor running.***
- ***In the interests of personal safety and equipment protection, many of the procedures in this Chapter suggest that the negative lead be removed from the battery terminal. This firstly eliminates the possibility of accidental short-circuits being caused as the vehicle is being worked upon, and secondly prevents damage to electronic components (eg, sensors, actuators, ECUs) which are particularly sensitive to the power surges caused by disconnection or reconnection of the wiring harness whilst they are still 'live'. Refer to* Disconnecting the battery *at the rear of this manual.***

2 Air cleaner and inlet system – removal and refitting

Removal

1 Where applicable and/or necessary for access, remove the plastic trim covers from the top of the engine and/or battery.

2 Release the securing clip and disconnect the wiring plug from the air mass meter **(see illustration)**.

3 On all models (except AMU, APX and BAM engine codes), release the securing clip and disconnect the breather hose from the front upper part of the air cleaner cover **(see illustration)**.

4 Slacken the securing clip from the air mass meter to the air inlet trunking **(see illustration)**.

5 Remove the two bolts securing the air cleaner base to the inner wing panel, and then lift out the air cleaner assembly releasing it from the air inlet ducting in the inner wing panel **(see illustrations)**. Also note the locating peg that also secures the position of the air cleaner assembly in the inner wing panel.

6 If required, the rest of the inlet trunking can be removed by releasing the hose clips and disconnecting any wiring connections. Before removal, make a note of the fitted locations of all the hoses prior to disconnection – label the hoses if necessary, to aid refitting.

Refitting

7 Refitting is a reversal of removal, noting the following points:

a) Where applicable, ensure that the air filter element is correctly refitted, referring to Chapter 1 Section 30 if necessary.

b) Make sure the locating peg and air inlet ducting at the outer edge of the air cleaner housing locates correctly on refitting.

c) It is most important that an airtight seal is made between the air mass meter and the air inlet trunking. Either check the condition of the seal as described in paragraph 7, or tighten the hose clip securely.

3 Fuel system components – removal and refitting

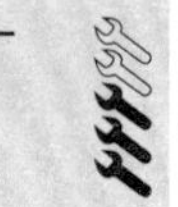

Note: *Observe the precautions in Section 1 before working on any component in the fuel system. Information on the engine management system sensors which are more directly related to the ignition system will be found in Chapter 5B.*

Throttle valve control unit

1 On all models (except AMU, APX and BAM engine codes) the throttle valve control unit is fitted to the right-hand end of the inlet manifold. On models with engine codes AMU,

2.2 Disconnect the wiring connector

2.3 Disconnect breather hose (arrowed) – where fitted

2.4 Slacken the inlet trunking securing clip (arrowed)

2.5a Undo the retaining bolts (arrowed)...

2.5b ... and remove the air cleaner assembly

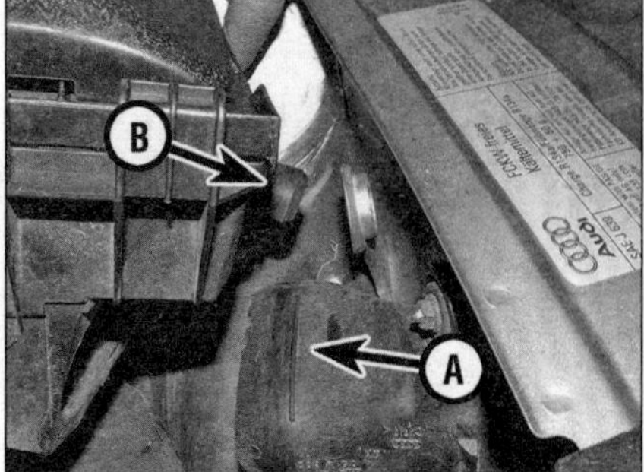

2.5c Air inlet ducting (A) and locating peg (B)

3.1a Throttle valve control unit (arrowed) – all models except AMU, APX and BAM engine codes

3.1b Throttle valve control unit (arrowed) – AMU, APX and BAM engine codes

APX and BAM, the throttle valve control unit is fitted to the left-hand end of the inlet manifold **(see illustrations)**.

2 Disconnect the battery negative lead and position it away from the terminal. **Note:** *Refer to* Disconnecting the battery *at the rear of this manual first.*

3 Slacken the retaining clips and disconnect the air intake hose and vacuum hose from the throttle valve control unit. Also disconnect the wiring connector from the lower part of the control unit **(see illustrations)**.

4 Slacken and remove the withdraw the Allen key bolts **(see illustration)**, then withdraw the throttle valve control unit away from

3.3a Air intake hose (A) and vacuum hose (B) – all models (except AMU, APX and BAM engine codes)

3.3b Disconnect wiring connector (arrowed)

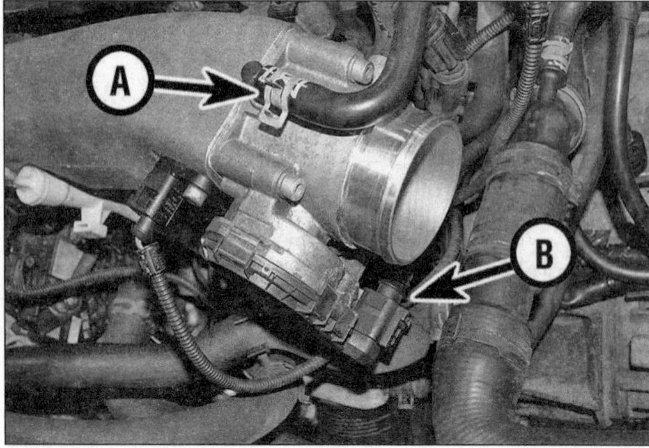

3.3c Vacuum hose (A) and wiring connector (B) – AMU, APX and BAM engine codes

3.4 Undo the four retaining bolts (arrowed)

3.7a Release the fasteners (arrowed) – all models except AMU, APX and BAM engine codes

3.7b Release the fasteners (arrowed) – AMU, APX and BAM engine codes

the inlet manifold. Recover and discard the gasket/O-ring seal.

5 Refitting is a reversal of removal, noting the following:

a) Use a new throttle valve control unit-to-inlet manifold gasket/seal.

b) Tighten the bolts evenly to the specified torque, to prevent air leaks.

c) Ensure that all hoses and electrical connectors are refitted securely.

Fuel injectors and fuel rail

Note: *Observe the precautions in Section 1 before working on any component in the fuel system. If a faulty injector is suspected, before removing the injectors, it is worth trying the effect of one of the proprietary injector-cleaning treatments. These can be added to the petrol in the tank, and are intended to clean the injectors as you drive.*

6 Disconnect the battery negative lead, and position it away from the terminal. **Note:** *Refer to* Disconnecting the battery *at the rear of this manual first.*

7 Release the fasteners and remove the plastic trim cover from the top of the engine **(see illustrations)**.

8 On all models (except AMU, APX and BAM engine codes), release the fasteners are remove the trim panel from along the front of the inlet manifold **(see illustration)**.

9 Release the securing clips and unplug the wiring connectors from the top of the injector. Release the wiring harness clips from the top of the fuel rail, and lay the harness back over the inlet manifold **(see illustrations)**.

10 Refer to Section 7 and depressurise the fuel system. Then with no pressure in the fuel lines, release the spring clips, securing the hoses to the fuel rail **(see illustration)**. Wrap some cloth around the connections to soak up any spilt fuel, when the hoses are disconnected. Note the fitted positions of the hoses – the supply hose is marked with a white arrow on the end, and the return hose is marked with a blue arrow.

11 Disconnect the vacuum hose from the top of the fuel pressure regulator **(see illustration)**.

3.8 Remove the trim panel – all models except AMU, APX and BAM engine codes

3.9a Disconnect the wiring plugs from the injectors...

3.9b ...then release the wiring harness from the fuel rail...

3.9c ...and lay the harness back over the inlet manifold

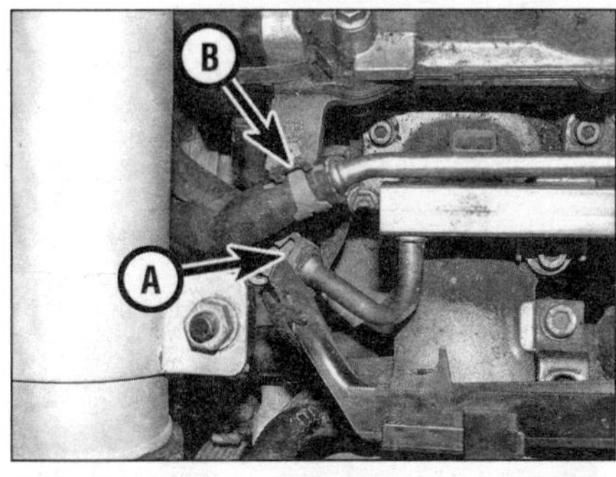

3.10 Disconnect supply hose (A) and return hose (B)

3.11 Disconnecting the vacuum hose (arrowed)

3.12 Fuel rail mounting bolts (arrowed)

3.27 Move the relays to one side

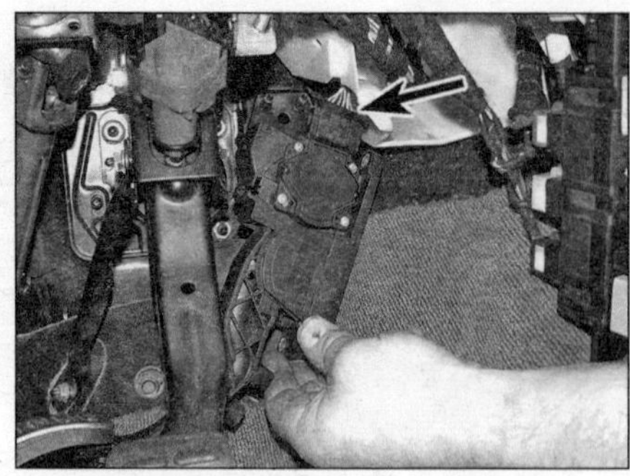
3.28 Disconnect the wiring connector (arrowed)

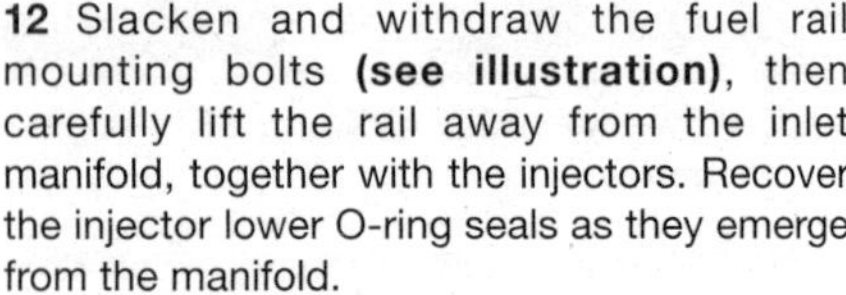

12 Slacken and withdraw the fuel rail mounting bolts **(see illustration)**, then carefully lift the rail away from the inlet manifold, together with the injectors. Recover the injector lower O-ring seals as they emerge from the manifold.

13 The injectors can be removed individually from the fuel rail by extracting the relevant metal clip and easing the injector out of the rail. Recover the injector upper O-ring seals.

14 If required, remove the fuel pressure regulator, referring to the relevant sub-Section for guidance.

15 Check the electrical resistance of the injectors using a multimeter, and compare it with the Specifications.

16 Refit the injectors and fuel rail by following the removal procedure in reverse, noting the following points:

a) *Renew the injector O-ring seals if they appear worn or damaged.*
b) *Ensure that the injector retaining clips are securely seated.*
c) *Check that the fuel supply and return hoses are reconnected correctly – refer to the colour coding described in removal.*
d) *Check that all vacuum and electrical connections are remade correctly and securely.*
e) *On completion, check exhaustively for fuel leaks before bringing the vehicle back into service.*

Fuel pressure regulator

Note: *Observe the precautions in Section 1 before working on any component in the fuel system.*

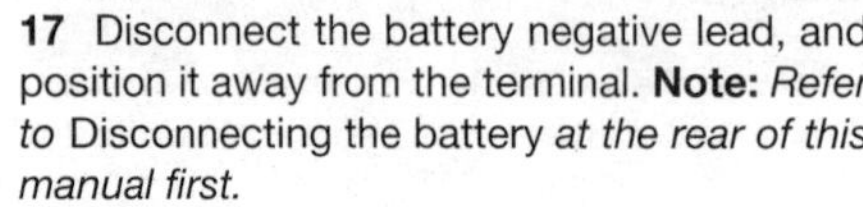

17 Disconnect the battery negative lead, and position it away from the terminal. **Note:** *Refer to* Disconnecting the battery *at the rear of this manual first.*

18 Refer to Section 7 and depressurise the fuel system.

19 Release the fasteners and remove the plastic trim cover from the top of the engine **(see illustrations 3.7a and 3.7b).**

20 Disconnect the vacuum hose from the port on the top of the fuel pressure regulator **(see illustration 3.11)**.

21 Release the spring clip and temporarily disconnect the fuel supply hose from the end of the fuel rail **(see illustration 3.10)**. This will allow the majority of fuel in the regulator to drain out. Be prepared for an amount of fuel loss – position a small container and some old rags underneath the fuel regulator housing. Reconnect the hose once the fuel has drained. **Note:** *The supply hose is marked with a black or white arrow.*

22 Withdraw the retaining spring clip from the top of the regulator housing and lift the regulator body out from the end of the fuel rail. Recover the O-ring seal(s) and check for any damage, fit new ones if required.

23 Refit the fuel pressure regulator by following the removal procedure in reverse, noting the following points:

a) *Renew the O-ring seal(s) if they appear worn or damaged.*
b) *Ensure that the regulator is securely seated in the fuel rail and the retaining clip is fitted correctly.*
c) *Refit the fuel supply hose and regulator vacuum hose securely.*

Throttle valve potentiometer/ positioner

24 The potentiometer (or motor/positioner) is matched to the throttle valve control unit during manufacture, and is not available separately – if defective, a complete throttle valve control unit will be required. Although it looks as if the potentiometer can be removed from the control unit by removing the retaining screws, doing so will damage the seal between the two, and it does not appear that a new seal is available as a new part.

Throttle position sensor

25 Disconnect the battery negative lead, and position it away from the terminal. **Note:** *Refer to* Disconnecting the battery *at the rear of this manual first.*

26 The position sensor is integral with the accelerator pedal. The pedal assembly can be removed (once access has been gained by removing the driver's lower facia panel – Chapter 11 Section 26).

27 To make access easier undo the two retaining nuts and remove the lower section of relays and move them to one side **(see illustration)**.

28 Undo the nuts securing the pedal to its mounting bracket, then as the pedal assembly is withdrawn, disconnect the wiring plug connector from the top of the pedal assembly **(see illustration)**.

Inlet air temperature/ pressure sensors

29 All models have an air temperature sensor built into the air mass meter. This sensor is an integral part of the air mass meter, and cannot be renewed separately. An additional air temperature sensor is fitted to the inlet manifold, and this can be renewed as described below.

30 On all models (except AMU, APX and BAM engine codes) the sensor is attached to the right-hand rear side of the inlet manifold, next to the throttle valve control unit **(see illustration)**.

31 On engine codes AMU, APX and BAM, it is fitted to the left-hand end front of the inlet manifold, next to the throttle valve control unit **(see illustration)**.

3.30 Air temperature sensor (arrowed)

3.31 Air temperature sensor (arrowed)

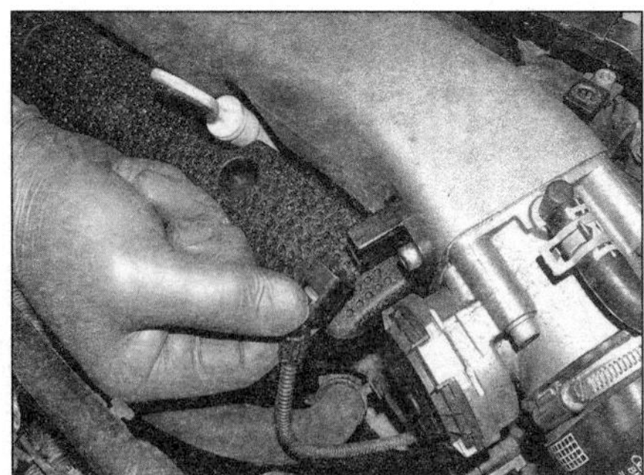

3.33a Disconnect the wiring connector...

32 Switch off the ignition and all electrical consumers, before disconnecting the sensor.
33 Disconnect the wiring connector, remove the securing screw, and pull the sensor from the manifold **(see illustrations)**. Recover the O-ring seal.
34 Refitting is a reversal of removal. Renew the O-ring seal, if necessary. Tighten the sensor retaining screws securely.

Roadspeed sensor

35 The roadspeed sensor is mounted on the rear of the transmission, on the differential housing – refer to Chapter 7A. Do not confuse the sensor with the reversing light switch, which is fitted to the front of the transmission housing.
36 Disconnect the wiring connector, remove the retaining bolt, and pull the sensor from the housing **(see illustration)**. Recover the O-ring seal.
37 Refitting is a reversal of removal. Renew the O-ring seal, if necessary. Tighten the sensor retaining screws securely.

Coolant temperature sensor

38 Refer to Chapter 3 Section 6.

Oxygen (lambda) sensor(s)

39 All models have a sensor threaded into the exhaust front downpipe, ahead of the catalytic converter and on most models an additional second oxygen sensor, mounted downstream of the converter (second sensor not fitted to AJQ, AMU and APX engine codes). Refer to Chapter 4B for more details.
40 Disconnect the battery negative lead and position it away from the terminal. Note: *Refer to* Disconnecting the battery *at the rear of this manual first.*

Warning: Working on the sensor(s) is only advisable with the engine (and therefore the exhaust system) completely cold. The catalytic converter in particular will be very hot for some time after the engine has been switched off.

41 On all models, undo the two retaining nuts and remove the plastic cover from under the drivers side front floor panel **(see illustration)**. Disconnect the wiring connector(s) from inside the cover. On AJQ, AMU, APX and BAM engine codes, there will only be one wiring connector. On all ohter engine codes, there will be two wiring connectors. **Note:** *On models with two wiring connectors inside the plastic cover, check the colour of the connectors for refitting. Typically, the wiring plug is coloured black for the front sensor, and brown for the rear sensor.*
42 On models with engine codes AMU, APX and BAM, the wiring connector for the sensor threaded into the exhaust front downpipe, ahead of the catalytic converter, can be accessed at the rear of the engine compartment, on the bulkhead **(see illustration)**.
43 On models with engine codes AMU, APX and BAM, remove the charge air pipe from around the top, right-hand side of the engine, as described in Chapter 4B Section 7, to access the sensor in the top of the exhaust front pipe.

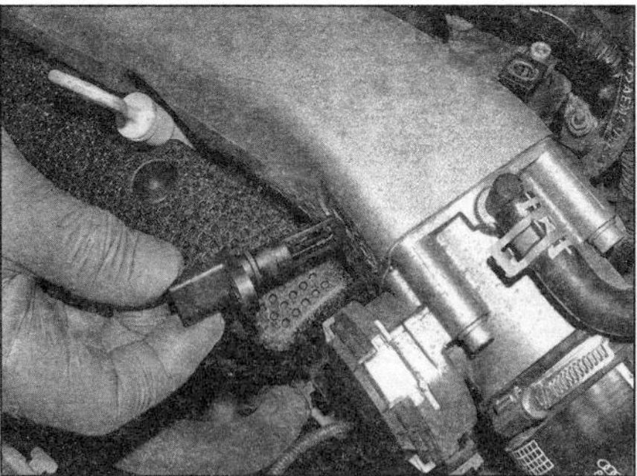

3.33b ...undo the bolt and remove the sensor

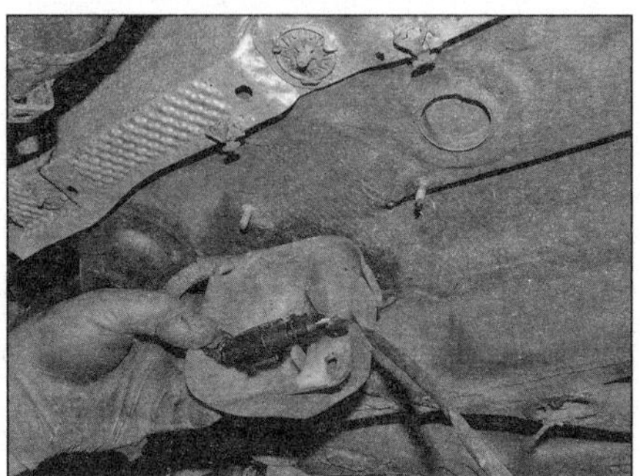

3.41 Disconnect the wiring connector – BAM engine code shown

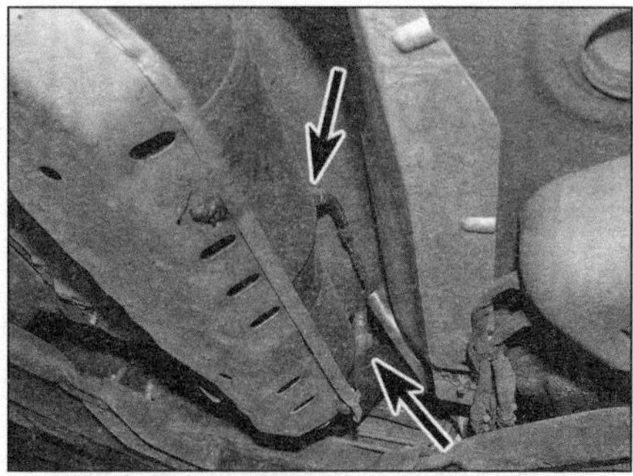

3.45a Front and rear oxygen sensor location – All except AJQ, AMU, APX and BAM engine codes

3.36 Roadspeed sensor at rear of transmission

3.42 Location of wiring connector (arrowed)

44 Trace the wiring harness from the connector back to the oxygen sensor, and unclip it from the retaining clips along the way, noting how it was routed.
45 Access to the front sensor is only possible on AMU, APX and BAM engine codes from above. All other sensors (where fitted) are only accessible from below **(see illustrations)**.
46 Slacken and withdraw the sensor, taking care to avoid damaging the sensor probe as it is removed. **Note:** *As a flying lead remains connected to the sensor after it has been disconnected,if the correct-size spanner is not available, a slotted socket will be required to remove the sensor.*
47 Apply a little high-temperature anti-seize grease to the sensor threads – avoid contaminating the probe tip.
48 Refit the sensor, tightening it to the correct torque. Restore the harness connection.

3.45b Rear oxygen sensor location – BAM engine code shown

3.50 Engine speed sensor (A) and wiring connector (B)

3.51 Sensor retaining bolt (arrowed)

3.54 Realise the securing clip (arrowed)

Engine speed sensor

49 The engine speed sensor is mounted on the front, left-hand side of the cylinder block, adjacent to the mating surface of the block and transmission bellhousing, next to the oil filter.

50 Trace the wiring back from the sensor, and unplug the harness connector **(see illustration)**.

51 Unscrew the retaining bolt **(see illustration)**, and withdraw the sensor from the cylinder block.

52 Refitting is a reversal of removal.

Camshaft position sensor

53 Remove the timing belt outer cover with reference to Chapter 2A Section 6.

54 Release the clip and disconnect the wiring multiplug from the sensor **(see illustration)**.

55 Unscrew the mounting bolts **(see illustration)**and withdraw the sensor from the cylinder head. If required, unscrew the central bolt and remove the inner element and hood from the end of the camshaft, noting how they are fitted.

56 Refitting is a reversal of removal; tighten the mounting bolts securely.

Clutch pedal switch

57 The clutch switch is mounted on the clutch pedal, and sends a signal to the ECU. The purpose of the switch is to disable the throttle closing damper during gearchanges, allowing the engine revs to die down more quickly than would otherwise happen when the accelerator is released. The switch also deactivates the cruise control system (where fitted) when the pedal is pressed.

58 To remove the switch, first remove the facia lower trim panel on the driver's side, as described in Chapter 11 Section 28.

59 Locate the clutch pedal switch, at the top of the clutch pedal **(see illustration)**. Disconnect the wiring connector, then turn the switch a quarter of a turn anti-clockwise, and withdraw it from the pedal mounting bracket.

60 When refitting the switch, first extend the switch plunger to its fullest extent, then hold the clutch pedal depressed when offering the switch into position. Fit the switch by turning it through a quarter of a turn clockwise and release the pedal – this sets the switch adjustment. Refit the wiring connector to the switch and then further refitting is a reversal of removal.

Power steering pressure switch

61 When the steering is at or near full left or right lock, this places a greater load on the power steering pump. Since the pump is driven by the engine, this could result in the engine idle speed dropping, risking the engine stalling. The pressure switch fitted to the pump detects the rise in system fluid pressure, and signals the ECU, which raises the idle speed temporarily to compensate for the extra load.

62 The pressure switch is screwed into the top of the steering pump fluid supply union **(see illustration)**, and is most easily accessed from below.

63 Disconnect the wiring plug from the top of the switch.

64 Hold the (slim) union nut against rotation with one spanner, and use another to unscrew the pressure switch from the union. Recover the sealing washers. Anticipate some fluid spillage as the switch is unscrewed. Once the switch has been removed, cover the open connection to prevent dirt from entering.

65 Refitting is a reversal of removal, noting the following points:

a) *Use new sealing washers. Tighten the switch securely, holding the union nut as for removal.*

b) *Top-up the power steering system as described in ' Weekly checks '. If a large amount of fluid was lost, bleed the system as described in Chapter 10 Section 23.*

c) *On completion, start the engine and have an assistant turn the steering wheel from lock-to-lock, while you check around the switch for leaks.*

Electronic control unit (ECU)

Caution: Always wait at least 30 seconds after switching off the ignition before disconnecting the wiring from the ECU. When the wiring is disconnected, all the learned values are erased, although any contents of the fault memory are retained. After reconnecting the wiring, the basic settings must be reinstated by an Audi dealer using a special test instrument. Note also that if the ECU is renewed, the identification of the new ECU must be transferred to the immobiliser control unit by an Audi dealer.

3.55 Sensor securing bolts (arrowed)

3.59 Clutch pedal switch (arrowed)

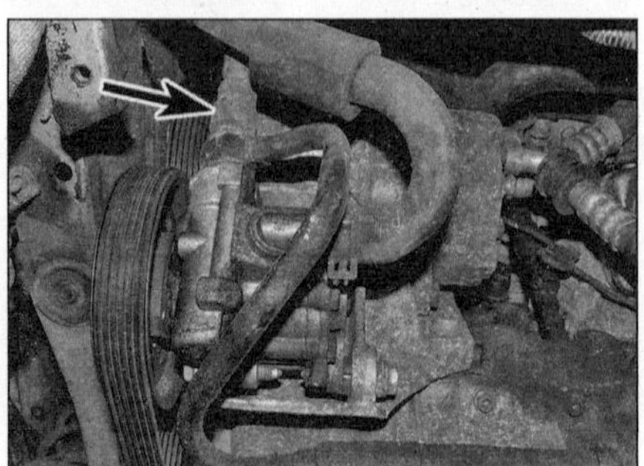
3.62 Power steering pressure switch (arrowed)

3.67 Disconnecting the right-hand wiring plug

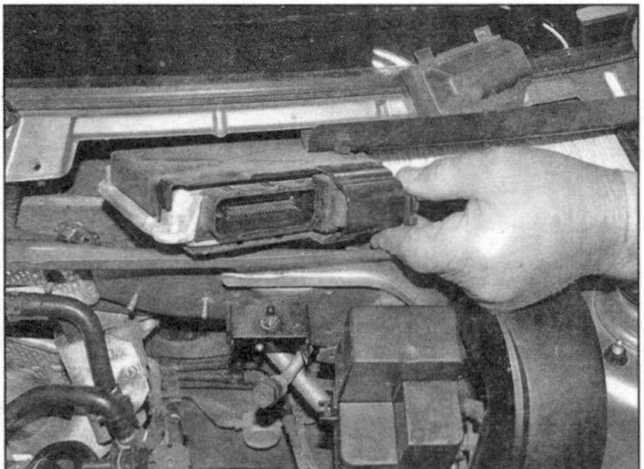

3.68 Removing the ECU from its location

3.69 Security/shear bolts (arrowed)

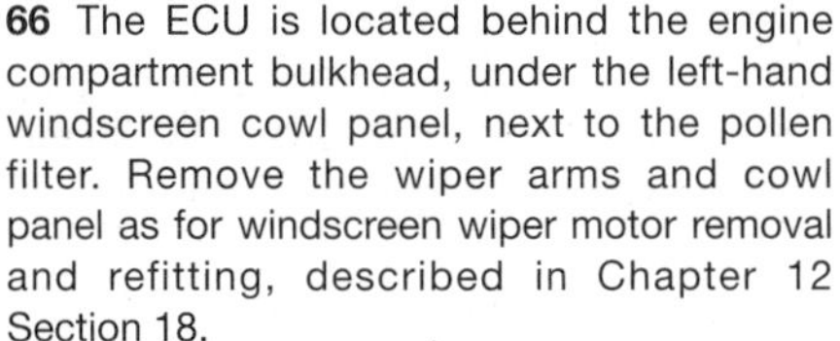

66 The ECU is located behind the engine compartment bulkhead, under the left-hand windscreen cowl panel, next to the pollen filter. Remove the wiper arms and cowl panel as for windscreen wiper motor removal and refitting, described in Chapter 12 Section 18.

67 Pull out the locking sliding clip on the side of the wiring connector, and disconnect it from the ECU **(see illustration)**. **Note:** *On most models, there are two separate plugs to be disconnected, the one on the left-hand side of the ECU cannot be removed until the security plate has been removed from around the ECU.*

68 Release the retaining tab and withdraw the control unit from inside the scuttle panel **(see illustration)**.

69 To remove the security plate from around the ECU, the two security (shear) bolts will need to be drilled out **(see illustration)**. New ones will be required for refitting.

70 Once the security plate has been removed, the second wiring connector can now be removed from the ECU.

71 Refitting is a reversal of removal, noting the following points:

a) *Fit new shear bolts to the security cover plate.*
b) *Make sure the ECU is secure in its position in the bulkhead.*
c) *Bear in mind the comments made in the Caution above – the ECU will not work correctly until it has been electronically coded.*

Camshaft chain adjuster solenoid valve

72 The solenoid valve is an integral part of the inlet camshaft drive chain adjuster/tensioner. At the time of writing it was unclear if the solenoid valve was available separately or whether it is an integral part of the adjuster/tensioner assembly. Refer to your Audi dealer for solenoid valve availability. The chain adjuster/tensioner assembly is removed with the camshafts (see Chapter 2A Section 10 for details).

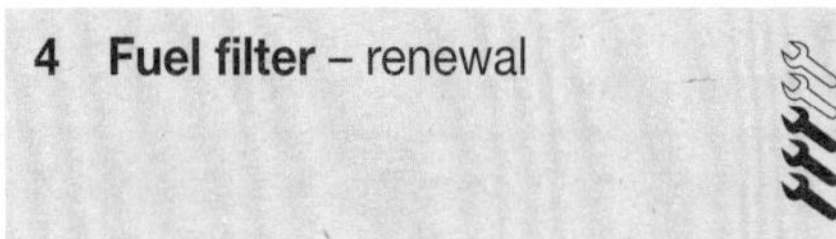

4 Fuel filter – renewal

Note: *Observe the precautions in Section 1 before working on any component in the fuel system.*

1 Depressurise the fuel system as described in Section 7. Remember, however, that this procedure merely relieves the fuel pressure, reducing the risk of fuel spraying when the connections are disturbed – fuel will still be spilt during filter renewal, so take precautions accordingly.

2 The fuel filter is located at the front, right-hand side of the fuel tank, under the car **(see illustration)**

3 Jack up the right-hand rear of the car, and support it on an axle stand (see *Jacking and vehicle support*). When positioning the axle stand, ensure that it will not inhibit access to the filter.

4 To further improve access, unhook the handbrake cable from the adjacent wire clip.

5 Disconnect the fuel hoses at either end of the filter, noting their locations for refitting. The connections are of quick-release type, disconnected by squeezing the catch on each **(see illustration)**. It may be necessary to release the hoses from the clips on the underside of the car, to allow greater movement. Both filter hoses should be black.

6 The filter is held in position by a large-diameter worm-drive clip. Before removing the filter, look for an arrow marking, which points in the direction of fuel flow – in this case, towards the front of the car. The new filter must be fitted the same way round.

7 Loosen the worm-drive clip, and slide the filter out of position **(see illustration)**. Try to keep it as level as possible, to reduce fuel spillage. Dispose of the old filter carefully – even if the fuel inside is tipped out, the filter element will still be soaked in fuel, and will be highly flammable.

8 Offer the new filter into position, ensuring that the direction-of-flow arrow is pointing towards the front of the car. Tighten the worm-drive clip securely, but without risking crushing the filter body.

9 Connect the fuel hoses to each end of the filter, in the same positions as noted on removal. Push the hoses fully onto the filter stubs, and if necessary, clip them back to the underside of the car. Hook the handbrake cable back in place, if it was disturbed.

10 Lower the car to the ground, then start the engine and check for signs of fuel leakage at both ends of the filter.

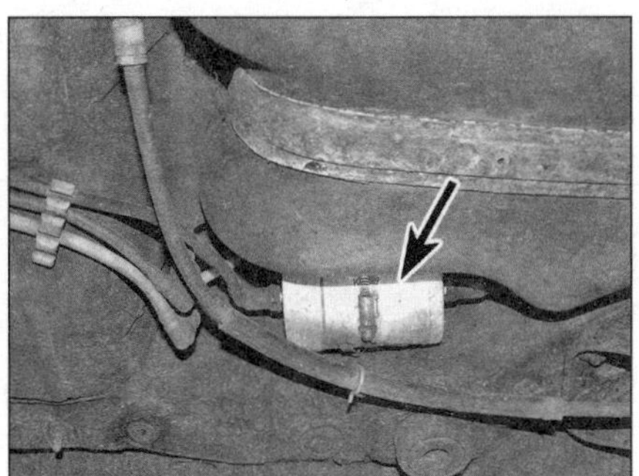

4.2 Fuel filter location (arrowed)

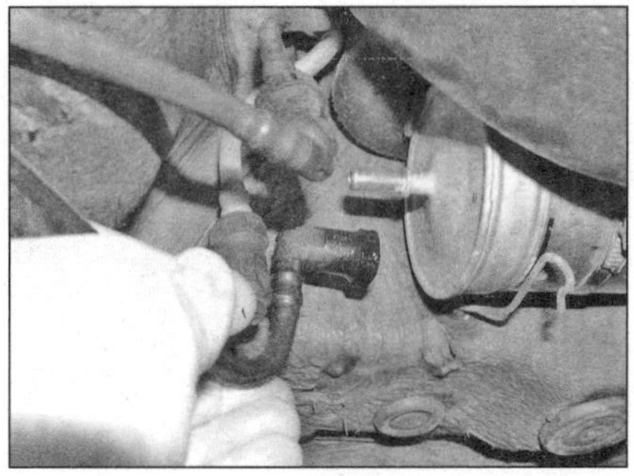

4.5 Disconnecting the fuel hose at the front of the filter

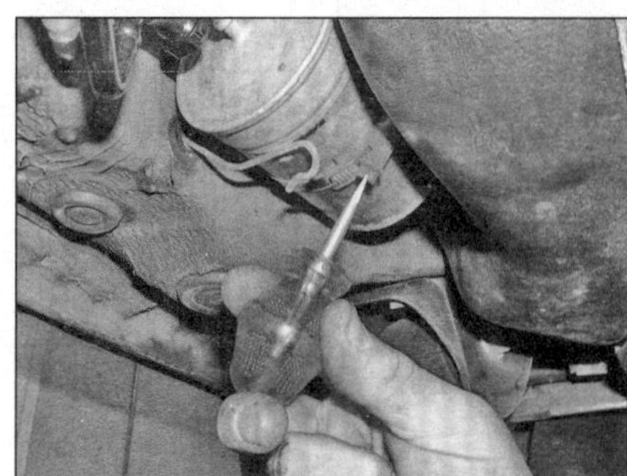

4.7 Loosening the filter securing clip

5.5 Remove the access cover

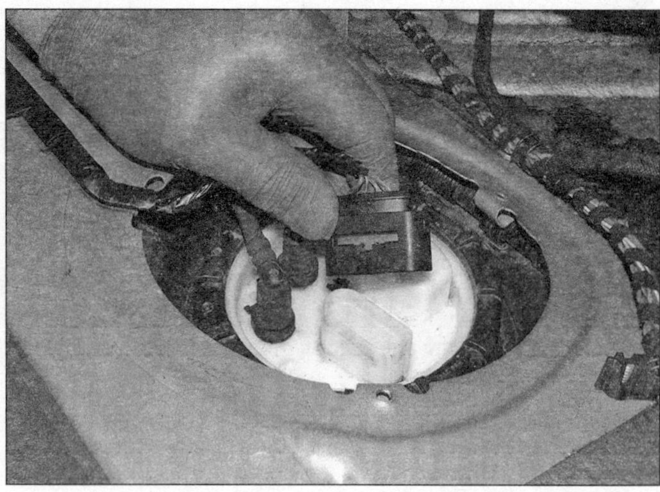
5.6 Unplug the pump/sender unit wiring connector

5 Fuel pump and gauge sender unit – removal and refitting

Note: *Observe the precautions in Section 1 before working on any component in the fuel system.*

Warning: Avoid direct skin contact with fuel – wear protective clothing and gloves when handling fuel system components. Ensure that the work area is well-ventilated to prevent the build-up of fuel vapour.

General information

1 The fuel pump and gauge sender unit are combined in one assembly, which is mounted on the top of the fuel tank. Access is via a hatch provided in the load space floor. The unit protrudes into the fuel tank, and its removal involves exposing the contents of the tank to the atmosphere.

Removal

2 Depressurise the fuel system (Section 7).

3 Ensure that the vehicle is parked on a level surface, then disconnect the battery negative lead and position it away from the terminal. **Note:** *Refer to* Disconnecting the battery *at the rear of this manual first.*

4 Remove the rear trim panels (convertible/roadster models) and rear seat base (coupe models) as described in Chapter 11.

5 Slacken and withdraw the access hatch screws, and lift the cover/hatch away from the floorpan **(see illustration)**.

6 Unplug the wiring harness connector from the pump/sender unit **(see illustration)**.

7 Pad the area around the supply and return fuel hoses with rags to absorb any spilt fuel, then squeeze the catch to release the hose clips and disconnect them from the ports at the sender unit **(see illustration)**. Observe the supply and return arrow markings on the ports – label the fuel hoses accordingly to ensure correct refitting later. The supply pipe is black, and may have white markings, while the return pipe is blue, or has blue markings.

8 Note the position of the alignment marks on the fuel tank, securing ring and sender unit before removal. Then using a special tool, unscrew the plastic securing ring from the top of the fuel tank **(see illustrations)**. Recover the seal.

9 On two wheel drive models, lift out the pump/sender unit, holding it above the level of the fuel in the tank until the excess fuel has drained out **(see illustration)**. Then remove the pump/sender unit from the car, and lay it on an absorbent card or rag. Inspect the float at the end of the sender unit swinging arm for punctures and fuel ingress – renew the unit if it appears damaged.

10 On four wheel drive (Quattro) models, the fuel tank is raised down the centre to allow access for the propeller shaft to the rear wheels. On these models there is a second pump (suction pump) fitted to the left-hand side of the fuel tank. When the fuel sender

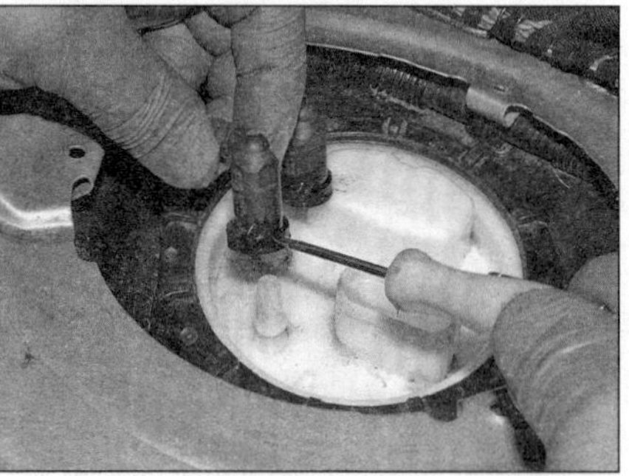
5.7 Releasing the securing clip with a small screwdriver

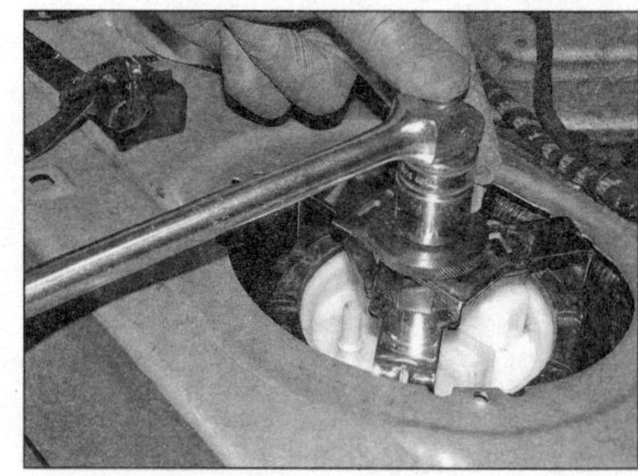
5.8a Using a special tool...

5.8b ...to remove the securing ring

5.9 Lift out the unit, and let the fuel drain into the tank

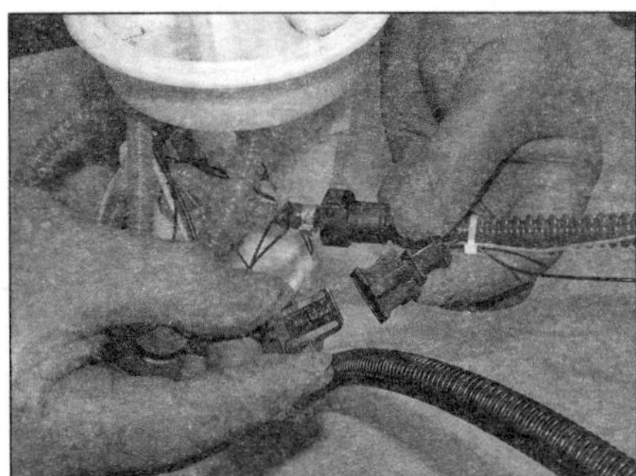
5.10a Disconnect the wiring connector...

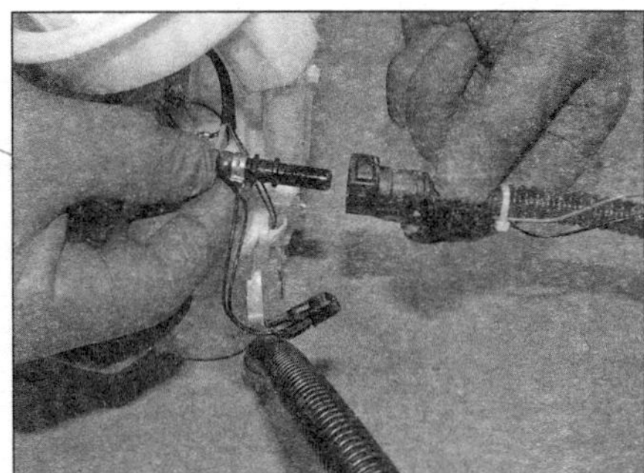
5.10b ...release the hose clip...

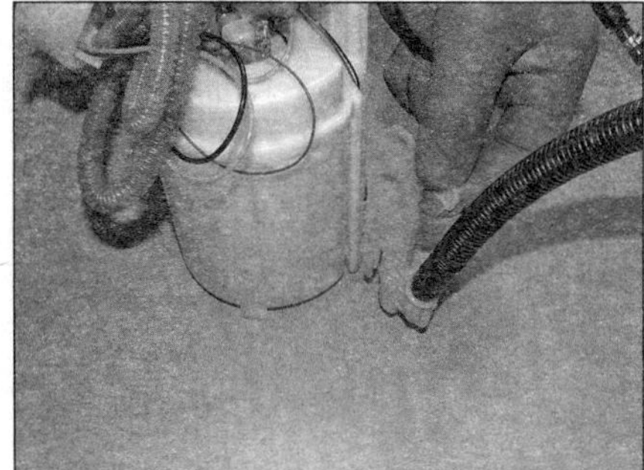
5.10c ...and unhook the lower hose – (pump removed for clarity)

5.12 If not removed with the unit, recover the rubber seal and check its condition

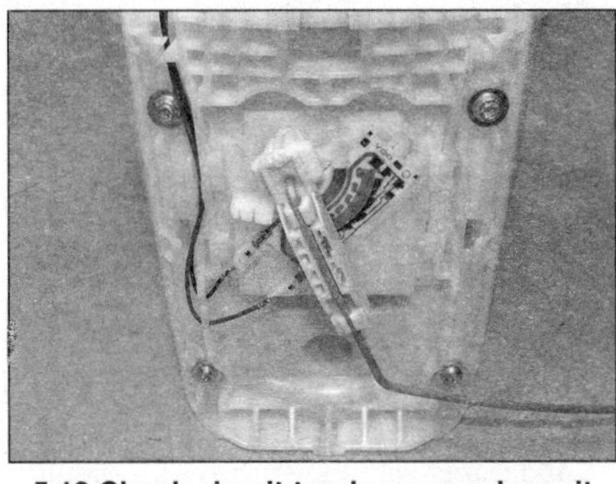
5.13 Check circuit tracks on sender unit

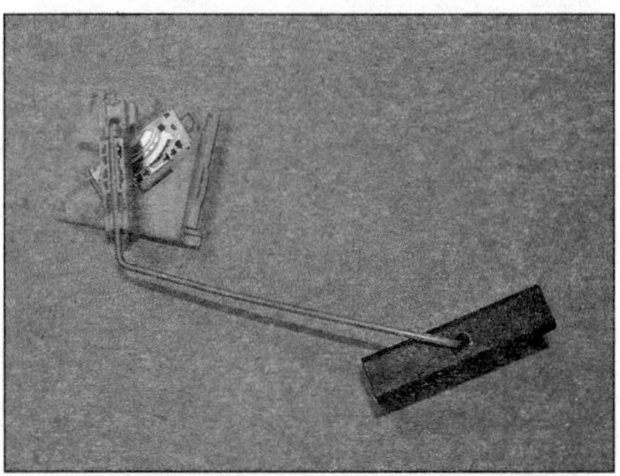
5.14 Sender unit removed from pump

unit is withdrawn from fuel tank, reach inside the tank and disconnect the wiring connector and two hoses from inside the tank. Remove the pump/sender unit from the car, and lay it on an absorbent card or rag. Inspect the float at the end of the sender unit swinging arm for punctures and fuel ingress – renew the unit if it appears damaged **(see illustrations)**.

11 The fuel pick-up incorporated in the assembly is spring-loaded to ensure that it always draws fuel from the lowest part of the tank. Check that the pick-up is free to move under spring tension with respect to the sender unit body.

12 Inspect the rubber seal from the fuel tank aperture for signs of fatigue – renew it if necessary **(see illustration)**.

13 Inspect the sender unit wiper and track; clean off any dirt and debris that may have accumulated, and look for breaks in the track **(see illustration)**.

14 If required, the sender unit can be separated from the assembly, as follows. Disconnect the two small wires (note their positions), then release the securing clips and slide the sender unit downwards to remove **(see illustration)**.

15 The tracks on the circuit board can be checked using an ohmmeter, with the probes connected to each side of the circuit (where the two wires where connected), the resistance should alter as the float arm is moved up and down **(see illustrations)**. This can also be checked whilst the sender unit is still fitted to the pump assembly.

16 On four-wheel drive (Quattro) models, if required the suction pump fitted to the left-hand side of the fuel tank can also be removed (after the removal of the main fuel pump sender unit on the right-hand side). Remove the access cover and note the position of the alignment marks on the sender

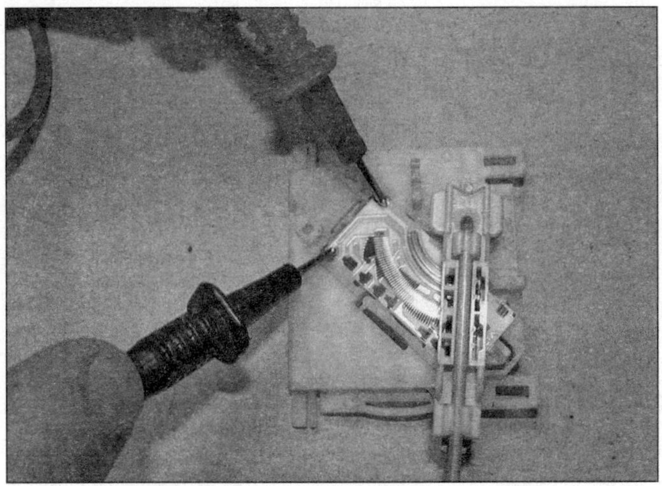
5.15a Checking circuit with sender removed...

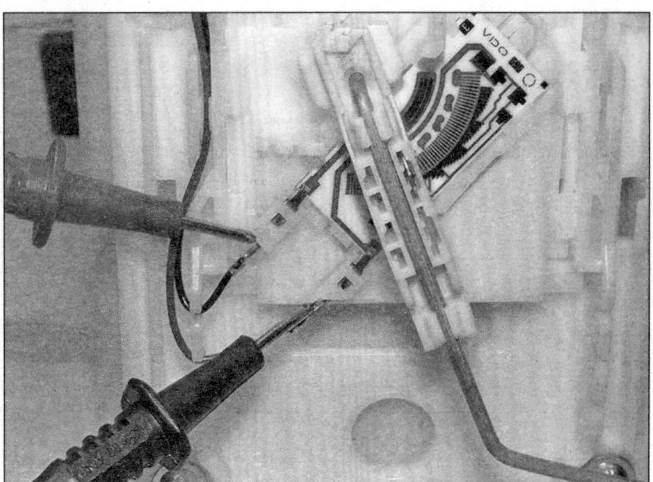

5.15b ... and still fitted to pump

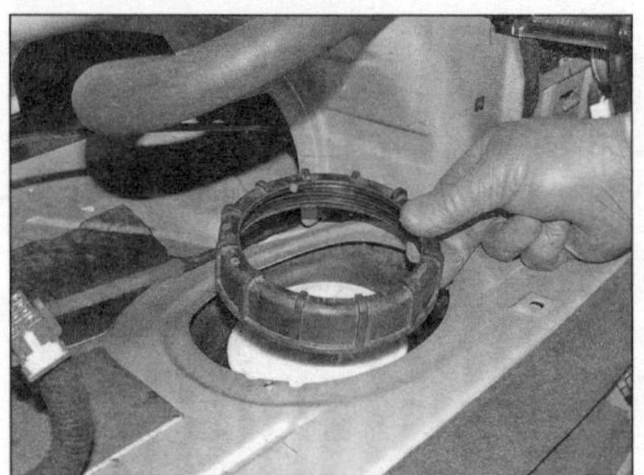
5.16a Remove the securing ring...

5.16b ...lift out the suction pump...

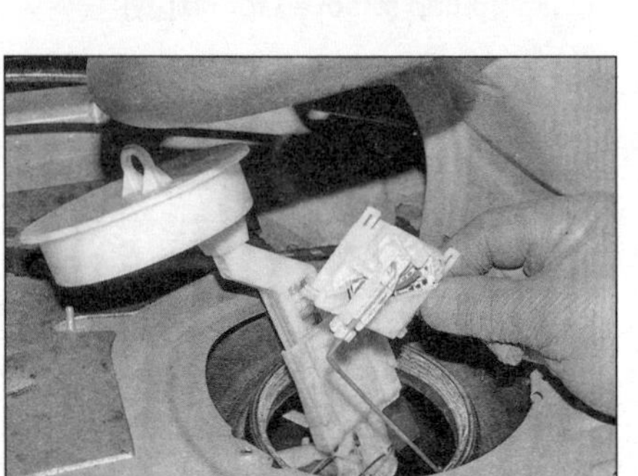
5.16c ...remove the float sender arm...

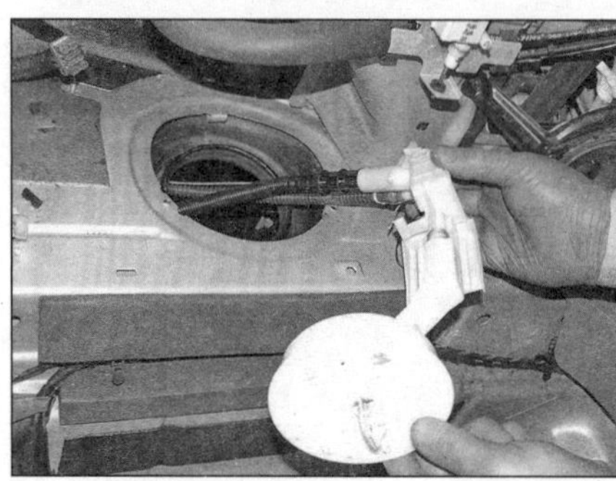
5.16d ...and withdraw pump with wiring/ hoses

unit. Then using a special tool, unscrew the plastic securing ring from the top of the fuel tank. Lift out the suction pump, removing the float sender arm to make removal easier, and then withdraw it complete with wiring and hoses from inside the fuel tank to the main pump sender unit **(see illustrations)**. Recover the seal.

Refitting

17 Refit the pump/sender unit by following the removal procedure in reverse, noting the following points:

a) Take care not to bend the float arm as the unit is refitted.

b) On four-wheel drive (Quattro) models, refit the wiring connector and two hoses before fitting fuel pump into its final position in the fuel tank.

c) Smear the outside of tank aperture rubber seal with clean fuel or lubricating spray, to ease fitting. Unless a new seal is required, the seal should be left on the pump unit before fitting. When the unit is almost fully in place, slide the seal down and locate it on the rim of the tank aperture, then slide the unit fully home.

d) The arrow markings on the sender unit body and the access aperture must be aligned (see illustration).

e) Reconnect the fuel hoses to the correct ports – observe the direction-of-flow arrow markings, and refer to paragraph 7. Ensure that the fuel hose fittings click fully into place.

f) On completion, check that all associated pipes are securely clipped to the tank.

g) Before refitting the access hatch and rear seat, run the engine and check for fuel leaks.

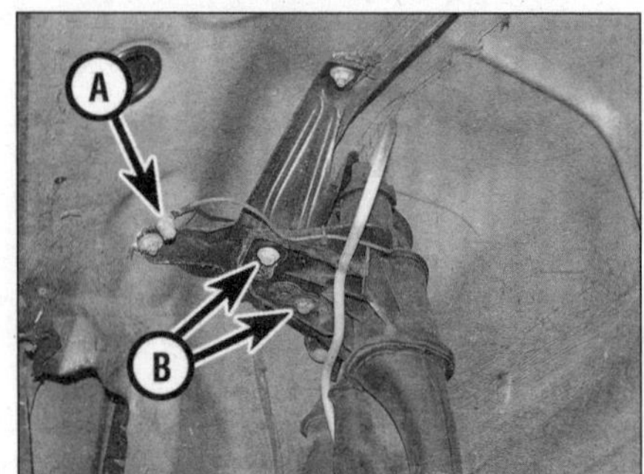

6.6 Disconnect earth wire (A) and undo bolts (B)

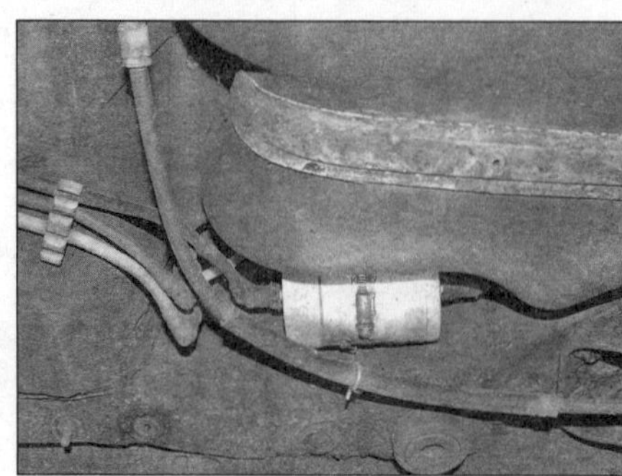
6.11 Disconnect the three fuel hose connections at the right-hand side of the fuel tank

6 Fuel tank – removal and refitting

Note: *Observe the precautions in Section 1 before working on any component in the fuel system.*

Removal

1 Before the tank can be removed, it must be drained of as much fuel as possible. As no drain plug is provided, it is preferable to carry out this operation with the tank almost empty.

2 Disconnect the battery negative lead and position it away from the terminal. **Note:** *Refer to* Disconnecting the battery *at the rear of this manual first.*

3 Open the fuel filler flap, and unscrew the fuel filler cap. If required, using a hand pump or syphon, remove any remaining fuel from the bottom of the tank.

4 Jack up the rear of the car, and support it on an axle stand (see *Jacking and vehicle support*). When positioning the axle stands, ensure that they will not inhibit access to the removal of the fuel tank. **Note:** *The fuel filler neck/pipe is fixed to the fuel tank and cannot be removed separately, so there will need to be enough height to allow for this, as it is being removed.*

5 Remove the right-hand rear wheel and inner wheel arch liner to access the fuel filler pipe/ neck.

6 Working inside the top of the wheel arch, undo the retaining nut and disconnect the earth wire from the inner wing panel. Then undo the two retaining bolts from the top of the filler neck/pipe **(see illustration)**.

7 Gain access to the top of the fuel pump/ sender unit as described in Section 5, and disconnect the wiring harness from the top of the pump/sender unit **(see illustration 5.6)**.

8 On four-wheel drive (Quattro) models, remove the propeller shaft, as described in Chapter 8A.

9 Referring to Chapter 4B Section 9, unbolt the rear section of the exhaust system. Given that the rear axle assembly has to be removed (or at least lowered) to allow the tank to be removed, it is preferable to remove the rear section of the exhaust system completely.

10 Where applicable, release the nuts or washer-type fasteners securing the fuel tank exhaust heat shields, and remove the shield.

11 At the front right-hand side of the fuel tank, disconnect the three fuel hoses. The fuel return hose (blue), the breather pipe (white), and the fuel supply hose (black) from the filter to the engine, noting their locations for refitting. The connections are of quick-release type, disconnected by squeezing the catch on each **(see illustration)**.

12 Refer to Chapter 10 and remove the rear axle assembly. In order to remove the tank, it is possible to just lower the axle out of position, rather than completely removing it.

6.14 Remove bolt (arrowed)

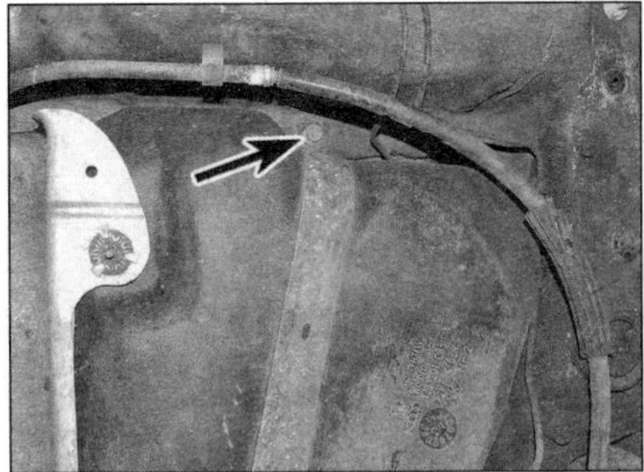

6.15a One of the fuel tank straps front bolt (arrowed)...

6.15b ...and strap rear bolt (arrowed)

13 Position a trolley jack under the centre of the tank. Insert a block of wood between the jack head and the tank to prevent damage to the tank surface. Raise the jack until it just takes the weight of the tank.

14 Undo the bolt at the right-hand rear of the fuel tank, where the filler neck/pipe enters the fuel tank **(see illustration)**.

15 Loosen and remove the retaining bolts and detach the tank straps at the front and rear of the tank **(see illustrations)**. Note that the straps are of different lengths, so do not confuse them when they are finally removed.

16 Lower the jack and tank away from the underside of the vehicle; check around the fuel tank to make sure that there isn't anything still attached. If required, disconnect the charcoal canister vent pipe from the port on the filler neck as it is exposed.

17 If the tank is contaminated with sediment or water, remove the fuel pump/sender unit (see Section 5) and swill the tank out with clean fuel. The tank is injection-moulded from a synthetic material, and if damaged, it should be renewed. However, in certain cases it may be possible to have small leaks or minor damage repaired. Seek the advice of a suitable specialist before attempting to repair the fuel tank.

Refitting

18 Refitting is the reverse of the removal procedure, noting the following points:

a) *When lifting the tank back into position, make sure the mounting rubbers are correctly positioned, and take care to ensure none of the hoses get trapped between the tank and vehicle body.*
b) *Ensure that all pipes and hoses are correctly routed, are not kinked, and are securely held in position with their retaining clips.*
c) *Reconnect the earth strap to its terminal on the filler neck.*
d) *Tighten the tank strap retaining bolts to the specified torque.*
e) *On completion, refill the tank with fuel, and exhaustively check for signs of leakage prior to taking the vehicle out on the road.*

7.2 Location of fuel pump relay (arrowed)

7 Fuel injection system – depressurisation

Note: *Observe the precautions in Section 1 before working on any component in the fuel system.*

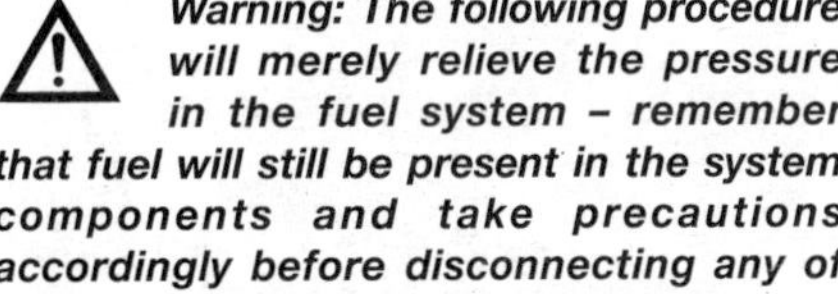

Warning: The following procedure will merely relieve the pressure in the fuel system – remember that fuel will still be present in the system components and take precautions accordingly before disconnecting any of them.

1 The fuel system referred to in this Section is defined as the tank-mounted fuel pump, the fuel filter, the fuel injectors, the fuel pressure regulator, and the metal pipes and flexible hoses of the fuel lines between these components. All these contain fuel, which will be under pressure while the engine is running and/or while the ignition is switched on. The pressure will remain for some time after the ignition has been switched off, and must be relieved before any of these components are disturbed for servicing work. Ideally, the engine should be allowed to cool completely before work commences.

2 Remove the driver's side lower facia panel (Chapter 11 Section 28) to locate the fuel pump relay **(see illustration)**. Remove the fuel pump relay or alternatively, identify and remove the fuel pump fuse from the fusebox, see Chapter 12.

3 With the fuel pump disabled, crank the engine for about ten seconds. The engine may fire and run for a while, but let it continue running until it stops. The fuel injectors should have opened enough times during cranking to considerably reduce the line fuel pressure, and reduce the risk of fuel spraying out when a fuel line is disturbed.

4 Disconnect the battery negative lead and position it away from the terminal. **Note:** *Refer to* Disconnecting the battery *at the rear of this manual first.*

5 Place a suitable container beneath the relevant connection/union to be disconnected, and have a large rag ready to soak up any escaping fuel not being caught by the container.

6 Slowly open the connection to avoid a sudden release of pressure, and position the rag around the connection to catch any fuel spray which may be expelled. Once the pressure has been released, disconnect the fuel line. Insert plugs to minimise fuel loss and prevent the entry of dirt into the fuel system.

8 Inlet manifold and associated components – removal and refitting

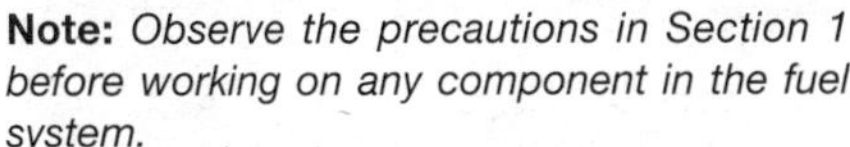

Note: *Observe the precautions in Section 1 before working on any component in the fuel system.*

Removal

1 Disconnect the battery negative lead and position it away from the terminal. **Note:** *Refer to* Disconnecting the battery *at the rear of this manual first.*

2 On models with engine codes AMU, APX and BAM, remove the charge air pipe from around the top, right-hand side of the engine, as described in Chapter 4B Section 7.

3 With reference to Section 3, remove the throttle housing from the inlet manifold. If preferred, the housing need not be completely unbolted from the end of the manifold, and can be removed with it, but all the hoses and electrical connectors to the housing must be disconnected.

4 Remove the fuel rail and injectors as described in Section 3. However, if the manifold is being removed as part of another procedure (such as cylinder head or engine removal), the fuel rail can be left in place, and the manifold just moved to one side.

8.6a Disconnect vacuum hose (arrowed) – AMU, APX and BAM engine codes

8.6b Disconnect vacuum hoses (arrowed) – All engine codes except AMU, APX and BAM

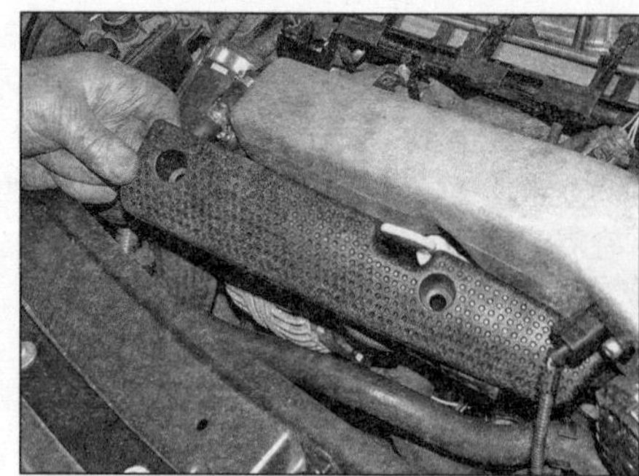

8.7 Remove the trim panel – AMU, APX and BAM engine codes shown

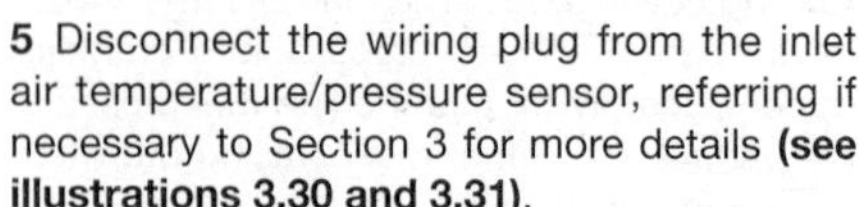

5 Disconnect the wiring plug from the inlet air temperature/pressure sensor, referring if necessary to Section 3 for more details **(see illustrations 3.30 and 3.31)**.

6 On models with engine codes AMU, APX and BAM, disconnect the vacuum hose from the right-hand end of the manifold. On all other models, disconnect the vacuum hose from the left-hand end of the manifold **(see illustrations)**.

7 If not already done, release the fasteners and remove the plastic trim panel from along the front edge of the inlet manifold **(see illustration)**.

8 On models with secondary air injection, undo the two retaining nuts and release the mounting brackets for the secondary air injection pipe **(see illustration)**.

9 On models with engine codes AMU, APX and BAM, disconnect the wiring connector from the exhaust gas temperature sender **(see illustration)**.

10 Undo the two retaining bolts and remove the mounting bracket from across the front of the manifold, releasing it from the locating peg at the top of the oil level dipstick tube **(see illustrations)**. Where applicable, disconnect the wiring connectors from the turbo recirculation valve and secondary air inlet valve (where fitted), on the underside of the mounting bracket.

11 On models with engine codes AMU, APX and BAM, undo the retaining bolts and remove the exhaust gas temperature sender from under the front of the manifold **(see illustration)**.

12 On all models (except AMU, APX and BAM engine codes), unbolt and remove the manifold support bracket from the engine block to the underside of the manifold.

13 Check around the manifold to check all is disconnected, then progressively slacken the ten manifold mounting bolts, and withdraw the manifold from the cylinder head. Recover the gasket and discard as a new one will be required for refitting.

Refitting

14 Refitting is a reversal of removal. Use a new gasket or seals, as applicable, and tighten the retaining bolts to the specified torque. It is most important that there are no air leaks at the joint.

8.8 Secondary air injection pipe mounting bracket nuts (arrowed)

8.9 Disconnect temperature sender connector – AMU, APX and BAM engine codes

9 Fuel injection system – testing and adjustment

1 If a fault appears in the fuel injection system, first ensure that all the system wiring connectors are securely connected and free of corrosion. Then ensure that the fault is not due to poor maintenance; ie, check that the air cleaner filter element is clean, the spark plugs are in good condition and correctly gapped, the cylinder compression pressures are correct, the ignition system wiring is in good condition and securely connected, and the engine breather hoses are clear and undamaged, referring to Chapter 1, Chapter 2A and Chapter 5B.

2 If these checks fail to reveal the cause of the problem, the vehicle should be taken to

8.10a Remove the mounting bracket

8.10b Disconnect wiring connectors (arrowed) – where applicable

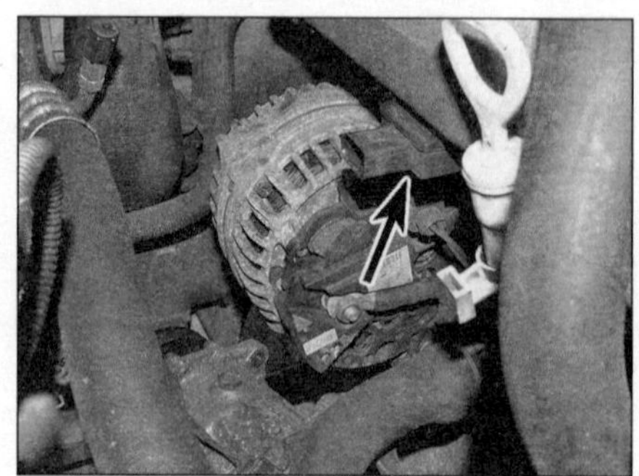

8.11 Exhaust gas temperature sender (arrowed)

a suitably-equipped Audi dealer for testing. A diagnostic connector is incorporated in the engine management system wiring harness, into which dedicated electronic test equipment can be plugged. The connector is located at the right-hand side of the lower facia next to the bonnet release lever **(see illustration)**. The test equipment is capable of 'interrogating' the engine management system ECU electronically and accessing its internal fault log (reading fault codes).

3 Fault codes can only be extracted from the ECU using a dedicated fault code reader. An Audi dealer will obviously have such a reader, but they are also available from other suppliers. It is unlikely to be cost-effective for the private owner to purchase a fault code reader, but a well-equipped local garage or auto-electrical specialist will have one.

4 Using this equipment, faults can be pinpointed quickly and simply, even if their occurrence is intermittent. Testing all the system components individually in an attempt to locate the fault by elimination is a time-consuming operation that is unlikely to be fruitful (particularly if the fault occurs dynamically), and carries a high risk of damage to the ECU's internal components.

5 Experienced home mechanics equipped with an accurate tachometer and a carefully-calibrated exhaust gas analyser may be able to check the exhaust gas CO content and the engine idle speed; if these are found to be out of specification, then the vehicle must be taken to a suitably-equipped VW dealer for assessment. Neither the air/fuel mixture (exhaust gas CO content) nor the engine idle speed are manually adjustable; incorrect test results indicate the need for maintenance (possibly, injector cleaning) or a fault within the fuel injection system.

10 Unleaded petrol - general information and usage

Note: *The information given in this Chapter is correct at the time of writing, and applies only to petrol's currently available in the UK. Check with an Audi dealer as more up-to-date information may be available. If travelling abroad, consult one of the motoring organisations (or a similar authority) for advice on the petrol's available and their suitability for your vehicle.*

1 The fuel recommended by Audi is given in the Specifications of this Chapter.

2 RON and MON are different testing standards; RON stands for Research Octane Number (also written as RM), while MON stands for Motor Octane Number (also written as MM).

11 Cruise control system - general information

1 Certain models may be equipped with a cruise control system, in which the driver can set a chosen speed, which the system will then try to maintain regardless of gradients, etc.

2 Once the desired speed has been set, the system is entirely under the control of the engine management ECU, which regulates the speed via the throttle housing.

9.2 Location of diagnostic connector (arrowed)

3 The system refers to signals from the engine speed sensor (see Section 3) and roadspeed sensor (on the transmission).

4 The system is deactivated if the clutch or brake pedals are pressed, signalled by the clutch pedal switch (Section 3) or the brake stop-light switch (Chapter).

5 The cruise control switch is part of the steering column combination switch assembly, which can be removed as described Chapter 12 Section 4.

6 Any problems with the system which are not caused by wiring faults or failure of the components mentioned in this Section should be referred to an Audi dealer. In the event of a problem occurring, it is advisable to first take the car to a suitably-equipped dealer for electronic fault diagnosis, using a fault code reader – refer to Section 9.

Notes

Chapter 4 Part B
Emission control and exhaust systems

Contents

Degrees of difficulty

Easy, suitable for novice with little experience 	**Fairly easy,** suitable for beginner with some experience	**Fairly difficult,** suitable for competent DIY mechanic	**Difficult,** suitable for experienced DIY mechanic	**Very difficult,** suitable for expert DIY or professional 

Specifications

Torque wrench settings	Nm	lbf ft
Coolant pipe banjo bolts	35	26
EGR pipe flange bolts to throttle housing	10	7
EGR pipe mounting bolts	10	7
Exhaust clamp nuts	40	30
Exhaust manifold nuts*	25	18
Exhaust manifold support bracket to engine	25	18
Exhaust manifold-to-downpipe nuts*	40	30
Exhaust mounting bracket nuts and bolts	25	18
Intercooler mounting bolts	10	7
Oil supply pipe banjo bolts	30	22
Oxygen sensor	50	37
Secondary air adaptor plate mounting bolts	10	7
Secondary air combi-valve mounting bolts	10	7
Secondary air pipe union nuts	25	18
Turbocharger support bracket to engine	25	18
Turbocharger-to-downpipe nuts**	40	30
Turbocharger-to-manifold bolts**	30	22
Turbocharger-to-support bracket bolt	30	22

** Use new nuts*
*** Use thread-locking compound*

1 General Information

Emission control systems

1 All engines covered are designed to use unleaded petrol, and are controlled by engine management systems that are programmed to give the best compromise between driveability, fuel consumption and exhaust emission production. In addition, a number of systems are fitted that help to minimise other harmful emissions. A crankcase emission control system is fitted, which reduces the release of pollutants from the engine's lubrication system, and a catalytic converter is fitted which reduces exhaust gas pollutant. An evaporative loss emission control system is fitted which reduces the release of gaseous hydrocarbons from the fuel tank.

Crankcase emission control

2 To reduce the emission of unburned hydrocarbons from the crankcase into the atmosphere, the engine is sealed and the blow-by gases and oil vapour are drawn from inside the crankcase, through a wire-mesh oil separator, into the inlet tract to be burned by the engine during normal combustion.

3 Under conditions of high manifold depression, the gases will be sucked positively out of the crankcase. Under conditions of low manifold depression, the gases are forced out of the crankcase by the (relatively) higher crankcase pressure. If the engine is worn, the raised crankcase pressure (due to increased blow-by) will cause some of the flow to return under all manifold conditions.

Exhaust emission control

4 To minimise the amount of pollutants which escape into the atmosphere, all petrol models are fitted with a three-way catalytic converter in the exhaust system. The fuelling system is of the closed-loop type, in which an oxygen (lambda) sensor in the exhaust system provides the engine management system ECU with constant feedback, enabling the ECU to adjust the air/fuel mixture to optimise combustion.

5 The oxygen (Lambda) sensor has a built-in heating element, controlled by the ECU through the oxygen sensor relay, to quickly bring the sensor's tip to its optimum operating temperature. The sensor's tip is sensitive to oxygen, and sends a voltage signal to the ECU that varies according on the amount of oxygen in the exhaust gas. If the inlet air/fuel mixture is too rich, the exhaust gases are low in oxygen so the sensor sends a low-voltage signal, the voltage rising as the mixture weakens and the amount of oxygen rises in the exhaust gases. Peak conversion efficiency of all major pollutants occurs if the inlet air/fuel mixture is maintained at the chemically-correct ratio for the complete combustion of petrol of 14.7 parts (by weight) of air to 1 part of fuel (the stoichiometric ratio). The sensor output voltage alters in a large step at this point, the ECU using the signal change as a reference point and correcting the inlet air/fuel mixture accordingly by altering the fuel injector pulse width.

6 Most later models have two oxygen (Lambda) sensors – one before and one after the main catalytic converter. This enables more efficient monitoring of the exhaust gas, allowing a faster response time. The overall efficiency of the converter itself can also be checked. Details of the oxygen sensor removal and refitting are given in Chapter 4A Section 3.

7 An Exhaust Gas Recirculation (EGR) system where fitted (not fitted to 1.8 litre turbo petrol engines). This reduces the level of nitrogen oxides produced during combustion by introducing a proportion of the exhaust gas back into the inlet manifold, under certain engine operating conditions, via a plunger valve. The system is controlled electronically by the engine management ECU.

8 Some engines are equipped with a secondary air system, to reduce cold-start emissions when the catalytic converter is still warming-up. The system comprises an electric air pump, fed with air from the air cleaner, and a system of valves. When the engine is cold, air is pumped into additional pipework on the exhaust manifold, and mixes with the exhaust gas – this has the effect of raising the temperature of the exhaust, which helps to 'burn' the pollutants. The extra heat produced also helps to bring the catalytic converter to its working temperature more quickly. When the engine coolant temperature is high enough, and the converter is operating normally, the system is switched off by the engine management ECU.

Evaporative emission control

9 To minimise the escape of unburned hydrocarbons into the atmosphere, an evaporative loss emission control system is fitted to all petrol models. The fuel tank filler cap is sealed and a charcoal canister is mounted underneath the right-hand wing to collect the petrol vapours released from the fuel contained in the fuel tank. It stores them until they can be drawn from the canister (under the control of the fuel injection/ignition system ECU) via the purge valve(s) into the inlet tract, where they are then burned by the engine during normal combustion.

10 To ensure that the engine runs correctly when it is cold and/or idling and to protect the catalytic converter from the effects of an over-rich mixture, the purge control valve(s) are not opened by the ECU until the engine has warmed-up, and the engine is under load; the valve solenoid is then modulated on and off to allow the stored vapour to pass into the inlet tract.

Exhaust systems

11 The exhaust system comprises the exhaust manifold, front pipe (with oxygen sensor), catalytic converter (with second oxygen sensor – on most models), intermediate pipe and rear silencer. The systems fitted may differ in detail depending on the engine fitted – for example, in how the catalytic converter is incorporated into the system. On turbocharged models, the turbocharger is mounted on the exhaust manifold, and is driven by the exhaust gases.

12 The system is supported by various metal brackets screwed to the vehicle floor, with rubber vibration dampers fitted to suppress noise **(see illustration)**.

2 Evaporative loss emission control system – information and component renewal

1 The evaporative loss emission control system consists of the solenoid (purge) valve, the activated charcoal filter canister and a series of connecting vacuum hoses.

2 The solenoid (purge) valve and canister are located on the right-hand side of the engine compartment, in front of the coolant expansion tank **(see illustration)**.

3 To remove the solenoid (purge) valve, unclip it from the mounting bracket on the top of the charcoal canister and move it to one side **(see illustration)**. If required, ensure that the ignition is switched off, then unplug the wiring harness from the solenoid valve and disconnect the hose connections.

4 Release the retaining clip and remove the hose to the solenoid (purge) valve from the top of the charcoal canister. Then prise out the round end fitting to which the smaller (tank breather) hose is attached.

5 Unscrew the mounting bolt, from lower part of the canister at the front. Then lift the charcoal canister out of its lower mounting,

1.12 Exhaust rubber mounting (arrowed)

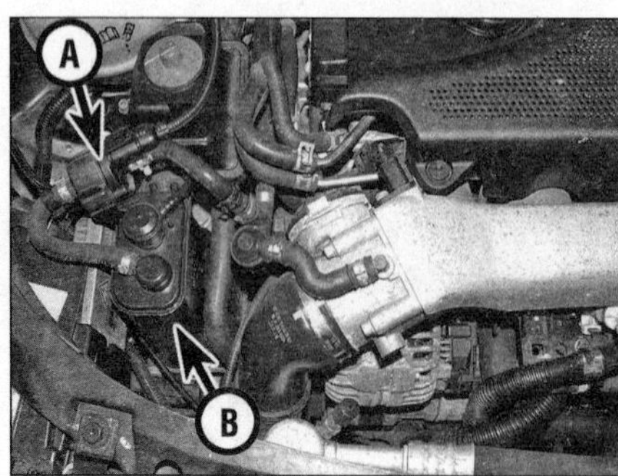

2.2 Solenoid (purge) valve (A) and charcoal canister (B)

2.3 Unclip the solenoid (purge) valve from the bracket

2.5a Undo the mounting bolt (arrowed)...

2.5b ...and remove the charcoal canister

noting how it is fitted, and remove it from the engine compartment **(see illustrations)**.

6 Refitting is a reversal of removal.

3 Crankcase emission system - general information

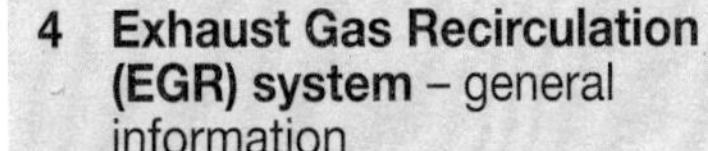

1 The crankcase emission control system consists of hoses connecting the crankcase to the air cleaner or inlet manifold. Oil separator units are fitted to some petrol engines, usually at the back of the engine.

2 The system requires no attention other than to check at regular intervals that the hoses, valve and oil separator are free of blockages and in good condition.

4 Exhaust Gas Recirculation (EGR) system - general information

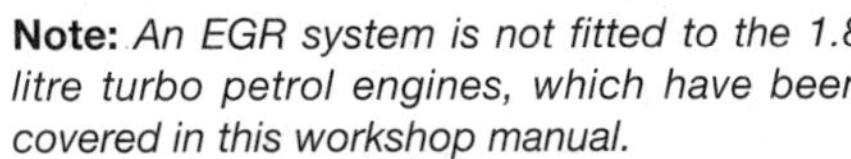

Note: *An EGR system is not fitted to the 1.8 litre turbo petrol engines, which have been covered in this workshop manual.*

1 Where fitted, the EGR system consists of the EGR valve, the modulator (solenoid) valve and a series of connecting vacuum hoses.

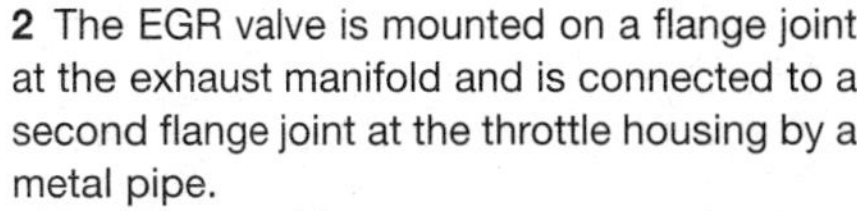

2 The EGR valve is mounted on a flange joint at the exhaust manifold and is connected to a second flange joint at the throttle housing by a metal pipe.

3 To improve access, remove the engine top cover(s). Removal details vary according to model, but the cover retaining nuts are concealed under circular covers, which are prised out of the main cover. Where plastic screws or turn-fasteners are used, these can be removed using a wide-bladed screwdriver. Remove the nuts or screws, and lift the cover from the engine, releasing any wiring or hoses attached.

5 Secondary air injection system - information and component renewal

1 The secondary air injection system (also known as a 'pulse-air' system) comprises an electrically-operated air pump (fed with air from the air cleaner), a relay for the air pump, a vacuum-operated air supply combi-valve, a solenoid valve to regulate the vacuum supply, and pipework to feed the air into the exhaust manifold. For more information on the principles of operation, refer to Section 1**(see illustration)**.

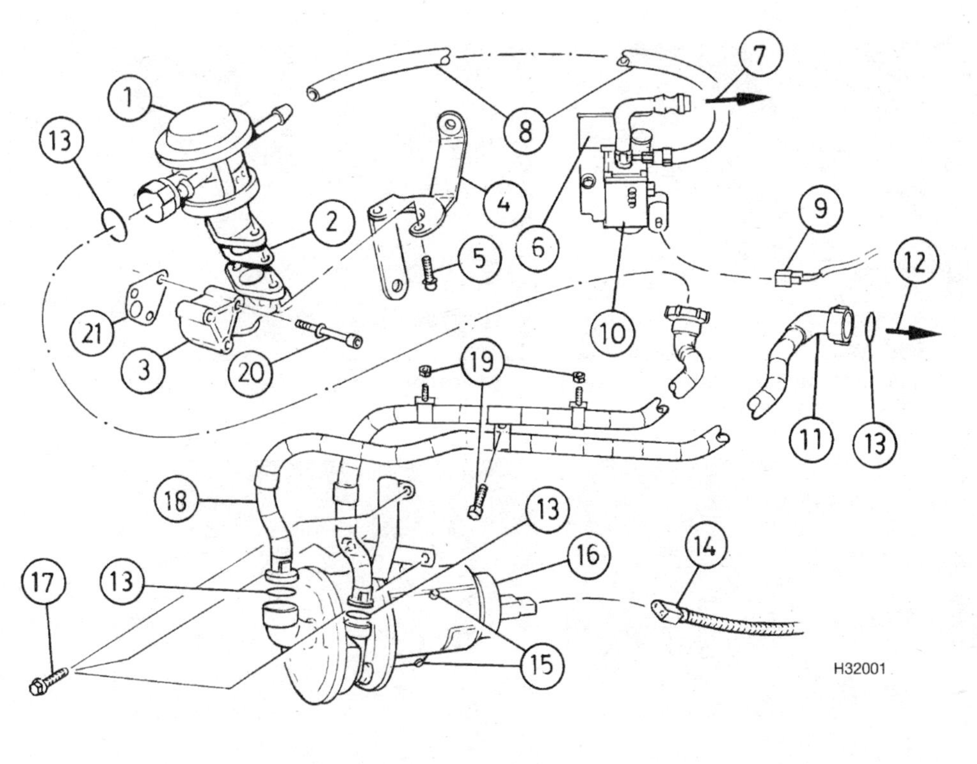

5.1 Secondary air injection system components

5.2 Location of air pump (arrowed)

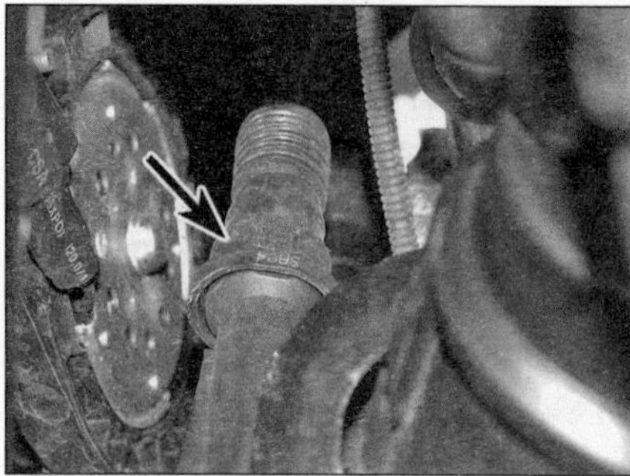
5.4 Disconnect air hose (arrowed)

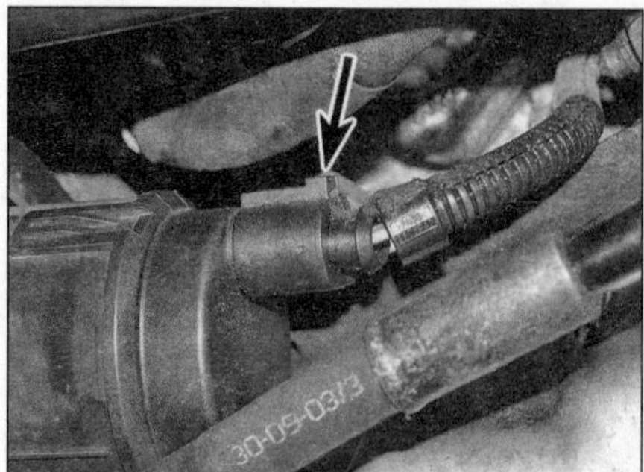
5.5 Disconnect the wiring connector (arrowed)

Air pump

2 The secondary air pump is mounted on a bracket, below the inlet manifold, at the rear of the power steering pump **(see illustration)**.

3 To improve access, remove the charge air pipe from across the front of the engine compartment, as described in Section 7.

4 Disconnect the air hoses on top of the pump by squeezing together the lugs on the hose end fittings **(see illustration)**, and pulling the hoses upwards. Recover the O-ring seal from each hose – new seals should be used when refitting. The hoses are of different sizes, and so cannot be refitted incorrectly.

5 Disconnect the wiring plug from the rear of the air pump **(see illustration)**.

6 Unscrew the pump-to-mounting bracket retaining nuts and slide the pump out of the mounting bracket **(see illustration)**. The pump is mounted to the bracket by small rubber mountings, if damaged they will need to be replaced.

7 If required, the mounting bracket can be removed from the cylinder block. The bracket is secured by two bolts and a nut, or by three bolts, depending on model. Where three bolts are used, they are of different lengths, so note their locations.

8 Refitting is a reversal of removal.

Air pump relay

9 The relay is located in the engine compartment fuse/relay box, at the left-hand rear of the engine compartment **(see illustration)** – refer to Chapter 12 for more details.

Air supply combi-valve

10 The secondary air supply combination valve is mounted on top of the exhaust manifold. To improve access to the valve, remove the engine top cover.

11 Disconnect the vacuum hose and the large-diameter air hose from the valve – the air hose is released by squeezing together the lugs on the hose end fitting.

12 Remove the two valve mounting bolts from below the valve, and lift the valve off its mounting flange. Recover the gasket.

13 Refitting is a reversal of removal. Use a new gasket, and tighten the mounting bolts to the specified torque.

Vacuum solenoid valve

14 The secondary air injection solenoid valve is mounted at the front of the engine compartment, under the mounting bracket on the front of the inlet manifold **(see illustration)**.

15 Release the fasteners and remove the plastic trim panel from across the front of the inlet manifold**(see illustration)**.

16 Disconnect the wiring plug and vacuum pipes from the valve – note which ports the pipes are fitted to, to avoid confusion when refitting.

17 Unscrew the bolts, or unclip the valve, and remove it from its mounting bracket.

18 Refitting is a reversal of removal.

5.6 Undo the mounting nuts (arrowed) – other nuts around other side

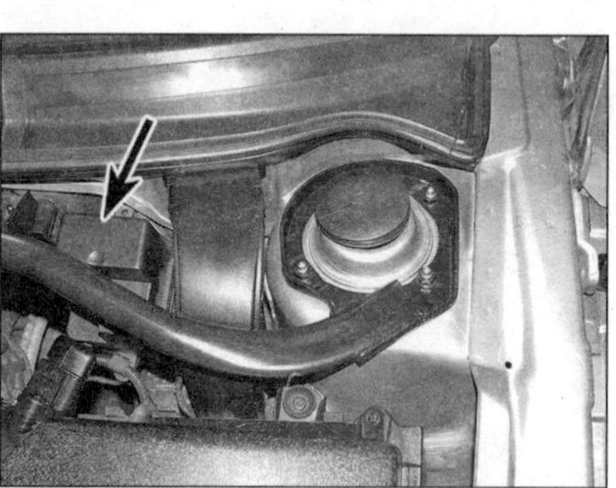
5.9 Location of air pump relay (arrowed)

5.14 Location of solenoid valve (arrowed)

5.15 Remove the trim panel

6 Turbocharger – general information, precautions, removal and refitting

General information

1 A turbocharger is mounted directly on the exhaust manifold**(see illustrations)**. Lubrication is provided by an oil supply pipe that runs from the engine oil filter mounting to the top of the turbocharger. Oil is then returned to the sump via a return pipe that connects to the rear of the sump, from the bottom of the turbocharger. The turbocharger unit has a wastegate valve and vacuum actuator

6.1a Turbocharger and associated components – All models (except AMU, APX and BAM engine codes)

1 Exhaust downpipe nuts
2 Exhaust downpipe gasket
3 Wastegate setting locknut
4 Wastegate
5 Circlip
6 Turbocharger
7 O-ring
8 Mounting bolt
9 Air inlet pipe stub
10 Gasket
11 Heat shield mounting bolt
12 Heat shield
13 Mounting bolt
14 Banjo bolt
15 Oil supply pipe
16 Turbo mounting bolts
17 Exhaust manifold
18 Manifold gasket
19 Mounting bolt
20 Banjo bolt
21 Manifold mounting nuts
22 Banjo bolt
23 Coolant return pipe
24 Mounting bolt
25 Spacer sleeve
26 Banjo bolt
27 Mounting bolt
28 Coolant supply pipe
29 Banjo bolt
30 Turbo-to-support bracket bolt
31 Turbo support bracket
32 Support bracket bolt
33 Gasket
34 Gasket
35 Oil return pipe flange bolt
36 Oil return pipe
37 Oil return pipe flange bolt

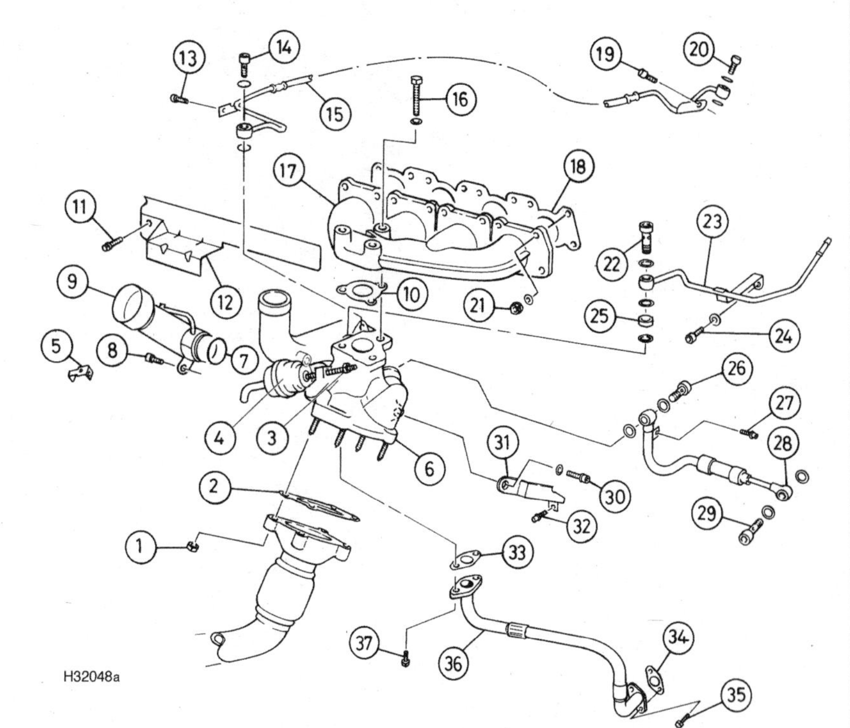

6.1b Turbocharger and associated components - AMU, APX and BAM engine codes

1 Bolt
2 Oil return pipe
3 Bolt
4 Gasket
5 Bolt
6 Nut
7 Vacuum unit for charge pressure control valve
8 Turbocharger
9 Nut
10 Gasket
11 Bolt
12 Banjo bolt
13 Oil supply pipe
14 Bolt
15 Exhaust manifold
16 Bolt
17 Banjo bolt
18 Gasket
19 Banjo bolt
20 Coolant return hose/pipe
21 Bolt
22 Banjo bolt
23 Bolt
24 Coolant supply pipe
25 Banjo bolt
26 Lambda probe before catalytic converter
27 Nut
28 Front exhaust pipe
29 Bolt
30 Bolt
31 Bracket
32 Gasket

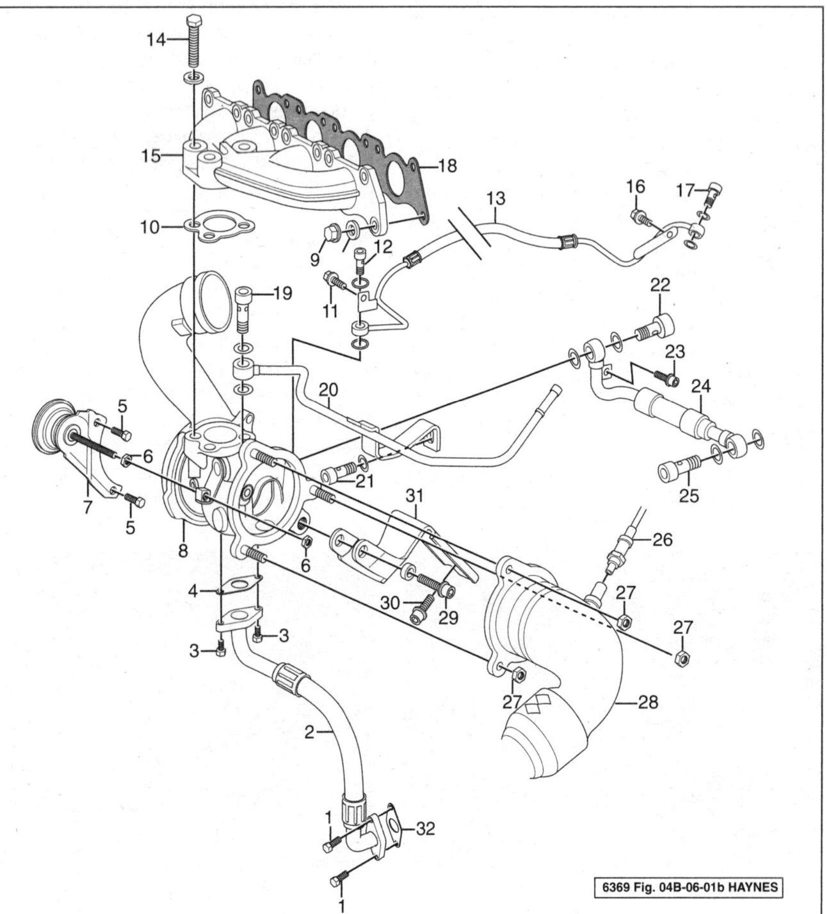

diaphragm, which is used to control the boost pressure applied to the inlet manifold.

2 The turbocharger is cooled by a coolant pipe that runs from the rear of the cylinder block to the lower part of the turbocharger. Coolant is returned to the cooling system via a return pipe that connects to the top of the turbocharger.

3 The turbocharger's internal components rotate at a very high speed, and as such are sensitive to contamination; a great deal of damage can be caused by small particles of dirt, particularly if they strike the delicate turbine blades.

Precautions

4 The turbocharger operates at extremely high speeds and temperatures. Certain precautions must be observed to avoid premature failure of the turbo, or injury to the operator.

5 Do not operate the turbo with any parts exposed. Foreign objects falling onto the rotating vanes could cause excessive damage and (if ejected) personal injury.

6 Cover the turbocharger air inlet ducts to prevent debris entering, and clean using lint-free cloths only.

7 Do not race the engine immediately after start-up, especially if it is cold. Give the oil a few seconds to circulate.

8 Always allow the engine to return to idle speed before switching it off – do not blip the throttle and switch off, as this will leave the turbo spinning without lubrication.

9 Allow the engine to idle for several seconds before switching off after a high-speed run.

10 Observe the recommended intervals for oil and filter changing, and use a reputable oil of the specified quality. Neglect of oil changing, or use of inferior oil, can cause carbon formation on the turbo shaft and subsequent failure. Thoroughly clean the area around all oil pipe unions before disconnecting them, to prevent the ingress of dirt. Store dismantled components in a sealed container to prevent contamination.

Removal

Caution: Thoroughly clean the area around all oil pipe unions before disconnecting them, to prevent the ingress of dirt. Store dismantled components in a sealed container to prevent contamination. Cover the turbocharger air inlet ducts to prevent debris entering, and clean using lint-free cloths only.

6.14 Remove air intake pipe (arrowed)

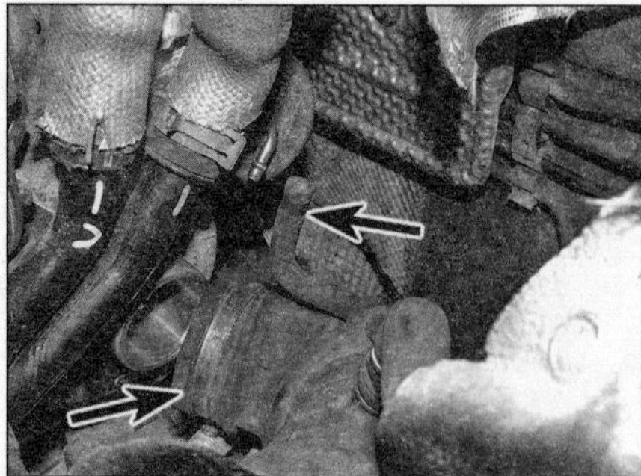

6.15 Disconnect the air intake and vacuum hoses (arrowed)

11 Apply the handbrake, then jack up the front of the vehicle and support it on axle stands (see *Jacking and vehicle support*). Remove the engine compartment undershield, and also release the fasteners and lift the plastic trim covers from the top of the engine.

12 The turbocharger is water cooled, so the cooling system will need to be drained before removal of the turbocharger. Drain the cooling system, as described in Chapter 1 Section 39.

13 On models with engine codes AMU, APX and BAM, remove the charge air pipe from around the top, right-hand side of the engine, as described in Section 7.

14 On all models (except for AMU, APX and BAM engine codes) slacken the hose clips, undo the bracket securing bolts and remove the air intake pipe from the turbocharger **(see illustration)**.

15 Slacken the securing clips and disconnect the air/vacuum hoses leading to the turbocharger unit from the air cleaner assembly **(see illustration)**. To make access easier, remove the air cleaner assembly, as described in Chapter 4A Section 2.

16 On all models (except with engine codes AMU, APX and BAM), unscrew the two bolts securing the heat shield above the turbocharger, and remove the shield.

17 On models with engine codes AMU, APX and BAM, remove the heat cover from around the hose and then slacken the securing clip and remove the hose from the top of the turbocharger **(see illustration)**.

18 On two-wheel drive models, remove the right-hand driveshaft, as described in Chapter 8A Section 3. Also undo the retaining bolts and remove the shield from around the right-hand driveshaft inner joint **(see illustration)**.

19 On four-wheel drive models, remove the transfer/bevel box, as described in Chapter 8B.

20 Undo the retaining bolts/nuts and remove the exhaust front pipe from the turbocharger, as described in Section 9.

21 Unscrew the union bolt and disconnect the oil supply pipe from the top of the turbocharger; recover the sealing washers, noting their order of fitting. Anticipate some oil spillage as the pipe is removed. Plug or cover the pipe and aperture to prevent entry of dust and dirt. Remove the small bolt securing the pipe mounting bracket **(see illustration)**, and move the pipe to one side.

22 The turbocharger housing is water-cooled, so removing it entails disconnecting two coolant pipes. Even if the cooling system is drained as described in Chapter 1, it is likely that the pipes will not be drained, and spillage will result. If the coolant is not due for renewal therefore, it may be preferable not to drain the system, but be prepared to plug the pipes once they have been disconnected.

23 Access to the coolant supply pipe union

6.17 Slacken the hose clip (arrowed)

6.18 Shield retaining bolts (arrowed)

6.21 Oil supply pipe securing bolt (arrowed)

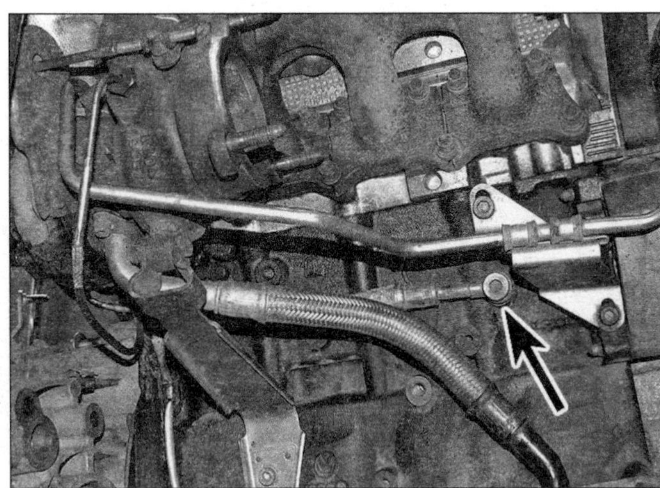

6.23 Coolant supply pipe (arrowed)

6.24 Coolant return pipe (A) and oil return pipe (B)

on the turbocharger is particularly poor – it will be easier to unscrew the pipe union bolt at the other end, on the rear of the cylinder block. The coolant supply pipe can then be removed with turbocharger **(see illustration)**.

24 Unscrew the union bolts and disconnect the coolant return from the top of the turbocharger and the oil return pipe from the bottom of the turbocharger **(see illustration)**. Anticipate some coolant/oil spillage as the pipes are disconnected, and recover the gaskets (obtain new ones for refitting).

25 Unscrew the nut and bolt securing the support bracket to the bottom of the turbocharger, and also the two bolts to the cylinder block **(see illustration)**, then remove the support bracket.

26 The turbocharger is secured to the exhaust manifold by three bolts **(see illustration)**, removed from above. Supporting the turbocharger (which is a heavy assembly), loosen and remove the three bolts (new bolts should be fitted on reassembly). Manoeuvre the turbocharger and wastegate assembly out from behind the engine, and remove it from the engine compartment. Recover the manifold-to-turbocharger gasket, and discard it – a new one must be used when refitting.

27 It is not advisable to separate the wastegate assembly from the turbocharger without first consulting an Audi dealer or turbocharger specialist, as the setting may be lost. Interfering with the wastegate setting may lead to a reduction in performance, or could result in engine damage.

Refitting

28 Refit the turbocharger by following the removal procedure in reverse, noting the following points:

a) Renew all gaskets, sealing washers and O-rings.

b) Renew the three turbocharger mounting bolts, and any self-locking nuts.

c) Before reconnecting the oil supply pipe, fill the turbocharger with fresh oil using an oil can.

d) Tighten all nuts and bolts to the specified torque, where given.

e) Ensure that the air hose clips are securely tightened, to prevent air leaks.

f) Refill the cooling system, with reference to Chapter 1 Section 39.

g) Check the engine oil level, with reference to Chapter 0 Section 5.

h) When the engine is started after refitting, allow it to idle for approximately one minute to give the oil time to circulate around the turbine shaft bearings. Check for signs of oil or coolant leakage from the relevant unions.

7 Intercoolers and charge air hoses/pipes – general information, removal and refitting

1 Intercoolers are effectively an 'air radiator', used to cool the pressurised inlet air before it enters the engine. On all engine codes (except AMU, APX and BAM), there is one

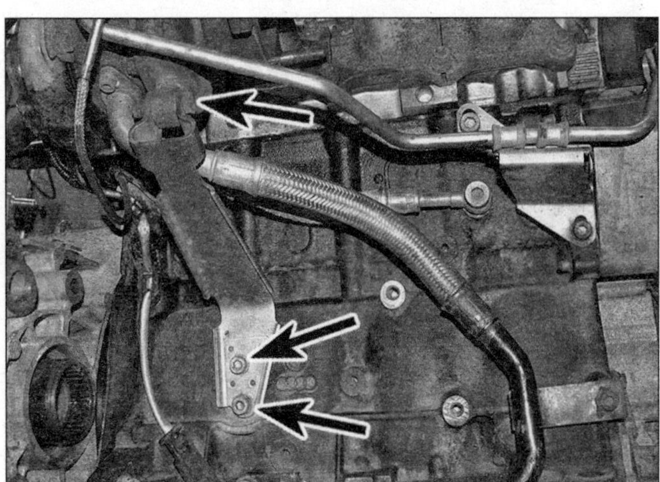

6.25 Undo the support bracket bolts (arrowed)

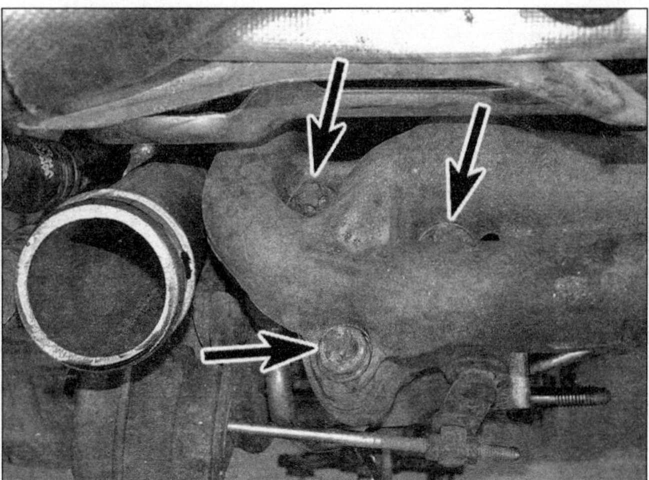

6.26 Turbo-to-manifold mounting bolts (arrowed)

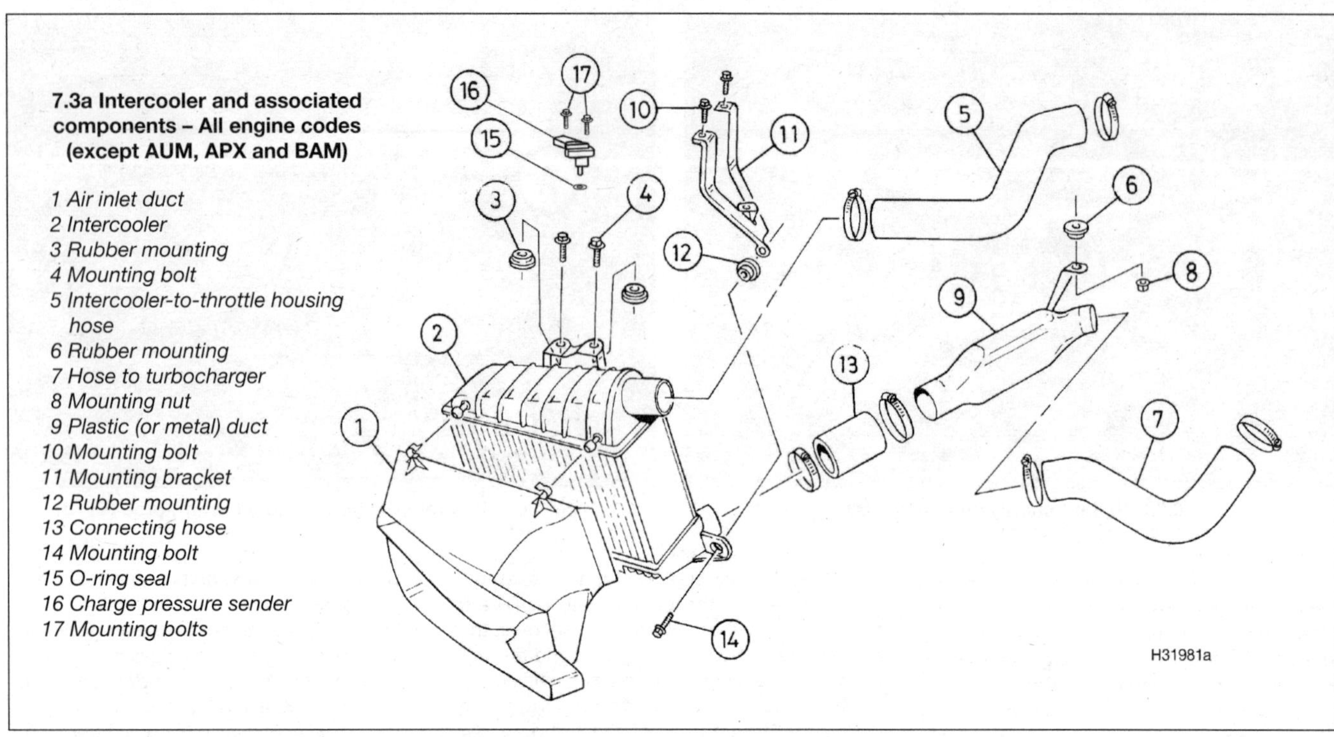

7.3a Intercooler and associated components – All engine codes (except AUM, APX and BAM)

1 Air inlet duct
2 Intercooler
3 Rubber mounting
4 Mounting bolt
5 Intercooler-to-throttle housing hose
6 Rubber mounting
7 Hose to turbocharger
8 Mounting nut
9 Plastic (or metal) duct
10 Mounting bolt
11 Mounting bracket
12 Rubber mounting
13 Connecting hose
14 Mounting bolt
15 O-ring seal
16 Charge pressure sender
17 Mounting bolts

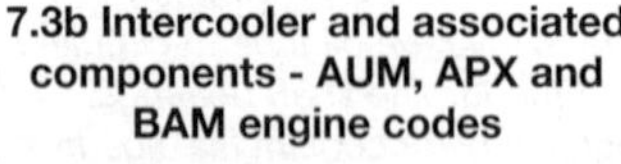

7.3b Intercooler and associated components - AUM, APX and BAM engine codes

1 Air intake hose
2 Air duct
3 Charge air cooler (right-hand side)
4 Rubber grommet
5 Bolt
6 To turbocharger
7 Bolt
8 Bracket
9 To intake manifold
10 Rubber grommet
11 Bolt
12 Bracket
13 Sleeve
14 Rubber grommet
15 Air intake hose
16 Bolt
17 Bolt
18 Charge pressure sender
19 Air pipe
20 Air intake hose
21 Rubber grommet
22 Bolt
23 Charge air cooler (left-hand side)
24 Rubber grommet
25 Bolt
26 Bracket
27 Air duct
28 Connecting pipe for charge air coolers
29 Connecting hose

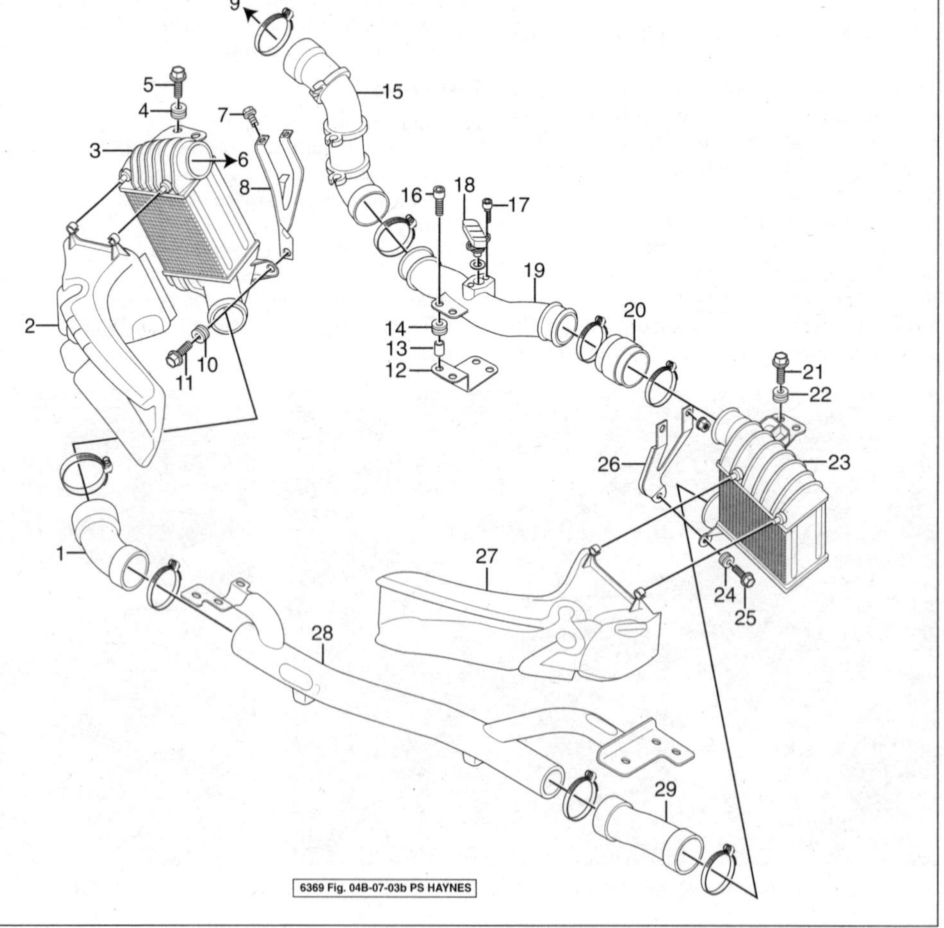

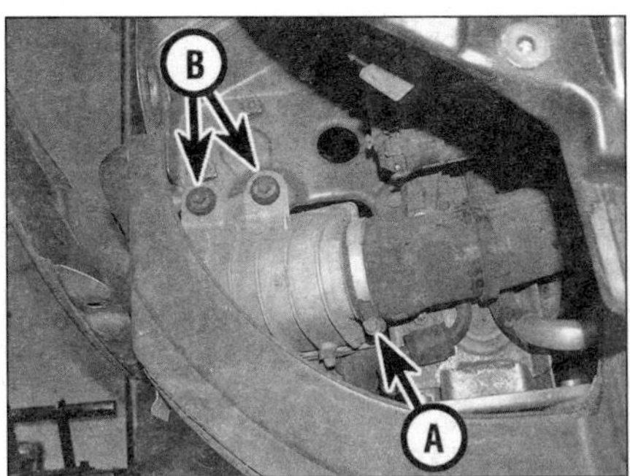

7.5 Slacken the retaining clip (A) and undo the mounting bolts (B)

intercooler fitted to the right-hand side front wheel arch of the vehicle behind the front bumper. On engine codes AMU, APX and BAM, there are two intercoolers fitted behind the front bumper, one to the right and another to the left-hand side front wheel arches of the vehicle.

2 When the turbocharger compresses the inlet air, one side-effect is that the air is heated, causing the air to expand. If the inlet air can be cooled, a greater effective volume of air will be inducted, and the engine will produce more power.

3 The compressed air from the turbocharger, which would normally be fed straight into the inlet manifold, is instead ducted around the engine to the base of the intercooler(s) **(see illustrations)**. Intercoolers are mounted at the front of the car, in the air flow. The heated air entering the base of the unit rises

7.6 Unclip the air duct from the front of the intercooler

upwards, and is cooled by the air flow over the intercooler fins, much as with the radiator. When it reaches the top of the intercooler, the cooled air is then ducted into the throttle housing.

Removal

4 To gain access to the intercooler(s), remove the bumper, as described in Chapter 11 Section 6, and the headlight unit(s), as described in Chapter 12 Section 7.

All engine codes (except AUM, APX and BAM)

5 Working in the engine compartment, through the headlight aperture, slacken the charge hose retaining clip leading to the top of the intercooler, and undo the two upper mounting bolts **(see illustration)**. Disconnect the wiring connector from the charge pressure sender in the top of the intercooler (where fitted).

6 Unclip the air duct from the locating pegs at the front of the intercooler **(see illustration)**.

7 Release the lower charge air hose retaining clip **(see illustration)**, then undo the intercooler lower mounting bolt from the mounting bracket.

8 The intercooler can now be released from the charge air hoses, then manoeuvre it out from under the wheel arch, taking care not to damage the cooling fins. Recover the three rubber grommets from the mounting bolts.

Charge air pipes/hoses

9 If required, the charge air duct from along the right-hand chassis leg can be removed, unscrew the nut at the rear, and the washer-type fasteners further forward, then release the air duct from under the wheel arch **(see illustrations)**. **Note:** *There is a charge air pipe which also acts as a brace between the two chassis legs at the front of the vehicle. It is fitted to ALL models, but is only used as a charge air pipe on engines with two intercoolers fitted (for removal of this charge air pipe, see paragraph 15).*

Engine codes AUM, APX and BAM

10 Working in the engine compartment, through the headlight aperture, slacken the charge hose retaining clips leading to the top of the intercoolers, and then undo the two upper mounting bolts **(see illustration)**. See illustration 7.5 for the upper bolts and retaining clip for right-hand side intercooler.

7.7 Release the charge air hose retaining clip (arrowed)

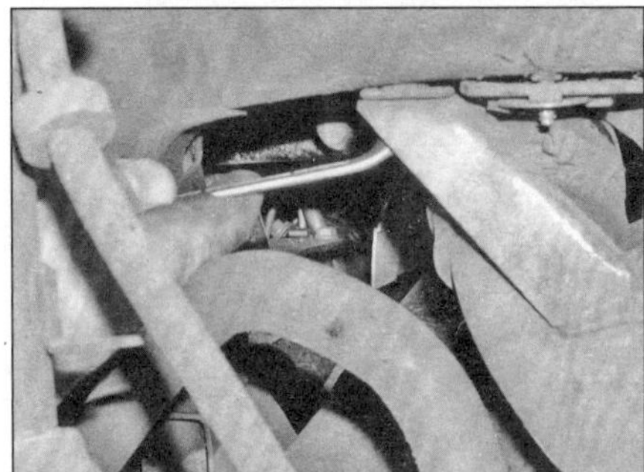

7.9a Unscrew the nut at the rear ...

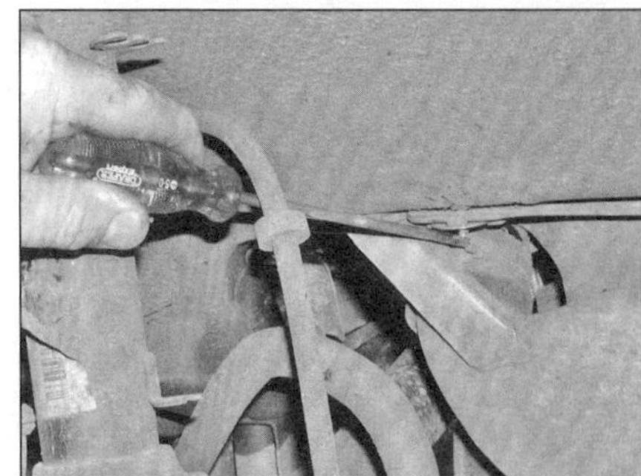

7.9b ... and the washer-type fasteners further forward ...

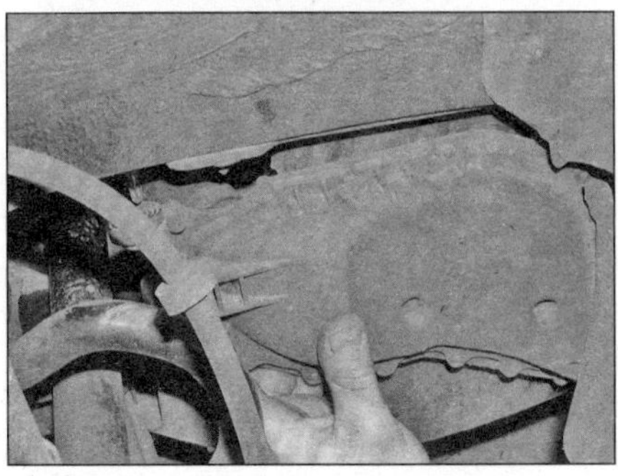

7.9c ... and manipulate the air duct ...

7.9d ... out from under the car

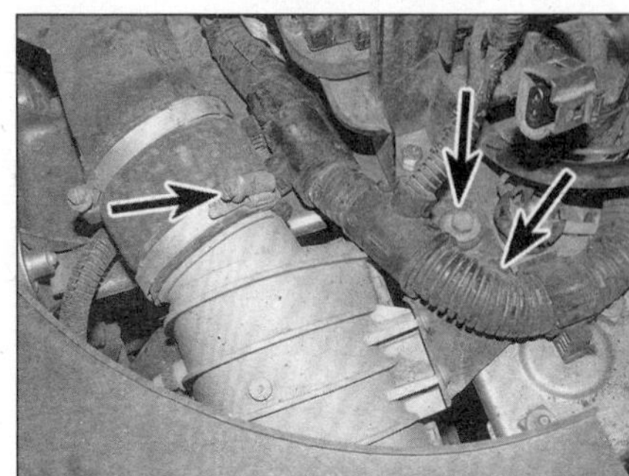

7.10 Undo the two bolts and the retaining clip (arrowed) – left-hand side shown

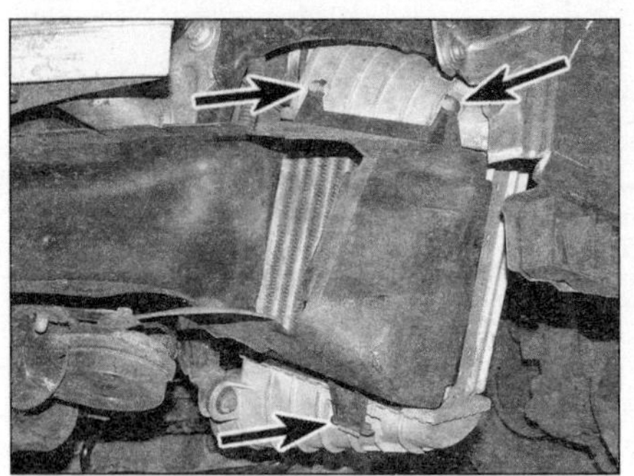

7.11 Unclip air duct from locating pegs (arrowed)

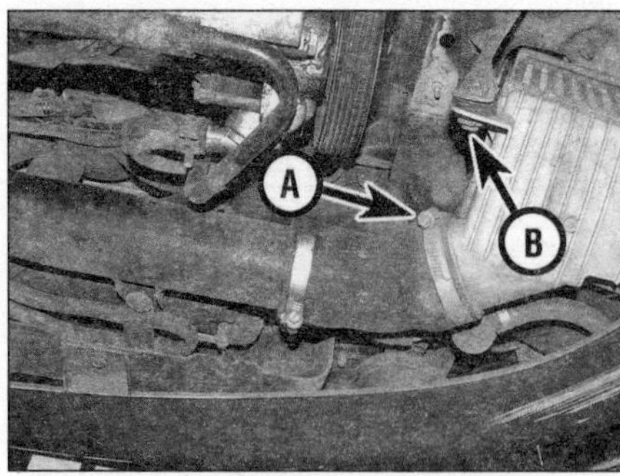

7.12a Retaining clip (A) and mounting bolt (B) – right-hand intercooler

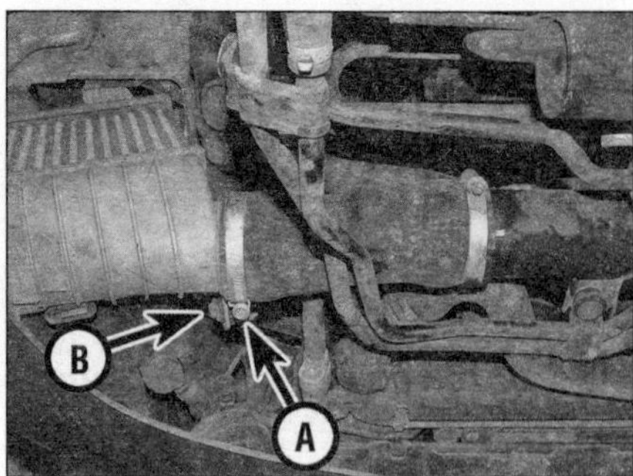

7.12b Retaining clip (A) and mounting bolt (B) – left-hand intercooler

11 Unclip the air ducts from the locating pegs at the front of the intercoolers **(see illustration)**.

12 Release the lower charge air hose retaining clips **(see illustrations)**, then undo the intercooler lower mounting bolts from the mounting brackets.

13 The intercoolers can now be released from the charge air hoses, then manoeuvred out from under the wheel arch, taking care not to damage the cooling fins. Recover the rubber grommets from the mounting bolts.

Charge air pipes/hoses

14 If required, the air ducts and charge air pipes/hoses can be removed from the vehicle, see the following procedures.

15 To remove the charge air pipe from across the front lower part of the engine compartment, first remove the engine undershield and two inner wheel arch trim panels. Slacken the retaining clips and disconnect the charge air hoses from each end of the charge pipe. Then undo the two retaining bolts and disconnect the power steering fluid cooler pipe from the charge air pipe. Finally undo the three bolts at each end of the charge air pipe and manoeuvre it out from under the front of the engine compartment, taking care not to damage the radiator, condenser or intercoolers **(see illustrations)**. **Note:** *This charge air pipe also acts as a brace between the two chassis legs at the front of the vehicle. It is fitted to ALL models, but is only used as a charge air pipe on engines with two intercoolers fitted.*

16 To remove the charge air pipe from the top right-hand side of the engine compartment, first remove the two plastic trim panels from the top of the engine and from over the coolant reservoir. Working at the rear of the engine, pull back the heat cover and slacken the retaining clip, then remove the two hoses and undo the rear mounting bracket nut. Working at the front part of the charge air pipe, slacken the retaining clip and undo the front mounting bracket retaining nut. Release the mounting brackets and withdraw the charge air pipe from the hoses at each end, and remove from the engine compartment **(see illustrations)**.

17 To remove the charge air pipe from the top left-hand side, from the left-hand side intercooler, first remove the battery,

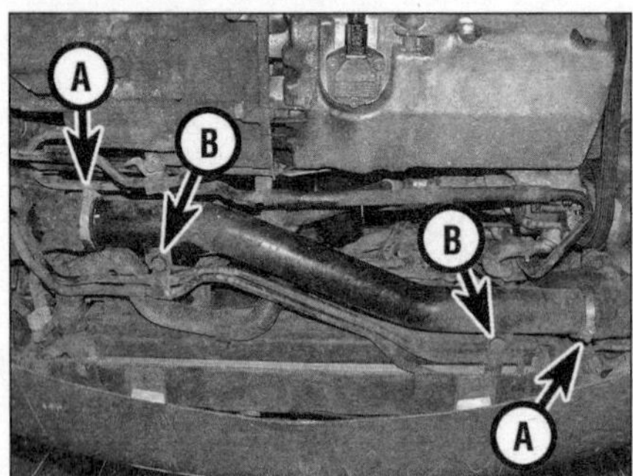

7.15a Slacken retaining clips (A) and undo PAS cooler mounting bolts (B)

7.15b Undo the mounting bolts (left-hand side shown)

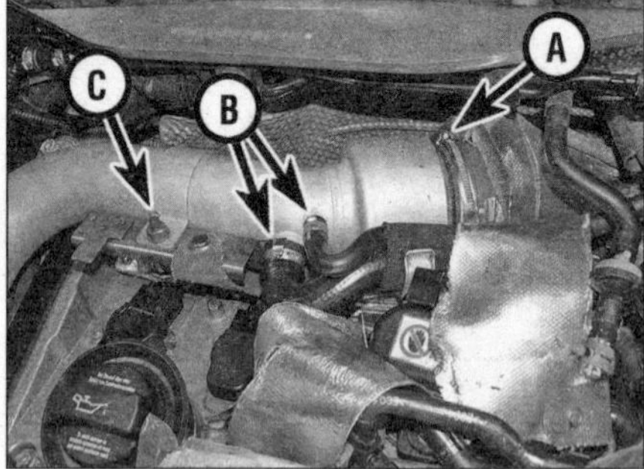

7.16a Slacken clip (A) disconnect hoses (B) and undo nut (C)

7.16b Slacken the clip (arrowed) and remove the mounting bracket

7.16c Remove the charge air pipe...

7.16d...and recover the lower part of the mounting bracket

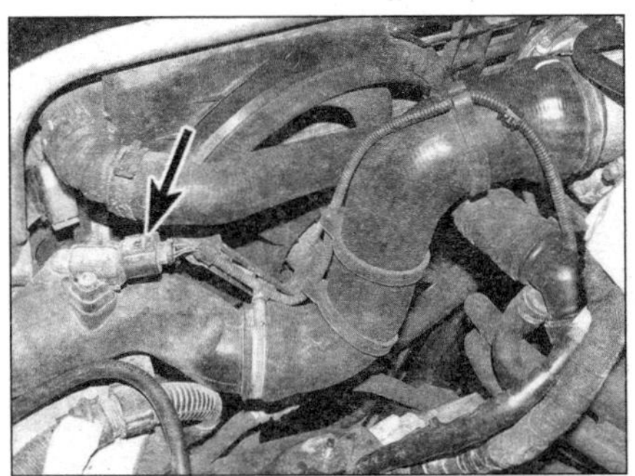
7.17a Disconnect the wiring connector (arrowed)

7.17b Undo the mounting bolts (arrowed)...

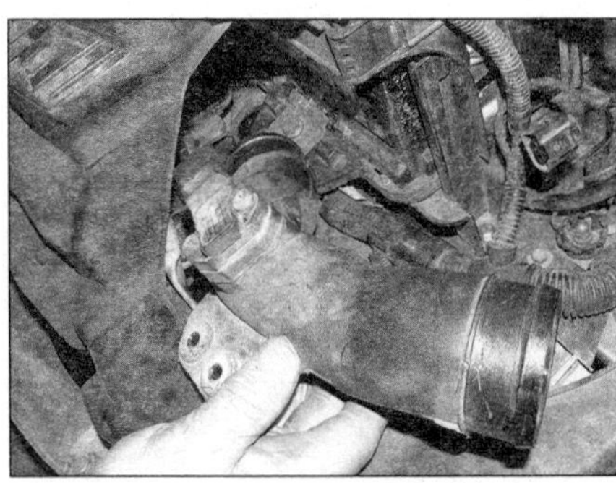
7.17c ...and withdraw the charge air pipe

as described in Chapter 5A Section 3. Disconnect the wiring connector from the charge pressure sensor on the top of the charge air pipe. Slacken the retaining clips at each end of the charge air pipe, then undo the mounting bracket bolts and withdraw the charge air pipe from the hoses at each end, and remove from the engine compartment **(see illustrations)**.

Refitting

18 Examine the intercooler for any damage, and check the charge air pipes/hoses and ducting for any cracks or splits, before refitting.

19 Refitting is a reversal of removal. Ensure that the charge air hose clips are correctly fitted and tightened, to prevent any air leaks. Where disconnected, make sure the wiring connector to the charge pressure sensor is fitted securely.

8 Exhaust manifold – removal and refitting

Removal

1 Working as described in Section 6, undo the retaining bolts and remove the turbocharger from the exhaust manifold. The turbocharger does not need to be completely removed from the engine compartment, just release from manifold and lower out of its position.

2 Unscrew and remove the three bolts from above which secure the turbocharger to the exhaust manifold; recover the washers. Note that new bolts must be used when refitting.

8.4 Manifold retaining nuts shown

3 Where applicable, disconnect the secondary air hose and vacuum hose from the valve mounted above the manifold heat shield. The larger hose fitting is released by squeezing the lugs together; recover the sealing O-ring, which must be renewed when refitting. Unscrew and remove the two bolts from below securing the secondary air valve to its mounting bracket on the exhaust manifold, and lift the valve clear. Recover the gasket – a new one must be used when refitting.

4 Unscrew and remove the manifold retaining nuts **(see illustration)**. Use plenty of penetrating oil if the studs are rusty. If a nut appears to be sticking, do not try to force it; tighten the nut back half a turn, apply some more penetrating oil to the stud threads, wait several seconds for it to soak in, then gradually unscrew the nut by one turn. Repeat this process until the nut is free.

5 In some cases, the manifold studs will come out with the nuts – this poses no great problem, and the studs can be refitted if they are in good condition. For preference, however, a complete set of manifold studs and nuts should be obtained, as the old ones are likely to be in less-than-perfect condition.

6 Remove the washers, then withdraw the manifold from the cylinder head, separating it from the turbocharger, and recover the gaskets from the studs and turbocharger mating face.

7 If the proximity of the turbocharger prevents the manifold from being withdrawn, unscrew the nut and bolt securing the turbocharger to the cylinder block mounting bracket, and lower the turbocharger slightly. If this is done, note that the weight of the turbocharger will be taken by the exhaust front pipe – also note that no great strain should be placed on the turbocharger oil and coolant pipes. If absolutely necessary, refer to Section 6 and remove the turbocharger completely.

Refitting

8 Refitting is a reversal of the removal procedure, noting the following points:

a) *Always fit new gaskets and seals, as applicable.*
b) *If any studs were broken when removing, drill out the remains of the stud, and fit new studs and nuts.*
c) *It is recommended that new studs and nuts are used as a matter of course – even if the old ones came off without difficulty, they may not stand being retightened. New components will be much easier to remove in future, should this be necessary.*
d) *If the old studs are re-used, clean the threads thoroughly to remove all traces of rust.*
e) *Tighten the manifold securing nuts to the specified torque.*

9 Exhaust system – component renewal

Warning: Allow ample time for the exhaust system to cool before starting work. In particular, note that the catalytic converter runs at very high temperatures. If there is any chance that the system may still be hot, wear suitable gloves. When removing the exhaust front section, take care not to damage the oxygen sensor(s) if they are not removed from their locations.

Removal

1 The original Audi system fitted in the factory depending on model, could have either a two, three or four section system. The front down pipe (includes flexible section and catalytic converter on 2-wheel drive models), the middle section (which includes the catalytic converter or silencer), and the rear exhaust silencer. On two wheel drive models (except engine codes AMU, APX and BAM), the catalytic converter is part of the front flexible pipe and the middle section incorporates a silencer.

2 To remove part of the system, first jack up the front or rear of the car and support it on axle stands (see *Jacking and vehicle support*). Alternatively, position the car over an inspection pit or on car ramps.

3 Before removing the front section of the exhaust or the catalytic converter, establish how many oxygen sensors are fitted – most models have two. Trace the wiring back from each sensor, and disconnect the wiring connectors. Unclip the oxygen sensor wiring from any clips or brackets, noting how it is routed for refitting. If a new front pipe or catalytic converter are being fitted, the oxygen sensor(s) will need to be removed from the exhaust pipe. If two sensors are fitted, note which fits where, as they should not be interchanged. Refer to Chapter 4A Section 3, for further information on the oxygen sensors.

Front flexible pipe and catalytic converter

Note: *Handle the braided section of the front pipe very carefully, do not bend it more than 10°, as this could damage it.*

4 On four-wheel drive models, disconnect the front of the propeller shaft from the transfer 'bevel' box and move it away from the exhaust front pipe. Refer to Chapter 8B, for further information on the propeller shaft. **Note:** *Mark the position of the propeller shaft on the flange from the bevel box before removal. Take care not to damage the seal in the centre of the coupling as it is being removed and refitted.*

5 On models with engine codes AMU, APX and BAM, remove the right-hand front driveshaft, as described in Chapter 8A Section 3. Remove the heat shield from over the right-hand driveshaft inner flange **(see illustration)**.

6 Remove the two bolts that secure the lower rear engine mounting to the subframe **(see illustration)**, this will allow the engine/transmission assembly to move slightly forwards to allow more room to access the front pipe securing bolts.

7 Loosen and remove the nuts securing the front flange to the turbocharger **(see illustration)**. On some models, the shield over the right-hand driveshaft inner CV joint must be removed to improve access. Separate the front joint, and move it down sufficiently to clear the mounting studs.

8 Support the front of the pipe, then undo the two clamp bolts and slide the clamp behind the catalytic converter either forwards or backwards to separate the joint **(see illustration)**. Twist the front pipe slightly from side-to-side, while pulling towards the front to release it from the rear section. When the pipe is free, lower it to the ground and remove it from under the car. **Note:** *The bolts/nuts securing the clamp may have rusted, so be prepared to replace them with new ones.*

9.5 Remove the heat shield

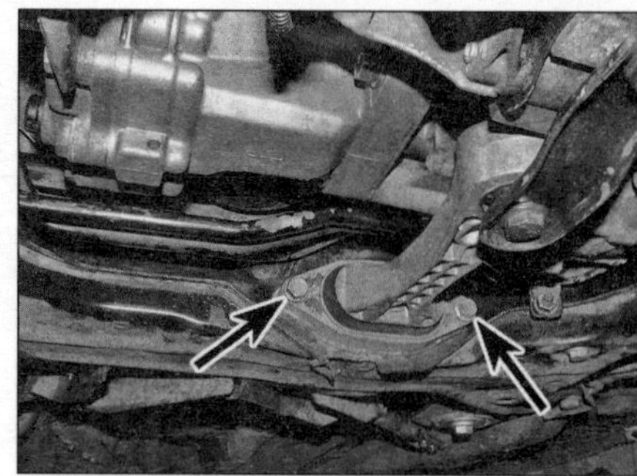

9.6 lower rear mounting securing bolts (arrowed)

9 Where applicable, undo the six retaining nuts to separate the front flexible pipe from the catalytic converter. **Note:** *The nuts securing the front pipe to the catalytic converter may have rusted, so be prepared to replace them with new ones. New gaskets will also be required for refitting.*

Rear pipe and silencers – 2-wheel drive models

Note: *On 2-wheel drive models the exhaust has to be split into two before removing from the vehicle, as the exhaust passes over the top of the rear axle. The rear axle would need to be removed first, before the complete exhaust system could be removed in one piece.*

10 If the factory-fitted Audi rear section is being worked on, examine the pipe between the two silencers for three pairs of punch marks, or three line markings. The centre marking indicates the point at which to cut the pipe, while the outer marks indicate the position of for the ends of the new clamp required when refitting. Cut through the pipe, making the cut as square to the pipe as possible if either resulting section is to be re-used **(see illustration)**. **Note:** *If the markings on the exhaust cannot be seen due to corrosion, purchase the new section of exhaust required first, and then measure it against the old exhaust to check where to cut.*

11 If the factory-fitted rear section has already been renewed, loosen the nuts securing the clamp in front of the rear silencer, so that the clamp can be moved.

Rear pipe and silencers – 4-wheel drive models

Note: *On 4-wheel drive models the exhaust does not need to be split into two before removing from the vehicle, as the exhaust passes under the rear axle.*

12 If the factory-fitted Audi rear section is being worked on, examine the pipe just in front of the rear silencer for an indentation on the outside of the exhaust pipe. Cut through the pipe, making the cut as square to the pipe as possible if either resulting section is to be re-used. **Note:** *If the markings on the exhaust cannot be seen due to corrosion, purchase the new section of exhaust required first, and then measure it against the old exhaust to check where to cut.*

13 If the factory-fitted rear section has already been renewed, loosen the nuts securing the clamp in front of the rear silencer, so that the clamp can be moved.

Catalytic converter – 4-wheel drive models

14 Undo the two clamp bolts and slide the clamp behind the catalytic converter either forwards or backwards to separate the joint **(see illustration 9.8)**. Twist the pipe slightly from side-to-side, while pulling towards the rear to release it from the rear section. **Note:** *The bolts/nuts securing the clamp may have*

9.7 Exhaust front pipe securing nuts (arrowed) – all models except AMU, APX and BAM shown

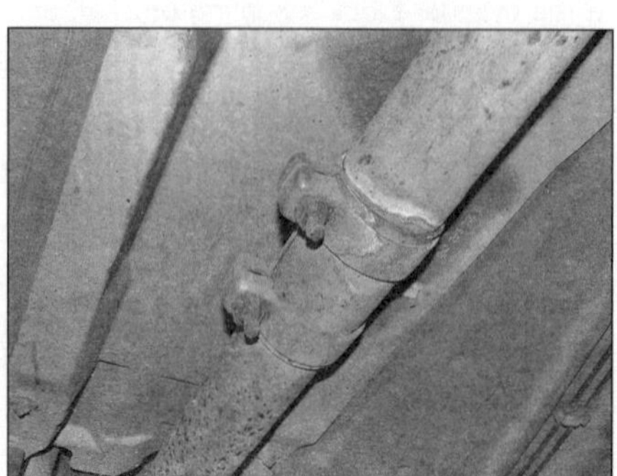

9.8 Slacken the clamp retaining bolts

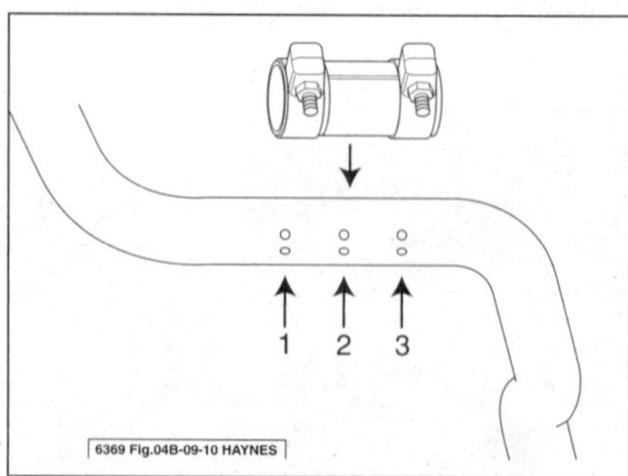

9.10 Cut exhaust at centre marking (2) and clamp will align between markings (1 and 3)

rusted, so be prepared to replace them with new ones.

15 Undo the six retaining nuts and separate the front flexible pipe from the catalytic converter **(see illustration)**. When the catalytic converter is free, lower it to the ground and remove it from under the car. **Note:** *The nuts securing the front pipe to the catalytic converter may have rusted, so be prepared to replace them with new ones. New gaskets will also be required for refitting.*

Rear silencer

16 Depending on model, the rear silencer is supported either just at the very back, or in front and behind, by a rubber mounting which is bolted to the underside of the car **(see illustration)**. The silencer is attached to these mountings by metal pegs which push into the rubber section of each mounting.

17 Unscrew the bolts, and release the mounting(s) from the underside of the car. On models with two silencer mountings, it may prove sufficient to unbolt only one, and to prise the silencer from the remaining mounting, but for preference, both should be removed, where applicable.

18 Check with the previous parts of this section, about the possibility of cutting the section of exhaust pipe between rear silencer and middle section. Where applicable, slide the clamp at the front end of the silencer section to release the pipe ends, and lower the silencer out of position.

Refitting

19 Each section is refitted by a reversal of the removal sequence, noting the following points:

a) *Ensure that all traces of corrosion have been removed from the flanges or pipe ends, and renew all necessary gaskets* ***(see illustrations).***
b) *The design of the clamps used between the exhaust sections means that they play a greater role in ensuring a gas-tight seal – fit new clamps if they are in less than perfect condition (see illustration).*
c) *When fitting the clamps, use the markings on the pipes as a guide to the clamp's correct fitted position.*
d) *Inspect the mountings for signs of damage or deterioration, and renew as necessary.*
e) *If using exhaust assembly paste, make sure this is only applied to joints downstream of the catalyst.*
f) *Prior to tightening the exhaust system mountings and clamps, ensure that all rubber mountings are correctly located and that there is adequate clearance between the exhaust system and vehicle underbody. Try to ensure that no unnecessary twisting stresses are applied to the pipes – move the pipes relative to each other at the clamps to relieve this.*

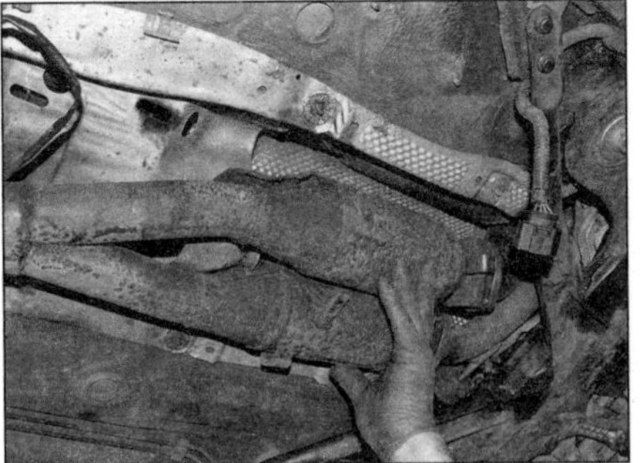

9.15 Disconnect the front pipe from the catalytic converter

9.16 Rear silencer mounting – 2-wheel drive shown

10 Catalytic converter – general information and precautions

1 The catalytic converter is a reliable and simple device which needs no maintenance in itself, but there are some facts of which an owner should be aware if the converter is to function properly for its full service life:

a) *DO NOT use leaded or lead-replacement petrol in a car equipped with a catalytic converter – the lead (or other additives) will coat the precious metals, reducing their converting efficiency and will eventually destroy the converter.*
b) *Always keep the ignition and fuel systems well-maintained in accordance with the manufacturer's schedule (see Chapter 1).*
c) *If the engine develops a misfire, do not drive the car at all (or at least as little as possible) until the fault is cured.*
d) *DO NOT push- or tow-start the car – this will soak the catalytic converter in unburned fuel, causing it to overheat when the engine does start.*
e) *DO NOT switch off the ignition at high engine speeds – ie do not 'blip' the throttle immediately before switching off the engine.*
f) *DO NOT use fuel or engine oil additives – these may contain substances harmful to the catalytic converter.*
g) *DO NOT continue to use the car if the engine burns oil to the extent of leaving a visible trail of blue smoke.*
h) *Remember that the catalytic converter operates at very high temperatures. DO NOT, therefore, park the car in dry undergrowth, over long grass or piles of dead leaves after a long run.*
i) *Remember that the catalytic converter is FRAGILE – do not strike it with tools during servicing work, and take care handling it when removing it from the car for any reason.*
j) *In some cases, a sulphurous smell (like that of rotten eggs) may be noticed from the exhaust. This is common to many catalytic converter-equipped cars, and has more to do with the sulphur content of the brand of fuel being used than the converter itself.*
k) *The catalytic converter, used on a well-maintained and well-driven car, should last for between 50 000 and 100 000 miles – if the converter is no longer effective, it must be renewed.*

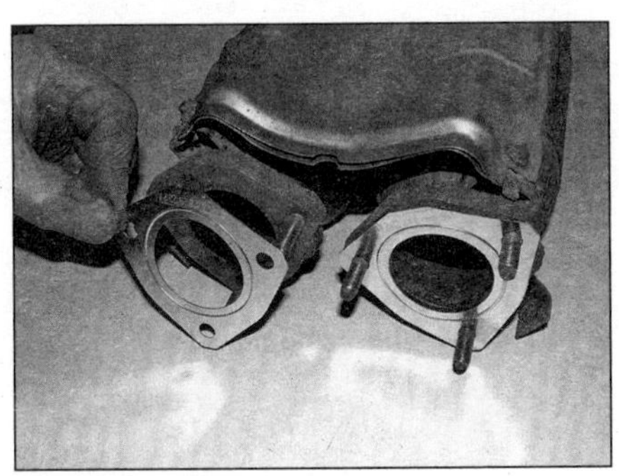

9.19a Fit new gaskets to catalytic converter-to-front pipe

9.19b Fit new gasket to front pipe-to-turbo

9.19c Fit new exhaust clamp

Chapter 5 Part A
Starting and charging systems

Contents

Degrees of difficulty

Easy, suitable for novice with little experience 	**Fairly easy,** suitable for beginner with some experience	**Fairly difficult,** suitable for competent DIY mechanic	**Difficult,** suitable for experienced DIY mechanic	**Very difficult,** suitable for expert DIY or professional 

Specifications

General

System type	12 volt, negative earth

Starter motor

Rating	12V, 1.1 kW

Battery

Ratings	36 to 72 Ah (depending on model and market)

Alternator

Rating	55, 60, 70 or 90 amp
Minimum brush length	5.0 mm

Torque wrench settings

	Nm	lbf ft
Alternator mounting bolts	25	18
Alternator mounting bracket	45	33
Battery clamping plate bolt	22	16
Starter mounting bolts	65	48

1 General information and precautions

General information

1 The engine electrical system consists mainly of the charging and starting systems. Because of their engine-related functions, these are covered separately from the body electrical devices such as the lights, instruments, etc (which are covered in Chapter 12). Refer to Part B of this Chapter for information on the ignition system.

2 The electrical system is of the 12 volt negative earth type.

3 The battery may be of the low maintenance or maintenance-free (sealed for life) type and is charged by the alternator, which is belt-driven from the crankshaft pulley.

4 The starter motor is of the pre-engaged type, with an integral solenoid. On starting, the solenoid moves the drive pinion into engagement with the flywheel ring gear before the starter motor is energised. Once the engine has started, a one-way clutch prevents the motor armature being driven by the engine until the pinion disengages from the flywheel.

5 Further details of the various systems are given in the relevant Sections of this Chapter. While some repair procedures are given, the usual course of action is to renew the compo-nent concerned. The owner whose interest extends beyond mere component renewal should obtain a copy of the Automotive Electrical & Electronic Systems Manual

Precautions

Warning: It is necessary to take extra care when working on the electrical system to avoid damage to semi-conductor devices (diodes and transistors), and to avoid the risk of personal injury. In addition to the precautions given in 'Safety first!', observe the following when working on the system:

• Always remove rings, watches, etc, before working on the electrical system. Even with the battery disconnected, capacitive discharge could occur if a component's live terminal is earthed through a metal object. This could cause a shock or nasty burn.

• Do not reverse the battery connections. Components such as the alternator, electronic control units, or any other components having semi-conductor circuitry could be irreparably damaged.

• Never disconnect the battery terminals, the alternator, any electrical wiring or any test instruments when the engine is running.

• Do not allow the engine to turn the alternator when the alternator is not connected.

• Never test for alternator output by flashing the output lead to earth.

• Always ensure that the battery negative lead is disconnected when working on the electrical system.

• If the engine is being started using jump leads and a slave battery, connect the batteries positive-to-positive and negative-to-negative (see Jump starting at the beginning of the manual). This also applies when connecting a battery charger.

• Before using electric-arc welding equipment on the car, disconnect the battery, alternator and components such as the electronic control units (where applicable) to protect them from the risk of damage.

Caution: Certain radio/cassettes fitted as standard equipment by Audi have a built-in security code to deter thieves. If the power source to the unit is cut, the anti-theft system will activate. Even if the power source is immediately reconnected, the radio/cassette unit will not function until the correct security code has been entered. Therefore, if you do not know the correct security code for the radio/cassette unit do not disconnect the battery negative terminal or remove the radio/cassette unit from the vehicle. Refer to your Audi dealer for further information on whether the unit fitted to your car has a security code. Refer to 'Disconnecting the battery' in the Reference section at the rear of this manual.

2 Battery – testing and charging

Testing

Standard and low-maintenance battery

1 If the vehicle covers a small annual mileage, it is worthwhile checking the specific gravity of the electrolyte every three months to determine the state of charge of the battery. Remove the battery (see Section 3) then remove the cell caps/cover (as applicable) and use a hydrometer to make the check, comparing the results with the following table. Note that the specific gravity readings assume an electrolyte temperature of 15°C (60°F); for every 10°C (18°F) below 15°C (60°F) subtract 0.007. For every 10°C (18°F) above 15°C (60°F) add 0.007. If the electrolyte level of any cell is low, top it up to the MAX level mark with distilled water.

	Above 25°C	Below 25°C
Fully-charged	1.210 to 1.230	1.270 to 1.290
70% charged	1.170 to 1.190	1.230 to 1.250
Discharged	1.050 to 1.070	1.110 to 1.130

2 If the battery condition is suspect, first check the specific gravity of electrolyte in each cell. A variation of 0.040 or more between any cells indicates loss of electrolyte or deterioration of the internal plates.

3 If the specific gravity variation is 0.040 or more, the battery should be renewed. If the cell variation is satisfactory but the battery is discharged, it should be charged as described later in this Section.

Maintenance-free battery

4 In cases where a sealed for life maintenance-free battery is fitted, topping-up and testing of the electrolyte in each cell is not possible. The condition of the battery can therefore only be tested using a battery condition indicator or a voltmeter.

5 Certain models may be fitted with a maintenance-free battery with a built-in charge condition indicator. The indicator is located in the top of the battery casing, and indicates the condition of the battery from its colour. If the indicator shows green, then the battery is in a good state of charge. If the indicator turns darker, eventually to black, then the battery requires charging, as described later in this Section. If the indicator shows clear/yellow, then the electrolyte level in the battery is too low to allow further use, and the battery should be renewed. Do not attempt to charge, load or jump start a battery when the indicator shows clear/yellow.

6 If testing the battery using a voltmeter, connect the voltmeter across the battery and note the voltage. The test is only accurate if the battery has not been subjected to any kind of charge for the previous six hours. If this is not the case, switch on the headlights for 30 seconds, then wait four to five minutes before testing the battery after switching off the headlights. All other electrical circuits must be switched off, so check that the doors and tailgate are fully shut when making the test.

7 If the voltage reading is less than 12.2 volts, then the battery is discharged, whilst a reading of 12.2 to 12.4 volts indicates a partially-discharged condition.

8 If the battery is to be charged, remove it from the vehicle and charge it as described later in this Section.

Charging

Note: *The following is intended as a guide only. Always refer to the manufacturer's recommendations (often printed on a label attached to the battery) before charging a battery.*

Standard and low maintenance battery

9 Charge the battery at a rate equivalent to 10% of the battery capacity (eg, for a 45 Ah battery charge at 4.5 A) and continue to charge the battery at this rate until no further rise in specific gravity is noted over a four-hour period.

10 Alternatively, a trickle charger charging at the rate of 1.5 amps can safely be used overnight.

11 Specially rapid boost charges which are

claimed to restore the power of the battery in 1 to 2 hours are not recommended, as they can cause serious damage to the battery plates through overheating.

12 While charging the battery, note that the temperature of the electrolyte should never exceed 37.8°C (100°F).

Maintenance-free battery

13 This battery type takes considerably longer to fully recharge than the standard type, the time taken being dependent on the extent of discharge, but it can take anything up to three days.

14 A constant voltage type charger is required, to be set, when connected, to 13.9 to 14.9 volts with a charger current below 25 amps. Using this method, the battery should be useable within three hours, giving a voltage reading of 12.5 volts, but this is for a partially-discharged battery and, as mentioned, full charging can take far longer.

15 If the battery is to be charged from a fully-discharged state (condition reading less than 12.2 volts), have it recharged by your local automotive electrician, as the charge rate is higher and constant supervision during charging is necessary.

3 Battery and tray – removal and refitting

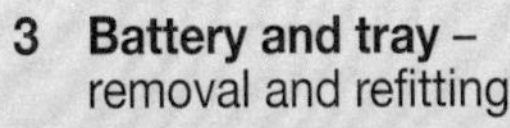

Note: *If the vehicle has a security-coded radio, make sure that you have the code number before disconnecting the battery. If necessary, a 'code-saver' or 'memory-saver' can be used to preserve the radio code and any other relevant memory values whilst the battery is disconnected (see* Disconnecting the battery *in the Reference Section).*

3.1 Remove the cover from the battery

3.2 Disconnect the negative terminal

Removal

1 The battery is located in the front, left-hand corner of the engine compartment. Where an insulator cover is fitted over the top of the battery, release the fasteners and remove the cover to gain access to the battery **(see illustration)**.

2 Loosen the clamp nut and disconnect the battery negative (–) lead from the terminal **(see illustration)**.

3 Slacken the clamp nut and disconnect the positive (+) lead from the battery terminal **(see illustration)**.

4 Lift the plastic cover/fuse holder on top of the battery, by releasing the securing clips at each side of the battery **(see illustration)**. Then hinge the cover/fuse holder backwards from over the top of the battery. **Note:** *On some models, the securing clip for the plastic cover/fuse holder may be at the front centre of the battery.*

5 Unscrew the bolt and remove the battery clamp from the front of the battery, and then lift the battery from its position in the battery tray **(see illustrations)**.

6 If required, to remove the battery tray, undo the four retaining screw (two each side), and with draw the plastic box from around the battery tray **(see illustrations)**.

3.3 Undo the positive terminal retaining nut (arrowed)

3.4 Release the tabs at each side (arrowed)

3.5a Unscrew the clamp bolt (arrowed)...

3.5b ...and remove the battery

3.6a Undo the retaining screws (arrowed) – one side shown

3.6b Remove the plastic box

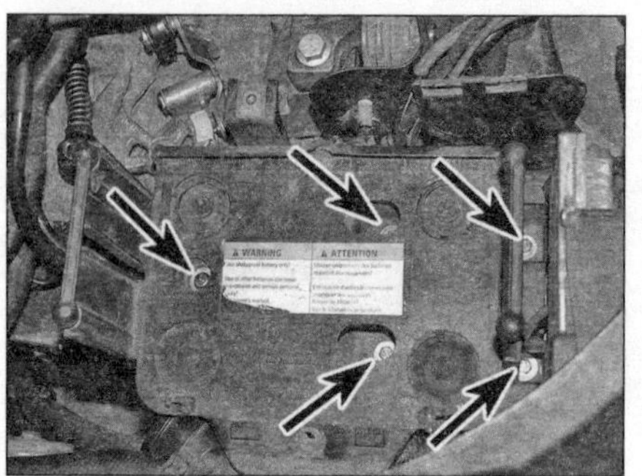

3.7a Undo the bolts (arrowed)...

3.7b ...and remove the battery tray

7 Unscrew the five retaining bolts, and remove the battery tray **(see illustrations)**.

Refitting

8 Refit the battery and battery tray, by following the removal procedure in reverse. Tighten the battery clamp bolt and battery terminals securely.

4 Alternator/charging system – testing in vehicle

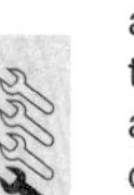

Note: *Refer to Section 1 of this Chapter before starting work.*

1 If the charge warning light fails to illuminate when the ignition is switched on, first check the alternator wiring connections for security. If the light still fails to illuminate, check the continuity of the warning light feed wire from the alternator to the bulbholder. If all is satisfactory, the alternator is at fault and should be renewed or taken to an auto-electrician for testing and repair.

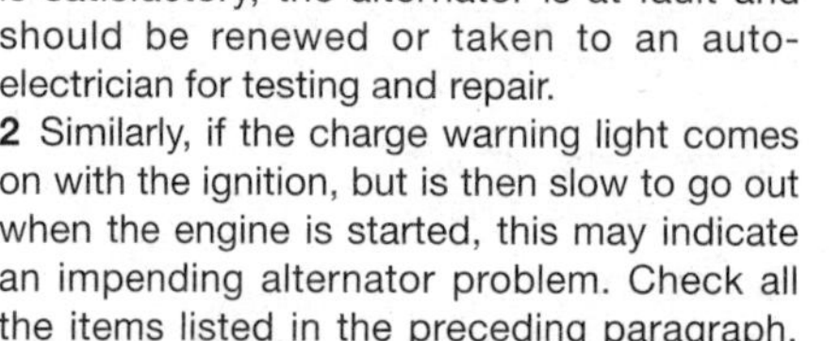

2 Similarly, if the charge warning light comes on with the ignition, but is then slow to go out when the engine is started, this may indicate an impending alternator problem. Check all the items listed in the preceding paragraph, and refer to an auto-electrical specialist if no obvious faults are found.

3 If the charge warning light illuminates when the engine is running, stop the engine and check that the drivebelt is correctly tensioned (see Chapter 1 Section 32) and that the alternator connections are secure. If all is so far satisfactory, check the alternator brushes and slip-rings as described in Section 6. If the fault persists, the alternator should be renewed, or taken to an auto-electrician for testing and repair.

4 If the alternator output is suspect even though the warning light functions correctly, the regulated voltage may be checked as follows.

5 Connect a voltmeter across the battery terminals, and start the engine.

6 Increase the engine speed until the voltmeter reading remains steady; the reading should be approximately 12 to 13 volts, and no more than 14 volts.

7 Switch on as many electrical accessories (eg, the headlights, heated rear window and heater blower) as possible, and check that the alternator maintains the regulated voltage at around 13 to 14 volts.

8 If the regulated voltage is not as stated, this may be due to worn brushes, weak brush springs, a faulty voltage regulator, a faulty diode, a severed phase winding or worn or damaged slip-rings. The brushes and slip-rings may be checked (see Section 6), but if the fault persists, the alternator should be renewed or taken to an auto-electrician.

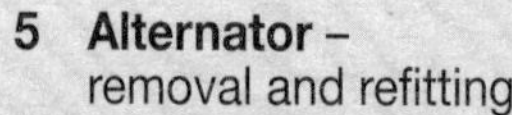

5 Alternator – removal and refitting

Removal

1 Disconnect the battery negative lead and position it away from the terminal. **Note:** *Before disconnecting the battery, refer to* Disconnecting the battery *in the reference section at the rear of this manual.*

2 Remove the auxiliary drivebelt from the alternator pulley (see Chapter 1 Section 32). Mark the drivebelt for direction to ensure it is refitted in the same position.

3 Release the fasteners and remove the plastic trim panel from across the front of the inlet manifold **(see illustration)**.

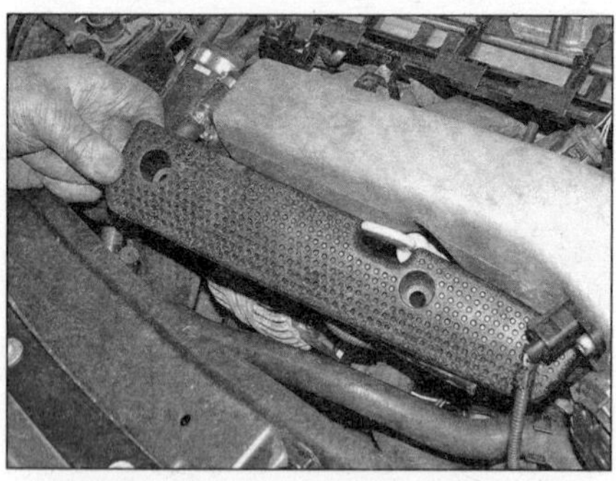

5.3 Remove the plastic trim cover

4 On models with engine codes AMU, APX and BAM disconnect the wiring connector from the exhaust gas temperature sender **(see illustration)**.

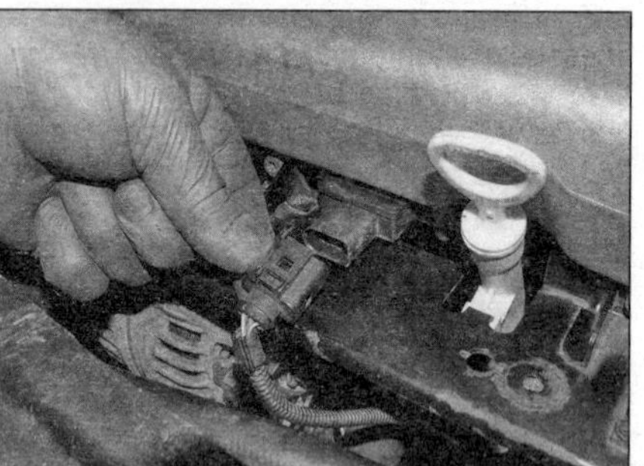

5.4 Disconnect the wiring connector

5 On models with secondary air injection, undo the retaining nuts from the two mounting brackets and disconnect the pipe from across the front of the intake manifold, and move it to one side **(see illustration)**.

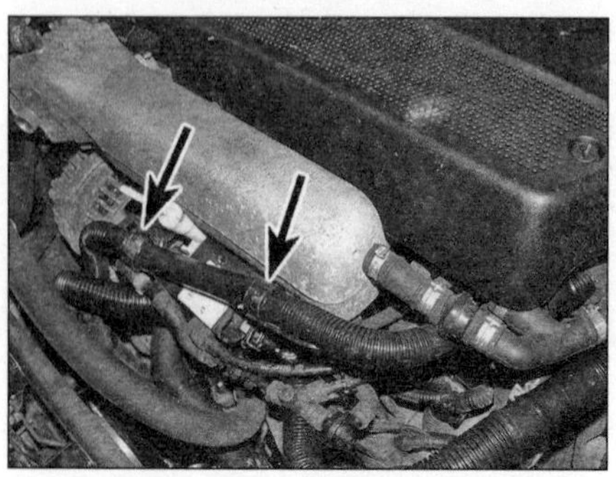

5.5 Undo the two clamp securing nuts (arrowed)

6 Undo the two retaining bolts and remove the mounting bracket from the front of the intake manifold **(see illustration)**. As the mounting bracket is withdrawn, unclip the top of the dipstick tube from the bracket. As the mounting bracket is withdrawn, also disconnect the wiring connectors from the turbocharger air recirculation valve and secondary air inlet valve (where fitted), which may be bolted to the underside of the mounting bracket.

5.6 Remove the mounting bracket

7 Release the retaining clip and pull the

5.7 Disconnect the wiring connector (arrowed)

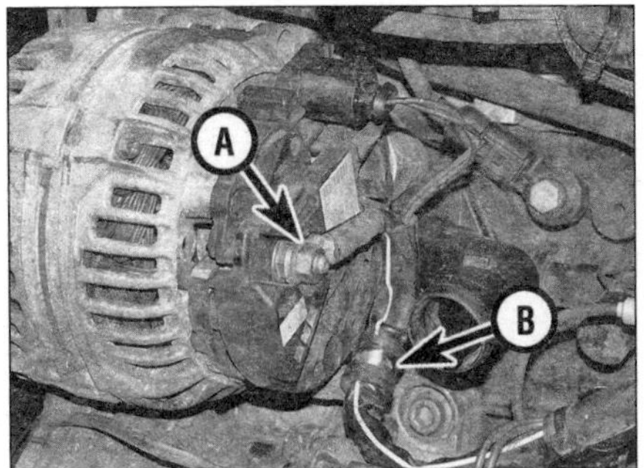

5.8 Disconnect the positive lead (A) and release cable guide (B)

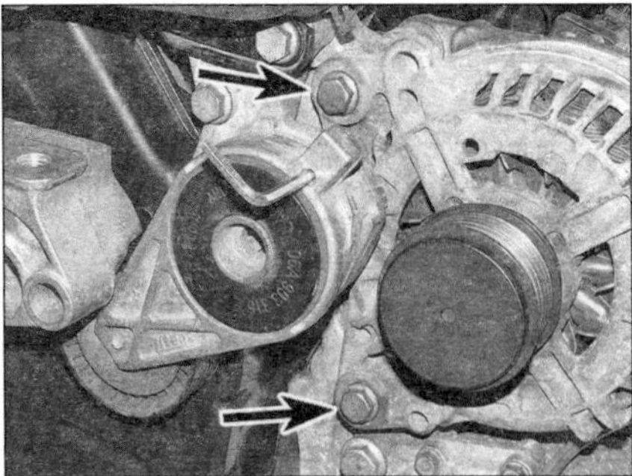

5.9 Undo the mounting bolts (arrowed)

2-pin push-in connector from the rear of the alternator **(see illustration)**.

8 Remove the protective cap (where fitted), unscrew and remove the nut and washers, then disconnect the battery positive cable from the alternator terminal. Where applicable, unscrew the nut and remove the cable guide **(see illustration)**.

9 Unscrew and remove the lower and upper bolt, from the alternator mounting bracket, then lift the alternator away from the front of the engine **(see illustration)**. Make sure the auxiliary belt tensioner is in the locked position, so the lower mounting bolt can be removed.

Refitting

10 Refitting is a reversal of removal, noting the following points:

a) Press the spacers back slightly in the alternator rear mounting bracket, to allow for easier fitting.

b) Refer to Chapter 1 Section 32, as applicable for details of refitting and tensioning the auxiliary drivebelt.

c) Tighten the alternator mounting bolts to the specified torque.

6 Alternator – brush holder/ regulator module renewal

1 Remove the alternator, as described in Section 5.

2 Place the alternator on a clean work surface, with the pulley facing down.

3 Where fitted, undo the screw and the two retaining nuts, and lift away the outer plastic cover **(see illustration)**.

4 Unscrew the three securing screws, and remove the voltage regulator **(see illustrations)**.

5 Measure the free length of the brush contacts **(see illustration)**. Check the measurement with the Specifications; renew the module if the brushes are worn below the minimum limit.

6 Clean and inspect the surfaces of the slip-rings, at the end of the alternator shaft. If they are excessively worn, or damaged, the alternator must be renewed.

7 Reassemble the alternator by following the dismantling procedure in reverse. On completion, refer to Section 5 and refit the alternator.

7 Starting system – testing

Note: *Refer to Section 1 of this Chapter before starting work.*

1 If the starter motor fails to operate when the ignition key is turned to the appropriate position, the following possible causes may be to blame:

a) The battery is faulty.

b) The electrical connections between the switch, solenoid, battery and starter motor are somewhere failing to pass the necessary current from the battery through the starter to earth.

c) The solenoid is faulty.

d) The starter motor is mechanically or electrically defective.

2 To check the battery, switch on the headlights. If they dim after a few seconds, this indicates that the battery is discharged – recharge (see Section 2) or renew the battery. If the headlights glow brightly, operate the ignition switch and observe the lights. If they dim, then this indicates that current is reaching the starter motor, therefore the fault must lie in the starter motor. If the lights continue to glow brightly (and no clicking sound can be heard from the starter motor solenoid), this indicates that there is a fault in the circuit or solenoid – see following paragraphs. If the starter motor turns slowly when operated, but the battery is in good condition, then this indicates that

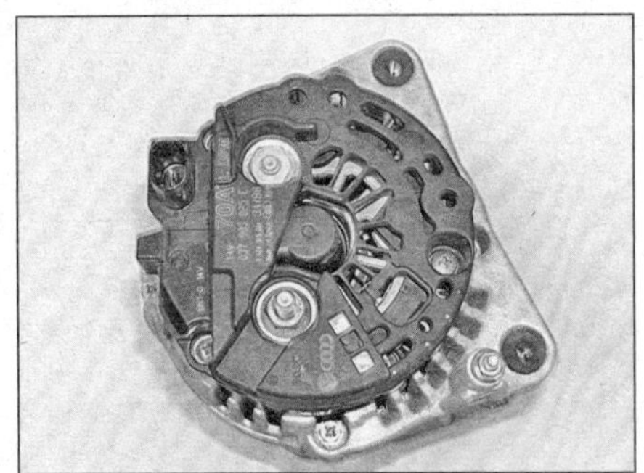

6.3 Remove the outer cover

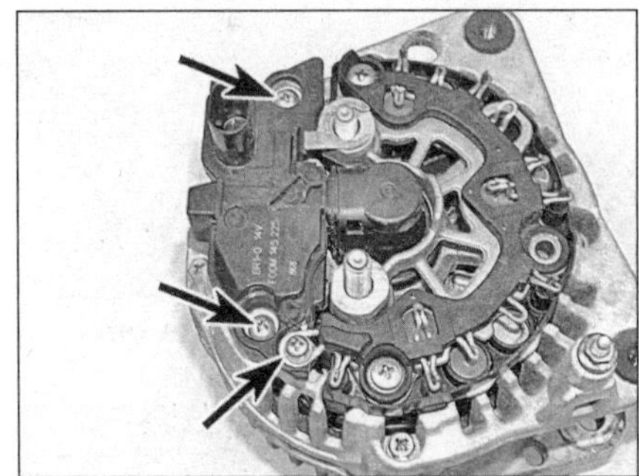

6.4a Undo the screws (arrowed) ...

6.4b ... and remove the brush holder/ regulator

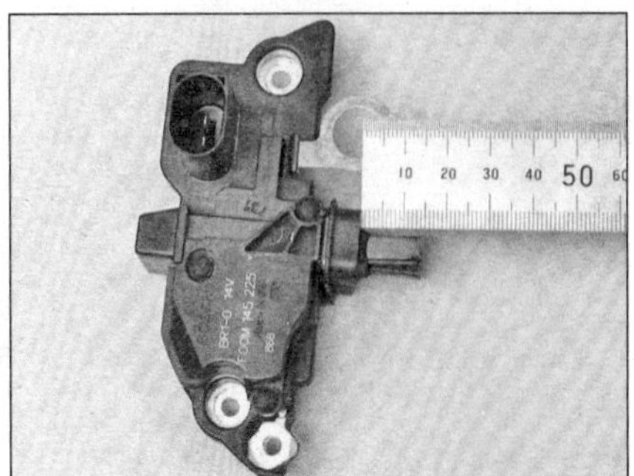

6.5 Measure the brush length

8.2 Disconnect wiring connector

either the starter motor is faulty, or there is considerable resistance somewhere in the circuit.

3 If a fault in the circuit is suspected, disconnect the battery leads (including the earth connection to the body), the starter/solenoid wiring and the engine/transmission earth strap. **Note:** *Before disconnecting the battery, refer to* Disconnecting the battery *in the Reference section at the rear of this manual. Thoroughly clean the connections, and reconnect the leads and wiring, then use a voltmeter or test light to check that full battery voltage is available at the battery positive lead connection to the solenoid, and that the earth is sound.*

4 If the battery and all connections are in good condition, check the circuit by disconnecting the wire from the solenoid blade terminal. Connect a voltmeter or test light between the wire end and a good earth (such as the battery negative terminal), and check that the wire is live when the ignition switch is turned to the start position. If it is, then the circuit is sound – if not the circuit wiring can be checked as described in Chapter 12.

5 The solenoid contacts can be checked by connecting a voltmeter or test light between the battery positive feed connection on the starter side of the solenoid, and earth. When the ignition switch is turned to the start position, there should be a reading or lighted bulb, as applicable. If there is no reading or lighted bulb, the solenoid is faulty and should be renewed.

6 If the circuit and solenoid are proved sound, the fault must lie in the starter motor. It may be possible to have the starter motor overhauled by a specialist, but check on the availability and cost of spares before proceeding, as it may prove more economical to obtain a new or exchange motor.

8 Starter motor – removal and refitting

Removal

1 Remove the battery and battery tray, with reference to Section 3.

2 Disconnect the wiring connector from the cable guide on top of the starter motor **(see illustration)**.

3 Note their fitted position, and disconnect the two wiring connectors from the rear of the solenoid **(see illustrations)**.

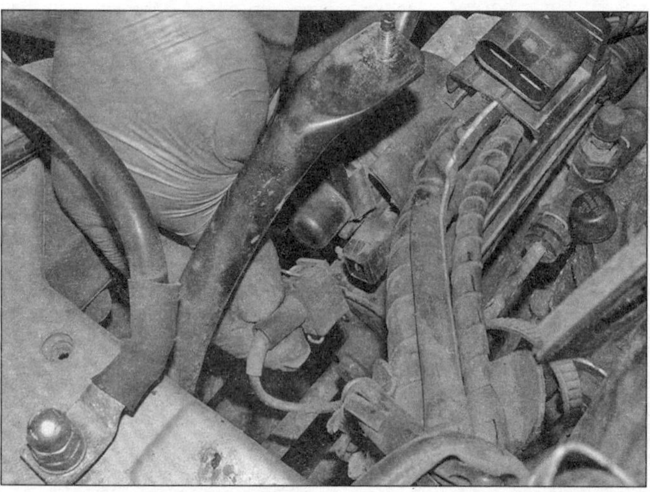
8.3a Disconnect the wiring connector...

8.3b ...remove the plastic cap...

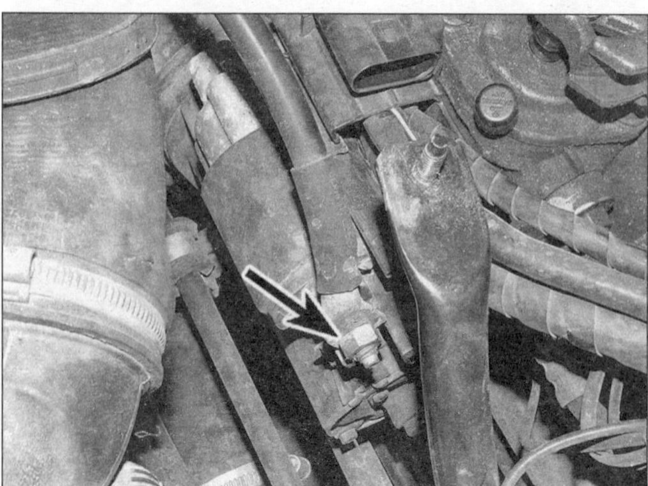
8.3c ...undo the retaining nut (arrowed)...

8.3d ...and remove the positive cable

8.4 Undo the cable guide securing nut (arrowed)

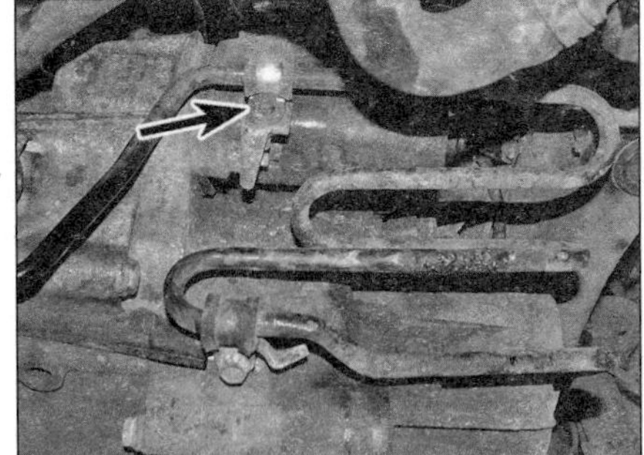
8.5a Undo the cooler retaining bolt (arrowed)

8.5b Remove the mounting bracket

4 Undo the retaining nut and withdraw the cable guide from the upper starter motor bolt, and move it to one side **(see illustration)**.

5 Where fitted, undo the retaining bolt and move the power steering cooler pipe away from the front of the transmission. Then undo the nut and withdraw the mounting bracket from the lower starter motor bolt **(see illustrations)**.

6 Remove the upper and lower starter motor-to-bellhousing bolts, then guide the starter/solenoid assembly out of the bellhousing aperture, and out from the engine compartment **(see illustrations)**.

Refitting

7 Refit the starter motor by following the removal procedure in reverse. Tighten the mounting bolts to the specified torque.

9 Starter motor – testing and overhaul

1 If the starter motor is thought to be defective, it should be removed from the vehicle and taken to an auto-electrician for assessment. In the majority of cases, new starter motor brushes can be fitted at a reasonable cost. However, check the cost of repairs first as it may prove more economical to purchase a new or exchange motor.

8.6a Remove the starter upper bolt (arrowed)...

8.6b ... the lower starter bolt...

8.6c ...and remove the starter motor

Notes

Chapter 5 Part B
Ignition system

Contents

Degrees of difficulty

Easy, suitable for novice with little experience 

Fairly easy, suitable for beginner with some experience

Fairly difficult, suitable for competent DIY mechanic

Difficult, suitable for experienced DIY mechanic

Very difficult, suitable for expert DIY or professional 

Specifications

System type*

1.8 litre engines	Bosch Motronic ME7.5

** Refer to Chapter 2A for engine code listings.*

Ignition coil

Type	One coil per spark plug

Spark plugs

See Chapter 1, Section 1

Torque wrench settings

Torque wrench settings	Nm	lbf ft
Knock sensor mounting bolt	20	15
Spark plugs	30	22

1 General Information

1 The Bosch Motronic systems are self-contained engine management systems, which control both the fuel injection and ignition. This Chapter deals with the ignition system components only – refer to Chapter 4A for details of the fuel system components.

2 The ignition system fitted to all models is of the increasingly popular 'distributorless' (DIS – Distributorless Ignition System) or 'static' type (there are no moving parts). Despite the many different system names and designations, as far as the ignition system fitted to the 1.8 litre engine, these have four separate coils, one fitted to each spark plug. Therefore, these systems have no distributor cap, rotor arm, or even HT leads, resulting in a simpler, more reliable system requiring even less maintenance.

3 Because there is no distributor to adjust, the ignition timing cannot be adjusted by conventional means, and the advance and retard functions are carried out by the Electronic Control Unit (ECU).

4 The ignition system comprises of the spark plugs, four separate coils and the ECU together with its associated sensors and wiring.

5 The ECU supplies a voltage to the input stage of the ignition coils, which causes the primary windings in the coils to be energised. The supply voltage is periodically interrupted by the ECU and this results in the collapse of primary magnetic field, which then induces a much larger voltage in the secondary coil, called the HT voltage. This voltage is directed to the spark plug in the cylinder currently on its ignition stroke. The spark plug electrodes form a gap small enough for the HT voltage to arc across, and the resulting spark ignites the fuel/air mixture in the cylinder. The timing of this sequence of events is critical, and is regulated solely by the ECU.

6 The ECU calculates and controls the ignition timing primarily according to engine speed, crankshaft position, camshaft position, and inlet air flow rate information, received from sensors mounted on and around the engine. Other parameters that affect ignition timing are throttle position and rate of opening, inlet air temperature, coolant temperature and engine knock, monitored via sensors mounted on the engine. Note that most of these sensors have a dual role, in that the information they provide is equally useful in determining the fuelling requirements as in deciding the optimum ignition or firing point – therefore, removal of some of the sensors mentioned below is described in Chapter 4A.

7 The ECU computes engine speed and crankshaft position from toothed impulse rotor attached to the engine flywheel, with an engine speed sensor whose inductive head runs just above rotor. As the crankshaft (and flywheel) rotate, the rotor 'teeth' pass the engine speed sensor, which transmits a pulse to the ECU every time a tooth passes it. At the top dead centre (TDC) position, there is one missing tooth in the rotor periphery, which results in a longer pause between signals from the sensor. The ECU recognises the absence of a pulse from the engine speed sensor at this point, and uses it to establish the TDC position for No 1 piston. The time interval between pulses, and the location of the missing pulse, allow the ECU to accurately determine the position of the crankshaft and its speed. The camshaft position sensor enhances this information by detecting whether a particular piston is on an inlet or an exhaust cycle.

8 Information on engine load is supplied to the ECU via the air mass meter (or via the inlet manifold pressure sensor, as applicable), and from the throttle position sensor. The engine load is determined by computation based on the quantity of air being drawn into the engine. Further engine load information is sent to the ECU from the knock sensor(s). These sensors are sensitive to vibration, and detect the knocking which occurs when the engine starts to 'pink' (pre-ignite). If pre-ignition occurs, the ECU retards the ignition timing of the cylinder that is pre-igniting in steps until the pre-ignition ceases. The ECU then advances the ignition timing of that cylinder in steps until it is restored to normal, or until pre-ignition occurs again.

9 Sensors monitoring coolant temperature, throttle position, roadspeed, and (where applicable) automatic transmission gear position and air conditioning system operation, provide additional input signals to the ECU on vehicle operating conditions. From all this constantly-changing data, the ECU selects, and if necessary modifies, a particular ignition advance setting from a map of ignition characteristics stored in its memory.

10 The ECU also uses the ignition timing to finely adjust the engine idle speed, in response to signals from the power steering switch or air conditioning switch (to prevent stalling), or if the alternator output voltage falls too low.

11 In the event of a fault in the system due to loss of a signal from one of the sensors, the ECU reverts to an emergency ('limp-home') program. This will allow the car to be driven, although engine operation and performance will be limited. A warning light on the instrument panel will illuminate if the fault is likely to cause an increase in harmful exhaust emissions.

12 It should be noted that comprehensive fault diagnosis of all the engine management systems described in this Chapter is only possible with dedicated electronic test equipment. In the event of a sensor failing or other fault occurring, a fault code will be stored in the ECU's fault log, which can only be extracted from the ECU using a dedicated fault code reader. An Audi dealer will obviously have such a reader, but they are also available from other suppliers. It is unlikely to be cost-effective for the private owner to purchase a fault code reader, but a well-equipped local garage or auto-electrical specialist will have one. Once the fault has been identified, the removal/refitting sequences detailed in the following Sections will then allow the appropriate component(s) to be renewed as required.

Ignition coil(s)

13 Each spark plug has its own dedicated 'plug-top' HT coil which fits directly onto the spark plug (no HT leads are therefore needed). Unlike the 'wasted spark' system, on these models a spark is only generated at each plug once every engine cycle.

2 Ignition system – testing

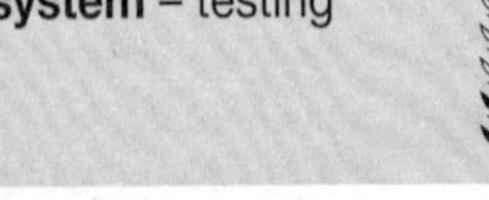

Warning: Extreme care must be taken when working on the system with the ignition switched on; it is possible to get a substantial electric shock from a vehicle's ignition system. Persons with cardiac pacemaker devices should keep well clear of the ignition circuits, components and test equipment. Always switch off the ignition before disconnecting or connecting any component and when using a multimeter to check resistances.

1 If a fault appears in the engine management (fuel injection/ignition) system which is thought to ignition related, first ensure that the fault is not due to a poor electrical connection or poor maintenance; i.e. check that the air cleaner filter element is clean, the spark plugs are in good condition and correctly gapped, that the engine breather hoses are clear and undamaged, referring to Chapter 1 for further information. Also check that the accelerator cable (where fitted) is correctly adjusted as described in Chapter 4A. If the engine is running very roughly, check the compression pressures as described in Chapter 2A.

2 If these checks fail to reveal the cause of the problem the vehicle should be taken to a suitably-equipped Audi dealer for testing. A diagnostic connector **(see illustration)** is incorporated in the engine management circuit into which a special electronic diagnostic tester can be plugged (see Chapter 4A). The tester will locate the fault quickly and simply, alleviating the need to test all the system components individually which is a time consuming operation that carries a high risk of damaging the ECU.

3 The only ignition system checks which can be carried out by the home mechanic are those described in Chapter 1, relating to the spark plugs. If necessary, the system wiring and wiring connectors can be checked as described in Chapter 12 ensuring that the ECU wiring connector(s) have first been disconnected.

3 Ignition coils – removal and refitting

Removal

1 Undo the securing screws and lift the plastic trim cover from the top of the engine, releasing it from the locating pegs at the rear.

All engine codes except AMU, APX and BAM

2 Undo the retaining nut and move

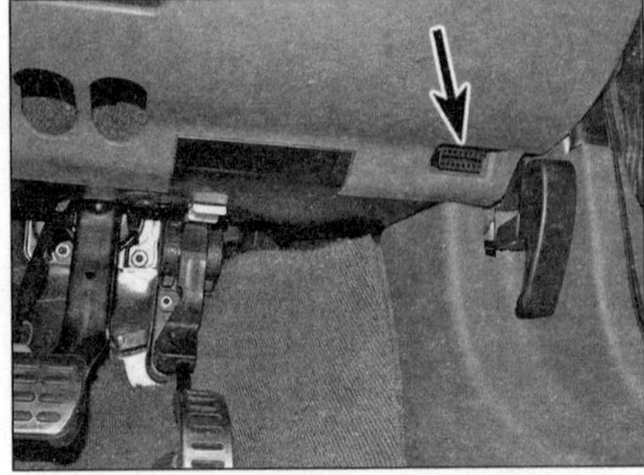

2.2 Location of diagnostic connector

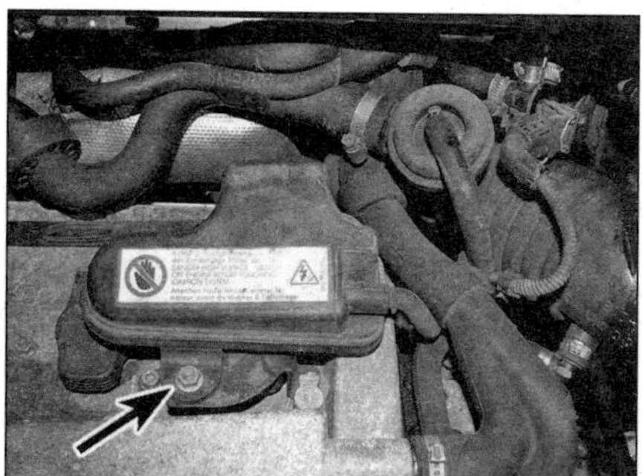
3.2 Undo the reservoir retaining nut (arrowed)

3.3 Unclip the heat protective covers (arrowed)

3.4a Disconnect the wiring connector...

3.4b...and unclip the valve from the mounting bracket

3.5 Remove the reservoir from the bracket

3.6 Remove the mounting bracket from over the coils

the vacuum reservoir to one side **(see illustration)**, then undo the retaining bolts and remove the mounting bracket.

Engine codes AMU, APX and BAM

3 Unclip and remove the heat protective covers from around the turbocharger divert valve and vacuum reservoir **(see illustration)**.

4 Disconnect the wiring connector from the turbocharger divert air valve, release the valve from the mounting bracket and then move it to one side **(see illustrations)**. Note you will need to unclip the hoses from the securing clips as it is moved to one side.

5 Undo the retaining nut and move the vacuum reservoir to one side **(see illustration)**.

6 Unbolt and remove the reservoir bracket from over number 3 and 4 coils **(see illustration)**.

All engine codes

7 Release the securing clips and disconnect the wiring connectors from the four ignition coils **(see illustration)**.

8 With all the wiring connectors disconnected pull the ignition coils straight upwards to release them from the top of the spark plugs **(see illustration)**.

Refitting

9 Refit the ignition coils back to the top of the spark plugs, making sure they are firmly pressed into position and the locating lug is aligned correctly **(see illustration)**. When in position, reconnect the wiring connectors to the ignition coils, making sure they secured by the retaining clip.

10 Refit the vacuum reservoir and mounting bracket using a reversal of the removal procedure.

11 On engine codes AMU, APX and BAM, refit the turbocharger divert air valve, using a reversal of the removal procedure.

12 When complete refit the engine plastic trim cover back to the top of the engine.

4 Ignition timing – checking and adjusting

1 The ignition timing is under the control of the engine management system ECU and is

3.7 Disconnect the wiring connectors

3.8 Remove the ignition coils from the spark plugs

3.9 Align locating lug arrowed

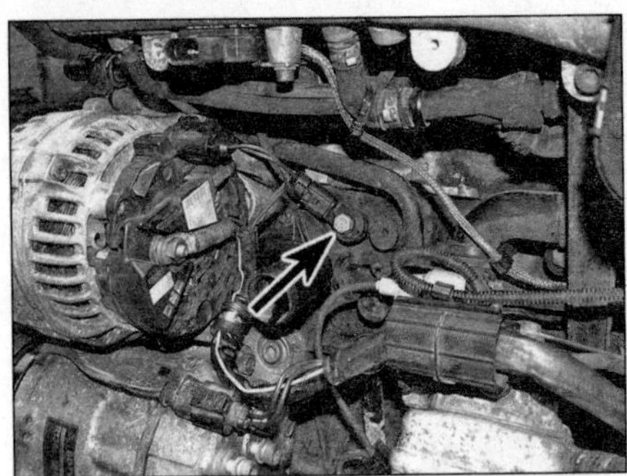
5.1 Location of knock sensor (arrowed)

5.3a Remove the plastic trim cover – all models except AMU, APX and BAM engine codes

5.3b Remove the plastic trim cover – AMU, APX and BAM engine codes

not manually adjustable without access to dedicated electronic test equipment. A basic setting cannot be quoted because the ignition timing is constantly being altered to control engine idle speed (see Section 1 for details).

2 The vehicle must be taken to an Audi dealer if the timing requires checking or adjustment.

5 Knock sensor – removal and refitting

Removal

1 The knock sensor is located on the front of the cylinder block, below the inlet manifold and to the rear of the alternator **(see illustration)**.

2 Disconnect the battery negative lead and position it away from the terminal. **Note:** *Before disconnecting the battery, refer to* Disconnecting the battery *in the reference section at the rear of this manual.*

3 Release the fasteners and remove the plastic trim panel from across the front of the inlet manifold **(see illustrations)**.

4 On models with engine codes AMU, APX and BAM disconnect the wiring connector from the exhaust gas temperature sender **(see illustration)**.

5 On models with secondary air injection, undo the retaining nuts from the two mounting brackets and disconnect the pipe from across the front of the intake manifold, and move it to one side **(see illustration)**.

6 Undo the two retaining bolts and remove the mounting bracket from the front of the intake manifold **(see illustration)**. As the mounting bracket is withdrawn, unclip the top of the dipstick tube from the bracket. As the mounting bracket is withdrawn, also disconnect the wiring connectors from the turbocharger air recirculation valve and secondary air inlet valve (where fitted), which may be bolted to the underside of the mounting bracket.

7 Disconnect the wiring connector from the sensor or trace the wiring back from the sensor and disconnect its wiring connector (as applicable). Unscrew the mounting bolt and remove the sensor from the cylinder block **(see illustration)**. Note the fitted position of the knock sensor for refitting.

Refitting

8 Refitting is the reverse of removal. Ensure the mating surfaces of the sensor and cylinder block are clean and dry. Refit the knock sensor in the same position as noted on removal, and ensure the mounting bolt is tightened to the specified torque to ensure correct operation.

5.4 Disconnect the wiring connector

5.5 Undo the two clamp securing nuts (arrowed)

5.6 Remove the mounting bracket

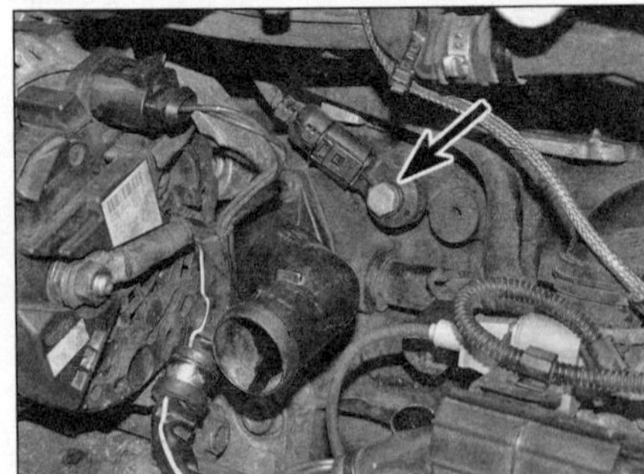
5.7 Knock sensor mounting bolt (arrowed)

Chapter 6
Clutch

Contents

Degrees of difficulty

Easy, suitable for novice with little experience 	**Fairly easy,** suitable for beginner with some experience	**Fairly difficult,** suitable for competent DIY mechanic	**Difficult,** suitable for experienced DIY mechanic	**Very difficult,** suitable for expert DIY or professional 

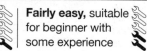

Specifications

General

Type	Single dry plate, diaphragm spring
Operation	Hydraulic with master and slave cylinders
Application:	
2-wheel drive	Transmission 02M and 02J
4-wheel drive	Transmission 02M and 02Y
Friction disc diameter:	
02J transmission	Diameter not stated
02M transmission	240 mm
02Y transmission	240 mm

Torque wrench settings	Nm	lbf ft
Clutch master cylinder mounting nuts*	25	18
Clutch pedal mounting bracket nuts*	25	18
Clutch pedal pivot nut*	25	18
Clutch pressure plate-to-flywheel bolts:		
02J transmission:		
Single-piece flywheel	20	15
Two-piece flywheel	13	10
02M and 02Y transmission	22	16
Clutch release bearing/slave cylinder mounting bolts:		
02M and 02Y transmission	12	9
Clutch slave cylinder mounting bolts:		
02J transmission	25	18

** Use new bolts/nuts*

2.2 Using pressure bleeding equipment

2.3a Bleed screw (arrowed)...

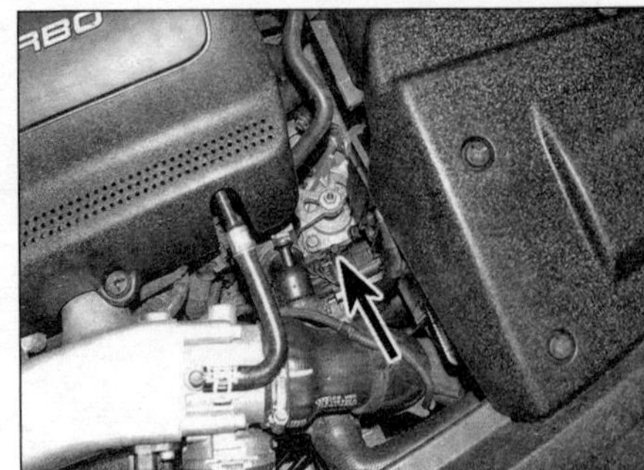
2.3b ...can be accessed with battery in place – 02M transmission shown

1 General Information

1 The clutch is of single dry plate type, incorporating a diaphragm spring pressure plate, and is hydraulically-operated.

2 The pressure plate is bolted to the rear face of the flywheel, and the friction disc is located between the pressure plate and the flywheel friction surface. The friction disc hub is splined to the transmission input shaft and is free to slide along the splines. Friction lining material is riveted to each side of the disc, and the disc hub incorporates cushioning springs to absorb transmission shocks and ensure a smooth take-up of drive.

3 On 02J transmissions, when the clutch pedal is depressed, the slave cylinder pushrod moves the release lever forwards. On 02M and 02Y transmissions, the slave cylinder is part of the release bearing and comes as a complete assembly **(see illustration 4.1a)**. The release bearing is forced onto the pressure plate diaphragm spring fingers. As the centre of the diaphragm spring is pushed in, the outer part of the spring moves out and releases the pressure plate from the friction disc. Drive then ceases to be transmitted to the transmission.

4 When the clutch pedal is released, the diaphragm spring forces the pressure plate into contact with the linings on the friction disc, and at the same time pushes the disc slightly forward along the input shaft splines into engagement with the flywheel. The friction disc is now firmly sandwiched between the pressure plate and flywheel. This causes drive to be taken up.

5 As the linings wear on the friction disc, the pressure plate rest position moves closer to the flywheel resulting in the 'rest' position of the diaphragm spring fingers being raised. The hydraulic system requires no adjustment since the quantity of hydraulic fluid in the circuit automatically compensates for wear every time the clutch pedal is operated.

2 Hydraulic system – bleeding

Warning: Hydraulic fluid is poisonous; thoroughly wash off spills from bare skin without delay. Seek immediate medical advice if any fluid is swallowed or gets into the eyes. Certain types of hydraulic fluid are inflammable and may ignite when brought into contact with hot components. Hydraulic fluid is also an effective paint stripper. If spillage occurs onto painted bodywork or fittings, it should be washed off immediately, using copious quantities of cold water. It is also hygroscopic (ie, it can absorb moisture from the air) which then renders it useless. Old fluid may have suffered contamination, and should never be re-used.

Note: *Suitable pressure-bleeding equipment will be required for this operation.*

1 If any part of the hydraulic system is dismantled, or if air has accidentally entered the system, the system will need to be bled. The presence of air is characterised by the pedal having a spongy feel and it results in difficulty in changing gear.

2 The design of the clutch hydraulic system does not allow bleeding to be carried out using the conventional method of pumping the clutch pedal. In order to remove all air present in the system, it is necessary to use pressure bleeding equipment **(see illustration)**. This is available from auto accessory shops at relatively low cost.

3 The pressure bleeding equipment should be connected to the brake/clutch hydraulic fluid reservoir in accordance with the manufacturer's instructions. The system is bled through the bleed screw of the clutch slave cylinder, which is located at the top of the transmission housing **(see illustrations)**. Access to the bleed screw can be achieved with the battery in place, but if required, remove the battery and battery tray, as described in Chapter 5A Section 3.

4 Bleed the system until the fluid being ejected is free from air bubbles. Close the bleed screw, then disconnect and remove the bleeding equipment.

5 Check the operation of the clutch to see that it is satisfactory. If air still remains in the system, repeat the bleeding operation.

6 Discard any fluid which is bled from the system, even if it looks clean. Hydraulic fluid absorbs water and its re-use can cause internal corrosion of the master and slave cylinders, leading to excessive wear and failure of the seals.

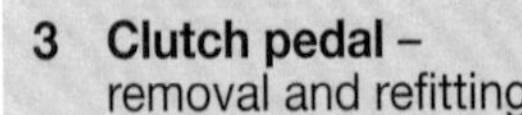

3 Clutch pedal – removal and refitting

Removal

1 Remove the driver's side lower facia trim panel, with reference to Chapter 11 Section 28.

2 Make up a tool similar to that shown, press it into position over the spring to hold the clutch pedal over-centre spring in the compressed position **(see illustration)**.

3 Fully depress the clutch pedal until the tool can be fitted to the over-centre spring **(see illustration)**, to retain it in the compressed position.

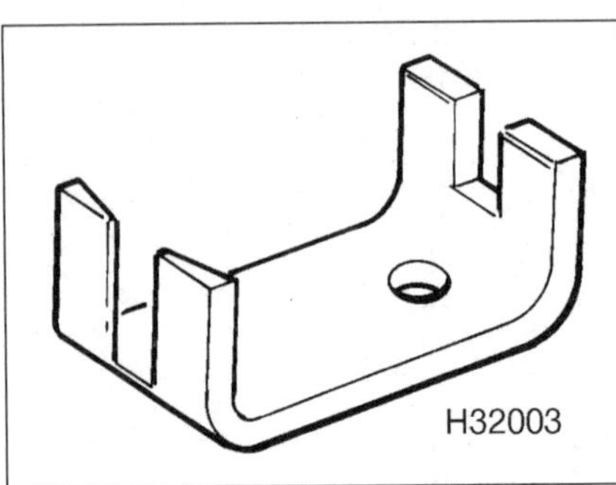

3.2 Over-centre spring retaining tool

3.3 Over-centre spring (arrowed)

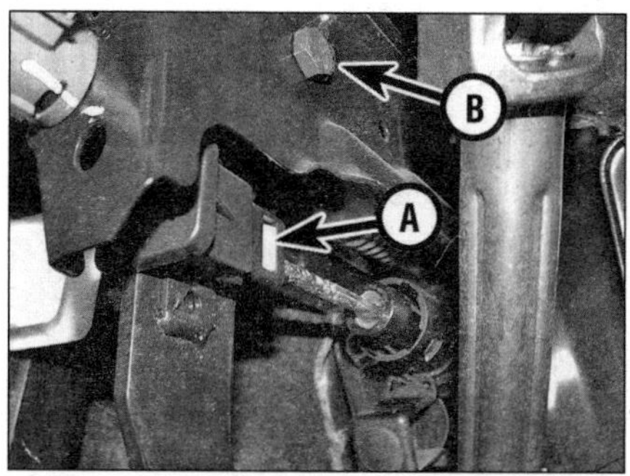

3.6 Pushrod retaining clip (A) and pedal pivot bolt (B)

4 Release the clutch pedal back to its normal position, and lift out the tool, complete with the over-centre spring.

5 Remove the clutch pedal switch from the top of the pedal mounting bracket, as described in Chapter 4A Section 3.

6 Squeeze together the tabs of the pushrod retaining clip, and separate the pedal from the pushrod **(see illustration)**.

7 Unscrew the nut and pull out the pedal pivot bolt at the top of the mounting bracket, until the pedal can be removed from the bracket assembly into the driver's footwell.

Refitting

8 Refitting is a reversal of removal, bearing in mind the following points:

a) *Before commencing refitting, make sure that the white plastic pedal retaining clip is fitted to the master cylinder pushrod.*
b) *Use a new pedal pivot bolt nut, and tighten the nut to the specified torque.*
c) *Make sure that the pedal-to-master cylinder pushrod retaining clip is fitted to the master cylinder pushrod before attempting to reconnect the pushrod to the pedal.*
d) *Push the pedal onto the pushrod to engage the retaining clip. Make sure that the clip is securely engaged.*
e) *On completion, check the brake/clutch fluid level, and top-up if necessary.*

4 Master cylinder – removal, overhaul and refitting

Note: *Refer to the warning at the beginning of Section 2 regarding the hazards of working with hydraulic fluid.*

Removal

1 The clutch master cylinder is located inside the car on the clutch and brake pedal mounting bracket. Hydraulic fluid for the unit is supplied from the brake master cylinder reservoir **(see illustrations)**.

2 Before proceeding, place cloth rags on the carpet inside the car to prevent damage from spilt hydraulic fluid.

1 Clutch master cylinder
2 Pushrod retaining clip
3 Clutch pedal
4 Self-locking nut
5 O-ring seals
6 Securing clips
7 Brake fluid resevoir
8 Fluid pipe retaining clip
9 T-piece connector
10 Clutch bleed valve
11 Dust cap
12 Slave cylinder connection

H45337

4.1a Clutch hydraulic system layout – 02M/02Y transmission

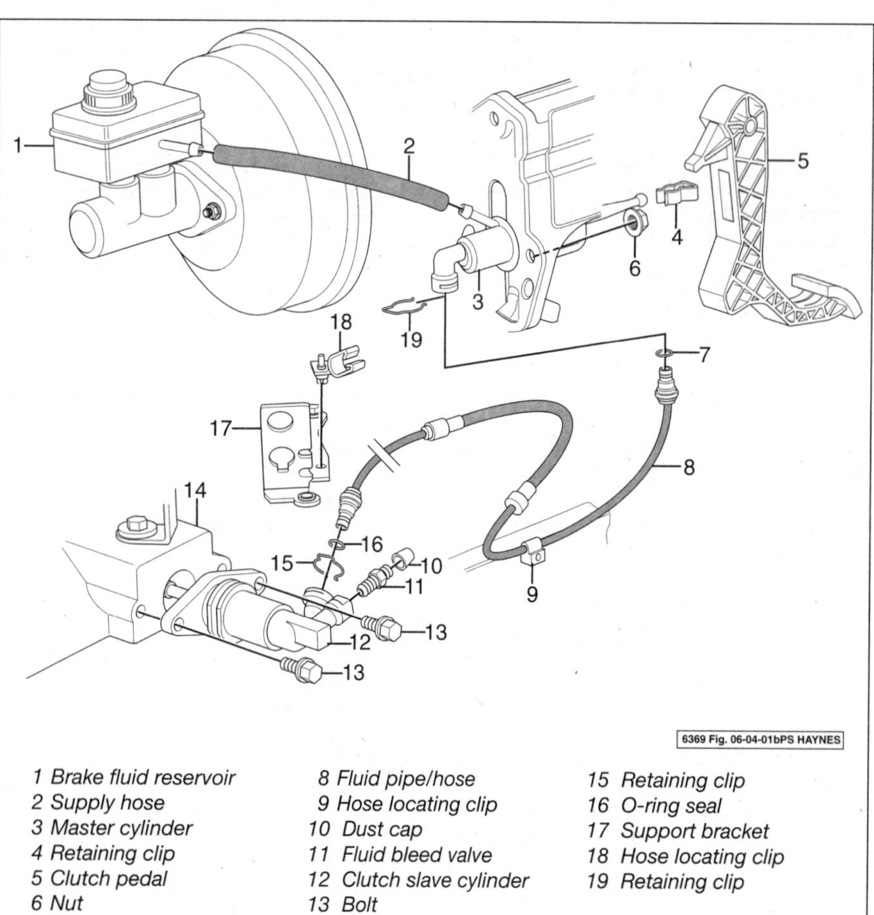

6369 Fig. 06-04-01bPS HAYNES

1 Brake fluid reservoir
2 Supply hose
3 Master cylinder
4 Retaining clip
5 Clutch pedal
6 Nut
7 O-ring seal
8 Fluid pipe/hose
9 Hose locating clip
10 Dust cap
11 Fluid bleed valve
12 Clutch slave cylinder
13 Bolt
14 Transmission
15 Retaining clip
16 O-ring seal
17 Support bracket
18 Hose locating clip
19 Retaining clip

4.1b Clutch hydraulic system layout – 02J transmission

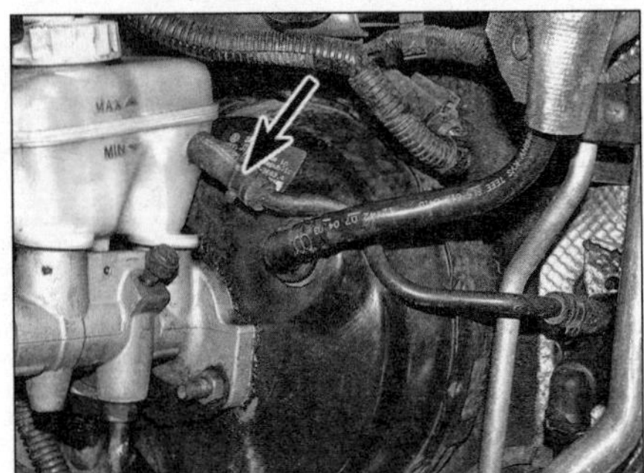
4.3 Hydraulic fluid hose (arrowed)

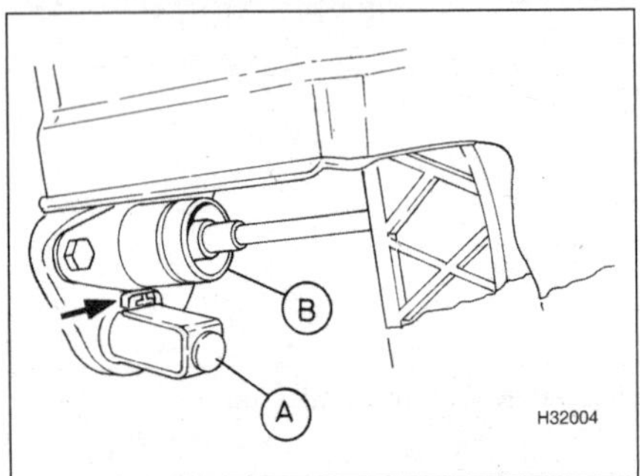

4.14 When refitting the pedal stop, ensure that the stop (A) is positioned with the lug (arrowed) nearest the master cylinder (B)

3 Working in the engine compartment, disconnect the clutch hydraulic fluid supply hose from the side of the brake fluid reservoir, plug the ends to prevent fluid loss **(see illustration)**.

4 Release the securing clip and pull the hydraulic supply hose from the clutch master cylinder on the bulkhead **(see illustration)**. Position a suitable container, or a wad of clean cloth, beneath the master cylinder to catch escaping hydraulic fluid.

5 Pull the fluid outlet hose retaining clip from the union on the master cylinder, then remove the pipe connection from the master cylinder. Again, be prepared for fluid spillage.

6 Remove the driver's side lower facia trim panel, with reference to Chapter 11 Section 28.

7 Where fitted, unscrew the securing bolts, and remove the plate connecting the clutch pedal mounting bracket to the brake pedal mounting bracket.

8 Unscrew the three nuts securing the clutch pedal mounting bracket to the bulkhead, then release the mounting bracket from the bulkhead **(see illustration)**.

9 The pedal must now be disconnected from the master cylinder pushrod by squeezing together the tabs of the retaining clip, and moving the pushrod away from the pedal **(see illustration 3.6)**.

10 Twist the clutch pedal stop anti-clockwise, and remove it from the bulkhead.

11 Push the master cylinder downwards until it covers the pedal stop mounting. Make sure that the upper end of the master cylinder flange is not covered by the pedal over-centre spring mounting.

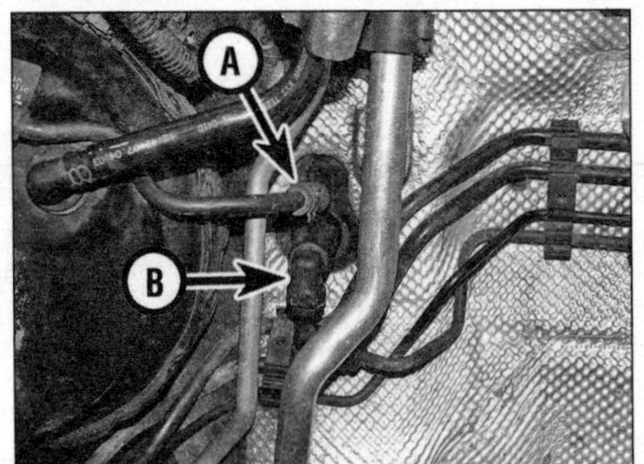

4.4 Fluid supply hose (A) and outlet hose to slave cylinder pipe (B)

12 Tilt the pushrod end of the master cylinder downwards, and manipulate the master cylinder out from the pedal mounting bracket. Lift the master cylinder out from the footwell, taking care to minimise fluid spillage.

Overhaul

13 No spare parts are available from Audi for the master cylinder. If the master cylinder is faulty or worn, the complete assembly must be renewed.

Refitting

14 Refitting is a reversal of removal, bearing in mind the following points:

a) *Ensure that the pedal-to-master cylinder pushrod retaining clip is fitted to the master cylinder pushrod before attempting to reconnect the pushrod to the pedal.*
b) *Push the pedal onto the pushrod to engage the retaining clip. Make sure that the clip is securely engaged.*
c) *When refitting the pedal stop, ensure that the stop is positioned with the lug nearest the master cylinder **(see illustration)**.*
d) *On completion, bleed the clutch hydraulic system as described in Section 2.*

5 Slave cylinder – removal, overhaul and refitting

Note: *Refer to the warning at the beginning of Section 2 regarding the hazards of working with hydraulic fluid.*

02J transmission

Removal

1 The slave cylinder is located on the top of the transmission casing **(see illustration)**. Access is gained from the engine compartment.

2 Remove the air cleaner assembly, as described in Chapter 4A Section 2.

3 Disconnect the gear selector cable from the gear selector lever, as described in Chapter 7A Section 2.

4 Place a wad of clean rag beneath the fluid line connection on the slave cylinder to catch escaping fluid.

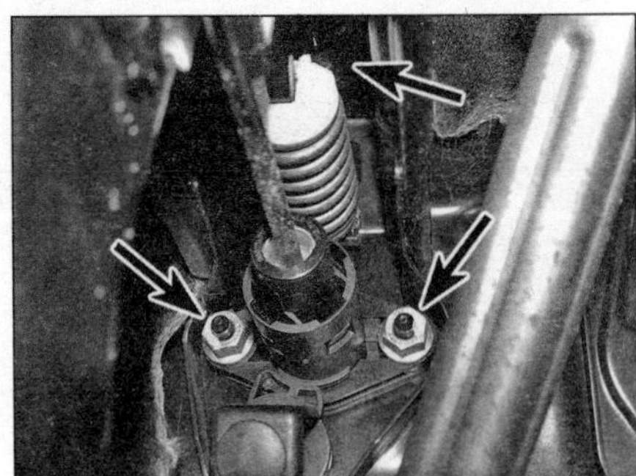
4.8 Undo the pedal bracket nuts (arrowed)

5 Pull the fluid pipe retaining clip from the union on the slave cylinder, then pull the pipe from the union. Release the fluid line from the bracket, and position it clear of the slave cylinder. Be prepared for fluid spillage.

6 Unscrew the two bolts securing the slave cylinder to the transmission casing, and withdraw the slave cylinder from the transmission.

Overhaul

7 No spare parts are available from Audi for the slave cylinder. If the slave cylinder is faulty or worn, the complete assembly must be renewed.

Refitting

8 Refitting is a reversal of removal, bearing in mind the following points:

a) *Tighten the slave cylinder securing bolts to the specified torque.*
b) *Reconnect the gear selector cable to the gear selector lever as described in Chapter 7A Section 2.*
c) *On completion, bleed the clutch hydraulic system as described in Section 2.*

02M and 02Y transmissions

Removal

9 The slave cylinder is part of the release bearing unit and is located inside the transmission bellhousing. For the removal and refitting procedure of the clutch release bearing/slave cylinder, see Section 7 in this Chapter.

5.1 Location of slave cylinder (arrowed)

6 Clutch friction disc and pressure plate – removal, inspection and refitting

Warning: Dust created by clutch wear and deposited on the clutch components may contain asbestos, which is a health hazard. DO NOT blow it out with compressed air or inhale any of it. DO NOT use petrol or petroleum-based solvents to clean off the dust. Brake system cleaner or methylated spirit should be used to flush the dust into a suitable receptacle. After the clutch components are wiped clean with clean rags, dispose of the contaminated rags and cleaner in a sealed container.

Note: *New clutch pressure plate securing bolts will be required on refitting. It is recommended that a friction disc centralising tool be used when refitting the clutch.*

Removal

1 Access to the clutch is obtained by removing the transmission as described in Chapter 7A Section 3.

2 Mark the clutch pressure plate and flywheel in relation to each other.

3 Hold the flywheel stationary, and then unscrew the clutch pressure plate bolts ¼ of a turn at a time, working clockwise **(see illustration)**. With the bolts unscrewed two or three turns, check that the pressure plate is not binding on the dowel pins. If necessary, use a screwdriver to release the pressure plate. On models with the Sachs clutch, as the bolts are removed the stop pin must slacken. If it doesn't, press the pin towards the flywheel **(see illustration)**.

4 Remove all the bolts, then lift the clutch pressure plate and friction disc from the flywheel.

Inspection

Note: *Due to the amount of work necessary to remove and refit clutch components, it is usually considered good practice to renew the clutch friction disc, pressure plate assembly and release bearing as a matched set, even if only one of these is actually worn enough to require renewal. It is also worth considering the renewal of the clutch components on a preventative basis if the engine and/or transmission have been removed for some other reason.*

5 Clean the pressure plate friction surface, clutch friction disc and flywheel. Do not inhale the dust, as it may contain asbestos which is dangerous to health.

6 Examine the fingers of the diaphragm spring for wear or scoring. If the depth of wear exceeds half the thickness of the fingers, a new pressure plate assembly must be fitted.

7 Examine the pressure plate for scoring, cracking, distortion and discoloration. Light scoring is acceptable, but if excessive, a new pressure plate assembly must be fitted. If the distortion of the friction surface exceeds 1.0 mm, renew it.

8 Examine the friction disc linings for wear and cracking, and for contamination with oil or grease. The linings are worn excessively if they are worn down to, or near, the rivets. Check the disc hub and splines for wear by temporarily fitting it on the transmission input shaft. Renew the friction disc as necessary.

9 Examine the flywheel friction surface for scoring, cracking and discoloration (caused by overheating). If excessive, it may be possible to have the flywheel machined by an engineering works, otherwise it should be renewed.

10 Ensure that all parts are clean, and free of oil or grease, before reassembling. Apply just a small amount of lithium-based grease to the splines of the friction disc hub. Do not use copper-based grease. Note that new pressure plates and clutch covers may be coated with protective grease. It is only permissible to clean the grease away from the friction disc lining contact area. Removal of the grease from other areas will shorten the service life of the clutch.

6.3a Undo the pressure plate retaining screws (arrowed)

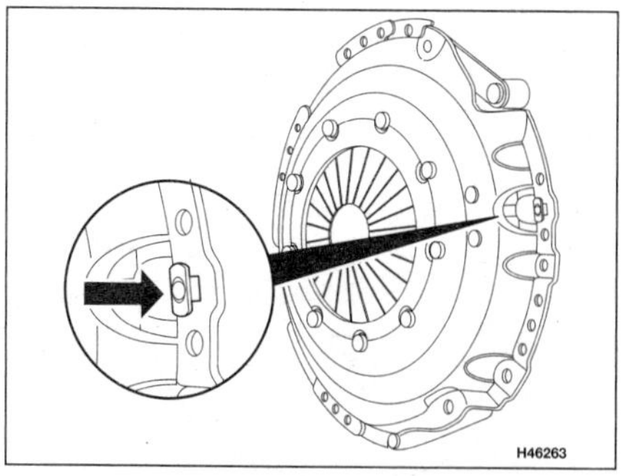

6.3b Ensure the stop pin is free to move

Refitting

11 Commence reassembly by locating the friction disc on the flywheel, with the raised side of the hub facing outwards (normally marked 'Getriebeseite' or 'Gearbox side'). If possible, the centralising tool (see paragraph 20) should be used to hold the disc on the flywheel at this stage **(see illustration)**.

6.11 The friction disc should be marked 'Getriebeseite' or 'Gearbox side'

Models with self-adjusting clutch (SAC)

12 On models with a Self-adjusting clutch (SAC), where a new friction disc is fitted, but the pressure plate is to be re-used, it is necessary to reset the pressure plate adjusting ring prior to assembly as follows.

13 Insert three 8 mm bolts into the pressure plate mounting holes at intervals of 120°. The bolts should be inserted from the flywheel side, and retained by nuts **(see illustration)**.

14 Place the pressure plate face down on the bed of an hydraulic press so that only the heads of the bolts make contact with the press bed, then place a circular spacer over the ends of the diaphragm springs fingers.

15 Use 2 screwdrivers to attempt to rotate the adjuster ring anti-clockwise. Apply just enough pressure with the hydraulic press until

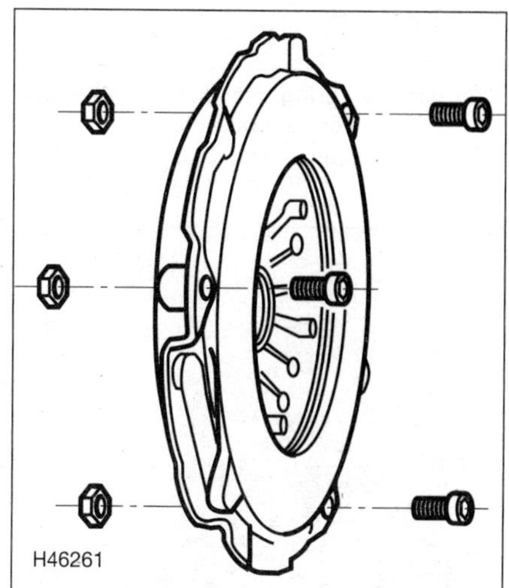

6.13 Insert three 8 mm bolts from the flywheel side, and secure with nuts

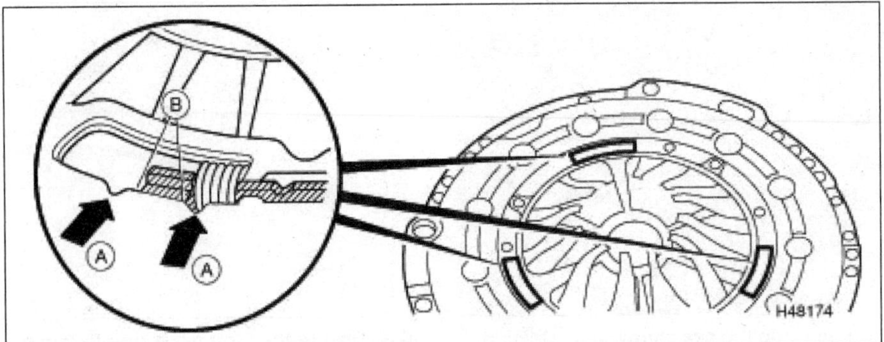

6.15 The edges of the adjuster ring (B) must be between the notches (A)

6.17 Fit the pressure plate over the locating dowel pins (arrowed)

6.20 With the pressure plate screws tightened, remove the centralising tool

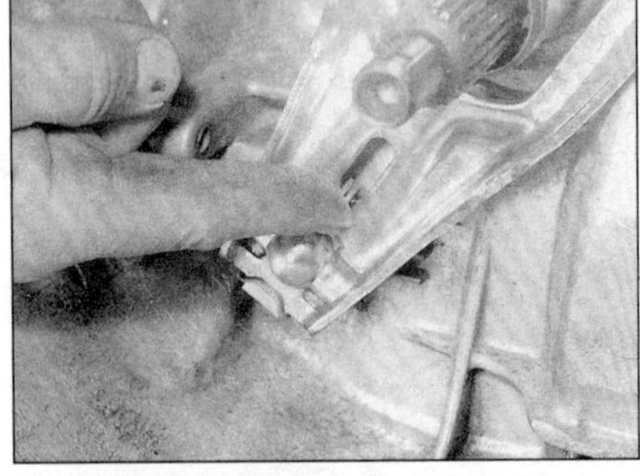

7.2 Push the spring clip to release the arm from the ball-stud

it's just possible to move the adjuster ring **(see illustration)**.

16 Once the adjuster ring edges are between the notches, relieve the pressure. The ring is now reset. **Note:** *New pressure plates are supplied in this reset position.*

All models

17 Locate the clutch pressure plate on the disc, and fit it onto the location dowels **(see illustration)**. If refitting the original pressure plate, make sure that the previously-made marks are aligned.

18 Insert the bolts finger-tight to hold the pressure plate in position.

19 The friction disc must now be centralised, to ensure correct alignment of the transmission input shaft with the disc centre. To do this, a proprietary tool may be used, or alternatively, use a wooden mandrel made to fit inside the friction disc and the hole in the centre of the crankshaft. Insert the tool through the friction disc into the crankshaft, and make sure that it is central.

20 Hold the flywheel stationary, and then tighten the clutch pressure plate bolts ¼ of a turn at a time, working clockwise. Tighten the pressure plate bolts progressively, until the specified torque setting is achieved, then remove the centralising tool **(see illustration)**.

21 Check the release bearing in the transmission bellhousing for smooth operation, and if necessary renew it with reference to Section 7.

22 Refit the transmission with reference to Chapter 7A Section 3.

7 Release bearing and lever – removal, inspection and refitting

02J transmission

Removal

1 Remove the transmission as described in Chapter 7A Section 3.

2 Using a screwdriver, prise the release lever from the ball-stud on the transmission housing. If this proves difficult, push the retaining spring from the release lever first **(see illustration)**. Where applicable, remove the plastic pad from the stud.

3 Slide the release bearing, together with the lever, from the guide sleeve, and withdraw it over the transmission input shaft.

4 Separate the release bearing from the lever **(see illustrations)**.

5 If the guide sleeve is worn excessively, or there is oil around the outer part of the sleeve, unbolt it and remove the O-ring seal **(see illustration)**. Renew as required.

7.4a Use a screwdriver to depress the retaining tags ...

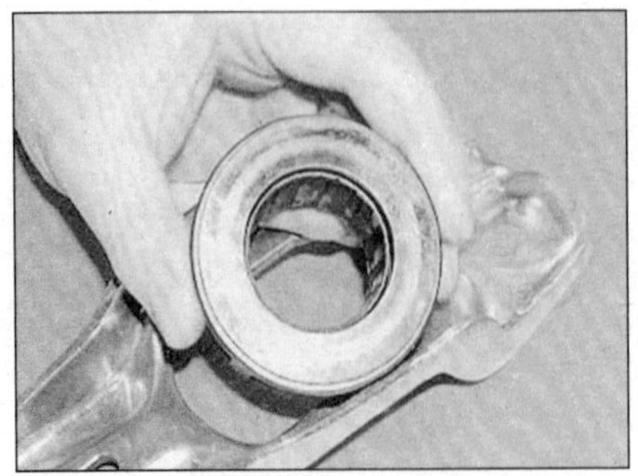

7.4b ... then remove the release bearing from the arm

7.5 Guide sleeve (arrowed)

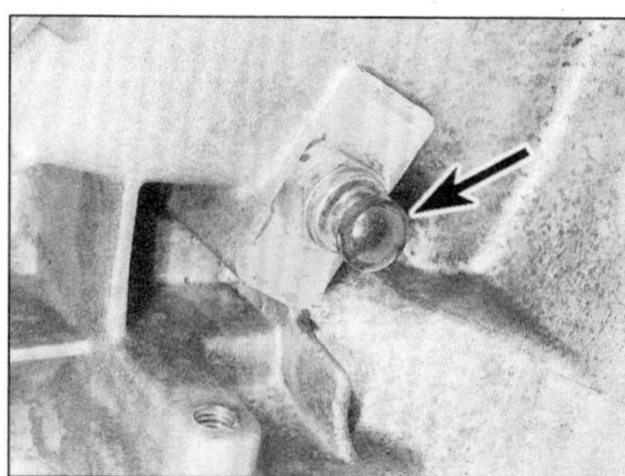
7.9 Lubricate the ball-stud (arrowed) with a little grease

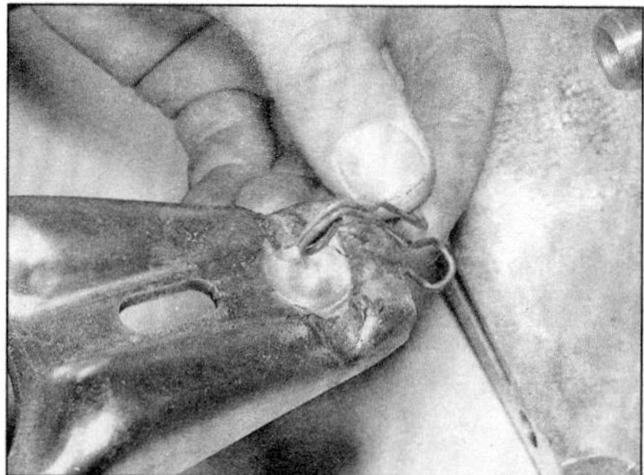
7.11a Locate the spring over the end of the release lever ...

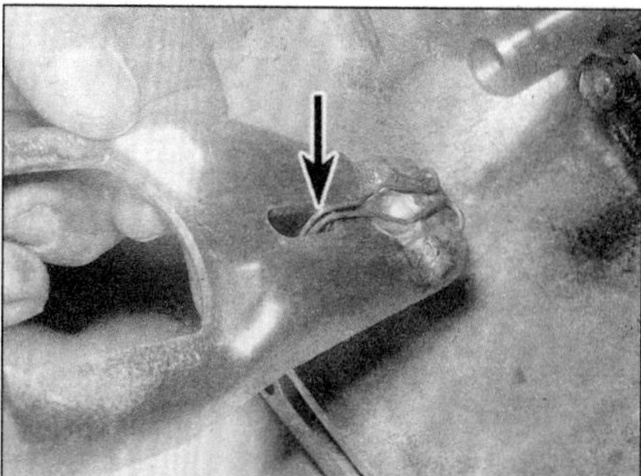
7.11b ... and press the spring into the hole ...

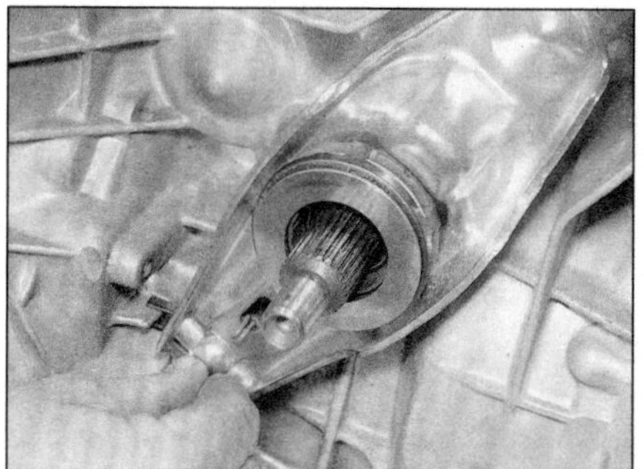
7.11c ... then press the release lever onto the ball-stud until the spring clip holds it in position

7.14 Fluid bleeder securing clip (arrowed)

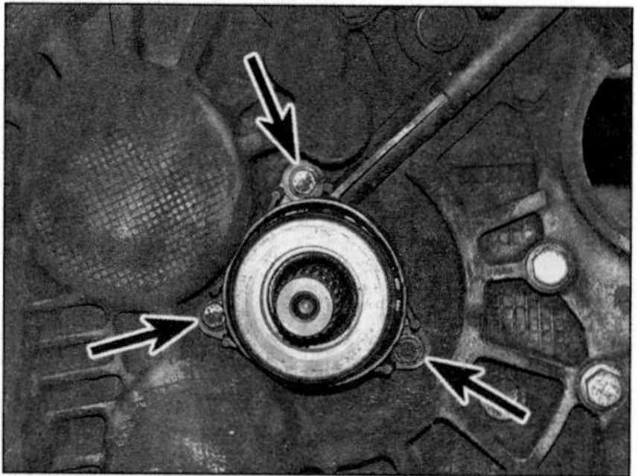
7.15 Slave cylinder/release bearing bolts (arrowed)

Inspection

6 Spin the release bearing by hand, and check it for smooth running. Any tendency to seize or run rough will necessitate renewal of the bearing. If the bearing is to be re-used, wipe it clean with a dry cloth; the bearing should not be washed in a liquid solvent, as this will remove the internal grease.

7 Clean the release lever, ball-stud and guide sleeve.

Refitting

8 If the guide sleeve was removed, locate a new O-ring seal over the input shaft, then fit the guide sleeve and tighten the bolts to the specified torque.

9 Lubricate the ball-stud in the transmission bellhousing with molybdenum sulphide-based grease **(see illustration)**. Also smear a little grease on the release bearing surface which contacts the diaphragm spring fingers in the clutch cover.

10 Push the release bearing into position on the release lever.

11 Fit the retaining spring onto the release lever, then press the release lever onto the ball-stud until the retaining spring holds it in position **(see illustrations)**.

12 Refit the transmission as described in Chapter 7A Section 3.

02M and 02Y transmission

Note: *The release bearing and slave cylinder are one unit which cannot be renewed separately.*

Removal

13 Remove the transmission as described in Chapter 7A Section 3.

14 Release the retaining clip and pull the fluid bleeder connection from the outside of the transmission casing **(see illustration)**.

15 Undo the three retaining bolts from the release bearing/slave cylinder unit, from inside the bell housing **(see illustration)**.

16 Withdraw the release bearing/slave cylinder unit from the transmission housing, and remove it over the input shaft **(see illustration)**.

17 Remove the O-ring and input shaft seal and discard, new ones will be required for refitting.

Inspection

18 Spin the release bearing by hand, and check it for smooth running. Any tendency to seize or run rough will necessitate renewal of the bearing. If the bearing is to be re-used, wipe it clean with a dry cloth; the bearing should not be washed in a liquid solvent, as this will remove the internal grease.

19 Check for fluid leaks around the slave cylinder and hose connection.

Refitting

20 Lubricate slave cylinder hose connection O-ring with some clean brake fluid for refitting.

21 Press the new input shaft seal into position, making sure it sits squarely in the housing.

22 Refit the release bearing/slave cylinder and tighten the retaining bolts to the specified torque setting.

23 Refit the transmission as described in Chapter 7A Section 3.

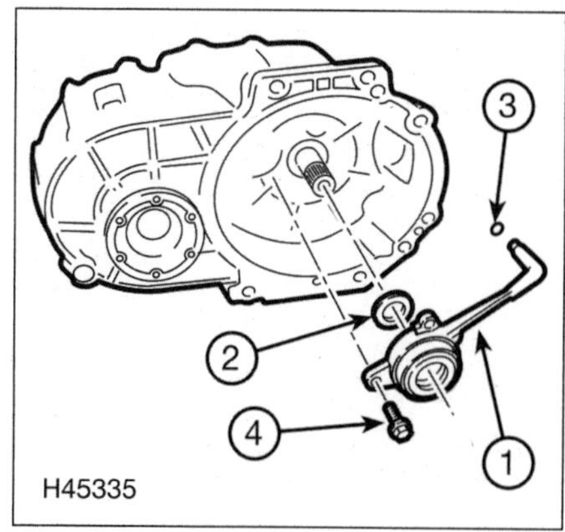

7.16 Release bearing/slave cylinder unit – 02M/02Y transmissions

1 Release bearing/slave cylinder unit
2 Input shaft seal
3 O-ring seal
4 Bolt

Chapter 7 Part A
Manual transmission

Contents

Degrees of difficulty

Easy, suitable for novice with little experience 

Fairly easy, suitable for beginner with some experience

Fairly difficult, suitable for competent DIY mechanic

Difficult, suitable for experienced DIY mechanic

Very difficult, suitable for expert DIY or professional 

Specifications

General

Type	Transversely-mounted, two-wheel-drive or four-wheel-drive layout with integral transaxle differential/final drive. 5 or 6 forward speeds, 1 reverse.
Application:	
2-wheel drive models	Transmissions 02J or 02M
4-wheel drive models	Transmissions 02M or 02Y

Torque wrench settings

	Nm	lbf ft
Gearchange rod to selector rod (02K transmission)	20	15
Release bearing guide to transmission	20	15
Reversing light switch	20	15
Transmission to engine:		
M12 bolts	80	59
M10 bolts	40	30
M7 bolts	10	7

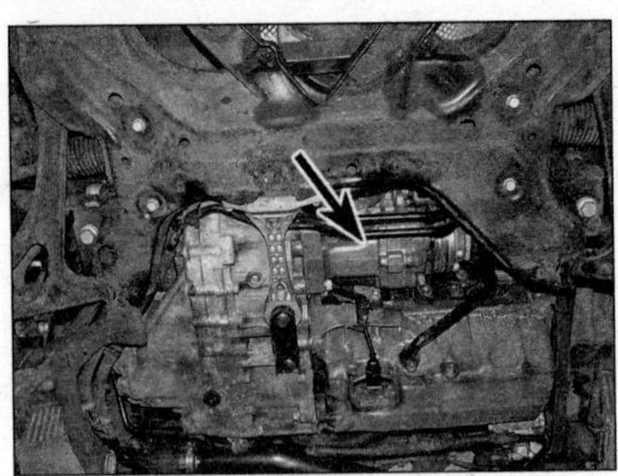

1.2 Location of transfer 'bevel' box (arrowed)

1 General Information

1 The manual transmission is bolted directly to the left-hand end of the engine. This layout has the advantage of providing the shortest possible drive path to the front wheels, as well as locating the transmission in the airflow through engine bay, optimising cooling. The unit is cased in aluminium alloy.

2 On four-wheel-drive models, it is the same layout as two-wheel-drive models, except there is a transfer 'bevel' box fitted at the rear of the engine **(see illustration)**. It is bolted to the transmission/differential casing where the right-hand side front driveshaft is fitted. This transfer 'bevel' box has a flange fitted to the rear, which takes the drive to the rear wheels, via the propeller shaft and final drive unit on the rear axle.

3 Drive from the crankshaft is transmitted via the clutch to the gearbox input shaft, which is splined to accept the clutch friction disc.

4 All forward gears are fitted with synchro-mesh. The floor-mounted gear lever is connected to the gearbox either by a selector rod, or selector and shift cables, depending on the transmission type **(see illustration)**. This in turn actuates selector forks inside the gearbox which are slotted onto the synchromesh sleeves. The sleeves, which are locked to the gearbox shafts but can slide axially by means of splined hubs, press baulk rings into contact with the respective gear/pinion. The coned surfaces between the baulk rings and the pinion/gear act as a friction clutch, that progressively matches the speed of the synchromesh sleeve (and hence the gearbox shaft) with that of the gear/pinion. This allows gear changes to be carried out smoothly.

5 Drive is transmitted to the differential crownwheel, which rotates the differential case and planetary gears, thus driving the sun gears and driveshafts. The rotation of the differential planetary gears on their shaft allows the inner roadwheel to rotate at a slower speed than the outer roadwheel during cornering.

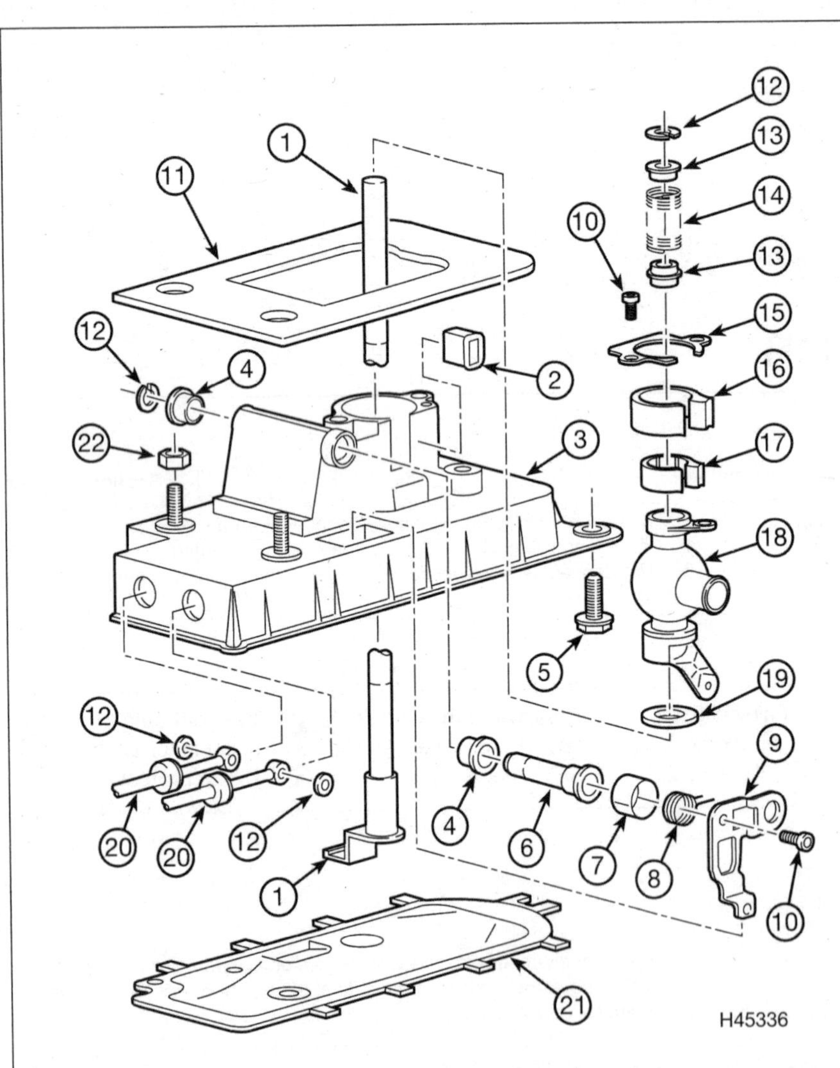

1.4 Gear linkage layout

1 Selector lever
2 Damper
3 Selector lever housing
4 Bush – bearing
5 Bolt
6 Fulcrum pin
7 Bush – guide
8 Spring
9 Selector lever gate
10 Retaining screw
11 Housing seal
12 Securing clip
13 Bush
14 Spring
15 Cover plate
16 Damper collar
17 Bearing
18 Selector lever ball/ guide
19 Damping washer
20 Gear selector cable
21 Baseplate
22 Securing nut

2 Gearchange linkage – adjustment

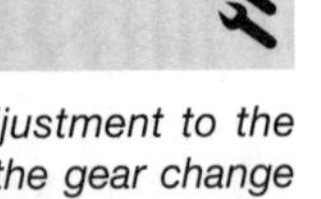

Note: *Before making any adjustment to the gear linkage, make sure that the gear change cables and gear mechanism is in good working condition.*

1 Remove the air cleaner assembly, as described in Chapter 4A, Section 2.

2 If required to make access easier, remove the battery and battery tray, as described in Chapter 5A Section 3.

3 With the gearchange set in the neutral position, push the two locking collars (one on each cable) forwards to compress the springs, turn them clockwise (looking from the driver's seat) to lock into position **(see illustration)**.

2.3 Push the collar down and lock in position

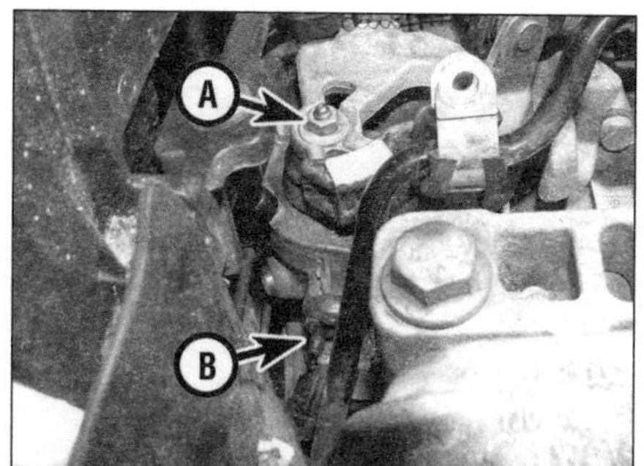

2.4a Press down on (A), then push in locking pin (B) – early models

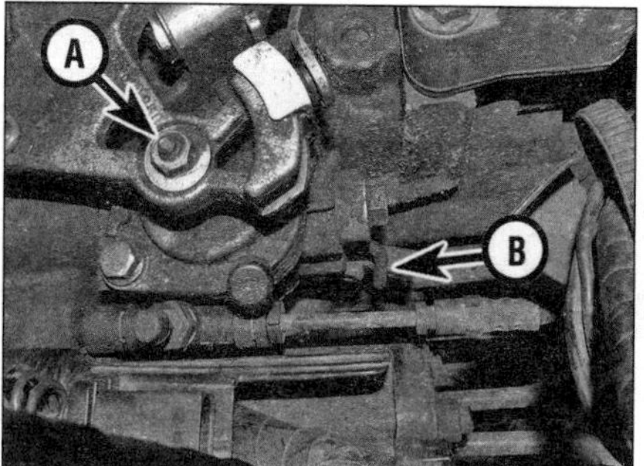

2.4b Press down on (A), then push in locking pin and turn (B) – later models

2.5 Locking the gear lever in position using a drill bit (arrowed)

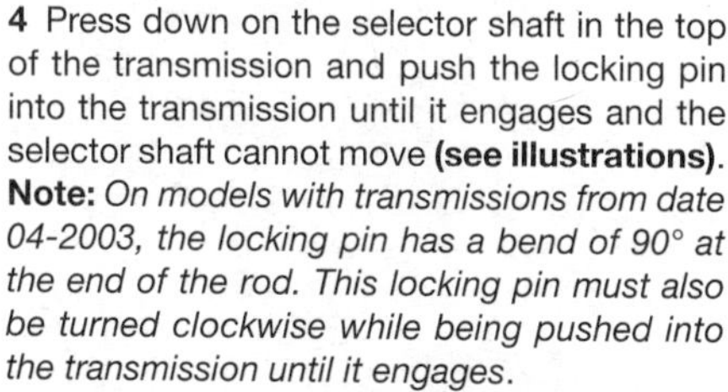

4 Press down on the selector shaft in the top of the transmission and push the locking pin into the transmission until it engages and the selector shaft cannot move **(see illustrations)**. **Note:** *On models with transmissions from date 04-2003, the locking pin has a bend of 90° at the end of the rod. This locking pin must also be turned clockwise while being pushed into the transmission until it engages.*

5 Working inside the vehicle, unscrew the gear lever, remove the bolts from round the outer ring and remove the gear lever gaiter from the centre console. Still in the neutral position, move the gear lever as far to the left as possible and insert the locking pin (or drill bit – take care of sharp edges if using drill bit) through the hole in the base of the gear lever and into the hole in the housing **(see illustration)**.

6 Working back in the engine bay, turn the two locking collars on the cables anti-clockwise so that the springs will release them back into position and lock the cables **(see illustration)**.

7 With the cable adjustment set, the locking pin can now be pulled back out of the transmission into its original position. **Note:** *On models with transmissions from date 04-2003, the locking pin must also be turned anti-clockwise while being pulled out, until it disengages.*

8 Inside the vehicle, remove the locking pin from the gear lever, then check the operation of the selector mechanism. When the gear lever is at rest in neutral, it should be central ready to select 3rd or 4th. The gear lever gaiter can now be refitted to the centre console.

9 Refit the air cleaner assembly with reference to the relevant Chapter 4A Section 2.

10 If removed, refit the battery and battery tray with reference to Chapter 5A Section 3.

3 Manual transmission – removal and refitting

Removal

1 Select a solid, level surface to park the vehicle upon. Give yourself enough space to move around it easily. Apply the handbrake and chock the rear wheels.

2 Raise the front of the vehicle and support it securely on axle stands (see *Jacking and vehicle support*). Where fitted, remove the engine/transmission undertray centre and left-hand sections. Position a suitable container beneath the transmission, then unscrew the drain plug and drain the transmission oil.

3 Release the fasteners, and remove the plastic trim covers from the top of the engine compartment, as required.

4 Remove the battery and battery tray, as described in Chapter 5A Section 3. **Note:** *Before disconnecting the battery, refer to* Disconnecting the battery *in the Reference section at the rear of this manual.*

5 Remove the air cleaner housing and intake hoses, as described in Chapter 4A Section 2.

2.6 Release the two locking collars (arrowed) back into position

6 Note the location of the gear selector cable ends and disconnect them, release the locking clips **(see illustrations)**, and disconnect the gear selector cables from the selector lever. On early models, there are no clips fitted, on these type carefully prise the end of the cable from the ball joint on the selector arm.

7 Unscrew the selector cable support bracket retaining bolts/nut **(see illustration)**, and lift the cables complete with bracket, clear of the transmission. Note the inner nut is fitted to the end of one of the bolts, in the outer edge of the bell housing, securing the transmission in position.

8 On 02J transmissions, undo the two retaining bolts and, with reference to Chapter 6 Section 5. Withdraw the clutch slave cylinder without disconnecting the hydraulic pipe, and move it to one side.

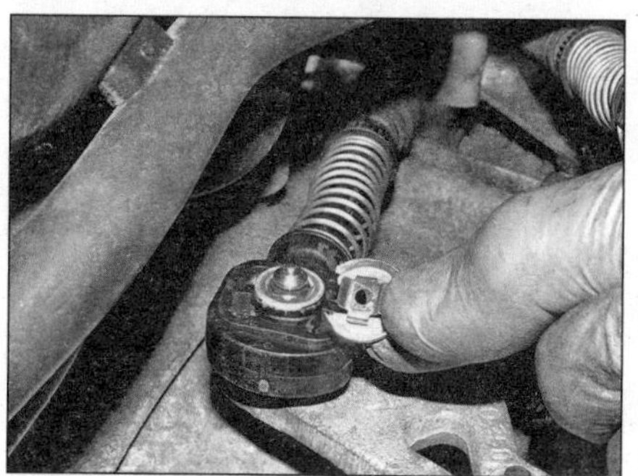

3.6a Remove the locking clips...

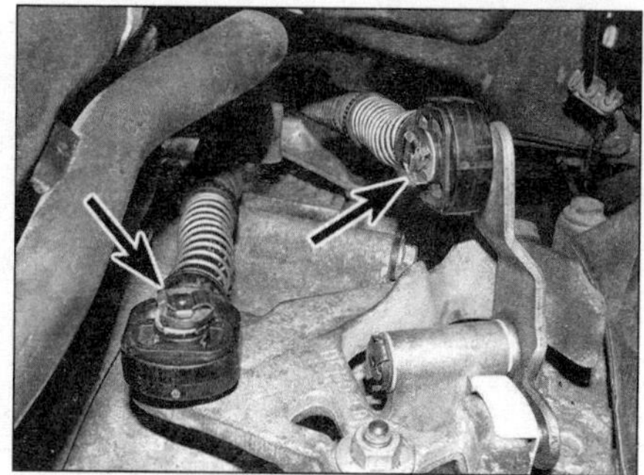

3.6b ...from the ends of the gear change cables (arrowed)

3.7 Support bracket retaining bolts/nut

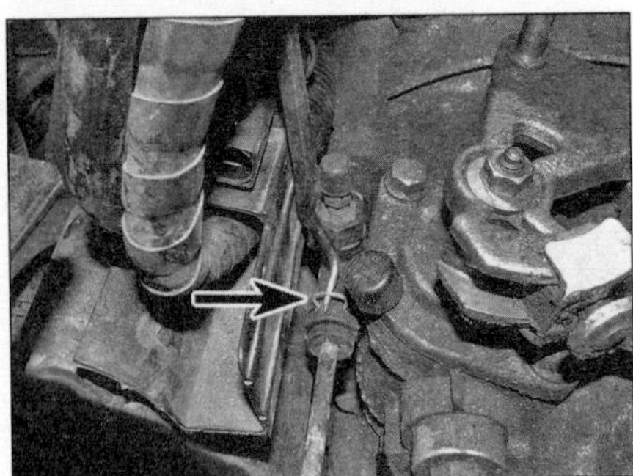
3.9 Release the locking clip (arrowed) – 02M and 02Y transmissions

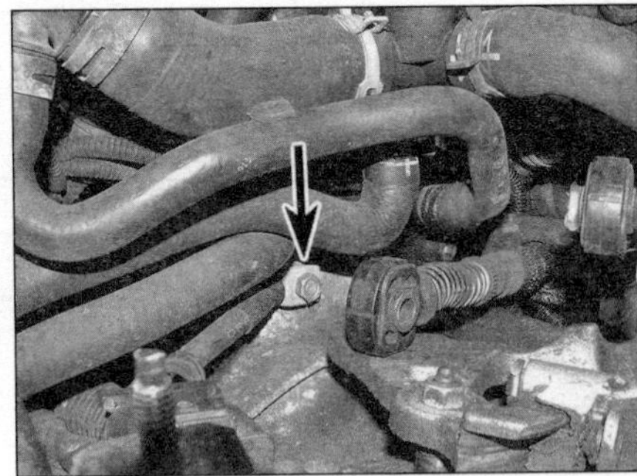
3.13a Undo the retraining nut (arrowed)...

3.13b ...and disconnect the earth cable

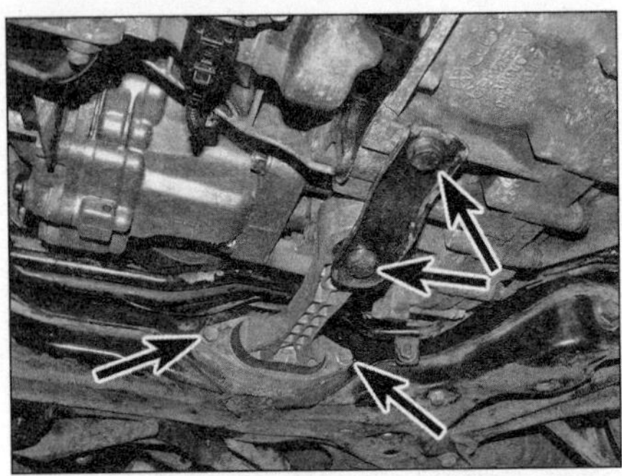
3.16 Lower mounting securing bolts (arrowed)

3.19a Hold the drive flange in position...

3.19b ...whilst removing the centre bolt...

9 On 02M and 02Y transmissions, release the locking clip and disconnect the clutch hydraulic hose from the bleed screw housing at the top of the bell housing **(see illustration)**. Plug the ends of the hydraulic hose when disconnected. Position some clean clean cloth, beneath the connection to catch escaping hydraulic fluid.

10 Disconnect the wiring connector from the reversing light switch, see Section 5, for further information.

11 Disconnect the wiring connector from the speedometer sender (Section 6), at the rear of the transmission/differential casing **(see illustration 6.5)**.

12 With reference to Chapter 5A Section 8, remove the starter motor.

13 Note the location of the earth cable on the transmission-to-engine mounting bolt **(see illustrations)**, then unscrew and remove the bolt.

14 Remove the both front driveshafts, as described in Chapter 8A Section 3. Note the driveshafts do not have to be disconnected from the wheel/hub side, and can be positioned to one side, away from the transmission.

15 Remove the charge air pipe from across the lower front part of the engine compartment, as described in Chapter 4B Section 7.

16 Unscrew the four retaining bolts, and remove the lower transmission support mounting bracket **(see illustration)**.

17 With reference to Chapter 4B Section 9, loosen the clamp securing the exhaust intermediate pipe to the rear section. This will allow the engine to be move forwards and backwards during the transmission removal and alignment procedures. Consequently, there is no need to separate the exhaust pipe sections.

18 On 4-wheel drive models, remove the transfer 'bevel' box, as described in Chapter 8B.

19 On 2-wheel drive models, it may be necessary to remove the right-hand driveshaft flange from the transmission**(see illustrations)**. This will make it easier for the removal of the transmission from around the edge of the flywheel.

20 Where applicable, remove the small plate covering the edge of the flywheel at the rear of the cylinder block **(see illustration)**.

3.19c ...then slide the flange from the transmission

3.20 Location of small plate (arrowed) – depending on model

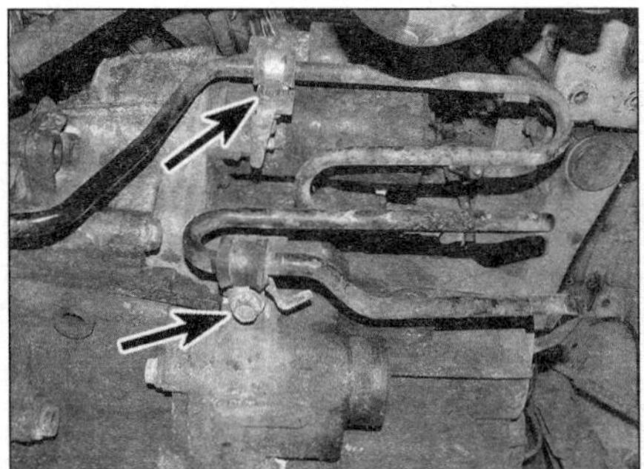
3.21a Undo the two front retaining bolts (arrowed)...

3.21b ...and the end bolt (arrowed)

21 Unbolt the power steering cooler pipe retaining brackets from the front and end of the transmission housing **(see illustrations)**. **Note:** *The upper mounting bracket is on the lower starter motor bolt, so may have been disconnected already.*

22 Using a suitable hoist, support the weight of the engine.

23 Unscrew and remove the upper transmission-to-engine mounting bolts, noting the two bolts that have a threaded section on the top to support the gear change bracket and earth cable **(see illustration)**.

24 Remove the left-hand mounting bracket from the transmission with reference to Chapter 2A Section 17. On models with 02J transmissions, unscrew the bolts retaining the left-hand transmission mounting support bracket, and the two transmission mounting bolts **(see illustration)**.

25 Lower the engine/transmission assembly slightly and, using a trolley jack, support the transmission. Position the jack so that it can be withdrawn from the left-hand side of the car.

26 Unscrew and remove the remaining lower transmission-to-engine mounting bolts.

27 With the aid of an assistant, carefully pull the transmission directly away from the engine, taking care not to allow its weight to rest on the clutch friction disc hub.

Warning: Support the transmission to ensure that it remains steady on the jack head. Keep the transmission level until the input shaft is fully withdrawn from the clutch friction disc.

28 When the transmission is clear of the locating dowels and clutch components, lower the transmission to the ground and withdraw from under the car.

Refitting

29 Refitting the transmission is essentially a reversal of the removal procedure, but note the following points:

a) *On models with 02J transmission, before refitting the gearbox, insert a M8x35 bolt into the hole above the slave cylinder aperture with the clutch release lever pressed towards the gearbox housing, to lock the lever in position. Remove the bolt once the gearbox has been fitted.*
b) *Apply a smear of high-melting-point grease to the clutch friction disc hub splines; take care to avoid contaminating the friction surfaces.*
c) *In order align the transmission with the flywheel, gently pull the engine forward as the transmission is manoeuvred into place.*
d) *Tighten the transmission-to-engine bolts to the specified torque.*
e) *Refer to Chapter 2A, and tighten the engine mounting bolts to the correct torque.*
f) *Refer to Chapter 8A, and tighten the driveshaft bolts to the specified torque.*
g) *On models with 02J, refer to Chapter 6 Section 5, and refit the slave cylinder.*
h) *On 4-wheel drive models, refit the transfer 'bevel' box as described in Chapter 8B.*
i) *On completion, refer to Section 2 and check the gearchange linkage/cable adjustment (where possible).*
j) *Refill the transmission with the correct grade and quantity of oil. Refer to 'Recommended lubricants and fluids' and Chapter 1.*

4 Manual transmission overhaul – general information

1 The overhaul of a manual transmission is a complex (and often expensive) task for the DIY home mechanic to undertake, which requires access to specialist equipment. It involves dismantling and reassembly of many small components, measuring clearances precisely and. if necessary, adjusting them by selecting shims and spacers. Internal transmission components are also often difficult to obtain and in many instances, extremely expensive. Because of this, if the transmission develops a fault or becomes noisy, the best course of action is to have the unit overhauled by a specialist repairer or to obtain an exchange reconditioned unit.

2 Nevertheless, it is not impossible for the more experienced mechanic to overhaul the transmission if the special tools are available and the job is carried out in a deliberate step-by-step manner, to ensure nothing is overlooked.

3 The tools necessary for an overhaul include internal and external circlip pliers, bearing pullers, a slide hammer, a set of pin punches,

3.23 Upper bolt with threaded top to support bracket

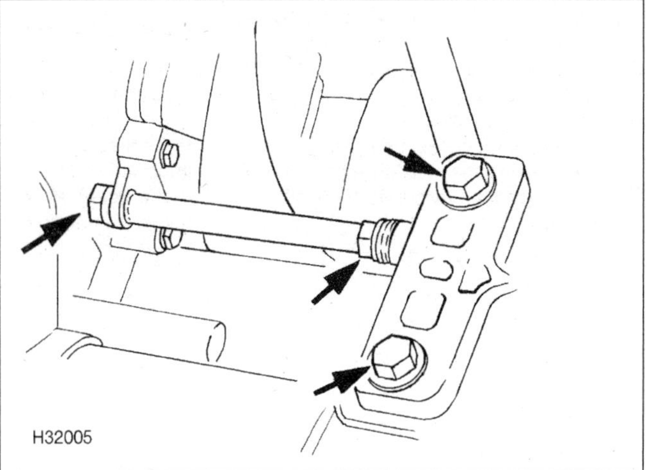

3.24 Remove the mounting and support bracket bolts (arrowed)

5.2a Reversing switch location (arrowed) – 02J transmission

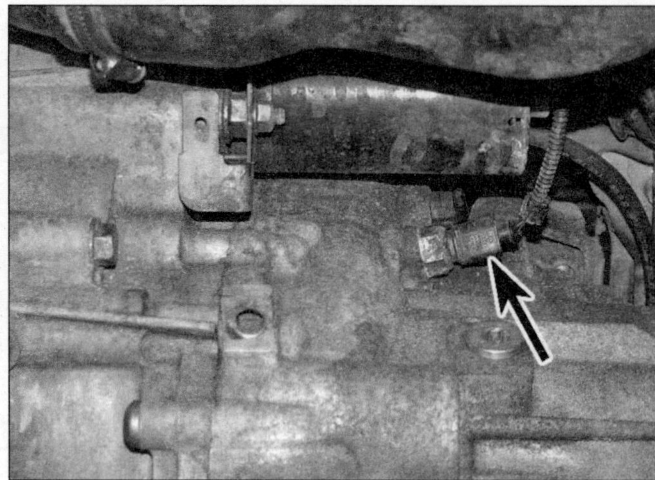

5.2b Reversing switch location (arrowed) – 02M/02Y transmissions

a dial test indicator and possibly a hydraulic press. In addition, a large, sturdy workbench and a vice will be required.

4 During dismantling of the transmission, make careful notes of how each component is fitted to make reassembly easier and accurate.

5 Before dismantling the transmission, it will help if you have some idea of where the problem lies. Certain problems can be closely related to specific areas in the transmission, which can make component examination and renewal easier. Refer to the Fault finding Section in this manual for more information.

5 Reversing light switch – testing, removal and refitting

Testing

1 Ensure that the ignition switch is turned to the OFF position.

2 Unplug the wiring harness from the reversing light switch at the connector. The switch is located on the top of the selector casing on 02J transmissions, and on the front of the transmission casing on 02M/02Y transmissions **(see illustrations)**.

3 Connect the probes of a continuity tester, or multimeter set to the resistance measurement function, across the terminals of the reversing light switch.

4 The switch contacts are normally open, so with any gear other than reverse selected, the tester/meter should indicate an open circuit or infinite resistance. When reverse gear is selected, the switch contacts should close, causing the tester/meter to indicate continuity or zero resistance.

5 If the switch does not operate correctly, it should be renewed.

Removal

6 Ensure that the ignition switch is turned to the OFF position.

7 Unplug the wiring harness from the reversing light switch at the connector.

8 Unscrew the switch from the transmission/ selector casing, and recover the sealing ring.

Refitting

9 Refitting is a reversal of removal.

6 Roadspeed sensor/ speedometer drive – removal and refitting

General information

1 All transmissions are fitted with an electronic speedometer transducer. This device measures the rotational speed of the transmission final drive and converts the information into an electronic signal, which is then sent to the speedometer module in the instrument panel. On certain models, the signal is also used as an input by the engine management system ECU.

Removal

2 Ensure that the ignition switch is turned to the OFF position.

3 Locate the speed transducer, at the rear of the transmission casing and unplug the wiring harness from the transducer at the connector.

4 On the 02J transmission, the road speed sensor is fitted directly on top of the drive pinion. If required, hold the housing with a spanner, then unscrew the transducer from the top of the differential housing and recover the washer.

5 On the 02M and 02Y transmissions, the transducer is in the rear of the transmission **(see illustration)**.

Refitting

6 Refitting is a reversal of removal.

6.5 Location of speed sensor

Chapter 7 Part B
Automatic transmission

Contents

Degrees of difficulty

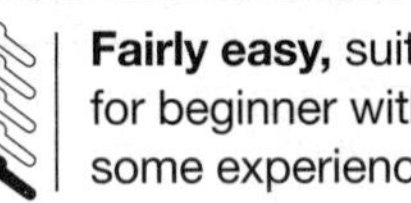

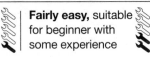

Easy, suitable for novice with little experience	**Fairly easy,** suitable for beginner with some experience	**Fairly difficult,** suitable for competent DIY mechanic	**Difficult,** suitable for experienced DIY mechanic	**Very difficult,** suitable for expert DIY or professional

Specifications

General

Description	Electro-hydraulically controlled planetary gearbox providing six forward speeds and one reverse speed. Drive transmitted through hydrokinetic torque converter. Lock-up clutch on all forward speeds, controlled by electronic control unit (ECU). Shift points controlled by the ECU using 'Fuzzy logic'
Transmission type	09G

Torque wrench settings	**Nm**	**lbf ft**
Multifunction switch:		
Outer spindle nut	13	10
Inner spindle nut	7	5
Mounting bolt	6	4
Selector cable locking bolt	8	6
Torque converter-to-driveplate nuts	60	44
Transmission bellhousing-to-engine bolts:		
M10 bolts	60	44
M12 bolts	80	59
Transmission bellhousing-to-engine sump M10 bolts	25	18
Transmission mounting spacer-to-casing bolts:		
Stage 1	40	30
Stage 2	Angle-tighten a further 90°	

1 General Information

1 The VAG type 09G automatic transmission has six forward speeds (and one reverse). The automatic gearchanges are electro-hydraulically controlled and the electronic control unit (ECU) has a 'self diagnosis' facility. The engine control unit gives information to the transmission control unit and exchanges signals with other control units. Some of the signals exchanged are engine speed, engine torque, throttle position, kickdown, ignition timing and cruise control. Any faults are stored in the memory and the transmission will remain in an emergency running mode. If a problem occurs, consult an Audi dealer or transmission specialist to test the electrical/electronic controls.

2 The ECU employs 'Fuzzy logic' to determine the gear up-shift and down-shift points. Instead of having predetermined points for up-shift and down-shift, the ECU takes into account several influencing factors before deciding to shift up or down. These factors include engine speed, driving 'resistance' (engine load), brake pedal position, throttle position, and the rate at which the throttle pedal position is changed. This results in an almost infinite number of shift points, which the ECU can tailor to match the driving style, be that sporty or economic. A kickdown facility is also provided, to enable a faster acceleration response when required.

3 The transmission consists of three main assemblies, these being the torque converter, which is directly coupled to the engine; the final drive unit, which incorporates the differential unit; and the planetary gearbox, with its multi-disc clutches and brake bands. The transmission is lubricated with automatic transmission fluid (ATF), and is regarded by the manufacturers as being 'filled for life', with no requirement for the fluid to be changed at regular intervals, although level checking procedures can be found in Chapter 1 Section 34.

4 The torque converter incorporates an automatic lock-up feature, which eliminates torque converter slip in 2nd, 3rd, 4th, 5th and 6th gears; this aids performance and economy.

5 The kickdown function of the transmission, which acts to select a lower gear (where possible) on full-throttle acceleration, is operated by the throttle pedal position sensor.

6 A starter inhibitor relay is fitted to prevent starter motor operation unless the transmission is in P or N. The relay is located above the main fuse/relay panel (see Chapter 11), and marked 175.

7 A fault diagnosis system is integrated into the control unit, but analysis can only be undertaken with specialised equipment. It is important that any transmission fault be identified and rectified at the earliest possible opportunity. An Audi dealer can 'interrogate' the ECU fault memory for stored fault codes, enabling him to pinpoint the fault quickly. Once the fault has been corrected and any fault codes have been cleared, normal transmission operation is restored.

8 Because of the need for special test equipment, the complexity of some of the parts, and the need for scrupulous cleanliness when servicing automatic transmissions, the work that the owner can do is limited. Most major repairs and overhaul operations should be left to an Audi dealer, who will be equipped with the necessary equipment for fault diagnosis and repair. The information in this Chapter is therefore limited to a description of the removal and refitting of the transmission as a complete unit. The removal, refitting and adjustment of the selector cable is also described.

9 In the event of a transmission problem occurring, consult an Audi dealer or transmission specialist before removing the transmission from the vehicle, since the majority of fault diagnosis is carried out with the transmission still fitted to the vehicle.

2 Automatic transmission – removal and refitting

Removal

1 The automatic transmission is removed downwards from the engine compartment. First, select a solid, level surface to park the vehicle upon. Give yourself enough space to move around it easily. Select P, apply the handbrake, and chock the rear wheels.

2 Loosen the front wheel bolts, and the left-hand driveshaft hub bolt, then raise the front of the vehicle and rest it securely on axle stands (see *Jacking and vehicle support*). Remove the front wheels. Allow a suitable working clearance underneath for the eventual withdrawal of the transmission.

3 Remove the battery and battery tray as described in Chapter 5A Section 3.

4 Remove the engine top cover/air cleaner and relevant air trunking. Remove the complete air filter housing and air inlet trunking with reference to Chapter 4A Section 2.

5 Using a screwdriver, lever off the end of the selector cable from the selector shaft lever, then squeeze together the clip and remove the outer cable from the support bracket. Position the cable to one side.

6 Clamp off the automatic transmission fluid cooler hoses with brake hose type clamps. Release the retaining clips and detach the hoses from the cooler (located on the top of the transmission).

7 Remove the starter motor as described in Chapter 5A Section 8.

8 Support the engine with a hoist or support bar located on the front wing inner channels. Depending on the engine, temporarily remove components as necessary to attach the hoist.

9 Remove the upper engine-to-transmission mounting bolts.

10 With reference to Chapter 8A Section 3, detach the right-hand driveshaft from the transmission, and remove the left-hand driveshaft completely. This procedure will involve detaching the front suspension lower arms from the hub carriers in order to pull out the driveshaft inner joints from the transmission. Tie the RH driveshaft to the underbody.

11 Note their locations, and then disconnect all wiring from the transmission.

12 Unbolt the engine rear mounting torque arm from the bottom of the transmission.

13 Unclip the blanking cap, located next to the right-hand transmission flange, and turn the engine to locate one of the torque converter-to-driveplate nuts. Unscrew and remove the nut whilst preventing the engine from turning by using a wide-bladed screwdriver engaged with the ring gear teeth on the driveplate visible through the starter aperture. Unscrew the remaining two nuts, turning the engine a third of a turn at a time to locate them.

14 With reference to the relevant part of Chapter 4B Section 9, separate the exhaust downpipe from the intermediate pipe.

15 Position a trolley jack underneath the transmission, and raise it to just take the weight of the unit.

16 Undo and remove the two bolts securing the left-hand gearbox mounting to the triangular mounting spacer. By controlling both the engine hoist/support bar and the trolley jack, lower the transmission approximately 60 mm. Unscrew the two remaining bolts and one nut, and remove the transmission mounting spacer.

17 Unscrew and remove the lower bolts securing the transmission bellhousing to the engine, noting the bolt locations, as they are of different sizes and lengths.

18 Check that all the fixings and attachments are clear of the transmission. Enlist the aid of an assistant to help in guiding and supporting the transmission during its removal.

19 The transmission is located on engine alignment dowels, and if stuck on them, it may be necessary to carefully tap and prise the transmission free of the dowels to allow separation. Once the transmission is disconnected from the location dowels, swivel the unit out and lower it out of the vehicle.

Warning: Support the transmission to ensure that it remains steady on the jack head. Ensure that the torque converter remains in position on its shaft in the torque converter housing.

20 With the transmission removed, bolt a suitable bar and spacer across the front face

of the torque converter housing, to retain the torque converter in position.

Refitting

21 Refitting is a reversal of the removal procedure, but note the following special points:

a) *When reconnecting the transmission to the engine, ensure that the location dowels are in position, and that the transmission is correctly aligned with them before pushing it fully into engagement with the engine. As the torque converter is refitted, ensure that the drive pins at the centre of the torque converter hub engage with the recesses in the automatic transmission fluid pump inner wheel.*

b) *Tighten all retaining bolts to their specified torque wrench settings.*

c) *Reconnect and adjust the selector cable, as described in Section 4.*

d) *On completion, check the transmission fluid level (see Chapter 1 Section 34).*

e) *If a new transmission unit has been fitted, it may be necessary to have the transmission ECU 'matched' to the engine management ECU electronically, to ensure correct operation – seek the advice of your Audi dealer.*

3 Automatic transmission overhaul – general information

1 In the event of a fault occurring, it will be necessary to establish whether the fault is electrical, mechanical or hydraulic in nature, before repair work can be contemplated. Diagnosis requires detailed knowledge of the transmission's operation and construction, as well as access to specialised test equipment, and so is deemed to be beyond the scope of this manual. It is therefore essential that problems with the automatic transmission be referred to an Audi dealer for assessment.

2 Note that a faulty transmission should not be removed before the vehicle has been assessed by a dealer, as fault diagnosis is carried out with the transmission still fitted to the vehicle.

4 Selector cable – removal, refitting and adjustment

Removal

1 Disconnect the battery negative lead and position It away from the terminal. **Note:** *Refer to* Disconnecting the battery *in the Reference section at the rear of this manual.*

2 Raise and support the vehicle at the front end on axle stands (see *Jacking and vehicle support*). Allow a suitable working clearance underneath the vehicle.

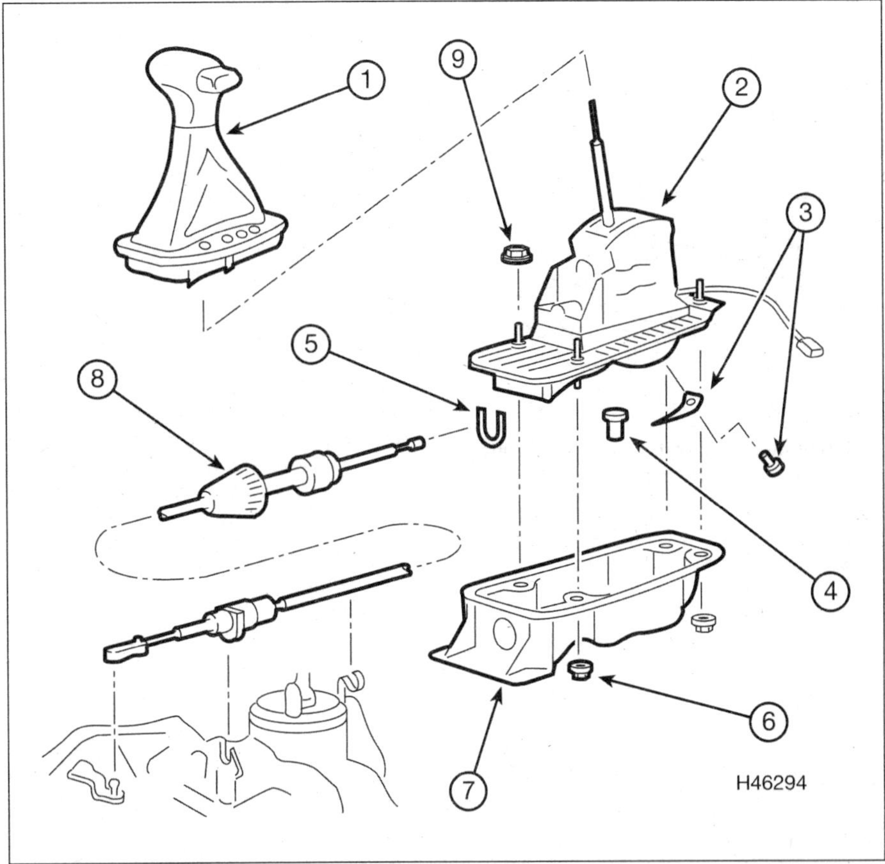

4.4 Selector lever components

1 Selector knob and gaiter
2 Selector lever and mechanism
3 Bolt and spring
4 Pin
5 Locking clip
6 Nut
7 Cover
8 Selector lever cable
9 Nut with washer

3 Move the selector lever to the S position.

4 Using a wide-bladed screwdriver, prise the end of the selector cable from the selector lever on the top of the transmission, then squeeze together the clip and detach the outer cable from the bracket **(see illustration)**. Position the cable to one side.

5 Separate the exhaust downpipe from the intermediate pipe with reference to Chapter 4B Section 9.

6 Remove the centre tunnel heat shield from the underside of the vehicle to gain access to the selector lever housing.

7 Undo the securing bolts and remove the cover from the selector lever housing.

8 Insert a screwdriver through the housing and push out the pin from the selector cable end fitting.

9 Remove the clip securing the outer cable to the selector lever housing, and withdraw the cable from the housing.

Refitting

10 Refit the selector cable by reversing the removal procedure, noting the following points:

a) *Do not grease the cable end fittings; this is stated by Audi.*

b) *Ensure that the cable is correctly routed, as noted on removal, and that it is securely held in position by its retaining clips.*

c) *Take care not to bend or kink the cable.*

d) *Carry out the cable adjustment procedure described below before reconnecting the cable at the transmission end.*

e) *When refitting the outer cable to the selector lever housing and the support bracket, use new clips.*

Adjustment

11 Inside the car, move the selector lever to the P position.

12 At the transmission, slacken the cable locking bolt at the ball socket. Check that both the selector lever inside the car and the lever on the transmission are in their P positions by gently rocking them backwards and forwards to settle the cable. Do not move either lever out of the P position.

13 Tighten the cable locking bolt to the specified torque.

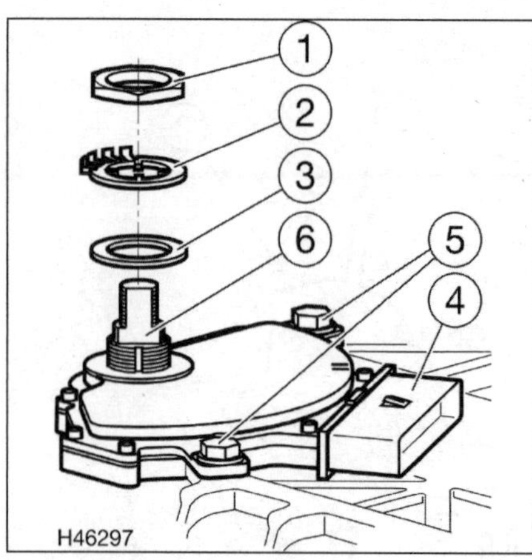

5.5 Multifunction switch spindle nut and washers

1 Nut
2 Lock washer
3 Plain washer
4 Multifunction switch
5 Mounting bolts
6 Spindle

14 Verify the operation of the selector lever by shifting through all gear positions and checking that every gear can be selected smoothly and without delay.

5 Multifunction switch – removal and refitting

Removal

1 The multifunction switch is located on the top of the transmission, and its purpose is to prevent inadvertent selection of certain forward and reverse gears while the vehicle is traveling forwards (for example, moving the selector lever into Reverse when moving forwards). First, switch off the ignition and move the selector lever to position N.

2 Using a wide-bladed screwdriver, prise the end of the selector cable from the selector lever on the transmission, then squeeze together the clip and detach the outer cable from the bracket.

3 Disconnect the wiring from the multifunction switch.

4 Unscrew the nut securing the lever to the switch spindle, and remove the lever.

5 Bend back the tabs of the lockwasher, and then unscrew the spindle nut **(see illustration)**.

6 Accurately mark the position of the switch in relation to the transmission housing.

7 Unscrew the mounting bolts, then pull the switch from the selector shaft together with the washers.

Refitting

8 Refitting is a reversal of removal, but tighten the spindle nut and switch mounting bolts to the specified torque. Note that Audi technicians use a setting gauge to adjust the multifunction switch accurately.

Chapter 8 Part A
Driveshafts

Contents

Degrees of difficulty

Easy, suitable for novice with little experience	**Fairly easy,** suitable for beginner with some experience 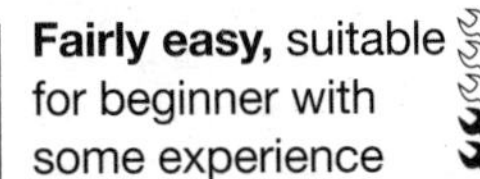	**Fairly difficult,** suitable for competent DIY mechanic	**Difficult,** suitable for experienced DIY mechanic	**Very difficult,** suitable for expert DIY or professional 

Specifications

Lubrication

Type of grease:	
CV joint (outer and inner joints)	VAG G 000 603 grease
Triple roller 'tripod' joint (inner joint)	VAG G 000 605 grease
Quantity of grease per joint:	
Outer CV joints:	
Joint diameter 88.0 and 90 mm	100 g
Joint diameter 98.0 mm	120 g
Inner CV joints:	
Joint diameter 100.0 and 108.0 mm	120 g
Inner triple roller (tripod) joint:	
Joint diameter 72.0 mm	110 g

Torque wrench settings	Nm	lbf ft
Driveshaft-to-transmission flange bolts:		
M8	40	30
M10	70	52
Hub bolt (without ribbing under head)*:		
Stage 1	240	177
Stage 2	Angle-tighten through 90°	
Stage 3	Slacken by one-half turn (90°)	
Stage 4	Raise vehicle and slacken a further 90°	
Stage 5	Tighten to 240 Nm	177
Stage 6	Lower vehicle to ground and angle-tighten through 90°	
Hub bolt (with ribbing under head)*:		
Stage 1	200	148
Stage 2	Angle-tighten through 180°	
Hub nut*:		
Stage 1	200	148
Stage 2	Slacken by one-half turn (180°)	
Stage 3	Rotate wheel one-half turn (180°)	
Stage 4	50	37
Stage 5	Angle-tighten through 60° (equivalent to 2 spaces on 12-point nut)	

**Use new nut/bolt*

1 General Information

1 Drive is transmitted from the differential to the wheels by means of steel driveshafts of either solid or hollow construction (depending on model, and which side of the vehicle). The driveshafts are splined at their outer ends, to accept the wheel hubs, and are secured to the hub by a large nut or bolt. The inner end of each driveshaft is bolted to the transmission drive flange.

2 The outer ends of each driveshaft are fitted with ball-bearing type constant velocity (CV) joints, to ensure the smooth and efficient transmission of drive at all the angles possible, as the roadwheels move up-and-down with the suspension, and as they turn from side to side under steering. The inner ends of each driveshaft are either fitted with ball and cage type constant velocity (CV) joint or a triple roller type (tripod) joint.

3 Rubber or Hytrel (thermoplastic elastomer) gaiters are fitted over the CV joints with steel clips. Hytrel gaiters combine the flexibility of rubber with the strength and durability of thermoplastics. The gaiters contain the grease that lubricates the joints, and also protect the joints from the entry of dirt and debris.

2 Driveshafts front – removal and refitting

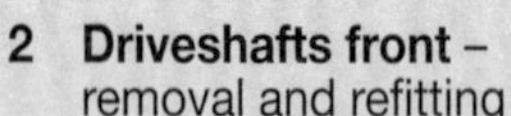

Note: *A new hub nut/bolt will be required on refitting. Where bolts are fitted, there are two different types fitted, one is ribbed* ***(see illustrations)*** *under the face of the bolt head and one is smooth. The torque setting is different for each type of bolt (see Specifications), so it is important to make sure you check which is fitted.*

Removal

1 Remove the wheel trim/centre cap (as applicable) then apply the handbrake, and partially unscrew the relevant nut/hub bolt with the vehicle resting on its wheels, by a maximum of 90° – note that the bolt is very tight, and a suitable extension bar will probably be required to aid unscrewing. Also slacken the road wheel securing bolts by half a turn. **Note:** *Do not loosen the bolt more than 90° with the vehicle standing on the ground, as the wheel bearings may be damaged.*

2 Apply the handbrake, then jack up the front of the vehicle and support it on axle stands (see *Jacking and vehicle support*). Remove the appropriate front roadwheel.

3 Remove the retaining screws and/or clips, and remove the undershields from beneath the engine/transmission unit to gain access to the driveshafts. On two wheel drive vehicles, also unbolt the heat shield from the rear of the cylinder block, to improve access to the driveshaft inner joint **(see illustration)**.

4 Unscrew and remove the hub nut/bolt **(see illustrations)**. **Note:** *Discard the nut/bolt and obtain a new one. Where bolts are fitted, there are two types fitted, see note at the beginning of this Section.*

5 Slacken the retaining nut, then disconnect the track rod end ball joint **(see illustration)**, refer to Chapter 10 Section 22, for further information. Discard the nut, as a new one must be used on refitting.

6 Slacken the retaining nut, then disconnect the lower ball joint from the hub **(see illustration)**, refer to Chapter 10 Section 6, for further information. Discard the nut, as a new one must be used on refitting.

7 Lever the lower arm downwards to release the lower balljoint, then pull the hub carrier outwards, and at the same time withdraw the driveshaft outer constant velocity joint from

2.0a Hub bolt with ribbed flange

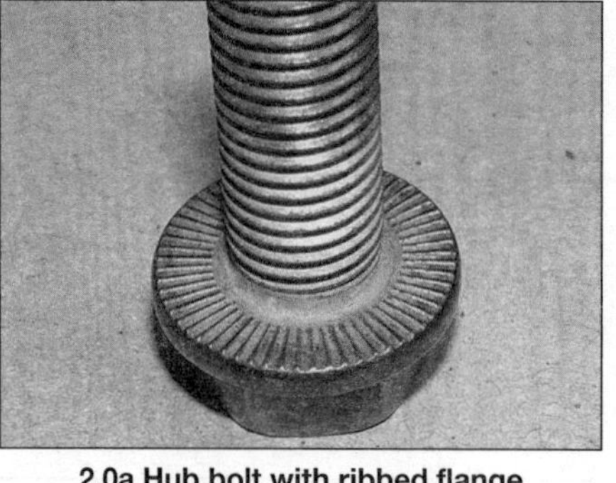

2.0b Hub bolt with smooth flange

2.3 Heat shield retaining bolts (arrowed)

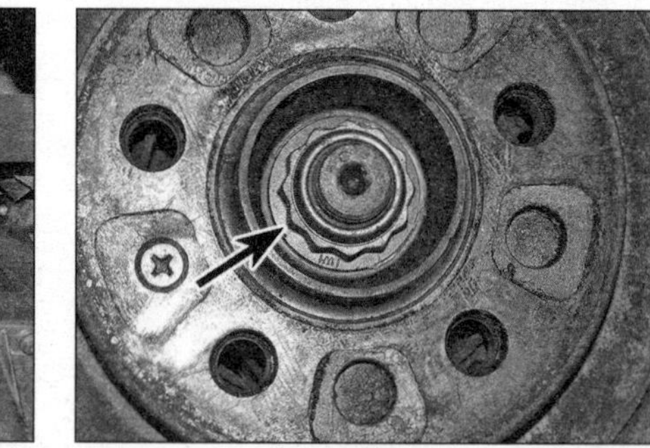

2.4a Remove the driveshaft/hub nut (arrowed)...

2.4b ...or driveshaft/hub bolt

2.5 Disconnect the track rod end

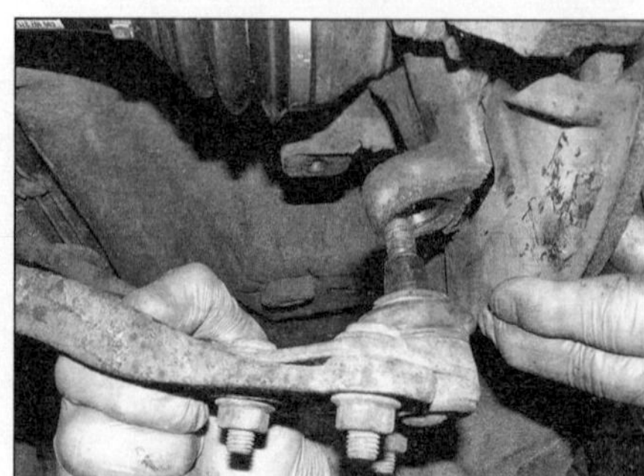

2.6 Disconnect the lower ball joint

2.7 Slide the driveshaft out from the hub assembly

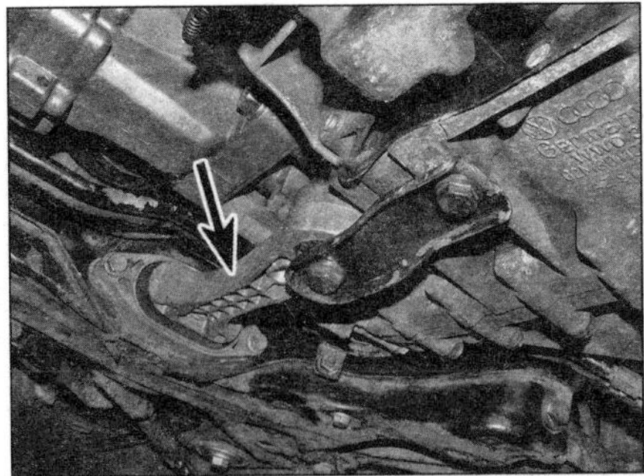
2.8 Lower rear mounting bracket (arrowed)

2.10a Remove the securing bolts...

the hub **(see illustration)**. If the joint splines are a tight fit in the hub, tap the joint out of the hub using a soft-faced mallet and drift. If this fails to free the driveshaft from the hub, the joint will have to be pressed out using a suitable tool bolted to the hub.

8 On some models, in order to gain the necessary clearance required to withdraw the left-hand driveshaft, it may be necessary to unbolt the lower rear engine transmission mounting from the subframe **(see illustration)**, and move the engine slightly forwards.

9 Proceed as follows according to driveshaft type.

Caution: Support the outer end of the driveshaft by suspending it with wire or string – do not allow it to hang under its own weight, or the joint may be damaged.

Inner joint with bolted drive flange

10 Mark the inner joint in relation to the drive flange for refitting. Using a multi-splined tool, unscrew and remove the six bolts securing the inner driveshaft joint to the transmission flange and, recover the retaining plates from underneath the bolts **(see illustrations)**.

Inner joint splined to differential drive shaft

11 Position a container beneath the transmission to catch any spilt oil, as the driveshaft is withdrawn. Pull the driveshaft from the splines, the internal driveshaft circlip may be tight in the transmission side gear, in which case careful use of a lever against the transmission casing will be required. Lever against a block of wood to prevent damage to the casing, and take care not to damage the oil seal as the driveshaft is being removed. **Note:** *Pull only on the inner joint body, not the driveshaft itself; otherwise the gaiter may be damaged.*

All types

12 Manoeuvre the driveshaft out from underneath the vehicle **(see illustrations)**. **Note:** *Where fitted, recover the gasket from the end of the inner constant velocity joint and discard, as a new one will be required for refitting.*

Caution: Caution: Do not allow the vehicle to rest on its wheels with one or both driveshaft(s) removed, as damage to the wheel bearings may result.

13 If moving the vehicle is unavoidable, temporarily insert the outer end of the driveshaft(s) in the hub(s), and tighten the driveshaft retaining nut/bolt(s); in this case, the inner end(s) of the driveshaft(s) must be supported, for example by suspending with string/wire from the vehicle underbody.

Refitting

14 On driveshafts which inner joints are splined onto the differential, check the condition of the circlip on the inner end of the driveshaft splines, and if necessary, renew it.

15 As applicable, clean the splines on each end of the driveshaft and in the hub and apply a little oil, and where applicable wipe clean the oil seal in the transmission casing. Check the oil seal and if necessary renew it, smear a

2.10b ...and rertaining plates

little oil on the lips of the oil seal before fitting the driveshaft.

Inner joint with bolted drive flange

16 Ensure that the transmission flange and inner joint mating surfaces are clean and dry. Where necessary, fit a new gasket to the joint by peeling off its backing foil and sticking it in position **(see illustration)**.

17 Manoeuvre the driveshaft into position, aligning the previously made marks, and then align the inner joint holes with those on the transmission flange. Refit the new retaining bolts and locking plates, and then tighten the retaining bolts to the specified torque.

Inner joint splined to differential drive shaft

18 Locate the inner end of the driveshaft into the transmission – turn the driveshaft as

2.12a Removing the left-hand driveshaft

2.12b Removing the right-hand driveshaft

2.16 Locate a new gasket on the inner joint

3.3 Remove the hub nut

necessary to engage the splines. Press in the driveshaft until the internal circlip engages the groove. Check that the circlip is engaged by attempting to pull out the driveshaft with only moderate force.

All types

19 With the lower arm levered downwards, engage the outer joint with the hub. Fit the new hub bolt and use it to draw the joint fully into position.

20 Align the balljoint studs with the holes in the lower arm, then release the arm and fit the three new nuts. Tighten the nuts to the specified torque.

21 Where applicable, refit the lower rear mounting-to-transmission bolts, and then tighten the new bolts to the specified torque.

22 Tighten the driveshaft nut/bolt to the Stage 1 torque setting. **Note:** *The nut/bolt must be tightened with the wheel clear of the ground. Where bolts are fitted, there are two different types fitted, one is ribbed* **(see illustration 2.0)** *under the face of the bolt head and one is smooth. See note at the beginning of this Section.*

23 Refit the roadwheel and lower the vehicle to the ground, then angle-tighten the driveshaft bolt through the Stage 2 angle (see Specifications).

24 Once the driveshaft bolt is correctly tightened, tighten the wheel bolts to the specified torque and refit the wheel trim/ centre cap.

3 Driveshafts rear – removal and refitting

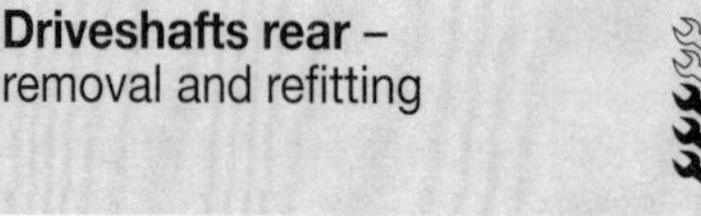

Note: *A new twelve-point hub nut will be required on refitting.*

Removal

1 Remove the wheel trim/centre cap (as applicable) then apply the handbrake, and partially unscrew the relevant driveshaft/hub nut with the vehicle resting on its wheels, by a maximum of 90°. Also slacken the road wheel securing bolts by half a turn. **Note:** *Do not loosen the nut more than 90° with the vehicle standing on the ground, as the wheel bearings may be damaged.*

2 Apply the handbrake, then jack up the rear of the vehicle and support it on axle stands (see *Jacking and vehicle support*). Remove the appropriate rear roadwheel.

3 Unscrew and remove the twelve-point driveshaft/hub nut **(see illustration)**.

4 Using a multi-splined tool, slacken and remove the bolts securing the inner driveshaft joint to the transmission flange and, recover the retaining plates from underneath the bolt heads, then lower the inner end of the driveshaft away from the flange on the final drive unit **(see illustrations)**.

Caution: Support the driveshaft by suspending it with wire or string – do not allow it to hang under its own weight, or the joint may be damaged.

5 When removing the left-hand driveshaft, it may be necessary to lever the exhaust over to one side to allow for the driveshaft inner joint to be lowered away from the flange on the final drive unit **(see illustration)**.

6 The outer end of the driveshaft can now be withdrawn from the hub, and the driveshaft removed completely out from under the vehicle. The joint may be a very tight fit in the hub; tap the joint out of the hub using a soft-faced mallet (refit the hub nut to the end of the driveshaft to protect the threads). If this fails to free the driveshaft from the hub, the joint will have to be pressed out using a suitable tool bolted to the hub **(see illustrations)**.

Caution: Do not allow the vehicle to rest on its wheels with one or both of the driveshafts removed, as damage to the wheel bearings may result.

3.4a Undo the driveshaft retaining bolts...

3.4b ...lower the driveshaft...

3.4c ...and support it with a thick piece of wire

3.5 Lever exhaust over to remove driveshaft

3.6a Remove the driveshaft

3.6b Using tool to remove shaft – (brake disc removed)

7 If moving the vehicle is unavoidable, temporarily insert the outer end of the driveshaft(s) in the hub(s), and tighten the driveshaft retaining nut(s)/bolt(s); in this case, the inner end(s) of the driveshaft(s) must be supported, for example by suspending with string/wire from the vehicle underbody.

Refitting

8 Ensure that the transmission flange and inner joint mating surfaces are clean and dry.

9 Ensure that the outer joint and hub splines are clean and dry. Coat the splines of the outer constant velocity joint, the threads on the end of the outer joint, the splines in the hub, and the contact face of the hub nut/bolt with a thin layer of oil.

10 Manoeuvre the driveshaft into position, and engage the outer joint with the hub. Fit the new driveshaft/hub nut and use it to draw the joint fully into position.

11 Align the driveshaft inner joint with the transmission flange, and refit the retaining bolts and (where necessary) plates. Tighten the retaining bolts to the specified torque.

12 Ensure that the outer joint is drawn fully into position, then refit the roadwheel and lower the vehicle to the ground.

13 Tighten the driveshaft nut/bolt in the Stages given in the Specifications.

14 Once the driveshaft nut/bolt is correctly tightened, tighten the wheel bolts to the specified torque (see relevant part of Chapter 1) and refit the wheel trim/hub cap.

4 Driveshaft rubber gaiters – renewal

1 Remove the driveshaft from the car, as described in Section 2 or Section 3. Continue as described under the relevant sub-heading. Driveshafts with a triple roller (tripod) type inner joint can be identified by the shape of the inner joint houisng; the driveshaft retaining bolt holes are in tabs extending from the joint, giving it a six-pointed star-shaped exterior, in contrast to the smooth, circular shape of the ball-and-cage CV joint **(see illustrations)**.

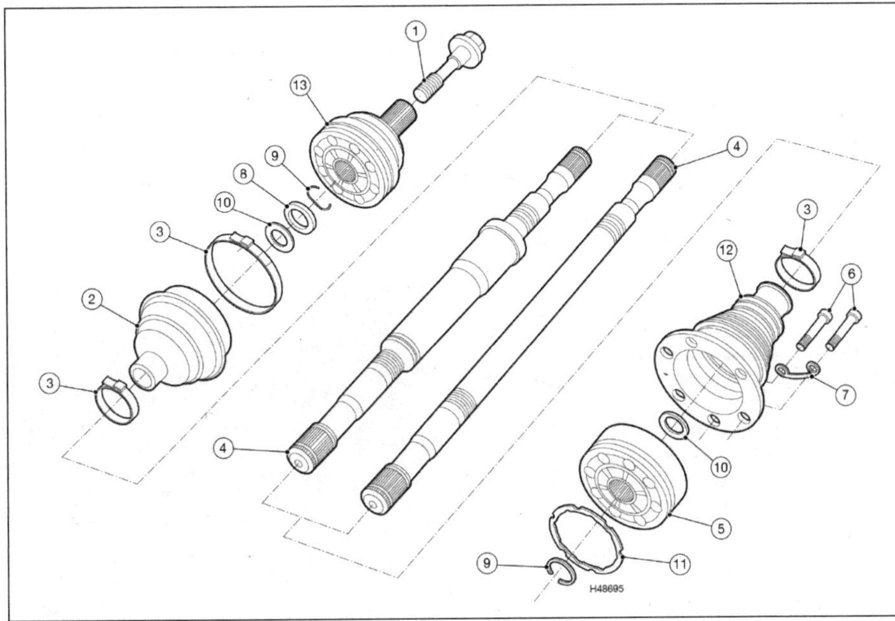

4.1a Driveshaft components – models with VL90 or VL100 CV joint

1 Hub nut
2 Outer joint gaiter
3 Gaiter securing clip
4 Driveshaft
5 Inner joint
6 Flange bolts
7 Bolt retaining plate
8 Thrust washer
9 Circlip
10 Washer
11 Gasket (where fitted)
12 Inner joint gaiter
13 Outer joint

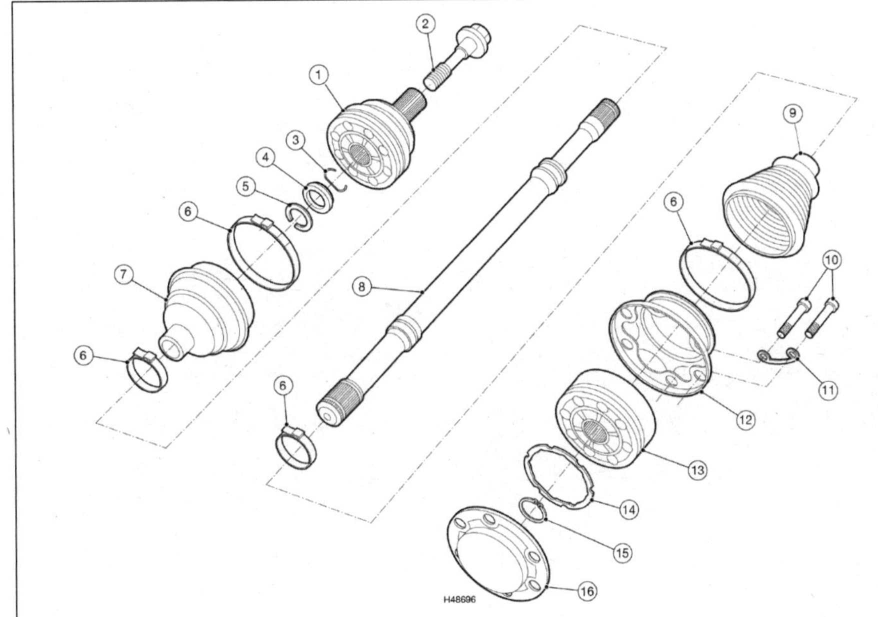

4.1b Driveshaft components – models with VL107 CV joint (bolt-on)

1 Outer joint
2 Hub bolt
3 Circlip
4 Thrust washer
5 Washer
6 Gaiter securing clip
7 Outer joint gaiter
8 Driveshaft
9 Inner joint gaiter
10 Flange bolts
11 Bolt retaining plate
12 Metal cover
13 Inner 'bolt-on' joint
14 Gasket
15 Circlip
16 Metal end cover

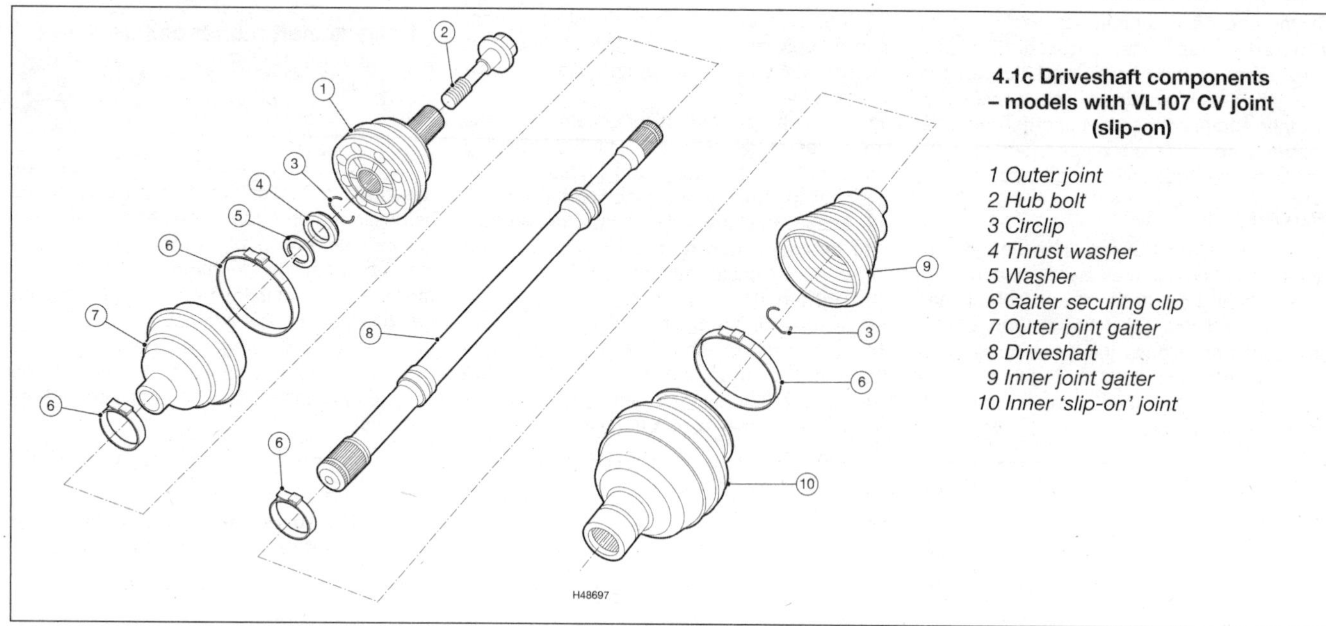

4.1c Driveshaft components – models with VL107 CV joint (slip-on)

1 Outer joint
2 Hub bolt
3 Circlip
4 Thrust washer
5 Washer
6 Gaiter securing clip
7 Outer joint gaiter
8 Driveshaft
9 Inner joint gaiter
10 Inner 'slip-on' joint

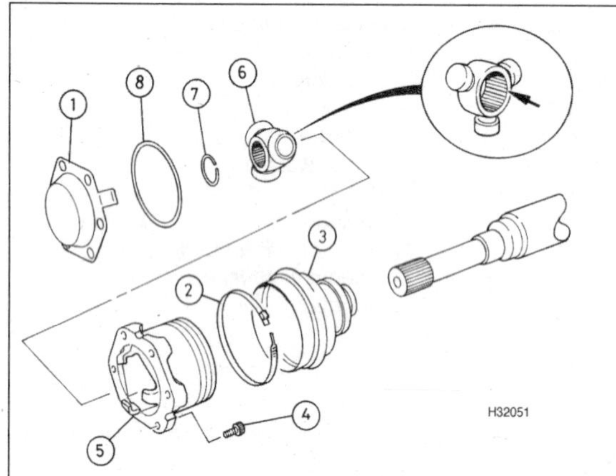

4.1d Inner triple roller (tripod) joint components

1 Metal cover
2 Gaiter securing clip
3 Inner joint gaiter
4 Driveshaft-to-transmission flange bolts
5 Inner joint
6 Tripod/roller assembly (chamfer arrowed faces towards driveshaft)
7 Circlip
8 Seal

4.2 Typical driveshaft gaiter kit – including new bolt

Outer CV joint gaiter

2 Check the driveshaft gaiter kit, to make sure all clips, grease and gaiter are present **(see illustration)**. A new nut/bolt may also be supplied for refitting of the driveshaft.

3 Release the two outer joint gaiter retaining clips **(see illustrations)**. If necessary, the retaining clips can be cut to release them.

4 Slide the rubber gaiter down the shaft to expose the constant velocity joint, and scoop out excess grease **(see illustration)**.

5 Secure the driveshaft in a vice (taking care not to damage the shaft in the jaws of the vice), then using a brass drift and hammer, tap

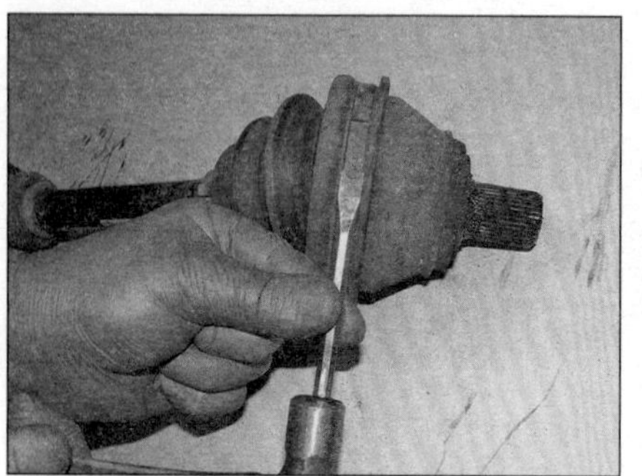

4.3a Remove the large outer clip...

4.3b ...and the smaller inner clip

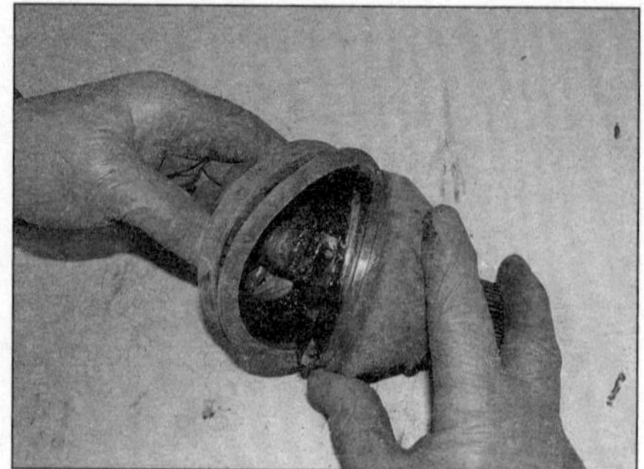

4.4 Pull back the gaiter

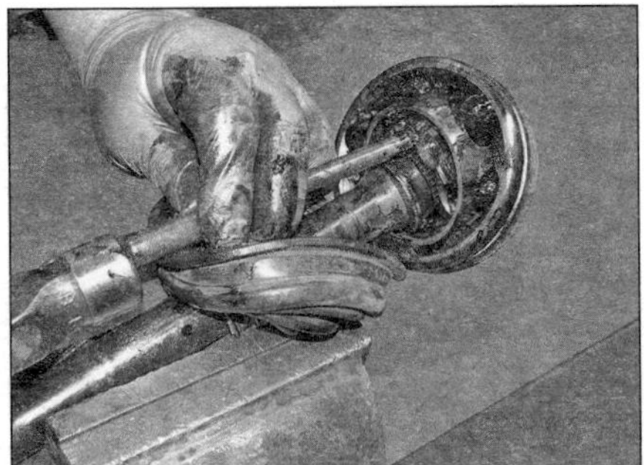
4.5a Tap joint on inner bearing race to release it ...

4.5b ...from circlip in splines (arrowed)

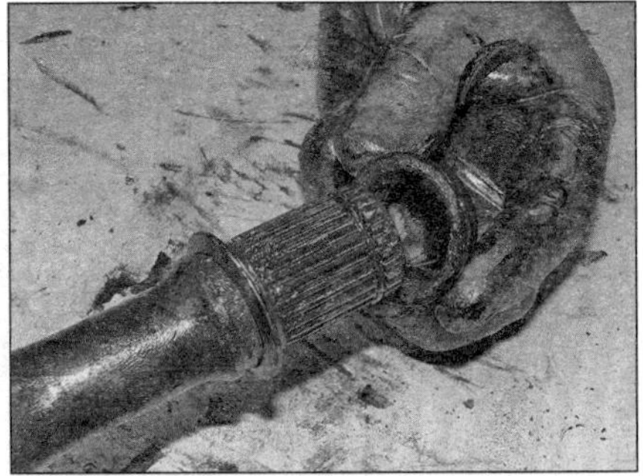
4.6a Remove plastic spacer...

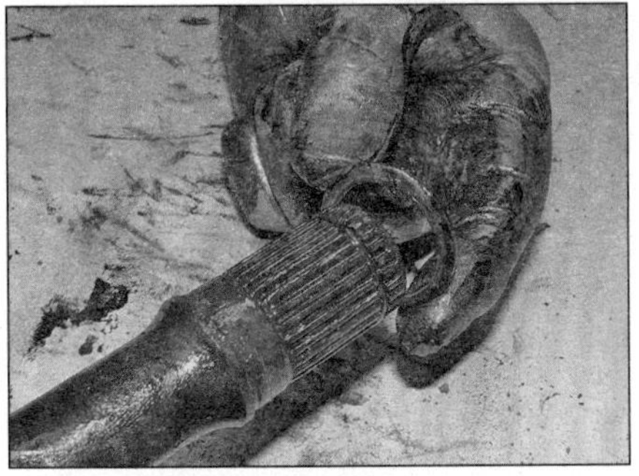
4.6b ...and dished washer – note which way fitted

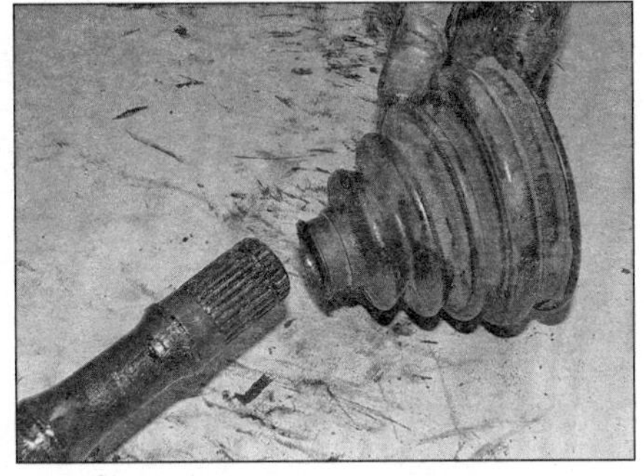
4.7a Remove the old gaiter...

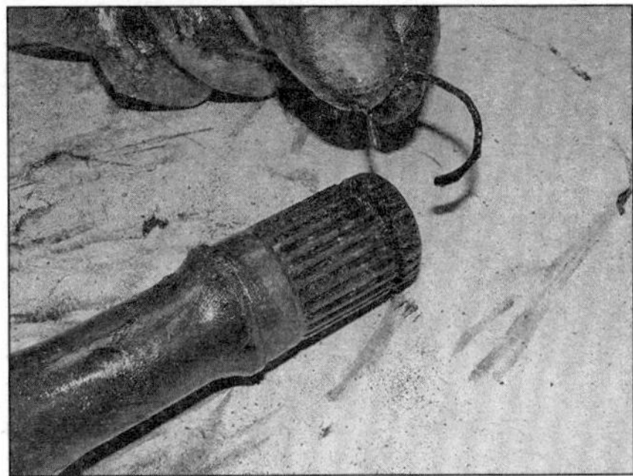
4.7b ...and circlip from the splines

the joint on the inner bearing race to release it from the circlip in the end of the driveshaft splines **(see illustrations)**.

6 Slide off the plastic thrust washer/spacer and dished washer, noting which way around it is fitted **(see illustrations)**.

7 Slide the rubber gaiter off the driveshaft and then remove the circlip from the groove in the end of the driveshaft splines **(see illustrations)**.

8 Thoroughly clean the constant velocity joint(s) using paraffin, or a suitable solvent, and dry thoroughly. Carry out a visual inspection as follows.

9 Move the inner splined driving member from side-to-side to expose each ball in turn at the top of its track. Examine the balls for cracks, flat spots or signs of surface pitting **(see illustration)**.

10 Inspect the ball tracks on the inner and outer members. If the tracks have widened, the balls will no longer be a tight fit. At the same time, check the ball cage windows for wear or cracking between the windows.

11 If on inspection any of the constant velocity joint components are found to be worn or damaged, it will be necessary to renew the complete joint assembly. If the joint is in satisfactory condition, obtain a new gaiter and retaining clips, a constant velocity joint circlip and the correct type of grease **(see illustration 4.2)**. Grease is often supplied with the joint repair kit – if not, use a good-quality molybdenum disulphide grease.

12 Slide the new small inner retaining clip onto the end of the driveshaft, followed by the new gaiter **(see illustrations)**.

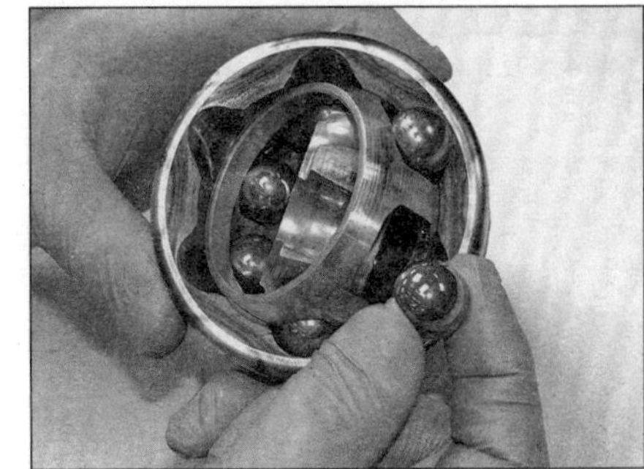
4.9 Check ball bearings for damage

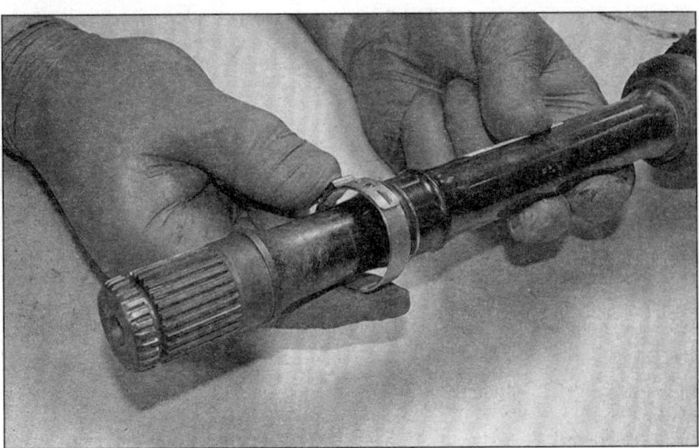
4.12a Slide on retaining clip...

4.12b ...followed by the gaiter

4.13a Slide on the dished washer, with its convex side innermost ...

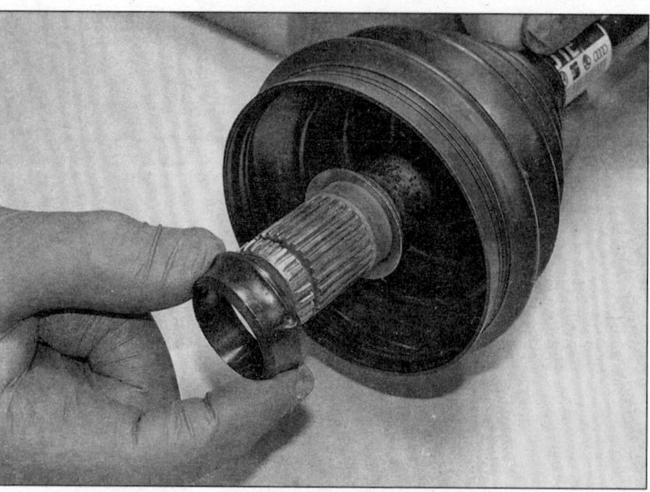
4.13b ... then slide on the thrustwasher

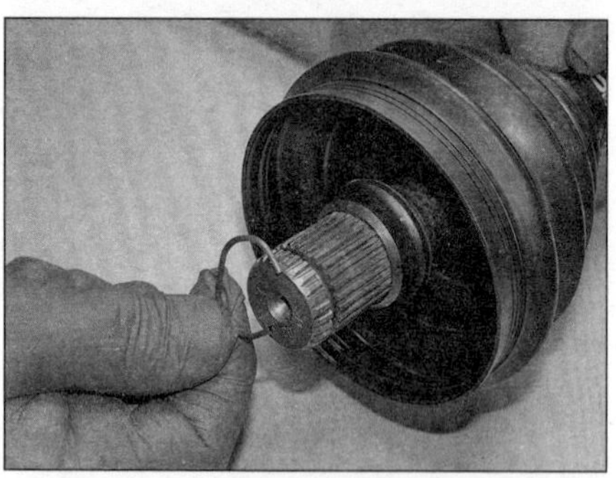
4.14a Fit the new circlip to the driveshaft groove

13 Slide the dished washer on to the end of the shaft, making sure its convex side is innermost, followed by the plastic thrustwasher **(see illustrations)**.

14 Fit a new circlip to the groove in the end of the driveshaft, making sure that it sits in the groove correctly **(see illustrations)**.

15 Pack the joint with approximately two thirds of the amount of grease recommended in the specifications at the beginning of this Chapter. Work the grease well into the bearing tracks whilst twisting the joint, and fill the rubber gaiter with the remainder **(see illustrations)**.

16 Engage the splines in the joint with the shaft, and then tap the joint onto the driveshaft until the circlip engages in its groove **(see illustrations)**. Make sure that the joint is securely retained by the circlip.

17 Ease the gaiter over the joint, and ensure that the gaiter lips are correctly located on both the driveshaft and constant velocity joint. Lift the outer sealing lip of the gaiter to release any air pressure within the gaiter **(see illustration)**.

18 Fit the retaining clips in position over the gaiter. Remove any slack in the gaiter retaining clip by carefully compressing the

4.14b Make sure washers and circlip are fitted correctly

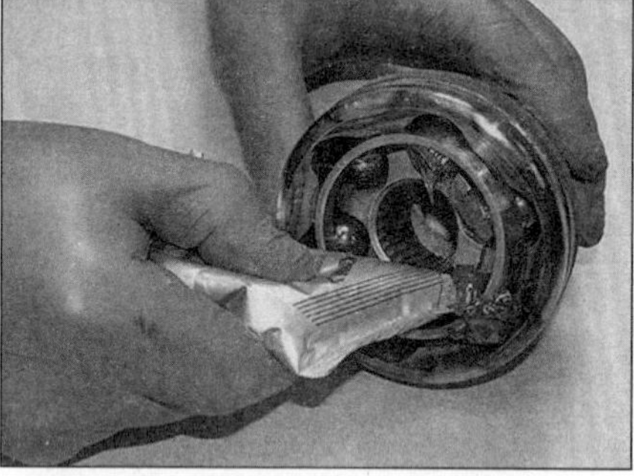
4.15a Squeeze the grease into the joint...

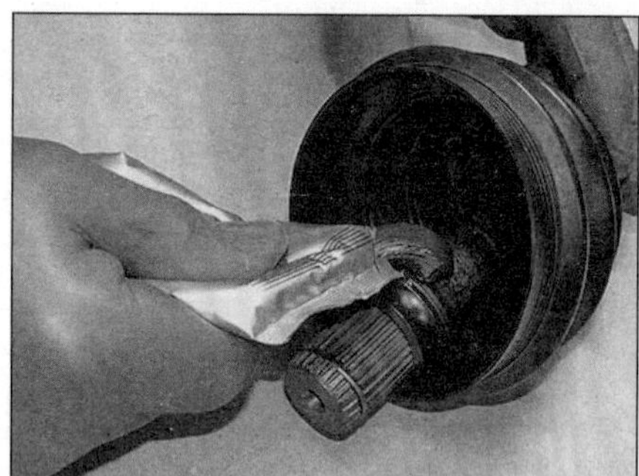
4.15b ...and the remainder into the gaiter

4.16a Align the joint on the splines...

4.16b ... and tap the joint onto the driveshaft

4.17 Seat the gaiter on the outer joint and driveshaft

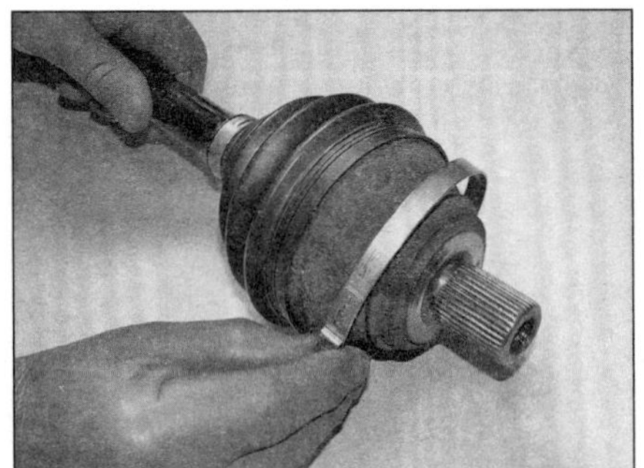
4.18a Fit the new retaining clips...

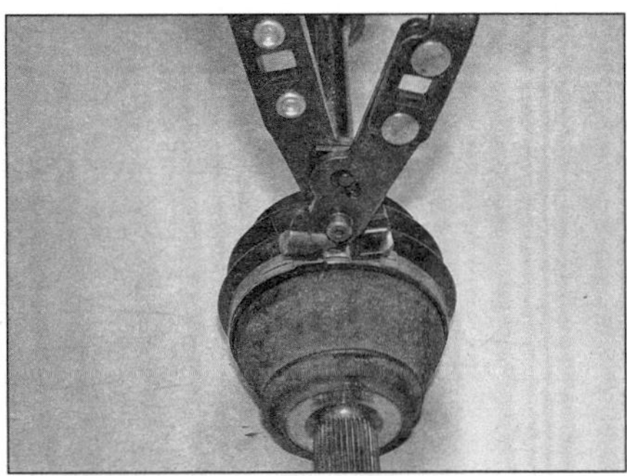
4.18b ...compress the raised section...

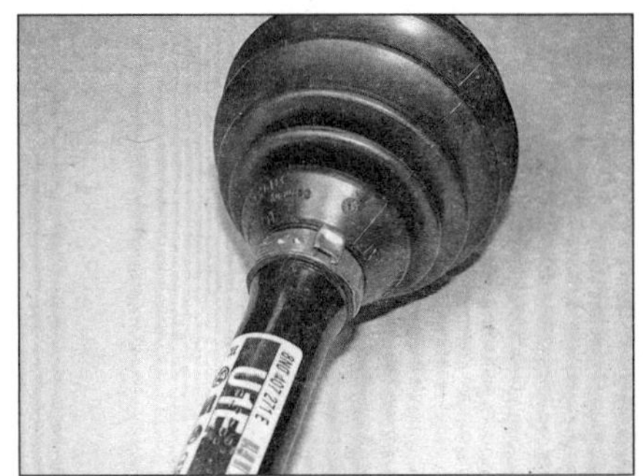
4.18c ... to secure the both clips in position

4.20 Typical driveshaft gaiter kit – including new bolt

4.21a Release the securing clip...

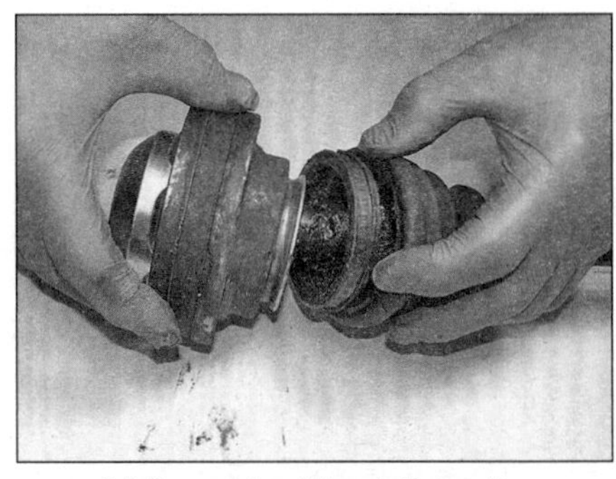
4.21b ...and pull back the gaiter

raised section of the clip. In the absence of the special tool, a pair of side-cutters may be used, taking care not to cut the clip **(see illustrations)**. **Note:** *Different types of retaining clips may be supplied depending on manufacturer.*

19 Check the constant velocity joint moves freely in all directions, then refit the driveshaft to the vehicle, as described in Section 2 or Section 3.

Ball-and-cage type inner CV joint

20 Check the driveshaft gaiter kit, to make sure all clips, grease and gaiter are correct **(see illustration)**. A new nut/bolt may also be supplied for refitting of the driveshaft.

21 Release the clip, securing the gaiter and pull it back from the inner joint **(see illustrations)**. If necessary, the clip can be cut to release it. It may be useful to secure the driveshaft in a vice equipped with soft jaws.

22 Using a hammer and a small drift, carefully drive the metal cover/cap from the end of the inner joint **(see illustrations)**.

23 Clean away the grease and remove the circlip from the end of the driveshaft **(see illustration)**.

24 Withdraw the inner CV joint along the splines from the shaft, then slide the gaiter from the end of the driveshaft **(see illustrations)**.

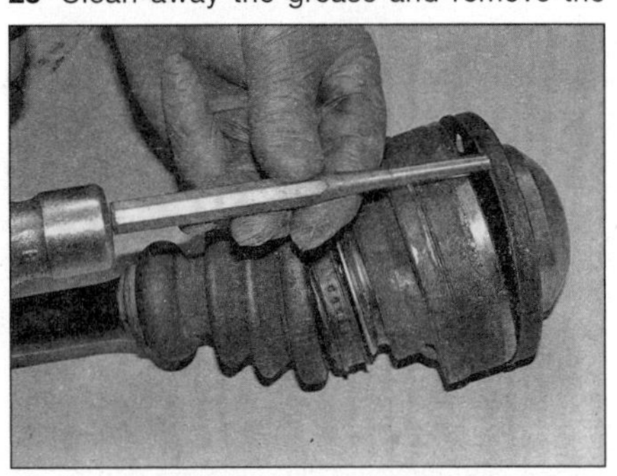
4.22a Using a drift...

4.22b ...to remove the metal cover

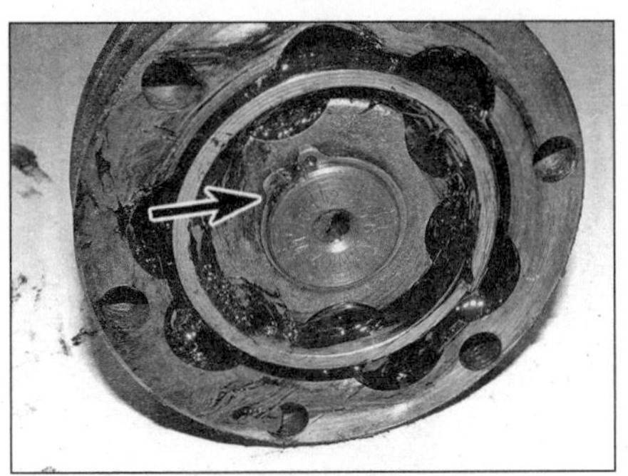
4.23 Remove circlip (arrowed)

4.24a Withdraw the inner joint...

4.24b ...and inner gaiter

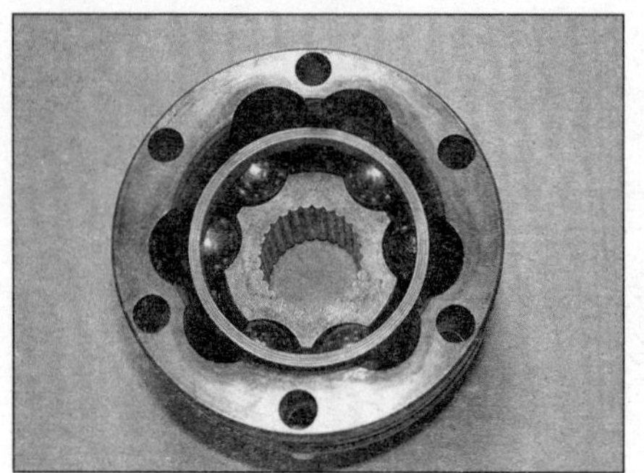
4.26 Examine the ball bearings for damage

4.30a Slide the gaiter into position...

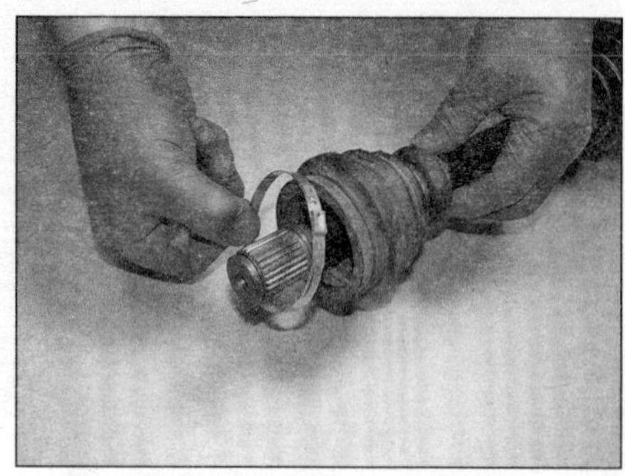
4.30b ...and locate the retaining clip on the gaiter

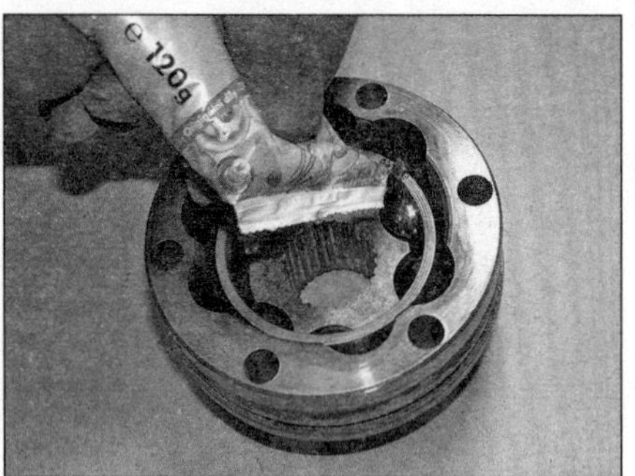

4.31a Squeeze the grease into the joint...

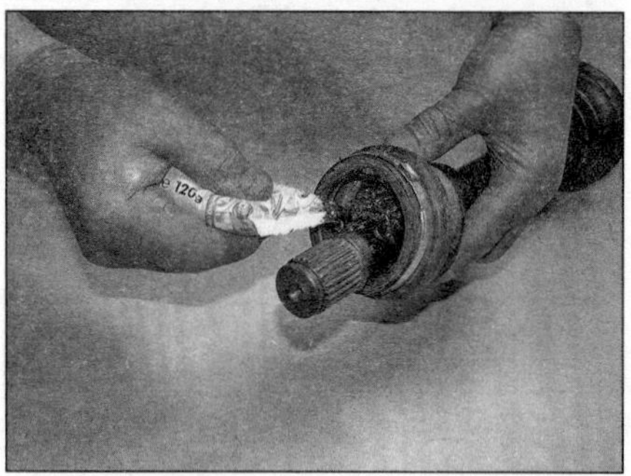
4.31b ...and the remainder into the gaiter

4.32a Slide the inner joint into place...

25 Thoroughly clean the constant velocity joint(s) using paraffin, or a suitable solvent, and dry thoroughly. Carry out a visual inspection as follows.

26 Move the inner splined driving member from side-to-side to expose each ball in turn at the top of its track. Examine the balls for cracks, flat spots or signs of surface pitting **(see illustration)**.

27 Inspect the ball tracks on the inner and outer members. If the tracks have widened, the balls will no longer be a tight fit. At the same time, check the ball cage windows for wear or cracking between the windows.

28 If on inspection any of the constant velocity joint components are found to be worn or damaged, it will be necessary to renew the complete joint assembly. If the joint is in satisfactory condition, obtain a new gaiter and retaining clips, a constant velocity joint circlip and the correct type of grease **(see illustration 4.20)**. Grease is often supplied with the joint repair kit – if not, use a good-quality molybdenum disulphide grease.

29 Fit the joint to the end of the driveshaft, noting that the chamfered edge of the internal splines on the joint should face towards the driveshaft. Drive or press the joint into position until it contacts the shoulder on the driveshaft.

30 Fit the new gaiter over the end of the shaft and slide it into position on the driveshaft. Fit the new retaining clip over the end of the gaiter **(see illustrations)**, ready for assembly.

31 Pack the joint with approximately two thirds of the amount of grease recommended in the specifications at the beginning of this Chapter. Work the grease well into the bearing tracks whilst twisting the joint, and fill the rubber gaiter with the remainder **(see illustrations)**.

32 Slide the inner joint back onto the driveshaft splines, and then secure in place using the new circlip **(see illustrations)**. Make sure the circlip has located correctly in the recess in the end of the driveshaft.

33 Slide the gaiter into position on the inner joint, then secure the securing clip in position **(see illustrations)**.

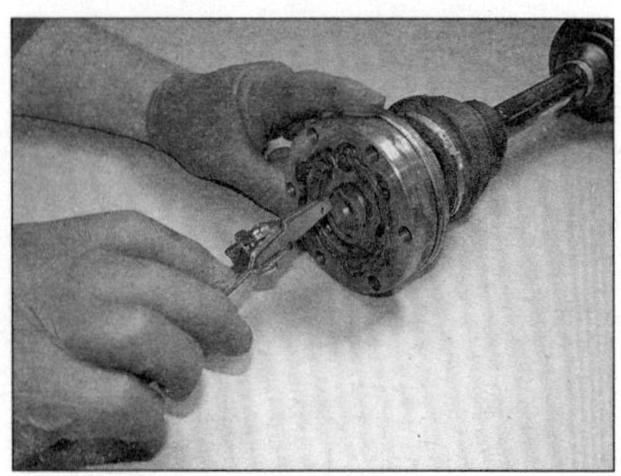
4.32b ...and secure with new circlip

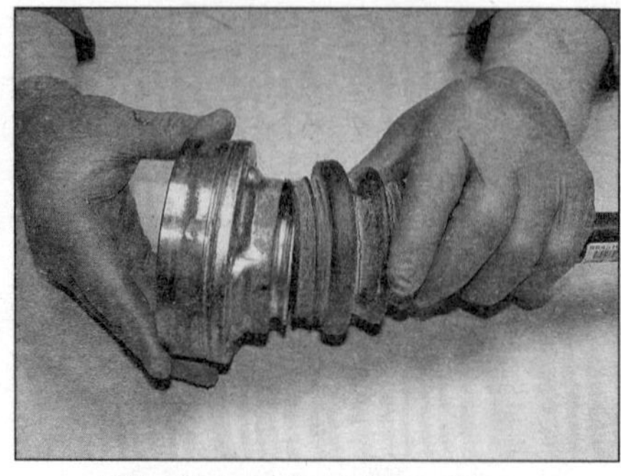
4.33a Slide gaiter into position...

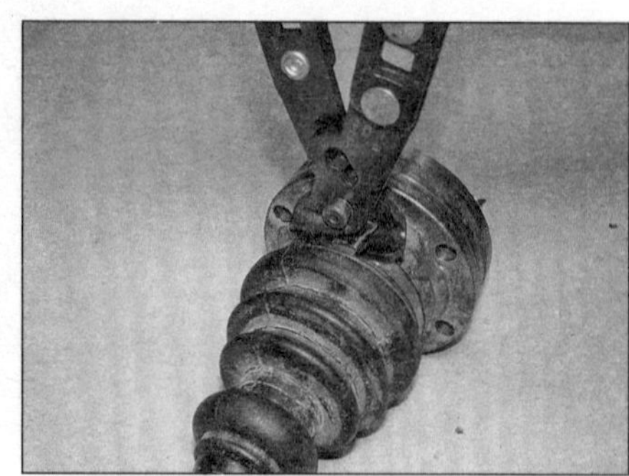
4.33b ...and secure with retaining clip

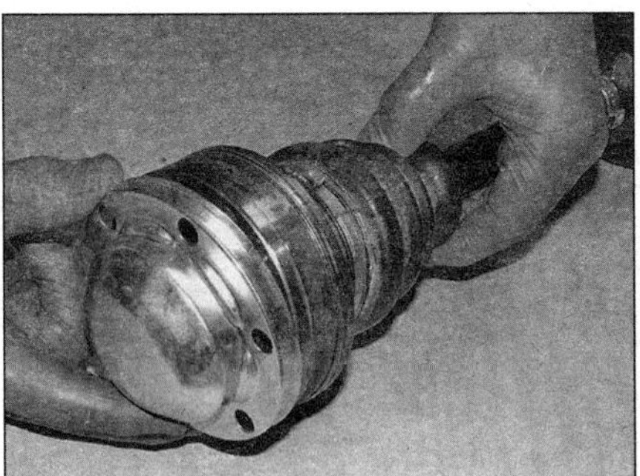

4.34a Fit the metal end cover...

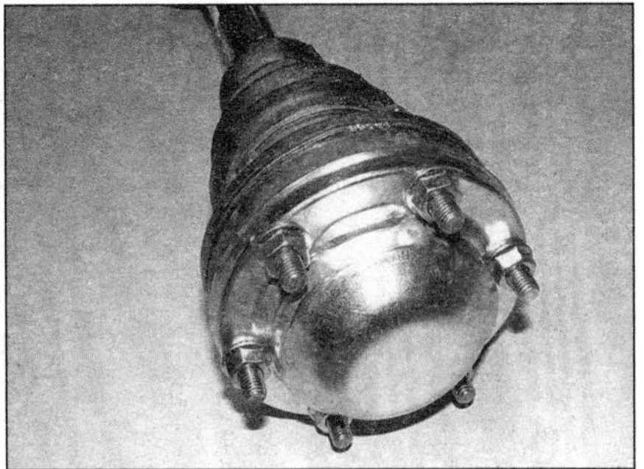

4.34b ...using nuts and bolts to pull on evenly

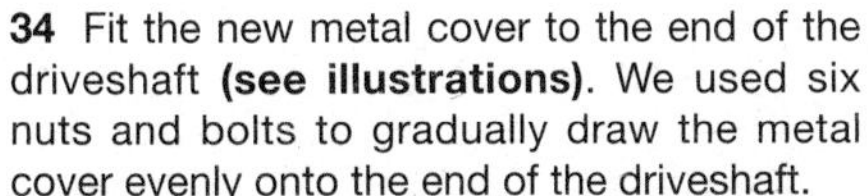

34 Fit the new metal cover to the end of the driveshaft **(see illustrations)**. We used six nuts and bolts to gradually draw the metal cover evenly onto the end of the driveshaft.

35 Check the driveshaft joint moves freely in all directions, then refit the driveshaft to the vehicle, as described in Section 2 or Section 3.

Triple roller (tripod) inner joint gaiter

36 This type of joint can be recognised from the metal cover fitted to the end of the CV joint outer member **(see illustration 4.1d)**. The cover fits over the end of the outer member flange, and the driveshaft-to-transmission flange bolts pass through the cover. The cover is secured to the outer member flange by three tabs.

37 Release the two outer joint gaiter retaining clips. If necessary, the retaining clips can be cut to release them. Slide the rubber gaiter down the shaft, away from the joint outer member.

38 Carefully secure the joint outer member in a vice equipped with soft jaws.

39 Using a screwdriver, prise up the tabs of the metal cap over the end of the joint outer member. Lever the cover from the joint outer member.

40 Scoop out excess grease from the joint, then remove the O-ring from the groove in the end of the joint outer member.

41 Using a suitable marker pen or a scriber, make alignment marks between the end of the driveshaft, the tripod roller assembly, and the outer member. The joint and rollers need to be refitted in exactly the same way when re-assembled.

42 Support the driveshaft and the inner tripod joint, and withdraw the outer housing. Slide the joint outer housing down the driveshaft, away from the tripod joint.

43 Remove the circlip from the end of the driveshaft.

44 Press or drive the driveshaft from the tripod, taking great care not to damage the rollers.

45 Slide the outer housing and the rubber gaiter from the end of the driveshaft.

46 Thoroughly clean the joint components using paraffin, or a suitable solvent, and dry thoroughly. Carry out a visual inspection as follows.

47 Inspect the tripod rollers and the joint outer member for signs of wear, pitting or scuffing on their mating surfaces. Check that the joint rollers rotate smoothly, with no traces of roughness.

48 If the rollers or outer member shown signs of wear or damage, it will be necessary to renew the complete driveshaft, since the joint is not available separately. If the joint is in satisfactory condition, obtain a repair kit, consisting of a new gaiter, retaining clips, circlip, and the correct type and quantity of grease.

49 Tape over the splines on the end of the driveshaft, to protect the new gaiter as it is slid into place, then slide the new gaiter and securing clips, and the joint outer housing over the end of the driveshaft. Remove the protective tape from the driveshaft splines.

50 Press or drive the tripod onto the end of the driveshaft until it contacts the stop, ensuring that the marks made on the end of the driveshaft and the tripod before dismantling are aligned. Note that the chamfered edge of the internal splines on the tripod should face towards the driveshaft.

51 Fit the new circlip to retain the tripod on the end of the driveshaft.

52 Work 60 grammes (half) of the grease supplied with the repair kit into the inner end of the joint outer housing, then slide the outer housing over the tripod, ensuring that the marks made during dismantling are aligned, and clamp the outer housing in the vice.

53 Work the rest of the grease supplied with the repair kit into the rear of the joint outer housing.

54 Slide the rubber gaiter up the driveshaft onto the joint outer housing, ensuring that the end of the gaiter seats in the groove in the joint outer housing, and secure with the large clip as described in paragraph 33.

55 Lift the gaiter outer end to equalise the air pressure in the gaiter, then secure the outer gaiter securing clip in position using the same method used previously.

56 Check that the grease in the joint outer housing is evenly distributed around the tripod rollers.

57 Wipe any excess grease from the inner face of the joint outer housing, then fit the O-ring provided in the repair kit into the groove in the inner face of the joint outer member.

58 Fit the new cover supplied in the repair kit to the inner end of the joint outer housing, ensuring that the bolt holes in the outer member and cover are aligned.

59 Secure the cover by bending the securing tabs around the edge of the outer houisng flange.

60 Check the driveshaft joint moves freely in all directions, then refit the driveshaft to the vehicle, as described in Section 2.

5 Driveshaft overhaul - general information

1 If any of the checks described in Chapter 1 reveal wear in any driveshaft joint, first remove the roadwheel trim or centre cap (as applicable) and check that the hub nut/bolt is tight. If the nut/bolt is loose, obtain a new nut/bolt, and tighten it to the specified torque (see Section 3). If the nut/bolt is tight, refit the centre cap/trim, and repeat the check on the other hub nut/bolt.

2 Road test the vehicle, and listen for a metallic clicking from the front of the vehicle as the vehicle is driven slowly in a circle on full-lock. If a clicking noise is heard, this indicates wear in the outer constant velocity joint; this means that the joint must be renewed.

3 If vibration consistent with roadspeed is felt through the car when accelerating, there is a possibility of wear in the inner constant velocity joints.

4 To check the joints for wear, remove the driveshafts, then dismantle them as described in Section 4. If any wear or free play is found, the affected joint must be renewed. Refer to an Audi dealer for information on the availability of driveshaft components.

Notes

Chapter 8 Part B
Transfer/bevel box, propeller shaft and final drive

Contents

Section number

Degrees of difficulty

Easy, suitable for novice with little experience 	**Fairly easy,** suitable for beginner with some experience	**Fairly difficult,** suitable for competent DIY mechanic	**Difficult,** suitable for experienced DIY mechanic	**Very difficult,** suitable for expert DIY or professional 

Specifications

Lubrication

Transfer/bevel box:
- Gear oil . . . . G51 SAE 75W90 (synthetic oil)
- Capacity (complete with transmission oil) . . . . 2.6 litres

Final drive:
- Gear oil . . . . G50 SAE 75W90 (synthetic oil)
- Capacity: . . . . 1.0 litre

Haldex coupling:
- Gear oil . . . . G 052 175 A1 – High performance oil
- Capacity:
  - Drain and refill (oil change) . . . . 0.25 litre
  - Total (from dry) . . . . 0.42 litre

Torque wrench settings	Nm	lbf ft
Centre bearing-to-body bolts	25	18
Flexible coupling bolts	60	45
Front propshaft-to-rear propshaft	40	30
Lower rear mounting bolts*:		
Stage 1	20	15
Stage 2	Angle-tighten through 90°	
Heat shield above right-hand driveshaft flange	25	18
Transfer/bevel box to transmission mounting bolts*:		
Stage 1	40	30
Satge 2	Angle-tighten through 45°	
Right-hand flange centre bolt	25	18
Transfer/bevel box rear mounting bracket:		
Pressed Steel bracket:		
Stage 1 – bolts to transfer/bevel box (initial torque)	5	3
Stage 2 – upper and lower bolts to cylinder block	35	26
Stage 3 – centre bolt to cylinder block	22	16
Stage 4 – bolts to transfer/bevel box (final torque)	45	32
Cast metal bracket:		
Stage 1 – bolts to transfer/bevel box (initial torque)	5	3
Stage 2 – bolts to cylinder block	35	26
Stage 3 – bolts to transfer/bevel box (final torque)	45	32
Final drive unit:		
Front mounting bolts-to-final drive casing*:		
Stage 1	40	30
Stage 2	Angle-tighten through 45°	
Rear mounting bracket bolts	60	45
Front and rear brackets-to-subframe	60	45
Final drive unit:		
Filler/level plug	25	18
Drain plug	30	22
Haldex coupling:		
Inspection plug	30	22
Drain plug	15	11

Use new nut/bolt

1 General Information

1 Drive is transmitted from the transmission differential to the left-hand front driveshaft in the normal manner. The transfer case, which is positioned to the rear of the engine, takes drive from the right-hand side of the transmission differential, and splits the drive between the right-hand front driveshaft and the propeller shaft to the rear wheel/final drive. The propeller shaft consists of a welded steel tube, with a centre support bearing, and universal joints at each end.

2 The rear driveshafts have constant velocity (CV) joints fitted to each end of the driveshafts, to ensure the smooth and efficient transmission of drive at all the angles possible as the roadwheels move up-and-down with the suspension. Both inner and outer constant velocity joints are protected by rubber gaiters, which are secured over both CV joints with steel clips. The gaiters contain the grease which lubricates the joints, and also protect the joints from the entry of dirt and debris. The inner end of the driveshafts are bolted to drive flanges at each side of the final drive unit. The outer ends of the shafts locate in splines in the rear hubs and are retained by non-reusable nuts.

2 Propeller shaft – removal and refitting

Note: *Before removing the propeller shaft, mark the positions of the front coupling, centre mounting and rear coupling to the flanges on the transfer/bevel box and final drive unit. If there is any imbalance when the propeller shaft is refitted, it will cause rumbling noise and possible damage to the centre bearing and mountings.*

Removal

1 Apply the handbrake, then jack up the vehicle and support it on axle stands (see *Jacking and vehicle support*). Remove the plastic shields from under the engine compartment and fuel tank (where fitted).

2 Remove the catalytic converter/centre section of the exhaust system, as described in Chapter 4B Section 9. Depending on model, it will make removal of the front section of the propeller shaft easier if the front pipe is removed also.

3 Undo the securing nuts and remove the heatshields from under the length of the propeller shaft.

Front section

4 Unbolt the lower rear engine/transmission mounting from the subframe **(see illustration)**, so as to allow the engine to move forwards slightly.

5 Working at the front end of the propeller shaft, undo the three retaining bolts from the flexible coupling and disconnect from

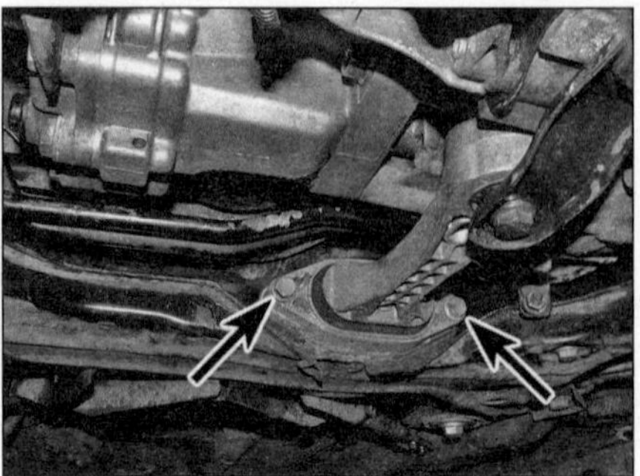

2.4 Undo the mounting bolts (arrowed)

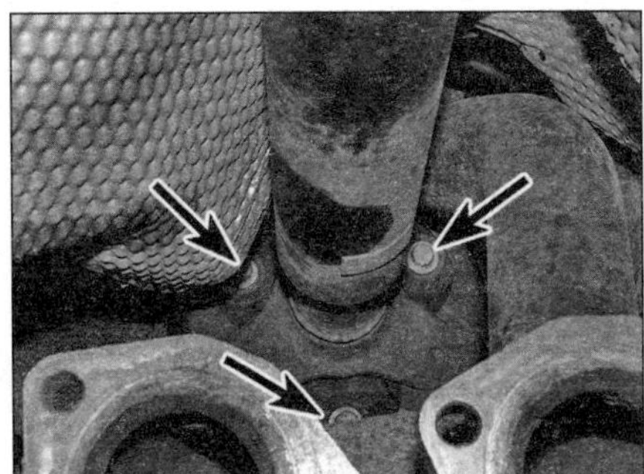

2.5a Front flexible coupling mounting bolts (arrowed)...

2.5b ... and viewed with the exhaust front pipe removed

2.6 Remove the six bolts and three retaining plates

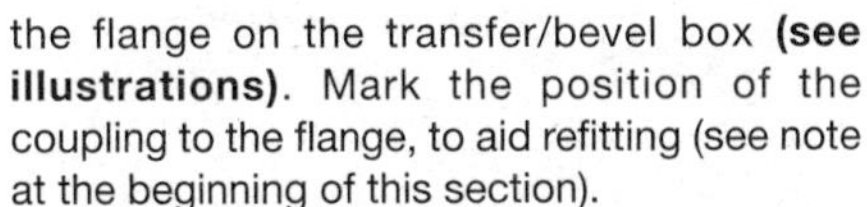

the flange on the transfer/bevel box **(see illustrations)**. Mark the position of the coupling to the flange, to aid refitting (see note at the beginning of this section).

6 Working at the centre of the propeller shaft, undo the six bolts and remove the retaining plates to split the front section of the propeller shaft from the rear section **(see illustration)**. Each pair of bolts has a retaining plate fitted under the heads of the bolts. Mark the position of the couplings, to aid refitting (see note at the beginning of this section)

7 With the bolts and retaining plates removed, slide the front section of propeller shaft forward to disengage it from the centre mounting. When separating the front and rear sections, pull them apart horizontally to prevent seal on centring pin being damaged.

8 Lower the propeller shaft downwards slightly and withdraw the front flexible coupling from the rear of the flange on the transfer/bevel box. As the front flexible coupling is withdrawn, take care not to damage the seal in the centre of the coupling **(see illustration)**.

9 If required, undo the three retaining bolts and remove the flexible coupling from the front end of the propeller shaft **(see illustration 2.8)**.

Rear section

Caution: Support the front section of the propeller shaft by suspending it with wire or similar – do not allow it to hang under its own weight, or the flexible coupling or centring seal may be damaged.

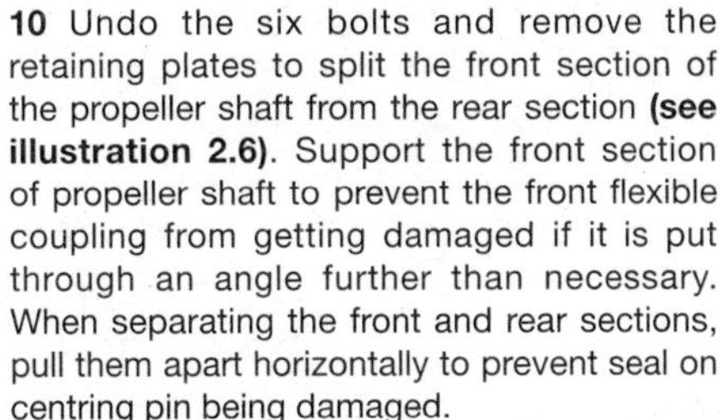

10 Undo the six bolts and remove the retaining plates to split the front section of the propeller shaft from the rear section **(see illustration 2.6)**. Support the front section of propeller shaft to prevent the front flexible coupling from getting damaged if it is put through an angle further than necessary. When separating the front and rear sections, pull them apart horizontally to prevent seal on centring pin being damaged.

11 Working at the rear end of the propeller shaft, undo the three retaining bolts from the rear flexible coupling and disconnect from the flange on the final drive unit **(see illustration)**. Mark the position of the coupling to the flange, to aid refitting (see note at the beginning of this section)

12 Working at the centre of the propeller shaft, undo the two retaining bolts from the centre bearing **(see illustration)**. With the two sections of the propeller shaft separated, remove the rear section from under the vehicle. Mark the position of the centre bearing mounting bracket, to aid refitting (see note at the beginning of this section)

Refitting

13 Check flexible couplings and centre bearing mounting for any damage.

14 At the time of writing the seal at the centre of the flexible coupling was not available. Audi recommend that the propeller shaft be renewed completely, if the seal is damaged.

15 Manoeuvre the propeller shafts into position, noting the alignment marks made on removal (see note at the beginning of this

2.8 Centring pin seal (arrowed)

Section). keep shafts horizontal when refitting, to prevent any damage to centring seal.

16 Tighten the flexible coupling mounting bolts to the specified torque setting, using a special tool to prevent the shaft from turning if required **(see illustration)**.

17 Before tightening the centre bearing mounting, make sure there is no stress on the propeller shaft or centre bearing.

18 Refit the heatshields under the propeller shaft, making sure they do not foul any moving parts.

19 Fit new rear engine/transmission mounting-to-subframe bolts, and tighten the bolts to the specified torque.

20 Refit exhaust system sections with reference to Chapter 4B Section 9.

21 Refit the undershields to the vehicle, then lower the vehicle to the ground.

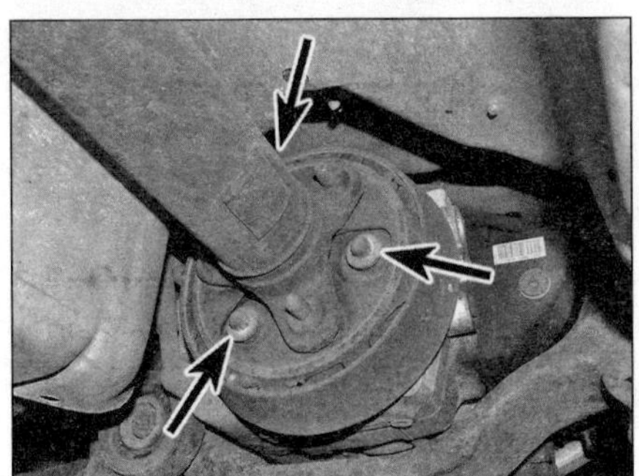

2.11 Rear flexible coupling mounting bolts (arrowed) – one bolt hidden

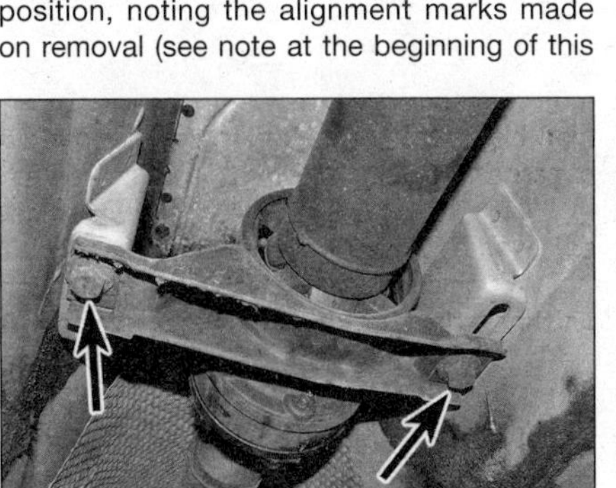

2.12 Centre mounting retaining bolts (arrowed)

2.16 Using a strap to prevent shaft from turning

3.2 Remove the right-hand side driveshaft

3.3 Remove the heat shield

3.4 Drain plug (arrowed)

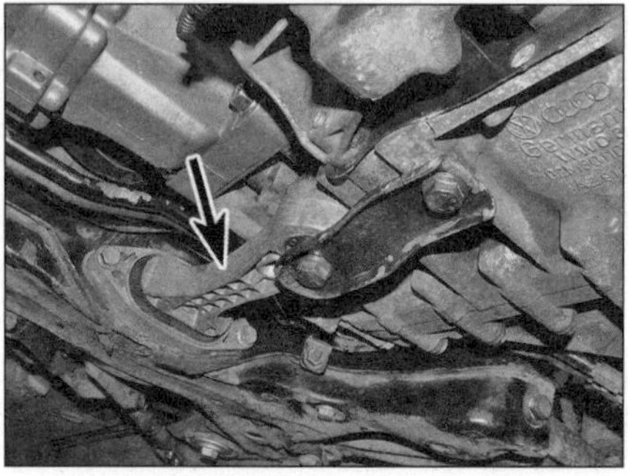
3.5 Lower rear mounting (arrowed)

3.7a Undo the retaining bolts (arrowed)...

3.7b ...and remove the mounting bracket

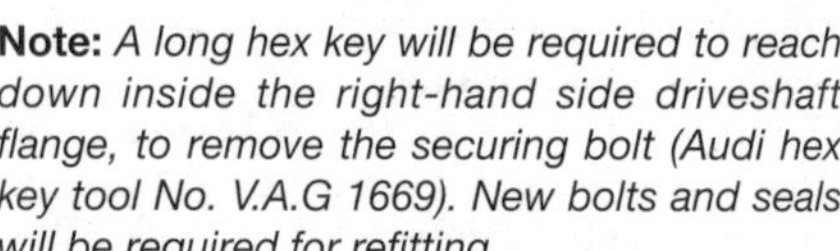

3 Transfer/bevel box – removal and refitting

Note: *A long hex key will be required to reach down inside the right-hand side driveshaft flange, to remove the securing bolt (Audi hex key tool No. V.A.G 1669). New bolts and seals will be required for refitting.*

Removal

1 Remove the front section of propeller shaft, as described in Section 2. Note the propeller shaft does not have to be completely removed, but will need to be moved backwards away from the rear flange on the transfer/bevel box. Take care not to damage centring seal, as the shaft is removed and refitted.

2 Remove the right-hand side front driveshaft **(see illustration)**, as described in Chapter 8A Section 2.

3 Undo the retaining nuts and remove the heats shield from above the right-hand side driveshaft flange **(see illustration)**.

4 Using a large Hex socket and wrench, slacken the drain plug about half a turn **(see illustration)**. Position the draining container under the drain plug, and then remove the plug completely. Recover the sealing ring from the drain plug. **Note:** *The transmission and transfer/bevel box share the same transmission oil, be prepared for up to 2.6 litres to drain from the transfer/bevel box.*

5 Undo the retaining bolts and remove the lower rear engine/transmission mounting **(see illustration)**.

6 To allow for the engine to move forward, remove the charge air pipe from across the front lower part of the engine compartment, as described in Chapter 4B Section 7.

7 Undo the retaining bolts and remove the mounting bracket from the rear of the transfer/bevel box **(see illustrations)**. There are two types of bracket fitted to the rear of the housing, either a pressed steel bracket or a cast metal bracket. **Note:** *On the model we where working on there was a pressed steel bracket fitted, see pics.*

8 Using a hex key long tool, undo the bolt from the centre of the right-hand driveshaft flange **(see illustrations)**. Insert a couple

3.8a Prevent the flange from turning...

3.8b ...and remove the flange centre bolt

3.9a Undo the upper bolts (arrowed)...

3.9b ...and lower bolts (arrowed)...

3.9c ...then withdraw the transfer/bevel box

3.10a Remove O-ring seals (arrowed)

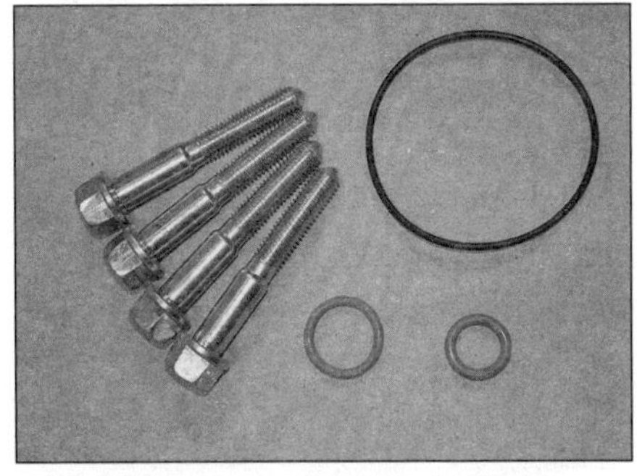
3.10b New seals and bolts for transfer/bevel box

of bolts into the driveshaft flange and use a lever to prevent the flange from turning. **Note:** *A long hex socket will be required to reach down inside the flange to remove the securing bolt (Audi hex key tool No. V.A.G 1669).*

9 Undo the four mounting bolts from the transmission casing, then withdraw the transfer/bevel box from the transmission **(see illustrations)**. Discard the four bolts, as new ones will be required for refitting.

10 With the transfer/bevel box on a clean work bench, remove the three O-ring seals from the transmission end of the housing **(see illustrations)**.

11 Lubricate the seals with clean oil and fit them to the end of the transmission **(see illustrations)**. Make sure the seals are sitting correctly around the dowels and in the groove in the casing.

Refitting

12 Refitting is the reversal of the removal procedure, noting the following points:

a) Bolts and O-ring seals must be renewed.

b) As the transfer/bevel box is offered up to the transmission housing, turn the driveshaft flange, so that the splines will align.

c) Make sure the transfer/bevel box housing is in full contact with the transmission housing and fit the new mounting bolts, then tighten to the specified torque setting. DO NOT use the bolts to pull the transfer/bevel box into position.

d) When fitting the mounting bracket to the rear of the housing, follow the correct tightening sequence and torque, in the specifications at the beginning of this section.

e) Tighten the flange centre hex bolt to the correct torque setting.

f) Refit the oil drain plug, using a new sealing washer, then refill the transmission, which includes the transfer/bevel box gear oil, as described in Chapter 1 Section 19.

4 Final drive unit and Haldex coupling – removal and refitting

Note: *The following procedure shows the removal of the Final drive unit and Haldex coupling as a complete assembly.*

Removal

1 Remove the rear section of the exhaust system, as described in Chapter 4B Section 9.

2 Remove the rear section of the propeller shaft, as described in Section 2. Take care not to damage centring seal, as the shaft is removed and refitted.

3 Using a Hex socket and wrench, slacken the drain plug about half a turn. Position the draining container under the drain plug, and then remove the plug completely. Recover the sealing ring from the drain plug. **Note:**

3.11a Lubricate the new seals...

3.11b ...and fit them to the dowels...

3.11c ...and into the groove (arrowed)

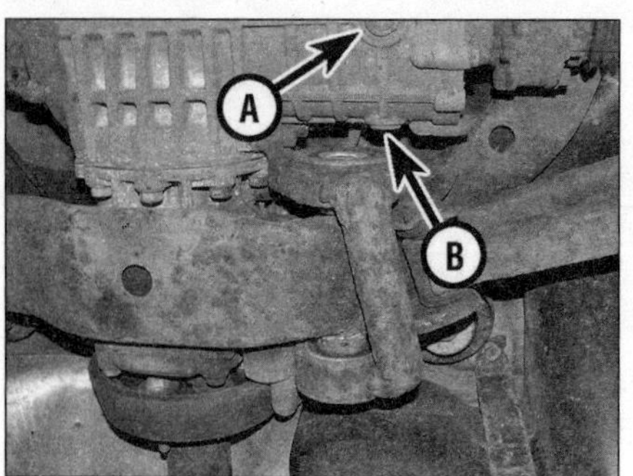

4.3a Drain plug (A) filler/level plug (B) – Final drive unit

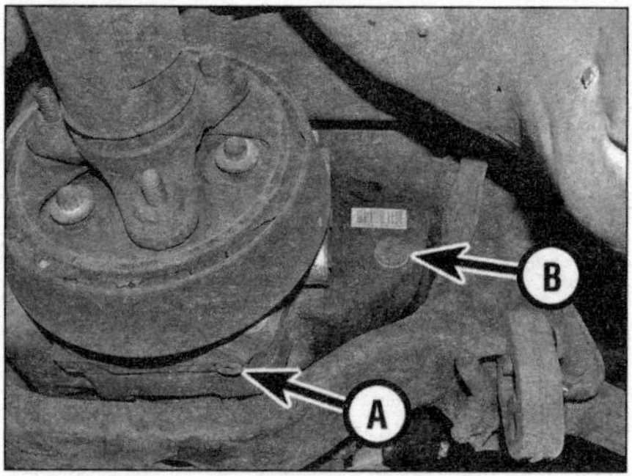

4.3b Drain plug (A) inspection plug (B) – Haldex unit

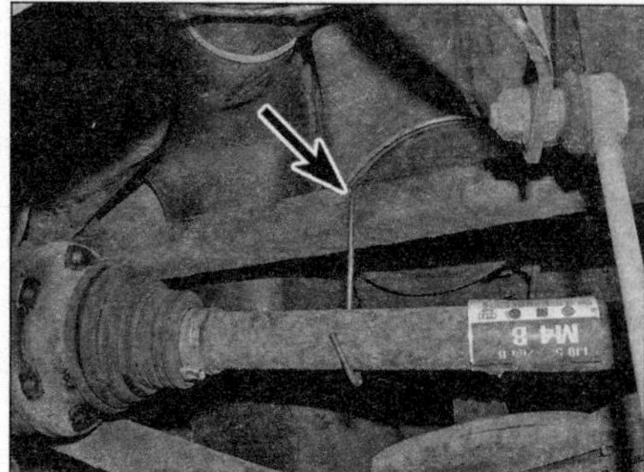
4.4 Bent piece of wire (arrowed) to support driveshaft

The Final drive unit and Haldex coupling have there own drain plugs **(see illustrations)**.

4 Undo the retaining bolts and disconnect both left and right-hand rear driveshafts from the flanges at each side of the final drive unit, with reference to Chapter 8A Section 3. **Note:** *The driveshafts do not have to be completely removed from the wheel hub end, but will need to be secured to one side* **(see illustration)**, *for the removal of the final drive unit.*

5 Undo the three mounting bolts from the final drive casing and the two bolts from the subframe, then remove the mounting bracket from the rear subframe **(see illustration)**.

6 Working at the rear of the final drive unit, release the securing clip and disconnect the wiring connector **(see illustration)**.

7 Using a trolley jack, support the weight of the final drive unit/Haldex unit. Slacken and remove the bolts, at each side of the rear of the final drive unit **(see illustrations)**.

8 Reaching to the top of the final drive unit, release the breather vent pipes from the underbody of the vehicle, as the final drive unit is lowered.

9 Make sure the final drive unit is secure on top of the trolley jack, then with the aid of an assistant, slowly lower the complete assembly down and out from under the rear of the vehicle.

10 If required, undo the four retaining bolts and remove the rear mounting bracket from across the rear of the final drive unit **(see illustration)**.

Refitting

11 Refitting is the reversal of the removal procedure, noting the following points:

a) *Tighten all bolts to the correct torque setting, where specified.*
b) *The oil level in the final drive unit and the Haldex coupling, should reach the lower edge of the filler/level/inspection plug hole. To ensure that a true level is established, wait until the initial trickle has stopped, then add oil as necessary until a trickle of new oil can be seen emerging. The level will be correct when the flow ceases; use only good-quality oil of the specified type.*
c) *Refit the driveshafts, propeller shaft and exhaust system with reference to the relevant Chapter.*

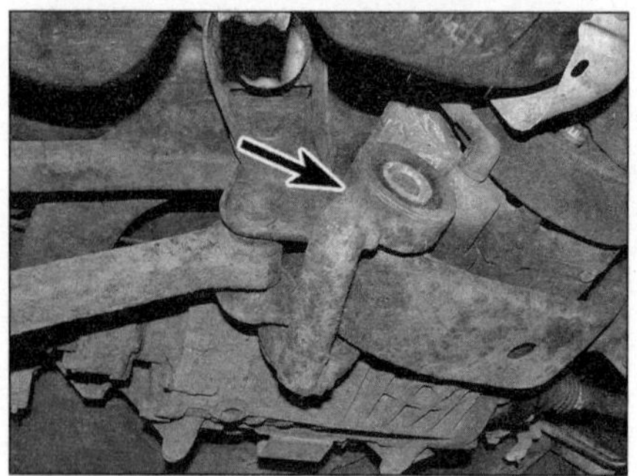
4.5 Remove mounting bracket (arrowed)

4.6 Disconnect the wiring connector

5 Haldex coupling – oil and filter change

Note: *The oil in the Haldex coupling must be between 20° and 40° for the following procedures.*

1 Apply the handbrake, then jack up the vehicle and support it on axle stands (see *Jacking and vehicle support*). Note the vehicle must be level, when checking the oil level in the Haldex coupling.

2 Place an oil drain tray under the Haldex coupling and remove the oil drain plug

4.7a Remove bolts (arrowed) from the right...

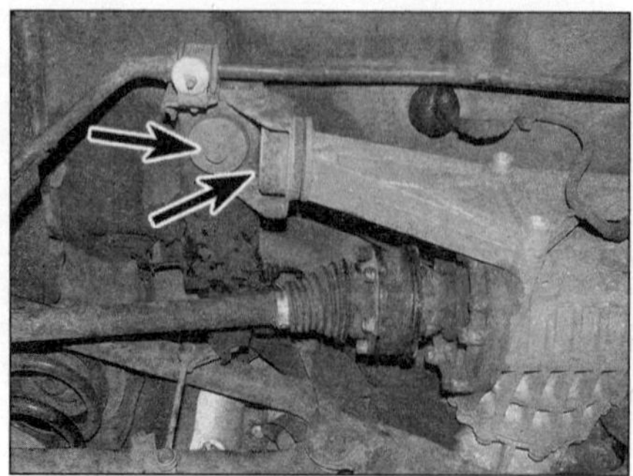
4.7b ...and left of the final drive unit

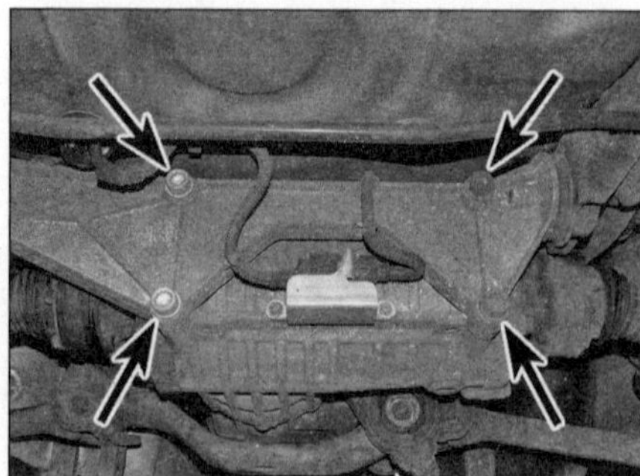
4.10 Mounting bracket bolts (arrowed)

5.2a Undo the drain plug...

5.2b ...and allow the oil to drain

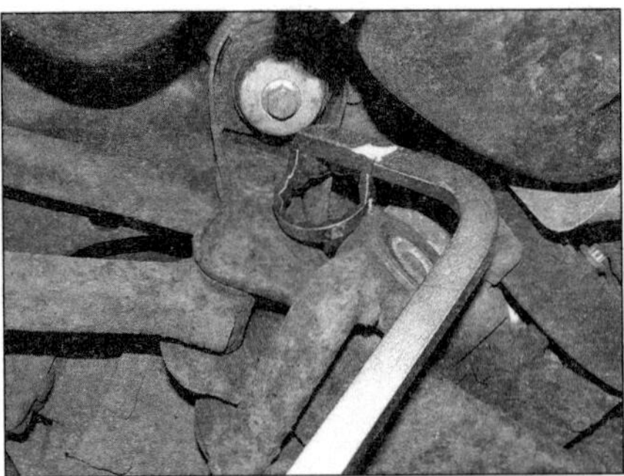
5.3a Using a special angled spanner...

from the lower part of the coupling **(see illustrations)**.

3 Whilst the oil is draining, remove the oil filter from the right-hand side of the Haldex coupling. The filter is awkward to get to and Audi technicians use a special angled spanner (T10066), to remove the filter **(see illustrations)**.

4 With the filter removed, clean around the filter area on the side of the Haldex coupling. Apply a small amount of oil on the O-ring seal of the new filter to lubrucate it, and then fit the new filter to the Haldex coupling **(see illustration)**. Tighten the filter using the special spanner (T10066)

5 Clean the drain plug and fit a new sealing washer **(see illustration)**.

6 The Haldex coupling is re-filled by using new oil in a cartridge, which is pumped up through the drain hole. Once the correct amount of oil (0.25 litre), is pumped up inside the coupling the cartridge is removed, and the oil drain plug (complete with new washer) needs to be to hand, to fit straight back into the drain hole **(see illustrations)**. Tighten the drain plug to the specified torque.

7 To check the oil level in the Haldex coupling, make sure the temperature of the oil is between 20° and 40°, then with the vehicle on level ground, remove the upper inspection plug **(see illustration 4.3b)**. The oil level should be upto (or within 2 mm of) the lower edge of the inspection hole. Once the level is correct, tighten the inspection plug to the specified torque.

5.3b ...remove the oil filter

5.4 Apply a small amount of oil to the seal

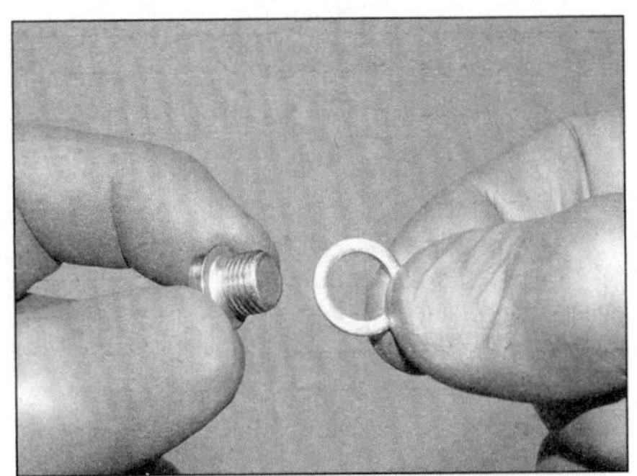
5.5 Fit a new sealing washer to the drain plug

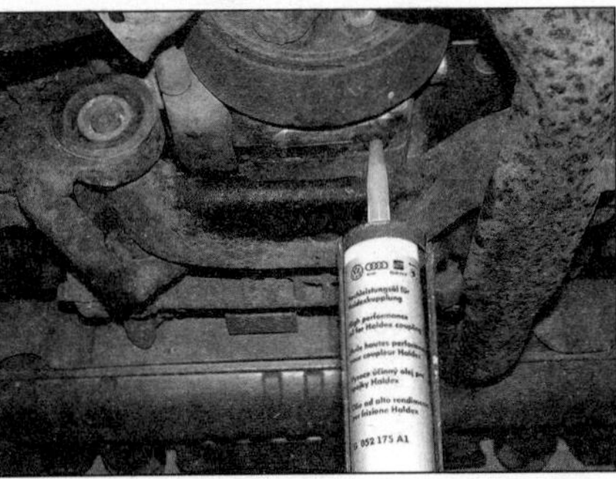
5.6a Pump the correct amount of oil into the coupling...

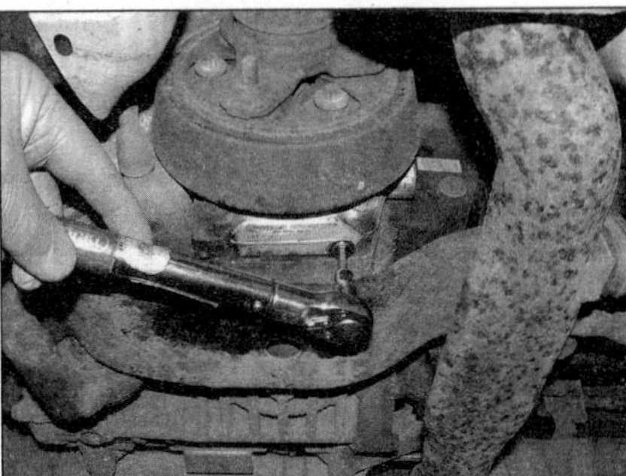
5.6b ...then refit and tighten the drain plug

Chapter 9
Braking system

Contents

Degrees of difficulty

Easy, suitable for novice with little experience	**Fairly easy,** suitable for beginner with some experience	**Fairly difficult,** suitable for competent DIY mechanic	**Difficult,** suitable for experienced DIY mechanic	**Very difficult,** suitable for expert DIY or professional

Specifications

Front brakes

Caliper:	
Type	FN3
Piston diameter	54 mm
Disc:	
Diameter	312 mm
Thickness (ventilated)	25 mm
Minimum permissible thickness	23 mm
Maximum run-out	0.1 mm
Brake pads (Thickness without backplate):	
New	14.0 mm
Minimum	2.0 mm

Rear disc brakes

Caliper:	
Type	C38
Piston diameter	38 mm
Disc:	
Diameter	232 mm
Thickness:	
Solid disc	9 mm
Vented disc	22 mm
Minimum permissible thickness:	
Solid disc	7 mm
Vented disc	20 mm
Maximum run-out	0.1 mm
Brake pads (Thickness without backplate):	
New	12.0 mm
Minimum	2.0 mm

Torque wrench settings

	Nm	lbf ft
ABS control unit retaining bolts	8	6
ABS control unit mounting bracket nuts	20	15
ABS wheel sensor retaining bolts	8	6
Brake pedal pivot shaft nut*	25	18
Brake disc shield bolts	12	9
Front brake caliper:		
Guide pins	28	20
Mounting bracket bolts	125	91
Hydraulic brake line to caliper banjo bolt	35	26
Hydraulic brake line union nuts	14	10
Master cylinder mounting nuts*	5	4
Rear brake caliper:		
Guide pin bolts*	35	26
Mounting bracket bolts	65	48
Handbrake lever mounting bolts	18	13
Brake pressure sender	14	10
Roadwheel bolts	120	89
Servo unit mounting bolts	28	20

** Use new bolts*

1 General information and precautions

General information

1 The braking system is of servo-assisted, diagonal dual-circuit hydraulic type. The arrangement of the hydraulic system is such that each circuit operates one front and one rear brake from a tandem master cylinder. Under normal circumstances, both circuits operate in unison, but, if there is hydraulic failure in one circuit, full braking force will still be available at two wheels. Vacuum for the servo unit is supplied from the inlet manifold.

2 All models covered by this manual are equipped with disc brakes at the front and rear. ABS is fitted as standard to all models (refer to Section for further information on ABS operation), with electronic brake pressure distribution (EBPD). Additional features are, electronic differential lock (EDL), traction control system (TCS) and electronic stability program (ESP), depending on model.

3 The front disc brakes are actuated by single-piston sliding type calipers, which ensure that equal pressure is applied to each disc pad.

4 The rear brakes are also actuated by single-piston sliding calipers, which incorporate independent mechanical handbrake mechanisms as well.

Precautions

• ***When servicing any part of the system, work carefully and methodically; also observe scrupulous cleanliness when overhauling any part of the hydraulic system. Always renew components in axle sets (where applicable) if in doubt about their condition, and use only genuine Audi parts, or at least those of known good quality. Note the warnings given in* Safety first! *and at relevant points in this Chapter concerning the dangers of harmfull dust and hydraulic fluid.***

2 Hydraulic system – bleeding

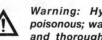

Warning: Hydraulic fluid is poisonous; wash off immediately and thoroughly in the case of skin contact, and seek immediate medical advice if any fluid is swallowed or gets into the eyes. Certain types of hydraulic fluid are flammable, and may ignite when allowed into contact with hot components; when servicing any hydraulic system, it is safest to assume that the fluid is flammable, and to take precautions against the risk of fire as though it is petrol that is being handled. Hydraulic fluid is also an effective paint stripper, and will attack plastics; if any is spilt, it should be washed off immediately, using copious quantities of fresh water. Finally, it is hygroscopic (it absorbs moisture from the air) – old fluid may be contaminated and unfit for further use. When topping-up or renewing the fluid, always use the recommended type, and ensure that it comes from a freshly opened sealed container.

Note: *Audi specify that at least 0.25 litre of brake fluid should be expelled from each caliper, when bleeding the system.*

General

1 The correct operation of any hydraulic system is only possible after removing all air from the components and circuit; this is achieved by bleeding the system. Since the clutch hydraulic system also uses fluid from the brake system reservoir, it should also be bled at the same time by referring to Chapter 6 Section 2.

2 During the bleeding procedure, add only clean, unused hydraulic fluid of the recommended type; never re-use fluid that has already been bled from the system. Ensure that sufficient fluid is available before starting work.

3 If there is any possibility of incorrect fluid being already in the system, the brake components and circuit must be flushed completely with uncontaminated, correct fluid, and new seals should be fitted to the various components.

4 If hydraulic fluid has been lost from the system, or air has entered because of a leak, ensure that the fault is cured before continuing further.

5 Park the vehicle on level ground, then chock the wheels and release the handbrake.

6 Check that all pipes and hoses are secure, unions tight and bleed screws closed. Clean any dirt from around the bleed screws.

7 Unscrew the master cylinder reservoir cap, and top the reservoir up to the MAX level line; refit the cap loosely, and remember to maintain the fluid level at least above the MIN level line throughout the procedure, or there is a risk of further air entering the system.

8 There is a number of one-man, do-it-yourself brake bleeding kits currently available from motor accessory shops. It is recommended that one of these kits is used whenever possible, as they greatly simplify the bleeding operation, and reduce the risk of expelled air and fluid being drawn back into the system. If such a kit is not available, the basic (two-man) method must be used, which is described in detail below.

9 If a kit is to be used, prepare the vehicle as described previously, and follow the kit manufacturer's instructions, as the procedure may vary slightly according to the type being used; generally, they are as outlined below in the relevant sub-section.

10 Whichever method is used, the same sequence must be followed (paragraph 12) to ensure the removal of all air from the system.

Bleeding sequence

11 If the system has been only partially disconnected, and suitable precautions were taken to minimise fluid loss, it should be necessary only to bleed that part of the system.

12 If the complete system is to be bled, then it should be done working in the following sequence:

Mark 20 IE system (see Section 19)

a) Right-hand rear brake.
b) Left-hand rear brake.
c) Right-hand front brake.
d) Left-hand front brake.

Mark 60 system (see Section 19)

a) Left-hand front brake.
b) Right-hand front brake.
c) Left-hand rear brake.
d) Right-hand rear brake.

13 If the hydraulic fluid has run dry in either chamber of the reservoir, the system must be pre-bled as follows, before carrying out the bleeding sequence described above:

a) On RHD models, bleed the primary and secondary circuit bleed screws on the brake master cylinder.
b) On RHD and LHD models, bleed the front left and right brakes simultaneously.
c) On RHD and LHD models, bleed the rear left and right brakes simultaneously.

Bleeding

Basic (two-man) method

14 Collect together a clean glass jar of reasonable size, a suitable length of plastic or rubber tubing which is a tight fit over the bleed screw, and a ring spanner to fit the screw. The help of an assistant will also be required.

15 Remove the dust cap from the first screw in the sequence **(see illustration)**. Fit the spanner and tube to the screw, place the other end of the tube in the jar, and pour in sufficient fluid to cover the end of the tube.

16 Ensure that the master cylinder reservoir fluid level is maintained at least above the MIN level line throughout the procedure.

17 Have the assistant fully depress the brake pedal several times to build-up pressure, and then maintain it on the final downstroke.

18 While pedal pressure is maintained, unscrew the bleed screw (approximately one turn) and allow the compressed fluid and air to flow into the jar. The assistant should maintain pedal pressure, following it down to the floor if necessary, and should not release it until instructed to do so. When the flow stops, tighten the bleed screw again, have the assistant release the pedal slowly, and recheck the reservoir fluid level.

19 Repeat the steps given in paragraphs 16 and 17 until the fluid emerging from the bleed screw is free from air bubbles. If the master cylinder has been drained and refilled, and air is being bled from the first screw in the sequence, allow approximately five seconds between cycles for the master cylinder passages to refill.

2.15 Remove the dust cap (arrowed)

20 When no more air bubbles appear, tighten the bleed screw securely, remove the tube and spanner, and refit the dust cap. Do not overtighten the bleed screw.

21 Repeat the procedure on the remaining screws in the sequence, until all air is removed from the system and the brake pedal feels firm again.

Using a one-way valve kit

22 As their name implies, these kits consist of a length of tubing with a one-way valve fitted, to prevent expelled air and fluid being drawn back into the system; some kits include a translucent container, which can be positioned so that the air bubbles can be more easily seen flowing from the end of the tube.

23 The kit is connected to the bleed screw, which is then opened. The user returns to the driver's seat, depresses the brake pedal with a smooth, steady stroke, and slowly releases it; this is repeated until the expelled fluid is clear of air bubbles **(see illustration)**.

2.23 Bleeding a brake using a one-way valve kit

24 Note that these kits simplify work so much that it is easy to forget the master cylinder reservoir fluid level; ensure that this is maintained at least above the MIN level line at all times.

Using a pressure-bleeding kit

25 These kits are usually operated by the reservoir of pressurised air contained in the spare tyre. However, note that it will be probably necessary to reduce the pressure to less than 1.0 bar (14.5 psi); refer to the instructions supplied with the kit.

26 By connecting a pressurised, fluid-filled container to the master cylinder reservoir, bleeding can be carried out simply by opening each screw in turn (in the specified sequence), and allowing the fluid to flow out until no more air bubbles can be seen in the expelled fluid.

27 This method has the advantage that the large reservoir of fluid provides an additional safeguard against air being drawn into the system during bleeding.

28 Pressure-bleeding is particularly effective when bleeding 'difficult' systems, or when bleeding the complete system at the time of routine fluid renewal.

All methods

29 When bleeding is complete, and firm pedal feel is restored, wash off any spilt fluid, tighten the bleed screws securely, and refit their dust caps.

30 Check the hydraulic fluid level in the master cylinder reservoir, and top-up if necessary (see *Weekly checks*).

31 Discard any hydraulic fluid that has been bled from the system; it will not be fit for re-use.

32 Check the feel of the brake pedal. If it feels at all spongy, air must still be present in the system, and further bleeding is required. Failure to bleed satisfactorily after a reasonable repetition of the bleeding procedure may be due to worn master cylinder seals.

3 Hydraulic pipes and hoses – renewal

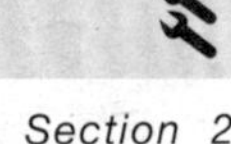

Note: *Refer to the note in Section 2 concerning the dangers of hydraulic fluid.*

1 If any pipe or hose is to be renewed, minimise fluid loss by first removing the master cylinder reservoir cap, then tightening it down onto a piece of polythene to obtain an airtight seal. Alternatively, flexible hoses can be sealed, if required, using a proprietary brake hose clamp; metal brake pipe unions can be plugged (if care is taken not to allow dirt into the system) or capped immediately they are disconnected. Place a wad of rag under any union that is to be disconnected, to catch any spilt fluid.

2 If a flexible hose is to be disconnected, where applicable unscrew the brake pipe union nut before removing the spring clip which secures the hose to its mounting bracket.

3 To unscrew the union nuts, it is preferable to obtain a brake pipe spanner of the correct size; these are available from most large motor accessory shops. Failing this, a close-fitting open-ended spanner will be required, though if the nuts are tight or corroded, their flats may be rounded-off if the spanner slips. In

3.6 Brake hose retaining clip (arrowed)

4.3a Use a screwdriver...

4.3b ...to release the spring from the caliper

such a case, a self-locking wrench is often the only way to unscrew a stubborn union, but it follows that the pipe and the damaged nuts must be renewed on reassembly. Always clean a union and surrounding area before disconnecting it. If disconnecting a component with more than one union, make a careful note of the connections before disturbing any of them.

4 If a brake pipe is to be renewed, it can be obtained, cut to length and with the union nuts and end flares in place, from Audi dealers. All that is then necessary is to bend it to shape, following the line of the original, before fitting it to the car. Alternatively, most motor accessory shops can make up brake pipes from kits, but this requires very careful measurement of the original, to ensure that the new pipe is of the correct length. The safest answer is usually to take the original to the shop as a pattern.

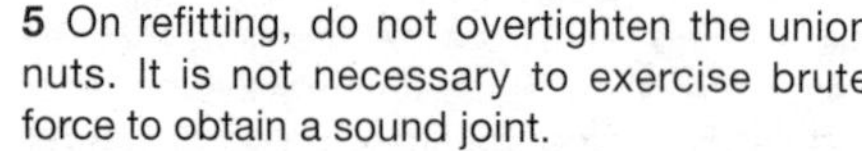

5 On refitting, do not overtighten the union nuts. It is not necessary to exercise brute force to obtain a sound joint.

6 Ensure that the pipes and hoses are correctly routed, with no kinks, and that they are secured in the clips or brackets provided **(see illustration)**. After fitting, remove the polythene from the reservoir, and bleed the hydraulic system as described in Section 2. Wash off any spilt fluid, and check carefully for fluid leaks.

4 Front brake pads – removal, inspection and refitting

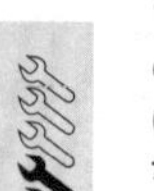

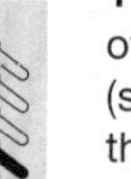

Warning: Renew both sets of brake pads at the same time – never renew the pads on only one wheel, as uneven braking may result. Note that the dust created by wear of the pads may be a health hazard. Never blow it out with compressed air, and do not inhale any of it. DO NOT use petrol or petroleum-based solvents to clean brake parts; use brake cleaner or methylated spirit only.

Removal

1 Apply the handbrake, then jack up the front of the vehicle and support it on axle stands (see *Jacking and vehicle support*). Remove the front roadwheels.

2 Trace the brake pad wear sensor wiring (where fitted) back from the pads, and disconnect it from the wiring connector. Note the routing of the wiring, and free it from any relevant retaining clips.

3 Using a screwdriver, lever the brake pad retaining spring from the caliper housing **(see illustrations)**.

4 Working at hte rear of the caliper, unclip the two protective rubber/plastic caps from over the ends of the guide pins **(see illustrations)**.

5 Using a hexagon key, slacken and remove the two caliper guide pins from the rear of the caliper **(see illustrations)**.

6 Lift the brake caliper away from over the brake pads and disc, and then unclip the inner brake pad from the piston in the caliper. Hook the caliper to the suspension strut using

4.4a Remove the upper...

4.4b ...and lower rubber/plastic cap

4.5a Use a hex socket...

4.5b ...to remove the lower...

4.5c ...and upper guide pins

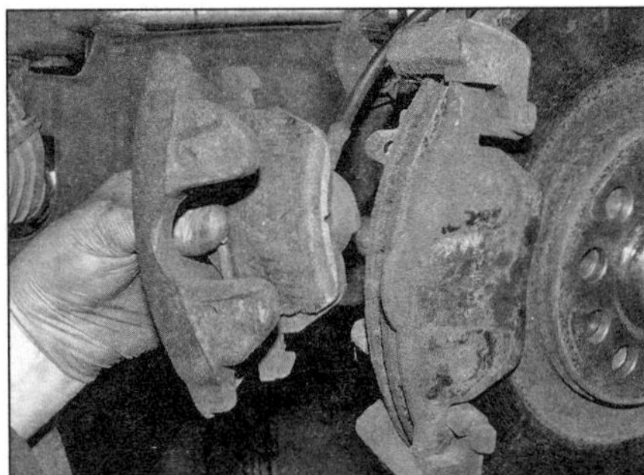

4.6a Withdraw the brake caliper...

4.6b ...unclip the inner brake pad...

4.6c ...and support the caliper with a piece of wire

4.7 Remove the outer brake pad

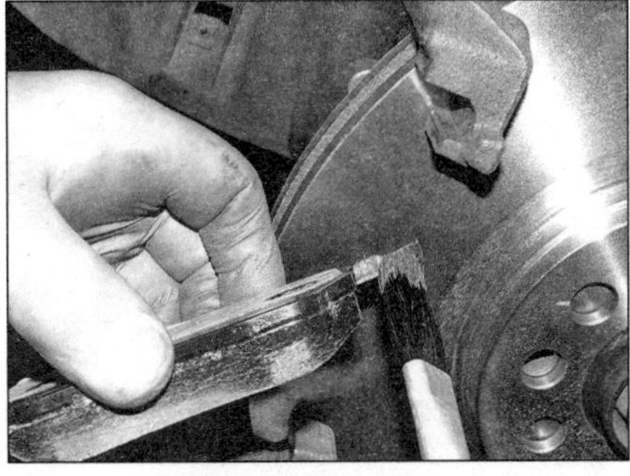

4.11a Applying high temperature grease to the ends of the brake pads

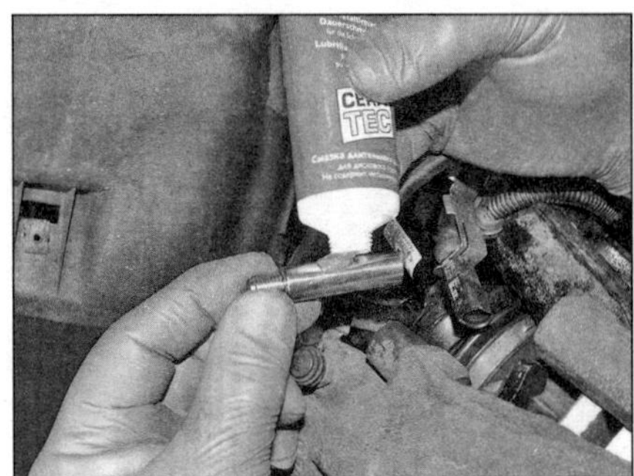

4.11b Applying special grease to the guide pins

a piece of strong wire **(see illustrations)**. Do not allow the caliper to hang unsupported on the flexible brake hose.

7 Withdraw the outer brake pad from the caliper mounting bracket **(see illustration)**. If the original pads are to be refitted, identify them so that they can be refitted in their original locations. Where applicable, disconnect the pad wear sensor wiring connector.

Inspection

8 First measure the thickness of each brake pad. If either pad is worn at any point to the specified minimum thickness or less, all four pads must be renewed. Also, the pads should be renewed if any are fouled with oil or grease; there is no satisfactory way of degreasing friction material, once contaminated. If any of the brake pads are worn unevenly, or are fouled with oil or grease, trace and rectify the cause before reassembly. New brake pad kits are available from Audi dealers.

9 If the brake pads are still serviceable, carefully clean them using a clean, fine wire brush or similar, paying particular attention to the sides and back of the metal backing. Clean out the grooves in the friction material (where applicable), and pick out any large embedded particles of dirt or debris. Carefully clean the pad locations in the caliper body/ mounting bracket.

10 Prior to fitting the pads, check that the guide pins are free to slide easily in the caliper body bushes, and are a reasonably tight fit. Brush the dust and dirt from the caliper and piston, but do not inhale it, as it is injurious to health. Inspect the dust seal around the piston for damage, and the piston for evidence of fluid leaks, corrosion or damage. If attention to any of these components is necessary, refer to Section 5.

11 Apply a small amount of high temperature grease to the edges of the brake pads that come into contact with the mounting bracket. Also use brake grease on the guide pins to help them slide in the caliper body **(see illustrations)**.

Refitting

12 If new brake pads are to be fitted, the caliper piston must be pushed back into the cylinder to make room for them. Either use a G-clamp or similar tool to press the piston back **(see illustration)**. To avoid any problems with the brake master cylinder or dirt entering the ABS solenoid valves, connect a pipe to the bleed screw and, as the piston is pushed back, open the bleed screw and allow the displaced fluid to flow through the pipe into a suitable container (see Section 2).

13 Remove the protective foil from the outer pad backplate (where applicable). Install the outer pad in the caliper mounting bracket **(see illustrations)**, ensuring that the friction material of the pad is against the brake disc. Lubricate the ends of the brake pads, as described in paragraph 11.

4.12 Pressing back the piston in the caliper

4.13a Remove the protective foil...

4.13b ...and fit the outer brake pad

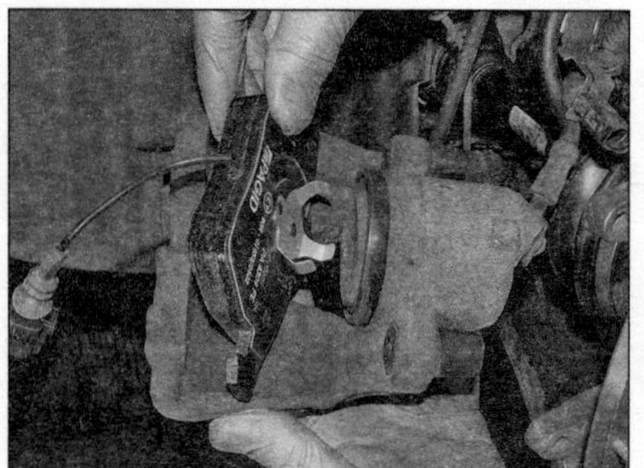
4.14 Fit the inner pad to the caliper piston

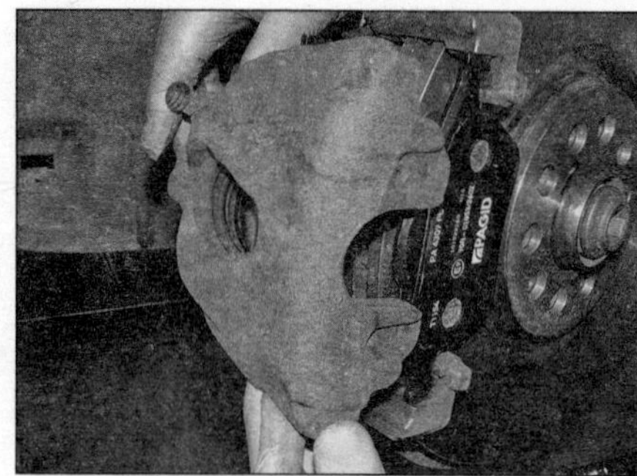
4.15a Position the caliper over the pads...

4.15b ...install the guide pins and tighten...

4.15c ...then refit the protective caps

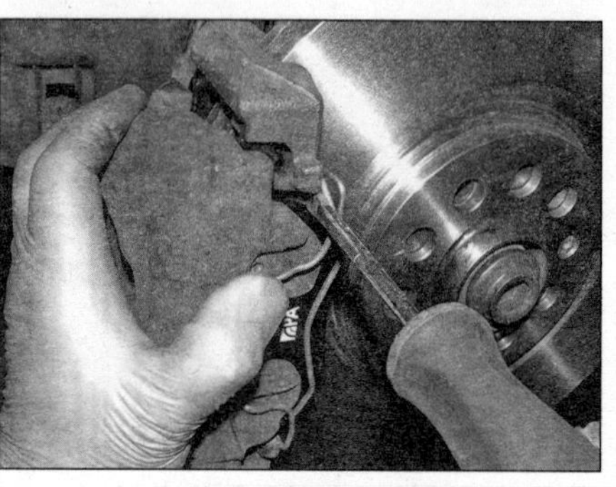
4.16a Refit the retaining spring...

4.16b ...making sure it is located correctly

14 Install the inner (piston side) pad into the caliper. The inner pad is fitted with a retaining clip, which engages with the recess in the piston **(see illustration)**. Where applicable, note that the pad with the wear sensor wiring should be installed as the inner pad. If the new pads are marked with an arrow on the backing plate, this identifies the direction of rotation. Lubricate the ends of the brake pads, as described in paragraph 11.

15 Press the caliper into position over the brake pads/disc and refit the upper and lower guide pins. Tighten the guide pins to the specified torque setting, and then refit the rubber/plastic protective caps **(see illustrations)**. Lubricate the guide pins as described in paragraph 11.

16 Refit the brake pad retaining spring to the caliper housing, making sure that the ends of the spring are located in the caliper in the correct place **(see illustrations)**.

17 Where applicable, reconnect the brake pad wear sensor wiring connector **(see illustration)**, ensuring that the wiring is correctly routed.

18 Depress the brake pedal repeatedly, until the pads are pressed into firm contact with the brake disc, and normal (non-assisted) pedal pressure is restored.

19 Repeat the above procedure on the remaining front brake caliper.

20 Refit the roadwheels, then lower the vehicle to the ground and tighten the roadwheel bolts to the specified torque.

21 Check the hydraulic fluid level as described in *Weekly checks*.

22 New pads will not give full braking efficiency until they have bedded-in. Be prepared for this and avoid hard braking (where possible) in the first hundred miles or so after pad renewal.

5 Front brake caliper - removal, overhaul and refitting

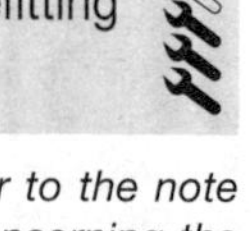

Note: *Before starting work, refer to the note at the beginning of Section 2 concerning the dangers of hydraulic fluid, and to the warning at the beginning of Section 4 concerning the dangers of hazardous brake dust.*

Removal

1 Apply the handbrake, then jack up the front of the vehicle and support it on axle stands (see *Jacking and vehicle support*). Remove the appropriate roadwheel.

2 Minimise fluid loss by first removing the master cylinder reservoir cap, and then tightening it down onto a piece of polythene, to obtain an airtight seal. Alternatively, use a brake hose clamp, a G-clamp or a similar tool to clamp the flexible hose.

3 Clean the area around the union, and then slacken and remove the brake hose union bolt **(see illustration)**. Place some cloth around the union to catch spilt fluid as the hose is disconnected.

4 Remove the brake pads as described in Section 4, and then remove the caliper from the vehicle.

Overhaul

Note: *Always check for the availability of parts, before stripping down the caliper.*

4.17 Brake pad sensor wiring connector (arrowed) – where fitted

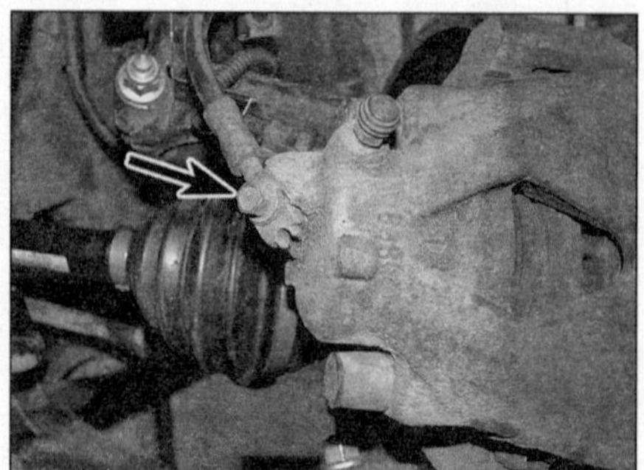
5.3 Undo the brake hose union bolt (arrowed)

5 With the caliper on the bench, wipe away all traces of dust and dirt, but avoid inhaling the dust, as it is injurious to health.

6 Withdraw the partially ejected piston from the caliper body, and remove the dust seal.

7 Using a small screwdriver, extract the piston hydraulic seal, taking great care not to damage the caliper bore **(see illustration)**.

8 Thoroughly clean all components, using only methylated spirit, isopropyl alcohol or clean hydraulic fluid as a cleaning medium. Never use mineral-based solvents such as petrol or paraffin, as they will attack the hydraulic system rubber components. Dry the components immediately, using compressed air or a clean, lint-free cloth. Use compressed air to blow clear the fluid passages. Always wear protective equipment (e.g. safety glasses), when using compressed air.

9 Check all components, and renew any that are worn or damaged. Check particularly the cylinder bore and piston; these should be renewed if they are scratched, worn or corroded in any way (note that this means the renewal of the complete caliper body assembly). Similarly check the condition of the spacers/guide pins and their bushes/bores (as applicable); both spacers/pins should be undamaged and (when cleaned) a reasonably tight sliding fit in their bores. If there is any doubt about the condition of any component, renew it.

10 If the assembly is fit for further use, obtain the appropriate repair kit; the components are available from Audi dealers in various combinations.

11 Renew all rubber seals, dust covers and caps disturbed on dismantling as a matter of course; these should never be re-used.

12 On reassembly, ensure that all components are clean and dry.

13 Thinly coat the piston and piston seal with brake fitting paste (VAG part no G 052 150 A2). This should be included in the Audi caliper overhaul/repair kit.

14 Fit the new piston (fluid) seal, using only your fingers (no tools) to manipulate it into the cylinder bore groove. Fit the new dust seal to the piston, and refit the piston to the cylinder bore using a twisting motion; ensure that the piston enters squarely into the bore. Press the piston fully into the bore, then press the dust seal into the caliper body.

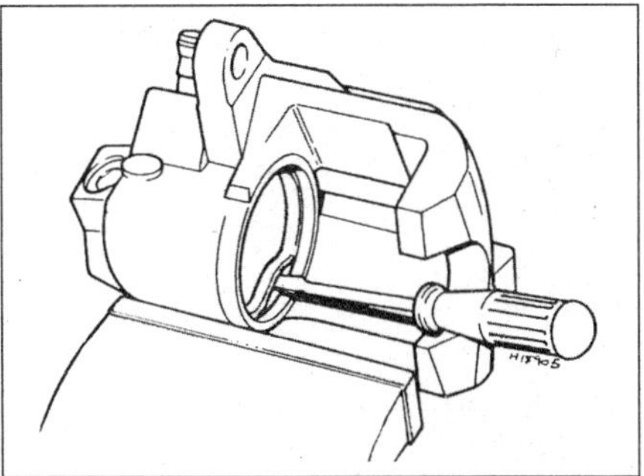

5.7 Use a small screwdriver to extract the caliper piston hydraulic seal

Refitting

15 Refit the brake pads as described in Section 4.

16 Refit the brake hose to the caliper, using new sealing washers. Make sure that the hose is not twisted, and then tighten the brake pipe union bolt to the specified torque setting.

17 Remove the brake hose clamp or polythene, as applicable, and bleed the hydraulic system as described in Section 2. Note that, providing the precautions described were taken to minimise brake fluid loss, it should only be necessary to bleed the relevant front brake.

18 Refit the roadwheel, then lower the vehicle to the ground and tighten the roadwheel bolts to the specified torque.

6 Brake disc – inspection, removal and refitting

Note: *Before starting work, refer to the note at the beginning of Section 4 concerning the dangers of hazardous brake dust.*

Note: *If either disc requires renewal, BOTH should be renewed at the same time, to ensure even and consistent braking. New brake pads should also be fitted.*

6.7a Undo the bolts (arrowed)...

6.7b ...and remove the mounting bracket

6.4 Using a DTI gauge to measure disc run-out

Front brake disc

Inspection

1 Apply the handbrake, then jack up the front of the car and support it on axle stands (see *Jacking and vehicle support*). Remove the appropriate front roadwheel.

2 Slowly rotate the brake disc so that the full area of both sides can be checked; remove the brake pads if better access is required to the inboard surface. Light scoring is normal in the area swept by the brake pads, but if heavy scoring or cracks are found, the disc must be renewed.

3 It is normal to find a lip of rust and brake dust around the perimeter of the disc; this can be scraped off if required. If, however, a lip has formed due to excessive wear of the brake pad swept area, then the disc thickness must be measured using a micrometer. Take measurements at several places around the disc, at the inside and outside of the pad swept area; if the disc has worn at any point to the specified minimum thickness or less, the disc must be renewed.

4 If the disc is thought to be warped, it can be checked for run-out. Either use a dial gauge mounted on any convenient fixed point, while the disc is slowly rotated, or use feeler blades to measure (at several points all around the disc) the clearance between the disc and a fixed point, such as the caliper mounting bracket. If the measurements obtained are at the specified maximum or beyond, the disc is excessively warped, and must be renewed; however, it is worth checking first that the hub bearings are in good condition. If the run-out is excessive, the disc must be renewed **(see illustration)**.

5 Check the disc for cracks, especially around the wheel bolt holes, and any other wear or damage, and renew if necessary.

Removal

6 Remove the brake pads as described in Section 4.

7 Unscrew the two bolts securing the brake caliper mounting bracket to the hub carrier **(see illustration)**, then slide it from over the brake disc.

8 Slacken and remove the screw securing

6.8 Undo the disc retaining screw

6.13 Caliper mounting bracket bolts (arrowed)

6.14 Brake disc securing screw (arrowed)

the brake disc to the hub, then remove the disc **(see illustration)**. If it is tight, apply penetrating fluid, and tap its rear face gently with a hide or plastic mallet. The use of excessive force could cause the disc to be damaged.

Refitting

9 Refitting is the reverse of the removal procedure, noting the following points:

a) *Ensure that the mating surfaces of the disc and hub are clean and flat.*
b) *Securely tighten the disc retaining screw.*
c) *If a new disc has been fitted, use a suitable solvent to wipe any preservative coating from the disc, before refitting the caliper.*
d) *Tighten the caliper bracket mounting bolts to the specified torque.*
e) *Refit the brake pads as described in Section 4.*
f) *Refit the roadwheel, then lower the vehicle to the ground and tighten the roadwheel bolts to the specified torque. On completion, repeatedly depress the brake pedal until normal (non-assisted) pedal pressure returns.*

Rear brake disc

Inspection

10 Apply the handbrake, then jack up the rear of the car and support it on axle stands (see *Jacking and vehicle support*). Remove the appropriate rear roadwheel.

11 Inspect the disc as described in paragraphs 2 to 5.

Removal

12 Remove the brake pads as described in Section 7.

13 Unscrew the two bolts securing the brake caliper mounting bracket to the hub carrier **(see illustration)**, then slide it from over the brake disc.

14 Slacken and remove the screw securing the brake disc to the hub, then remove the disc **(see illustration)**. If it is tight, apply penetrating fluid, and tap its rear face gently with a hide or plastic mallet. The use of excessive force could cause the disc to be damaged.

Refitting

15 Refitting is a reversal of the removal procedure, noting the following points:

a) *Ensure that the mating surfaces of the disc and hub are clean and flat.*
b) *Securely tighten the disc retaining screw.*
c) *If a new disc has been fitted, use a suitable solvent to wipe any preservative coating from the disc, before refitting the caliper.*
d) *Tighten the caliper bracket mounting bolts to the specified torque.*
e) *Refit the brake pads as described in Section 7.*
f) *Refit the roadwheel, then lower the vehicle to the ground and tighten the roadwheel bolts to the specified torque. On completion, repeatedly depress the brake pedal until normal (non-assisted) pedal pressure returns.*

7 Rear brake pads – removal, inspection and refitting

Note: *Before starting work, refer to the note at the beginning of Section 4 concerning the dangers of hazardous brake dust. New caliper mounting bolts will be required on refitting.*

Removal

1 Chock the front wheels, then jack up the rear of the vehicle and support it on axle stands (see *Jacking and vehicle support*). Remove the rear wheels.

2 Slacken the handbrake cable and detach it from the caliper as described in Section 15.

3 Slacken and remove the guide pin bolts, using a slim open-ended spanner to prevent the guide pins from rotating **(see illustration)**. Discard the bolts – new ones must be used on refitting.

4 Lift the caliper away from the brake pads, and tie it to the suspension strut using a piece of strong wire **(see illustrations)**. Do not allow the caliper to hang unsupported on the flexible brake hose.

7.3 Using a spanner to counterhold the guide pin

7.4a Remove the caliper...

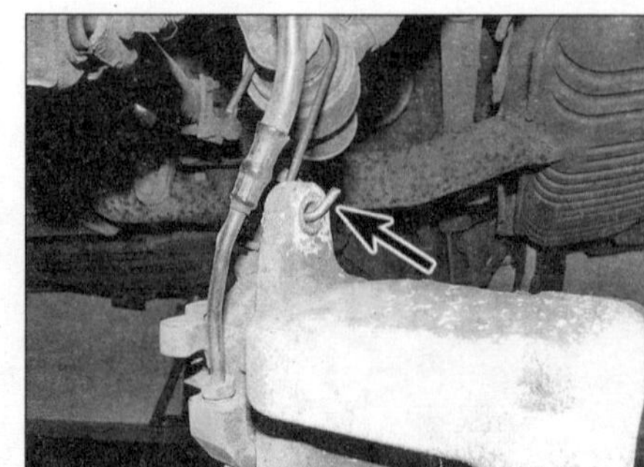
7.4b ...and hang it on a piece of wire (arrowed)

7.5a Remove the inner brake pad...

7.5b ...and outer brake pad

7.9a Applying high temperature grease to the ends of the brake pads

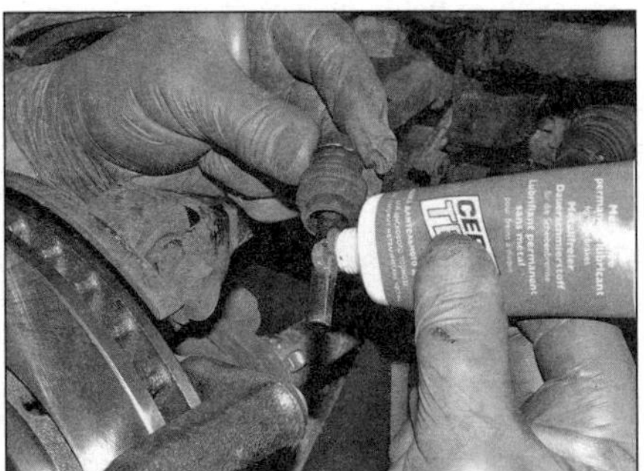

7.9b Applying special grease to the guide pins

7.10 Using special tool to push back piston

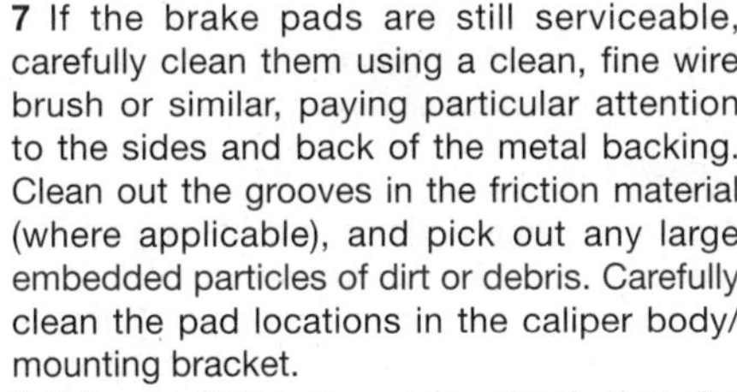

HAYNES HiNT

In the absence of the special tool, the piston can be screwed back into the caliper using a pair of circlip pliers.

5 Withdraw the two brake pads from the caliper mounting bracket **(see illustrations)**. **Note:** *The brake pad anti-rattle springs are attached to the top of the pads.*

Inspection

6 First measure the thickness of each brake pad. If either pad is worn at any point to the specified minimum thickness or less, all four pads must be renewed. Also, the pads should be renewed if any are fouled with oil or grease; there is no satisfactory way of degreasing friction material, once contaminated. If any of the brake pads are worn unevenly, or fouled with oil or grease, trace and rectify the cause before reassembly. New brake pads are available from your Audi dealer.

7 If the brake pads are still serviceable, carefully clean them using a clean, fine wire brush or similar, paying particular attention to the sides and back of the metal backing. Clean out the grooves in the friction material (where applicable), and pick out any large embedded particles of dirt or debris. Carefully clean the pad locations in the caliper body/ mounting bracket.

8 Prior to fitting the pads, check that the guide pins are free to slide easily in the caliper bracket, and check that the rubber guide pin gaiters are undamaged. Brush the dust and dirt from the caliper and piston, but do not inhale it, as it is injurious to health. Inspect the dust seal around the piston for damage, and the piston for evidence of fluid leaks, corrosion or damage. If attention to any of these components is necessary, refer to Section 8.

9 Apply a small amount of high temperature grease to the edges of the brake pads that come into contact with the mounting bracket. Also use brake grease on the guide pins to help them slide in the caliper body **(see illustrations)**.

Refitting

10 If new brake pads are to be fitted, it will be necessary to retract the piston fully. Use a special tool to rotate the piston in a clockwise direction, as it is pushed into the caliper bore **(see illustration)**. To avoid any damage to the brake master cylinder or dirt entering the ABS solenoid valves, connect a pipe to the bleed nipple, and as the piston is pushed back open the nipple and allow the displaced fluid to flow through the pipe into a suitable container, see Section 2.

11 Remove the protective foil from the outer pad backing plate, then install the pads in the mounting bracket, ensuring that each pad's friction material is against the brake disc **(see illustrations)**.

12 Make sure that the slots in the caliper piston are vertical, and then slide the caliper back into position over the pads **(see**

7.11a Remove the protective foil...

7.11b ...and install the brake pads

7.12a Align the slots in the piston...

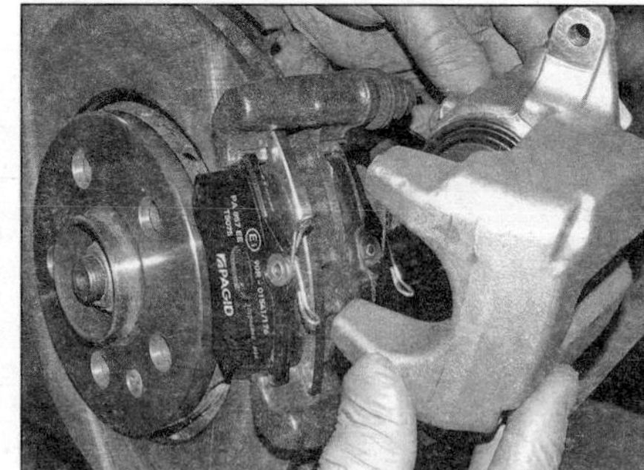
7.12b ...and slide the caliper into position

7.13 Fit new guide pin bolts

illustrations). **Note:** *On some models, the inner brake pad has a peg on the back that aligns with the slot in the caliper piston.*

13 Press the caliper into position, against the anti rattle springs on top of the brake pads, and then install the new guide pin bolts **(see illustration)**. Tighten them to the specified torque setting while retaining the guide pin with an open-ended spanner, as done on removal.

14 Depress the brake pedal repeatedly, until the pads are pressed into firm contact with the brake disc, and normal (non-assisted) pedal pressure is restored.

15 Repeat the above procedure on the remaining rear brake caliper.

16 Reconnect the handbrake cables to the calipers, and adjust the handbrake as described in Section 13.

17 Refit the roadwheels, then lower the vehicle to the ground and tighten the roadwheel bolts to the specified torque setting.

18 Check the hydraulic fluid level as described in *Weekly checks*.

19 New pads will not give full braking efficiency until they have bedded-in. Be prepared for this, and avoid hard braking as far as possible for the first hundred miles or so after pad renewal.

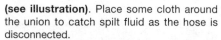

8.2 Using a brake hose clamp (arrowed)

8 Rear brake caliper – removal, overhaul and refitting

Note: *Before starting work, refer to the note at the beginning of Section 2 concerning the dangers of hydraulic fluid, and to the warning at the beginning of Section 4 concerning the dangers of hazardous dust.*

Removal

1 Chock the front wheels, then jack up the rear of the vehicle and support on axle stands (see *Jacking and vehicle support*). Remove the relevant rear wheel.

2 Minimise fluid loss by first removing the master cylinder reservoir cap, and then tightening it down onto a piece of polythene, to obtain an airtight seal. Alternatively, use a brake hose clamp, a G-clamp or a similar tool to clamp the flexible hose **(see illustration)**.

3 Clean the area around the union on the caliper, and then loosen the brake hose union bolt and disconnect the hose from the caliper **(see illustration)**. Place some cloth around the union to catch spilt fluid as the hose is disconnected.

4 Remove the caliper from over the brake pads **(see illustration)**, as described in Section 7, and then remove the caliper from the vehicle.

Overhaul

Note: *It is not possible to overhaul the brake caliper handbrake mechanism. If the mechanism is faulty, or fluid is leaking from the handbrake lever seal the caliper assembly must be renewed. Always check for the availability of parts, before stripping down the caliper.*

5 With the caliper on the bench, wipe away all traces of dust and dirt, but avoid inhaling the dust, as it is injurious to health.

6 Using a small screwdriver, carefully prise out the dust seal from the caliper, taking care not to damage the piston.

7 Remove the piston from the caliper bore by rotating it in an anti-clockwise direction. This can be achieved using a suitable pair of circlip pliers engaged in the caliper piston slots. Once the piston turns freely but does not come out any further, the piston can be withdrawn by hand.

8 Using a small screwdriver, extract the piston hydraulic seal(s), taking care not to damage the caliper bore.

9 Withdraw the guide pins from the caliper, and remove the guide sleeve gaiters.

10 Thoroughly clean all components, using only methylated spirit, isopropyl alcohol or clean hydraulic fluid as a cleaning medium. Never use mineral-based solvents such as petrol or paraffin, as they will attack the hydraulic system rubber components. Dry the components immediately, using compressed air or a clean, lint-free cloth. Use compressed air to blow clear the fluid passages.

11 Check all components, and renew any that are worn or damaged. Check particularly the cylinder bore and piston; these should be renewed (note that this means the renewal of the complete caliper body assembly) if they are scratched, worn or corroded in any way. Similarly check the condition of the spacers/guide pins and their bushes/bores (as applicable); both spacers/pins should be

8.3 Disconnect the brake hose

8.4 Removing the brake caliper

undamaged and (when cleaned) a reasonably tight sliding fit in their bores. If there is any doubt about the condition of any component, renew it.

12 If the assembly is fit for further uses obtain the appropriate repair kit; the components are available from Audi dealers in various combinations.

13 Renew all rubber seals, dust covers and caps disturbed on dismantling as a matter of course; these should never be re-used.

14 On reassembly, ensure that all components are clean and dry.

15 Smear a thin coat of brake fitting paste (VAG part no G 052 150 A2) on the piston, seal and caliper bore. This should be included in the overhaul/repair kit. Fit the new piston (fluid) seal, using only the fingers (no tools) to manipulate into the cylinder bore groove.

16 Fit the new dust seal to the piston groove, then refit the piston assembly. Turn the piston in a clockwise direction, using the method employed on dismantling, until it is fully retracted into the caliper bore.

17 Press the dust seal into position in the caliper housing.

18 Apply the grease supplied in the repair kit, or a copper-based brake grease or anti-seize compound, to the guide pins. Fit the new gaiters to the guide pins and fit the pins to the caliper ensuring that the gaiters are correctly located in the grooves on both the pins and caliper.

19 Prior to refitting, fill the caliper with fresh hydraulic fluid by slackening the bleed screw and pumping the fluid through the caliper until bubble-free fluid is expelled from the union hole.

Refitting

20 Refit the brake pads as described in Section 7.

21 Refit the brake hose to the caliper, using new sealing washers. Make sure that the hose is not twisted, and then tighten the brake pipe union bolt to the specified torque setting.

22 Remove the brake hose clamp or remove the polythene from the fluid reservoir, as applicable, and bleed the hydraulic system as described in Section 2. Note that, providing the precautions described were taken to minimise brake fluid loss, it should only be necessary to bleed the relevant rear brake.

23 Connect the handbrake cable to the caliper, and adjust the handbrake as described in Section 13.

24 Refit the roadwheel, then lower the vehicle to the ground and tighten the roadwheel bolts to the specified torque. On completion, check the hydraulic fluid level as described in *Weekly checks*.

9 Brake pedal – removal and refitting

Removal

1 Disconnect the battery negative lead. **Note:** *Before disconnecting the battery, refer to Disconnecting the battery in the reference section at the rear of this manual.*

2 With reference to Chapter 11 Section 28, remove the driver's side lower facia trim panel.

3 Undo the fasteners and remove the footwell trim panel from behind the pedal assembly **(see illustration)**.

4 Undo the retaining nuts and remove the support bracket from the pedal assembly **(see illustration)**.

5 Removed the brake light switch from the top of the brake pedal mounting bracket, as described in Section 17.

6 It is now necessary to release the brake pedal from the ball on the vacuum servo pushrod. To do this, an Audi special tool is available, but a suitable alternative can be improvised. Note that the plastic lugs in the pedal are very stiff, and it will not be possible to release them by hand. Depress and hold down the pedal, then, using the tool, release the securing lugs, and pull the pedal from the servo pushrod **(see illustrations)**.

7 Undo and remove the pivot shaft nut and bolt from the top of the mounting bracket **(see illustration)**. Slide the pivot shaft bolt out, until the pedal is free, and then remove the pedal.

8 Carefully clean all components, and renew any that are worn or damaged.

Refitting

9 Prior to refitting, apply a smear of multi-purpose grease to the pivot shaft and pedal bearing surfaces.

9.3 Remove the trim panel

9.4 Undo support bracket securing nuts (arrowed)

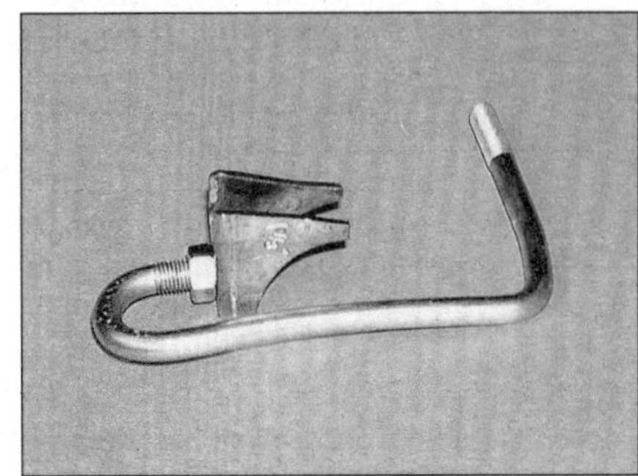

9.6a Improvised special tool constructed from a modified exhaust clamp, used to release the brake pedal from the servo pushrod

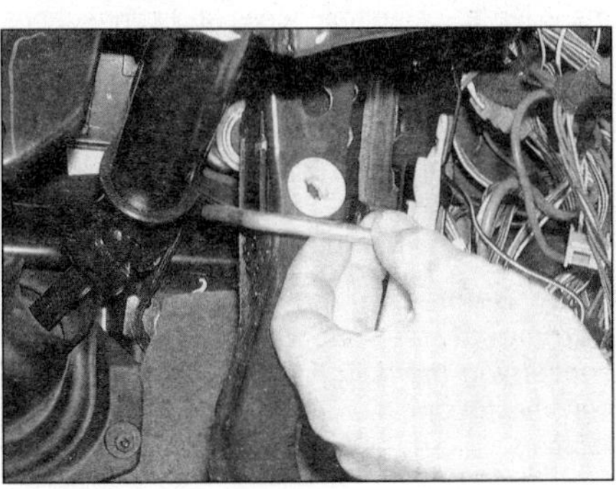

9.6b Using the tool to release the brake pedal from the servo pushrod

9.6c Rear view of the brake pedal showing plastic lugs (arrowed) securing pedal to servo pushrod

9.7 Brake pedal pivot bolt (arrowed)

10.9 Servo securing nuts (arrowed)

11.1 Non-return valve (arrowed) in vacuum pipe

11.2 Disconnect the hoses from the valve

10 Pull the servo unit pushrod down, and at the same time manoeuvre the pedal into position, ensuring that the pivot bush is correctly located.

11 Hold the servo unit pushrod, and push the pedal back onto the pushrod ball. Make sure the pedal is securely fastened to the pushrod.

12 Insert the pedal pivot bolt and tighten the retaining nut to the specified torque.

13 The remainder of the refitting procedure is the opposite of the removal; refer to the relevant Chapters where applicable.

10 Servo unit – testing, removal and refitting

Testing

1 To test the operation of the servo unit, depress the footbrake several times to exhaust the vacuum, then start the engine whilst keeping the pedal firmly depressed. As the engine starts, there should be a noticeable 'give' in the brake pedal as the vacuum builds-up. Allow the engine to run for at least two minutes, and then switch it off. If the brake pedal is now depressed, it should feel normal, but further applications should result in the pedal feeling firmer, with the pedal stroke decreasing with each application.

2 If the servo does not operate as described, first inspect the servo unit non-return valve as described in Section 11.

3 If the servo unit still fails to operate satisfactorily, the fault lies within the unit itself. Repairs to the unit are not possible – if faulty, the servo unit must be renewed.

Removal

4 Remove the master cylinder as described in Section 12.

5 Where applicable remove the heat shield from the servo, then carefully ease the vacuum hose out from the sealing grommet in the front of the servo. Where applicable, also disconnect the wiring from the servo vacuum sensor, then extract the retaining circlip with a screwdriver, and withdraw the sensor from the servo.

6 With reference to Chapter 11 Section 28, remove the driver's side lower facia trim panels, and the trim panel below the dash.

7 Where fitted, unscrew the two retaining screws and remove the support plate between the clutch and brake pedals. Also, where fitted, remove the air duct and cover for access to the servo mounting nuts.

8 It is now necessary to release the brake pedal from the ball on the vacuum servo pushrod, see Section 9.

9 Again working in the footwell, undo the nuts securing the servo unit to the bulkhead **(see illustration)**, then return to the engine compartment and manoeuvre the servo unit out of position, and recover the gasket where fitted. Note that, on some RHD models, it may be necessary to remove the inlet manifold to give sufficient clearance to withdraw the servo.

Refitting

10 Check the servo unit vacuum hose sealing grommet for signs of damage or deterioration, and renew if necessary.

11 Where applicable, fit a new gasket to the rear of the servo unit, and then reposition the unit in the engine compartment.

12 From inside the vehicle, ensure that the servo unit pushrod is correctly engaged with the brake pedal, and push the pedal onto the pushrod ball. Check the pushrod ball is securely engaged, then refit the servo unit mounting nuts and tighten them to the specified torque.

13 As applicable, refit the connecting plate, air duct and cover.

14 Refit the facia trim panels.

15 Carefully ease the vacuum hose back into position in the servo, taking great care not to displace the sealing grommet. Refit the heat shield to the servo and, where applicable, refit the vacuum sensor and wiring.

16 Refit the master cylinder as described in Section 12 of this Chapter.

17 Where applicable on RHD models, refit the inlet manifold.

18 On completion, start the engine and check for air leaks at the vacuum hose-to-servo unit connection; check the operation of the braking system.

11 Servo non-return valve – testing, removal and refitting

1 The non-return valve is located in the vacuum hose leading from the inlet manifold to the brake servo **(see illustration)**. Release the fasteners and remove the plastic trim cover from the top of the engine.

Removal

2 Slacken the retaining clips and disconnect the hoses from each side of the valve **(see illustration)**, then remove it from the engine compartment, noting the fitted direction of the valve.

Testing

3 Examine the check valve and vacuum hose for signs of damage, and renew if necessary.

4 The valve may be tested by blowing through it in both directions; air should flow through the valve in one direction only; when blown through from the servo unit end of the valve. Renew the valve if this is not the case.

Refitting

5 Make sure the valve is fitted the correct way around, as noted on removal. Ensure that the hoses are correctly routed, and are fitted to the valve securely by the retaining clips.

6 Refit the plastic trim cover to the top of the engine.

7 On completion, start the engine and check the valve-to-servo unit hoses and connections for signs of air leaks.

12 Master cylinder – removal, overhaul and refitting

Note: *Before starting work, refer to the warning at the beginning of Section 2 concerning the dangers of hydraulic fluid. A new master cylinder O-ring will be required on refitting.*

Removal

1 Disconnect the battery negative lead. **Note:** *Before disconnecting the battery, refer to*

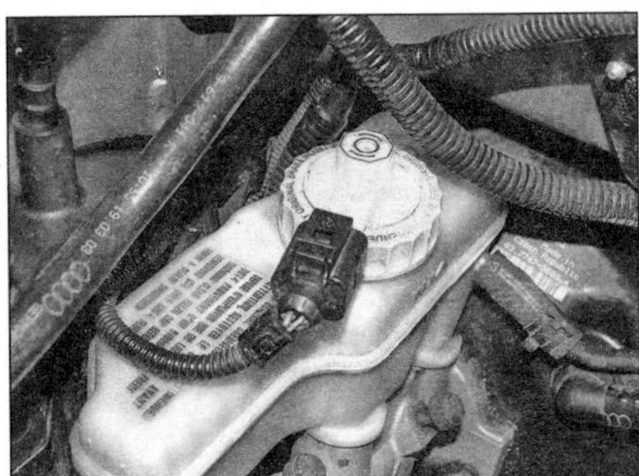
12.3 Filler cap incorporating brake fluid level warning switch

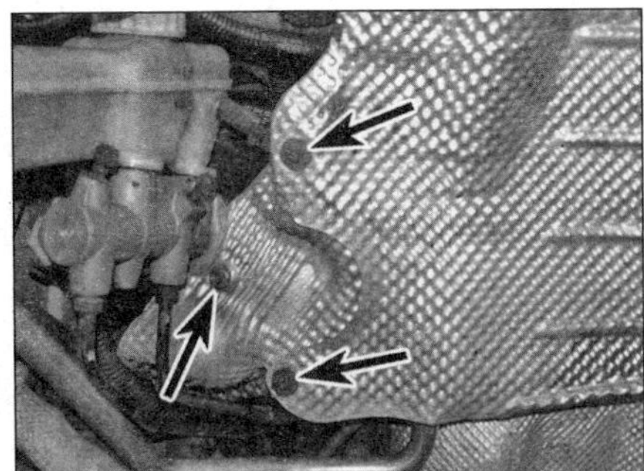
12.4 Undo the fasteners (arrowed)

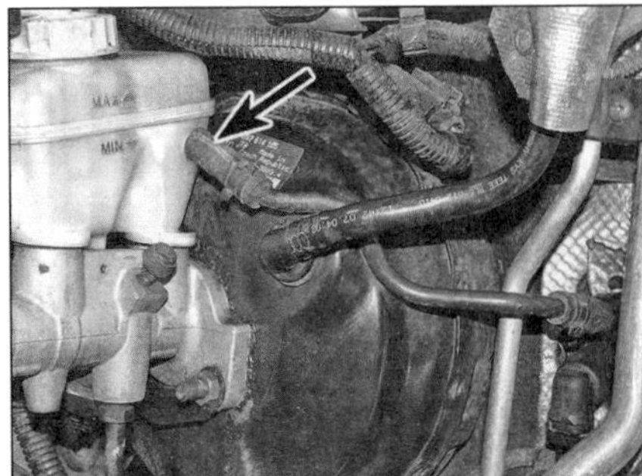
12.5 Clutch fluid supply hose (arrowed)

Disconnecting the battery *in the Reference section at the rear of this manual*. Remove the engine top cover and air inlet trunking.

2 On models with engine codes AMU, APX and BAM, remove the charge air pipe from around the top, right-hand side of the engine, as described in Chapter 4B Section 7.

3 Remove the master cylinder reservoir cap, disconnecting the wiring plug from the brake fluid level warning switch **(see illustration)**, and then syphon the hydraulic fluid from the reservoir. Note: *Do not syphon the fluid by mouth, as it is poisonous; use a syringe or an old antifreeze tester.*

4 Undo the two retaining screws and lower securing nut on the master cylinder and remove the lower part of the heat shield from the side of the master cylinder **(see illustration)**.

5 On manual transmission models, disconnect and plug the clutch master cylinder supply hose from the side of the brake fluid reservoir **(see illustration)**.

6 Disconnect the wiring connectors from the brake pressure senders, in the lower part of the master cylinder **(see illustration)**.

7 Wipe clean the area around the brake pipe unions on the side of the master cylinder, and place absorbent rags beneath the pipe unions to catch any leaking fluid **(see illustration)**. Make a note of the correct fitted positions of the unions, then unscrew the union nuts and carefully withdraw the pipes. Plug or tape over the pipe ends and master cylinder orifices, to minimise the loss of brake fluid, and to prevent the entry of dirt into the system. Wash off any spilt fluid immediately with cold water.

8 Unscrew and remove the two nuts and washers securing the master cylinder to the vacuum servo unit, then withdraw the unit from the engine compartment **(see illustration)**. Remove the O-ring from the rear of the master cylinder, and check it for damage, renew if required.

Overhaul

9 If the master cylinder is faulty, it must be renewed. Repair kits are not available from Audi dealer, so the cylinder must be treated as a sealed unit.

10 The only items that can be renewed are the mounting seals for the fluid reservoir; if these show signs of deterioration, undo the retaining screw and prise the reservoir from the top of the master cylinder. The mounting seals can then be prised out with a screwdriver. Lubricate the new seals with clean brake fluid, and press them into the master cylinder ports.

Refitting

11 Remove all traces of dirt from the master cylinder and servo unit mating surfaces, and fit a new O-ring to the groove on the master cylinder body.

12 If removed, refit the hydraulic fluid reservoir to the top of the master cylinder; making sure it is entered correctly in the rubber grommets.

13 Fit the master cylinder to the servo unit, ensuring that the servo unit pushrod enters the master cylinder bore centrally. Refit the master cylinder mounting nuts, then tighten them to the specified torque.

14 Wipe clean the brake pipe unions, then refit them to the master cylinder ports and tighten them securely.

15 On manual transmission models, reconnect the clutch master cylinder supply hose to the reservoir.

16 Refill the master cylinder reservoir with new fluid, and bleed the complete hydraulic system as described in Section 2.

17 Reconnect the wiring to the brake level switch and pressure sender switches, as applicable.

18 On models with engine codes AMU, APX and BAM, refit the charge air pipe to the top, right-hand side of the engine, as described in Chapter 4B Section 7.

19 Refit the engine cover and air trunking where necessary, and then reconnect the battery negative lead.

13 Handbrake – adjustment

1 To check the handbrake adjustment, first apply the footbrake firmly several times to establish correct pad-to-disc clearance, then apply and release the handbrake several times.

2 With the handbrake in the released position,

12.6 Brake pressure senders (arrowed)

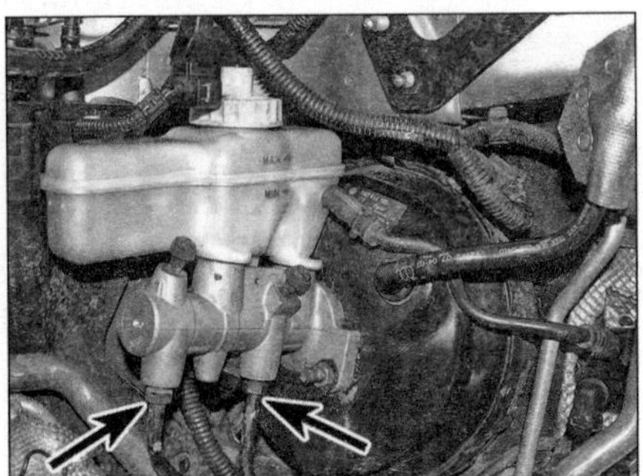
12.7 Brake pipe unions (arrowed)

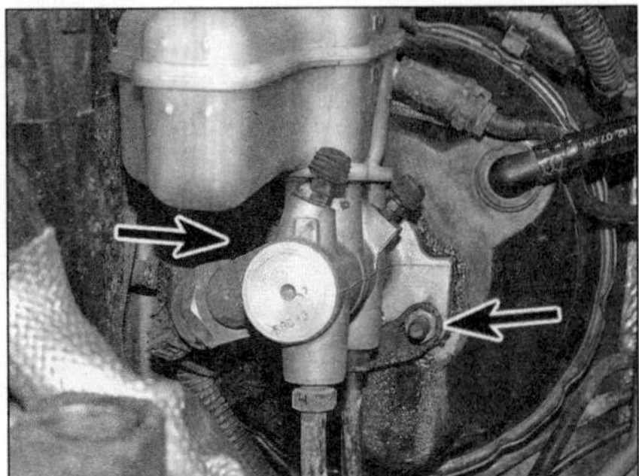
12.8 Master cylinder securing nuts (one side hidden)

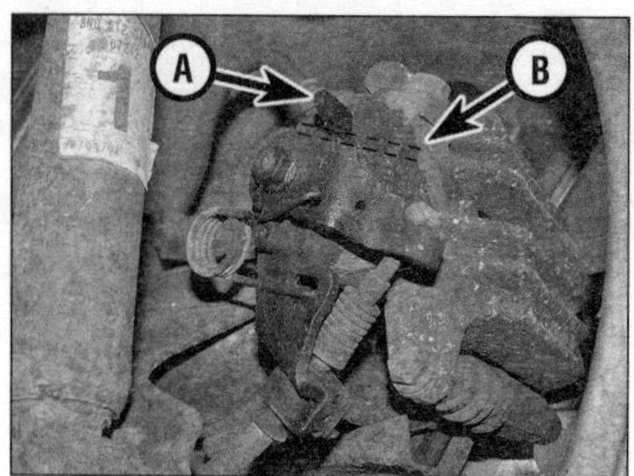

13.2 Caliper stop (A) – gap no more than 3.0 mm (B)

13.3a Unclip the trim from the centre console

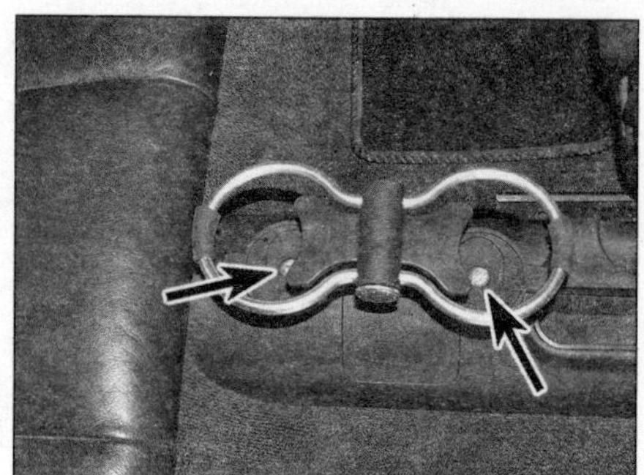

13.3b Where fitted, undo the retaining screws (arrowed)...

the measurement between the stop on the rear caliper and the handbrake lever should be no more than 3.0 mm **(see illustration)**. If adjustment is required, adjust as follows.

3 Depending on specification, it will be necessary to remove the rear trim from the rear of the centre console, and the cup holder where fitted **(see illustrations)**. On models with cup holder, remove the rubber mats, undo the retaining screws and remove the cup holder and trim.

4 With the handbrake in the fully released position, slacken the handbrake adjuster nut **(see illustration)**, until both the rear caliper handbrake levers are back against their stops. Make sure the handbrake cables are in good condition, and move freely.

5 Chock the front wheels, then jack up the rear of the vehicle and support it on axle stands, with reference to.

6 From this point, re-tighten the adjusting nut until the levers on the both rear calipers move off the caliper stops. Ensure that the gap between each caliper handbrake lever and its stop is between 1.0 and 3.0 mm **(see illustration 13.2)**.

7 Pull the handbrake on firmly three times and release it fully, then check that both wheels rotate freely.

8 Once adjustment is correct, refit the handbrake cover/cup holder (as applicable) and lower the vehicle to the ground.

14 Handbrake lever – removal and refitting

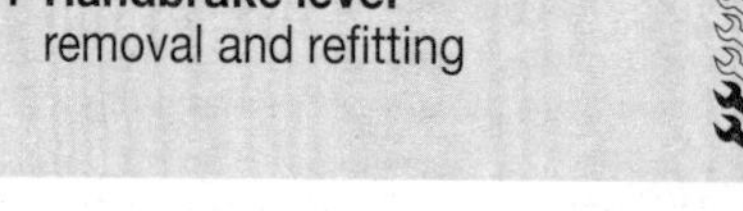

Removal

1 Remove the centre console as described in Chapter 11 Section 27. If desired, remove the handbrake lever cover sleeve by depressing the locating tag with a screwdriver, then sliding the sleeve from the lever.

2 Disconnect the wiring plug from the handbrake 'on' warning light switch **(see illustration)**.

3 Slacken the handbrake cable adjuster nut sufficiently to allow the ends of the cables to be disengaged from the equaliser plate **(see illustrations)**.

4 Unscrew the retaining nuts, and withdraw the lever and bracket assembly from the floor **(see illustration)**.

Refitting

5 Refitting is a reversal of removal, bearing in mind the following points.

a) Prior to refitting the handbrake cover, adjust the handbrake as described in Section 13.

b) Check the operation of the handbrake 'on' warning switch prior to refitting the centre console.

13.3c ...and remove the cup holder

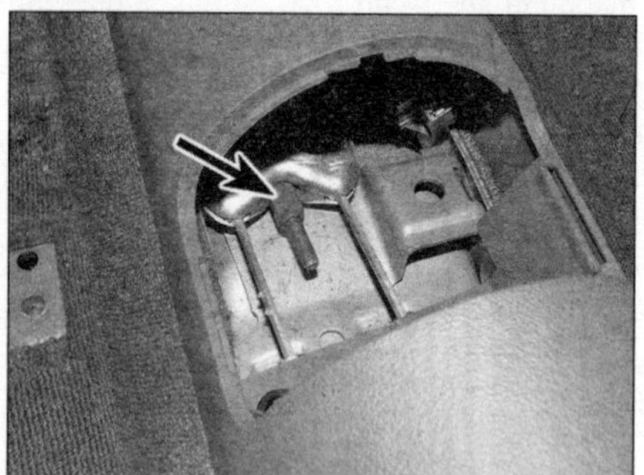

13.4 Slacken the adjuster nut (arrowed)

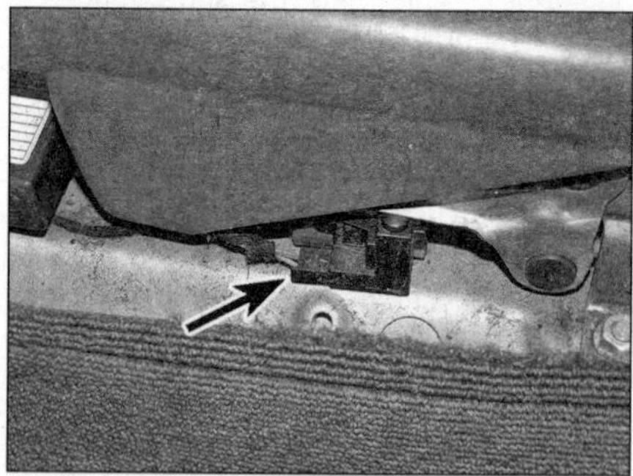

14.2 Handbrake warning light switch (arrowed)

14.3a Slacken the adjuster nut (arrowed)...

14.3b ...and disengage the inner cables (arrowed)

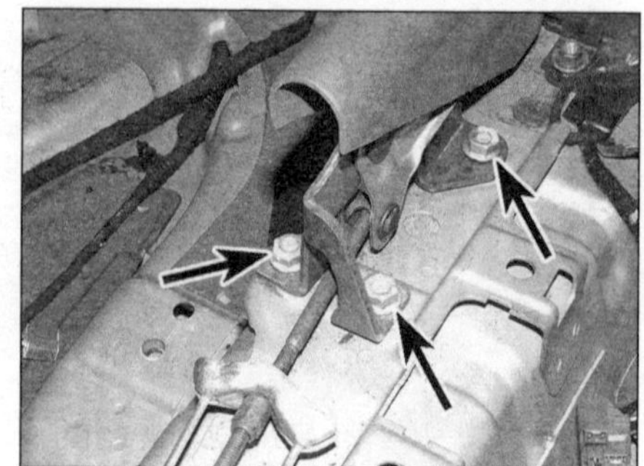

14.4 Handbrake lever bracket mounting nuts (arrowed)

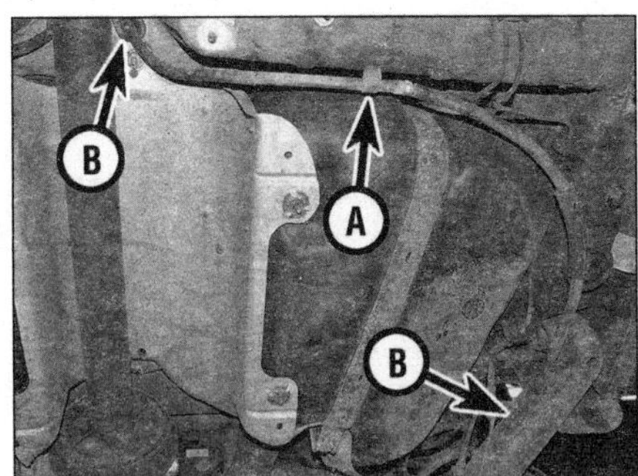

15.4 Note the routing of the cable – 4-wheel drive shown

(A) Retaining clip (B) Grommets

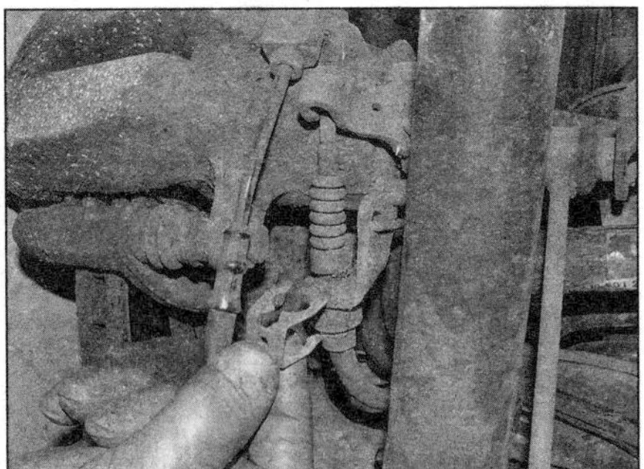

15.5a Remove the retaining clip...

15.5b ...release the inner cable...

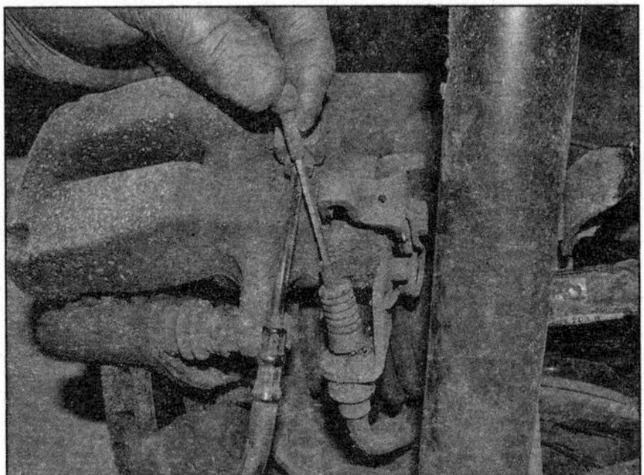

15.5c ...and remove the inner cable from its lever

15.6 Disengage grommet (arrowed) from floor panel

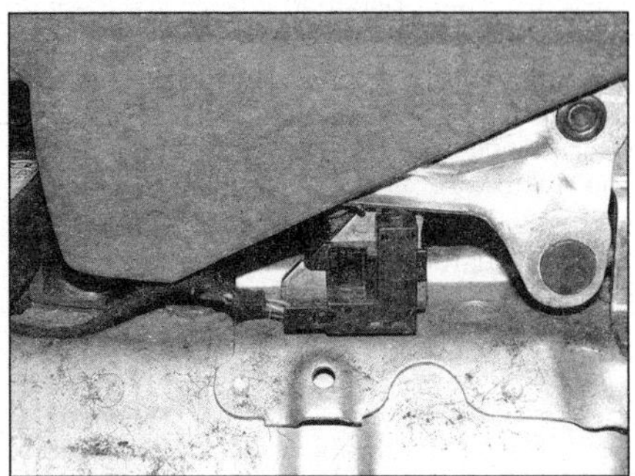

16.3 Handbrake warning light switch

15 Handbrake cables – removal and refitting

Removal

1 Remove the centre console as described in Chapter 11 Section 27, to gain access to the handbrake lever. There are two cables fitted, a right- and a left-hand section, which are linked to the lever by an equaliser plate. Each cable can be removed individually.

2 Slacken the handbrake cable adjuster nut sufficiently to allow the ends of the cables to be disengaged from the equaliser plate, see Section 14.

3 Chock the front wheels, then jack up the rear of the car and support it on axle stands, with reference to. Remove the undershields and heatshields, as required, to access the handbrake cables.

4 Working back along the length of the cable, note its correct routing, and free it from all the relevant guides and retaining clips **(see illustration)**. On 4-wheel drive models, the cable passes through the rear trailing arms. On 2-wheel drive models, the cable is clipped to the underside of the rear trailing arms.

5 Remove the outer cable retaining clip, then disengage the inner cable from the caliper handbrake lever and detach the cable from the caliper **(see illustrations)**.

6 Withdraw the cable from underneath the vehicle, releasing it from the grommets in the floor panel **(see illustration)**.

Refitting

7 Refitting is a reversal of removal, bearing in mind the following points.

a) *Make sure the handbrake cable is located securely to the underside of the vehicle, and the grommets are fitted correctly, as noted on removal.*

b) *Before refitting the centre console, adjust the handbrake as described in Section 13.*

c) *Once adjustment is correct, refit any undershields and lower the vehicle to the ground.*

16 Handbrake 'on' warning light switch – removal and refitting

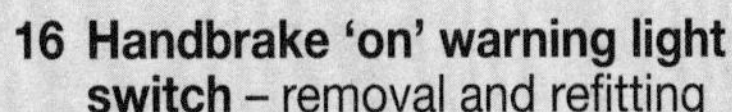

Removal

1 Disconnect the battery negative lead. **Note:** *Before disconnecting the battery, refer to* Disconnecting the battery *in the reference section at the rear of this manual.*

2 Remove the centre console, with reference to Chapter 11 Section 27, if necessary.

3 Disconnect the wiring plug from the switch **(see illustration)**.

4 Release the securing lugs, and remove the switch from the handbrake lever mounting bracket.

Refitting

5 Refitting is a reversal of removal.

17 Brake light switch – removal and refitting

Note: *There are two types of brake light switch fitted, one has a round housing, and the other has a square housing, follow the correct procedure for the type fitted.*

Note: *As the switch retaining clips are plastic, it is recommended by Audi that once the switch has been removed, a new one should be refitted.*

1 The brake light switch is mounted on the top of the brake pedal mounting bracket **(see illustration)**.

17.1 Brake light switch (arrowed)

18.1 Brake pressure senders (arrowed)

2 To remove the switch, first remove the facia lower trim panel on the driver's side, as described in Chapter 11 Section 28.

Switch with round housing

3 Disconnect the wiring connector, then turn the switch through 45° anti-clockwise, and withdraw it from the pedal mounting bracket.
4 When refitting the switch, first extend the switch plunger to its fullest extent. Fit the switch to the mounting bracket, aligning the two locating tabs and turning it through 45° clockwise. The brake pedal does not need to be depressed for this operation, as the plunger automatically adjusts when it is inserted. Refit the wiring connector to the switch and then further refitting is a reversal of removal.

Switch with square housing

5 Disconnect the wiring connector, then turn the switch through 90° anti-clockwise, and withdraw it from the pedal mounting bracket.
6 When refitting the switch, first extend the switch plunger to its fullest extent, then hold the brake pedal depressed when offering the switch into position. Fit the switch by turning it through 90° clockwise and release the pedal – this sets the switch adjustment. Refit the wiring connector to the switch and then further refitting is a reversal of removal.

18 Brake pressure sender(s) – removal and refitting

Removal

1 The brake pressure sender(s) are located on the lower part of the master cylinder **(see illustration)**.
2 Remove the engine top cover, and on models with engine codes AMU, APX and BAM, remove the charge air pipe from around the top, right-hand side of the engine, as described in Chapter 4B Section 7.
3 Remove the master cylinder reservoir cap, disconnecting the wiring plug from the brake fluid level warning switch, and then syphon the hydraulic fluid from the reservoir. **Note:** *Do not syphon the fluid by mouth, as it is poisonous; use a syringe or an old antifreeze tester.*
4 Disconnect the wiring from the pressure sender switch(es).
5 Unscrew the pressure sender switch(es) from the bottom of the master cylinder, place absorbent rags beneath the master cylinder to catch leaking fluid.

Refitting

6 Refitting is a reversal of removal, but tighten the pressure sender switches to the specified torque. Refill and bleed the brake system, as described in Section 2.

19 Anti-lock braking system (ABS) – general information and precautions

Note: *On models equipped with traction control, the ABS unit is a dual function unit, controlling both the anti-lock braking system (ABS) and the electronic differential locking (EDL) system functions.*
1 ABS is standard on models covered in this manual; the system may also be referred to as including EBD (Electronic Brake Distribution) which means it adjusts the front and rear braking forces according to the weight being carried. Two types of ABS are fitted: the Mark 20 IE and the Mark 60 **(see illustrations)**. The system comprises a hydraulic unit (which contains the hydraulic solenoid valves and accumulators), the electrically-driven fluid return pump, four roadwheel sensors (one fitted for each wheel), and the electronic control module (ECM). The purpose of the system is to prevent wheel(s) locking during heavy braking. This is achieved by automatic release of the brake on the relevant wheel, followed by re-application of the brake.
2 The solenoids are controlled by the ECM, which itself receives signals from the four wheel sensors, which monitor the speed of rotation of each wheel. By comparing these speed signals, the ECM can determine the speed at which the car is travelling. It can then use this speed to determine when a wheel is decelerating at an abnormal rate, compared to the speed of the car, and therefore predicts when a wheel is about to lock. During normal operation, the system functions in the same way as a non-ABS braking system.
3 If the ECM senses that a wheel is about to lock, it operates the relevant solenoid valve in the hydraulic unit, which then isolates the brake caliper on the wheel which is about to lock from the master cylinder, effectively sealing-in the hydraulic pressure.
4 If the speed of rotation of the wheel continues to decrease at an abnormal rate, the ECM switches on the electrically-driven

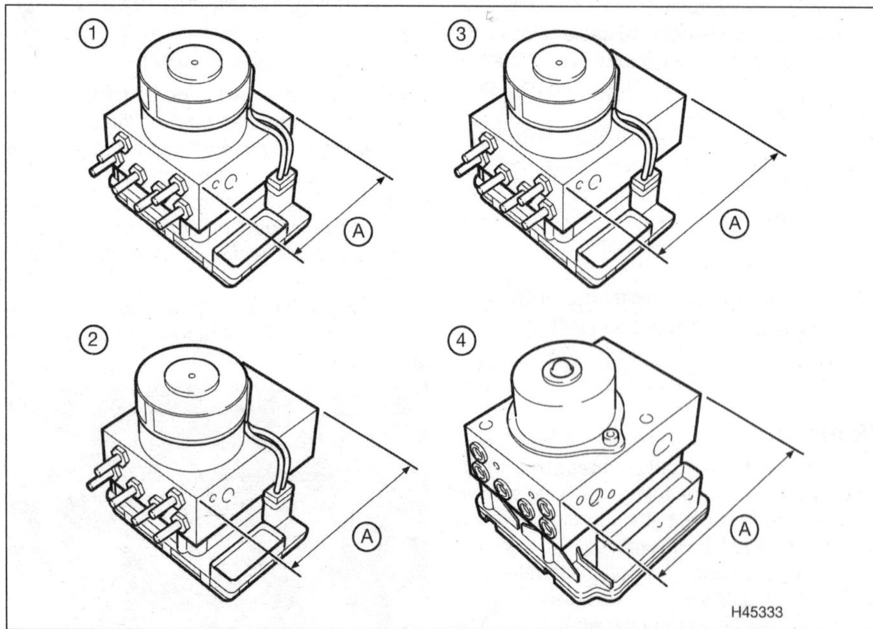

19.1a Distinguishing features of the Mark 20 IE ABS hydraulic unit

1 ABS version (A = 100 mm)
2 ABS/EDL version (A = 130 mm)
3 ABS/EDL/TCS version (A = 130 mm)
4 ABS/EDL/TCS/ESP version (A = 135 mm)

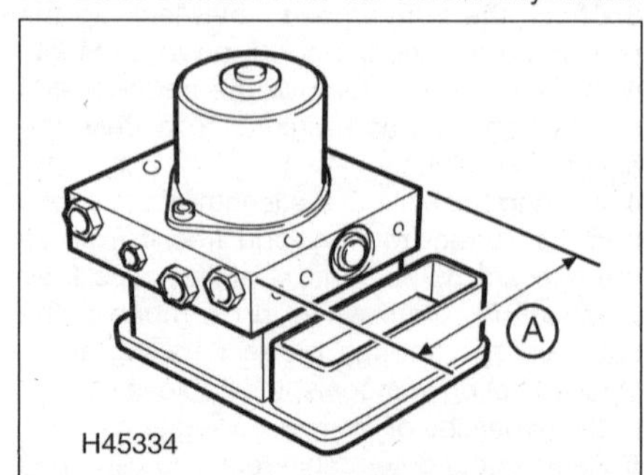

19.1b Distinguishing features of the Mark 60 ABS hydraulic unit

1 ABS/EDL/TCS/ESP version (A = 100 mm)

return pump, which pumps the hydraulic fluid back into the master cylinder, releasing pressure on the brake caliper so that the brake is released. Once the speed of rotation of the wheel returns to an acceptable rate, the pump stops; the solenoid valve opens, allowing the hydraulic master cylinder pressure to return to the caliper, which then re-applies the brake. This cycle can be carried out at up to 10 times a second.

5 The action of the solenoid valves and return pump creates pulses in the hydraulic circuit. When the ABS system is functioning, these pulses can be felt through the brake pedal.

6 The operation of the ABS system is entirely dependent on electrical signals. To prevent the system responding to any inaccurate signals, a built-in safety circuit monitors all signals received by the ECM. If an inaccurate signal or low battery voltage is detected, the ABS system is automatically shut down, and the warning light on the instrument panel is illuminated, to inform the driver that the ABS system is not operational. Normal braking should still be available, however.

7 If a fault does develop in the ABS system, the car must be taken to an Audi dealer for fault diagnosis and repair.

20 Anti-lock braking system (ABS) components – removal and refitting

Hydraulic unit

1 Removal and refitting of the hydraulic unit is best entrusted to an Audi dealer. It is positioned in the left-hand rear corner of the engine compartment, behind the battery **(see illustration)**. If the fluid is lost from the hydraulic unit, there is no guarantee that the unit can be sufficiently filled or the fluid bled through the unit. Also a fault diagnosis check must be performed on completion using specialist equipment.

Electronic control module (ECM)

2 The ECM is mounted at the rear of the hydraulic unit, secured by three Torx screws. Although it can be separated from the hydraulic unit, due to the delicacy of the components and the need for absolute cleanliness, it is recommended that the work be entrusted to a Audi dealer. See hydraulic unit information in paragraph 1.

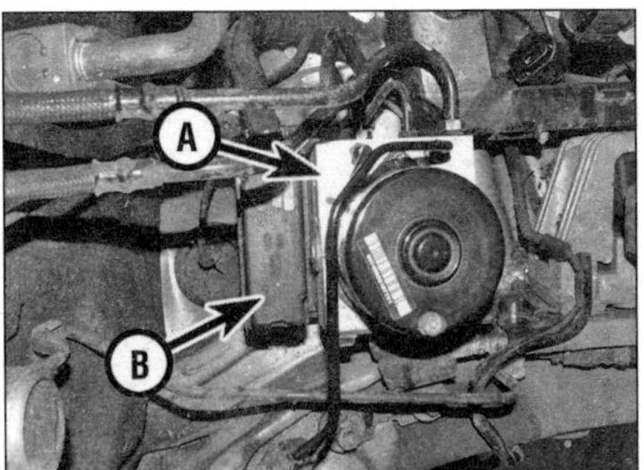

20.1 ABS hydraulic unit (A) and ECM (B)

Front wheel sensor

Removal

3 Chock the rear wheels, then firmly apply the handbrake, jack up the front of the car and support on axle stands (see *Jacking and vehicle support*). Remove the appropriate front roadwheel.

4 Disconnect the electrical connector from the sensor by carefully lifting up the retaining tag, and pulling the connector from the sensor **(see illustration)**.

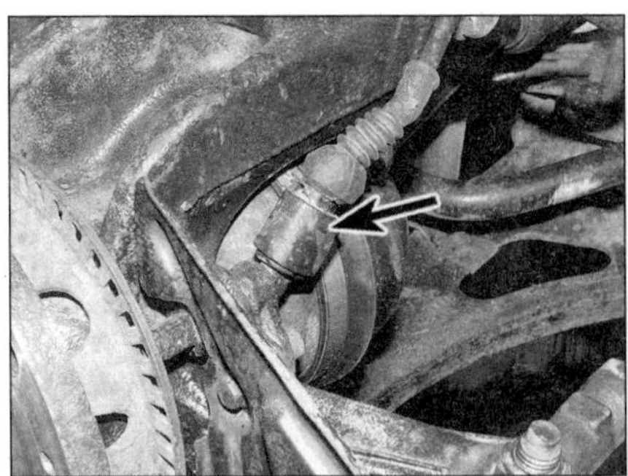

20.4 Disconnect the wiring connector (arrowed)

5 Slacken and remove the hexagon socket-head bolt securing the sensor to the hub carrier, and remove the sensor from the car.

Refitting

6 Ensure that the sensor and hub carrier sealing faces are clean.

7 Apply a thin coat of lubricating paste (Audi G 000 650) to the mounting hole inner surface, then fit the sensor to the hub carrier. Refit the retaining bolt and tighten it to the specified torque. The gap between the end of the sensor and the ABS rotor should be a constant 0.3 mm, as the rotor is turned **(see illustration)**.

20.7 Air gap (arrowed) should be 0.3 mm

8 Ensure that the sensor wiring is correctly routed and retained by all the necessary clips, and does not foul anything when the steering is turned, reconnect the wiring connector.

9 Refit the roadwheel, then lower the car to the ground and tighten the roadwheel bolts to the specified torque.

Rear wheel sensor

Removal

10 Chock the front wheels, then jack up the rear of the car and support it on axle stands (see *Jacking and vehicle support*). Remove the appropriate roadwheel.

11 Remove the rear sensor **(see illustration)**, as described in paragraphs 4 and 5, for front wheel speed sensor.

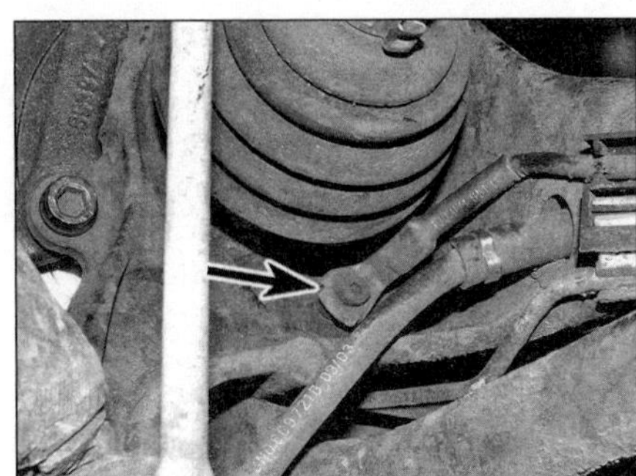

20.11 Rear wheel sensor (arrowed)

Refitting

12 Refit the sensor as described above in paragraphs 6 to 9.

Rotor ring

13 The ABS rotor rings are integral with the centre hub on the front wheels of all models. These can only be inspected after removal of the front brake disc, see Section 6.

14 On the rear of 4WD models, they are also integral with the centre hub **(see illustration)**. These can be inspected after removal of the front brake disc, see Section 6.

20.14 Rotor ring (arrowed) part of the centre hub

15 On the rear of FWD models they are part of the wheel bearing assembly.These can only be inspected after removal of the wheel bearing assembly.

16 If the ABS rotor is faulty, the bearings must be renewed as described in Chapter 10 Section 3 (front) and Chapter 10 Section 9 (rear).

Chapter 10
Suspension and steering systems

Contents

Degrees of difficulty

Easy, suitable for novice with little experience	**Fairly easy,** suitable for beginner with some experience	**Fairly difficult,** suitable for competent DIY mechanic	**Difficult,** suitable for experienced DIY mechanic	**Very difficult,** suitable for expert DIY or professional

Specifications

Front suspension

Type . . . Independent, with MacPherson struts incorporating coil springs and telescopic shock absorbers. Anti-roll bar fitted to all models

Rear suspension – FWD

Type . . . . . Transverse torsion beam axle with trailing arms. Separate gas-filled telescopic shock absorbers and coil springs. Anti-roll bar fitted to all models

Rear suspension – 4WD

Type . . . . . Dual link trailing arm (DLTA) axle connected to the rear subframe that supports the final drive assembly. Separate gas-filled telescopic shock absorbers and coil springs. Anti-roll bar fitted to all models

Steering

Type . . . . . Rack-and-pinion. Power assistance standard

Wheel alignment and steering angles*

Front wheel:

Toe setting at each wheel . . . . . +4' ± 3.5'
Total toe . . . . . +8' ± 7'
Toe-out on turns at 20 degrees steering angle . . . . . +1° 31' ± 20'
Camber:
  Standard suspension . . . . . -45' ± 30'
  Sports suspension . . . . . -58' ± 30'
Caster (non-adjustable)
  Standard suspension . . . . . +7° 58'
  Sports suspension . . . . . +8° 15'
Maximum permissible difference between left and right . . . . . 30°

Rear wheel (front wheel drive – FWD):

Toe setting at each wheel:
  Standard suspension . . . . . +14' ± 5'
  Sports suspension . . . . . +19.5' ± 5'
Total toe:
  Standard suspension . . . . . +28' ± 10'
  Sports suspension . . . . . +39' ± 10'
Maximum permissible difference between left and right . . . . . 15'
Camber . . . . . -2° ± 20'
Maximum permissible difference between left and right . . . . . 30°

Rear wheel (four wheel drive – 4WD):

Toe setting at each wheel . . . . . +7.5' ± 5'
Total toe . . . . . +15' ± 10'
Maximum permissible difference between left and right . . . . . 20'
Camber (tolerance ± 20') :
  Suspension height (standard suspension)*:
    352 mm . . . . . -2° 20'
    355 mm . . . . . -2° 04'
    360 mm . . . . . -1° 54'
    365 mm . . . . . -1° 44'
    370 mm . . . . . -1° 34'
    372 mm . . . . . -1° 30'
    375 mm . . . . . -1° 24'
    380 mm . . . . . -1° 14'
    382 mm . . . . . -1° 10'
  Suspension height (sports suspension)*:
    332 mm . . . . . -2° 48'
    335 mm . . . . . -2° 42'
    340 mm . . . . . -2° 32'
    345 mm . . . . . -2° 22'
    350 mm . . . . . -2° 12'
    352 mm . . . . . -2° 08'
    355 mm . . . . . -2° 02'
    360 mm . . . . . -1° 52'
    362 mm . . . . . -1° 48'

** Suspension height measured from the centre of the wheel to the upper inside edge of the wheel arch.*

Roadwheels

Type . . . . . Aluminium alloy

Tyres

Size . . . . . 205/55R16 and 225/45R17
Pressures . . . . . see *Lubricants, fluids and tyre pressures*

Torque wrench settings

	Nm	lbf ft
Front suspension		
Anti-roll bar:		
Mounting clamp-to-subframe bolts	25	18
Connecting link-to-anti-roll bar nut*	90	66
Connecting link-to-strut nut	90	66
Hub nut/bolt*	See Chapter 8	
Lower arm:		
Pivot/mounting bolts*:		
Stage 1	70	52
Stage 2	Angle-tighten a further 90°	
Balljoint-to-lower arm nuts*	75	55
Balljoint nut*	75	55
Suspension strut:		
Bottom clamp bolt nut*:		
Stage 1	60	44
Stage 2	Angle-tighten a further 90°	
Upper mounting nut*	60	44
Spring seat retaining nut	60	44
Splash plate to wheel housing	10	7
Subframe-to-underbody bolts*:		
Stage 1	100	74
Stage 2	Angle-tighten a further 90°	
Vehicle level sender:		
Sender to underbody (pop-rivet screw)	8	6
Sender link to lower arm	6	4
Steering		
Power steering pump mounting bolts	25	18
Power steering pump pressure hose union bolt	30	22
Steering column universal joint clamp bolt*	30	22
Steering column:		
Upper mounting bolts	22	16
Lower mounting bolt nut	10	7
Fluid pipe union bolts:		
M14 union bolt	40	30
M16 union bolt	45	33
Steering gear mounting bolts*:		
Stage 1	20	15
Stage 2	Angle-tighten a further 90°	
Steering wheel bolt	50	37
Track rod balljoint locknut	50	37
Track rod balljoint nut*	45	33
Track rod inner balljoint to steering rack	75	55
Rear suspension (front wheel drive – FWD)		
Hub nut (12-point nut)*	220	162
Axle mounting bracket bolts: *		
Stage 1	30	22
Stage 2	Angle-tighten a further 90°	.
Axle mounting bush nut and bolt: *		
Stage 1	45	33
Stage 2	Angle-tighten a further 90°	
Stub axle bolts: *		
Stage 1	50	37
Stage 2	Angle-tighten a further 90°	
Shockabsorber:		
Lower mounting bolt and nut*		
Stage 1	40	30
Stage 2	Angle-tighten a further 90°	
Upper mounting bolts*		
Stage 1	30	22
Stage 2	Angle-tighten a further 90°	
Vehicle level sender to trailing arm	20	15
Vibration damper weight-to-axle bolts*:		
Stage 1	20	15
Stage 2	Angle-tighten a further 45°	

Torque wrench settings (continued)

	Nm	lbf ft
Rear suspension (four wheel drive – 4WD)		
Hub nut/bolt*	See Chapter 8	
Axle mounting bracket bolts*	75	54
Axle mounting bush nut and bolt *	90	66
Upper transverse link arm bolts: *		
Stage 1	70	52
Stage 2	Angle-tighten a further 90°	
Lower transverse link arm bolts: *		
Stage 1	70	52
Stage 2	Angle-tighten a further 90°	
Shockabsorber:		
Upper bolt*	60	44
Lower bolt	110	81
Anti-roll bar to drop link nut*	25	18
Anti-roll bar clamp bolts:		
Stage 1	5	3
Stage 2	20	15
Rear subframe mounting bolts: *		
Stage 1	110	81
Stage 2	Angle-tighten a further 90°	
Subframe support to final drive:		
Stage 1	40	30
Stage 2	Angle-tighten a further 45°	
Subframe support bush bolt	60	44
Subframe rear alloy frame bolts	60	44
Subframe bush to final drive bolts	60	44
Roadwheels		
Roadwheel bolts	120	89

** Renew the nut/bolt every time it is removed*

1 General Information

1 The independent front suspension is of the MacPherson strut type, incorporating coil springs and integral telescopic shock absorbers. The struts are located by transverse lower suspension arms, which use rubber inner mounting bushes, and incorporate a balljoint at the outer ends. The front wheel bearing housings, which carry the wheel bearings, brake calipers and the hub/disc assemblies, are attached to the MacPherson struts by clamp bolts, and connected to the lower arms through the balljoints. A front anti-roll bar is fitted to all models. The anti-roll bar is rubber-mounted, and is connected to both lower suspension arms by short links.

2 On front wheel drive (FWD) models, the rear suspension consists of a torsion beam axle with telescopic shock absorbers and coil springs. An anti-roll bar is incorporated into the rear axle beam.

3 On four wheel drive (4WD) models, the rear suspension consists of a dual link trailing arm (DLTA) axle, which is connected to the rear subframe that supports the final drive unit and Haldex coupling. It has separate gas-filled telescopic shock absorbers and coil springs. An anti-roll bar fitted across the rear of the rear subframe.

4 The safety steering column incorporates an intermediate shaft at its lower end. The inter-mediate shaft is connected to both the steering column and steering gear by universal joints, although the shaft is supplied as part of the column assembly and cannot be separated. Both the inner steering column and intermediate shaft have splined sections which collapse during a major frontal impact. The outer column is also telescopic with two sections, to facilitate reach adjustment.

5 The steering gear is mounted onto the front subframe, and is connected by two track rods, with balljoints at their inner and outer ends, to the steering arms projecting rearwards from the wheel bearing housings. The track rod ends are threaded to the track rods in order to allow adjustment of the front wheel toe setting.

6 Power-assisted steering is fitted as standard on all models. The hydraulic steering system is powered by a belt-driven pump, which is driven off the crankshaft pulley.

7 All models are fitted with an Anti-lock Brake System (ABS), and can also be fitted with a Traction Control System (TCS), an Electronic Differential Lock (EDL) system and an Electronic Stability Program (ESP). The ABS may also be referred to as including EBD (Electronic Brake Distribution) which means it adjusts the front and rear braking forces according to the weight being carried, and the TCS may also be referred to as ASR (Anti Slip Regulation).

8 The TCS system prevents the front wheels from losing traction during acceleration by reducing the engine output. The system is switched on automatically when the engine is started, and it utilises the ABS system sensors to monitor the rotational speeds of the front wheels.

9 The ESP system extends the ABS, TCS and EDL functions to reduce wheel spin in difficult driving conditions. It does this by using highly-sensitive sensors which monitor the speed of the vehicle, lateral movement of the vehicle, the brake pressure, and the steering angle of the front wheels. If, for example, the vehicle is tending to oversteer, the brake will be applied to the front outer wheel to correct the situation. If the vehicle is tending to understeer, the brake will be applied to the rear inside wheel. The steering angle of the front wheels is monitored by an angle sensor on the top of the steering column.

10 The TCS/ESP systems should always be switched on, except when driving with snow chains, driving in snow or driving on loose surfaces, when some wheel spin may be

2.3 Removing the driveshaft retaining nut

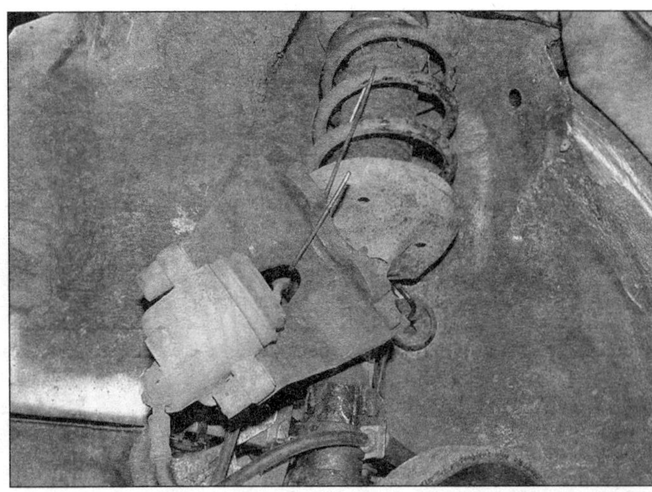

2.5 Support the caliper with a piece of wire

advantageous. The ESP switch is located in the centre of the facia.

11 Some models are also fitted with an Electronic Differential Lock (EDL) which reduces unequal traction from the front wheels. If one front wheel spins 100 rpm or more faster than the other, the faster wheel is slowed down by applying the brake to that wheel. The system is not the same as the traditional differential lock, where the actual differential gears are locked. Because the system applies a front brake, in the event of a brake disc overheating the system will shut down until the disc has cooled. No warning light is displayed if the system shuts down. As is the case with the TCS system, the EDL system uses the ABS sensors to monitor front wheel speeds.

2 Front wheel bearing housing - removal and refitting

Note: *All self-locking nuts and bolts disturbed on removal must be renewed as a matter of course.*

Note: *A new hub nut/bolt will be required on refitting. Where bolts are fitted, there are two different types fitted, one is ribbedunder the face of the bolt head and one is smooth (see Chapter 8A Section 2). The torque setting is different for each type of bolt (see Specifications), so it is important to make sure you check which is fitted.*

Removal

1 Remove the wheel trim/centre cap (as applicable) then apply the handbrake, and partially unscrew the relevant nut/hub bolt with the vehicle resting on its wheels, by a maximum of 90° – note that the bolt is very tight, and a suitable extension bar will probably be required to aid unscrewing. Also slacken the road wheel securing bolts by half a turn. **Note:** *Do not loosen the bolt more than 90° with the vehicle standing on the ground, as the wheel bearings may be damaged.*

2 Apply the handbrake, then jack up the front of the vehicle and support it on axle stands (see *Jacking and vehicle support*). Remove the relevant front roadwheel.

3 Unscrew and remove the driveshaft retaining nut/bolt **(see illustration)**.

4 Disconnect the wiring connector from the ABS wheel speed sensor, as described in Chapter 9 Section 20.

5 Remove the brake disc as described in Chapter 9 Section 6. This procedure includes removing the brake pads (see Chapter 9 Section 4). Using a piece of strong wire or similar, tie the caliper to the front suspension coil spring, to avoid placing any strain on the hydraulic brake hose **(see illustration)**.

6 Loosen the nut securing the steering track rod balljoint to the arm on the front wheel bearing housing **(see illustration)**. To do this, fit a ring spanner to the nut, then hold the balljoint pin stationary using a Torx/Allen key. With the nut removed, it may be possible to release the balljoint from the arm on the wheel bearing housing. If not, leave the nut on by a few turns to protect the threads, then use a universal balljoint separator to release the balljoint. Remove the nut completely once the taper has been released (see Section 22).

7 Loosen the nut securing the lower lower arm to the lower part of the front wheel bearing housing **(see illustration)**. To do this, fit a ring spanner to the nut, then hold the balljoint pin stationary using a Torx/Allen key. With the nut removed, it may be possible to release the taper on the balljoint from the wheel bearing housing. If not, leave the nut on by a few turns to protect the threads, then use a universal balljoint separator to release the balljoint. Remove the nut completely once the taper has been released (see Section 5).

8 Note which way round it is fitted, then unscrew the nut and remove the clamp bolt securing the top of the wheel bearing housing to the bottom of the strut **(see illustration)**.

2.6 Disconnect the track rod balljoint

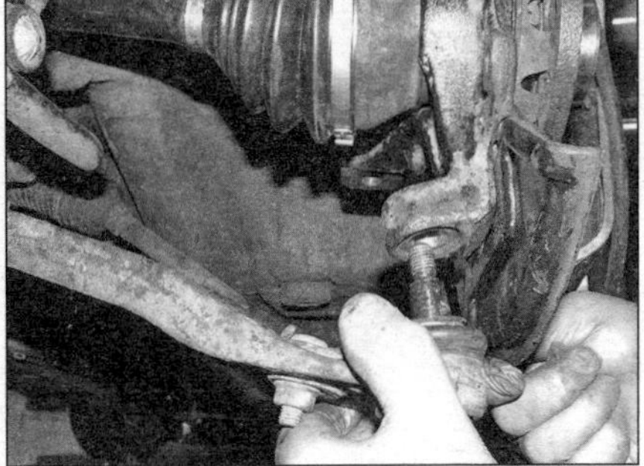

2.7 Disconnect the lower arm

2.8 Note the fitted position of the bolt (arrowed)

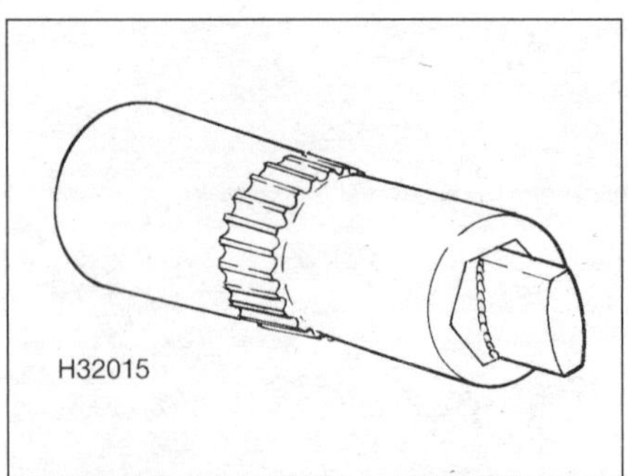

2.9a Tool used by Audi technicians...

2.9b ...to open up the split (arrowed) in the wheel bearing housing

2.9c Withdrawing the wheel bearing housing from the bottom of the suspension strut

2.10 Remove the splash shield

9 The wheel bearing housing must now be released from the strut. To do this, Audi technicians insert a special tool into the split at the upper rear part of the wheel bearing housing, where the strut is inserted. Turn the special tool through 90° to open up the clamp. A similar tool can be made out of an old screwdriver, or alternatively a suitable cold chisel can be driven into the split as a wedge. Slightly press inwards the top of the wheel bearing housing, then push it downwards from the bottom of the strut **(see illustrations)**.

10 Undo the three retaining bolts and remove the splash plate from the wheel bearing housing **(see illustration)**.

Refitting

11 Note that all self-locking nuts and bolts disturbed on removal must be renewed as a matter of course.

12 Ensure that the driveshaft outer joint and hub splines are clean and dry, then lubricate the splines with fresh engine oil. Also lubricate the threads and contact surface of the hub nut/bolt with oil.

13 Lift the wheel bearing assembly into position, and engage the hub with the splines on the outer end of the driveshaft. Fit the new hub nut/bolt, tightening it by hand only at this stage.

14 Engage the wheel bearing housing with the bottom of the suspension strut, making sure that the hole in the side plate aligns with the holes in the split housing. Remove the tool used to open the split.

15 Insert the new strut-to-wheel bearing housing clamp bolt from the rear, and fit the new retaining nut. Tighten the nut to the specified torque.

16 Refit the lower arm balljoint to the wheel bearing housing, and tighten the new nut to the specified torque. If necessary, hold the balljoint pin with a Torx/Allen key while tightening the nut.

17 Refit the track rod balljoint to the wheel bearing housing, then fit a new retaining nut and tighten it to the specified torque. If necessary, hold the balljoint pin with a Torx/Allen key while tightening the nut.

18 Refit the splash plate and tighten the bolts.

19 Refit the brake disc and caliper with reference to Chapter 9 Section 6.

20 Refit the wiring connector to the ABS wheel speed sensor.

21 Ensure that the outer joint is drawn fully into the hub, then refit the roadwheel. Lower the vehicle to the ground, and tighten the roadwheel bolts.

22 Tighten the driveshaft retaining nut/bolt in the stages given in the Specifications. It is recommended that an angle gauge is used to ensure the correct tightening angle.

3 Front hub bearings – renewal

Note: *The bearing is a sealed, pre-adjusted and pre-lubricated, double-row ball type, and requires no maintenance.A press will be required to remove the bearing, however, and if such a tool is not available, a large bench vice and spacers (such as large sockets) will serve as an adequate substitute. There are specialist tool kits available from different tool manufacturers* ***(see illustrations)****. The*

3.0a Wheel bearing, circlip and locking nuts

3.0b Bearing insertion and extraction kit

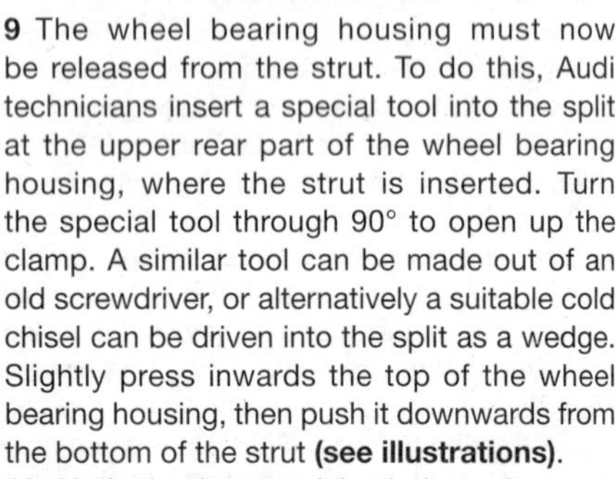

3.2a Drive the hub...

3.2b ...out of the bearing

3.3a Remove the circlip...

3.3b ...seal and ball bearings

3.4a Start the bearing moving...

3.4b ...then raise the housing to remove bearing

bearing's inner races are an interference fit on the hub, and if the inner race remains on the hub when the latter is pressed out, a knife-edged bearing puller will be required to remove it. Note that the bearing is rendered unserviceable when it is removed.

1 Remove the wheel bearing housing as described in Section 2.

2 Support the wheel bearing housing securely on blocks or in a vice. Using a metal tube which bears only on the inner end of the hub, press or drive out the hub from the bearing **(see illustrations)**. If the bearing's outboard inner race remains on the hub, remove it using a bearing puller. Take care not to damage the ABS rotor reluctor ring, which is welded to the hub.

3 Extract the bearing retaining circlip from the outside of the wheel bearing housing. At this point the seal and ball bearings from the outside of the bearing can be removed **(see illustrations)**.

4 Using a suitable metal tube, drive or press the complete bearing out of the wheel bearing housing. To start the bearing moving, you can initially start it on a flat surface, then raise it onto some wooden blocks to drive it all the way out **(see illustrations)**.

5 The inner race of the old bearing will be still attached to the centre hub, remove the old seal and then using a puller withdraw the inner race from the centre hub **(see illustrations)**. Take care not to damage the centre hub and ABS rotor, whilst removing the bearing inner race.

6 Thoroughly clean the centre hub and wheel bearing housing, removing all traces of dirt and grease, and polish away any burrs or raised edges which might hinder reassembly. Make sure the groove for the circlip is thoroughly cleaned out. Check both for cracks or any other signs of wear or damage, and renew them if necessary. It is recommended that the circlip is renewed, regardless of its apparent condition. Check for any damage to the ABS rotor wheel.

7 On reassembly, apply a light coating of molybdenum disulphide grease (Audi recommend Molykote – available from your dealer) to the bearing outer race and bearing surface of the wheel bearing housing.

8 Securely support the wheel bearing housing, and locate the bearing in the hub. Press the bearing fully into position, ensuring

3.5a Remove the old seal...

3.5b ...fit the bearing puller...

3.5c ...and withdraw the inner race

3.8a Position the bearing in the housing...

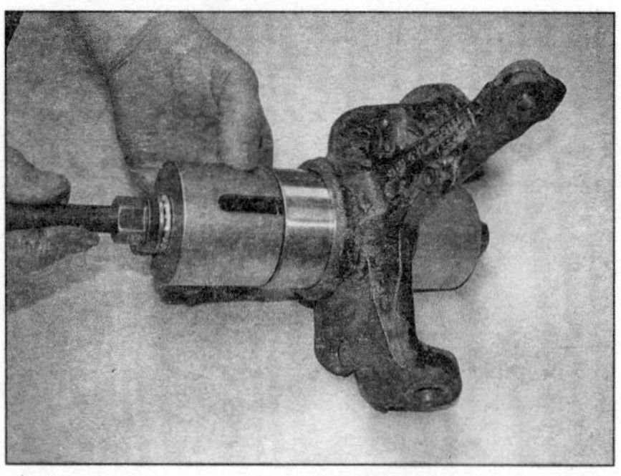

3.8b ...assemble metal tubes and threaded bar...

3.8c ...and press the bearing into the housing

that it enters the hub squarely. Using different sizes of metal tubes (or sockets) which bears only on the bearing outer race and threaded bar **(see illustrations)**. Do Not use a hammer to refit the bearing, as this could damage the new bearing.

9 Once the bearing is correctly seated, secure the bearing in position with the new circlip, ensuring that it is correctly located in the groove in the wheel bearing housing **(see illustrations)**.

10 Locate the wheel bearing housing bearing inner race over the end of the centre hub. Press the bearing onto the hub, using a metal tube (or socket) which bears only on the inner race of the hub bearing and threaded bar, until it seats against the hub shoulder **(see illustrations)**.

11 Check that the hub rotates freely, and wipe off any excess oil or grease. Make sure the ABS rotor does not foul the sensor in the wheel bearing housing, there should be a 0.3 mm air gap (see Chapter 9 Section 20), then refit the wheel bearing housing to the vehicle, as described in Section 2.

3.9a Fit the new circlip...

3.9b ...making sure it is located in the groove (arrowed)

3.10a Position the centre hub in the bearing...

3.10b ...and press the hub into the bearing

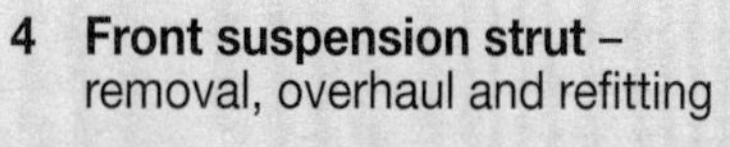

4 Front suspension strut – removal, overhaul and refitting

Note: *All self-locking nuts and bolts disturbed on removal must be renewed as a matter of course.*

Removal

1 Apply the handbrake, then jack up the front of the vehicle and support it on axle stands (see *Jacking and vehicle support*). Remove the appropriate roadwheel.

2 Refer to Chapter 9 Section 4 and unbolt the front brake caliper from the wheel bearing housing.Support or tie the caliper to one side, taking care to avoid placing any strain on the brake line.

3 Release the retaining clip and disconnect the brake hose from the lower part of the strut **(see illustrations)**.

4 Unclip the ABS wheel sensor wiring from

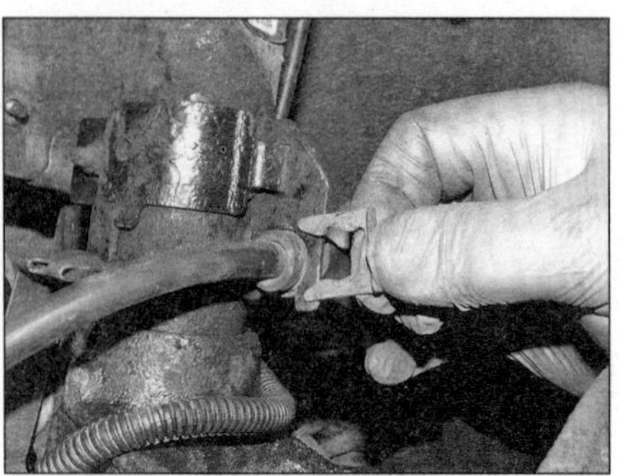

4.3a Remove the clip...

4.3b ...and disconnect the brake hose

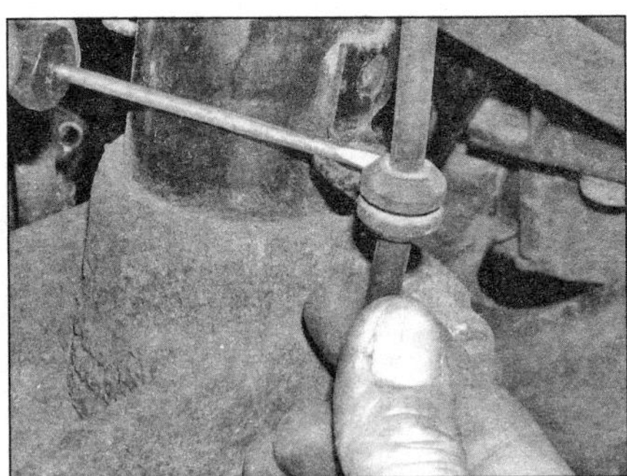
4.4a Detach the sensor wiring from the lower...

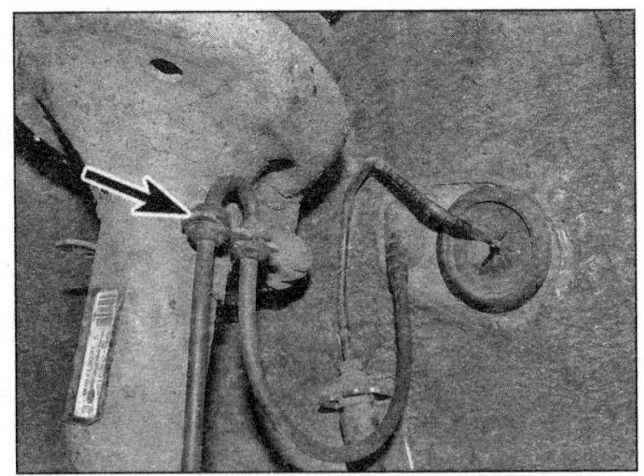
4.4b ... and upper part (arrowed) of the strut

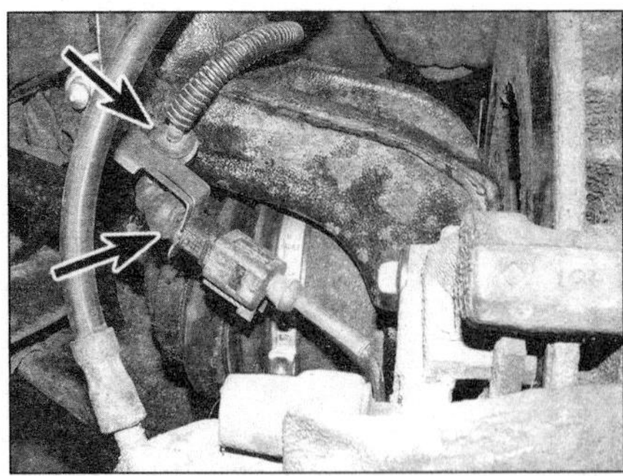
4.5 Detach the pad warning light wiring (arrowed)

the brackets on the upper and lower part of the suspension strut **(see illustrations)**.

5 Where fitted, unclip the wiring for the brake pad warning light from the bracket on the lower part of the strut **(see illustration)**.

6 Undo the retraining nuts and remove the vehicle level sender (for headlight range control), from the chassis leg, and then remove the plastic inner trim panel **(see illustration)**. Some models have an elongated slot in the bracket on the lower arm (this is for adjustment), on this type, mark the position of the retaining nut before removal.

7 Unscrew the retaining nut and detach the ball joint at the top of the drop link (coupling rod) from the front strut **(see illustration)**.

8 Undo the retaining bolts from around the inner flange of the driveshaft **(see illustration)**. This will allow for the movement of the hub assembly to remove the strut, without damaging the driveshaft. Once disconnected from the flange, support the driveshaft with a piece of strong wire to prevent the inner gaiter from getting damaged.

9 Note which way round it is fitted, then unscrew the nut and remove the clamp bolt securing the top of the wheel bearing housing to the bottom of the strut **(see illustration 2.8)**.

10 Release the wheel bearing housing from the bottom of the strut by slightly opening the split housing with reference to Section 2. Press inwards on the hub to keep aligned and then push the wheel bearing housing downwards, to release it from the bottom of the strut. Once the strut has been released from the wheel bearing housing, use a piece of wire to support the wheel bearing housing. Check the position of the driveshaft, to prevent any damage to the inner gaiter.

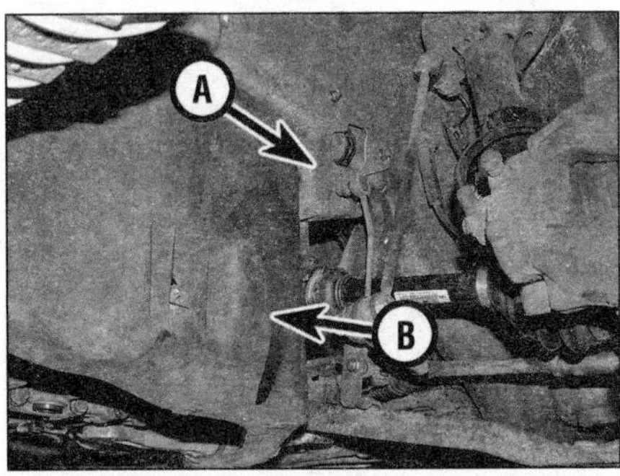

4.6 Vehicle level sender (A) and Inner trim panel (B)

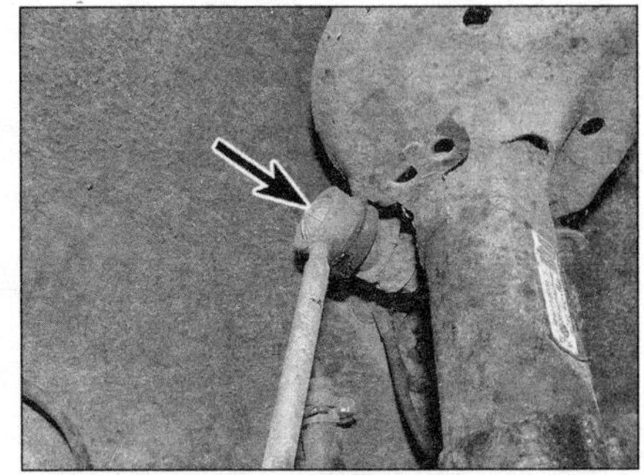
4.7 Upper drop link ball joint (arrowed)

11 Unclip the plastic cover from the strut upper mounting, and then support the suspension strut. With the strut supported, unscrew and remove the upper mounting nut and recover the mounting plate. Note that it may be necessary to retain the strut piston rod with a suitable Torx/Allen key, to prevent it from rotating as the nut is loosened **(see illustrations)**. Once the nut/mounting plate have been removed, withdraw the strut from underneath the wheel arch, and remove it from the vehicle.

Overhaul

Warning: Before attempting to dismantle the suspension strut, a suitable tool to hold the coil spring in compression must be obtained. Adjustable coil spring compressors are readily available, and are recommended for this operation. Any attempt to dismantle the strut without such a tool is likely to result in damage or personal injury.

12 With the strut removed from the car, clean away all external dirt. If necessary, mount it upright in a vice during the dismantling procedure.

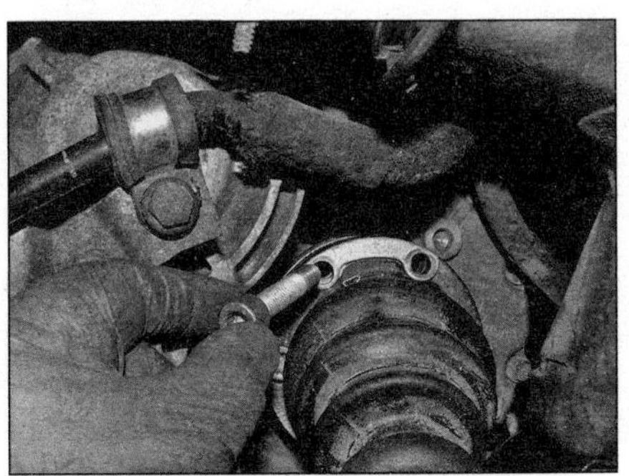
4.8 Remove the driveshaft inner bolts

4.11a Unclip the plastic cover...

4.11b ...and unscrew the upper mounting nut, whilst holding the strut piston

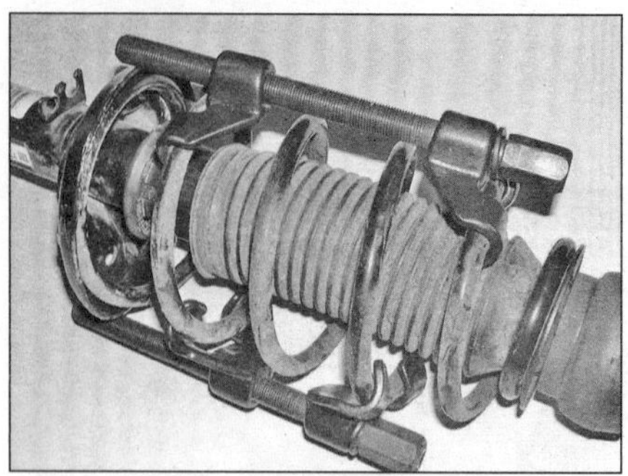
4.13 Compressor tool (double clamp type) fitted to the front suspension coil spring

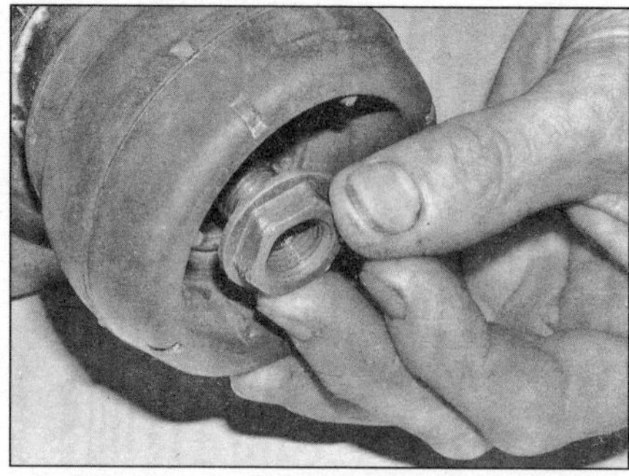
4.14a Unscrew the spring seat retaining nut ...

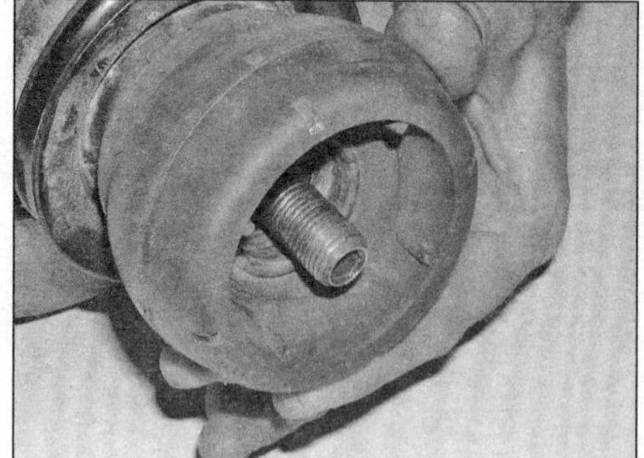
4.14b ... then remove the bearing and mounting rubber ...

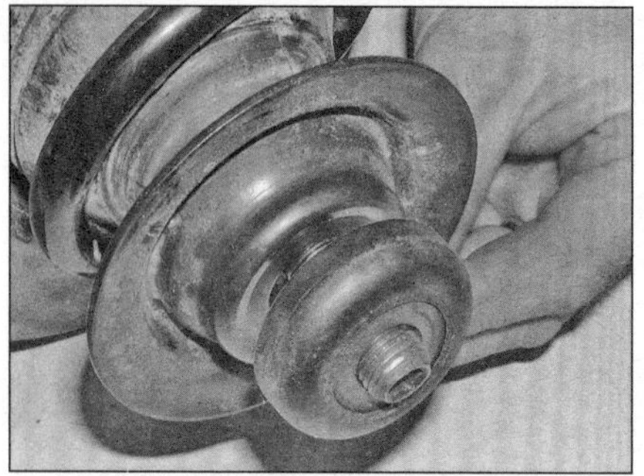
4.14c ... followed by the upper spring seat ...

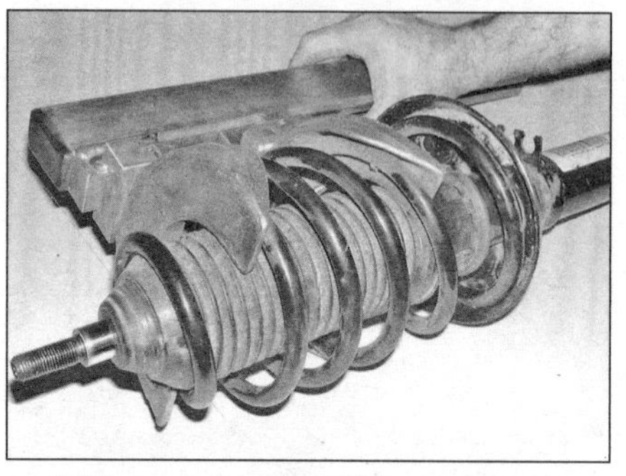
4.15a ... coil spring with compressor tool ...

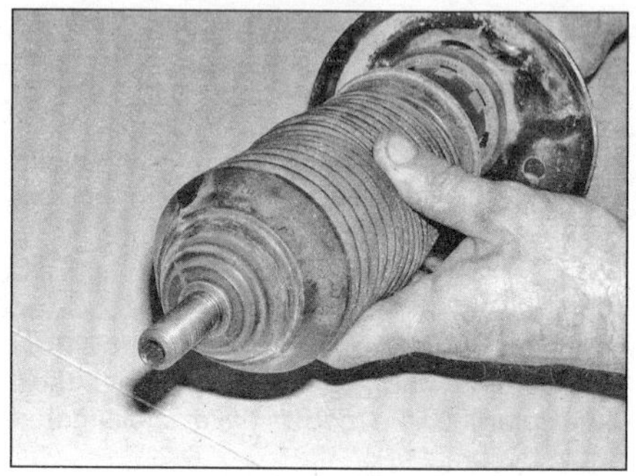
4.15b ... protective gaiter ...

13 Fit the spring compressor, and compress the coil spring until all tension is relieved from the upper spring seat **(see illustration)**.

14 Unscrew and remove the spring seat retaining nut, whilst retaining the strut piston with a suitable Torx/Allen key, then remove the bearing and mounting rubber, followed by the upper spring seat **(see illustrations)**. On models with heavy duty suspension, also remove the spacer/bush.

15 Remove the coil spring (together with the compressor tool), then slide off the protective gaiter and rubber damper stop **(see illustrations)**.

16 With the strut assembly now completely dismantled **(see illustration)**, examine all the components for wear, damage or deformation, and check the bearing for smoothness of operation. Renew any of the components as necessary.

17 Examine the strut for signs of fluid leakage. Check the strut piston for signs of pitting along its entire length, and check the strut body for signs of damage. While holding it in an upright position, test the operation of the strut by moving the piston through a full stroke, and then through short strokes of 50 to 100 mm. In both cases, the resistance felt should be smooth and continuous. If the resistance is jerky, or uneven, or if there is any visible sign of wear or damage to the strut, renewal is necessary.

18 If any doubt exists about the condition of the coil spring, carefully remove the spring compressors, and check the spring for distortion and signs of cracking. Renew the spring if it is damaged or distorted, or if there is any doubt as to its condition.

19 Inspect all other components for signs of damage or deterioration, and renew as necessary.

20 Slide the rubber damper and protective gaiter onto the strut piston.

21 Fit the coil spring (together with the compressor tool) onto the strut, making sure its lower end is correctly located against the spring seat stop **(see illustration)**.

22 Refit the upper spring seat (and spacer/bush where fitted), followed by the bearing and mounting rubber. Screw on the new retaining nut, and tighten to the specified torque setting whilst retaining the strut piston with the Allen key.

Refitting

23 Manoeuvre the strut into position under the wheel arch, then locate the mounting plate on the suspension strut turret and screw on

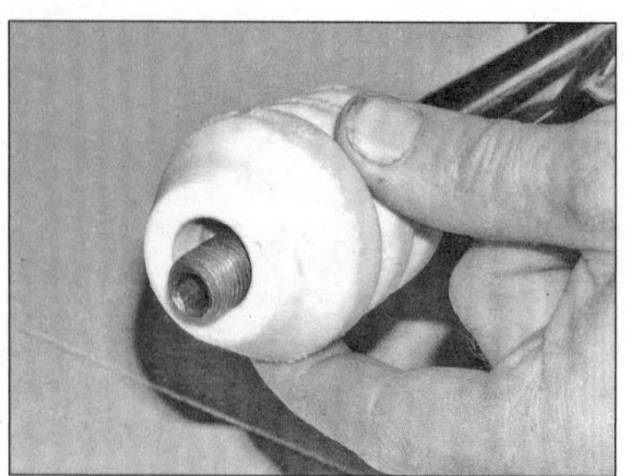
4.15c ... and rubber damper stop

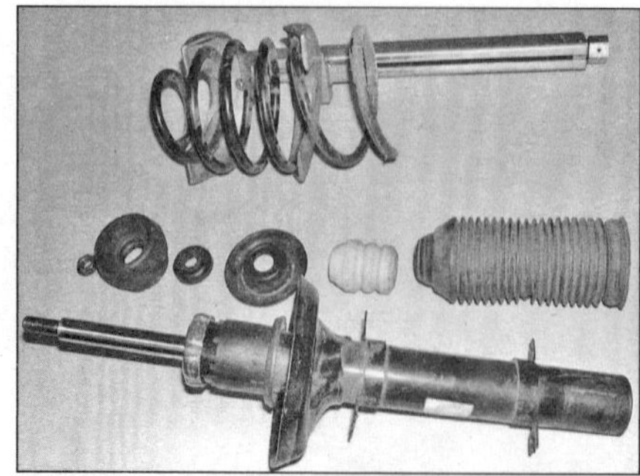
4.16 The front suspension strut completely dismantled

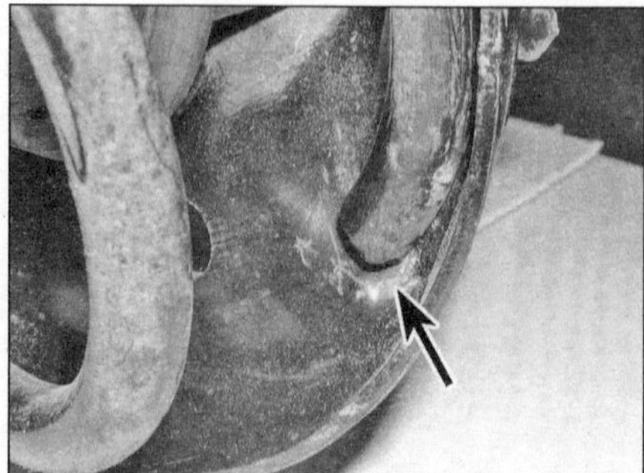
4.21 Make sure the lower end of the coil spring locates in the seat stop

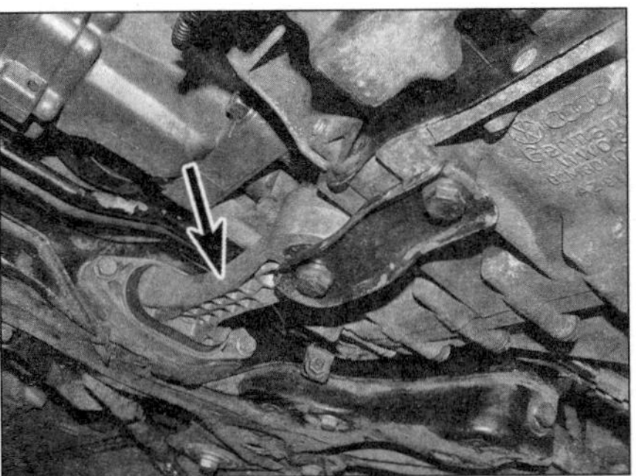
5.2 Lower rear engine mounting (arrowed)

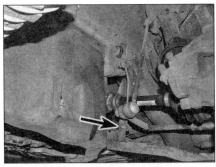

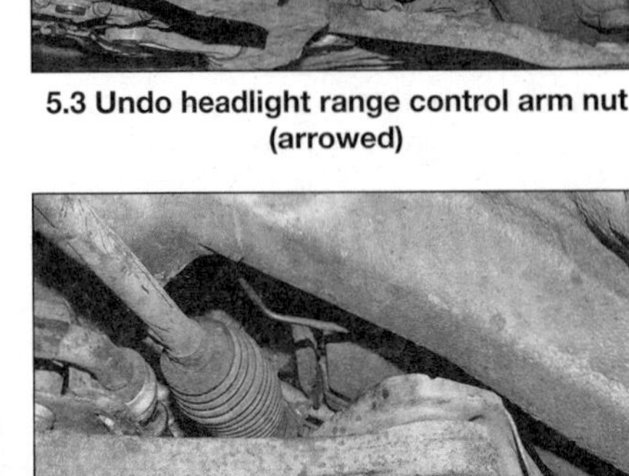
5.3 Undo headlight range control arm nut (arrowed)

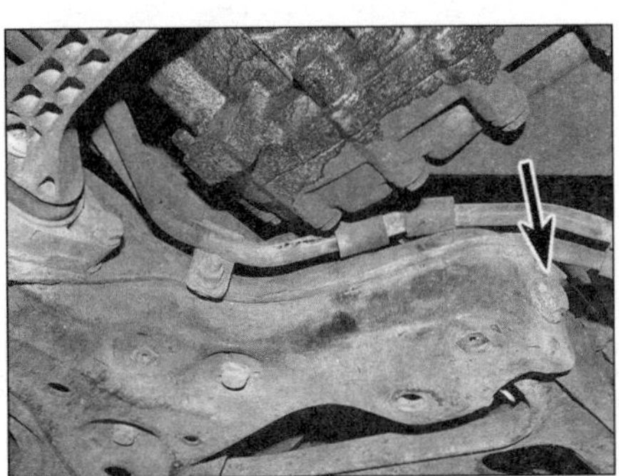
5.5a Lower arm front mounting bolt ...

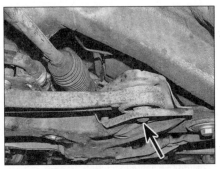

5.5b ... and rear mounting bolt (arrowed)

the new upper mounting nut. Tighten the nut to the specified torque, and refit the plastic cover.

24 Engage the wheel bearing housing with the bottom of the suspension strut, making sure that the hole in the side plate aligns with the holes in the split housing. Remove the tool used to open the split.

25 Insert the new strut-to-wheel bearing housing bolt from the rear, and fit the new retaining nut. Tighten the nut to the specified torque.

26 Refit the driveshaft inner flange bolts, and tighten to the specified torque. Where applicable, refit the headlight range control sender and plastic inner trim panel.

27 Refit the drop link upper ball joint to the suspension strut, and then tighten the new retaining nut to the specified torque.

28 Refit the wiring back into the support brackets on the strut, for the brake pad warning light and ABS wheel speed sensor.

29 Refit the brake hose back in it's bracket on the strut and secure in place with clip, then refer to Chapter 9 Section 4 and refit the front brake caliper.

30 Refit the roadwheel and lower the vehicle to the ground. Tighten the roadwheel bolts, too there specified torque.

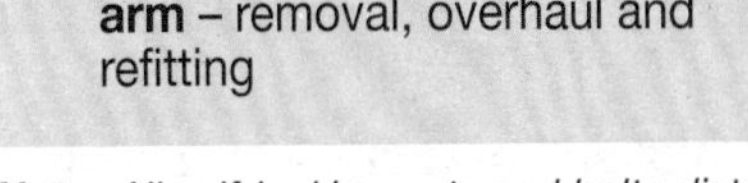

5 Front suspension lower arm – removal, overhaul and refitting

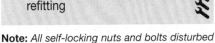

Note: *All self-locking nuts and bolts disturbed on removal must be renewed as a matter of course.*

Removal

1 Apply the handbrake, then jack up the front of the vehicle and support it on axle stands (see *Jacking and vehicle support*). Remove the appropriate front roadwheel and the engine compartment undershield.

2 If the left-hand lower arm is being removed on automatic transmission models, unscrew the bolts securing the engine/transmission lower rear mounting to the subframe **(see illustration)**. Discard the bolts, new ones should be used on refitting. This is necessary to allow the engine/ transmission unit to be moved slightly forwards when removing the lower arm front bolt.

3 If removing the left-hand lower arm, on models with an automatic headlight range control system, unscrew the nut and detach the sender link arm from the lower arm **(see illustration)**. Some models have an elongated slot in the bracket on the lower arm (this is for adjustment), on this type, mark the position of the retaining nut before removal.

4 Mark the position of the three balljoint retaining nuts to the lower suspension arm, then slacken and remove them from the lower arm.

5 Unscrew and remove the lower arm front pivot bolt and rear mounting bolt **(see illustrations)**. On automatic transmission models it may be necessary to lever the engine/transmission slightly forwards in order to remove the front pivot bolt.

6 Remove the arm from the subframe and withdraw from under the vehicle. If necessary, for additional working room, unbolt the driveshaft inner joint from the transmission drive flange with reference to Chapter 8A Section 2, and pull out the wheel bearing housing.

Overhaul

Note: *There are specialist tool kits available from different tool manufacturers, to remove and refit bearings and bushes* **(see illustration 3.0b).**

7 Thoroughly clean the lower arm, then check carefully for cracks or any other signs of wear or damage, paying particular attention to the pivot and rear mounting bushes. If either bush requires renewal, the lower arm should be taken to an Audi dealer or suitably-equipped garage. A hydraulic press and suitable spacers are required to press the bushes out of the arm and install the new ones. Always note the fitted position of the bushes before removal, so that the new bushes can be fitted correctly. When fitting a new rear mounting bush, make sure that it is located in the lower arm with the largest cavity/slot in the rubber, facing forwards, in the direction of travel.

Refitting

8 Locate the lower arm in the subframe, and insert the new front pivot and rear mounting bolts. Tighten the rear mounting bolt to the specified torque and angle, however only hand-tighten the front pivot bolt at this stage.

9 Where removed, refit the driveshaft inner joint to the transmission flange with reference to Chapter 8A Section 2.

10 Refit the balljoint to the lower arm in the position noted on removal, then using new nuts, tighten them to the specified torque.

11 On models equipped with automatic headlight range control, refit the sender link arm to its previously noted position on the left-hand lower arm plate, and tighten the nut.

12 If the left-hand lower arm is being refitted on automatic transmission models, align the engine/transmission rear mounting with the subframe and fit the new mounting bolts. Tighten the bolts to the specified torque.

13 Refit the roadwheel and undershield then lower the vehicle to the ground. With the weight of the vehicle on the suspension, tighten the lower arm front pivot bolt to the specified torque and angle.

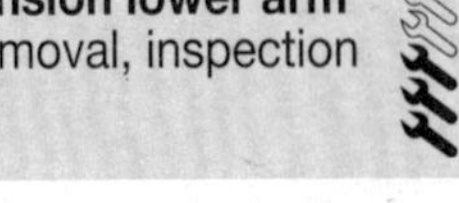

6 Front suspension lower arm balljoint – removal, inspection and refitting

Note: *All self-locking nuts and bolts disturbed on removal must be renewed as a matter of course.*

Removal

1 Apply the handbrake, then jack up the front of the vehicle and support it on axle stands (see *Jacking and vehicle support*). Remove the appropriate front roadwheel.

6.2a Use a Torx/Allen key to prevent the joint turning

6.2b Using a universal balljoint separator tool to remove the lower balljoint

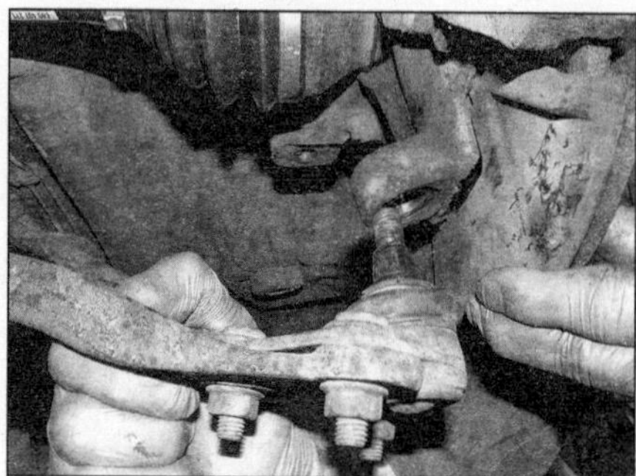
6.2c Pull the lower arm down to disengage the balljoint

2 Unscrew and remove the balljoint retaining nut, then release the balljoint from the wheel bearing housing using a universal balljoint separator **(see illustrations)**. Note that it may be necessary to retain the balljoint with a suitable Torx/Allen key, to prevent it from rotating as the nut is loosened.

3 Mark the position of the three balljoint retaining nuts to the lower suspension arm, then slacken and remove them from the lower arm.

4 With the wheel bearing housing moved to one side, remove the balljoint from the lower arm.

Inspection

5 With the balljoint removed, check that it moves freely, without any sign of roughness. Check also that the balljoint rubber gaiter shows no sign of deterioration, and is free from cracks and splits. Renew as necessary.

Refitting

6 Fit the balljoint to the wheel bearing housing and fit the new retaining nut. Tighten the nut to the specified torque setting, noting that the balljoint shank can be retained with a Torx/Allen key if necessary to prevent it from rotating **(see illustration 6.2a)**.

7 Move the wheel bearing housing into position over the suspension lower arm, then refit the balljoint to the lower arm in the position noted on removal, then using new nuts, tighten them to the specified torque.

8 Refit the roadwheel, and then lower the vehicle to the ground and tighten the wheel bolts to the specified torque.

7 Front anti-roll bar – removal and refitting

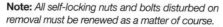

Note: *All self-locking nuts and bolts disturbed on removal must be renewed as a matter of course.*

Removal

1 Apply the handbrake, then jack up the front of the vehicle and support it on axle stands (see *Jacking and vehicle support*). Remove both front roadwheels.

2 Remove both anti-roll bar connecting links as described in Section 8.

3 To remove the anti-roll bar, the front subframe will need to be lowered, with reference to Section 21.

4 Mark the position of the anti-roll bar to indicate which way it is fitted, and the position of the rubber mounting bushes. Unscrew and remove the anti-roll bar mounting clamp bolts from the subframe **(see illustration)**, and release the clamps from the lower slots.

5 Remove the anti-roll bar from the top of the front subframe and remove the rubber mounting bushes from the anti-roll bar.

6 Carefully examine the anti-roll bar components for signs of wear, damage or deterioration, paying particular attention to the rubber mounting bushes. Renew worn components as necessary.

Refitting

7 Fit the rubber mounting bushes to the anti-roll bar, aligning them with the marks made prior to removal.

8 Offer up the anti-roll bar, and manoeuvre it into position. Refit the mounting clamps, ensuring that their ends are correctly located in the slots on the subframe, and refit the retaining bolts. Ensure that the bush markings are still aligned with the marks on the bars, then securely tighten the mounting clamp retaining bolts.

9 Refit and tighten the subframe mounting bolts to the specified torque, with reference to Section 21.

10 Refit the connecting links with reference to Section 8.

11 Refit the roadwheels, then lower the vehicle to the ground and tighten the wheel bolts to the specified torque.

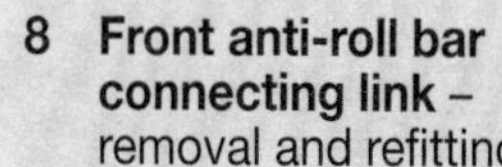

8 Front anti-roll bar connecting link – removal and refitting

Note: *All self-locking nuts and bolts disturbed on removal must be renewed as a matter of course.*

Removal

1 Apply the handbrake, then jack up the front of the vehicle and support it on axle stands (see *Jacking and vehicle support*). Remove the relevant front roadwheel.

2 Unscrew and remove the nut securing the drop link lower ball joint to the end of the ant-roll bar. Use an open ended spanner to counter hold the ball joint to prevent it from turning **(see illustration)**.

7.4 Anti-roll bar rubber bush and clamp

8.2a Using two spanners to counterhold the ball joint

8.2b Detach the lower ball joint

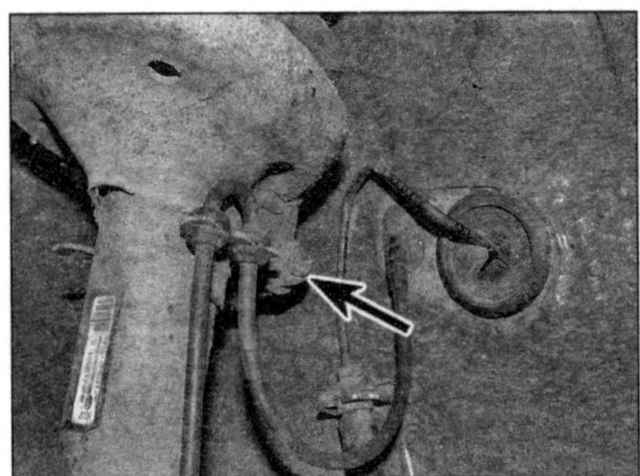

8.3 Connecting link upper ball joint securing nut (arrowed)

9.3 Undo the disc retaining screw

9.4 Remove centre cap from the hub

3 Unscrew the nut and detach the drop link upper ball joint, from the mounting bracket on the rear of the suspension strut **(see illustration)**. Use an open ended spanner to counter hold the ball joint to prevent it from turning.

4 Remove the connecting link from the vehicle and inspect the link rubbers and ball joints, for signs of damage or deterioration. If evident, renew the link complete.

Refitting

5 Refitting is a reversal of removal, tighten the ball joint retaining nuts to the specified torque.

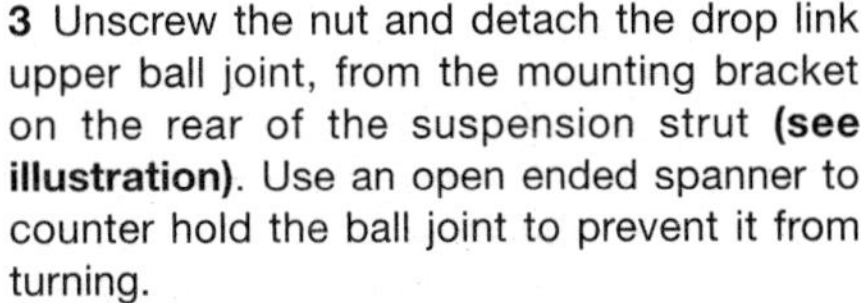

9 Rear hub bearing assembly – removal and refitting

Front wheel drive (FWD) models

Note: *The rear wheel bearings on front wheel drive (FWD) models, cannot be renewed independently of the rear hub, because the outer races are formed in the hub itself. If excessive wear is evident, the rear hub must be renewed complete. The rear hub nut must always be renewed after removal.*

1 Chock the front roadwheels, then jack up the rear of the vehicle and support on axle stands (see *Jacking and vehicle support*). Release the handbrake and remove the relevant rear roadwheel.

2 Remove the rear brake caliper and mounting bracket with reference to Chapter 9 Section 7. Do not disconnect the hydraulic brake pipe. Move the caliper just clear of the brake disc, without bending the hydraulic pipe excessively, and support it with piece of wire or on an axle stand.

3 Undo the crosshead screw then withdraw the brake disc from the hub **(see illustration)**.

4 Remove the dust cap from the centre of the hub using a screwdriver or cold chisel **(see illustration)**.

5 Unscrew and remove the hub nut **(see illustrations)**. Note that it is tightened to a high torque and a socket extension bar may be required to loosen it. It is recommended that the nut is renewed whenever removed.

6 Using a suitable puller, pull the hub and bearings from the stub axle, screw the old nut onto the threads (to prevent damage to the threads), to start the bearing moving. Once the bearing has started moving the nut can be removed. The bearing inner race will remain on the stub axle, and a puller will be required to remove it; use a sharp cold chisel to move the race away from the stub axle base so that the puller legs can fully engage the race. The ABS rotor may come off of the hub and remain on the inner race as the hub is being removed, and it should be removed over the race before pulling off the race **(see illustrations)**.

7 Examine the hub and bearings for wear, pitting and damage. It is highly likely that the bearing surfaces will be damaged as a result of the inner race remaining on the stub axle, however if all the bearing surfaces and balls appear to be in good order upon inspection, the hub may be refitted.

8 Wipe clean the stub axle, then check that the bearing races are adequately lubricated

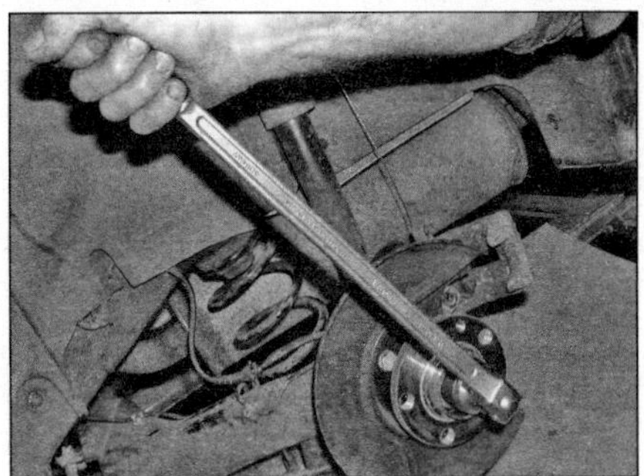

9.5a Use a socket extension bar to loosen the hub nut which is tightened to a high torque

9.5b Removing the hub nut

9.6a Using a puller to remove the rear hub

9.6b The ABS rotor may remain on the inner race – remove it before fitting the puller

9.6c Using a puller to remove the inner race from the stub axle

9.9a Locate the hub on the stub axle ...

9.9b ... then drive it on using a socket which locates only on the inner bearing race

9.10 Torque-tightening the rear hub nut

with suitable grease. Check that the inner bearing race is located correctly in the hub. Also make sure that the ABS rotor is pressed firmly onto the inner end of the hub.

9 Locate the hub as far as possible on the stub axle. Audi technicians use a special elongated hub nut to pull the hub onto the stub axle, since the normal retaining nut is not long enough to reach the threads. If the special nut is unavailable, carefully drive on the hub using a metal tube or socket located only on the inner bearing race **(see illustrations)**.

10 Screw on the new nut and tighten it to the specified torque **(see illustration)**.

11 Check the dust cap for damage and renew it if necessary. Use a hammer to carefully tap the cap into the hub **(see illustration)**. **Note:** *A badly fitting dust cap will allow moisture to enter the bearing, reducing its service life.*

12 Refit the brake disc and tighten the crosshead screw.

13 Refit the rear brake caliper and brake pads, with reference to Chapter 9 Section 7.

14 Refit the roadwheel and lower the vehicle to the ground, tighten the wheel bolts to the specified torque.

Four wheel drive (4WD) models

Note: *To remove and refit the bearing from the rear axle housing a special tool kit will be required. These are available from different tool manufacturers* **(see illustration 3.0b).**

15 Remove the rear driveshaft, as described in Chapter 8A Section 3.

16 Remove the rear brake caliper and brake pads, as described in Chapter 9 Section 8.

17 Undo the two retaining bolts and remove the caliper mounting bracket from the axle housing.

18 Remove rear brake disc, as described in Chapter 9 Section 6.

19 Using a puller, slide the centre hub and ABS rotor from the axle/wheel bearing housing **(see illustration)**.

20 The ABS speed sensor is fitted to the axle housing **(see illustration)**. Take care not to damage the sensor whilst removing the wheel bearing. If required, remove the sensor as described in Chapter 9 Section 20.

21 Remove the outer ball bearing race from the bearing and release the circlip **(see illustrations)**.

22 Undo the retaining bolts and remove the rear splash shield from the axle housing **(see illustration)**.

23 Press the wheel bearing from the axle housing, using a special tool, see note at begining of this section. Alternatively different sizes of metal tubes (or sockets) which bears

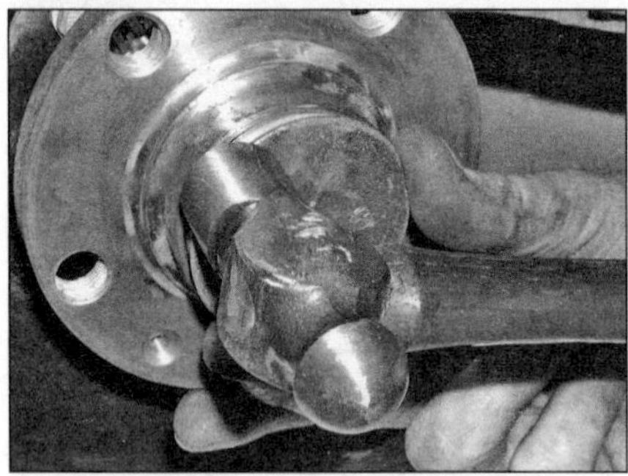
9.11 Tapping the cap into the hub

9.19 Using slide hammer to withdraw hub

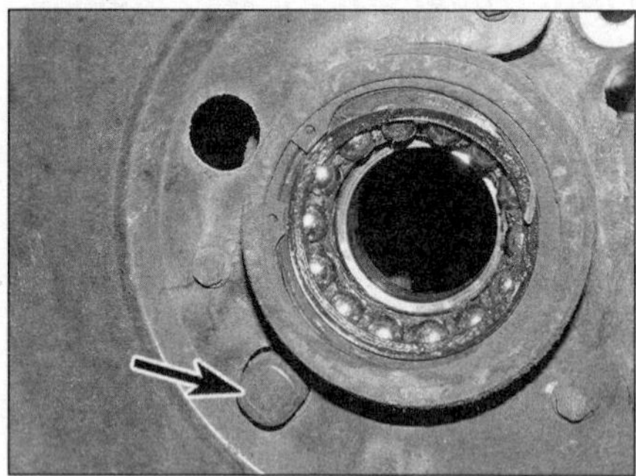
9.20 Speed sensor (arrowed)

9.21a Remove the outer ball bearings...

9.21b ...and release the circlip

9.22 Remove the splash shield

9.23a Using special tool...

9.23b ...to remove the bearing

9.25 Clean out the circlip groove

only on the axle housing on the outside, and on the bearing inner race on the inside can be used. Then using a threaded bar, washers and nuts press the bearing out from the housing **(see illustrations)**.

24 The inner race of the old bearing will be still attached to the centre hub, remove the old seal and then using a puller withdraw the inner race from the centre hub **(see illustrations 3.5a, 3.5b and 3.5c)**. Take care not to damage the centre hub and ABS rotor, whilst removing the bearing inner race.

25 Thoroughly clean the hub and wheel bearing housing, removing all traces of dirt and grease, and polish away any burrs or raised edges which might hinder reassembly. Make sure the groove for the circlip is thoroughly cleaned out **(see illustration)**. Check both for cracks or any other signs of wear or damage, and renew them if necessary. It is recommended that the circlip is renewed, regardless of its apparent condition. Check for any damage to the ABS rotor wheel.

26 On reassembly, apply a light coating of molybdenum disulphide grease (Audi recommend Molykote – available from your dealer) to the bearing outer race and bearing surface of the wheel bearing housing.

27 Locate the new bearing in the hub and press it fully into position, ensuring that it enters the hub squarely. Using different sizes of metal tubes (or sockets) which bears only on the bearing outer race and threaded bar **(see illustration)**. Do Not use a hammer to refit the bearing, as this could damage the new bearing.

9.27 Pressing the new bearing into the axle housing

9.28 Locate circlip in the groove (arrowed)

28 Once the bearing is correctly seated, secure the bearing in position with the new circlip, ensuring that it is correctly located in the groove in the axle housing **(see illustration)**.

29 Locate the wheel centre hub complete with ABS rotor to the inner race of the new fitted bearing. Press the wheel centre hub into the bearing, using a metal tube (or socket) which bears only on the inner race of the hub bearing at the rear and the centre hub on the outside. Tighten the nuts on the threaded bar, until it seats the centre hub fully into the bearing **(see illustrations)**.

30 Check that the hub rotates freely, and wipe off any excess oil or grease. Make sure the ABS rotor does not foul the sensor in the wheel bearing housing, there should be a 0.3 mm air gap, see Chapter 9 Section 20.

31 Refit the brake disc and tighten the retaining screw, then fit the brake caliper mounting bracket and tighten the two mounting bolts to the specified torque setting.

32 Refit the brake pads and caliper, with reference to Chapter 9 Section 7.

33 Refit the driveshaft, with reference to Chapter 8A Section 3.

34 Refit the roadwheel and lower the vehicle to the ground, tighten the wheel bolts to the specified torque.

10 Rear stub axle (Front wheel drive models) – removal and refitting

Note: *All self-locking nuts and bolts disturbed on removal must be renewed as a matter of course.*

Removal

1 Chock the front roadwheels, then jack up the rear of the vehicle and support on axle stands (see *Jacking and vehicle support*). Release the handbrake and remove the relevant roadwheel.

2 Remove the rear hub as described in Section 9.

3 Disconnect the wiring, then unscrew the bolt and remove the speed sensor (see Chapter 9 Section 20) from the rear axle trailing arm.

4 Unscrew the mounting bolts securing the stub axle and backplate to the rear axle

9.29a Position the centre hub squarely...

9.29b ...and press the bearing into the axle housing

10.4 Rear stub axle and mounting bolts

trailing arm **(see illustration)**. Withdraw the backplate and stub axle.

5 Inspect the stub axle for signs of damage and renew if necessary. Do not attempt to straighten the stub axle.

Refitting

6 Ensure the mating surfaces of the axle, stub axle and backplate are clean and dry. Check the backplate for signs of damage.

7 Refit the stub axle together with the backplate, then insert the new bolts and progressively tighten to the specified torque.

8 Refit the speed sensor, tighten the bolt, and reconnect the wiring.

9 Refit the rear hub with reference to Section 9.

10 Refit the roadwheel and lower the vehicle to the ground, tighten the wheel bolts to the specified torque.

11 Rear suspension shock absorber and coil spring – removal and refitting

Note: *All self-locking nuts and bolts disturbed on removal must be renewed as a matter of course.*

1 Before removing the shock absorber, an idea of how effective it is can be gained by depressing the rear corner of the car. If the shock absorber is in good condition, the body should rise then settle in its normal position. If the body oscillates more than this, the shock absorber is defective. **Note:** *To ensure even rear suspension, both rear shock absorbers should be renewed at the same time.*

2 Chock the front roadwheels, then jack up the rear of the vehicle and support on axle stands (see *Jacking and vehicle support*). Remove the relevant rear roadwheel.

Shock absorber

Removal

Front wheel drive (FWD) models

3 Position a trolley jack and block of wood beneath the coil spring position on the trailing arm, and raise the arm so that the shock absorber is slightly compressed **(see illustration)**. Note on some models, it may be necessary to remove the stone protection guard first, from under the lower arm.

4 Unscrew and remove the shock absorber lower mounting nut and bolt, and lever the bottom of the shock absorber from the trailing arm **(see illustrations)**.

5 Support the shock absorber, then unscrew the upper mounting bolts located in the rear wheel arch. Lower the shock absorber and withdraw from under the wheel arch **(see illustrations)**.

6 With the shock absorber on the bench, unscrew the nut from the top of the piston rod and remove the upper mounting bracket. The piston rod can be held stationary with a pair of grips on the raised peg on the top of the rod. Remove the rubber stop and protectors from the top of the rod.

7 If necessary, the action of the shock absorber can be checked by mounting it upright in a vice. Fully depress the rod, then pull it up fully. The piston rod must move smoothly over its complete length.

Four wheel drive (4WD) models

8 Position a trolley jack beneath the trailing arm, and raise the arm so that the shock absorber is slightly compressed **(see illustration)**. Note on some models, it may be necessary to remove the stone protection guard first, from under the lower arm.

9 Unscrew and remove the shock absorber lower mounting bolt, and move the bottom of

11.3 Position the trolley jack and block of wood beneath the trailing arm

11.4a Remove the lower mounting bolt ...

11.4b ... and withdraw the shock absorber from the trailing arm

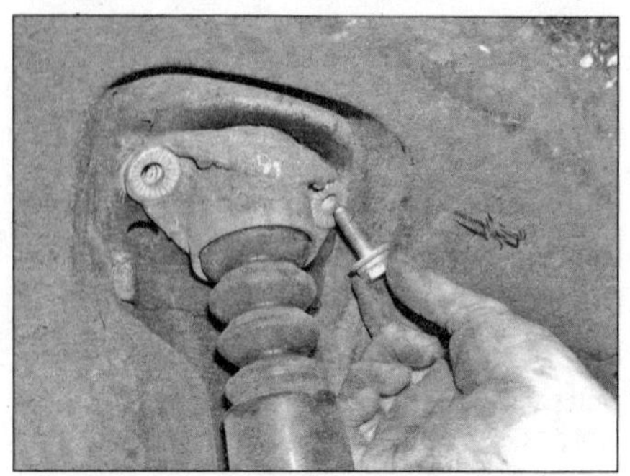

11.5a Unscrew the upper mounting bolts ...

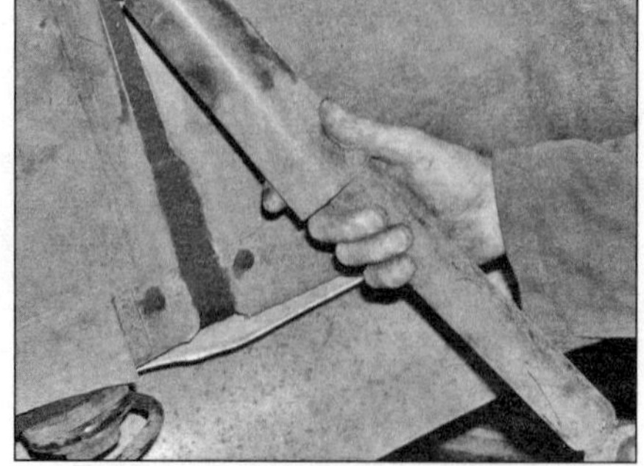

11.5b ... and withdraw the rear shock absorber from under the wheel arch

11.8 Position jack under the lower arm

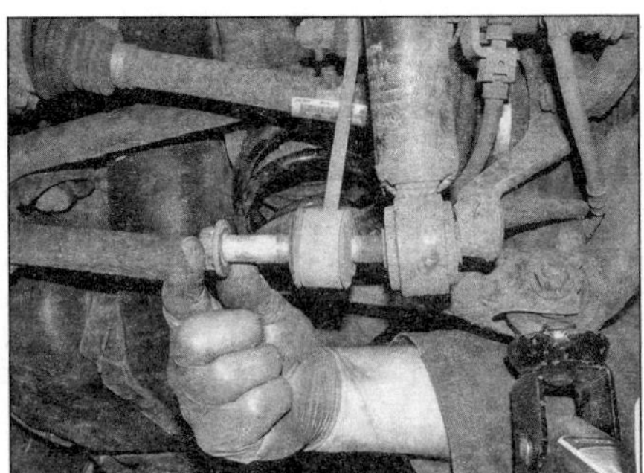

11.9 Remove bolt from connecting link and shockabsorber

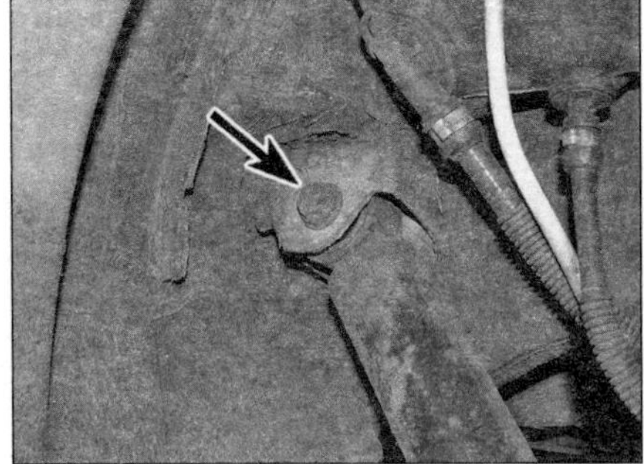

11.11 Shockabsorber upper mounting bolt (arrowed)

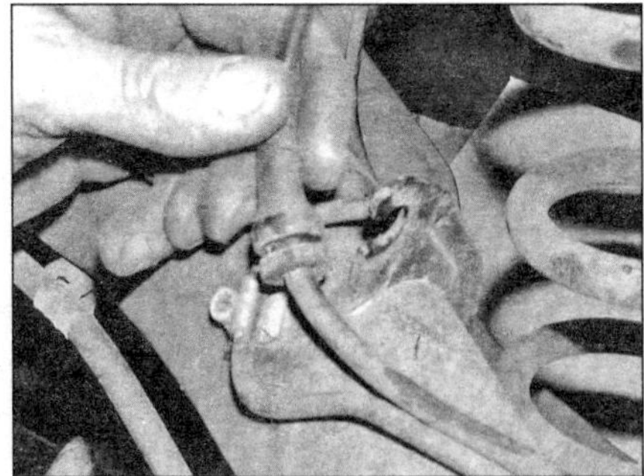

11.22 Release the handbrake cable from the bracket on the trailing arm

the shock absorber from the trailing arm **(see illustration)**. Note the lower mounting bolt also supports the lower part of the anti-roll bar connecting link.

10 Release the fasteners and remove the inner trim plastic liner from inside the wheel arch.

11 Support the shock absorber, then unscrew the upper mounting bolt located in the rear wheel arch. Lower the shock absorber and withdraw from under the wheel arch **(see illustration)**.

12 If necessary, the action of the shock absorber can be checked by mounting it upright in a vice. Fully depress the rod, then pull it up fully. The piston rod must move smoothly over its complete length.

Refitting

13 On front wheel drive (FWD) models, locate the rubber stop and protectors on the piston rod followed by the upper mounting bracket. Fit the new nut and tighten to the specified torque while holding the piston rod as for removal.

14 Locate the shock absorber in the rear wheel arch, then insert the upper mounting bolt(s) and tighten to the specified torque. Refit the inner wheel arch liner, where removed.

15 On front wheel drive (FWD) models, locate the bottom of the shock absorber in the trailing arm, insert the bolt from the outside, then screw on the nut. Raise the trailing arm with the jack to take the weight of the rear suspension, then tighten the lower mounting bolt to the specified torque.

16 On four wheel drive (4WD) models, locate the bottom of the shock absorber and the suspension connecting link and insert the bolt. Raise the trailing arm with the jack to take the weight of the rear suspension, then align and tighten the lower mounting bolt to the specified torque.

17 Lower the jack, from under the suspension and remove. Where necessary refit the stone protection guard under the rear trailing arm.

18 Refit the roadwheel and lower the vehicle to the ground, tighten the wheel bolts to the specified torque.

Coil spring

Removal

19 Chock the front roadwheels, then jack up the rear of the vehicle and support on axle stands (see *Jacking and vehicle support*). Remove the relevant rear roadwheel.

20 Position a trolley jack and block of wood beneath the coil spring position on the trailing arm, and raise the arm so that the shock absorber is slightly compressed, as previously described in this section. Note on some models, it may be necessary to remove the stone protection guard first, from under the lower arm.

21 Unscrew and remove the shock absorber lower mounting nut and bolt, and lever the bottom of the shock absorber from the trailing arm, as previously described in this section.

Front wheel drive (FWD) models

22 Release the handbrake cable from the bracket on the trailing arm **(see illustration)**.

23 Lower the trolley jack and remove it from under the trailing arm, then carefully lever the arm down until the coil spring can be removed. Lever against a block of wood to prevent damage to the underbody. Make sure that the vehicle is adequately supported on the axle stands **(see illustrations)**.

24 With the coil spring removed, recover the upper and lower zinc spring seats and check them for damage **(see illustration)**. Obtain new ones if necessary. Also clean the spring locations on the underbody and trailing arm.

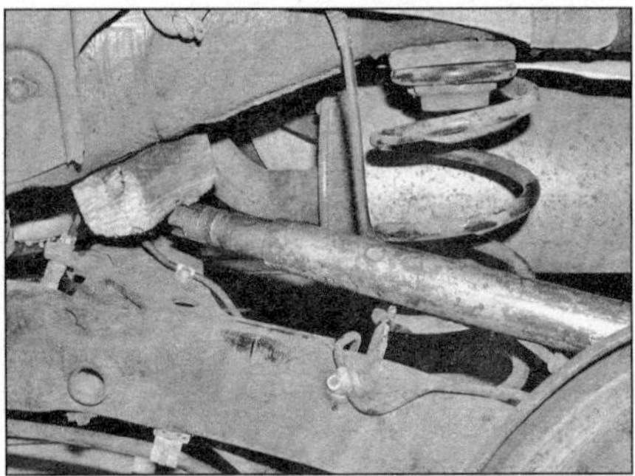

11.23a Lever down the trailing arm ...

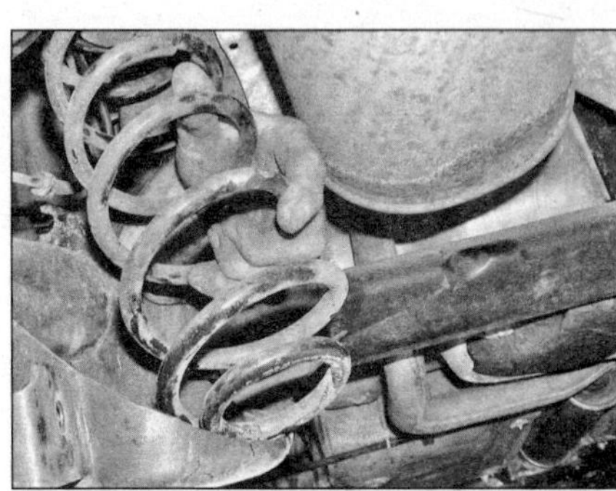

11.23b ... then release the coil spring from its lower seat ...

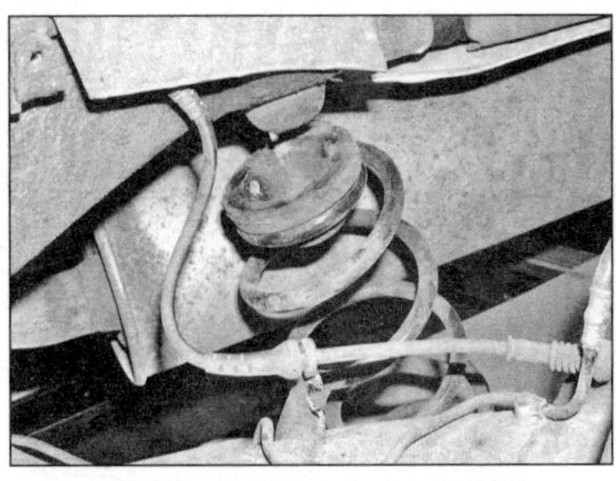

11.23c ... and underbody seat

11.24 Recovering the upper spring seat

11.25 Unclip the ABS sensor wiring from the trailing arm

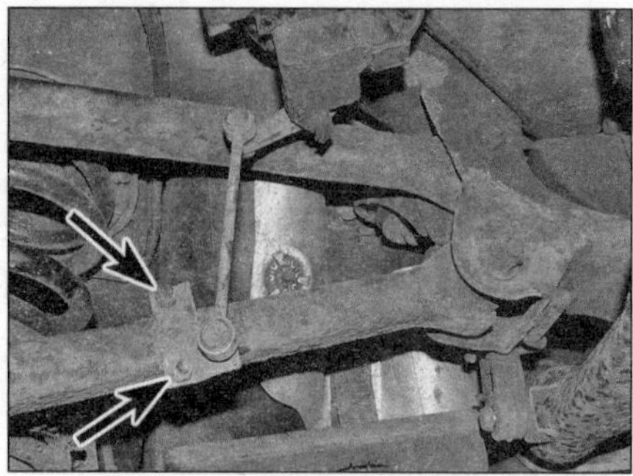
11.26 Undo the sender arm retaining nuts (arrowed)

11.27 Support the driveshaft with a piece of wire (arrowed)

Four wheel drive (4WD) models

25 Release the ABS speed sensor wiring from the bracket on the trailing arm **(see illustration)**.

26 If working on the left-hand suspension, undo the retaining nuts and disconnect the arm for the headlight range sender from the lower arm **(see illustration)**.

27 Undo the retaining bolts and disconnect the driveshaft from the flange on the final drive unit, with reference to Chapter 8A Section 3. **Note:** *The driveshafts do not have to be completely removed from the wheel hub end, but will need to be secured to one side* **(see illustration)**, *to allow the trailing arm to be lowered completely.*

28 Lower the trolley jack and remove it from under the trailing arm, then carefully lever the arm down until the coil spring can be removed. Lever against a block of wood to prevent damage to the underbody. Make sure that the vehicle is adequately supported on the axle stands **(see illustration)**.

29 With the spring removed, recover the upper and lower seat springs, noting how the lower seat is fitted. The lower seat is made up of two pieces (depending on model). There are locating pegs on the underside to fit into the axle trailing arm. The top of the lower seat has a lug that locates against the end of the spring **(see illustrations)**. Renew spring seats, as required.

Refitting

30 On front wheel drive (FWD) models, refitting is a reversal of removal, but make sure that the upper spring seat is located correctly on the top of the coil spring, with the spring end abutting the shoulder on the seat. The lower seat is circular and locates only in the centre of the spring. Before tightening the shock absorber lower mounting bolt to the specified torque, raise the trailing arm with the jack to take the weight of the rear suspension.

31 On four wheel drive (4WD) models, refitting is a reversal of removal, but make sure that the lower spring seat is located correctly on the top of the axle **(see illustrations 11.29b, 11.29c and 11.29d)**, with the spring end abutting the lug on the seat. The upper seat is circular and locates only in the centre of the spring **(see illustration)**. Before tightening the

11.28 Remove the coil spring

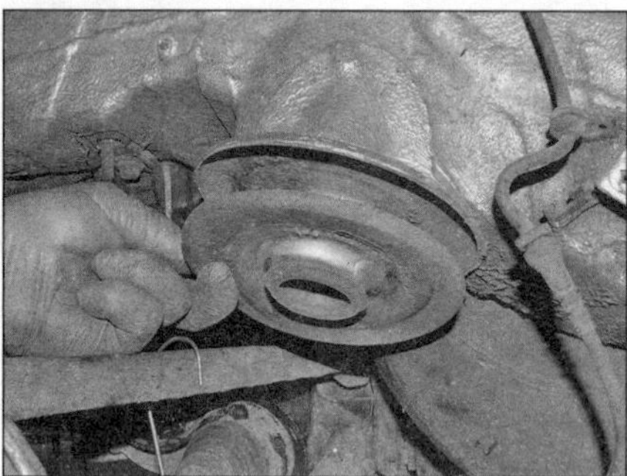
11.29a Recover the upper spring seat

11.29b Lower seat in two parts

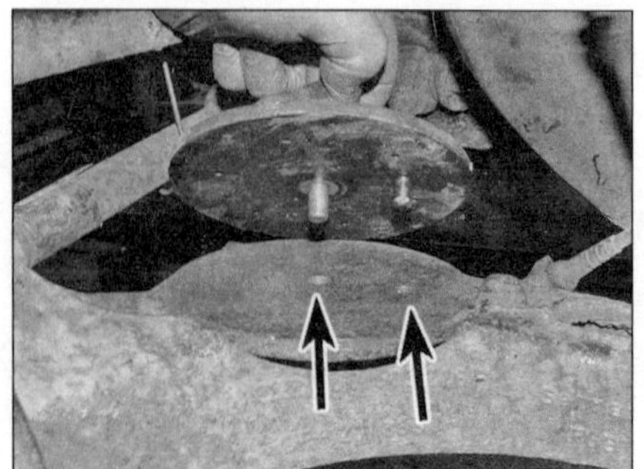
11.29c Align pegs with holes in axle (arrowed)

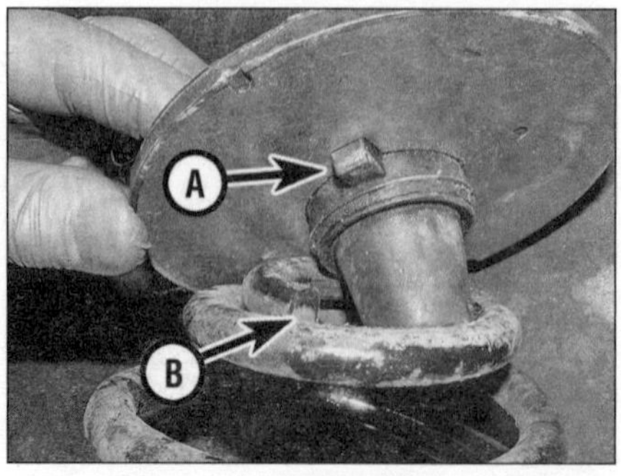

11.29d Locate end of spring (B) against lug (A) – when fitting

11.31 Fitting new upper spring seat

12.6 Connecting link upper retaining nut (arrowed)

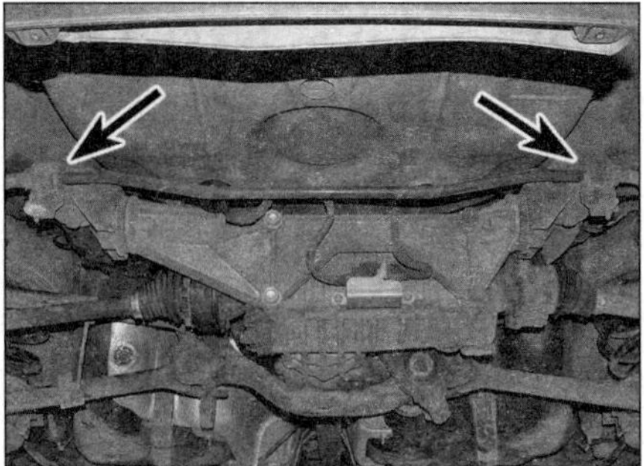
12.7 Anti-roll bar mounting brackets (arrowed)

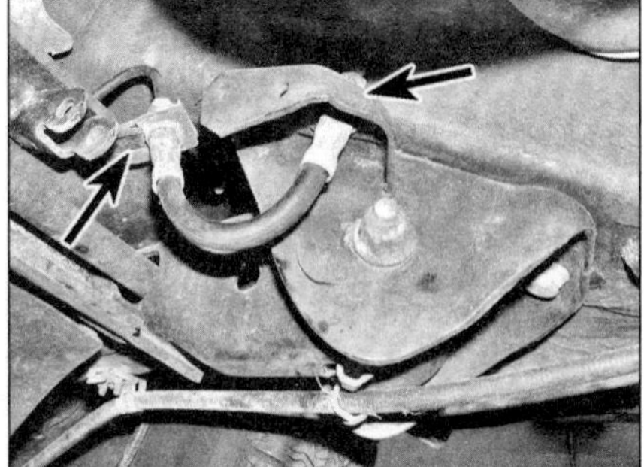
13.5 Flexible brake hose support brackets (arrowed) – one side shown

shock absorber lower mounting bolt to the specified torque, raise the trailing arm with the jack to take the weight of the rear suspension.

12 Rear anti-roll bar – removal and refitting

Front wheel drive (FWD) models

1 The rear anti-roll bar runs along the length of the rear axle beam. It is an integral part of the axle assembly, and cannot be removed. If the anti-roll bar is damaged, which is unlikely, the complete axle assembly must be renewed.

Four wheel drive (4WD) models

2 The rear anti-roll bar runs across the rear of the subframe. To make removal easier, remove the rear section of exhaust, as described in Chapter 4B Section 9.
3 Chock the front roadwheels, then jack up the rear of the vehicle and support on axle stands (see *Jacking and vehicle support*). Remove the relevant rear roadwheel.
4 Position a trolley jack beneath the trailing arm, and raise the arm so that the shock absorber is slightly compressed **(see illustration 11.8)**. Note on some models, it may be necessary to remove the stone protection guard first, from under the lower arm.
5 Unscrew and remove the shock absorber lower mounting bolt, and move the bottom of the shock absorber from the trailing arm **(see illustration 11.9)**. Note the lower mounting bolt also supports the lower part of the anti-roll bar connecting link.
6 Slacken the retaining nut and disconnect the top of the connecting link from the end of the anti-roll bar **(see illustration)**. The connecting links can stay fitted to the ends of the anti-roll bar, if required.
7 Slacken the retaining bolts from the two anti-roll bar mounting brackets **(see illustration)**, and then remove the anti-roll bar from across the rear of the final drive subframe.
8 Refitting is a reversal of removal, tighten all the retaining bolts/nuts to the specified torque.

13 Rear axle assembly (Front wheel drive models) – removal and refitting

Note: *All self-locking nuts and bolts disturbed on removal must be renewed as a matter of course.*

Removal

1 Chock the front roadwheels, then jack up the rear of the vehicle and support on axle stands positioned beneath the underbody (see *Jacking and vehicle support*). Remove both rear roadwheels.
2 On models fitted with a vehicle level/ headlight range sender system, unbolt the link and arm from the left-hand trailing arm.
3 Remove the rear shock absorbers and coil springs, as described in Section 11.
4 Release the handbrake cable from the supports/clips on the rear axle and underbody.
5 Pull out the clips and disconnect the flexible brake hoses from the supports on the rear axle and underbody bracket on both sides of the vehicle **(see illustration)**. The brake hoses do not have to bedisconnect from rigid brake lines, just carefully move them to one side, once the clips have been released.
6 Refer to Chapter 9 Section 7 and unbolt both brake calipers from the rear axle trailing arms. Release the rigid pipes from their clips and place the calipers to one side of the vehicle, together with the handbrake cables.
7 Disconnect the speed sensor wiring from the ABS speed sensors (see Chapter 9 Section 20), on each trailing arm and release the wiring from the retaining clips.
8 Undo the screws and remove the brake discs, then remove the hubs and unbolt the stub axles and backplates. Refer to Section 9, 10 if necessary.
9 Support the rear axle with a trolley jack, then unscrew and remove the rear axle front mounting bolts from the underbody brackets.
10 Manoeuvre the rear axle down from the underbody brackets and withdraw from under the vehicle. The help of an assistant is recommended.
11 Inspect the rear axle mountings for signs or damage or deterioration, and refer to Section 14, if renewal is necessary. Where fitted, unbolt the vibration damper block from the top of the rear axle.

Refitting

12 Apply a little brake grease or soapy water to the kidney-shaped cavity in the front mounting rubbers, then manoeuvre the rear axle into the underbody brackets and insert the mounting bolts from the outside. Screw on the nuts finger-tight at this stage.
13 Refer to Section 9, 10 and refit the backplates, stub axles and hubs, then refit the brake discs and secure with the screws tightened firmly.
14 Reconnect the wiring to the ABS speed sensors and clip the wiring in the supports.
15 Refit the brake calipers and secure the rigid hydraulic pipes in their clips with reference to Chapter 9 Section 7.
16 Refit the hydraulic brake hoses to the supports and secure with the clips.
17 Refit the handbrake cables and locate them in the supports/clips.
18 Refit the shock absorbers and coil springs, with reference to Section 11. Make sure the lower zinc spring seat is not damaged, before refitting.
19 Refit the stone protection plates (where applicable) under the trailing arms.
20 Check and if necessary adjust the handbrake as described in Chapter 9 Section 13.
21 On models fitted with a vehicle level/ headlight range sender system, refit the link and arm to the left-hand trailing arm and tighten the bolts to the specified torque.
22 Refit the roadwheels and lower the vehicle to the ground.

14 Rear axle rubber mountings (Front wheel drive models) – renewal

Note: *It is recommended that the rubber mountings are renewed on both sides at the same time to ensure the correct rear wheel alignment.*
1 Chock the front roadwheels, then jack up the rear of the vehicle and support on axle

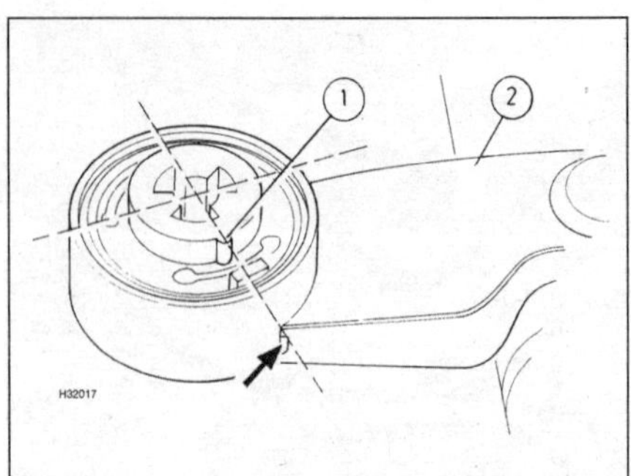

14.8 Fitting position of the rear axle rubber mounting

The cut-out (1) must align with the point indicated by the arrow on the trailing arm (2)

stands positioned beneath the underbody (see *Jacking and vehicle support*). Remove both rear roadwheels.

2 Release the handbrake cables from the supports/clips on the rear axle and underbody.

3 Pull out the clips and disconnect the flexible brake hoses from the supports on the rear axle and underbody brackets **(see illustration 13.7)**.

4 Unscrew and remove both rear axle front mounting bolts from the underbody brackets.

5 Working on one side at a time, pull the front end of the trailing arm down from the underbody bracket and retain it in this position by placing a block of wood between the arm and underbody.

6 Note the fitted position of the rubber mounting to aid refitting.

7 Audi technicians use a slide hammer tool to remove the rubber mounting from the rear axle. If a similar tool is not available, use a long bolt with suitable-sized metal tubing and washers to force out the mounting.

8 The new mounting must be located correctly in the rear axle **(see illustration)**. Using a suitable tool, pull the mounting into the rear axle until it is positioned as noted on removal.

9 Renew the mounting on the other side using the same procedure described in paragraphs 6 to 9 inclusive.

10 Apply a little brake grease or soapy water to the kidney-shaped cavity in the front mounting rubbers, then locate the rear axle in the underbody brackets. Insert the mounting bolts from the outside, hand-tight at this stage.

11 Refit the flexible brake hoses and handbrake cables, and secure with the clips.

12 Working on one side at a time, raise the trailing arm with a trolley jack until the weight of the car is taken on the coil spring, then fully tighten the front mounting bolt to the specified torque.

13 Refit the roadwheels and lower the vehicle to the ground.

15 Rear trailing arm and bracket (Four wheel drive models) – removal, overhaul and refitting

Removal

1 Chock the front roadwheels, then jack up the rear of the vehicle and support on axle stands (see *Jacking and vehicle support*). Remove the roadwheel.

2 Refer to Chapter 9 Section 7 and unbolt both brake calipers from the rear axle trailing arms. Release the rigid pipes from their clips and place the calipers to one side of the vehicle, together with the handbrake cables.

3 Disconnect the handbrake cable and release it from the trailing arm, with reference to Chapter 9 Section 15.

4 Remove the rear driveshaft, as described in Chapter 8A Section 3.

5 Remove the rear shockabsorber and coil spring, as described in Section 11.

6 Unscrew the bolts securing the upper and lower transverse links to the trailing arm.

7 Pull out the clips and disconnect the flexible brake hoses from the supports on the trailing arm and underbody brackets **(see illustration)**.

8 Mark the position of the trailing arm front mounting bracket in relation to the underbody **(see illustration)**. Note the holes for the bolts in the mounting bracket are elongated to allow for adjustment.

9 Support the front mounting bracket on a trolley jack, then unscrew the bolts, lower the assembly and withdraw the rear trailing arm and bracket from under the vehicle.

Overhaul

10 Thoroughly clean the trailing arm and bracket, then unscrew the front pivot bolt and separate the arm from the bracket. Check carefully for cracks or any other signs of wear or damage, paying particular attention to the rubber mounting bush.

11 If the bush requires renewal, take the arm to an Audi dealer or suitably equipped garage. Alternatively, a press and suitable spacers may be used to press the bush out of the arm, and to install the new one.

12 With the new bush in position, locate the front of the arm in the bracket, and insert the bolt. Position the arm in relation to the bracket as shown **(see illustration)** then tighten the bolt/nut to the specified torque.

Refitting

13 Raise the front mounting bracket and locate it on the underbody in its previously noted position. Insert the new bolts and tighten to the specified torque.

14 Fit the rear of the trailing arm to the upper and lower transverse links and insert the bolts loosely. These will need to be tightened to the specified torque, once the vehicle is sitting on its wheels with the vehicle weight on the suspension.

15 Refit the rear shockabsorber and coil spring with reference to Section 11.

16 Refit the driveshaft, with reference to Chapter 8A Section 3.

17 Refit the rear brake pads and caliper, with reference to Chapter 9 Section 7.

18 Refit the handbrake cable to the support brackets and re-connect to brake caliper. Adjust the handbrake, with reference to Chapter 9 Section 13.

19 Refit the brake hose/pipe back to the support brackets on the trailing arm and underbody and secure in place with retaining clips.

20 Refit the roadwheel and lower the vehicle to the ground. With the vehicle on level ground and the weight on the suspension, tighten the upper and lower transverse links to the specified torque. Also tighten the wheel bolts to the specified torque.

21 Have the rear wheel alignment checked and if necessary adjusted by an Audi dealer.

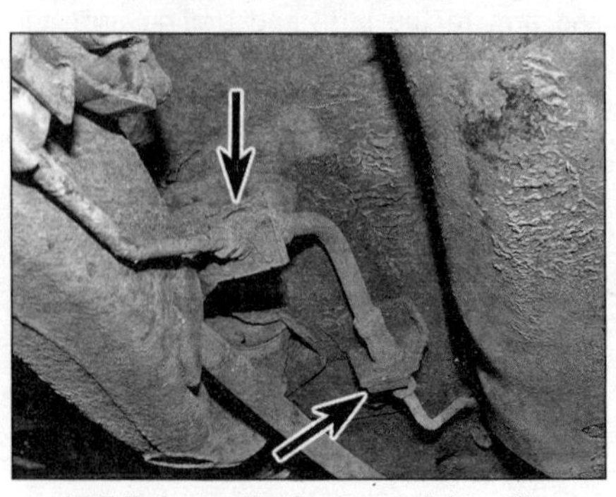

15.7 Release the hose retaining clips (arrowed)

15.8 Rear trailing arm mounting bracket

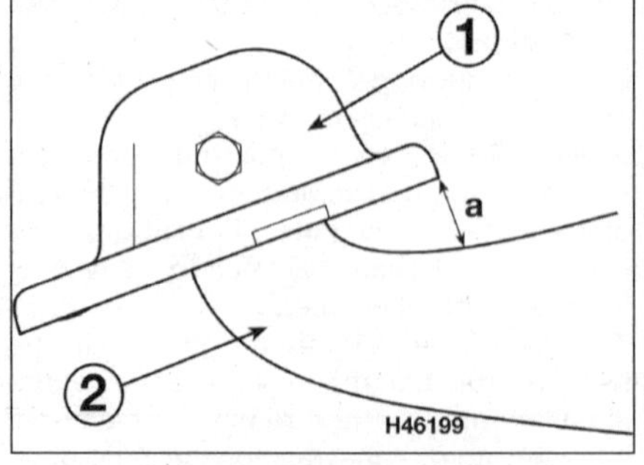

15.12 Mounting bracket assembly to trailing arm

1 Mounting bracket 2 Trailing arm
a = 53.5 mm

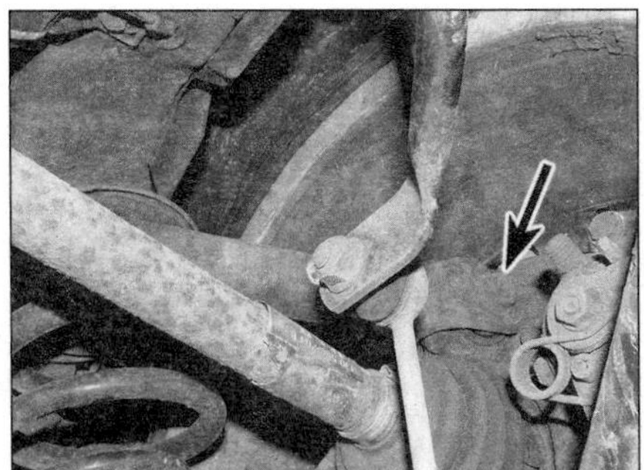

16.2 Upper transverse link outer bolt (arrowed)

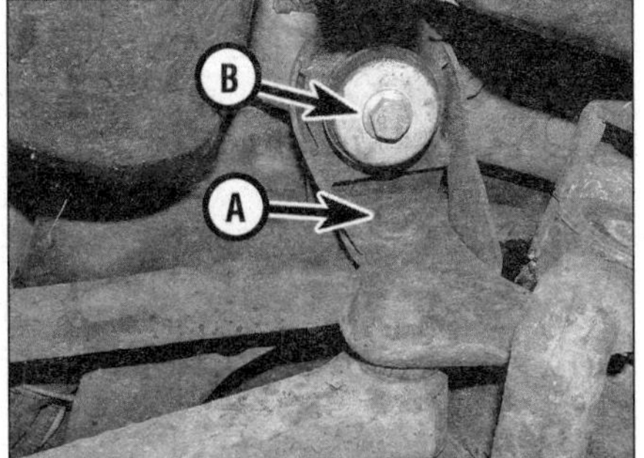

16.3 Upper link inner bolt (A) subframe mounting bolt (B)

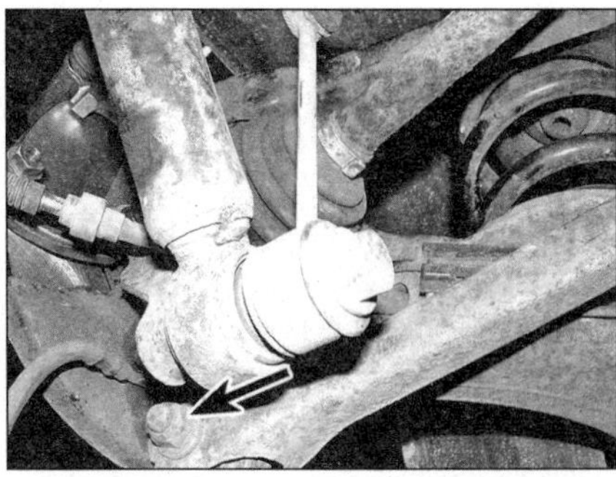

16.10 Lower transverse link outer bolt (arrowed)

16 Rear transverse links (Four wheel drive models) – removal and refitting

Upper link

Removal

1 Chock the front roadwheels, then jack up the rear of the vehicle and support on axle stands (see *Jacking and vehicle support*). Remove the roadwheel.

2 Support the rear trailing arm on a trolley jack, then slacken and remove the outer bolt on the upper transverse link **(see illustration)**. Discard the bolt as a new one will be required for refitting.

3 At the inner end of the upper link, slacken and remove the retaining bolt from the mounting bracket on the rear subframe **(see illustration)**. To withdraw the upper bolt, the subframe front mounting bolt may need to be removed, to allow the link bolt to be removed. Discard the bolts as a new ones will be required for refitting.

4 The upper link can now be withdrawn from under the vehicle. The trailing arm may need to be pulled outwards slightly to allow the transverse link to be removed. Take care not to damage any of the hoses, pipes or wiring as the link is being removed.

Refitting

5 Refitting is a reversal of removal, but delay fully-tightening the mounting bolts until the vehicle is sitting on its wheels, and the vehicle weight on the suspension. New bolts will be required for refitting.

6 Refit the roadwheel and lower the vehicle to the ground. Tighten the wheel bolts to the specified torque.

7 With the vehicle on level ground and the weight on the suspension, tighten the upper transverse link bolts and subframe bolt (if removed) to the specified torque. If required, have the rear wheel alignment checked and if necessary adjusted by an Audi dealer.

Lower transverse link

Removal

8 Chock the front roadwheels, then jack up the rear of the vehicle and support on axle stands (see *Jacking and vehicle support*). Remove the roadwheel.

9 If working on the left-hand suspension, undo the retaining nuts and disconnect the arm for the headlight range sender from the lower arm (see Section 17). Mark the position of the bracket, so that it can be fitted in the correct position on the link arm when refitting.

10 Support the rear trailing arm on a trolley jack, then slacken and remove the outer bolt on the lower transverse link **(see illustration)**. Discard the bolt as a new one will be required for refitting.

11 At the inner end of the upper link, slacken and remove the retaining bolt from the mounting bracket on the rear subframe **(see illustration)**. Discard the bolts as a new ones will be required for refitting.

12 The lower link can now be withdrawn from under the vehicle. The trailing arm may need to be pulled outwards slightly to allow the transverse link to be removed. Take care not to damage any of the hoses, pipes or wiring as the link is being removed.

Refitting

13 Refitting is a reversal of removal, but delay fully-tightening the mounting bolts until the vehicle is sitting on its wheels, and the vehicle weight on the suspension. New bolts will be required for refitting.

14 On left-hand lower transverse link, refit the vehicle level/headlight range sender. Align the marks made on removal, then tighten the mounting bracket retaining bolts.

15 Refit the roadwheel and lower the vehicle to the ground. Tighten the wheel bolts to the specified torque

16 With the vehicle on level ground and the weight on the suspension, tighten the upper transverse link bolts and subframe bolt (if removed) to the specified torque. If required, have the rear wheel alignment checked and if necessary adjusted by an Audi dealer.

17 Vehicle level sender – removal and refitting

Removal

1 The front sender for the vehicle level/ head-light range control system is located on the left-hand side of the underbody, and incorporates an arm and link attached to the left-hand front lower suspension arm **(see illustration)**.

2 The rear sender is bolted to the underbody, and an arm and link is attached to a bracket on the left-hand trailing arm **(see illustration)**.

16.11 Lower transverse link inner bolt (arrowed)

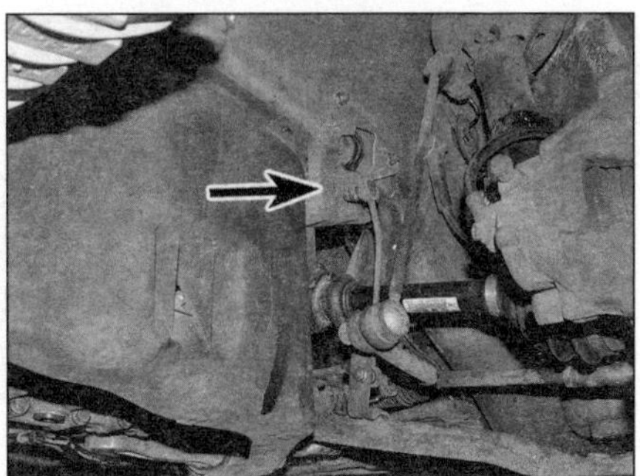

17.1 Front sender location (arrowed)

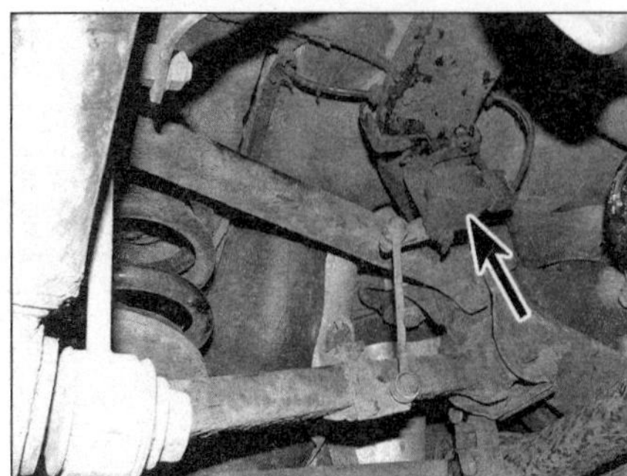

17.2 Rear sender location (arrowed) – 4WD model shown

3 To remove the front sender, apply the handbrake then jack up the front of the vehicle and support it on axle stands (see *Jacking and vehicle support*). Remove the front roadwheel, then mark the position of the sender link on the lower arm plate – this will aid refitting. Unscrew the nut and disconnect the link from the plate on the lower arm, some models have an elongated hole in the plate, if so mark the position for refitting. Disconnect the wiring then unscrew the nuts and remove the sender from the underbody.

4 To remove the rear sender, chock the front roadwheels then jack up the rear of the vehicle and support on axle stands (see *Jacking and vehicle support*). Unscrew the nuts and separate the link from the bracket on the rear axle. Disconnect the wiring then unbolt the sender from the underbody.

Refitting

5 Refitting is a reversal of removal, but tighten the mounting nuts/bolts to the specified torque. If necessary, have the front sender adjustment checked by an Audi dealer.

18 Steering wheel – removal and refitting

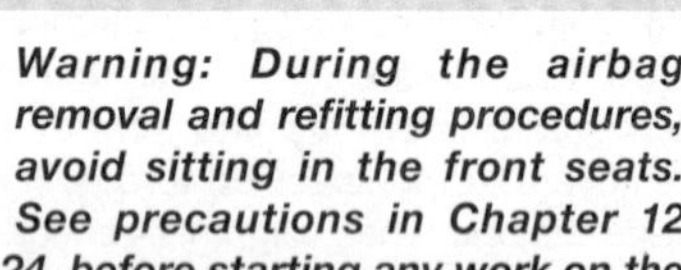

Warning: During the airbag removal and refitting procedures, avoid sitting in the front seats. See precautions in Chapter 12 Section 24, before starting any work on the airbag system.

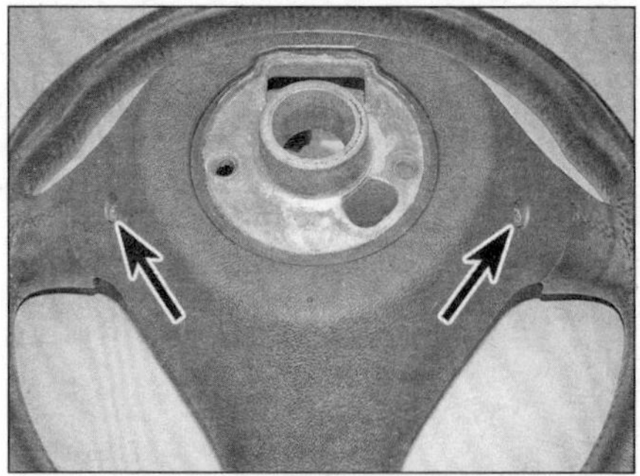

18.4a Position of screws (arrowed) in the rear of the steering wheel...

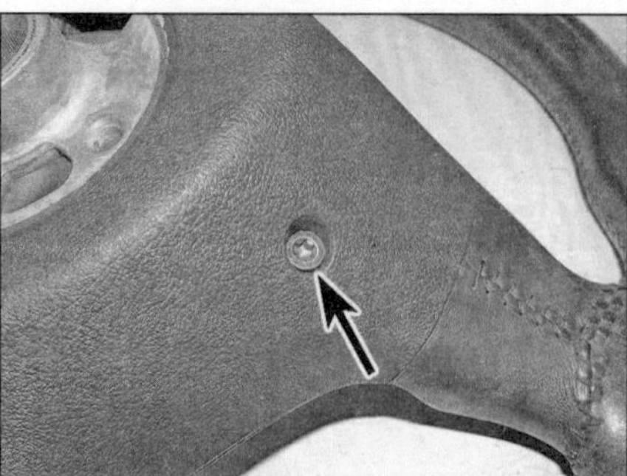

18.4b ...remove the Torx screw (arrowed)

Removal

1 Set the front wheels in the straight-ahead position, and release the steering lock by inserting the ignition key.

2 Disconnect the battery negative (earth) lead and position it away from the terminal.

3 Adjust the steering column to its lowest position by releasing the adjustment handle, then pull out the column and lower it as far as possible. Lock the column in this position by returning the adjustment handle.

4 With the spokes in the vertical position, undo the driver's airbag Torx screw at the rear of the steering wheel hub. Then turn the steering wheel through 180° and undo the remaining airbag Torx screw **(see illustrations)**. Note the screws stay in position in the steering wheel and do not need to be completely removed.

5 Carefully withdraw the driver's airbag from the centre of the steering wheel, release the locking clip and and disconnect the wiring connector **(see illustrations)**.

Warning: Position the airbag in a safe and secure place, away from the work area (refer to Chapter 12 Section 24).

6 Release the retaining clips and disconnect the wiring connector from the central contact unit **(see illustration)**. The steering angle sender, slip ring and return spring and built into the central contact unit.

7 Using a multi-spline socket, unscrew and remove the retaining bolt, while holding the steering wheel stationary **(see illustration)**.

8 Check if the steering wheel is marked in relation to the column **(see illustration)**. If not use a dab of paint to mark the steering wheel in relation to the column in order to aid refitting, then ease the steering wheel

18.5a Carefully withdraw from the steering wheel...

18.5b ...release the locking clip...

18.5c ...and remove the airbag module

18.6 Disconnect the wiring connector

18.7 Remove the multi-splined bolt

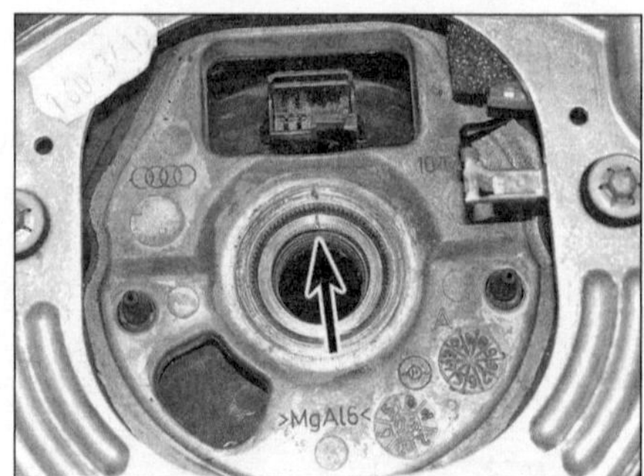

18.8 Alignment marks on steering wheel and column (arrowed)

19.4a Undo the two retaining screws (arrowed)...

19.4b ...and remove the upper shroud

19.5a Undo the retaining screws (arrowed)...

from the column splines by firmly rocking it side-to-side.

Refitting

9 Locate the steering wheel on the column splines making sure that the previously-made marks are correctly aligned.

10 Fit the new steering bolt (which has locking compound on the threads), and tighten to the specified torque, while holding the steering wheel stationary.

11 Reconnect the wiring connectors to the central contact unit and rear of the airbag. Carefully hold the airbag in position and tighten the two Torx screws at the rear of the steering wheel.

12 Reconnect the battery negative (earth) lead.

19 Steering column – removal, inspection and refitting

Removal

1 Disconnect the battery negative (earth) lead and position it away from the terminal.

2 Remove the steering wheel and driver's airbag, as described in Section 18, and return the steering to the straight-ahead position.

3 Remove the drivers side lower facia trim panel, as described in Chapter 11 Section 28.

4 Undo the two retaining screws, up through the lower part of the steering column, and then unclip the upper shroud from the top of the steering column **(see illustrations)**.

5 Undo the screws and remove the column height and reach adjustment handle **(see illustrations)**

6 Undo the three retaining screws and remove the lower shroud from under the steering column **(see illustrations)**. As the shroud is being removed, release it from the height and reach adjustment handle.

7 Remove the steering column combination switch/central control unit assembly from the top of the steering column, as described in Chapter 12 Section 4.

8 Undo the fasteners and remove the foot rest trim panel from the lower end of the steering column **(see illustration)**.

9 Disconnect the wiring from the rear of the ignition switch and from the ignition key sensor coil. Also undo the bolt and remove the earth wire from the steering lock housing **(see illustration)**.

10 On automatic transmission models, move the selector lever to position P, then turn the ignition key to the 'On' position. Release the wire clip by pressing it either up or down (according to type), then pull out the steering lock locking cable.

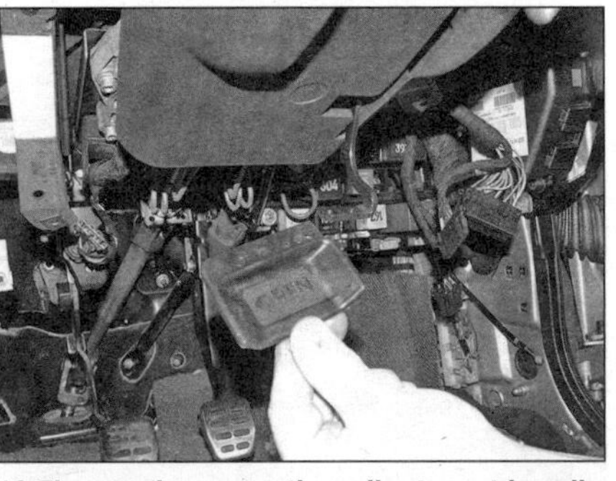

19.5b ...and remove the adjustment handle

19.6a Undo the lower screw (arrowed)...

19.6b ...and the two upper screws...

19.6c ...then remove the lower shroud

19.8 Remove the foot rest trim panel

19.9 Disconnect the wiring connectors at the ignition switch

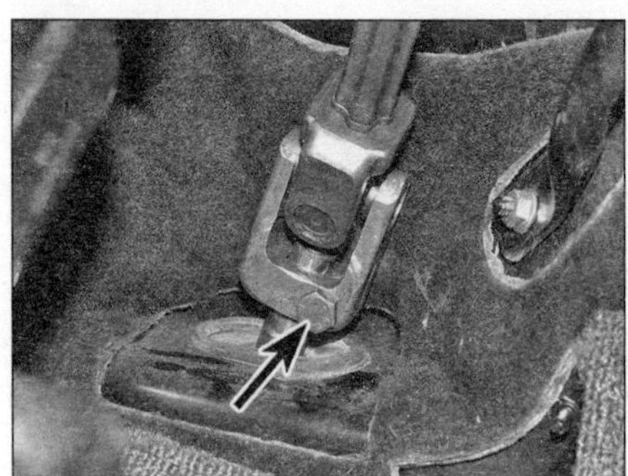
19.11 Remove the clamp bolt (arrowed)

19.12a Insert a dowel or plug (arrowed) to hold the steering column together (early models)...

19.12b ...or in hole in the upper housing (arrowed) – later models

19.13a Remove the lower retaining bolt (arrowed)...

19.13b ...and the upper mounting bolts (arrowed)

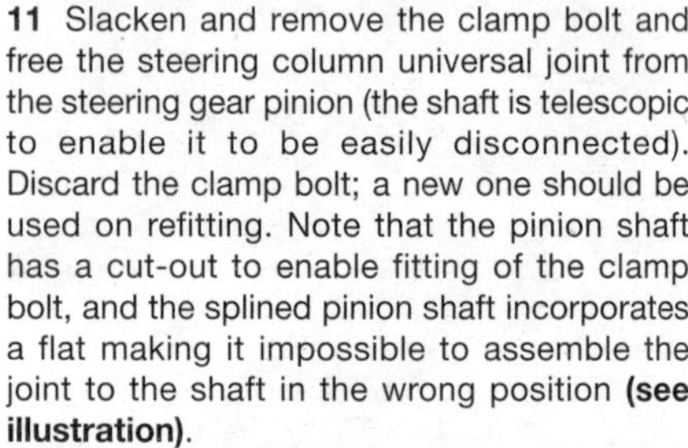

11 Slacken and remove the clamp bolt and free the steering column universal joint from the steering gear pinion (the shaft is telescopic to enable it to be easily disconnected). Discard the clamp bolt; a new one should be used on refitting. Note that the pinion shaft has a cut-out to enable fitting of the clamp bolt, and the splined pinion shaft incorporates a flat making it impossible to assemble the joint to the shaft in the wrong position **(see illustration)**.

12 Note that the inner and outer columns, and the intermediate shaft, are telescopic, to facilitate the reach adjustment. It is important to keep the splined sections of the inner steering column engaged with each other while the steering column is removed. If they become detached due to the outer column sections being separated, especially on a vehicle which has completed a high mileage, it is possible that rattling noises may occur. Audi technicians use a special plastic clip to hold the outer column sections together, although a retainer can be made out of a tapered wooden dowel, or the plastic end of a ballpoint pen can be put to good use. First, release the reach adjustment handle and position the outer column tubes so that the transportation holes are in alignment. Insert the dowel or plug to hold the sections of the column together during removal **(see illustrations)**.

13 Unscrew and remove the lower mounting bolt, then support the steering column and unscrew the upper mounting bolts. Withdraw the steering column from inside the vehicle **(see illustrations)**.

14 If necessary, remove the ignition switch/steering column lock with reference to Section.

Inspection

15 The steering column is designed to collapse in the event of a front-end crash, to prevent the steering wheel injuring the driver. Before refitting the steering column, examine the column and mountings for signs of damage and deformation. There are two types of steering column fitted, depending on model.

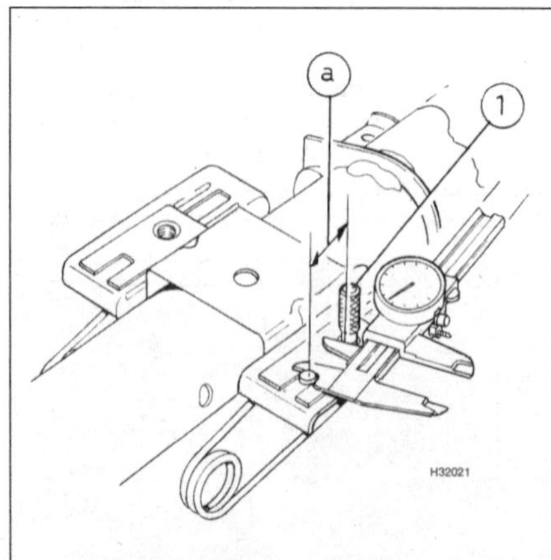

19.16 Using vernier calipers to measure the distance between the column mounting bolt hole and stop peg – earlier models

1 Mounting bolt a = 23.0 mm

16 On earlier models, using a vernier caliper, measure the distance between the bolt hole and the stop peg on the upper mounting plate **(see illustration)**. Insert the mounting bolt to make this check. If the distance is not 23.0 mm, the steering column is damaged and should be renewed.

17 On later models, when looking at the top of the upper mounting bracket housing, there must not be more than a 0.5 mm between the sliding part and the mounting bracket.

18 Check the inner column sections for signs of free play in the column bushes. If any damage or wear is found on the steering column bushes, the column must be renewed as an assembly.

19 The intermediate shaft is permanently attached to the inner column and cannot be renewed separately **(see illustration)**. Inspect the universal joints for excessive wear. If evident, the complete steering column must be renewed.

Refitting

20 On early models, if a new steering column is being fitted, the roller bracket must be removed from the old outer column and secured to the new one with a new

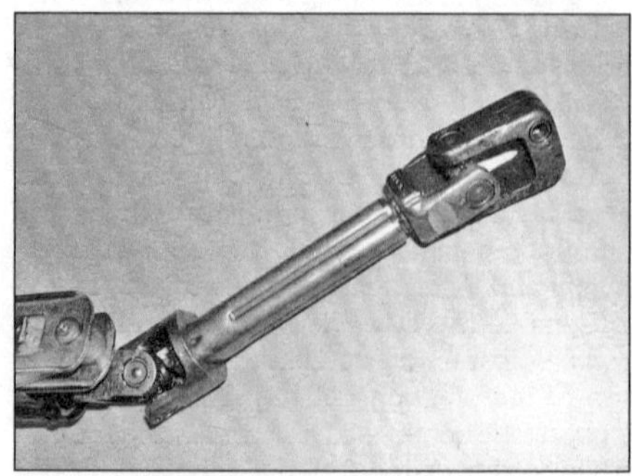
19.19 The intermediate shaft is permanently attached to the inner steering column – early model shown

shear-head bolt **(see illustration)**. Drill out the old shear-head bolt to remove the bracket, and unscrew the remains of the bolt. Locate the bracket on the new column and secure it with a new shear-head bolt. Tighten the bolt until its head breaks off.

21 If removed, refit the ignition switch/ steering column lock with reference to Section.

22 Apply a little locking fluid to the threads of the mounting bolts. Offer the steering column onto its mounting bracket and insert all of the mounting bolts loosely. Tighten the lower mounting bolt to the specified torque, then tighten the upper bolts to the specified torque.

23 Where applicable, remove the clip/peg securing the telescopic tube sections together to prevent them coming apart.

24 Locate the universal joint onto the steering gear pinion shaft so that the cut-out is aligned with the bolt holes. Insert the new clamp bolt and tighten to the specified torque.

25 Refit the plastic cover beneath the pedal bracket and secure with the fasteners.

26 On automatic transmission models, with the selector lever in position P and the ignition key in the 'On' position, slide the locking cable into the lock housing until the wire clip engages. Check that it is possible to move the selector lever out of the P position. If not, refer to Chapter and adjust the cable. Check also that it is only possible to remove the ignition key with the selector in the P position. With the ignition key in the 'Off' position, it must not be possible to move the selector lever out of the P position.

27 Locate the combination switch on the column with reference to Chapter 12 Section 4, align it with the previously made mark, and tighten the clamp bolt. **Note:** *The basic setting of the sensor must be checked by an Audi dealer whenever it is removed or whenever the steering wheel is re-positioned.*

28 Reconnect the wiring to the ignition switch and combination switch/central control unit.

29 Temporarily locate the steering wheel on the column splines and check that the clearance between the steering wheel and the clock spring housing is approximately 3.0 mm. If not, loosen the combination switch clamp bolt and reposition it, then retighten the bolt. Remove the steering wheel.

19.20 The roller bracket is secured to the steering column with a single shear-head bolt

30 Refit the upper and lower steering column shrouds and secure with the screws.

31 Refit the height and reach adjustment handle and tighten the screws.

32 Refit the lower trim panels on the driver's side of the facia, with reference to Chapter 11 Section 28.

33 Refit the steering wheel and driver's airbag, with reference to Section 18.

34 Reconnect the battery negative (earth) lead.

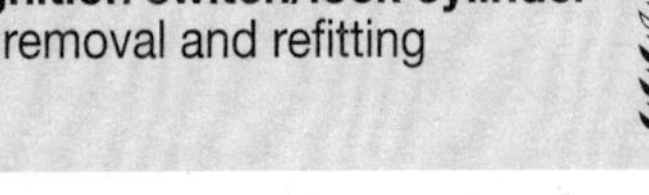

20 Ignition switch/lock cylinder – removal and refitting

Ignition switch

Removal

1 Disconnect the battery negative lead (see Reference at end of Manual), and position it away from the terminal.

2 Remove the steering wheel and airbag, as described in Section 18.

3 Undo the retaining screws and remove the upper and lower shrouds from around the upper part of the steering column, as described in Section 19.

20.4 Disconnect the wiring connector (arrowed)

4 Release the retaining clip and disconnect the wiring plug from the rear of the ignition switch **(see illustration)**.

5 Pull back the label, then using a small screwdriver prise the plastic cover from the rear of the switch. Then using two small screwdrivers in the slots in the outer housing release the two retaining clips, and withdraw the ignition electrical switch **(see illustrations)**. Note, this may not be possible on all models, check with your local dealer for the availability of parts, before removal.

Refitting

6 Refit the switch to the steering lock housing and press in until the two retaining clips engage. Making sure the slot in the rear of the switch is aligned correctly.

7 Refit the plastic cover to the rear of the switch and stick down the label.

8 Reconnect the wiring plug to the ignition switch.

9 Refit the upper and lower shrouds, and tighten the screws.

10 Refit the steering wheel and airbag, with reference to Section 18.

11 Reconnect the battery negative lead.

Lock cylinder

Removal

12 Carry out the procedures as described in paragraphs 1 to 3.

13 Release the securing clip and disconnect

20.5a Insert two thin screwdrivers in the recesses (arrowed) ...

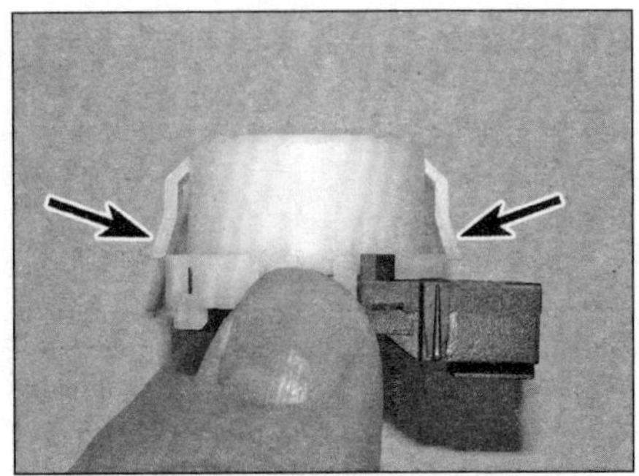

20.5b ...to release the two securing clips (arrowed)...

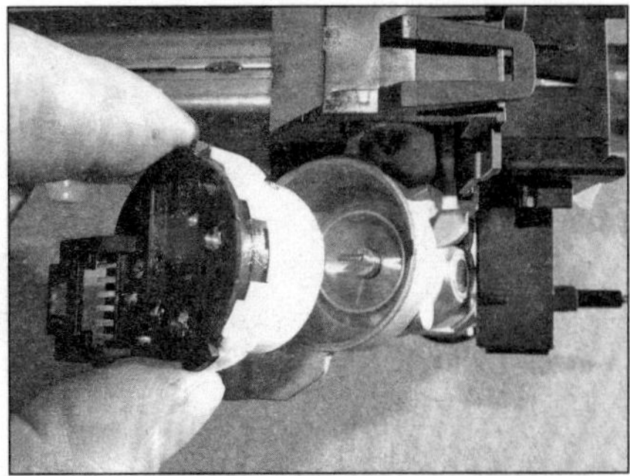

20.5c ...and withdraw the electrical switch

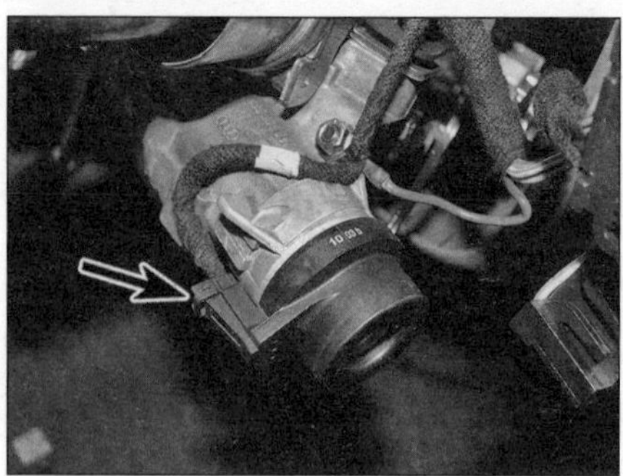
20.13 Disconnect the wiring connector (arrowed)

20.15a insert a thin rod through the hole ...

20.15b ...to release the lock cylinder

the wiring connector from the transponder around the ignition switch **(see illustration)**.

14 Insert the ignition key and turn the lock cylinder to the drive position (which is approx. 90° from off position).

15 Insert a piece of wire 1.2 mm in diameter in the drilling next to the ignition key, slide it in to release the locking lever, then withdraw the lock cylinder from the housing **(see illustrations)**. To make the piece of wire locate in the locking lever easier, file an angle on the end of the wire.

Refitting

16 Refit the lock cylinder with the ignition key in the Drive position, then remove the wire.

17 Reconnect the wiring connector to the transponder.

18 Refit the upper and lower shrouds, and tighten the screws.

19 Refit the steering wheel and airbag, with reference to Section 18.

20 Reconnect the battery negative lead.

Ignition switch/lock cylinder housing

Removal

21 The ignition switch/lock housing is integral with the switch assembly carrier, which is secured to the steering column with shear-head bolts **(see illustration)**.

22 To remove the housing, it may be necessary to first remove the steering column, as described in Section 19.

23 The switch/lock carrier is secured by shear-head bolts, and the heads are broken off in the tightening procedure. To remove the old bolts, either drill them out, or use a sharp cold chisel to cut off their heads or turn them anti-clockwise. Withdraw the carrier from the steering column.

24 When refitting locate the switch/lock carrier on the steering column, and insert the new shear-head bolts. Tighten the bolts until their heads break off.

25 The remaining procedure is a reversal of removal.

21 Steering gear assembly – removal, overhaul and refitting

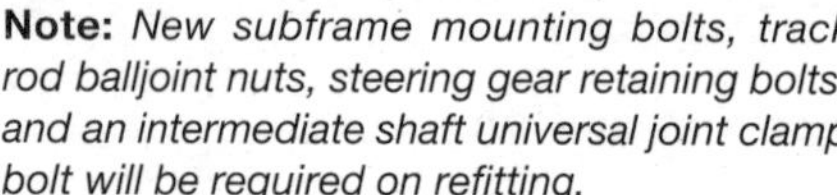

Note: *New subframe mounting bolts, track rod balljoint nuts, steering gear retaining bolts, and an intermediate shaft universal joint clamp bolt will be required on refitting.*

Removal

1 Apply the handbrake, then jack up the front of the vehicle and support it on axle stands positioned on the underbody, leaving the subframe free (see *Jacking and vehicle support*). Position the steering straight-ahead, then remove both front roadwheels. Also remove the engine compartment undershield.

2 Inside the vehicle, undo the screws and remove the plastic cover for access to the universal joint connecting the steering inner column to the steering gear pinion. Unscrew and remove the clamp bolt **(see illustration 19.11)**, and pull the universal joint from the pinion splines. **Note:** *The steering gear pinion incorporates a cut-out for the clamp bolt, and therefore the joint can only be fitted in one position. Discard the clamp bolt, a new one should be used on refitting.*

3 Fit a hose clamp to the fluid return hose leading from the steering gear to the power steering fluid reservoir. Also fit a hose clamp to the power steering pump fluid inlet hose.

4 Working on each side at a time, unscrew the nuts from the track rod ends, then use a balljoint separator tool to release the ends from the steering arms on the front wheel bearing housings (see Section 25).

5 Unscrew the two bolts securing the rear engine/transmission mounting to the underside of the transmission unit **(see illustration)**. Discard both bolts, new ones must be used on refitting, and leave the mounting attached to the subframe.

6 Unscrew the nut securing the power steering pipe bracket to the subframe **(see illustration)**.

7 On models with an automatic headlight range control system, unscrew the nut and detach the sender link arm from the left-hand

20.21 Steering lock housing shear bolts (arrowed)

21.5 Undo the rear mounting bolts (arrowed)

21.6 Undo the bracket nut (arrowed)

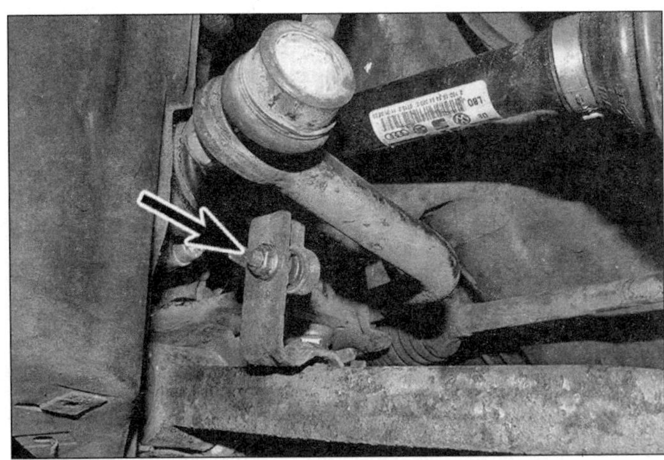

21.7 Link arm securing nut (arrowed)

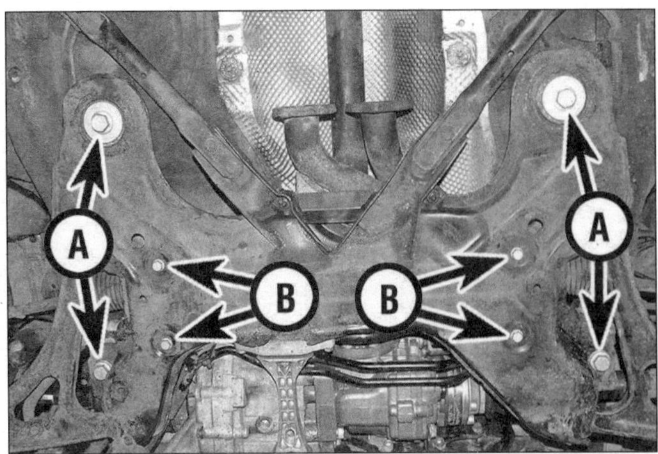

21.8 Subframe bolts (A) and steering rack mounting bolts (B)

side lower suspension arm **(see illustration)**. Some models have an elongated slot in the bracket on the lower arm (this is for adjustment), on this type, mark the position of the retaining nut before removal.

8 Support the weight of the subframe with a trolley jack, then unscrew the four bolts securing the subframe to the underbody, and also the four retaining bolts from the steering rack **(see illustration)**.

9 Lower the subframe a little to give sufficient access to the fluid supply and return unions on the steering gear, at the same time guiding the pinion shaft from the rubber grommet in the floor panel.

10 Position a suitable container beneath the steering gear to catch spilt fluid. Unscrew the union bolts and disconnect the lines, then recover the copper sealing washers **(see illustration)**. Tape over or plug the ends of the lines and the apertures in the steering gear to prevent entry of dust and dirt into the hydraulic system. The line ends can be wrapped in a plastic bag if preferred.

11 With the mounting bolts removed, carefully lever the steering gear away from the top of the subframe. Note the steering gear has a metal dowel fitted **(see illustration)**, to locate in the top of the subframe. Withdraw the steering gear from the subframe to the rear.

12 The mounting on the left-hand side (passenger side) of the gear incorporates a clamp and rubber mounting **(see illustration)**. Examine the mounting for wear and damage, and renew it if necessary. Discard the steering gear mounting bolts, new ones should be used on refitting.

Overhaul

13 Examine the steering gear assembly for signs of wear or damage, and check that the rack moves freely throughout the full length of its travel, with no signs of roughness or excessive free play between the steering gear pinion and rack. It is not possible to overhaul the steering gear assembly housing components, and if it is faulty, the assembly must be renewed. The only components which can be renewed individually are the steering gear gaiters, the track rod end balljoints and the track rods, as described later in this Chapter.

Refitting

14 Locate the steering gear on the subframe, and insert the new mounting bolts. Make sure that the location dowel is correctly fitted. Tighten the bolts to the specified torque and Stage 2 angle.

15 Attach the return line to the subframe/ steering gear and tighten the bolt/nut. The clearance between the fluid lines should be approximately 10 mm.

16 Reconnect the fluid supply and return lines to the steering gear, together with new copper washers on each side of the unions. Tighten the union bolts to the specified torque.

17 Raise the subframe and at the same time guide the steering gear pinion shaft through the rubber grommet in the floor. Insert the new subframe bolts and tighten them to the specified torque and angle.

18 Align the engine/transmission rear mounting with the transmission unit and fit the new mounting bolts. Tighten the bolts to the specified Stage 1 torque and through the specified Stage 2 angle (see Chapter 2A Section 17).

19 Refit the track rod ends to the steering arms, screw on the new nuts, and tighten them to the specified torque.

20 Remove the hose clamps from the fluid supply and return hoses.

21 Working inside the car, locate the steering column universal joint on the pinion shaft,

21.10 Hydraulic fluid line union bolts (arrowed)

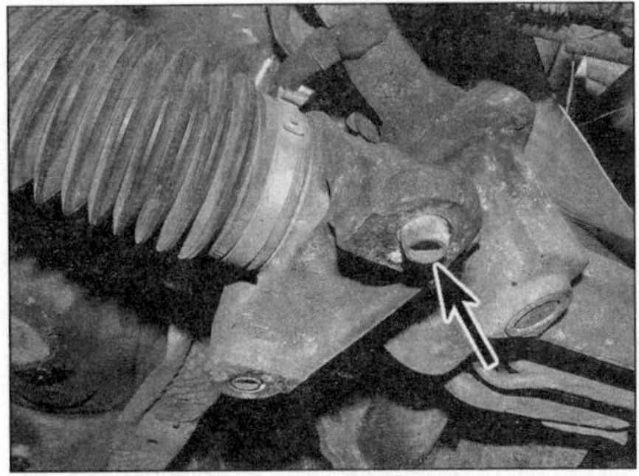

21.11 Steering gear metal dowel (arrowed)

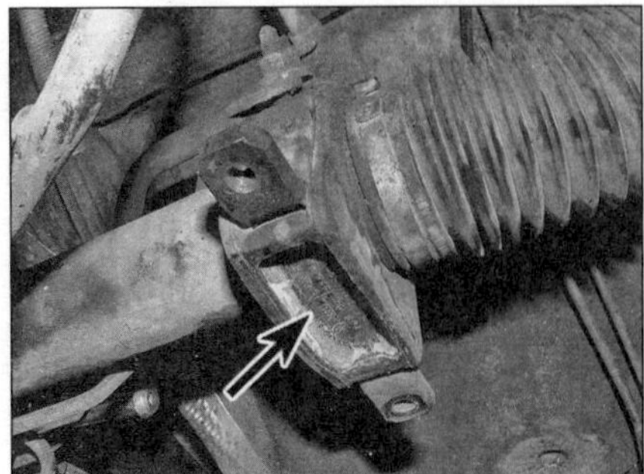

21.12 Check the rubber mounting (arrowed)

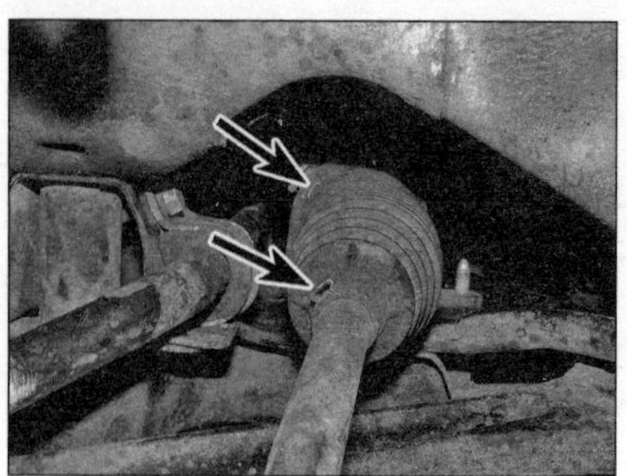

22.2 Gaiter retaining clips (arrowed)

making sure that the cut-out is aligned with the bolt holes. Insert the new bolt and tighten to the specified torque.

22 Check that the rubber grommet is located correctly in the floor, then refit the plastic cover and secure with the fasteners.

23 Refit the engine compartment undershield and roadwheels, then lower the vehicle to the ground. On completion check and, if necessary, adjust the front wheel alignment as described in Section 26.

22 Steering gear rubber gaiters and track rods – renewal

Steering gear rubber gaiters

1 Remove the track rod end balljoint as described in Section 25.

2 Note the fitted position of the gaiter on the track rod, then release the retaining clips and slide the gaiter off the steering gear housing and track rod **(see illustration)**.

3 Wipe clean the track rod and the steering gear housing, then apply a film of suitable grease to the surface of the rack. To do this, turn the steering wheel as necessary to fully extend the rack from the housing, then reposition it in its central position.

4 Carefully slide the new gaiter onto the track rod, and locate it on the steering gear housing. Position the gaiter as previously noted on removal, making sure that it is not twisted, then lift the outer sealing lip of the gaiter to equalise air pressure within the gaiter.

5 Secure the gaiter in position with new retaining clips. Where crimped-type clips are used, pull the clip as tight as possible, and locate the hooks in their slots. Remove any slack in the clip by carefully compressing the raised section. In the absence of the special crimping tool, a pair of side-cutters may be used, taking care not to actually cut the clip.

6 Refit the track rod end balljoint as described in Section 25.

Track rods

7 Remove the relevant steering gear rubber gaiter as described earlier. If there is insufficient working room with the steering gear mounted in the car, remove it as described in Section 21 and hold it in a vice while renewing the track rod.

8 Hold the steering rack stationary with one spanner on the flats provided, then loosen the balljoint nut with another spanner. Fully unscrew the nut and remove the track rod from the rack.

9 Locate the new track rod on the end of the steering rack and screw on the nut. Hold the rack stationary with one spanner and tighten the balljoint nut to the specified torque. A crow's foot adapter may be required since the track rod prevents access with a socket, and care must be taken to apply the exact torque in this situation.

10 Refit the steering gear or rubber gaiter with reference to the earlier paragraphs or Section 21. On completion check and, if necessary, adjust the front wheel alignment as described in Section 26.

23 Power steering system – bleeding

1 With the engine stopped, use a screwdriver to unscrew the cap from the top of the power steering hydraulic fluid container located on the right-hand side of the engine compartment. Wipe clean the dipstick which forms part of the cap, then fully screw on the cap again. Remove the cap once more, and check the level of the fluid on the dipstick **(see illustrations)**. Top-up the level to the MAX mark, using the fluid recommended in Lubricants and fluids at the beginning of this Manual.

2 Slowly move the steering from lock-to-lock several times to purge out the trapped air, then top-up the level in the fluid reservoir. Repeat this procedure until the fluid level in the reservoir does not drop any further.

3 Have an assistant start the engine, whilst you keep watch on the fluid level. Be prepared to add more fluid as the engine starts, as the fluid level may drop quickly. The fluid level must be kept above the MIN mark at all times.

4 With the engine running at idle speed, turn the steering wheel slowly from lock-to-lock 10 times. Do not hold the wheel on either lock, as this imposes excessive strain upon the hydraulic system. Repeat this procedure until bubbles cease to appear in the fluid reservoir.

5 If, when turning the steering, an odd noise is heard from the fluid lines, it indicates there is still air in the system. Check this by turning the wheels to the straight-ahead position and switching off the engine. If the fluid level in the reservoir rises, then air is present in the system, and further bleeding is necessary.

6 Once all traces of air have been removed from the power steering hydraulic system, switch off the engine and allow the system to cool. Once cool, check that the fluid level is up to the maximum mark on the power steering fluid reservoir, and top-up if necessary. Finally, tighten the cap onto the reservoir.

24 Power steering pump – removal and refitting

Note: *New feed pipe union copper sealing washers will be required on refitting*

Removal

1 Apply the handbrake, then jack up the front of the vehicle and support it on axle stands (see *Jacking and vehicle support*). Remove the right-hand side front wheel, and engine compartment undershields **(see illustration)**.

2 Using an Allen key loosen only the bolts

23.1a Use a screwdriver...

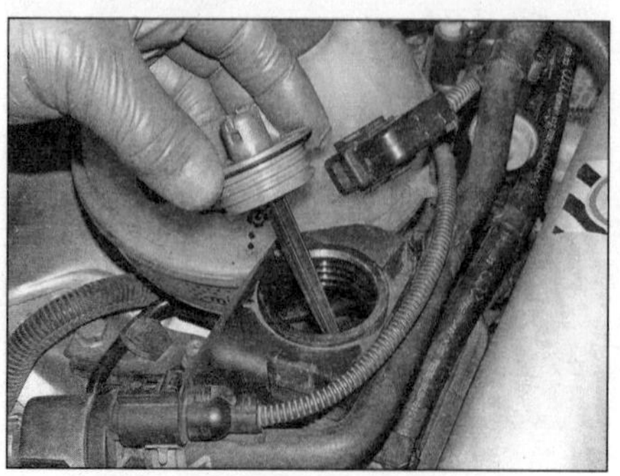

23.1b ...to remove the cap/dipstick

24.1 Remove the engine side trim cover

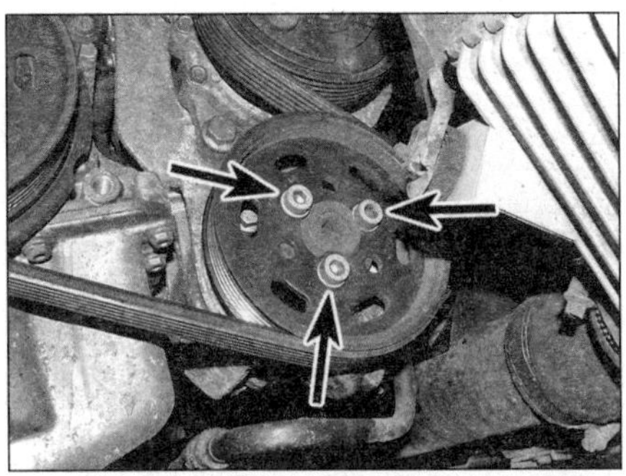
24.2 Slacken the pulley bolts (arrowed) – do not remove completely

24.4 Remove the pulley from the pump

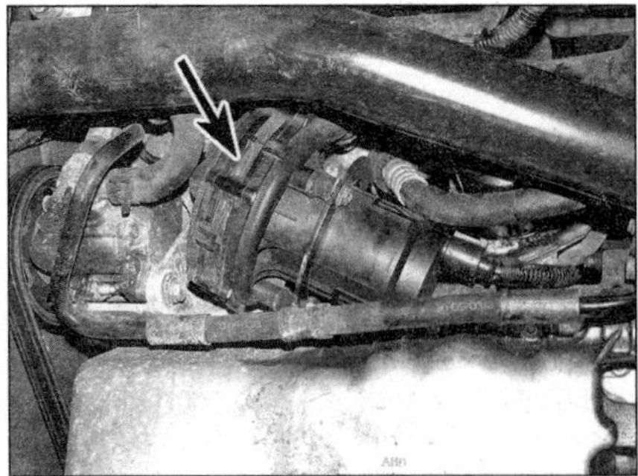
24.5 Secondary air injection pump (arrowed)

24.6 Pressure switch wiring connector (arrowed)

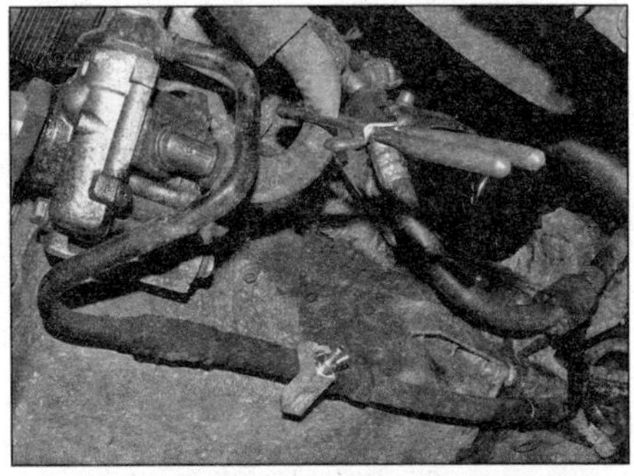
24.7 Clamps fitted to the power steering hoses

24.9 Remove the switch (arrowed) and then the pressure pipe

securing the pulley to the power steering pump **(see illustration)**. Do not remove them at this stage.

3 Mark the auxiliary drivebelt for direction of rotation, then remove it as described in Chapter 1 Section 32.

4 The pulley retaining bolts can now be completely removed, and the pulley removed from the flange on the power steering pump **(see illustration)**.

5 On models with secondary air injection fitted, remove the air pump **(see illustration)**, from the rear of the power steering pump, as described in Chapter 4B Section 5.

6 Disconnect the wiring connector from the pressure switch **(see illustration)**, which is located on the high pressure pipe union.

7 Fit a hose clamps to the hoses leading to the rear of the power steering pump **(see illustration)**. The high pressure pipe is made up of metal pipe and rubber hose sections, clamp the rubber hose section.

8 Before removing the pipe/hose, position a suitable container beneath the pump to catch spilt fluid from the pump and hoses.

9 With the wiring disconnected, unscrew the power steering system pressure switch from the union bolt **(see illustration)**. Then unscrew the union bolt and disconnect the pressure hose union from the pump. Recover the copper sealing washers. Tape over or plug the ends of the hoses and the apertures in the pump to prevent entry of dust and dirt into the hydraulic system. The end of the pressure line can be wrapped in a plastic bag if preferred.

10 Release the clip and disconnect the supply hose **(see illustration)**. Note that the hose and pump stub have alignment marks to ensure correct refitting. Audi technicians use a special tool to remove the clip, but it should be possible to remove it using a pair of pliers.

11 Unscrew and remove the three mounting bolts from the pulley end of the pump, and the single mounting bolt from the engine side of the pump **(see illustrations)**. Withdraw the power steering pump from the engine mounting bracket.

Refitting

12 Before refitting the pump (and especially if fitting a new pump), prime it with fresh fluid as follows. Place the pump in a container with the supply hose stub uppermost. Pour hydraulic fluid into the supply stub and turn

24.10 Note alignment marks (arrowed) for refitting

24.11a Undo the three bolts (arrowed)...

24.11b ...and the one (arrowed) at the rear of the pump

the pulley drive flange clockwise by hand until fluid emerges from the pressure hose aperture.

13 Tilt the pump to retain the fluid, then locate it in the engine compartment and fit the supply hose and clip. Make sure that the alignment mark on the hose is in line with the seam on the pump supply stub.

14 Locate the pump in its mounting bracket and secure with the mounting bolts, tightened to the specified torque.

15 Reconnect the pressure hose union, together with new copper sealing washers, and tighten to the specified torque. Refit the pressure switch and reconnect the wiring connector.

16 Remove the hose clamps from the hoses.

17 Locate the pulley on the pump, insert the bolts, and tighten them securely while holding the drive flange with an Allen key.

18 Refit the auxiliary drivebelt with reference to Chapter 1 Section 32.

19 Refit the engine compartment undershields and right-hand front wheel, then lower the vehicle to the ground. Tighten the wheel bolts to the specified torque.

20 Bleed the power steering hydraulic system as described in Section 23.

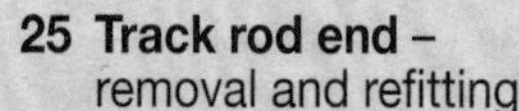

25 Track rod end – removal and refitting

Note: *A new balljoint retaining nut will be required on refitting.*

Removal

1 Apply the handbrake, then jack up the front of the vehicle and support it on axle stands (see *Jacking and vehicle support*). Remove the relevant roadwheel.

2 If the track rod end is to be re-used, mark its position in relation to the track rod to facilitate refitting.

3 Unscrew the track rod end locknut by a quarter of a turn **(see illustration)**. Do not move the locknut from this position, as it will serve as a handy reference mark on refitting.

4 Loosen and remove the nut securing the track rod end balljoint to the wheel bearing housing, and release the balljoint tapered shank using a universal balljoint separator. Note that the balljoint shank has a hexagon hole – hold the shank with an Allen key while loosening the nut **(see illustrations)**.

5 Counting the exact number of turns necessary to do so, unscrew the track rod end from the track rod **(see illustration)**.

6 Carefully clean the balljoint and the threads. Renew the balljoint if its movement is sloppy or too stiff, if excessively worn, or if damaged in any way; carefully check the stud taper and threads. If the balljoint gaiter is damaged, the complete balljoint assembly must be renewed; it is not possible to obtain the gaiter separately.

Refitting

7 Screw the track rod end onto the track rod by the number of turns noted on removal. This should bring the track rod end to within a quarter of a turn of the locknut, with the alignment marks that were made on removal (if applicable) lined up. Tighten the locknut.

8 Refit the balljoint shank to the steering arm on the wheel bearing housing, then fit a new retaining nut and tighten it to the specified torque. Hold the shank with an Allen key if necessary.

9 Refit the roadwheel, then lower the car to the ground and tighten the roadwheel bolts to the specified torque.

10 Check and, if necessary, adjust the front wheel toe setting as described in Section 26.

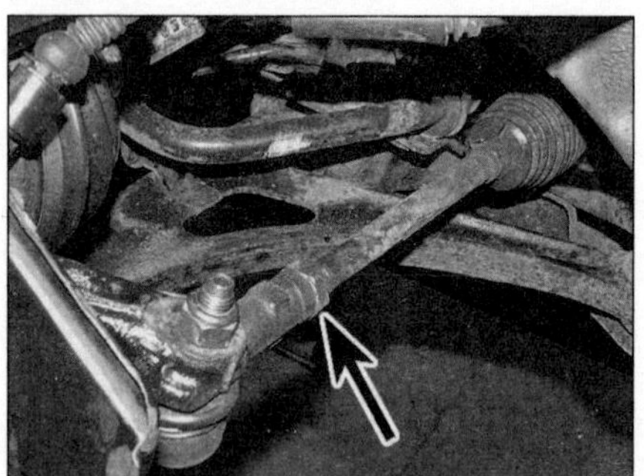

25.3 Track rod end locknut (arrowed)

25.4a Using an Allen key to hold the balljoint shank while loosening the nut

25.4b Using a balljoint separator...

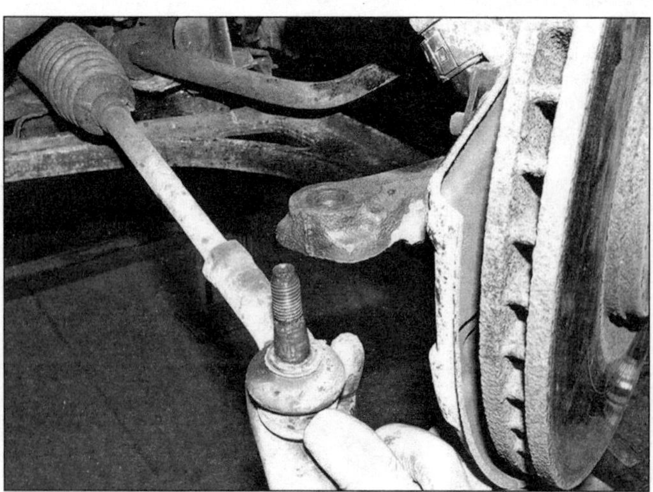

25.4c ...to release the track rod balljoint

25.5 Unscrewing the track rod end from the track rod

26 Wheel alignment and steering angles – general information

Definitions

1 A car's steering and suspension geometry is defined in three basic settings – all angles are expressed in degrees; the steering axis is defined as an imaginary line drawn through the axis of the suspension strut, extended where necessary to contact the ground.

2 Camber is the angle between each roadwheel and a vertical line drawn through its centre and tyre contact patch, when viewed from the front or rear of the car. Positive camber is when the roadwheels are tilted outwards from the vertical at the top; negative camber is when they are tilted inwards.

3 Camber angle is only adjustable by loosening the front suspension subframe mounting bolts and moving it slightly to one side. This also alters the Castor angle. The camber angle can be checked using a camber checking gauge.

4 Castor is the angle between the steering axis and a vertical line drawn through each roadwheel's centre and tyre contact patch, when viewed from the side of the car. Positive castor is when the steering axis is tilted so that it contacts the ground ahead of the vertical; negative castor is when it contacts the ground behind the vertical. Slight castor angle adjustment is possible by loosening the front suspension subframe bolts and moving it slightly to one side. This also alters the Camber angle.

5 Castor is not easily adjustable, and is given for reference only; while it can be checked using a castor checking gauge, if the figure obtained is significantly different from that specified, the car must be taken for careful checking by a professional, as the fault can only be caused by wear or damage to the body or suspension components.

6 Toe is the difference, viewed from above, between lines drawn through the roadwheel centres and the car's centre-line. Toe-in is when the roadwheels point inwards, towards each other at the front, while toe-out is when they splay outwards from each other at the front.

7 The front wheel toe setting is adjusted by screwing the track rod(s) in/out of the outer balljoint(s) to alter the effective length of the track rod assembly.

8 Rear wheel toe setting is not adjustable, and is given for reference only. While it can be checked, if the figure obtained is significantly different from that specified, the car must be taken for careful checking by a professional, as the fault can only be caused by wear or damage to the body or suspension components.

Checking and adjustment

Front wheel toe setting

9 Due to the special measuring equipment necessary to check the wheel alignment, and the skill required to use it properly, the checking and adjustment of these settings is best left to an Audi dealer or similar expert. Note that most tyre-fitting centres now possess sophisticated checking equipment.

10 To check the toe setting, a tracking gauge must first be obtained. Two types of gauge are available, and can be obtained from motor accessory shops. The first type measures the distance between the front and rear inside edges of the roadwheels, as previously described, with the car stationary. The second type, known as a 'scuff plate', measures the actual position of the contact surface of the tyre, in relation to the road surface, with the car in motion. This is achieved by pushing or driving the front tyre over a plate, which then moves slightly according to the scuff of the tyre, and shows this movement on a scale. Both types have their advantages and disadvantages, but either can give satisfactory results if used correctly and carefully.

11 Make sure that the steering is in the straight-ahead position when making measurements.

12 If adjustment is necessary, apply the handbrake, then jack up the front of the vehicle and support it securely on axle stands (see *Jacking and vehicle support*). Turn the steering wheel onto full-left lock, and record the amount of exposed thread on the right-hand track rod. Now turn the steering onto full-right lock, and record the number of threads on the left-hand track rod. If there is the same amount of thread visible on both sides, then subsequent adjustment should be made equally on both sides. If there are more thread is visible on one side than the other, it will be necessary to compensate for this during adjustment.

13 First clean the track rod threads; if they are corroded, apply penetrating fluid before starting adjustment. Release the rubber gaiter outer clips, peel back the gaiters and apply a smear of grease. This will ensure that both gaiters are free and will not be twisted or strained as their respective track rods are rotated.

14 Retain the track rod with a suitable spanner, and loosen the balljoint locknut fully. Alter the length of the track rod, by screwing it into or out of the balljoint. Rotate the track rod using an open-ended spanner fitted to the track rod flats provided; shortening the track rod (screwing it onto its balljoint) will reduce toe-in/increase toe-out.

15 When the setting is correct, hold the track rod and tighten the balljoint locknut to the specified torque setting. If after adjustment, the steering wheel spokes are no longer horizontal when the wheels are in the straight-ahead position, remove the steering wheel and reposition it (see Section 18).

16 Check that the toe setting has been correctly adjusted by lowering the car to the ground and rechecking the toe setting; re-adjust if necessary. Ensure that the rubber gaiters are seated correctly and are not twisted or strained, and secure them in position with the retaining clips; where necessary, fit a new retaining clip (refer to Section 22).

Rear wheel toe setting

17 The procedure for checking the rear toe setting is the same as described for the front setting in paragraph 10. The setting is not adjustable – see paragraph 8.

Front wheel camber and castor angles

18 Checking and adjusting the front wheel camber angle should be entrusted to an Audi dealer or other suitably-equipped specialist. Note that most tyre-fitting centres now possess sophisticated checking equipment. For reference, adjustments are made by loosening the front suspension subframe mounting bolts, and repositioning the subframe.

Notes

Chapter 11
Bodywork and fittings

Contents

Degrees of difficulty

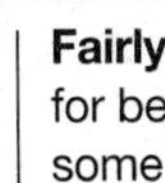

Easy, suitable for novice with little experience	**Fairly easy,** suitable for beginner with some experience	**Fairly difficult,** suitable for competent DIY mechanic	**Difficult,** suitable for experienced DIY mechanic	**Very difficult,** suitable for expert DIY or professional

Specifications

Torque wrench settings	**Nm**	**lbf ft**
Bonnet hinge retaining bolts	21	16
Bonnet lock retaining bolts	10	7
Door hinge bolts	30	22
Door lock/catch retaining bolts	20	15
Door lock striker plate bolts	20	15
Door regulator/assembly subframe lower retaining bolts	25	18
Door regulator/assembly subframe upper and centre lower retaining nuts	30	22
Door fixed side window clamp bolts	8	6
Door window glass clamp bolts	7	5
Front seat mounting retaining bolts	23	17
Seat belt anchorage bolts	40	30
Tailgate/boot lid catch retaining bolts	12	8
Tailgate/boot lid hinge retaining bolts	21	16

** Renew the bolt every time it is removed*

1 General Information

1 The body shell is made of pressed-steel sections, and is available in Coupe and Convertible ("Roadster") versions. Most components are welded together, and some use is made of structural adhesives; the front wings are bolted on.

2 The bonnet, door, and some other vulnerable panels are made of zinc-coated metal, and are further protected by being coated with an anti-chip primer before being sprayed.

3 Extensive use is made of plastic materials, mainly in the interior, but also in exterior components. The front and rear bumpers, and front grille, are injection-moulded from a synthetic material that is very strong and yet light. Plastic components such as wheel arch liners are fitted to the underside of the vehicle, to improve the body's resistance to corrosion.

2 Maintenance – bodywork and underframe

1 The general condition of a vehicle's bodywork is the one thing that significantly affects its value. Maintenance is easy, but needs to be regular. Neglect, particularly after minor damage, can lead quickly to further deterioration and costly repair bills. It is important also to keep watch on those parts of the vehicle not immediately visible, for instance the underside, inside all the wheel arches, and the lower part of the engine compartment.

2 The basic maintenance routine for the bodywork is washing – preferably with a lot of water, from a hose. This will remove all the loose solids which may have stuck to the vehicle. It is important to flush these off in such a way as to prevent grit from scratching the finish. The wheel arches and underframe need washing in the same way, to remove any accumulated mud, which will retain moisture and tend to encourage rust. Paradoxically enough, the best time to clean the underframe and wheel arches is in wet weather, when the mud is thoroughly wet and soft. In very wet weather, the underframe is usually cleaned of large accumulations automatically, and this is a good time for inspection.

3 Periodically, except on vehicles with a wax-based underbody protective coating, it is a good idea to have the whole of the underframe of the vehicle steam-cleaned, engine compartment included, so that a thorough inspection can be carried out to see what minor repairs and renovations are necessary. Steam-cleaning is available at many garages, and is necessary for the removal of the accumulation of oily grime, which sometimes is allowed to become thick in certain areas. If steam-cleaning facilities are not available, there are some excellent grease solvents available which can be brush-applied; the dirt can then be simply hosed off. Note that these methods should not be used on vehicles with wax-based underbody protective coating, or the coating will be removed. Such vehicles should be inspected annually, preferably just prior to Winter, when the underbody should be washed down, and any damage to the wax coating repaired. Ideally, a completely fresh coat should be applied. It would also be worth considering the use of such wax-based protection for injection into door panels, sills, box sections, etc, as an additional safeguard against rust damage, where such protection is not provided by the vehicle manufacturer.

4 After washing paintwork, wipe off with a chamois leather to give an unspotted clear finish. A coat of clear protective wax polish will give added protection against chemical pollutants in the air. If the paintwork sheen has dulled or oxidised, use a cleaner/polisher combination to restore the brilliance of the shine. This requires a little effort, but such dulling is usually caused because regular washing has been neglected. Care needs to be taken with metallic paintwork, as special non-abrasive cleaner/polisher is required to avoid damage to the finish. Always check that the door and ventilator opening drain holes and pipes are completely clear, so that water can be drained out. Brightwork should be treated in the same way as paintwork. Windscreens and windows can be kept clear of the smeary film which often appears, by the use of proprietary glass cleaner. Never use any form of wax or other body or chromium polish on glass.

3 Maintenance – upholstery and carpets

1 Mats and carpets should be brushed or vacuum-cleaned regularly, to keep them free of grit. If they are badly stained, remove them from the vehicle for scrubbing or sponging, and make quite sure they are dry before refitting. Seats and interior trim panels can be kept clean by wiping with a damp cloth. If they do become stained (which can be more apparent on light-coloured upholstery), use a little liquid detergent and a soft nail brush to scour the grime out of the grain of the material. Do not forget to keep the headlining clean in the same way as the upholstery. When using liquid cleaners inside the vehicle, do not over-wet the surfaces being cleaned. Excessive damp could get into the seams and padded interior, causing stains, offensive odours or even rot.

2 If the inside of the vehicle gets wet accidentally, it is worthwhile taking some trouble to dry it out properly, particularly where carpets are involved. Do not leave oil or electric heaters inside the vehicle for this purpose.

4 Minor body damage – repair

Scratches

1 If the scratch is very superficial, and does not penetrate to the metal of the bodywork, repair is very simple. Lightly rub the area of the scratch with a paintwork renovator, or a very fine cutting paste, to remove loose paint from the scratch, and to clear the surrounding bodywork of wax polish. Rinse the area with clean water.

2 Apply touch-up paint to the scratch using a fine paint brush; continue to apply fine layers of paint until the surface of the paint in the scratch is level with the surrounding paintwork. Allow the new paint at least two weeks to harden, then blend it into the surrounding paintwork by rubbing the scratch area with a paintwork renovator or a very fine cutting paste. Finally, apply wax polish.

3 Where the scratch has penetrated right through to the metal of the bodywork, causing the metal to rust, a different repair technique is required. Remove any loose rust from the bottom of the scratch with a penknife, then apply rust-inhibiting paint to prevent the formation of rust in the future. Using a rubber or nylon applicator, fill the scratch with bodystopper paste. If required, this paste can be mixed with cellulose thinners to provide a very thin paste which is ideal for filling narrow scratches. Before the stopper-paste in the scratch hardens, wrap a piece of smooth cotton rag around the top of a finger. Dip the finger in cellulose thinners, and quickly sweep it across the surface of the stopper-paste in the scratch; this will ensure that the surface of the stopper-paste is slightly hollowed. The scratch can now be painted over as described earlier in this Section.

Dents

4 When deep denting of the vehicle's bodywork has taken place, the first task is to pull the dent out, until the affected bodywork almost attains its original shape. There is little point in trying to restore the original shape completely, as the metal in the damaged area will have stretched on impact, and cannot be reshaped fully to its original contour. It is better to bring the level of the dent up to a point which is about 3 mm below the level of the surrounding bodywork. In cases where the dent is very shallow anyway, it is not worth trying to pull it out at all. If the underside of the dent is accessible, it can be hammered out gently from behind, using a mallet with a wooden or plastic head. Whilst doing this, hold a suitable block of wood firmly against the outside of the panel, to absorb the impact from the hammer blows and thus prevent a large area of the bodywork from being 'belled-out'.

5 Should the dent be in a section of the bodywork which has a double skin, or some other factor making it inaccessible from behind, a different technique is called for. Drill several small holes through the metal inside the area – particularly in the deeper section. Then screw long self-tapping screws into the holes, just sufficiently for them to gain a good purchase in the metal. Now the dent can be pulled out by pulling on the protruding heads of the screws with a pair of pliers.

6 The next stage of the repair is the removal of the paint from the damaged area, and from an inch or so of the surrounding 'sound' bodywork. This is accomplished most easily by using a wire brush or abrasive pad on a power drill, although it can be done just as effectively by hand, using sheets of abrasive paper. To complete the preparation for filling, score the surface of the bare metal with a screwdriver or the tang of a file, or alternatively, drill small holes in the affected area. This will provide a really good 'key' for the filler paste.

7 To complete the repair, see the Section on filling and respraying.

Rust holes or gashes

8 Remove all paint from the affected area, and from an inch or so of the surrounding 'sound' bodywork, using an abrasive pad or a wire brush on a power drill. If these are not available, a few sheets of abrasive paper will do the job most effectively. With the paint removed, you will be able to judge the severity of the corrosion, and therefore decide whether to renew the whole panel (if this is possible) or to repair the affected area. New body panels are not as expensive as most people think, and it is often quicker and more satisfactory to fit a new panel than to attempt to repair large areas of corrosion.

9 Remove all fittings from the affected area, except those which will act as a guide to the original shape of the damaged bodywork (eg headlight shells etc). Then, using tin snips or a hacksaw blade, remove all loose metal and any other metal badly affected by corrosion. Hammer the edges of the hole inwards, in order to create a slight depression for the filler paste.

10 Wire-brush the affected area to remove the powdery rust from the surface of the remaining metal. Paint the affected area with rust-inhibiting paint, if the back of the rusted area is accessible, treat this also.

11 Before filling can take place, it will be necessary to block the hole in some way. This can be achieved by the use of aluminium or plastic mesh, or aluminium tape.

12 Aluminium or plastic mesh, or glass-fibre matting, is probably the best material to use for a large hole. Cut a piece to the approximate size and shape of the hole to be filled, then position it in the hole so that its edges are below the level of the surrounding bodywork. It can be retained in position by several blobs of filler paste around its periphery.

13 Aluminium tape should be used for small or very narrow holes. Pull a piece off the roll, trim it to the approximate size and shape required, then pull off the backing paper (if used) and stick the tape over the hole; it can be overlapped if the thickness of one piece is insufficient. Burnish down the edges of the tape with the handle of a screwdriver or similar, to ensure that the tape is securely attached to the metal underneath.

Filling and respraying

14 Before using this Section, see the Sections on dent, deep scratch, rust holes and gash repairs.

15 Many types of bodyfiller are available, but generally speaking, those proprietary kits which contain a tin of filler paste and a tube of resin hardener are best for this type of repair. A wide, flexible plastic or nylon applicator will be found invaluable for imparting a smooth and well-contoured finish to the surface of the filler.

16 Mix up a little filler on a clean piece of card or board – measure the hardener carefully (follow the maker's instructions on the pack), otherwise the filler will set too rapidly or too slowly. Using the applicator, apply the filler paste to the prepared area; draw the applicator across the surface of the filler to achieve the correct contour and to level the surface. As soon as a contour that approximates to the correct one is achieved, stop working the paste – if you carry on too long, the paste will become sticky and begin to 'pick-up' on the applicator. Continue to add thin layers of filler paste at 20-minute intervals, until the level of the filler is just proud of the surrounding bodywork.

17 Once the filler has hardened, the excess can be removed using a metal plane or file. From then on, progressively-finer grades of abrasive paper should be used, starting with a 40-grade production paper, and finishing with a 400-grade wet-and-dry paper. Always wrap the abrasive paper around a flat rubber, cork, or wooden block – otherwise the surface of the filler will not be completely flat. During the smoothing of the filler surface, the wet-and-dry paper should be periodically rinsed in water. This will ensure that a very smooth finish is imparted to the filler at the final stage.

18 At this stage, the dent should be surrounded by a ring of bare metal, which in turn should be encircled by the finely 'feathered' edge of the good paintwork. Rinse the repair area with clean water, until all of the dust produced by the rubbing-down operation has gone.

19 Spray the whole area with a light coat of primer – this will show up any imperfections in the surface of the filler. Repair these imperfections with fresh filler paste or bodystopper, and once more smooth the surface with abrasive paper. Repeat this spray-and-repair procedure until you are satisfied that the surface of the filler, and the feathered edge of the paintwork, are perfect. Clean the repair area with clean water, and allow to dry fully.

If bodystopper is used, it can bemixed with cellulose thinners toform a really thin paste which isideal for filling small holes.

20 The repair area is now ready for final spraying. Paint spraying must be carried out in a warm, dry, windless and dust-free atmosphere. This condition can be created artificially if you have access to a large indoor working area, but if you are forced to work in the open, you will have to pick your day very carefully. If you are working indoors, dousing the floor in the work area with water will help to settle the dust which would otherwise be in the atmosphere. If the repair area is confined to one body panel, mask off the surrounding panels; this will help to minimise the effects of a slight mis-match in paint colours. Bodywork fittings (eg chrome strips, door handles etc) will also need to be masked off. Use genuine masking tape, and several thicknesses of newspaper, for the masking operations.

21 Before commencing to spray, agitate the aerosol can thoroughly, then spray a test area (an old tin, or similar) until the technique is mastered. Cover the repair area with a thick coat of primer; the thickness should be built up using several thin layers of paint, rather than one thick one. Using 400-grade wet-and-dry paper, rub down the surface of the primer until it is really smooth. While doing this, the work area should be thoroughly doused with water, and the wet-and-dry paper periodically rinsed in water. Allow to dry before spraying on more paint.

22 Spray on the top coat, again building up the thickness by using several thin layers of paint. Start spraying at one edge of the repair area, and then, using a side-to-side motion, work until the whole repair area and about 2 inches of the surrounding original paintwork is covered. Remove all masking material 10 to 15 minutes after spraying on the final coat of paint.

23 Allow the new paint at least two weeks to harden, then, using a paintwork renovator, or a very fine cutting paste, blend the edges of the paint into the existing paintwork. Finally, apply wax polish.

Plastic components

24 With the use of more and more plastic body components by the vehicle manufacturers (eg bumpers. spoilers, and in some cases major body panels), rectification of more serious damage to such items has become a matter of either entrusting repair work to a specialist in this field, or renewing complete components. Repair of such damage by the DIY owner is not really feasible, owing to the cost of the equipment and materials required for effecting such repairs. The basic technique involves making a groove along the line of the crack in the plastic, using a rotary burr in a power drill. The damaged part is then welded back together, using a hot-air gun to heat up and fuse a plastic filler rod into the groove. Any excess plastic is then removed, and the area rubbed down to a smooth finish. It is important that a filler rod of the correct plastic is used, as body components can be made of a variety of different types (eg polycarbonate, ABS, polypropylene).

25 Damage of a less serious nature (abrasions, minor cracks etc) can be repaired by the DIY owner using a two-part epoxy filler repair material. Once mixed in equal proportions, this is used in similar fashion to the bodywork filler used on metal panels. The filler is usually cured in twenty to thirty minutes, ready for sanding and painting.

26 If the owner is renewing a complete component himself, or if he has repaired it with epoxy filler, he will be left with the problem of finding a suitable paint for finishing which is compatible with the type of plastic used. At one time, the use of a universal paint was not possible, owing to the complex range of plastics encountered in body component applications. Standard paints, generally speaking, will not bond to plastic or rubber satisfactorily. However, it is now possible to obtain a plastic body parts finishing kit which consists of a pre-primer treatment, a primer and coloured top coat. Full instructions are normally supplied with a kit, but basically, the method of use is to first apply the pre-primer to the component concerned, and allow it to dry for up to 30 minutes. Then the primer is applied, and left to dry for about an hour before finally applying the special-coloured top coat. The result is a correctly-coloured component, where the paint will flex with the plastic or rubber, a property that standard paint does not normally possess.

5 Major body damage – repair

1 Where serious damage has occurred, or large areas need renewal due to neglect, it means that complete new panels will need welding-in, and this is best left to professionals. If the damage is due to impact, it will also be necessary to check completely the alignment of the body shell, and this can only be carried out accurately by an Audi dealer using special jigs. If the body is left misaligned, it is primarily dangerous, as the car will not handle properly, and secondly, uneven stresses will be imposed on the steering, suspension and possibly transmission, causing abnormal wear, or complete failure, particularly to such items as the tyres.

6 Front bumper – removal and refitting

Note: *Depending on the model, it is possible that slight changes to the removal and refitting procedures may be necessary.*

Removal

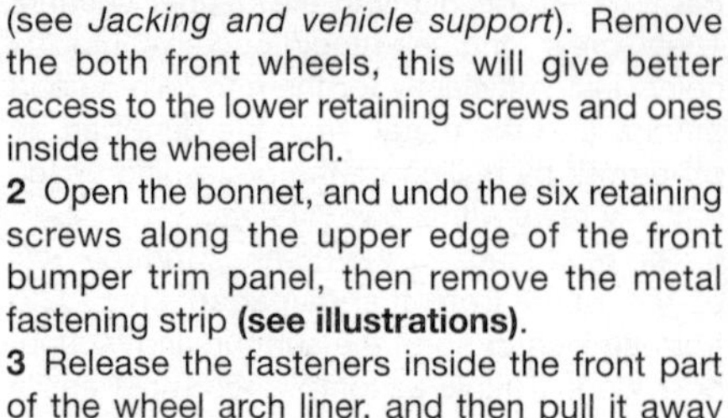

1 Apply the handbrake, then jack up the front of the vehicle and support it on axle stands (see *Jacking and vehicle support*). Remove the both front wheels, this will give better access to the lower retaining screws and ones inside the wheel arch.

2 Open the bonnet, and undo the six retaining screws along the upper edge of the front bumper trim panel, then remove the metal fastening strip **(see illustrations)**.

3 Release the fasteners inside the front part of the wheel arch liner, and then pull it away from the ends of the front bumper.

4 Working inside the lower part of the front bumper, at the left-hand side, release the securing clip and disconnect the headlamp washer hose to the washer reservoir **(see illustration)**. Be prepared for some washer fluid spillage, plug the ends of the pipes once disconnected.

5 Remove the four nuts (two each side) and two securing screws (one each side) from inside each end of the front bumper **(see illustration)**.

6 Working under the front lower edge of the front bumper remove the two securing screws **(see illustration)**.

7 With the aid of an assistant, carefully release the bumper left- and right-hand ends from the wing panels, and then pull the bumper away from the vehicle in a forwards direction **(see illustration)**.

8 On models with headlamp washers, remove the washer jets as described in Chapter 12 Section 19.

6.2a Undo the retaining screws (arrowed)...

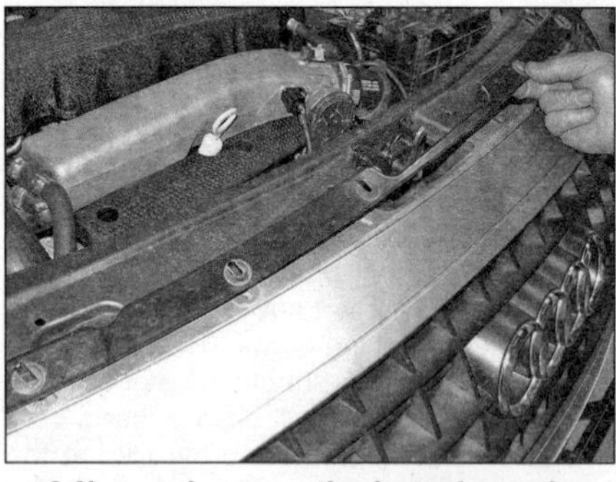

6.2b ...and remove the fastening strip

6.4 Disconnect the headlamp washer hose

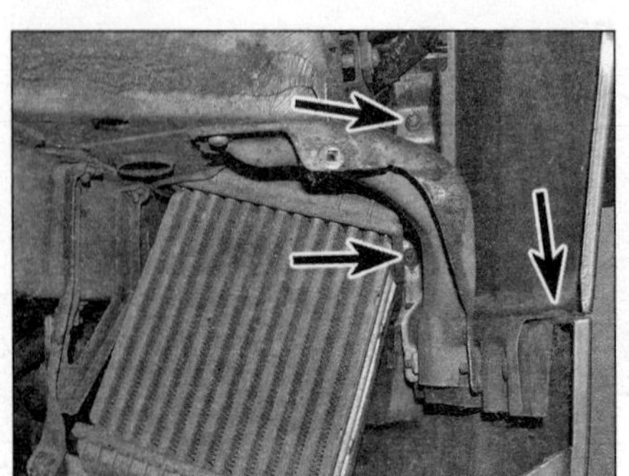

6.5 Undo the two nuts and one screw (arrowed) – right-hand side shown

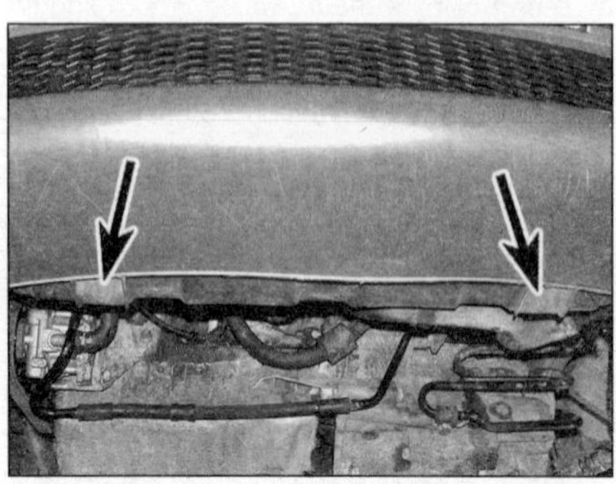

6.6 Remove the two lower securing screws (arrowed)

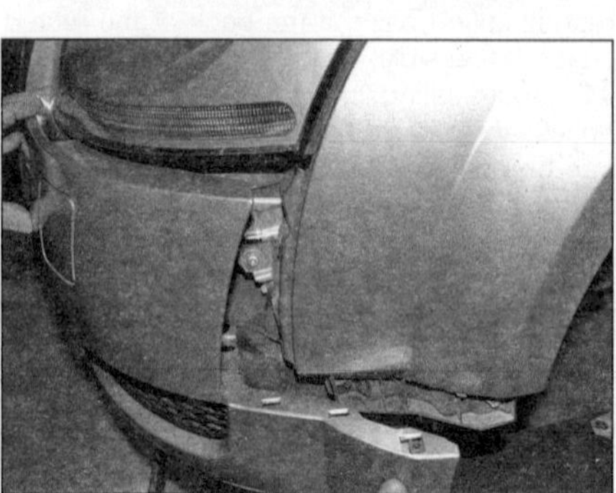

6.7 Release the ends of the bumper

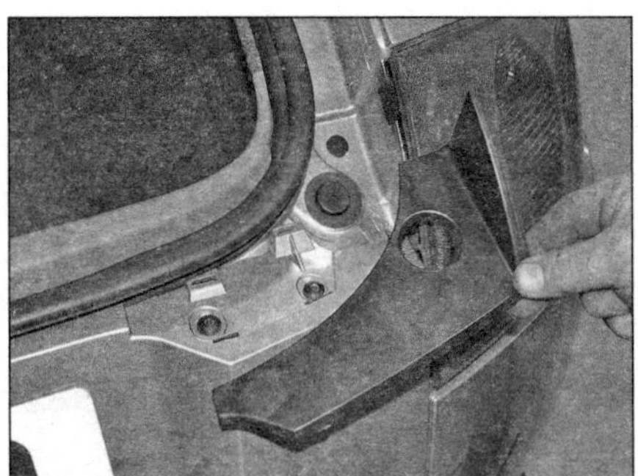
7.3a Unclip the trim panels...

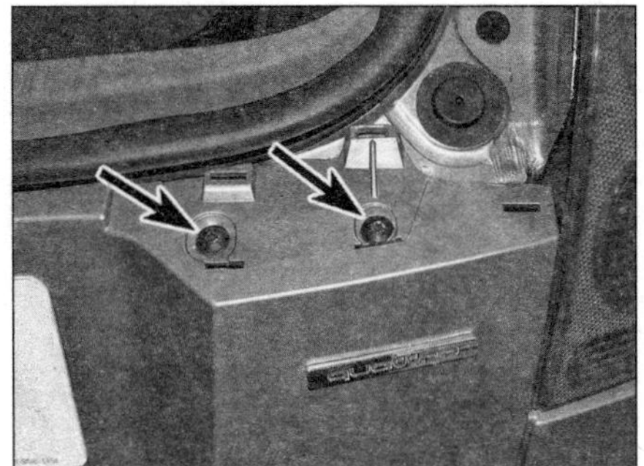
7.3b ...and remove the retaining screws (arrowed)

7.4 Lower bumper retaining screws (arrowed)

Refitting

9 Refitting is a reverse of the removal procedure, ensuring that the bumper ends engage correctly with the locating guides as the bumper is refitted.

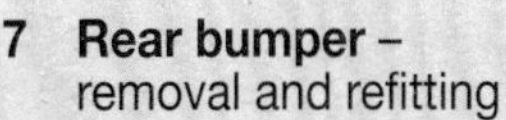

7 Rear bumper – removal and refitting

Note: *Depending on the model, it is possible that slight changes to the removal and refitting procedures may be necessary.*

Removal

1 To improve access, chock the front wheels, then jack up the rear of the vehicle and support it on axle stands (see *Jacking and vehicle support*). Remove the both rear wheels, this will give better access to the lower retaining screws and ones inside the wheel arch.

2 Release the fasteners inside the rear part of the wheel arch liner, and then pull it away from the ends of the rear bumper.

3 Open the boot lid/tailgate and remove the two trim panels (one each side) from the upper corners of the rear bumper. Then undo the four retaining screws (two at each side) from under the trim panels **(see illustrations)**.

4 Slacken and remove the two screws securing the lower edge of the bumper in position **(see illustration)**.

5 Remove the four bolts (two at each side) from inside each end of the rear bumper **(see illustration)**.

6 With the aid of an assistant, carefully release the bumper left- and right-hand ends from the wing panels, and then pull the bumper away from the vehicle **(see illustration)**.

Refitting

7 Refitting is a reverse of the removal procedure, ensuring that the bumper ends engage correctly with the slides as the bumper is refitted. Retrieve the centre pins for the plastic rivets from the plastic slides before refitting the bumper – renew if necessary.

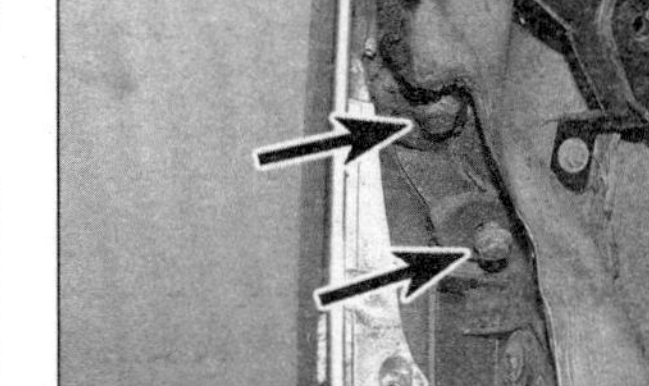
7.5 Remove rear bumper bolts (arrowed) – one side shown

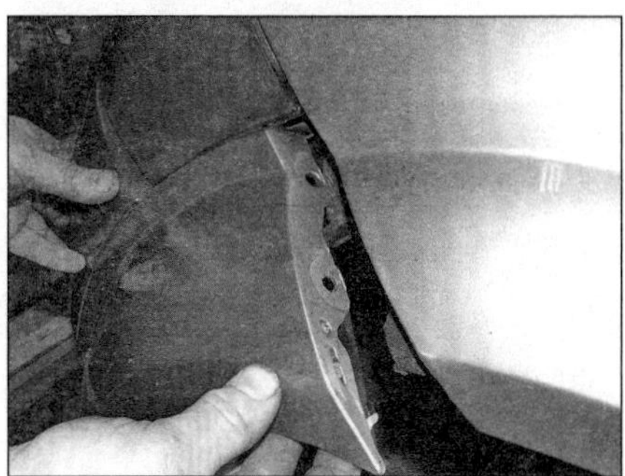
7.6 Release the ends of the bumper

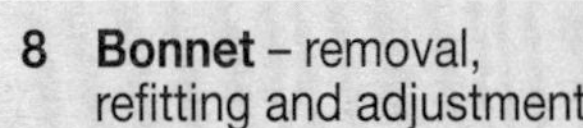

8 Bonnet – removal, refitting and adjustment

Removal

1 Open the bonnet and using a pencil or felt tip pen, mark the outline of each bonnet hinge relative to the bonnet, to use as a guide on refitting.

2 With the aid of an assistant to help support the bonnet, undo the bonnet retaining bolts **(see illustration)** and carefully lift the bonnet clear. Store the bonnet out of the way in a safe place.

3 Inspect the bonnet hinges for signs of wear and free play at the pivots, and if necessary renew. Check the operation of the gas struts and the ball joint connections at each end. The hinges are secured to the body by three bolts **(see illustration)**, mark the position of the hinge on the body then undo the retaining bolts and remove it from the vehicle. On refitting, align the new hinge with the marks and tighten the retaining bolts.

Refitting and adjustment

4 With the aid of an assistant, offer up the bonnet and loosely fit the retaining bolts. Align the hinges with the marks made on removal, then tighten the retaining bolts securely.

5 Close the bonnet, and check for alignment with the adjacent panels. If necessary, slacken the hinge bolts and re-align the bonnet. Once the bonnet is correctly aligned, tighten the hinge bolts. Check that the bonnet fastens and releases satisfactorily.

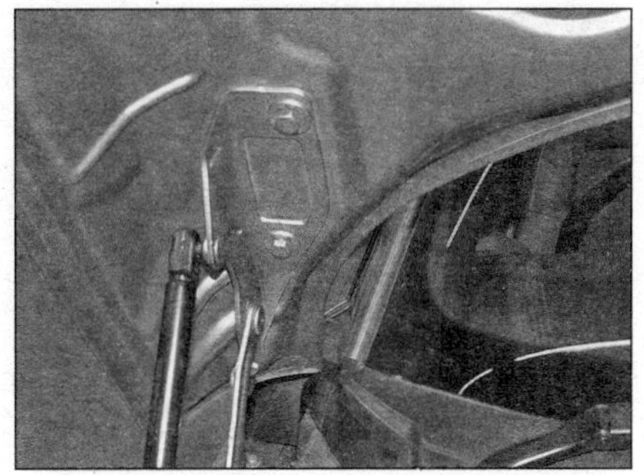
8.2 Remove the bonnet securing bolts

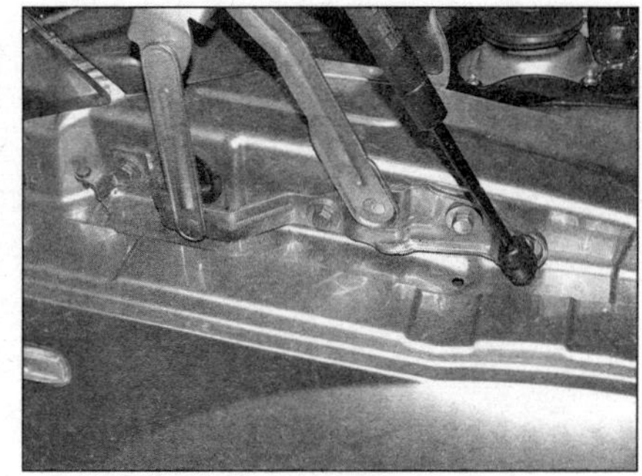
8.3 Hinge to body securing bolts

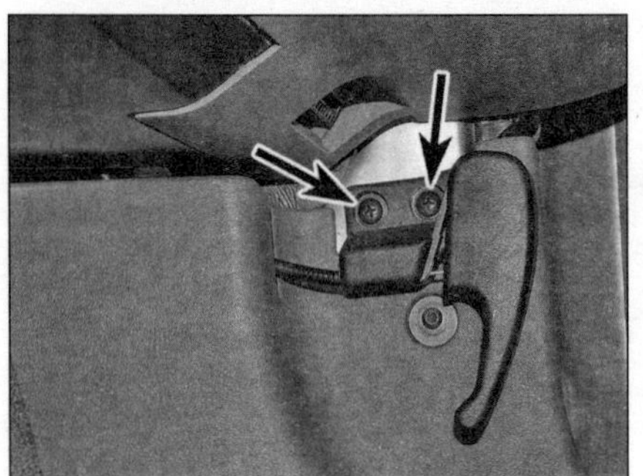
9.1a Undo the retaining screws (arrowed)...

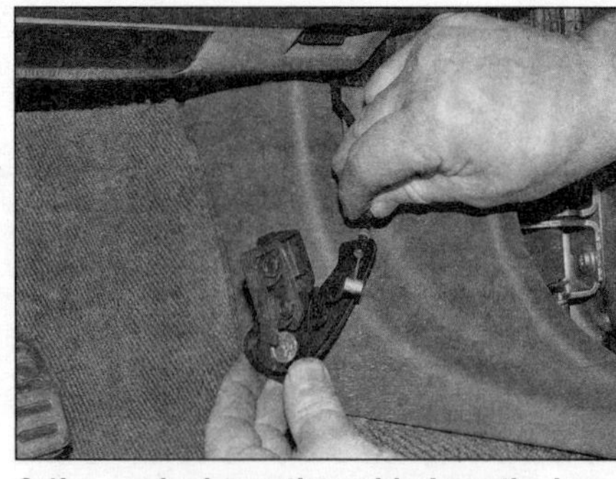
9.1b ...and release the cable from the lever

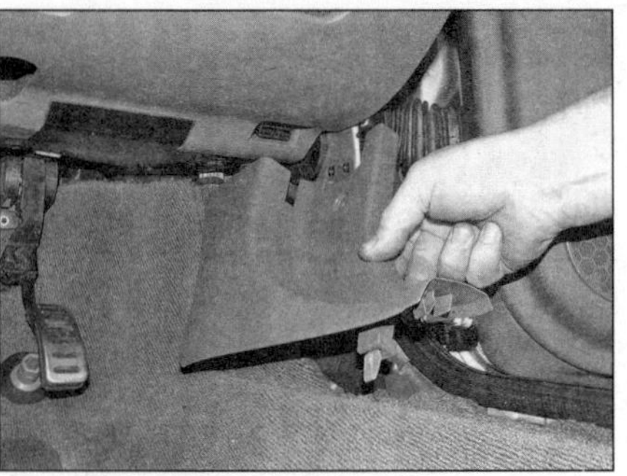
9.2 Remove the side trim panel

9.4 Remove bonnet lock (arrowed)

9 Bonnet lock and release cable – removal and refitting

Removal

1 Working inside the vehicle, locate the bonnet release lever and pull it to open the bonnet. Then undo the two retaining screws and remove the release lever from the trim panel. Unclip the outer cable from the mounting bracket and release the inner cable from the lever **(see illustrations)**.

2 Undo the retaining screw, then lift the side trim panel upwards, to unclip it's lower locating peg from the sill panel to remove **(see illustration)**.

3 Release the cable sealing grommet from the bulkhead. If required remove the facia lower trim panel, with reference to Section 28.

4 Open the bonnet, undo the four retaining bolts and withdraw the bonnet lock **(see illustration)** from the front crossmember. Disconnect the outer cable from the lock housing and detach the inner cable from the lock mechanism.

5 Work along the length of the cable, noting its correct routing, and free it from the retaining clips and ties.

6 Tie a length of string to the end of the cable inside the vehicle, then withdraw the cable through into the engine compartment.

7 Once the cable is free, untie the string and leave it in position in the vehicle; the string can then be used to draw the new cable back into position.

Refitting

8 Refitting is a reversal of the removal, noting the following points:

9 Tie the inner end of the string to the end of the cable, then use the string to draw the bonnet release cable back from the engine compart-ment. Once the cable is through, untie the string.

10 Ensure the rubber grommet in the bulkhead is fitted correctly, and the cable is correctly routed and secured to all the relevant retaining clips.

11 Before closing the bonnet, check the operation of the lock, release lever and cable.

10 Door – removal, refitting and adjustment

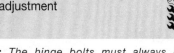

Note: *The hinge bolts must always be renewed if loosened.*

Removal

1 Disconnect the battery negative terminal. **Note:** *Before disconnecting the battery, refer to* Disconnecting the battery *at the rear of this manual.*

2 Open the door, undo the retaining screw and unclip the lower trim from the front door pillar, carefully pull away and lift upwards to disengage the lower locating peg from the sill panel (on the driver's door, remove the bonnet release lever as described in Section 9).

3 Disconnect the wiring connector from behind the trim **(see illustration)**.

4 Remove the gaiter from the door pillar, then guide wiring out through the hole in the pillar.

5 Mark the position of the hinges on the pillar and door panel, and have an assistant to hold the door in position. Then remove the bolts from the upper and lower hinges and remove the door from the vehicle, with the aid of an assistant **(see illustrations)**.

6 Examine the hinges for signs of wear or damage. If renewal is necessary, mark the position of the hinge(s) then undo the retaining bolts and remove them from the vehicle. If there is a requirement to remove the top hinge from the front pillar, then the facia panel must be removed as described in Section 28. Fit the new hinge(s), aligning with the marks made before removal then tighten the retaining bolts and top hinge pin to the specified torque.

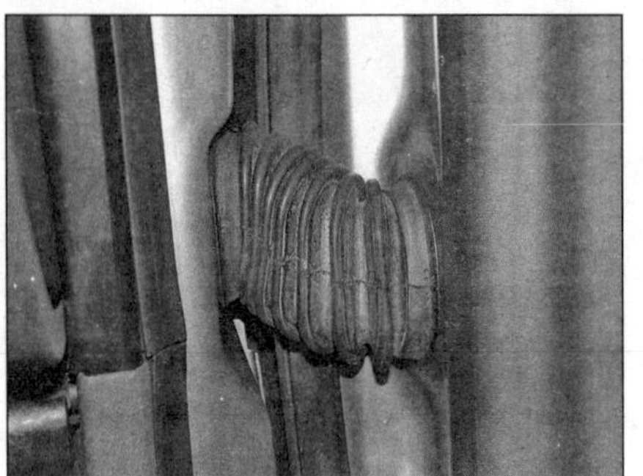
10.3 Wiring gaiter between door and pillar

10.5a Upper hinge

10.5b Lower hinge

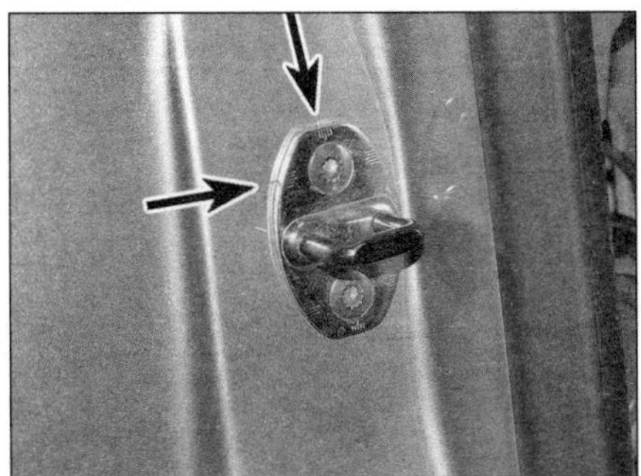

10.11 Alignment marks (arrowed) on body and striker plate

11.2a Carefully prise the trim off...

11.2b ...and remove the Torx screw

Refitting

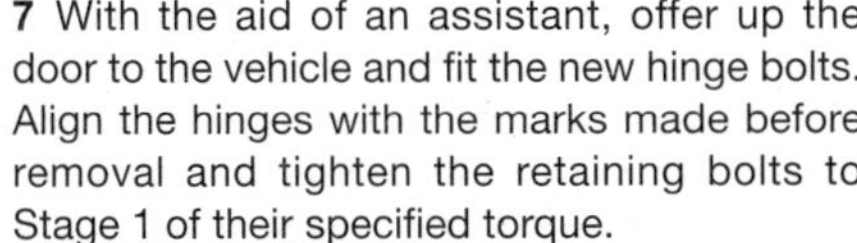

7 With the aid of an assistant, offer up the door to the vehicle and fit the new hinge bolts. Align the hinges with the marks made before removal and tighten the retaining bolts to Stage 1 of their specified torque.

8 Guide the wiring back through the hole in the pillar and reconnect the wiring block connector, then refit the gaiter.

9 Refit the lower trim securely back into the retaining clips (on the driver's door, refit the bonnet release lever as described in Section 9).

10 Check the door alignment and if necessary adjust. If the paintwork around the hinges has been damaged, paint the area with a suitable touch-in brush to prevent corrosion. Reconnect the battery negative terminal.

Adjustment

Note: *Always renew the hinge bolts after loosening.*

11 Close the door and check the door alignment with the surrounding body panels. Adjustment can be made by slackening and moving the striker plate slightly **(see illustration)**. If necessary, slight adjustment of the door position can be made by slackening the hinge retaining bolts and repositioning the hinge/door as necessary. Once the door is correctly positioned, tighten the hinge bolts to their specified torque. If the paintwork around the hinges has been damaged, paint the affected area with a suitable touch-in brush to prevent corrosion.

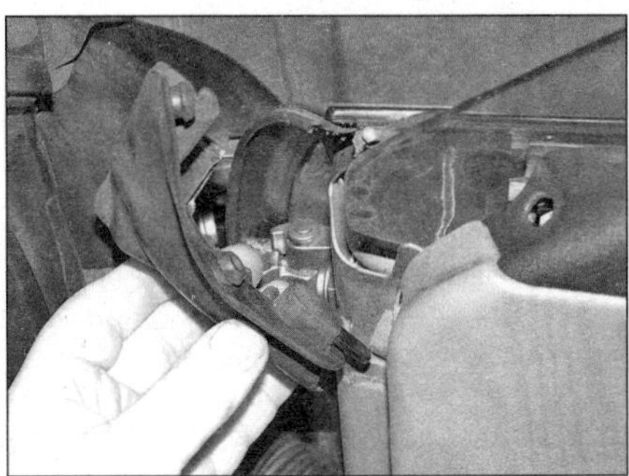

11.3a Unclip the front...

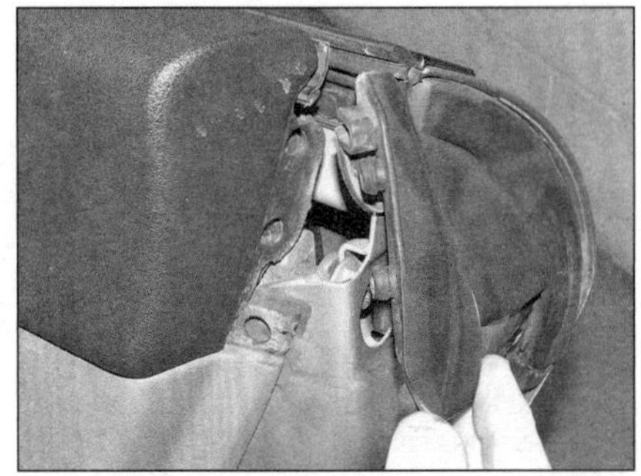

11.3b ...and rear rubber covers

11 Door inner trim panel – removal and refitting

Removal

1 Make sure the keys are not inside the vehicle, then disconnect the battery negative terminal, refer to *Disconnecting the battery* at the rear of this manual.

2 Open the door, then carefully unclip the round trim cover from the door grab handle taking care not to damage it. Undo the Torx screw and withdraw it from the grab handle **(see illustrations)**.

3 Unclip the rubber covers from the front and rear upper edges of the door panel **(see illustrations)**.

4 Release the door trim panel studs, carefully levering between the panel and door with a flat-bladed lever. Work around the outside of the panel, and when all the studs are released, lift the door trim panel upwards and off the window slot **(see illustration)**.

5 As the panel is being removed disconnect the outer cable from the release handle housing, then unhook the inner cable from the lever **(see illustration)**.

6 Disconnect wiring block connectors, as they become accessible **(see illustration)**.

Refitting

7 Before refitting, check whether any of the trim panel retaining studs were broken on removal, renew them as necessary. Refitting of the trim panel is then a reverse of removal. After connecting the battery, check the operation of the door electrical equipment.

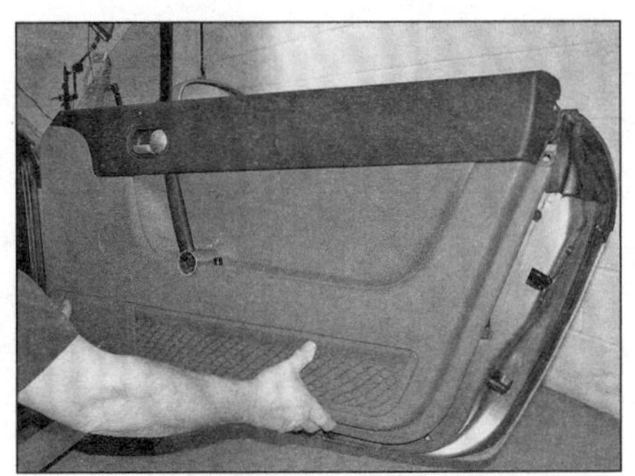

11.4 Release the trim panel carefully

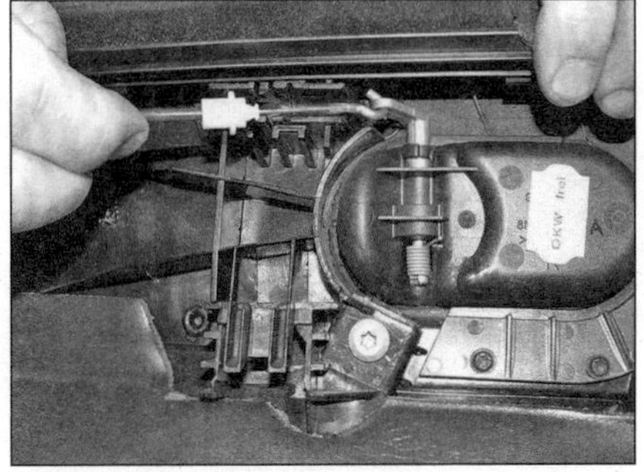

11.5 Unclip the outer cable, then unhook the inner cable

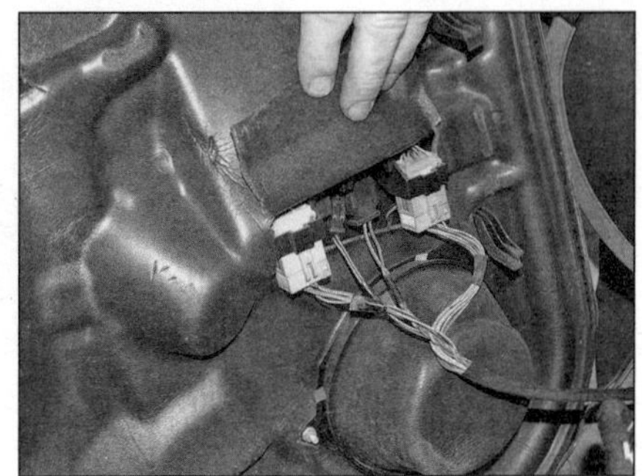

11.6 Disconnect the wiring connectors

12.2 Remove the screws on the inside of the trim panel

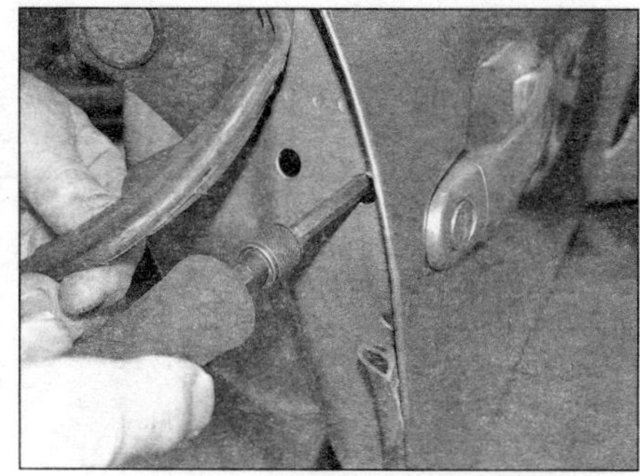
12.4 Pull back rubber seal and insert screwdriver

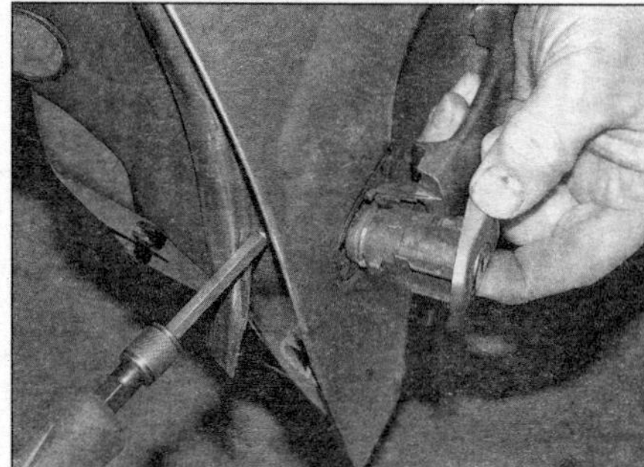
12.5 Hold the door handle in the open position while loosening the screw to the stop

12 Door handle and lock components – removal and refitting

Removal

Interior door handle

1 Remove the door inner trim panel as described in Section 11.

2 Undo the screw on the inside of the door trim panel, then unclip the door handle to remove it **(see illustration)**.

Door lock cylinder

3 Note: *This task can be performed with the door inner trim panel in position.*

4 Open the door, then pull back the rubber seal at the rear edge of the door to locate the retaining screw **(see illustration)**.

5 Pull the door handle out, hold it in this position whilst undoing the Torx retaining screw until it comes to its stop. Do not remove the screw too far or the locking ring may fall into the door **(see illustration)**.

6 Pull the lock cylinder housing out of the door handle, and release the handle to the original position **(see illustration)**. **Note:** *Do not drop the locking ring into the door, as it will be necessary to remove the inner trim panel to recover it.*

Exterior door handle

7 On the front door, remove the door lock cylinder housing as described in paragraphs 3 to 5. Working via the lock cylinder aperture, disconnect the lock release cable from the handle then manoeuvre the handle out from the door. Recover the gasket **(see illustrations)**.

Door lock

8 Remove the door inner trim panel as described in Section 11, and then carry out the operations described in paragraphs 3 to 6.

9 Release the retaining clip and remove the plastic protective cover from over the door lock assembly **(see illustrations)**.

10 Disconnect the wiring connector from

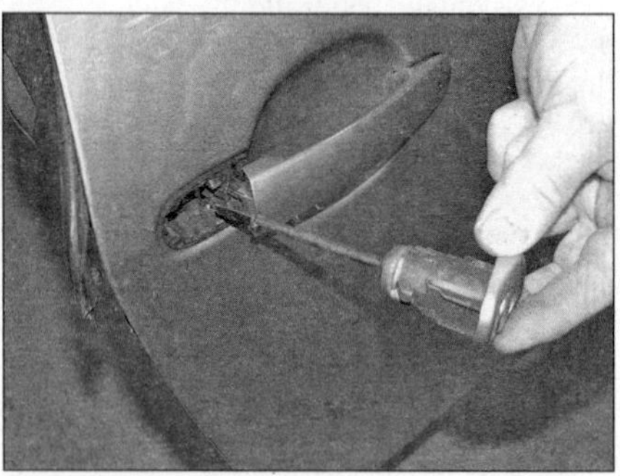
12.6 Withdraw the lock cylinder from the handle

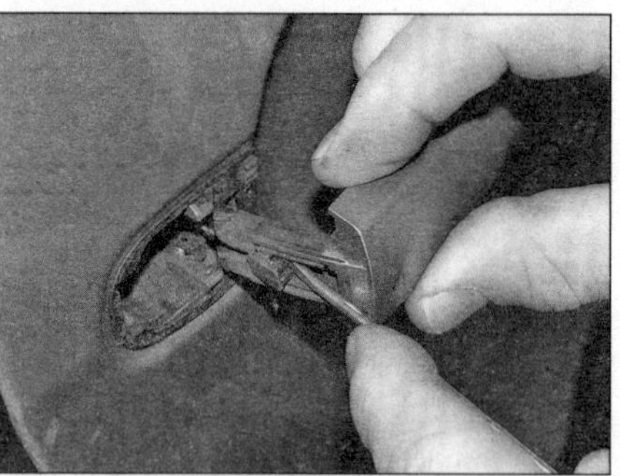
12.7a Detach the release cable from the door handle ...

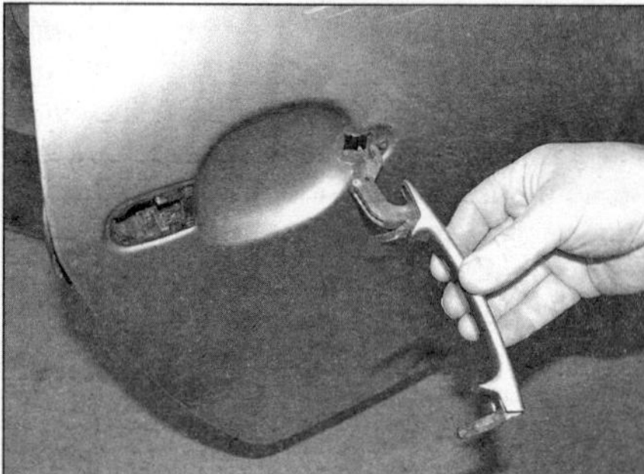
12.7b ... then pivot the handle from the door

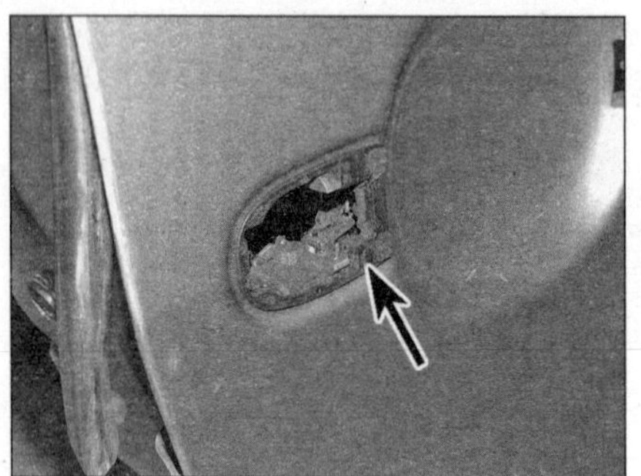
12.7c Recover the gasket (arrowed)

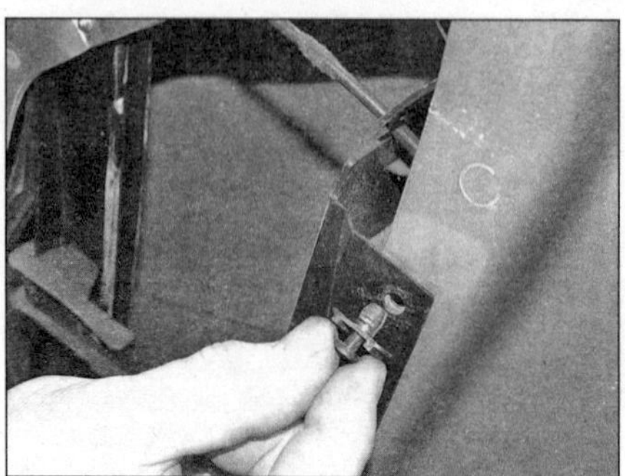
12.9a Remove the retaining clip...

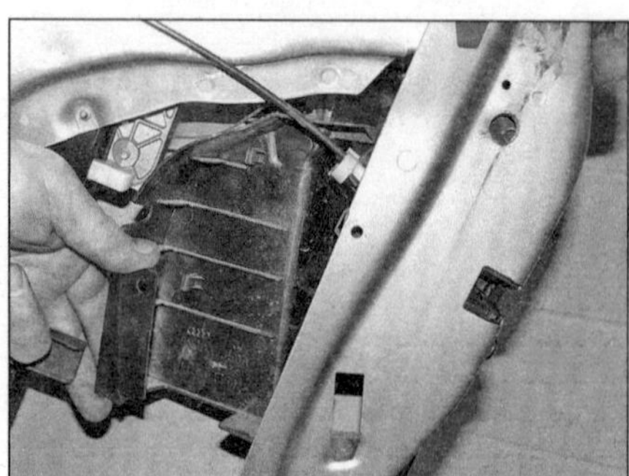
12.9b ...and remove the protective cover

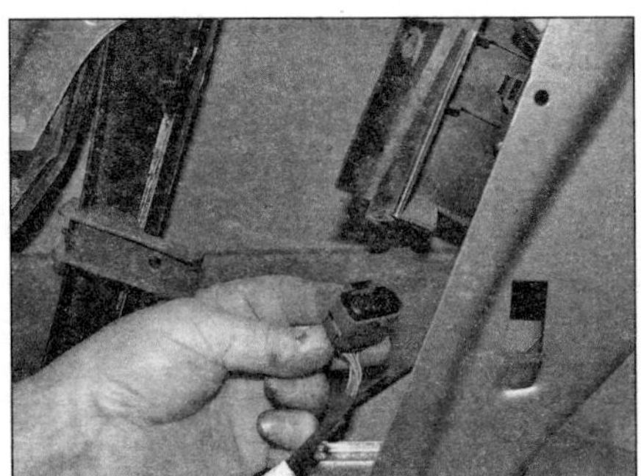
12.10 Disconnect the wiring connector

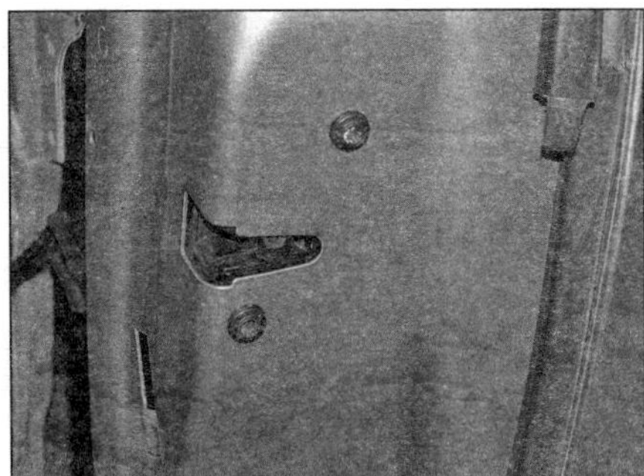
12.11a Undo the two retaining screws...

12.11b ...and remove the door lock assembly

the base of the door lock assembly **(see illustration)**.

11 Unscrew the two bolts on the rear edge of the door from the door lock, and then manoeuvre the door lock assembly from out of the door aperture **(see illustrations)**. Unclip the cable for the interior door handle from the door frame and remove with door lock assembly.

12 The cable can now be removed from the lock assembly by releasing the outer cable from the lock housing, then unclip the end of the inner cable from the operating lever **(see illustrations)**.

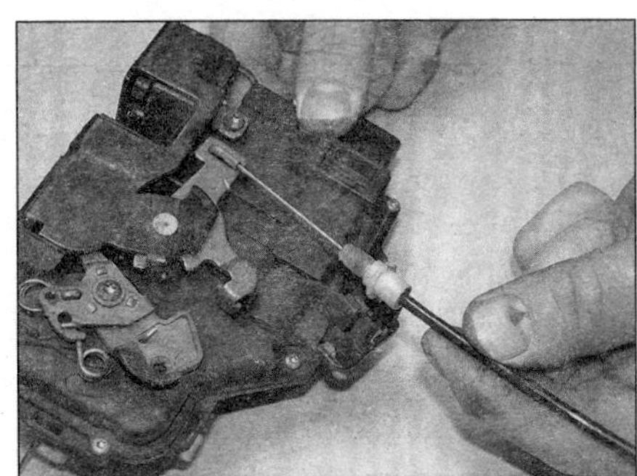
12.12a Release the outer cable...

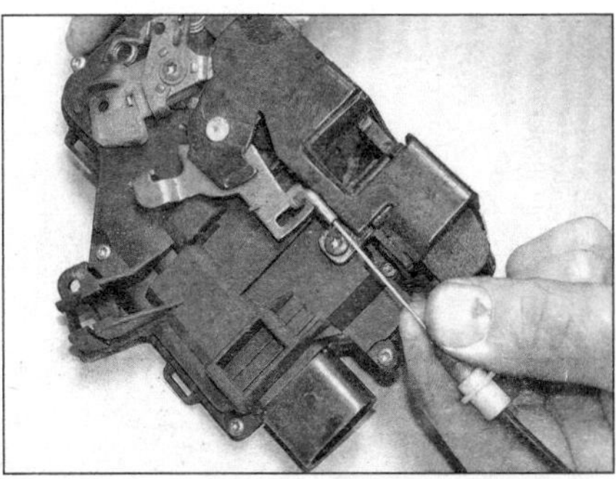
12.12b ...and unclip the inner cable

Refitting

Interior door handle

13 Clip the handle back into position and secure with the screws on the inside of the door trim. Refit the door trim panel as described in Section 11.

Exterior door handle

14 Locate the door handle into the door at the front end, then pivot the handle into position. Refit the cable into the door handle and clip into recess **(see illustration)**. Refit the lock cylinder housing (drivers door) or housing and end cap (passenger door) to the handle and secure it in position with the retaining screw. Refit rubber cover over screw aperture.

Door lock cylinder

15 Refit the lock cylinder into the door handle housing, then tighten the screw in the rear edge of the door to secure door lock cylinder. Refit the rubber cover over the screw aperture.

Door lock

16 Refitting is a reversal of removal as described in paragraphs 8 to 11. When fitting the plastic protective cover over the lock assembly, make sure the locating peg at the top of the cover locates in the door frame **(see illustration)**. Tighten all the bolts to the specified torque, where given.

13 Door window glass and regulator – removal and refitting

1 The window glass and window regulator mechanism are secured to the door subframe,

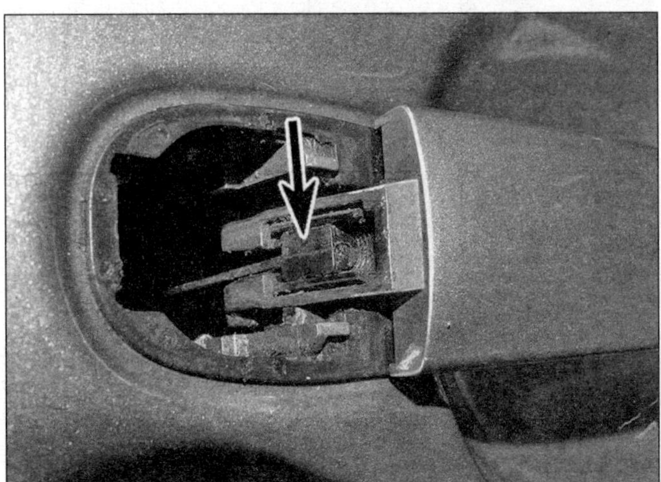
12.14 End of cable (arrowed) fitted into door handle

12.16 Align locating peg with opening (arrowed) in door frame

13.1 Removing the complete assembly

13.2 Unclip the release cable from the subframe

13.3a Disconnect he wiring connectors...

13.3b ...and unclip the wiring loom from the subframe

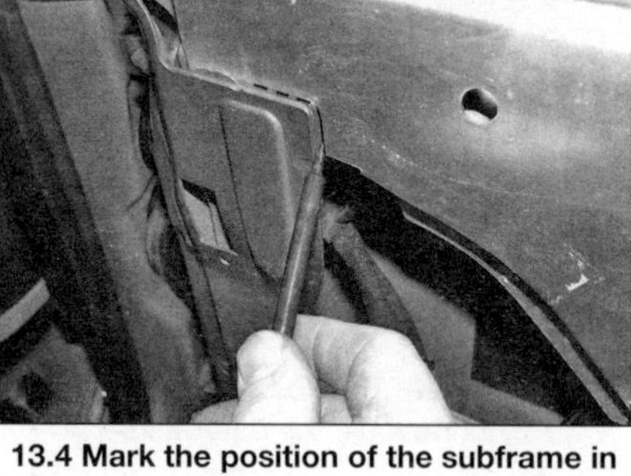

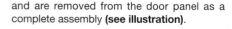

13.4 Mark the position of the subframe in the door panel

13.5a Pull back the rubber cover...

13.5b ...then remove the rear mounting/ adjustment nut...

and are removed from the door panel as a complete assembly **(see illustration)**.

Removal

Door subframe assembly

2 Remove the door inner trim panel as described in Section 11, and then unclip the inner door handle release cable from the top of the door subframe **(see illustration)**.

3 Disconnect the wiring connector from the window regulator motor, then unclip the wiring loom from the door subframe **(see illustrations)**.

4 Before removing the subframe assembly, mark the position of the subframe in the door panel, at the front and rear upper edges **(see illustration)**. This will aid in the refitting of the subframe.

5 Working at the upper part of the door panel, pull back the rubber cover and remove the mounting/adjusting nuts from the rear and front edges of the door panel **(see illustrations)**. Note, if there is a slot in the top of the door panel, then the nuts can be slackened a couple of turns and not have to be removed completely.

6 Working along the lower edge of the door panel remove the plastic trim covers from over the lower mounting bolts **(see illustrations)**.

7 Undo the bolts securing the lower part of

13.5c ...and the front mounting/adjustment nut

13.6a Unclip the outer plastic covers...

13.6b ...and the one at the centre

13.7a Undo the lower mounting bolts (arrowed)...

13.7b ...and the centre mounting/ adjustment nut (arrowed)

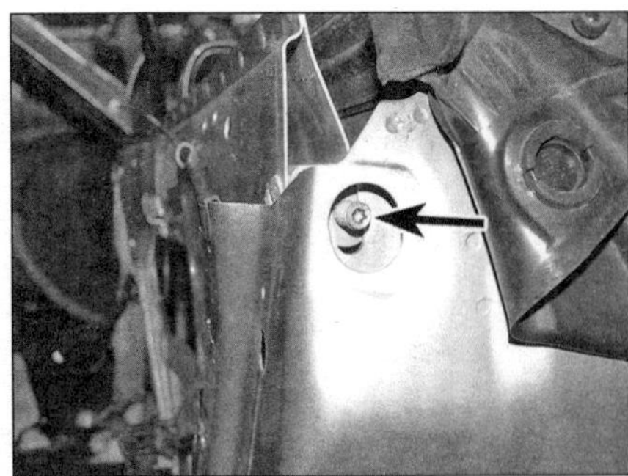
13.8a Adjuster screw (arrowed) – note how many turns

13.8b Remove the subframe assembly from the door panel

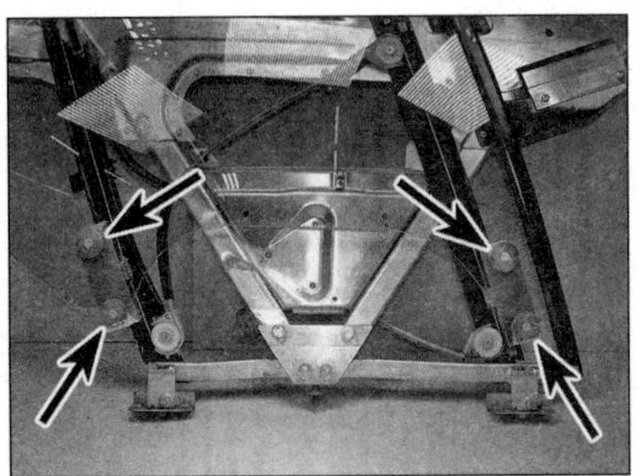
13.10a Window glass mountings (arrowed)

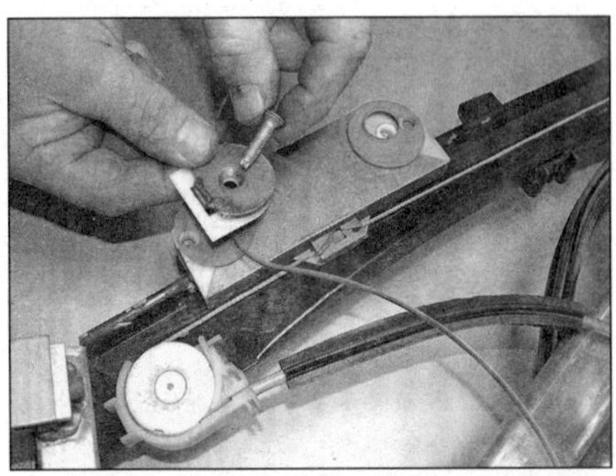
13.10b Remove the mounting screws and washers...

the subframe to the door and the mounting/ adjusting nut at the centre **(see illustrations)**.

8 With all the mounting bolts/nuts removed, lift the subframe from the door panel. If the top of the subframe is tight inside the door panel, turn the adjuster screws in a couple of turns at the front and rear of the door panel **(see illustrations)**. Make a note of how many turns, to aid refitting.

Door window glass

9 Carry out the operations described in previously in this section, and remove the door subframe assembly (see paragraphs 2 to 8).

10 The door window glass can now be removed from the subframe assembly, undo the Torx screws and remove the washers and spacers, noting there fitted position **(see illustrations)**. If the old glass is being re-used mark the position of the glass to the mounting bolts and washers, to aid refitting.

Small fixed side window

11 Carry out the operations described in previously in this section, and remove the door subframe assembly (see paragraphs 2 to 8).

12 The small fixed side window glass can now be removed from the subframe assembly, undo the Torx screws and remove the glass from the subframe **(see illustration)**. If the old glass is being re-used mark the position of the glass/mounting bracket, to aid refitting.

Window lifter mechanism

Note: *The window lifter mechanism is riveted to the subframe, these will need to be drilled out and replaced with new ones on refitting.*

13 Carry out the operations described in previously in this section, and remove the door subframe assembly and door window glass (see paragraphs 2 to 10).

14 Undo the three retaining screws and remove the window motor from the subframe assembly **(see illustration)**.

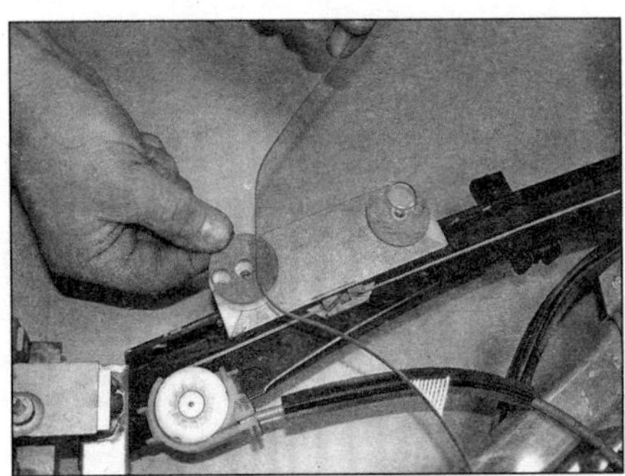
13.10c ...and also the spacers – noting there fitted position

13.12 Window glass mounting screws (arrowed)

13.14 Window motor retaining screws (arrowed)

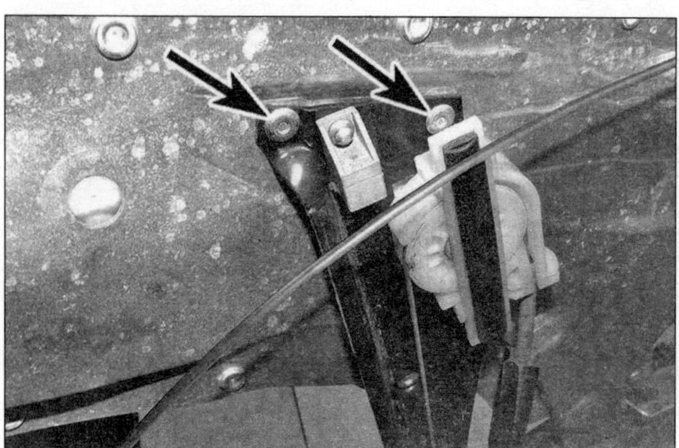
13.15a Upper rivets (arrowed)

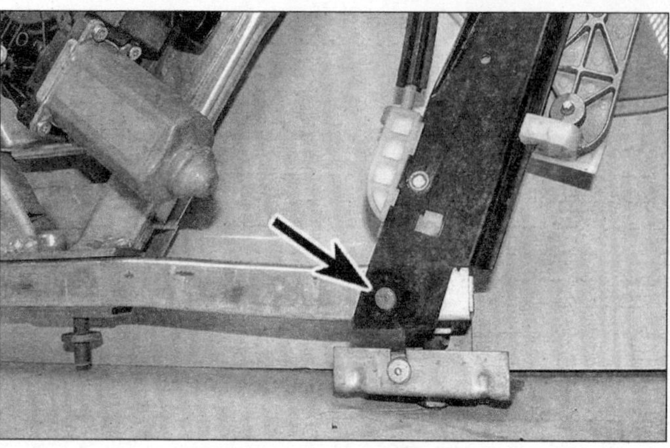
13.15b Lower rivet (arrowed)

15 With the subframe on a flat surface, drill out the rivets from the window lifter mechanism **(see illustrations)**, and then remove it from the subframe.

Refitting

Door subframe assembly

16 Manoeuvre the subframe back into position and engage it with mounting points. Make sure the subframe is correctly seated, with the alignment marks made on removal **(see illustration)**. Refit the mounting bolts/ nuts and lightly tighten. Once the subframe is located in the door correctly, tighten the bolts/ nuts to the specified torque. Refit the door inner trim panel as described in Section 11.

17 If once the door has been completely re-assembled the window glass does not fit right in the aperture, when the door is closed, adjustment can be made by adjusting the front, rear and lower adjusting nuts/screws. If adjustment is required, slacken the adjuster retaining nuts at the front and rear of the door panel. Also slacken the nut on the adjuster under the centre of the door. Once adjustment has been made, tighten the securing nuts to there specified torque.

18 Turn the adjusters at the front and rear of the door panel to centralise the subframe/ window assembly **(see illustrations)**.

19 Turn the adjusters under the centre of the door panel to move the window assembly up or down **(see illustration 13.7b)**.

20 Turn the adjusters at the lower edge of door panel to move the window assembly inwards or outwards at the top **(see illustrations)**.

Door window glass

21 Manoeuvre the window glass into position on the window lifter mechanism and into the window guide, then fit the spacers into position under the glass. Make sure the glass is correctly seated and aligned with the marks made on removal. Fit the washers and retaining screws, then tighten to the specified torque.

22 Refit the door subframe assembly as described previously in this section, see paragraphs 16 to 20.

Small fixed side window glass

23 Manoeuvre the window glass into position on the subframe, making sure the glass is correctly seated and aligned with the marks made on removal. Fit the retaining screws and tighten to the specified torque.

24 Refit the door subframe assembly as described previously in this section, see paragraphs 16 to 20.

Window lifter mechanism

25 Refitting is a reversal of removal, using new rivets to secure the window lifter mechanism to the subframe. Refit the window motor to the subframe and tighten the retaining bolts.

26 Refit the door subframe assembly as described previously in this section, see paragraphs 16 to 20.

13.16 Alignment marks (arrowed) – made before removal

13.18a Adjusting the front...

13.18b ...and rear adjusters

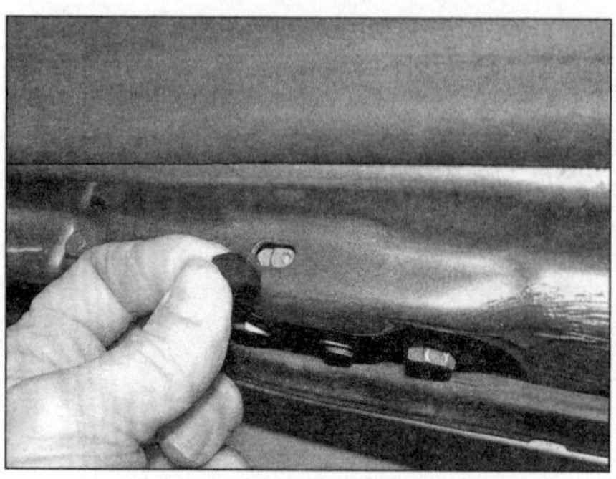
13.20a Remove the plastic plugs...

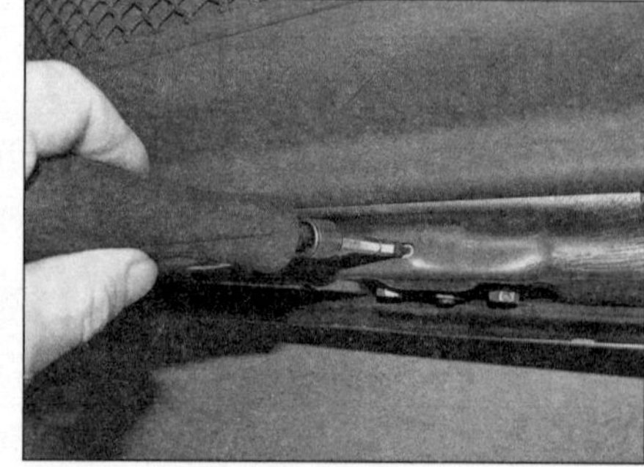
13.20b ...and turn the adjustment screws

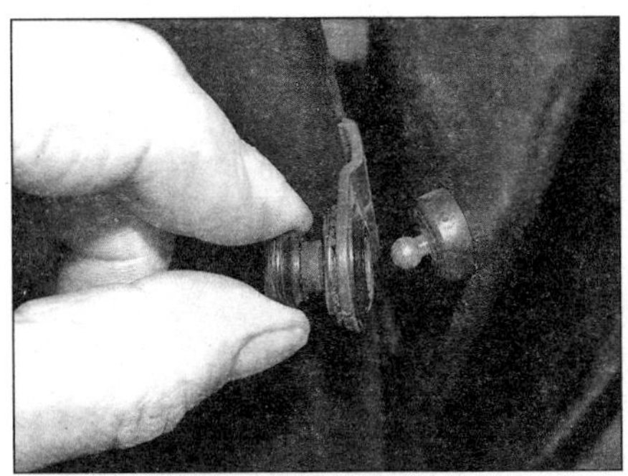
14.2a Unclip the side fasteners...

14.2b ...and then remove the shelf panel

14.3 Remove plastic trim

14 Tailgate and support struts – removal and refitting

Removal

Tailgate

1 Open up the tailgate then disconnect the battery negative terminal, refer to *Disconnecting the battery* at the rear of this manual.

2 Where fitted unclip the ball joint fittings at each side of the shelf trim panel and then unclip and remove it from inside the tailgate **(see illustrations)**.

3 Unclip the plastic trim from over the tailgate lock striker plate **(see illustration)**.

4 Unclip the interior light unit from the trim panel and disconnect the wiring connector **(see illustration)**.

5 The tailgate trim panel is made up of two parts and can be removed in one piece. Working around the trim panel, carefully release the retaining clips and remove the trim panel from the tailgate **(see illustration)**.

6 Disconnect any wiring connectors situated behind the trim panel and the heated rear screen terminals, and then free the rubber wiring sleeve/grommets from the tailgate **(see illustrations)**.

14.4 Remove the interior light

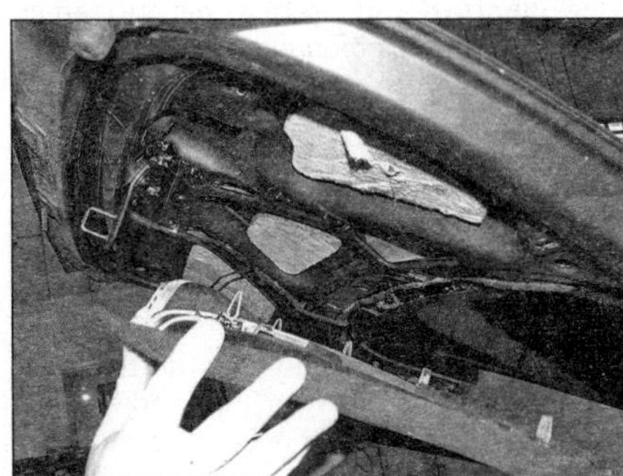
14.5 Unclip the trim panel from the tailgate

7 Tie a piece of string to each end of the wiring then, noting the correct routing of the wiring harness, release the harness rubber grommets from the tailgate and withdraw the wiring. When the end of the wiring appears, untie the string and leave it in position in the tailgate; it can then be used on refitting to draw the wiring into position.

8 Using a suitable marker pen, draw around the outline of each hinge marking its correct position on the tailgate.

9 With the help of an assistant to support the tailgate, remove the support struts as described below.

10 Slacken and remove the bolts securing the hinges to the tailgate **(see illustration)**. Where necessary, recover the gaskets which are fitted between the hinge and vehicle body.

11 Inspect the hinges for signs of wear or damage and renew if necessary. The hinges are secured to the vehicle by nuts or bolts (depending on model) which can be accessed once the headlining rear cover strip has been removed.

Support struts

Warning: The support struts are filled with a gas and must be disposed of safely.

12 With the help of an assistant, support the tailgate in the open position.

13 Using a small flat-bladed screwdriver lift the locking clip (this does not need to be completely removed), and pull the gas support

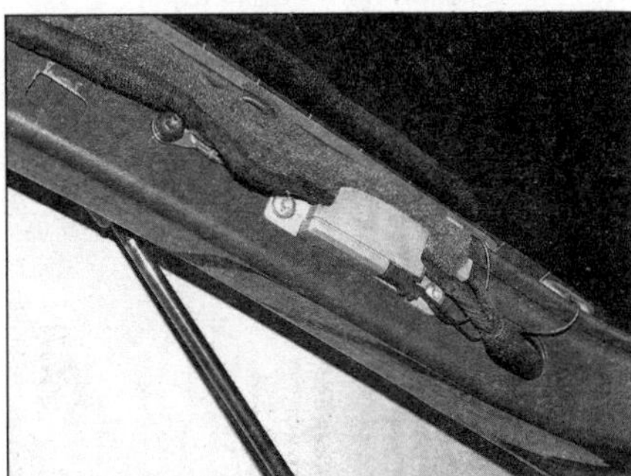
14.6a Disconnect the wiring connectors...

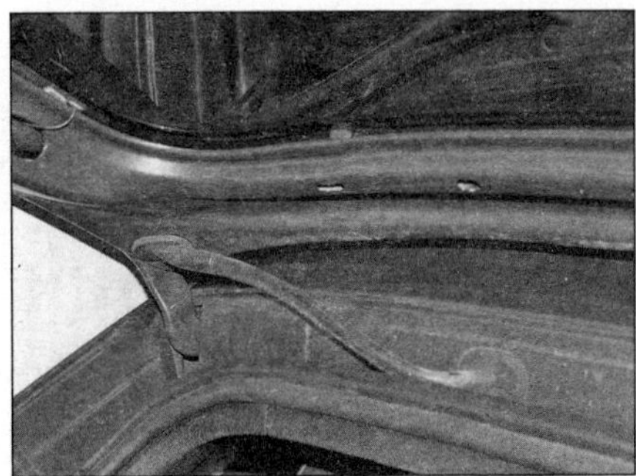
14.6b ... then pull rubber grommet from tailgate to release the wiring

14.10 Remove tailgate hinge securing bolts (arrowed)

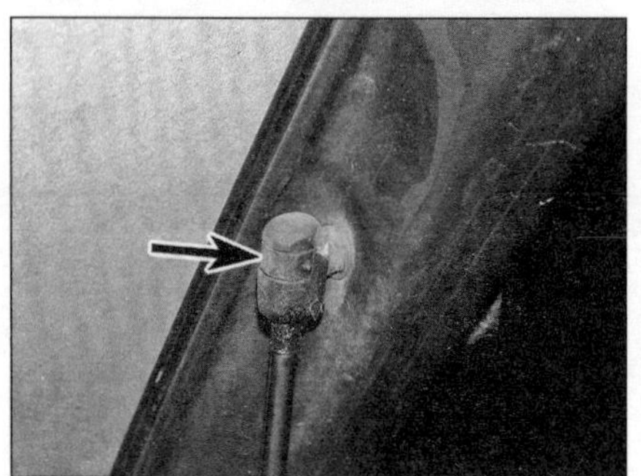
14.13a Upper securing clip (arrowed)

14.13b Lower securing clip (arrowed)

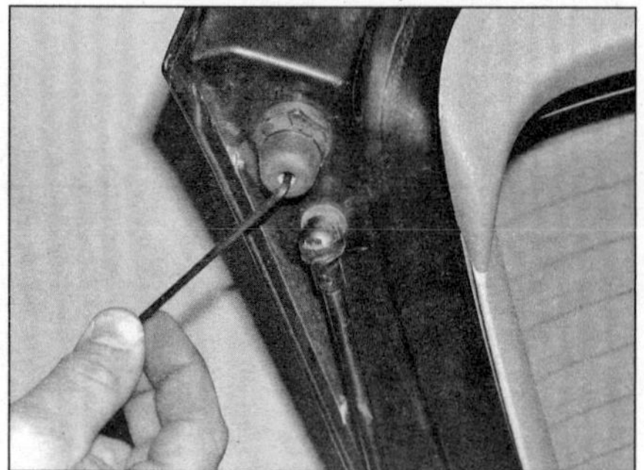
14.16 Slacken the centre screw to adjust the tailgate buffer

strut off its balljoint mounting on the tailgate **(see illustrations)**. Repeat the procedure on the lower strut mounting and remove the strut from the vehicle body. **Note:** *If the gas strut is to be re-used, the locking clip must not be taken all the way out, or the clip will be damaged.*

Refitting

Tailgate

14 Refitting is the reverse of removal, aligning the hinges with the marks made before removal. Tighten retaining bolts to the specified torque.

15 On completion, close the tailgate and check its alignment with the surrounding panels. If necessary slight adjustment can be made by slackening the retaining bolts and repositioning the tailgate on its hinges. If the tailgate buffers are not in contact with the rear cross panel, they will need to be adjusted, continue as follows.

16 Locate the adjustment buffers on the tailgate. Through the hole in the rubber cap, insert an Allen key and slacken the screw until the centre notched slide will move freely in or out, in the housing. Slide the buffer out, and then carefully close the tailgate, to push the centre part of the buffer in to set to the correct position. When the buffer has been set to the correct position tighten the centre screw **(see illustration)**.

Support struts

17 Refitting is a reverse of the removal procedure, ensuring that the strut is securely retained by its retaining clips.

15 Boot lid and support struts - removal and refitting

Removal

Boot lid

1 Open up the boot lid then disconnect the battery negative terminal, refer to *Disconnecting the battery* at the rear of this manual.

2 Disconnect the wiring connectors from the number plate lights, tie a piece of string to each end of the wiring. Noting the correct routing of the wiring harness, release the harness rubber grommet **(see illustration)**, from the boot lid and withdraw the wiring. When the end of the wiring appears, untie the string and leave it in position in the boot lid; it can then be used on refitting to draw the wiring into position

3 Draw around the outline of each hinge with a suitable marker pen then slacken and remove the hinge retaining nuts and remove the boot lid from the vehicle. Note the position of the alignment marks on the boot lid **(see illustration)**.

4 Inspect the hinges for signs of wear or damage and renew if necessary; the hinges are secured to the vehicle body by bolts **(see illustration)**. Remove the support struts as described below.

Support struts

Warning: The support struts are filled with a gas and must be disposed of safely.

5 With the help of an assistant, support the boot lid in the open position.

6 Using a small flat-bladed screwdriver lift the locking clip, and pull the gas support strut off its balljoint mounting on the boot lid hinge. Repeat the procedure on the lower strut mounting and remove the strut from the vehicle body **(see illustrations)**. **Note:** *If the*

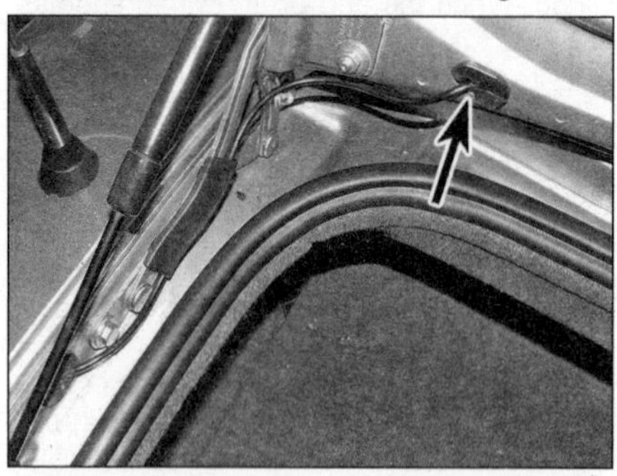
15.2 Release the wiring grommet (arrowed)

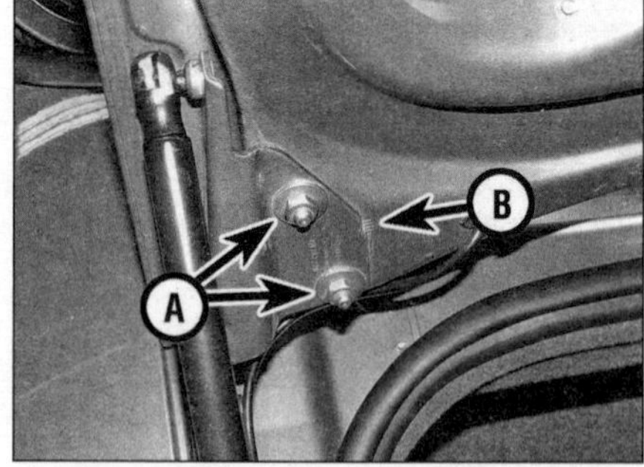

15.3 Undo the hinge nuts (A) and check alignment marks (B)

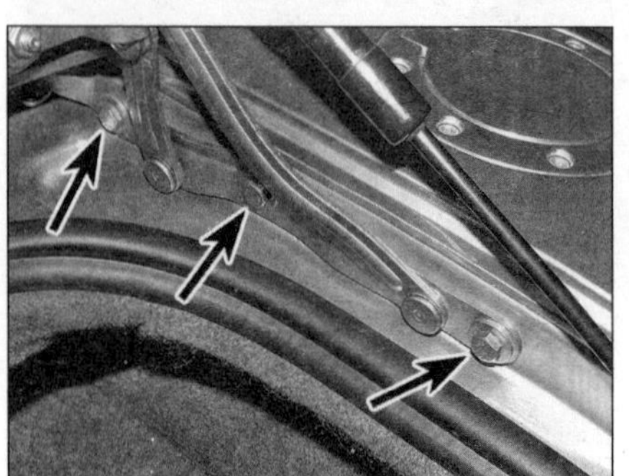
15.4 Hinge mounting bolts (arrowed)

15.6a Strut upper locking clip (arrowed)

15.6b Strut lower locking clip (arrowed)

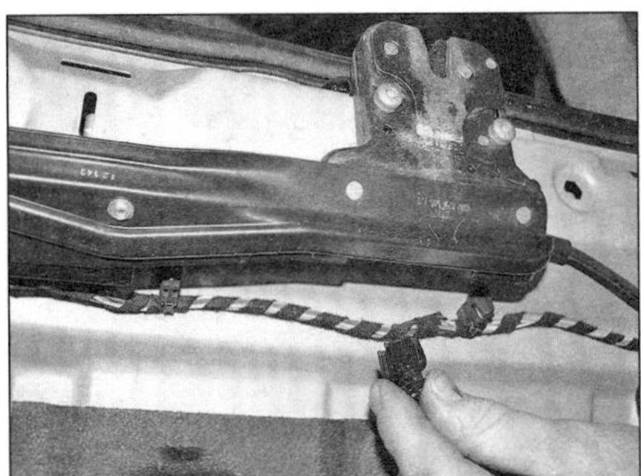
16.2a Disconnect the wiring from the lock...

16.2b ...and the solenoid motor

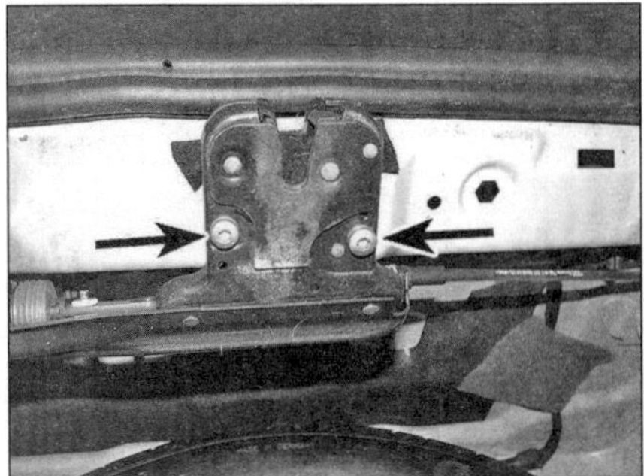
16.3a Removing the two screws (arrowed)

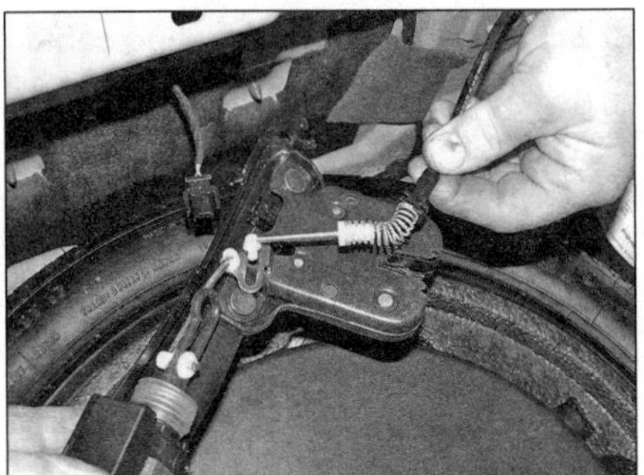
16.3b Unclip the operating cable from the lock

16.4a Remove the plastic trim from the boot lid

16.4b Remove the plastic trim from the tailgate

gas strut is to be reused, the locking clip must not be taken all the way out, or the clip will be damaged.

Refitting

Boot lid

7 Refitting is the reverse of removal, aligning the hinges with the marks made before removal.

8 On completion, close the boot lid and check its alignment with the surrounding panels. If necessary slight adjustment can be made by slackening the retaining nuts and repositioning the boot lid on its hinges. If further adjustment is required see the buffer adjustment in the tailgate refitting procedure in Section 14.

Support struts

9 Refitting is a reverse of removal, ensuring the strut is securely retained by its clips.

16 Boot lid/tailgate lock components – removal and refitting

Removal

Boot lid/tailgate lock

1 Open up the boot lid/tailgate, and remove the trim panel from across the rear of the luggage compartment, as described in Section 26.

2 Disconnect the wiring connectors from the lock unit and the solenoid motor **(see illustrations)**.

3 Undo the two retaining screws and remove the lock assembly mounting bracket from inside the rear panel. Release the outer cable from the housing, and then unclip the inner cable from the lever on the lock assembly **(see illustrations)**.

Boot lid/tailgate striker plate

4 Open up the boot lid, remove the plastic trim panel from the striker plate **(see illustrations)**.

5 Mark the position of the striker plate and then undo the two retaining screws, and remove the striker from the boot lid/tailgate **(see illustrations)**. **Note:** *The mounting holes in the striker plate are elongated to allow for adjustment.*

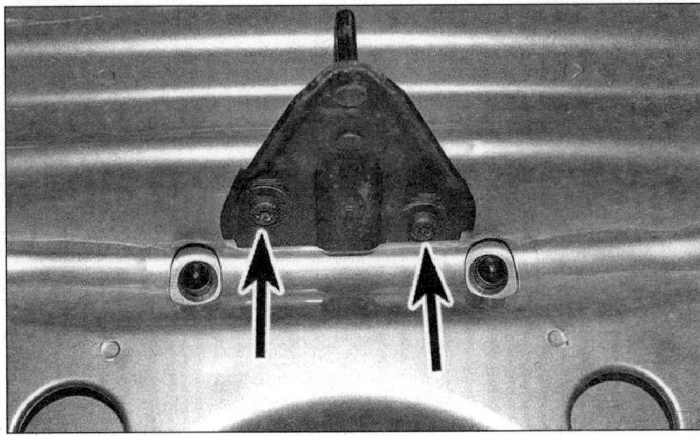
16.5a Remove the screws (arrowed) from the boot lid

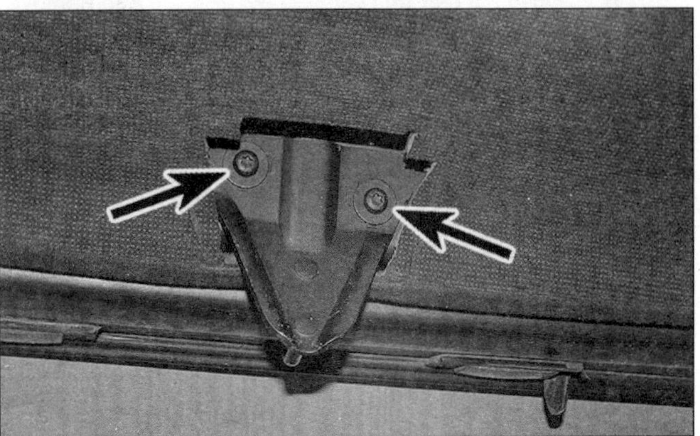
16.5b Remove the screws (arrowed) from the tailgate

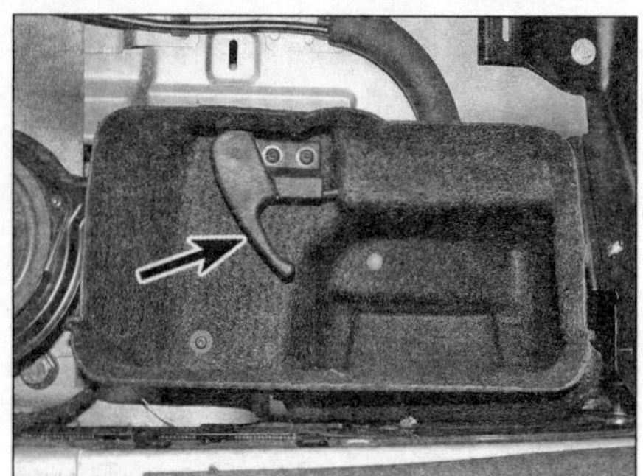
16.6a Boot lid opening lever (arrowed) – Roadster models

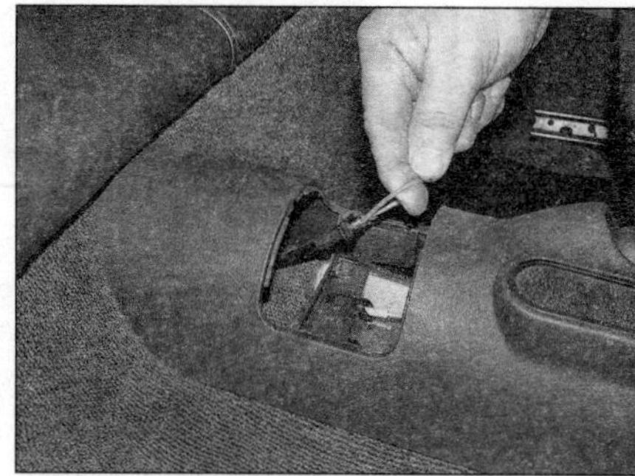
16.6b Release tailgate lock – Coupe model

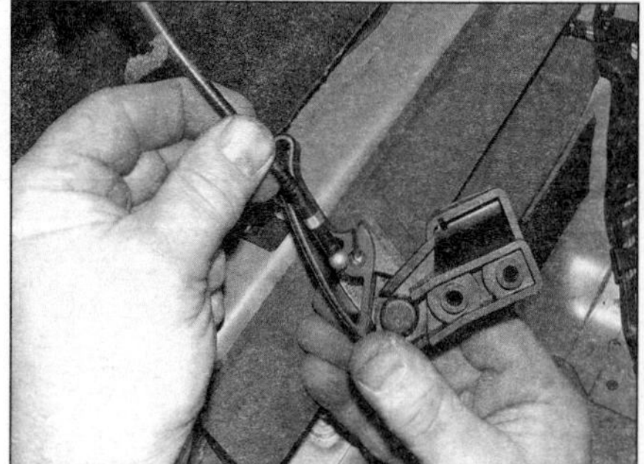
16.9 Remove the release lever from the end of the cable

Boot lid/tailgate lock operating cable

6 There is an operating cable connected to the rear lock assembly, that can be manually operated in the event of the electrics not working, from inside the passenger compartment. To access the operating cable on Roadster (convertible) models, open the compartment behind the drivers seat. On Coupe models, remove the plastic cover at the rear of the centre console **(see illustrations)**.
7 Remove the boot lid/tailgate lock and disconnect the operating cable, as described previously in this section, see paragraphs 1 to 3.
8 The cable will now need to be traced behind trim panels and on Coupe models under the rear seat. Refer to the relevant sections in this manual, then trace the operating cable and release it from the retaining clips along the way.
9 On Roadster (convertible) models, undo the retaining screws and remove the release lever from inside the compartment behind the drivers seat. Release the outer cable from the mounting bracket and then unclip the inner cable from the lever **(see illustration)**.

Refitting

Boot lid/tailgate lock

10 Refit the operating cable to the lock assembly, then refit the lock mounting bracket back to the rear panel and tighten the retaining screws. Reconnect the wiring connectors and refit the trim panel back to the rear of the luggage compartment.

Boot lid/tailgate striker plate

11 Refitting is a reversal of removal. Check the operation of the boot lid/tailgate and adjust the striker plate accordingly.

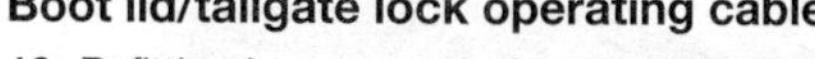

Boot lid/tailgate lock operating cable

12 Refitting is a reversal of removal. Refit the lock assembly as described in paragraph 10.

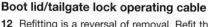

17 Central locking components – removal and refitting

1 Before working on the central locking components, disconnect the battery negative terminal. **Note:** *Before disconnecting the battery, refer to* Disconnecting the battery *at the rear of this manual.*

Removal

Internal central locking switch

2 Unclip the trim panel from the rear of the centre console **(see illustration)**. On models with cup holder fitted, undo the two retaining screws, and then remove the trim panel.
3 Reach inside the rear of the centre console and push the switch panel upwards and disconnect the wiring connectors **(see illustrations)**.
4 Release the securing clips and remove the central locking switch from the switch panel.

17.2 Unclip the rear trim panel

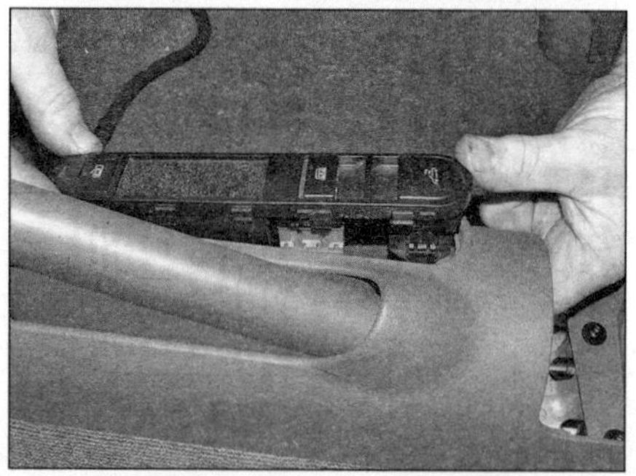
17.3a Remove the switch panel...

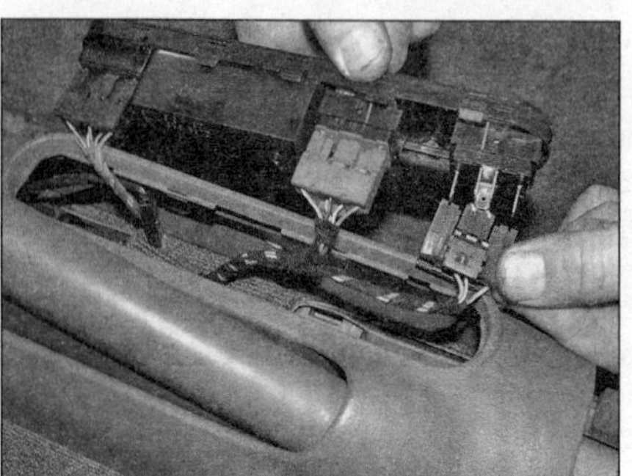
17.3b ...and disconnect the wiring connectors

17.6 Central locking control unit – Coupe model

Central locking control unit

Note: *On models fitted with the 'convenience system', this is the central control unit which also operates the alarm, sunroof and the electric windows and exterior mirrors (via the separate control unit in each door).*

Coupe models

5 The central locking control unit is located inside the left-hand rear of the vehicle, behind the left-hand side trim panel. Remove the rear left-hand side trim panel, with reference to Section 26.
6 Disconnect the wiring connectors, undo the securing screws and remove the control unit from the mounting bracket **(see illustration)**.

Roadster 'convertible' models

7 The central locking control unit is located inside the left-hand rear of the vehicle, inside the storage compartment behind the rear wind deflector glass. Unclip the access panel

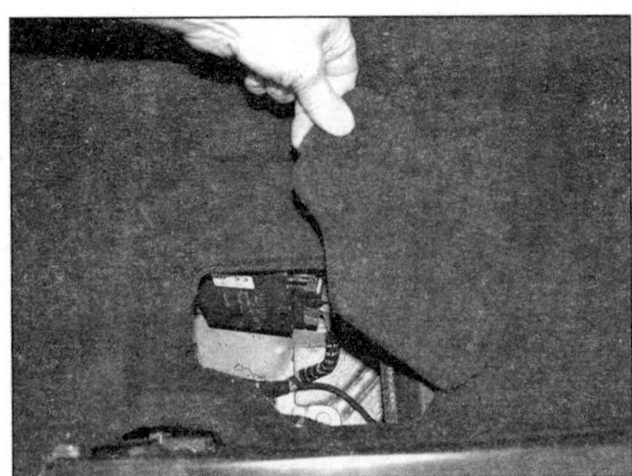
17.7 Unclip the access panel...

17.8 ...to access the control unit

17.12 Disconnect the linkage rod

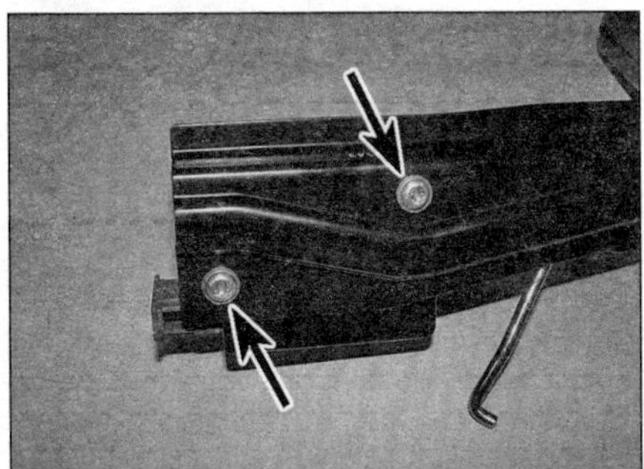
17.13 Lock solenoid motor retaining screws (arrowed)

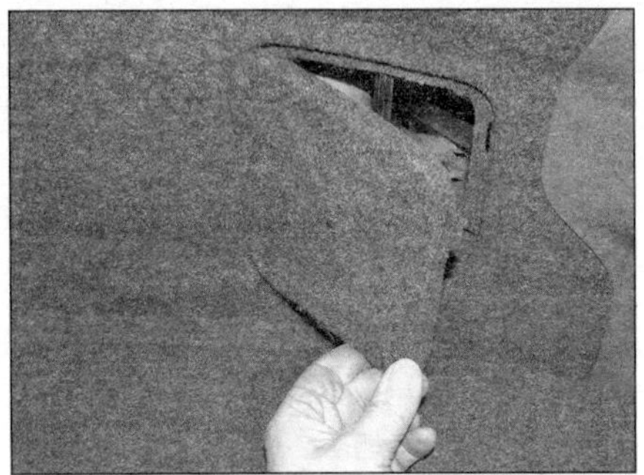
17.14 Open the access panel

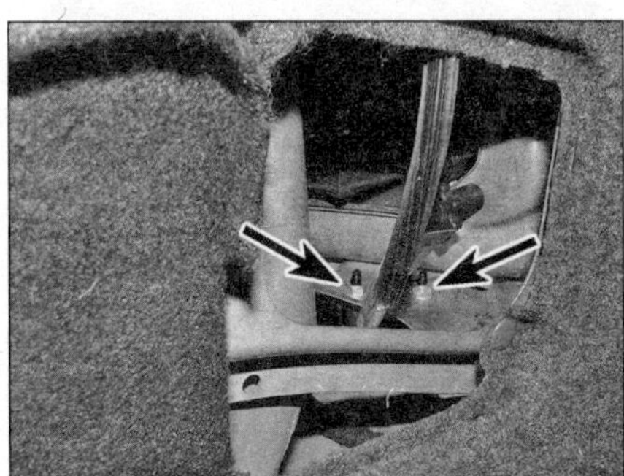
17.15 Undo the two mounting nuts (arrowed)

in the bottom of the storage compartment **(see illustration)**.

8 Disconnect the wiring connectors, undo the securing screws and remove the control unit from the mounting bracket **(see illustration)**.

Door locking motor/actuator

9 Remove the door lock as described in Section 12.

10 The locking motors are part of the door lock assembly and cannot be obtained separately.

Boot lid/tailgate lock motor/actuator

11 Remove the boot lid/tailgate lock assembly, as described in Section 16.

12 Disconnect the linkage rod from the lock solenoid motor **(see illustration)**.

13 Undo the retaining screws, and remove the lock solenoid motor from the mounting bracket **(see illustration)**.

Fuel filler flap lock motor/actuator

14 Open the tailgate/boot lid and open the access trim panel on the right-hand side of the luggage compartment, behind the right-hand rear light unit **(see illustration)**.

15 Undo the two retaining nuts and manoeuvre the the locking motor/actuator and bracket from inside the rear panel **(see illustration)**. Disconnect the wiring connector and operating cable from the motor. If required, slacken the retaining screws and remove the lock motor/actuator out of the elongated holes in the mounting bracket.

Rear compartment lock motor/actuator – Roadster 'convertible' models

16 There are two lock motors/actuators fitted to the rear panel behind the front seats, for the storage compartments. One is for the upper central compartment and one for the lower left-hand side compartment **(see illustration)**.

17 Tilt the seat back forwards and remove the trim panels from behind the seats, with reference to Section 26, **(see illustration)**.

18 Disconnect the wiring connectors, undo

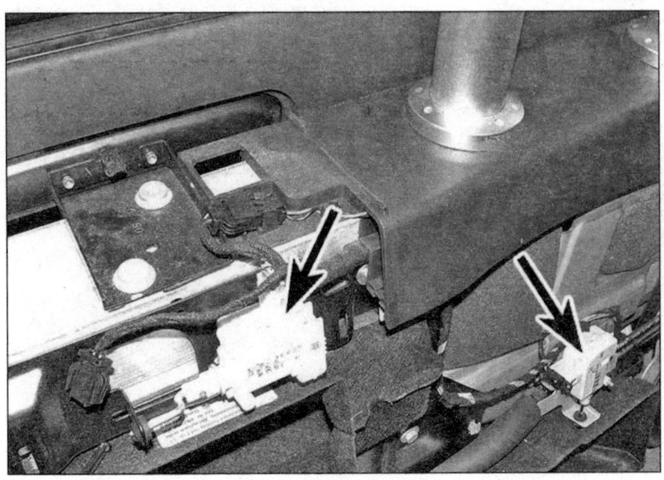
17.16 Location of locking motors/actuators (arrowed)

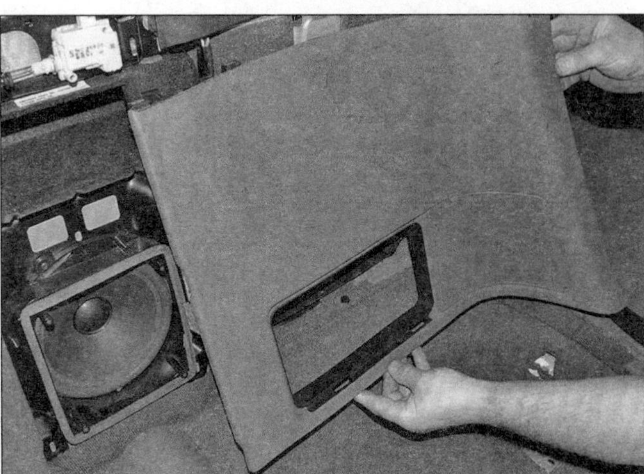
17.17 Remove the rear trim panels

17.18a Disconnect the wiring connector...

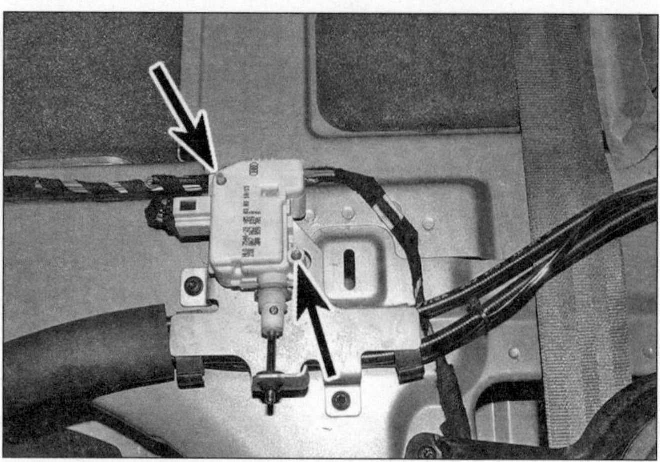
17.18b ...and slacken the two screws (arrowed)

the securing screws and remove the motor/actuator from the mounting bracket. The two screws holding the motor/actuator to the mounting bracket do not have to be removed completely, slacken them a couple of turns, by turning the ends of the screws, and then slide them out from the elongated holes in the mounting bracket **(see illustrations)**.

Refitting

19 Refitting is a reverse of the relevant removal procedure making sure all connections are securely remade. On completion check the operation of all central locking system components.

18 Electric window components - removal and refitting

Window switches

1 Remove the door inner trim panel, as described in Section 11.

2 Pull back the grab handle and remove the cover from over the switches **(see illustration)**.

3 Working at the rear of the trim panel, release the fasteners and then unclip the weathershield/insulation cover from the door trim panel **(see illustration)**.

4 Withdraw the switch locating sleeve and remove the window switch from the rear of the trim panel. Release the securing clips and disconnect the wiring connectors from the switch **(see illustrations)**.

5 Refitting of the switch is then a reversal of removal. Refit the door inner trim panel, with reference to Section 11.

Window winder motors

Removal

6 Remove the door inner trim panel, as described in Section 11.

7 Undo the three retaining screws, disconnect the wiring connector and remove the motor from the window regulator **(see illustration)**. Note the screws may be of the tamper proof type, so a special tool may be needed.

Refitting

8 If a new motor is being fitted, remove the protective cover from the gearing.

9 Make sure that the motor drive gear components are sufficiently lubricated (recommend grease G 000 450 02 – available from your Audi dealer) and free from dust and dirt.

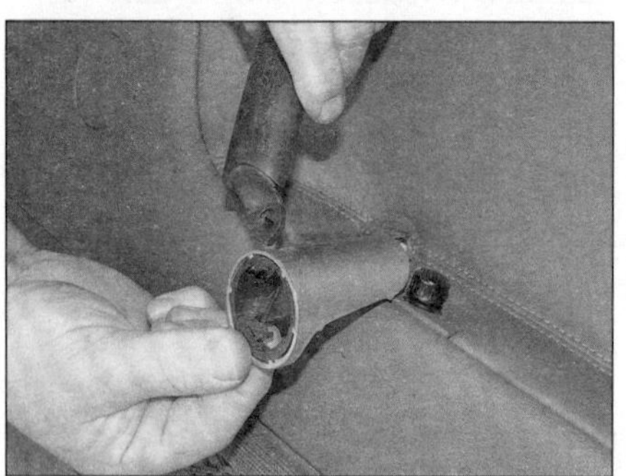
18.2 Remove the switch trim cover

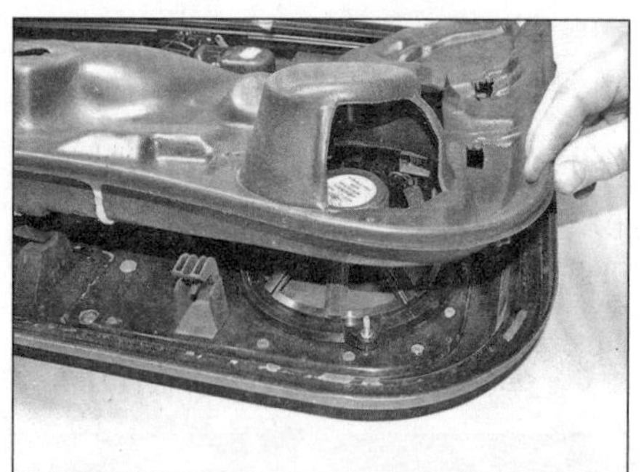
18.3 Unclip the inner weathershield

18.4a Remove the switch...

18.4b ...and disconnect the wiring connectors

18.7 Remove retaining screws (arrowed) and disconnect the wiring

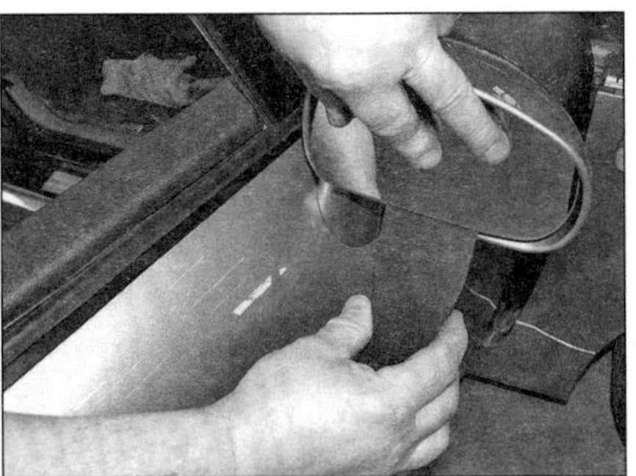

19.1a Carefully lever out the mirror glass...

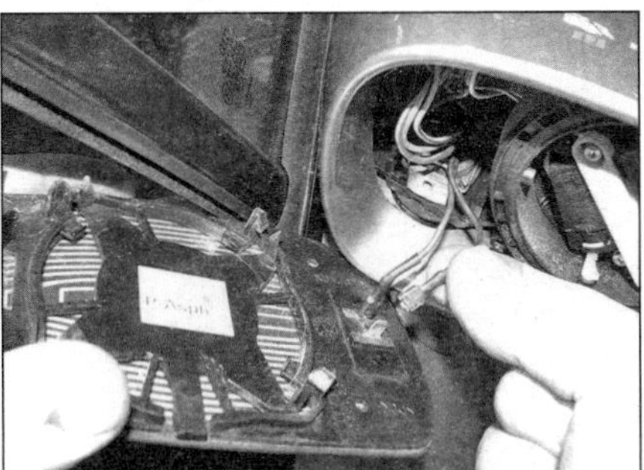

19.1b ...and disconnect the wiring connectors

19.4 Release the securing clip

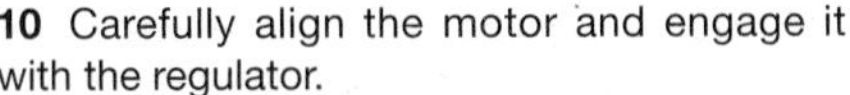

10 Carefully align the motor and engage it with the regulator.

11 Refit the window motor retaining screws and screw them in loosely; when the motor drive gears engage correctly, tighten the screws. Refit the wiring connector to the window motor.

12 Refit the door inner trim panel, with reference to Section 11.

19 Exterior mirrors and associated components – removal and refitting

Removal

Mirror glass

1 Insert a flat lever and carefully slide it between the lower part of the mirror glass and mirror housing. First press the mirror inwards at the top and carefully prise the glass from the motor. Disconnect the wiring connectors from the mirror heating element **(see illustrations)**. Take great care when removing the glass; do not use excessive force as the glass is easily broken.

2 When refitting the mirror glass, press firmly at the centre taking care not to use excessive force, as the glass is easily broken. Either use a piece of cloth or wear gloves to prevent any harm to your hands.

Mirror motor and housing

3 Remove the mirror glass as described previously in this section (see paragraphs 1 & 2)

4 Using long nose pliers release the securing clip from the mounting bracket inside the mirror housing **(see illustration)**. Hinge the clip upwards and move it away from the mounting.

5 Insert a screw into the threads in the retaining clamp, and then tighten the screw to withdraw the retaining clamp from the mounting **(see illustrations)**.

6 Disconnect the wiring connectors from inside the mirror housing and then remove the housing assembly from the mirror mounting **(see illustrations)**.

7 To remove the mounting post on the door panel, undo the two retaining screws **(see illustration)**. Then remove the door inner trim panel as described in Section 11, and disconnect the mirror wiring connectors from inside the door trim panel.

8 Refitting is the reverse of the relevant removal procedure. Making sure that the securing clip is located correctly on the retaining clamp and mounting post **(see illustration)**.

19.5a Tighten the screw...

19.5b ...to withdraw the retaining clamp

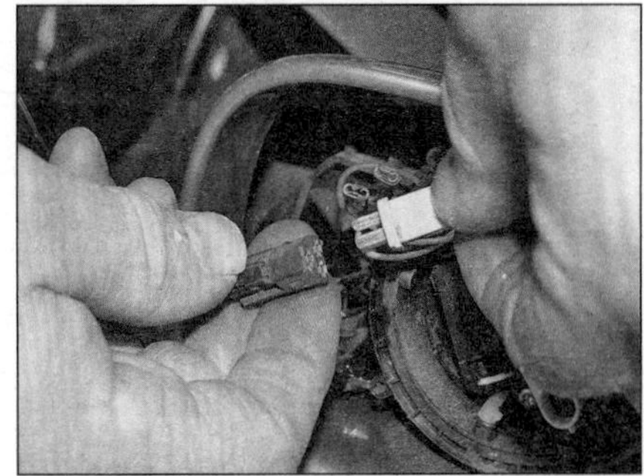

19.6a Disconnect the wiring connectors...

19.6b ...and remove the housing assembly

19.7 Mirror mounting post retaining screws

19.8 Securing clip (arrowed)

Mirror switch

9 Remove the door inner trim panel, as described in Section 11. Working at the rear of the trim panel, release the fasteners and then unclip the weathershield/insulation cover from the door trim panel **(see illustration 18.3)**.

10 Release the securing clips at the rear of the switch and push it out through the door trim panel, then disconnect the wiring connector **(see illustrations)**.

11 Refitting of the switch is then a reversal of removal. Refit the door inner trim panel, with reference to Section 11.

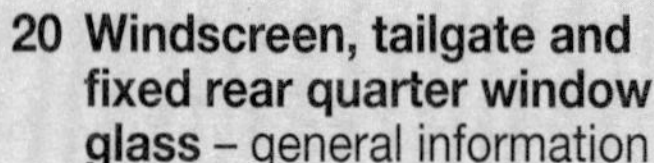

20 Windscreen, tailgate and fixed rear quarter window glass – general information

1 These areas of glass are secured by the tight fit of the weather-strip in the body aperture, and are bonded in position with a special adhesive. Renewal of such fixed glass is a difficult, messy and time-consuming task, which is beyond the scope of the home mechanic. It is difficult, unless one has plenty of practice, to obtain a secure, waterproof fit. Furthermore, the task carries a high risk of breakage; this applies especially to the laminated glass windscreen. In view of this, owners are strongly advised to have this sort of work carried out by one of the many specialist windscreen fitters.

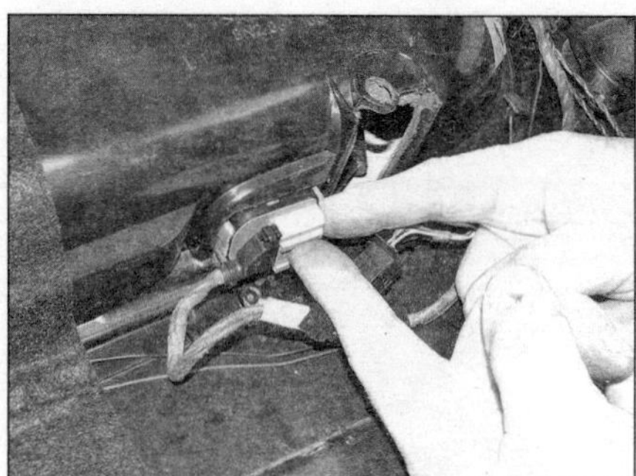

19.10a Remove the switch...

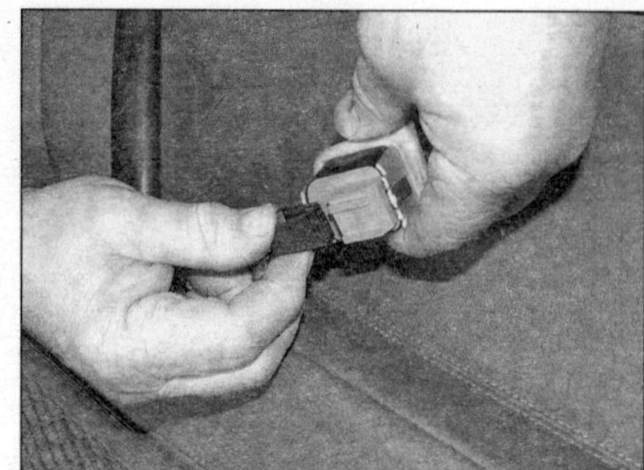

19.10b ...and disconnect the wiring connectors

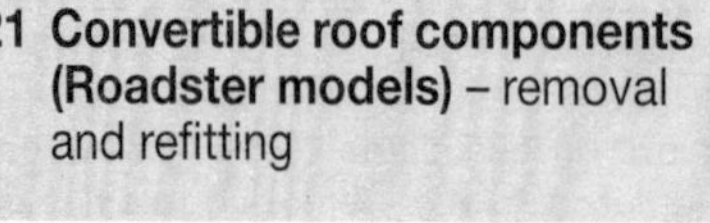

21 Convertible roof components (Roadster models) – removal and refitting

Convertible roof assembly

1 Before working on the convertible top components, disconnect the battery negative terminal. **Note:** *Before disconnecting the battery, refer to* 'Disconnecting the battery' *at the rear of this manual.*

2 Tilt the front seat backs forward and remove the trim panels from the front of the glass wind deflector, with reference to Section 26.

3 With the convertible roof in the closed position, reach behind the glass wind deflector assembly and release the lower part of the trim panel inside the front of the convertible roof compartment. With the lower part released, open the convertible roof and withdraw the trim panel from the rear of the glass wind deflector assembly **(see illustrations)**.

4 Close the convertible roof, then release the securing clips on the two gas struts (one at each side) and disconnect the upper part of the gas strut from the roof frame mechanism **(see illustrations)**.

5 Working around the rear of the convertible roof compartment, release the inner trim from the inside rear of the convertible roof **(see illustration)**.

6 Lower the convertible roof and undo the retaining bolts and remove the inner catches from inside the rear of the convertible roof

21.3a Release the trim (with roof up)...

21.3b ...lower roof and remove trim panel

21.4a Use a small screwdriver...

21.4b ...to release the securing clip...

21.4c ...then disengage the gas strut from the frame

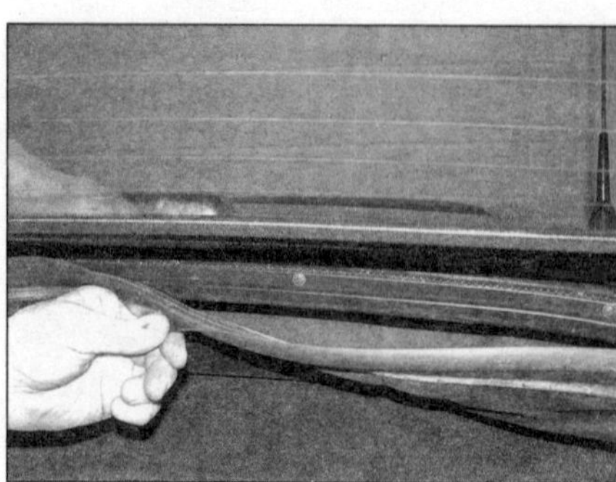

21.5 Release the trim from the convertible roof

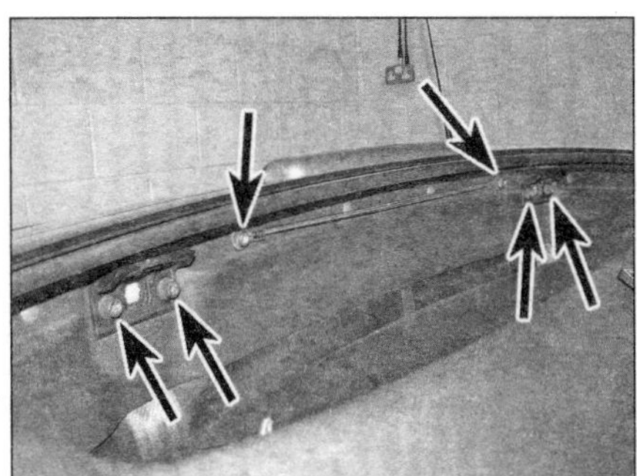
21.6a Undo the retaining bolts (arrowed)

21.6b Mark the position of the catches before removal

21.7a Release the retaining clips...

compartment. Also undo the two retaining screws and remove the elastic cord **(see illustrations)**. Mark the position of the catches on the rear panel before removing, to aid refitting.

7 Working around the inner edge of the convertible roof compartment, release the retaining clips and remove the trim panel from inside the compartment **(see illustrations)**.

8 Undo the six mounting bolts (three at each side) for the roof frame **(see illustration)**.

9 Working inside the left and right-hand sides of the convertible roof frame compartment, release the rubber covers and undo the four retaining screws (two at each side) from the roof frame mechanism **(see illustrations)**.

10 With the frame mounting point disconnected remove the rubber covers from the convertible roof mechanism **(see illustrations)**.

21.7b ...and remove the inner trim panel

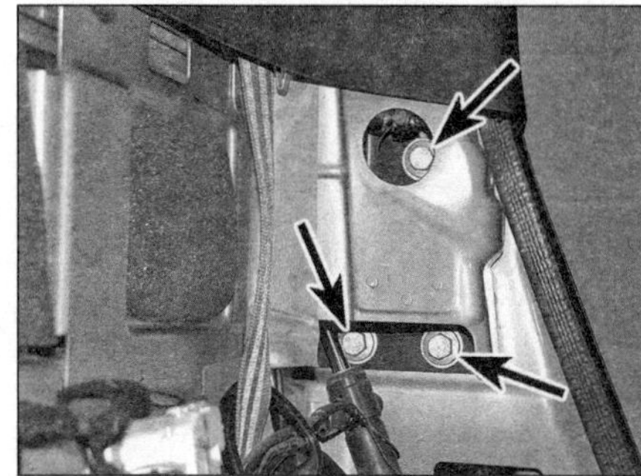
21.8 Roof frame mounting bolts (arrowed)

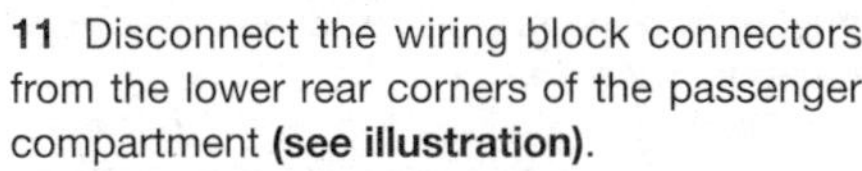
11 Disconnect the wiring block connectors from the lower rear corners of the passenger compartment **(see illustration)**.

12 With the aid of an assistant, remove the convertible roof assembly from the rear of the vehicle **(see illustration)**. One side of the convertible roof assembly should be pushed down as far as it will go into one side of the

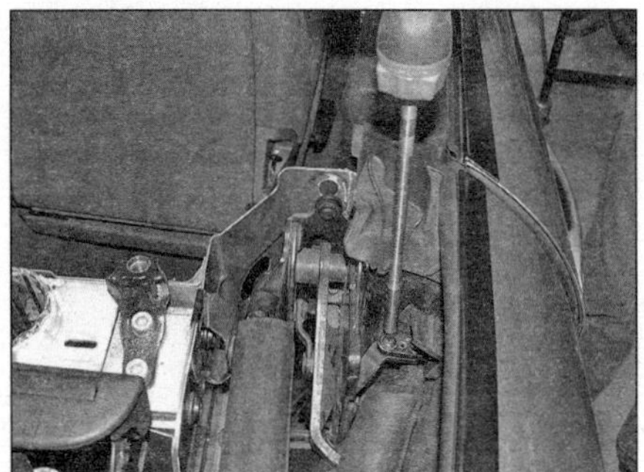
21.9a Undo the right-hand side retaining screws...

21.9b ...and left-hand side retaining screws (arrowed)

21.10a Release the frame mounting point...

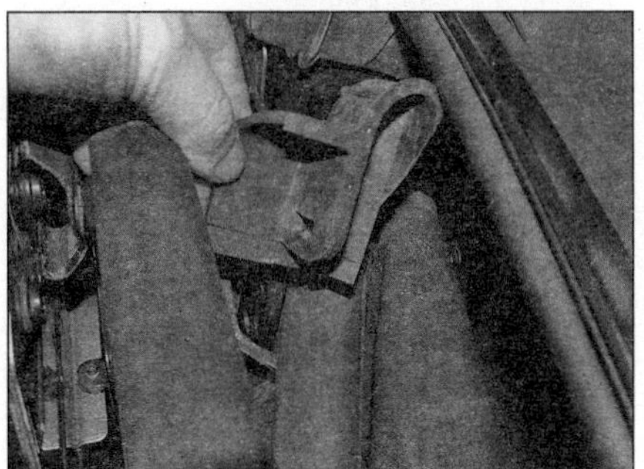
21.10b ...and remove the rubber covers

21.11 Disconnect the wiring block connector (one side shown)

21.12 Removing the roof assembly

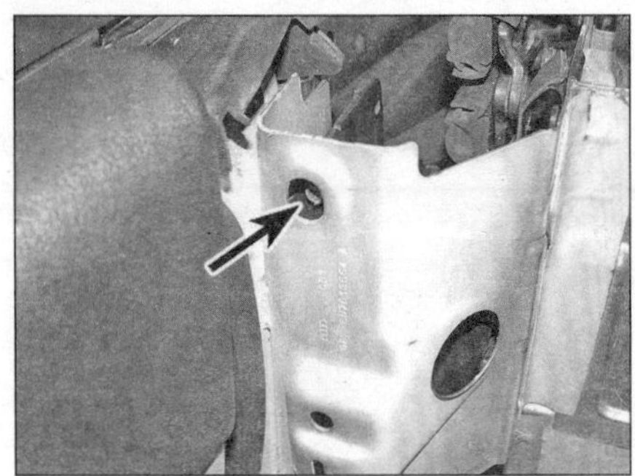

21.13a Upper adjustment grub screw (arrowed)

21.13b Lower adjustment grub screw (one arrowed)

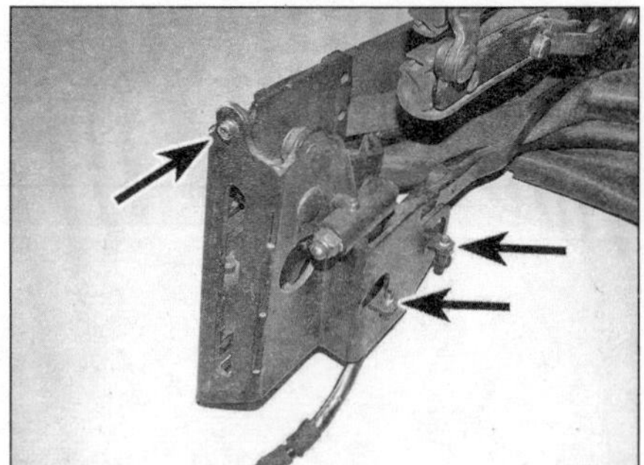

21.13c Adjustment grub screws (arrowed) – roof frame removed

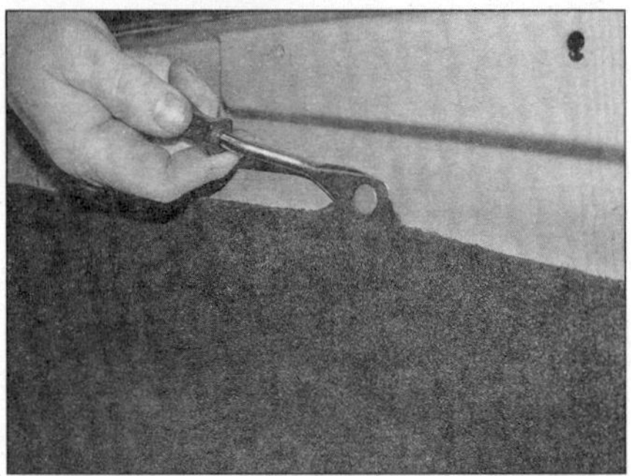

21.15a Release the retaining clips...

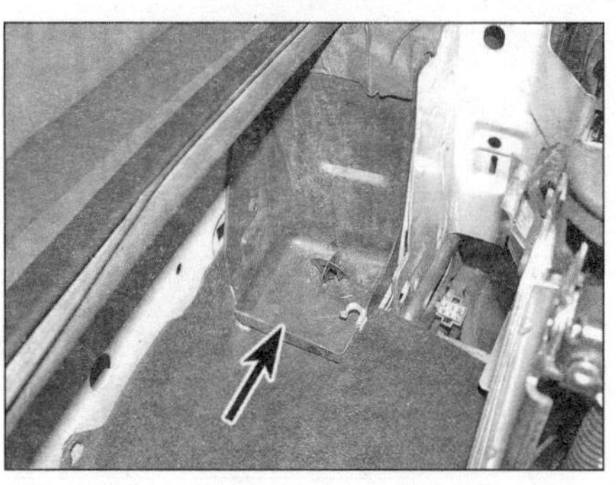

21.15b ...unclip from the water drip trays (arrowed)...

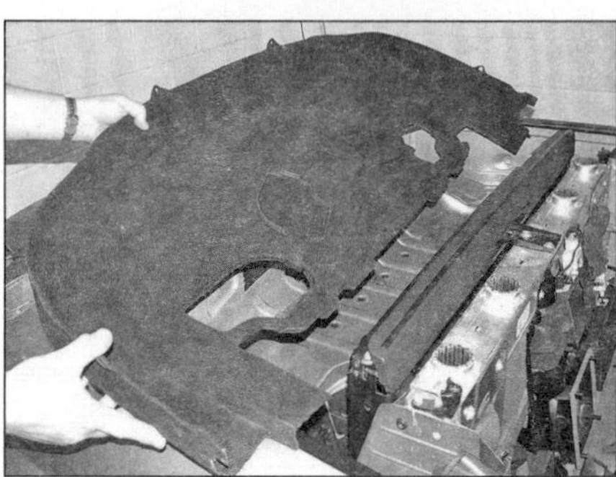

21.15c ...and remove the carpet trim panel

rear compartment, to allow for the other side to be removed. When the one side has been lifted out from the rear compartment then the complete assembly can be withdrawn.

Caution: When removing the convertible roof assembly, take care not to damage any of the paintwork/bodywork as it is being withdrawn.

13 Refitting is a reversal of removal. Making sure any alignment marks made on removal are aligned. Check the operation of the convertible roof and adjust accordingly **(see illustrations)**.

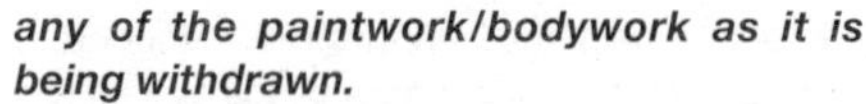

21.16 Disconnect the motor wiring connector (arrowed)

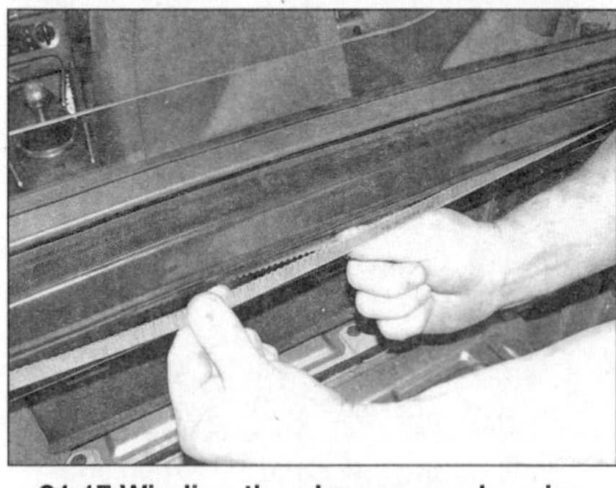

21.17 Winding the glass upwards using drive belt

Glass wind deflector assembly

14 Remove the convertible roof assembly first, as described previously in this section (see paragraphs 1 to 13).

15 Working around the inside of the convertible roof compartment, release the retaining clips and remove the carpet trim panel from the lower part of the compartment, releasing the ends of the carpet from the water drip trays **(see illustrations)**.

16 Disconnect the wiring connector from the glass wind deflector motor **(see illustration)**.

17 Wind the glass wind deflector up, by pulling on the drive belt under the top edge of the assembly **(see illustration)**.

18 Undo the six mounting bolts, two at the front upper edge, two at the right-hand rear and two at the left-hand rear of the assembly. With the aid of an assistant lift the glass wind deflector assembly out from the rear of the vehicle **(see illustrations)**.

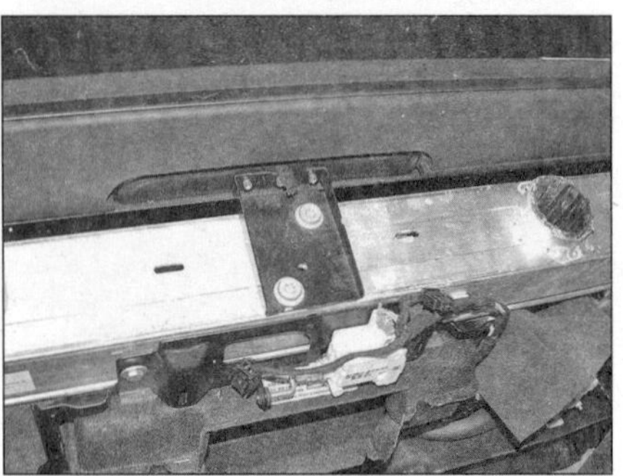

21.18a Undo the upper bolts...

21.18b ...the right-hand side bolts...

21.18c ...and the left-hand side bolts

19 Refitting is a reversal of removal. Check the operation of the glass wind deflector and clean out the water drip trays at each corner of the rear compartment **(see illustration)**.

22 Body exterior fittings – removal and refitting

Wheel arch liners and body under-panels

1 The various plastic covers fitted to the underside of the vehicle are secured in position by a mixture of screws, nuts and retaining clips and removal will be fairly obvious on inspection. Work methodically around the panel removing its retaining screws and releasing its retaining clips until the panel is free and can be removed from the underside of the vehicle. Most clips used on the vehicle are simply prised out of position. Remove the wheels to ease the removal of the wheel arch liners.

2 On refitting, renew any retaining clips that may have been broken on removal, and ensure that the panel is securely retained by all the relevant clips and screws.

Body trim strips and badges

3 The various body trim strips and badges are held in position with a special adhesive tape and locating lugs. Removal requires the trim/badge to be heated, to soften the adhesive, and then carefully lifted away from the surface. Due to the high risk of damage to the vehicle's paintwork during this operation, it is recommended that this task should be entrusted to an Audi dealer.

23 Seats – removal and refitting

Note: *Refer to the warnings in Chapter 12 Section 24, if side airbags are fitted to the vehicle. Before disconnecting the battery, refer to* Disconnecting the battery *at the rear of this manual.*

21.19 Cleaning out the water drain tube with a piece of wire

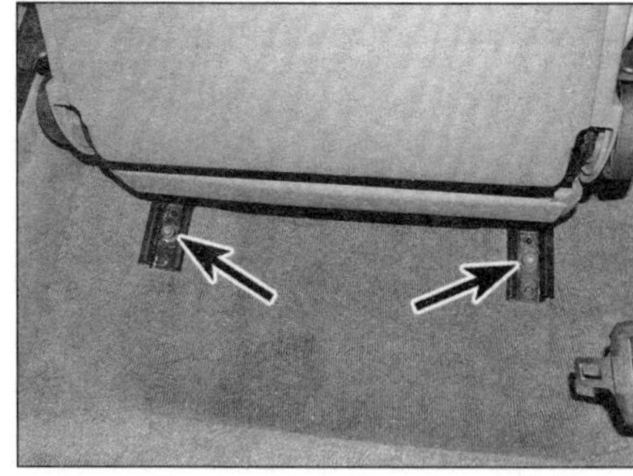

23.2 Undo the mounting bolts (arrowed)

Removal

Front seats

Note: *The amount of wiring connectors under the seat may vary depending on the vehicle specification.*

1 Disconnect the battery negative terminal.

2 Slide the seat forwards and remove the two bolts from the rear of the seat guide rails **(see illustration)**.

3 Slide the seat backwards, and unclip the plastic caps from the seat runner guide rails. Remove the two bolts from the front of the seat guide rails **(see illustrations)**.

4 Tilt the seat backwards and disconnect the wiring connectors from under the front of the seat **(see illustrations)**. Unclip the wiring loom from the underside of the seat and carefully remove it from the vehicle. Take care not to damage the vehicle paintwork, as the seat is withdrawn out through the door aperture.

Rear seat assembly – Coupe models

5 Pull the front of the rear seat cushion upwards at the front at each side. This will release the wire clip on the underside of the seat from the plastic peg in the floor panel. Slide the seat cushion forwards, disengaging

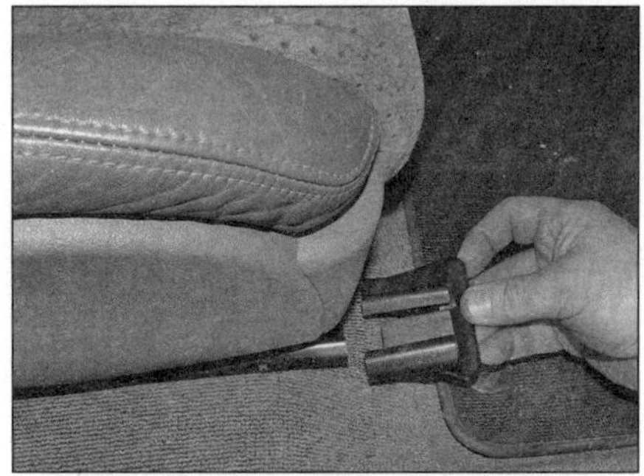

23.3a Remove the inner rail trim...

23.3b ...and the outer rail trim...

23.3c ...and remove the mounting bolts (arrowed)

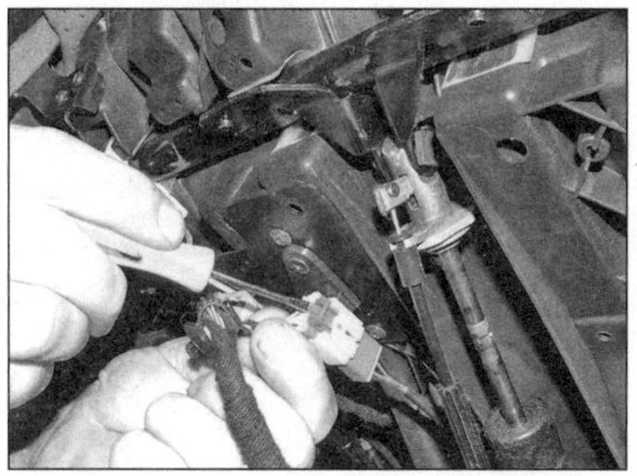

23.4a Release the locking clips...

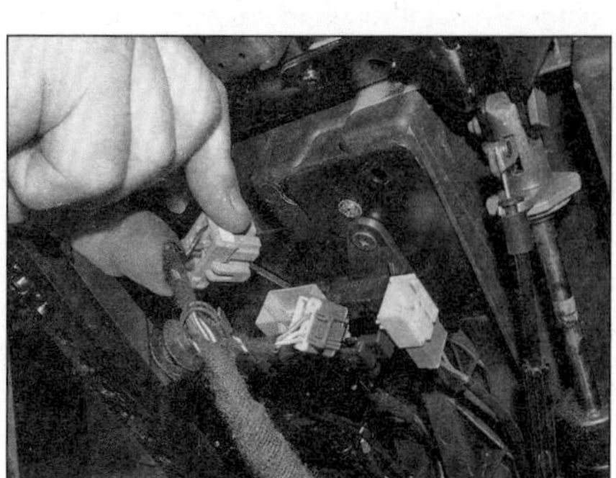

23.4b ...and disconnect the wiring connectors

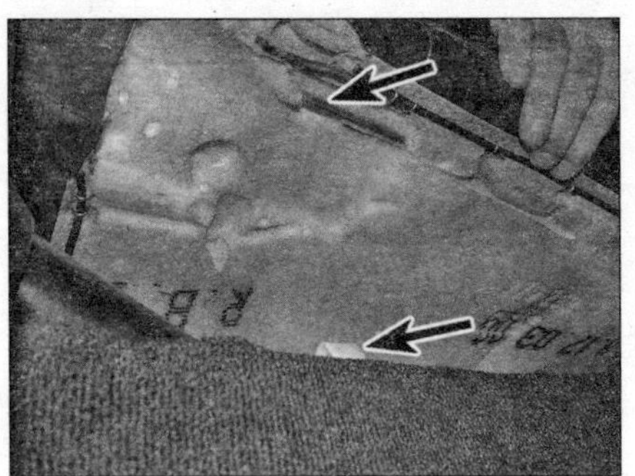
23.5a Release the seat securing clips (arrowed)

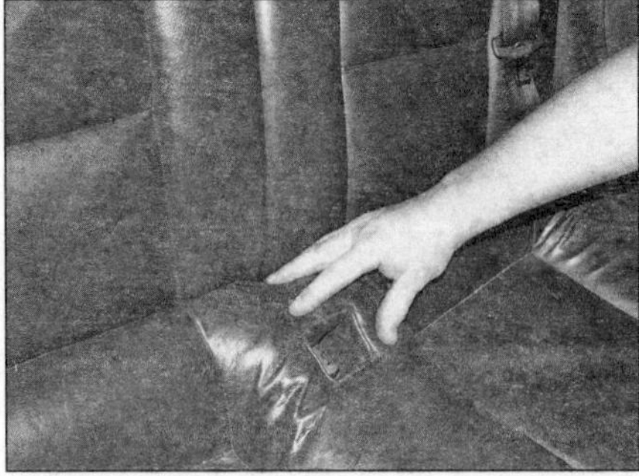
23.5b Release the seat belt stalks from the seat cushion

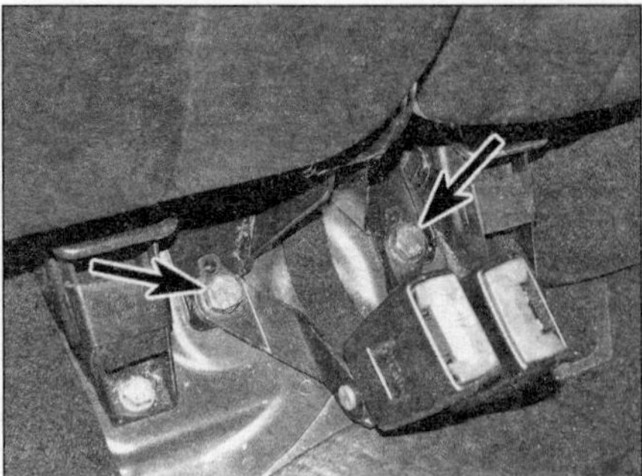
23.6a Undo the mounting bolts (arrowed)...

23.6b ...and remove the seat belt stalks

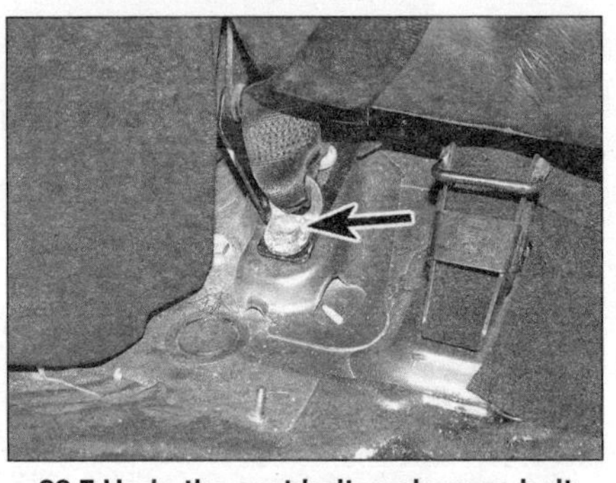
23.7 Undo the seat belt anchorage bolt (arrowed)

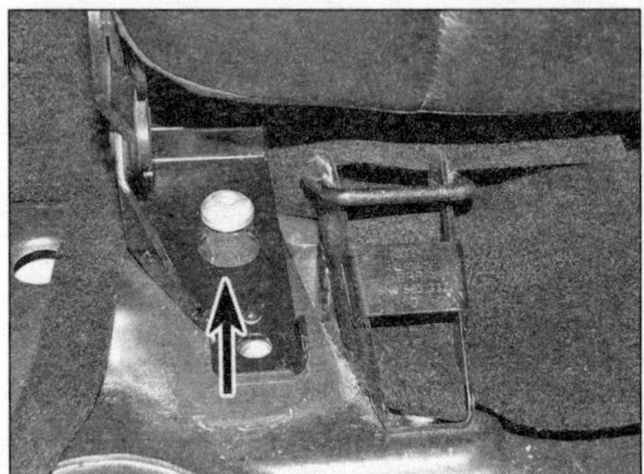
23.8 Elongated hole (arrowed) to remove seat bracket from bolt

the seat belt stalks as it is removed **(see illustrations)**.

6 With the seat cushion removed, undo the retaining bolts and remove the seat belt stalks from the centre seat mounting brackets **(see illustrations)**.

7 Undo the retaining bolts and remove the seat belt anchorage bracket from the outer seat mounting brackets **(see illustration)**.

8 The rear bolts on the mounting brackets can now be slackened **(see illustration)**. Do not remove the bolts completely, the seat bracket have elongated holes, so the bracket can be removed from the bolts.

9 Release the upper seat catch and then move the lower seat brackets rearwards to disengage from the mounting bolts. The rear seat backs can then be removed from the passenger compartment. Take care not to damage the vehicle paintwork, as the seat is withdrawn out through the door aperture.

Refitting

Front seats

10 Before refitting examine the seat guide rails for signs of wear or damage and renew if necessary. Refitting is a reverse of the removal procedure. Ensure that the seat adjustment lever engages correctly with the centre guide rail when the seat has been refitted and the seat bolts are tightened to their specified torque.

Rear seat assembly – Coupe models

11 Refitting is the reverse of removal, making sure the seat backs are clipped securely in position and the seat bolts are tightened securely.

24 Front seat belt tensioning mechanism – general information

1 Most models covered in this manual are fitted with a front seat belt tensioner system. The system is designed to instantaneously take up any slack in the seat belt in the case of a sudden frontal impact, therefore reducing the possibility of injury to the front seat occupants. Each front seat is fitted with its system, the tensioner being situated behind the sill trim panel.

2 The seat belt tensioner is triggered by a frontal impact above a predetermined force. Lesser impacts, including impacts from behind, will not trigger the system.

3 When the system is triggered, the explosive gas in the tensioner mechanism retracts and locks the seat belt through a cable which acts on the inertia reel. This prevents the seat belt moving and keeps the occupant firmly in position in the seat. Once the tensioner has been triggered, the seat belt will be permanently locked and the assembly must be renewed.

4 There is a risk of injury if the system is triggered inadvertently when working on the vehicle, and it is therefore strongly recommended that any work involving the seat belt tensioner system is entrusted to an Audi dealer. Note the following warnings before contemplating any work on the front seat belts.

Warning: Do not expose the tensioner mechanism to temperatures in excess of 100°C (212°F).

- ***If the tensioner mechanism is dropped, it must be renewed, even it has suffered no apparent damage.***
- ***Do not allow any solvents to come into contact with the tensioner mechanism.***
- ***Do not attempt to open the tensioner mechanism as it contains explosive gas.***
- ***Tensioners must be discharged before they are disposed of, but this task should be entrusted to an Audi dealer.***
- ***If the battery is to be disconnected, refer to* Disconnecting the battery *at the rear of this manual.***

25 Seat belt components – removal and refitting

Warning: On models equipped with seat belt tensioners refer to Section 24 before proceeding; under no circumstances should you attempt to separate the tensioner assembly from the inertia reel.

Front seat belt removal

Roadster (convertible) models

Note: *Before disconnecting the battery, refer to* Disconnecting the battery *at the rear of this manual.*

1 Disconnect the battery negative lead, then

25.1 Remove rear trim panel – drivers side shown

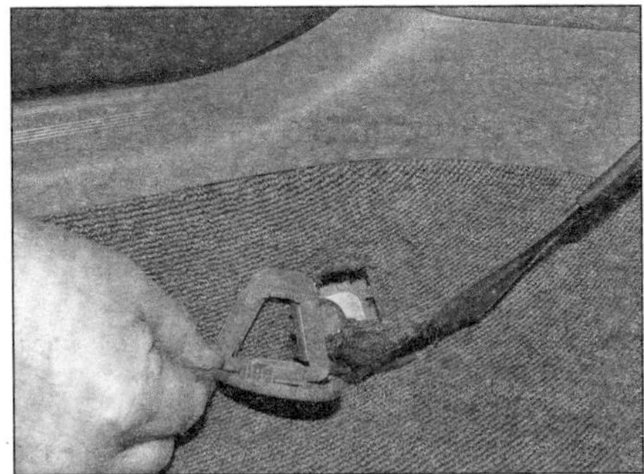
25.2a Unclip the plastic trim...

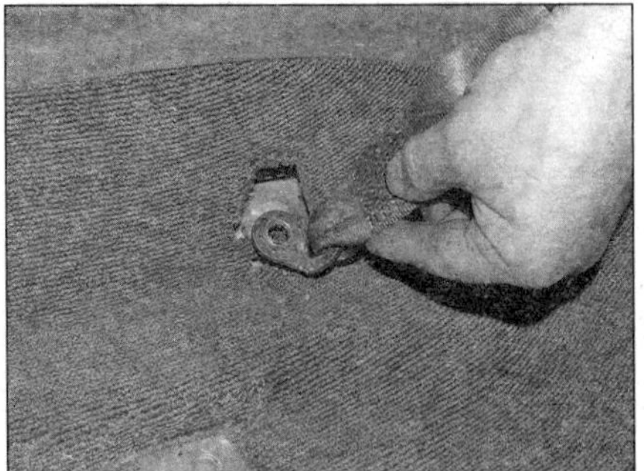
25.2b ...and remove the seat belt lower anchorage

tilt the seat back forwards and remove the trim panel from behind the seat **(see illustration)**, with reference to Section 26.

2 Unclip the plastic trim and then slacken and remove the seat belt lower mounting bolt and free the seat belt from its lower anchorage **(see illustrations)**.

3 Undo the retaining screws and remove the speaker from in front of the inertia reel seat belt assembly **(see illustration)**.

4 Unclip the cover on the upper seat belt mounting and remove the securing bolt **(see illustrations)**.

5 Slide the collars upwards for the roll bars, then slide the upper plastic trim panel upwards, so that the seat belt can be withdrawn **(see illustrations)**.

6 On vehicles with side airbags, disconnect the wiring connector from the seat belt tensioner reel **(see illustration)**.

7 Slacken and remove the inertia reel mounting bolt and remove the seat belt assembly from the vehicle **(see illustration)**. To remove the inertia reel from the vehicle body, lift it up slightly and move it backwards, to release the locating peg, just above the mounting bolt.

Coupe models

8 Remove the relevant rear seat as described in Section 23.

9 With the rear seat removed, slacken and

25.3 Speaker retaining screws (arrowed)

25.4a Unclip the trim cover...

25.4b ...and remove the upper mounting bolt

25.5a Slide the collars upwards...

25.5b ...then withdraw the seat belt through the trim panel

25.6 Disconnect the wiring connector (arrowed)

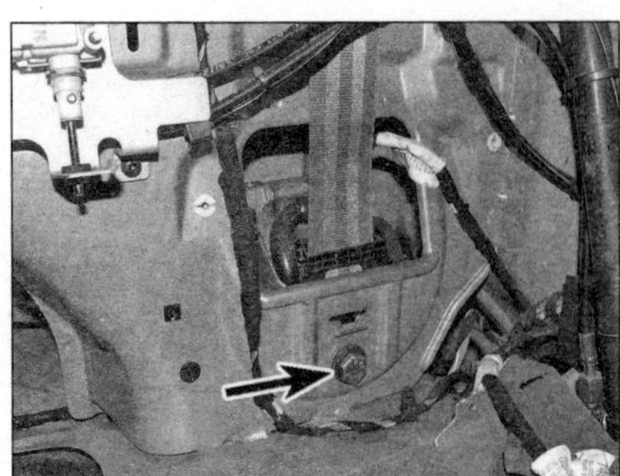
25.7 Inertia reel mounting bolt (arrowed)

25.9a Remove the seat catch post...

25.9b ...and unclip the side trim panel

remove the rear seat catch post and unclip the rear inner side trim panel **(see illustrations)**.

10 Undo the four mounting bolts and two nuts and remove the B-pillar brace from over the inertia reel seat belt **(see illustrations)**.

11 Unclip the plastic trim and then slacken and remove the seat belt lower mounting bolt and free the seat belt from its lower anchorage **(see illustrations 25.2a and 25.2b)**.

12 Undo the two retaining bolts and remove the belt guide from the top of the side body panel **(see illustration)**.

13 On vehicles with side airbags, disconnect the wiring connector from the seat belt tensioner reel **(see illustration)**.

14 Slacken and remove the inertia reel mounting bolt and remove the seat belt assembly from the vehicle **(see illustration)**.

Front seat belt stalk removal

15 Remove the front seat assembly as

25.10a Undo the three bolts (arrowed)...

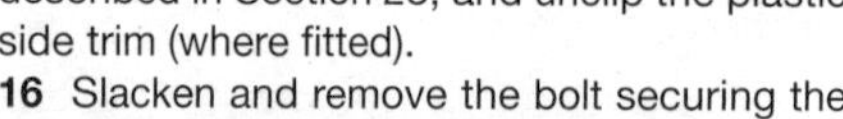
described in Section 23, and unclip the plastic side trim (where fitted).

16 Slacken and remove the bolt securing the stalk to the seat, and remove the stalk.

Rear seat side belt removal – Coupe models

17 Remove the rear seat assembly as described in Section 23.

18 The rear inertia seat belts can only be removed from the seat back if the seat cover and padding is removed first. The seat belt reel can then be unbolted from the seat frame.

Rear seat belt stalk removal – Coupe models

19 Remove the rear seat cushion, as described in Section 23.

20 Slacken and remove the bolts securing the seat belt stalk/buckle assembly to the

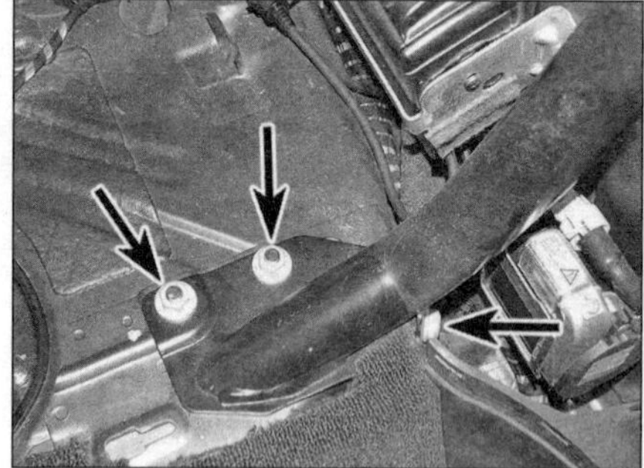
25.10b ...and the two nuts and one bolt (arrowed)

floor, and remove it from the vehicle **(see illustrations 23.6a and 23.6b)**.

Refitting

21 Refitting is a reversal of the removal procedure, ensuring that all the seat belt units are located correctly and mounting bolts are securely tightened to their specified torque. Check all the trim panels are securely retained by all the relevant retaining clips.

26 Interior trim – removal and refitting

Interior trim panels

1 The interior trim panels are secured using either screws or various types of trim fasteners, usually studs or clips.

2 Check that there are no other panels overlapping the one to be removed; usually there is a sequence that has to be followed, and this will only become obvious on close inspection.

3 Remove all obvious fasteners, such as screws. If the panel will not come free, it is held by hidden clips or fasteners. These are usually situated around the edge of the panel and can be prised up to release them; note, however that they can break quite easily so new ones should be available. The best way of releasing such clips, without the correct type of tool, is to use a large flat-bladed screwdriver. Note in many cases that the adjacent sealing strip must be prised back to release a panel.

4 When removing a panel, never use excessive force or the panel may be damaged; always check carefully that all fasteners or other relevant components have been removed or released before attempting to withdraw a panel.

5 Refitting is the reverse of the removal procedure; secure the fasteners by pressing them firmly into place and ensure that all disturbed components are correctly secured to prevent rattles.

Glovebox

6 Working at the left-hand end of the facia, remove the end trim panel and remove the

25.12 Remove the seat belt guide from the body panel

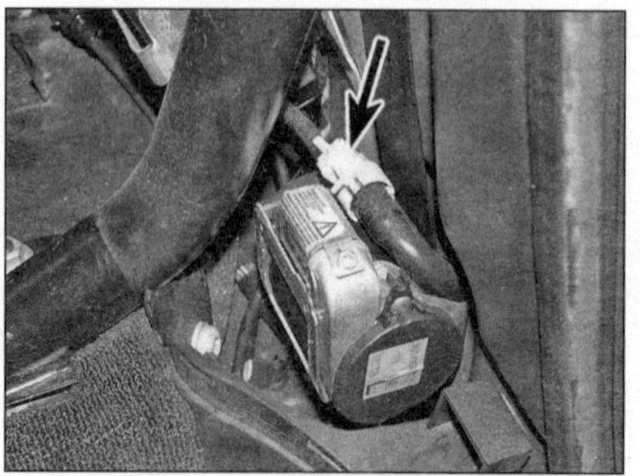
25.13 Disconnect the wiring connector (arrowed)

25.14 Inertia reel mounting bolt (arrowed)

26.6a Remove the end trim cover...

26.6b ...and remove the screws (arrowed)

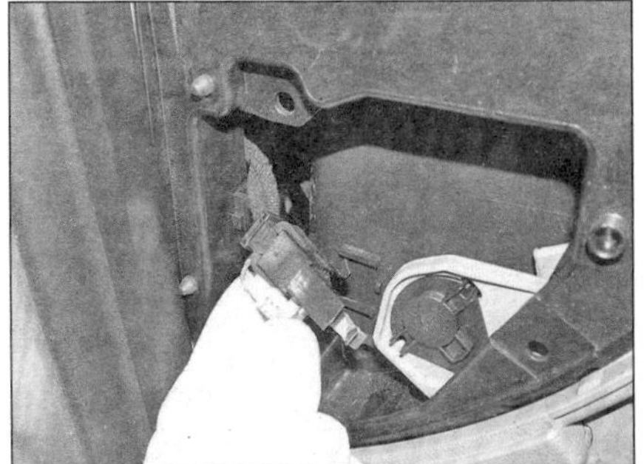

26.7 Disconnect the glove box light wiring connector

26.8 Remove the retaining screws (arrowed)

26.9a Disconnect the light wiring connector...

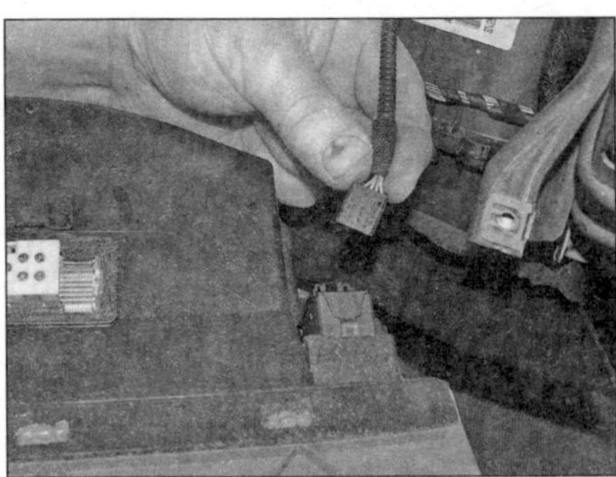

26.9b ...and the airbag switch wiring connector

three retaining screws from the end of the glovebox **(see illustrations)**.

7 Disconnect the wiring plug for the glovebox light from inside the end of the facia **(see illustration)**.

8 Open up the glovebox lid then slacken and remove the three upper retaining screws and one to the lower right-hand front of the glovebox **(see illustration)**.

9 Slide the glovebox out of position, disconnecting the wiring connectors from the glovebox illumination light and passenger airbag switch, as they become accessible **(see illustrations)**.

10 If required, the glovebox lock can be removed by carefully unclipping the lock assembly from the glovebox lid. With the lock assembly removed, retrieve the spring from the glovebox lid, and put to one side for refitting. Insert the key into the lock and then release the securing clips at the rear and withdraw the lock from the housing. Take care, if the key is removed from the lock, the tumblers inside the lock will fall out with there springs **(see illustrations)**.

11 Refitting is the reverse of removal.

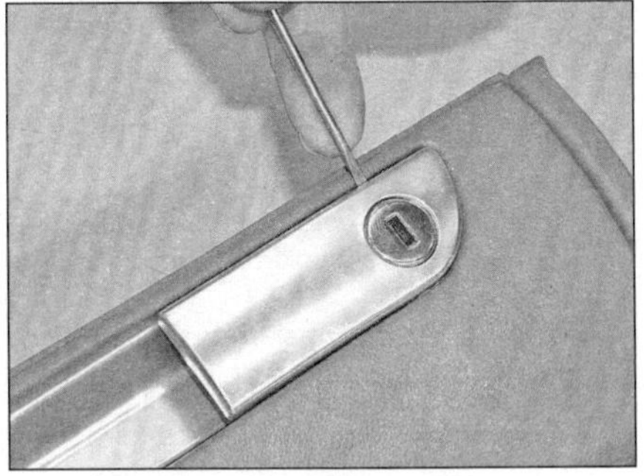

26.10a Carefully prise...

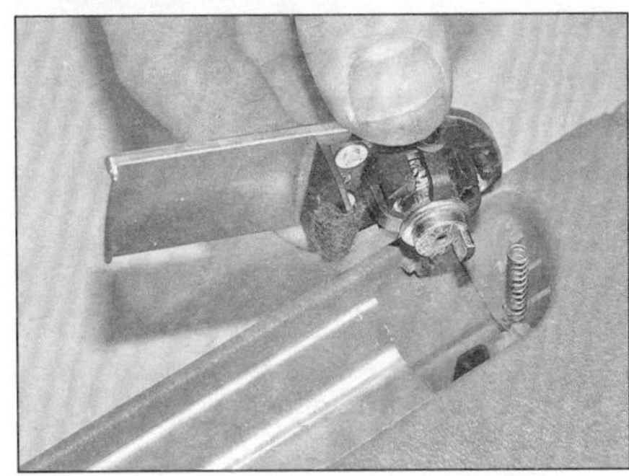

26.10b ...the lock from the glovebox lid...

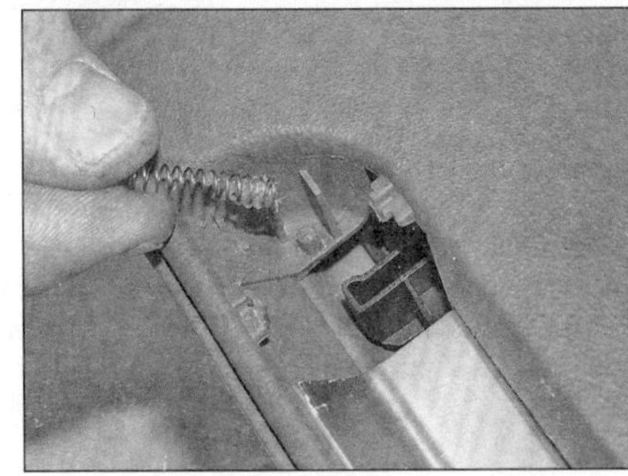

26.10c ...and retrieve the spring

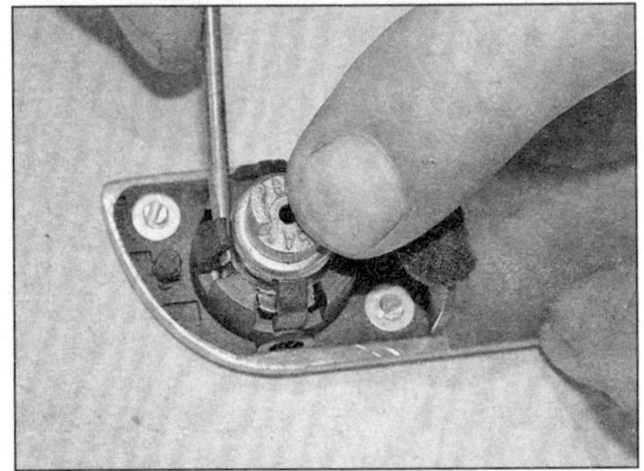

26.10d Unclip the securing clips...

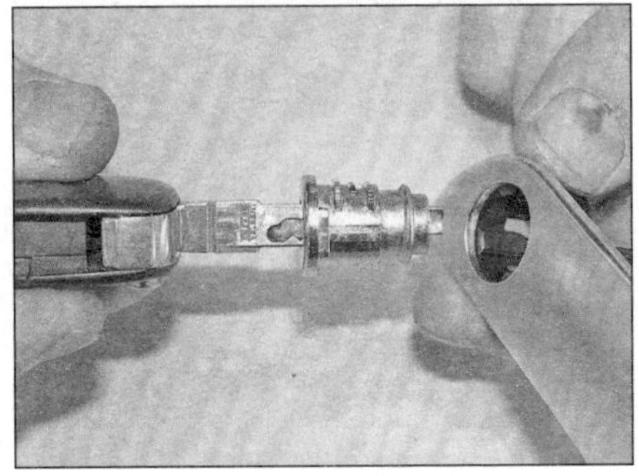

26.10e ...and withdraw the lock...

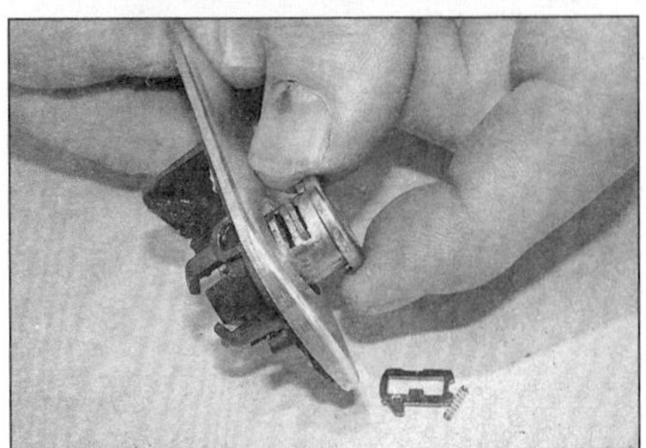

26.10f ...taking care not to lose the tumblers and springs

26.18a Unclip the speaker grille...

26.18b ...and undo the four retaining screws

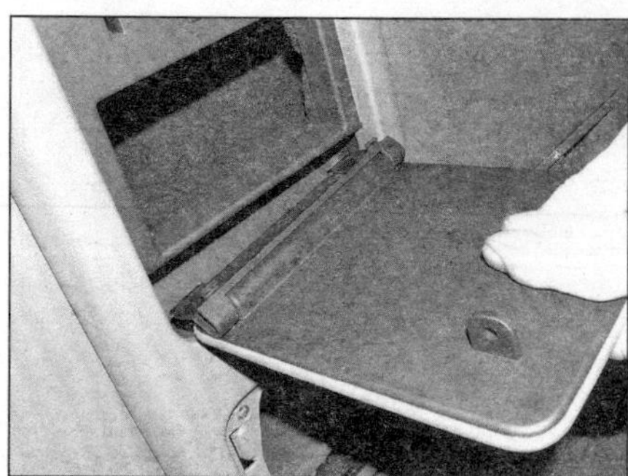
26.19 Pull the compartment door to release the hinge

Carpets

12 The passenger compartment floor carpet is in one piece and is secured at its edges by screws or clips, usually the same fasteners used to secure the various adjoining trim panels.

13 Carpet removal and refitting is reasonably straightforward but very time-consuming because all adjoining trim panels must be removed first, as must components such as the seats, the centre console and seat belt lower anchorages.

Headlining

14 The headlining is clipped to the roof and can be withdrawn only once all fittings such as the grab handles, sun visors, sunroof (if fitted), and related upper trim panels have been removed and the door, tailgate and sunroof aperture sealing strips have been prised clear. To remove the sun visors and grab handles the plastic covers have to be unclipped first, to gain access to the securing screws.

15 Note that headlining removal requires considerable skill and experience if it is to be carried out without damage and is therefore best entrusted to an expert.

Interior mirror

16 Turn the mirror through approx. 90° anti-clockwise to remove from the mounted position on the windscreen. When refitting, place the mirror at approx. 90° to the mounted position; then turn clockwise until the locking clip locks into place to secure the mirror. On models fitted with rain sensor, unclip the trim around the stem of the mirror and disconnect the wiring connector.

Rear trim panels – Roadster 'convertible' models

17 Slide the two front seats as far forward as possible and tilt them forwards.

18 Unclip the speaker grille from the centre of the trim panels, and undo the four retaining screws **(see illustrations)**.

19 Open the upper central compartment door, hinge it downwards and pull it, to release the hinged part from the central trim panel **(see illustration)**.

20 Using a lever, release the fasteners and carefully unclip the centre trim panel from the rear panel **(see illustrations)**.

21 Remove the compartment access panel from the left-hand side rear panel, by releasing the fasteners and carefully unclip the trim from the rear panel **(see illustrations)**.

22 Carefully release the fasteners and unclip the right-hand side trim from the rear panel **(see illustration)**.

23 To remove the upper trim panels, from across the front of the rear wind deflector glass panel, First unclip the plastic cover, then

26.20a Carefully lever the panel...

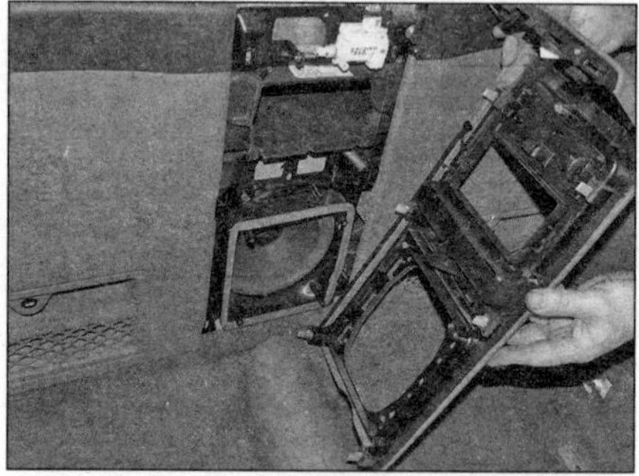
26.20b ...to release the fasteners on the trim panel

26.21a Remove the lower compartment door...

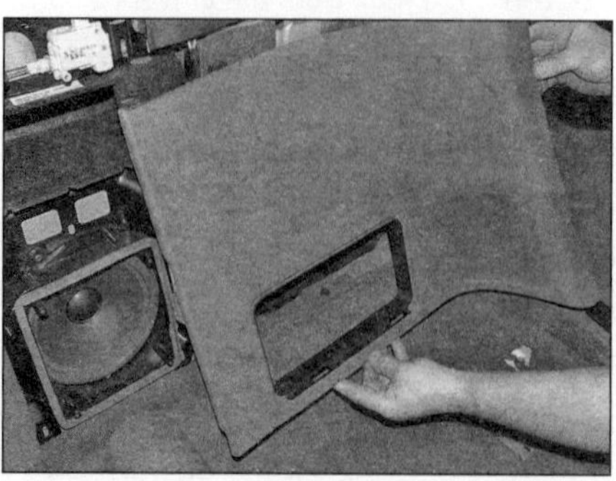
26.21b ...and carefully release the trim panel

26.22 Remove the right-hand trim panel

26.23a Unclip the plastic cover...

26.23b ...and undo the seat belt bolt

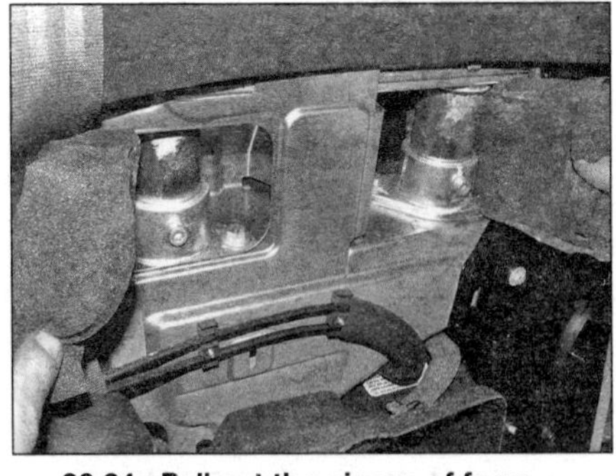
26.24a Pull out the pieces of foam...

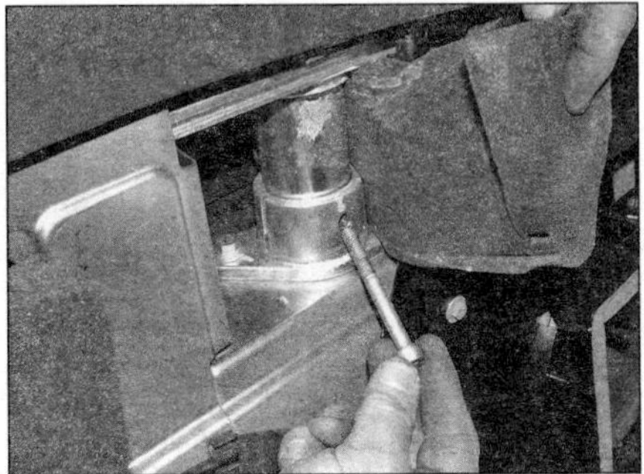
26.24b ...remove the securing bolts...

26.24c ...and withdraw the rollover bars

undo the retaining bolt for the seat belt upper anchorage point **(see illustrations)**.

24 Undo the retaining bolts and remove the rollover bars **(see illustrations)**. **Note:** *It will be necessary to have the convertible in the down position, to allow for the rollover bars to be withdrawn from the rear panel.*

25 Disconnect the wiring connectors at the upper centre of the trim panels, then unclip the trim panel and remove it from the rear panel **(see illustrations)**. To remove the trim panel completely from the vehicle, the seat belt lower anchorage point will need to be disconnected and the seat belt passed through the slot in the top of the trim panel.

Facia lower trim panels

26 See Section 28.

27 Centre console – removal and refitting

Removal

1 Unclip the trim panel from the rear of the centre console and undo the two retaining screws. On models with cup holder, remove the rubber mats, undo the retaining screws and remove the cup holder and trim **(see illustrations)**.

26.25a Disconnect the wiring connectors...

26.25b ...and remove the trim panel

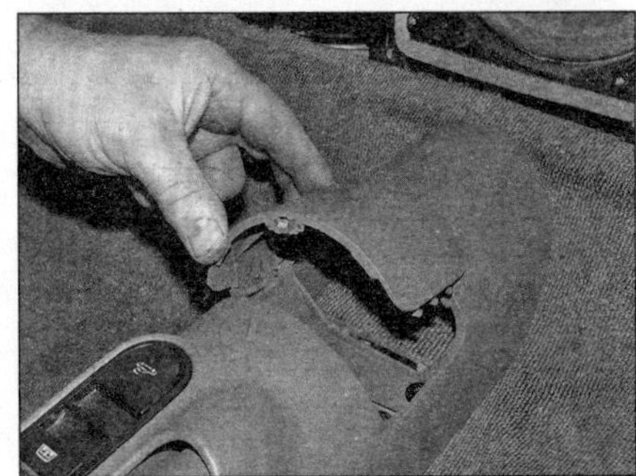
27.1a Unclip the trim cover...

27.1b ...where applicable, undo the retaining screws (arrowed)...

27.1c ...and remove the cup holder (where fitted)

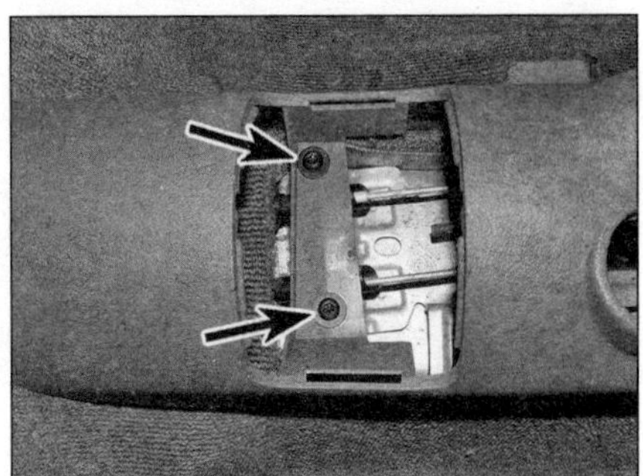
27.1d Remove the two retaining screws (arrowed)

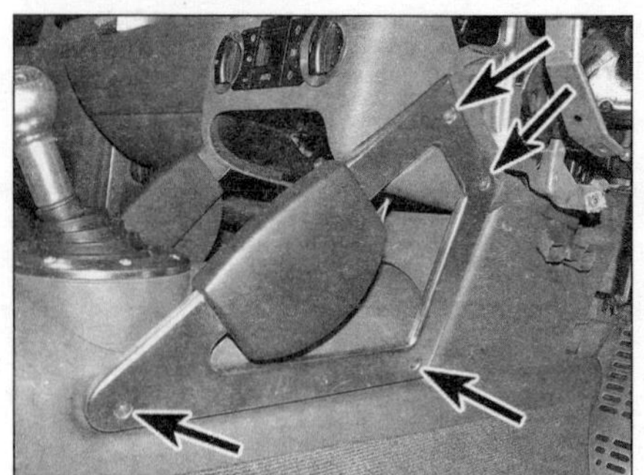
27.2a Undo the retaining bolts...

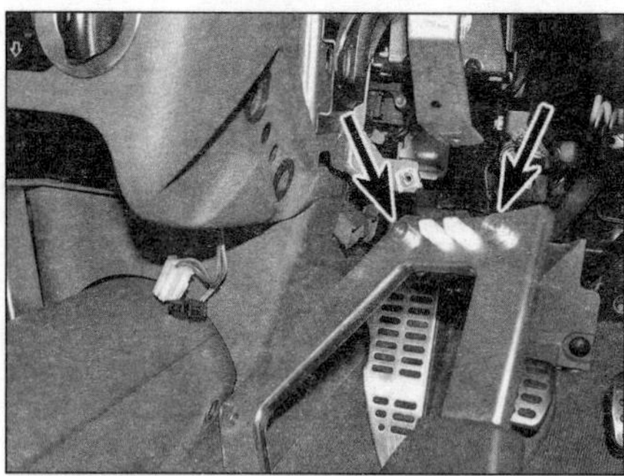
27.2b Check the spacers (arrowed)

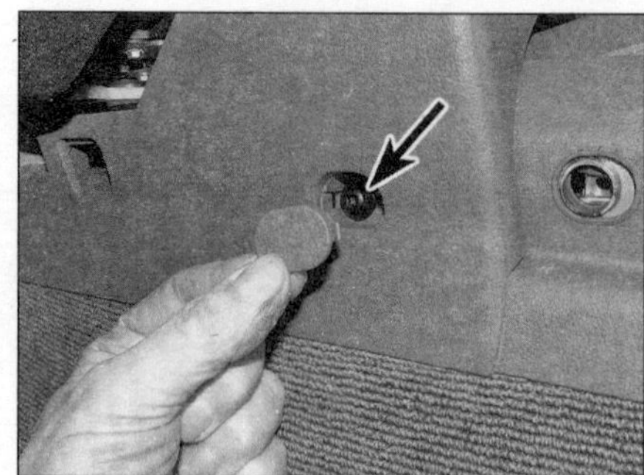
27.3a Undo the screw (arrowed) on the left-hand side...

27.3b ...and the screw (arrowed) on the right-hand side...

27.3c ...then withdraw the vent trims from under the facia

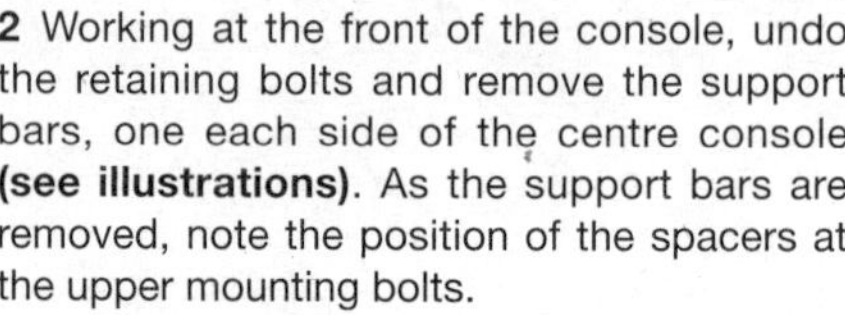
2 Working at the front of the console, undo the retaining bolts and remove the support bars, one each side of the centre console **(see illustrations)**. As the support bars are removed, note the position of the spacers at the upper mounting bolts.

3 Remove the plastic caps and remove the retaining screws (one each side) from the front vent trim panels. With the screws removed, withdraw the trim panels from each side of the front console and from under the facia panel **(see illustrations)**.

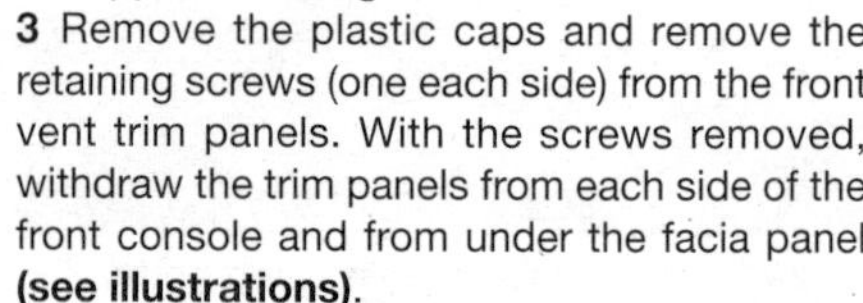
4 With the handbrake in the raised position, unclip the trim panel from the top of the console **(see illustration)**.

5 Reaching inside the rear of the console, push the switch panel upwards and out from the centre console **(see illustration)**. Disconnect the wiring connectors and remove the switch panel from the console.

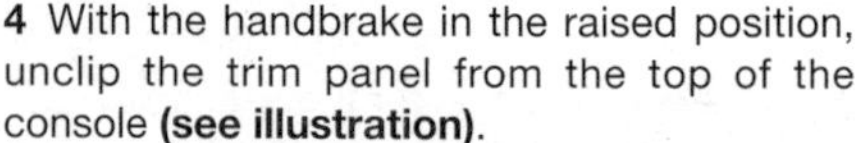
6 At the front of the console, carefully unclip the trim frame from over the console, then disconnect the airbag warning lamp from the trim as it is removed **(see illustrations)**.

7 Open the compartment at the front of the centre console and unclip the switch panel, then disconnect the wiring connectors and remove **(see illustration)**. Close the compartment, once the switch panel has been removed.

8 Pull the centre console off upwards at the rear from over the handbrake and gear lever,

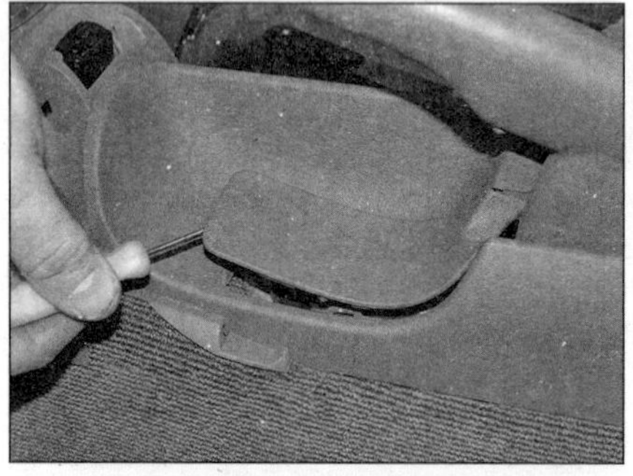
27.4 Unclip the trim panel

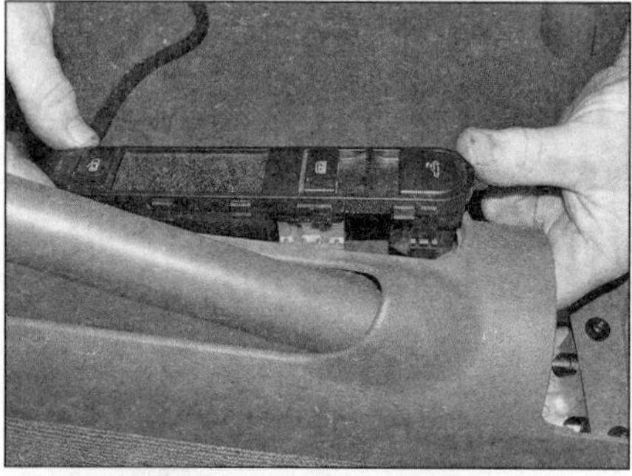
27.5 Remove the switch panel

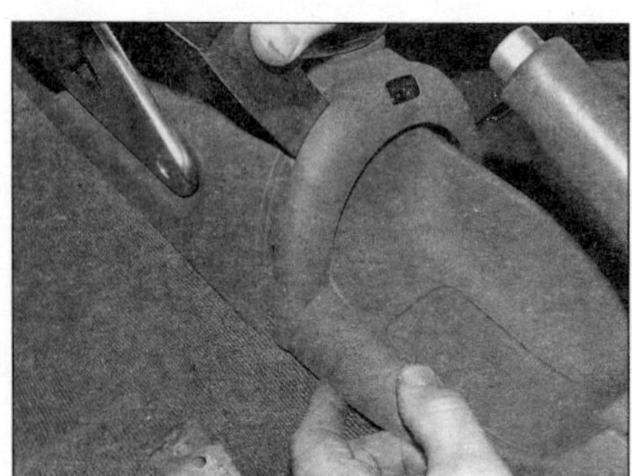
27.6a Remove the trim panel...

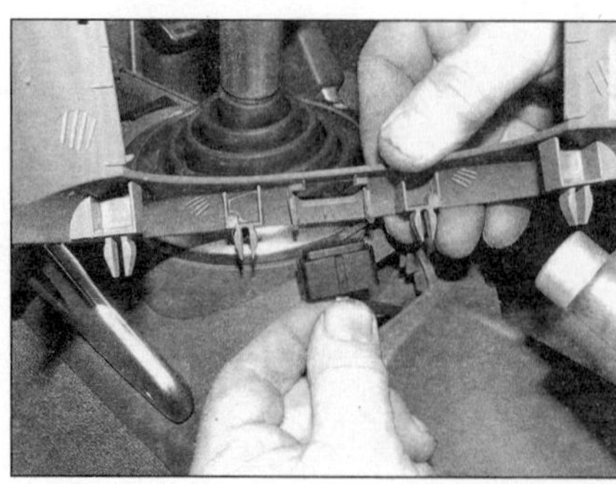
27.6b ...and disconnect the airbag warning light

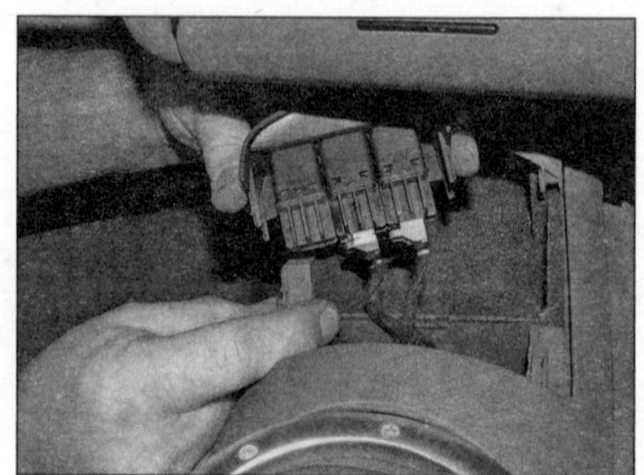
27.7 Remove the front switch panel

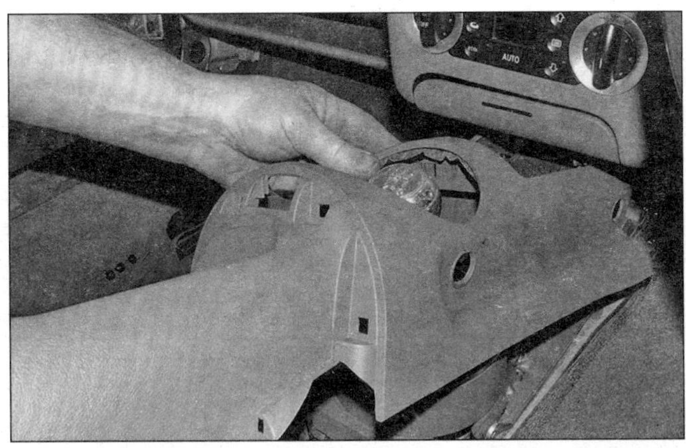

27.8a Lift the console up over the gear lever ...

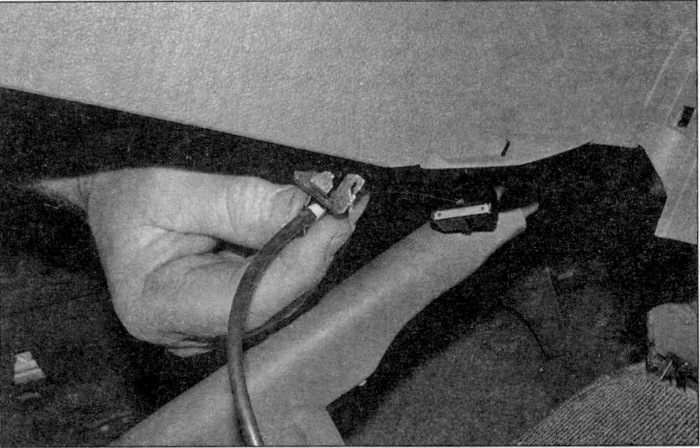

27.8b ... release the wiring clip from under the console

release the metal clip for the wiring from under the console as it is being removed **(see illustrations)**.

Refitting

9 Refitting is the reverse of removal making sure all fasteners are securely tightened.

28 Facia panel assembly – removal and refitting

1 Note : Refer to the warnings in Chapter 12 Section 24 for airbags.

Note: *Before disconnecting the battery, refer to* Disconnecting the battery *at the rear of this manual.*

Label each wiring connector as it is disconnected from its component. The labels will prove useful on refitting, when routing the wiring and feeding the wiring through the facia apertures.

Removal

2 Disconnect the battery negative terminal.

3 Remove the centre console, as described in Section 27.

4 Remove the steering wheel and steering column shrouds, as described in Chapter 10 Section 18.

5 Remove the instrument panel, as described in Chapter 12 Section 10. Then release the wiring loom cable ties from the facia panel **(see illustration)**.

6 Remove the glovebox, as described in Section 26.

7 Using a flat-bladed screwdriver, unclip the right-hand end panel from the facia panel, then undo the retaining screws from the end of the facia **(see illustrations)**.

8 Remove the bonnet release lever and footwell side trim panel, as described in Section 9.

9 Remove the lighting switch, as described in Chapter 12 Section 4.

10 Undo the three retaining screws and remove the lower trim panel from under the facia on the drivers side. As the trim panel is removed, disconnect the diagnostic plug from the lower right-hand corner of the panel **(see illustrations)**.

28.5 Release the cable ties (arrowed)

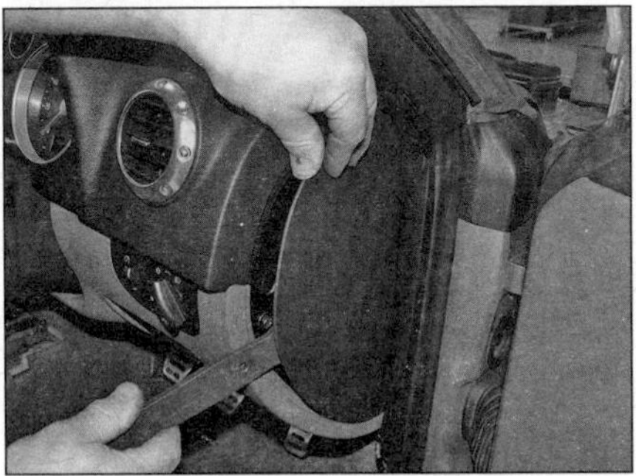

28.7a Unclip the facia end panel...

28.7b ...and undo the retaining screws (arrowed)

28.10a Undo the screws (arrowed)...

28.10b ...remove the trim panel...

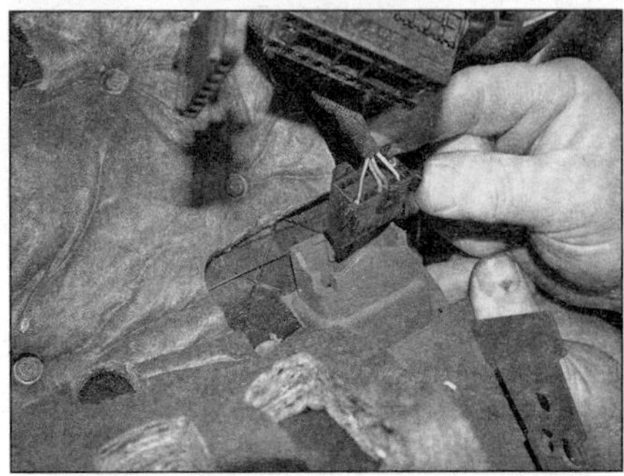

28.10c ...and release the diagnostic plug

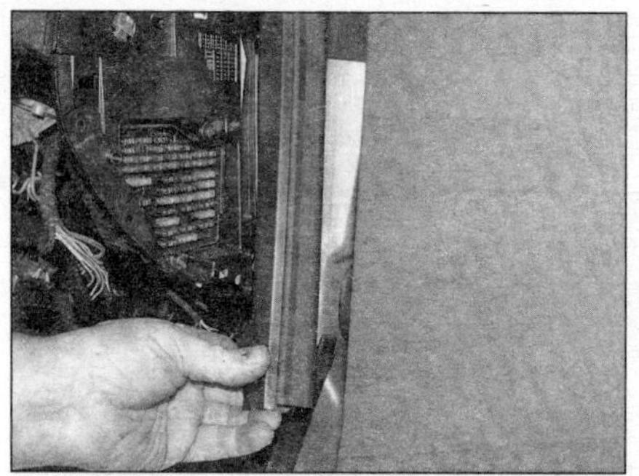
28.14a Pull back the door seals...

28.14b ...undo the screws (arrowed)...

28.14c ...and remove the right-hand panel

28.14d Undo the screws (arrowed)

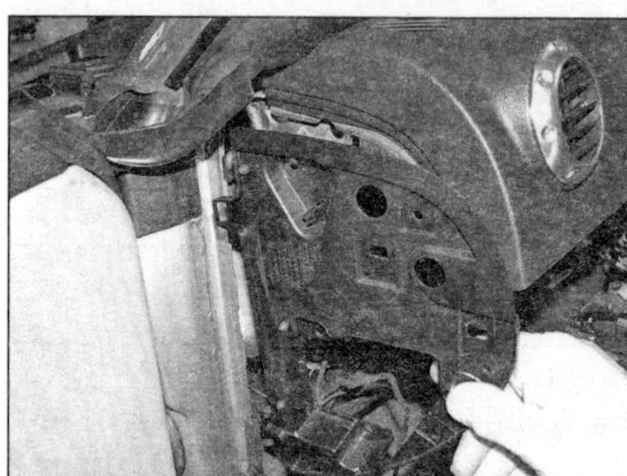
28.14e ...and remove the left-hand panel

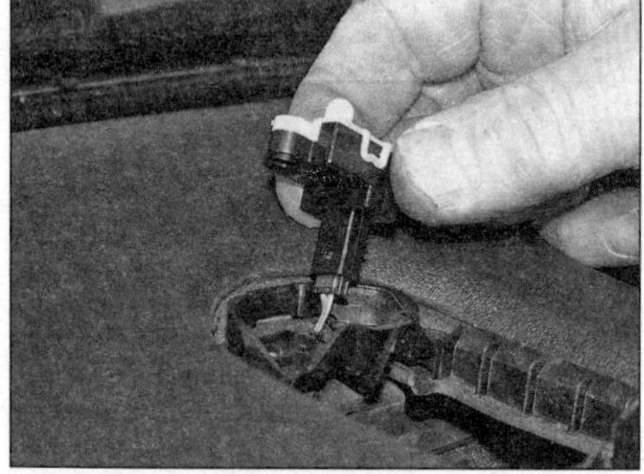
28.15a Remove the sunlight sensor...

28.15b ...and fasten a piece of wire to the connector – for refitting

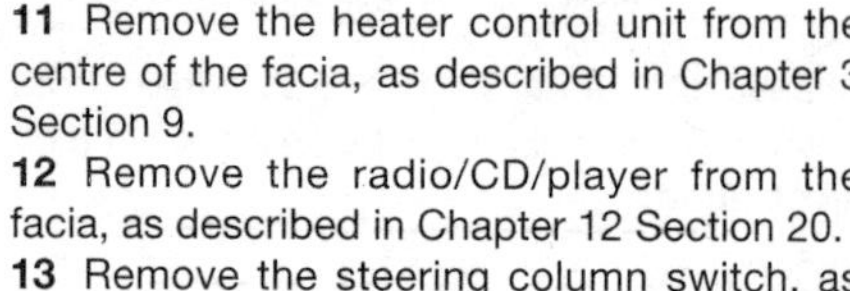

11 Remove the heater control unit from the centre of the facia, as described in Chapter 3 Section 9.

12 Remove the radio/CD/player from the facia, as described in Chapter 12 Section 20.

13 Remove the steering column switch, as described in Chapter 12 Section 4.

14 Working at each end of the facia, pull back the door seals, undo the retaining screws and remove the two panels (one each side) from the ends of the facia panel **(see illustrations)**. Note the panel on the driver's side of the facia, houses the fusebox.

15 Remove the two vent trims from the top of the facia panel, as described in Chapter 3 Section 10. Then undo the retaining screw and remove the sunlight sensor **(see illustrations)**. Disconnect the wiring connector and tie a piece of string (or similar) to the wiring, and pass it through the top of the facia, so as to aid refitting. Depending on model, also remove the speaker from the top of the facia, and follow the same procedure with the wiring.

16 Undo the retaining bolts and remove the mounting bracket from the facia cross member **(see illustration)**.

17 Disconnect the wiring connectors from the facia switches **(see illustration)**.

18 Undo the retaining screw and remove the footwell air vent, from the drivers side of the heater unit **(see illustration)**.

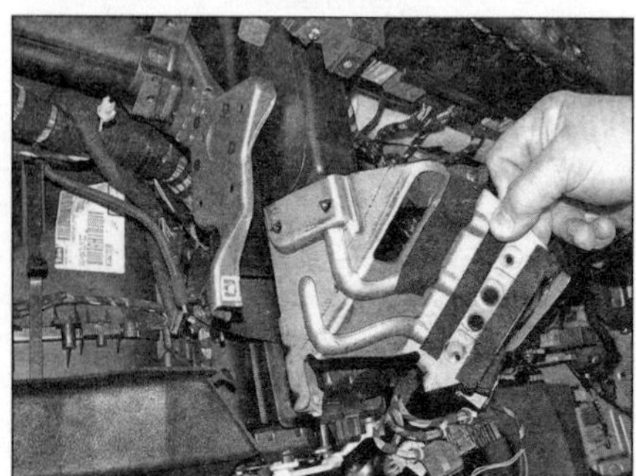
28.16 Remove the mounting bracket

28.17 Disconnect the wiring connecotrs

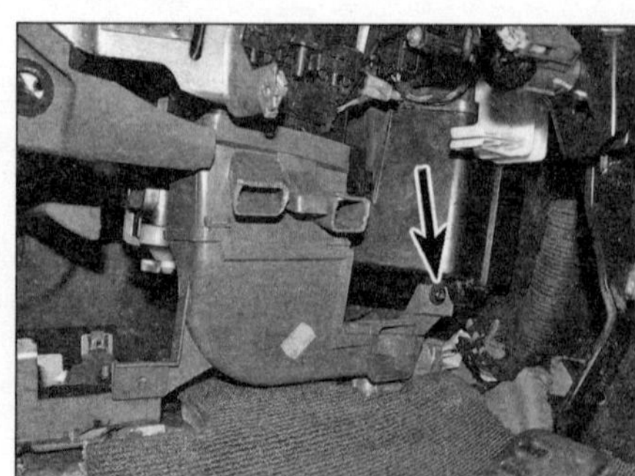
28.18 Undo the screw (arrowed) and remove air vent

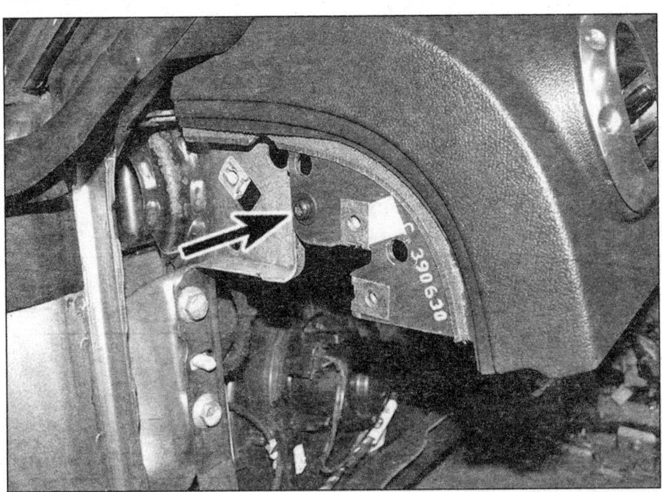
28.20a Undo the left-hand end screw (arrowed)...

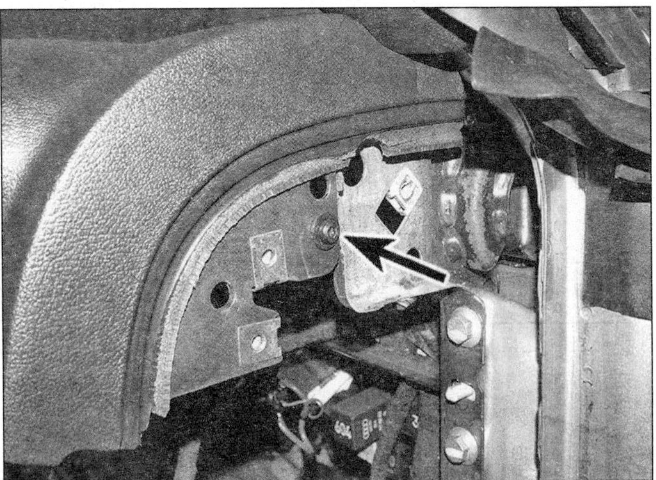
28.20b ...and the right-hand end screw (arrowed)

28.21a Undo the left-hand side screws (arrowed)...

28.21b ...and right-hand side screws (arrowed)

19 Remove the passenger side airbag, as described in Chapter 12 Section 25.

20 Working at each end of the facia, undo the retaining screws (one each side) from the ends of the facia panel **(see illustrations)**.

21 Undo the retaining screws from the under centre of the facia, at each end of the central switch panel **(see illustrations)**.

22 With the aid of an assistant, release the facia panel from the crossmember, by pulling it away from the locating clips on the bulkhead. Check around the facia trim panel to make sure that everything is disconnected. Then remove the facia panel out through the door aperture, taking care not to cause any damage to the paintwork or facia panel.

Refitting

23 Refitting is a reversal of the removal procedure, noting the following points:

a) Clip the facia back into position, making sure all the wiring connectors are fed through their respective apertures, then refit all the facia fasteners, and tighten them securely.

b) On completion, reconnect the battery and check that all the electrical components and switches function correctly.

c)

Chapter 12
Body electrical system

Contents

Degrees of difficulty

Easy, suitable for novice with little experience 	**Fairly easy,** suitable for beginner with some experience	**Fairly difficult,** suitable for competent DIY mechanic	**Difficult,** suitable for experienced DIY mechanic	**Very difficult,** suitable for expert DIY or professional 

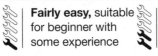

Specifications

System type	12 volt negative earth	
Fuses	See *Wiring diagrams*	
Bulbs	**Wattage**	**Type**
Direction indicators	21	Bayonet
Front foglight	55	H3 Halogen
Rear foglight (drivers side)	21	Bayonet
Headlight:		
Halogen:		
Main beam	55	H7 Halogen
Dipped beam	55	H1 Halogen
Gas discharge:		
Main beam	55	H7 Halogen
Dipped beam	35	D2S (80-117 volt)
Interior light	3	Festoon
Sidelight	6	H6
Brake light/tail light	21/5	Bayonet
Reversing light (passenger side)	21	Bayonet

1 General information and precautions

Warning: Before carrying out any work on the electrical system, read through the precautions given in 'Safety first!' at the beginning of this manual, and in Chapter 5A Section 1.

1 The electrical system is of 12 volt negative earth type. Power for the lights and all electrical accessories is supplied by a lead-acid type battery, which is charged by the alternator.

2 This Chapter covers repair and service procedures for the various electrical components not associated with the engine. Information on the battery, alternator and starter motor can be found in Chapter 5A.

3 It should be noted that prior to working on any component in the electrical system, the ignition and all electrical consumers must be switched off. Additionally, where stated, the battery negative lead must be disconnected, however, note the information given in *Disconnecting the battery* in the Reference section at the end of this manual, as special procedures have to be carried out when reconnecting the battery.

4 Audi TT models have halogen headlights fitted, however, some models may be fitted with gas discharge headlight systems. These vehicles are also equipped with automatic range control, to reduce the possibility of dazzling oncoming drivers. Note the special precautions which apply to these systems as given in Section 5.

2 Electrical fault finding – general information

Note: *Refer to the precautions given in 'Safety first!' and in Chapter 5A Section 1 before starting work. The following tests relate to testing of the main electrical circuits, and should not be used to test delicate electronic circuits (such as anti-lock braking systems), particularly where an electronic control module is used.*

General

1 A typical electrical circuit consists of an electrical component, any switches, relays, motors, fuses, fusible links or circuit breakers related to that component, and the wiring and connectors which link the component to both the battery and the chassis. To help to pinpoint a problem in an electrical circuit, wiring diagrams are included at the end of this Chapter.

2 Before attempting to diagnose an electrical fault, first study the appropriate wiring diagram to obtain a complete understanding of the components included in the particular circuit concerned. The possible sources of a fault can be narrowed down by noting if other components related to the circuit are operating properly. If several components or circuits fail at one time, the problem is likely to be related to a shared fuse or earth connection.

3 Electrical problems usually stem from simple causes, such as loose or corroded connections, a faulty earth connection, a blown fuse, a melted fusible link, or a faulty relay (refer to Section 3 for details of testing relays). Visually inspect the condition of all fuses, wires and connections in a problem circuit before testing the components. Use the wiring diagrams to determine which terminal connections will need to be checked in order to pinpoint the trouble spot.

4 The basic tools required for electrical fault finding include a circuit tester or voltmeter (a 12 volt bulb with a set of test leads can also be used for certain tests); a self-powered test light (sometimes known as a continuity tester); an ohmmeter (to measure resistance); a battery and set of test leads; and a jumper wire, preferably with a circuit breaker or fuse incorporated, which can be used to bypass suspect wires or electrical components. Before attempting to locate a problem with test instruments, use the wiring diagram to determine where to make the connections.

5 To find the source of an intermittent wiring fault (usually due to a poor or dirty connection, or damaged wiring insulation), a wiggle test can be performed on the wiring. This involves wiggling the wiring by hand to see if the fault occurs as the wiring is moved. It should be possible to narrow down the source of the fault to a particular section of wiring. This method of testing can be used in conjunction with any of the tests described in the following sub-Sections.

6 Apart from problems due to poor connections, two basic types of fault can occur in an electrical circuit – open-circuit, or short-circuit.

7 Open-circuit faults are caused by a break somewhere in the circuit, which prevents current from flowing. An open-circuit fault will prevent a component from working, but will not cause the relevant circuit fuse to blow.

8 Short-circuit faults are caused by a short somewhere in the circuit, which allows the current flowing in the circuit to escape along an alternative route, usually to earth. Short-circuit faults are normally caused by a breakdown in wiring insulation, which allows a feed wire to touch either another wire, or an earthed component such as the bodyshell. A short-circuit fault will normally cause the relevant circuit fuse to blow.

Finding an open-circuit

9 To check for an open-circuit, connect one lead of a circuit tester or voltmeter to either the negative battery terminal or a known good earth.

10 Connect the other lead to a connector in the circuit being tested, preferably nearest to the battery or fuse.

11 Switch on the circuit, bearing in mind that some circuits are live only when the ignition switch is moved to a particular position.

12 If voltage is present (indicated either by the tester bulb lighting or a voltmeter reading, as applicable), this means that the section of the circuit between the relevant connector and the battery is problem-free.

13 Continue to check the remainder of the circuit in the same fashion.

14 When a point is reached at which no voltage is present, the problem must lie between that point and the previous test point with voltage. Most problems can be traced to a broken, corroded or loose connection.

Finding a short-circuit

15 To check for a short-circuit, first disconnect the load(s) from the circuit (loads are the components which draw current from a circuit, such as bulbs, motors, heating elements, etc).

16 Remove the relevant fuse from the circuit, and connect a circuit tester or voltmeter to the fuse connections.

17 Switch on the circuit, bearing in mind that some circuits are live only when the ignition switch is moved to a particular position.

18 If voltage is present (indicated either by the tester bulb lighting or a voltmeter reading, as applicable), this means that there is a short circuit.

19 If no voltage is present, but the fuse still blows with the load(s) connected, this indicates an internal fault in the load(s).

Finding an earth fault

20 The battery negative terminal is connected to earth – the metal of the engine/transmission and the car body – and most systems are wired so that they only receive a positive feed, the current returning through the metal of the car body. This means that the component mounting and the body form part of that circuit. Loose or corroded mountings can therefore cause a range of electrical faults, ranging from total failure of a circuit, to a puzzling partial fault. In particular, lights may shine dimly (especially when another circuit sharing the same earth point is in operation), motors (eg, wiper motors or the radiator cooling fan motor) may run slowly, and the operation of one circuit may have an apparently unrelated effect on another. Note that on many vehicles, earth straps are used between certain components, such as the engine/transmission and the body, usually where there is no metal-to-metal contact between components due to flexible rubber mountings, etc.

21 To check whether a component is properly earthed, disconnect the battery (refer to the warnings given in the Reference section at the rear of the manual) and connect one lead of an ohmmeter to a known good earth point. Connect the other lead to the wire or earth connection being tested. The resistance reading should be zero; if not, check the connection as follows.

22 If an earth connection is thought to be faulty, dismantle the connection and clean back to bare metal both the bodyshell and the wire terminal or the component earth connection mating surface. Be careful to remove all traces of dirt and corrosion, then use a knife to trim away any paint, so that a clean metal-to-metal joint is made. On reassembly, tighten the joint fasteners securely; if a wire terminal is being refitted, use serrated washers between the terminal and the bodyshell to ensure a clean and secure connection. When the connection is remade, prevent the onset of corrosion in the future by applying a coat of petroleum jelly or silicone-based grease or by spraying on (at regular intervals) a proprietary ignition sealer or a water dispersant lubricant.

3 Fuses and relays – general information

Fuses and fusible links

1 Fuses are designed to break a circuit when a predetermined current is reached, in order to protect the components and wiring which could be damaged by excessive current flow. Any excessive current flow will be due to a fault in the circuit, usually a short-circuit (see Section 2).

2 The main fuses are located in the fusebox on the driver's side of the facia. Open the driver's door and unclip the fusebox cover from the end of the facia to gain access to the fuses **(see illustration)**. The fuse locations are marked onto the rear of the fusebox cover.

3 To remove a fuse, first switch off the circuit concerned (or the ignition), then pull the fuse out of its terminals **(see illustration)**.

4 The wire within the fuse should be visible; if the fuse has blown it will be broken or melted.

5 Always renew a fuse with one of the correct rating, never use a fuse with a different rating from that specified.

6 Refer to the wiring diagrams for details of the fuse ratings and the circuits protected. The fuse rating is stamped on the top of the fuse, the fuses are also colour-coded as follows.

Colour	Rating
Light brown	5A
Red	10A
Blue	15A
Yellow	20A
Green	30A

7 Never renew a fuse more than once without tracing the source of the trouble. If the new fuse blows immediately, find the cause before renewing it again; a short to earth as a result of faulty insulation is most likely. Where a fuse protects more than one circuit, try to isolate the fault by switching on each circuit in turn (where possible) until the fuse blows again. Always carry a supply of spare fuses of each relevant rating on the vehicle.

8 Additional heavy-duty fusible links (and 30A fuses) are located in the fuse holder which is fitted to the top of the battery **(see illustration)**. Unclip and open the fuse holder cover to gain access to these links.

9 To renew a fusible link, first disconnect the battery negative terminal. Unscrew the retaining nuts then remove the blown link from the holder. Fit the new link to its terminals and reconnect the lead. Ensure the link and lead are correctly seated then refit the retaining nuts and tighten securely. Clip the cover back into position then reconnect the battery.

Relays

10 A relay is an electrically-operated switch, which is used for the following reasons:

a) A relay can switch a heavy current remotely from the circuit in which the current is flowing, allowing the use of lighter-gauge wiring and switch contacts.
b) A relay can receive more than one control input, unlike a mechanical switch.
c) A relay can have a timer function – for example, the intermittent wiper relay.

11 Most of the relays are located on the relay plate behind the driver's side facia.

12 Access to the relays can be obtained after removing the driver's side lower facia panel as described in Chapter 11 Section 28 **(see illustration)**. Identification details of the relays are given at the start of the wiring diagrams.

13 If a circuit or system controlled by a relay develops a fault, and the relay is suspect, operate the system. If the relay is functioning, it should be possible to hear it click as it is energised. If this is the case, the fault lies with the components or wiring of the system. If the relay is not being energised, then either the relay is not receiving a main supply or a switching voltage, or the relay itself is faulty. Testing is by the substitution of a known good unit, but be careful – while some relays are identical in appearance and in operation, others look similar but perform different functions.

14 To remove a relay, first ensure that the relevant circuit is switched off. The relay can then simply be pulled out from the socket, and pushed back into position.

15 The direction indicator/hazard flasher relay is integral with the hazard warning switch. Refer to Section 4 for the switch removal procedure.

4 Switches – removal and refitting

Ignition switch/ steering column lock

Note: *Disconnect the battery negative lead (refer to* Disconnecting the battery *in the Reference section at the end of this manual) before removing this switch, and reconnect the lead after refitting.*

3.2 Unclip the fusebox cover

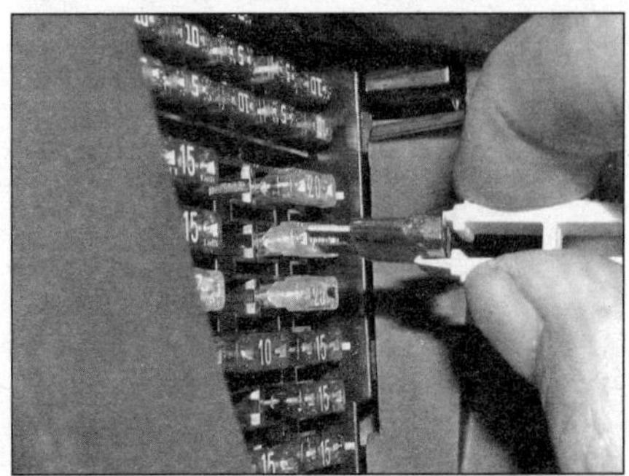

3.3 Removing a fuse from the facia fusebox

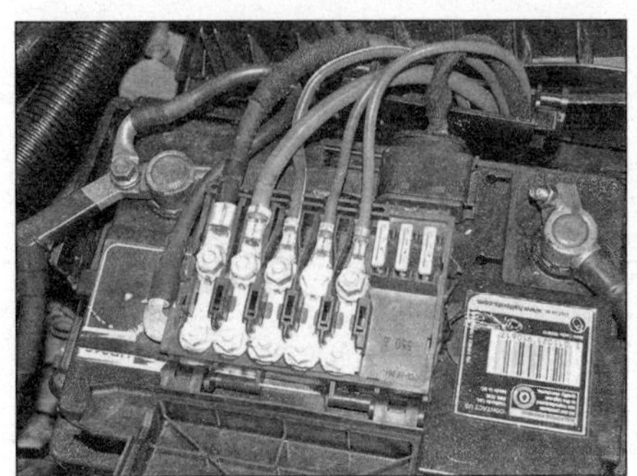

3.8 Fuses and fusible links located on battery

3.12 Relays located behind the facia

4.4a Disconnect the two wiring connectors ...

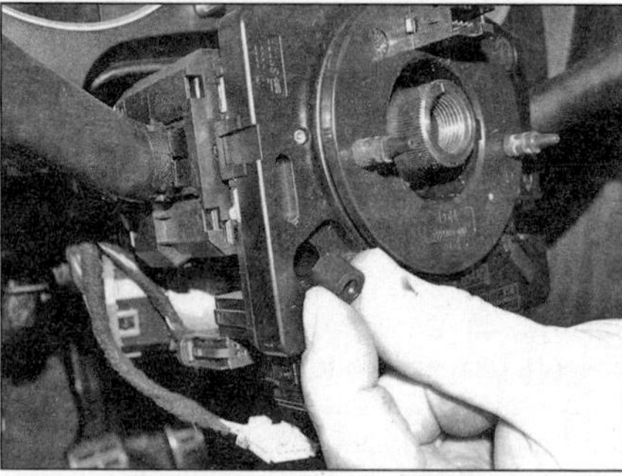

4.4b ...recover the spacer...

4.4c ...and withdraw the return ring with slip ring

1 The ignition switch/steering column lock is covered when removing the steering column, refer to Chapter 10 Section 20.

Steering column switch

Note: *Disconnect the battery negative lead (refer to* Disconnecting the battery *in the Reference section at the end of this manual) before removing this switch, and reconnect the lead after refitting.*

2 Remove the steering wheel, as described in Chapter 10 Section 18.

3 Remove the upper and lower steering column shrouds, as described in Chapter 10 Section 19.

4 Disconnect the two wiring connectors from the return ring with slip ring. Recover the spacer from the screw recess at the front of the unit, and then withdraw it from the top of the steering column **(see illustrations)**. Do not turn the return ring with slip ring, whilst removed from the vehicle as it needs to go back in the same position.

4.5a Release the switch...

4.5b ...and disconnect the wiring connector

5 Release the securing clip and slide the wiper switch from the right-hand side of the steering column. Disconnect the wiring connector and remove the switch **(see illustrations)**.

6 Disconnect the wiring connector, slacken the switch clamp screw and pull the indicator switch assembly from the column **(see illustrations)**.

7 Refitting is a reversal of removal, but the switch assembly and return ring with slip ring must be accurately positioned as follows:

a) Refit the indicator switch to the column, but only lightly tighten the clamp screw.

b) Refit the wiper switch, making sure it is located fully with the securing clip

c) Refit the return ring with slip ring to the top of the switch. There should be a yellow dot showing in the window in the right-hand top of the unit, and alignment lines on the lower part ***(see illustrations)****.*

4.6a Disconnect the wiring connector...

4.6b ...slacken the clamp screw...

4.6c ...and remove the switch

4.7a Align the yellow dot (arrowed)

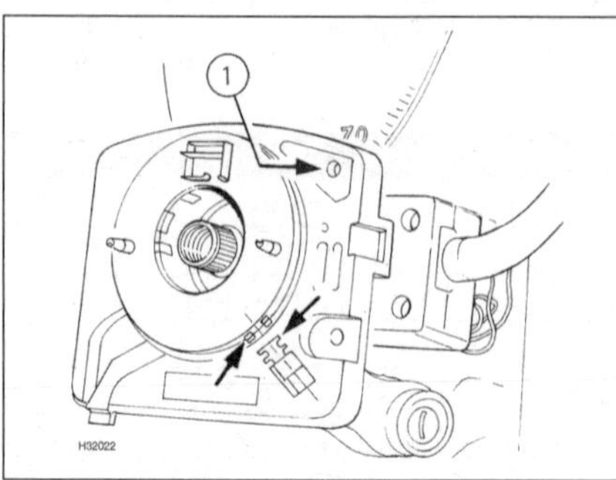

4.7b The yellow dot must be visible through the hole (1) with the alignment markings (arrowed) in line

4.8 In the correct position, pull the switch from the facia...

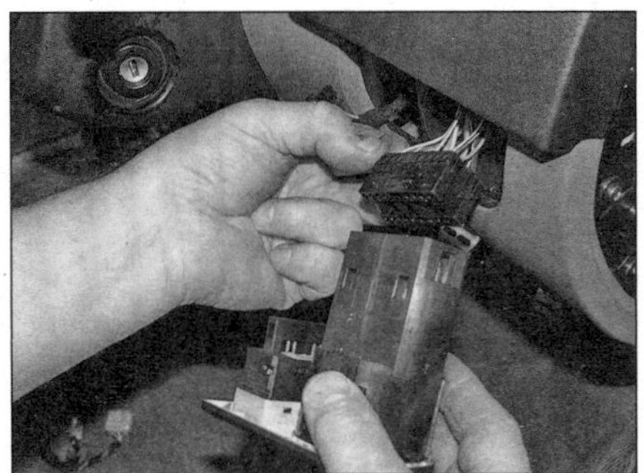
4.9 ...and disconnect the wiring connectors

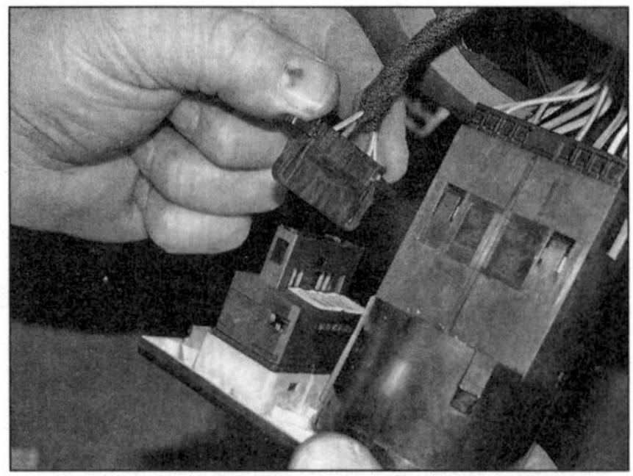
4.12 Disconnect the wiring connector

d) Temporarily refit the steering wheel, and measure the clearance between the wheel and return ring with slip ring. The correct clearance should be approximately 3.0 mm.

e) Once the correct clearance is achieved, tighten the switch clamp screw securely.

Lighting switch

Note: *Disconnect the battery negative lead (refer to* Disconnecting the battery *in the Reference section at the end of this manual) before removing this switch, and reconnect the lead after refitting.*

8 With the light switch in position O, press the switch centre inwards and turn it slightly to the right. Hold this position and pull the switch from the dash **(see illustration)**.

9 As the switch is withdrawn from the dash, disconnect the wiring plug **(see illustration)**.

10 On refitting, first reconnect the wiring connectors, then Insert the switch into the dash, turn the rotary part to position O and release. Check the switch for correct operation.

Headlamp range control switch

Note: *Switch off the ignition and all electrical consumers before commencing work.*

11 Remove the light switch with reference to paragraphs 8 and 9.

12 Disconnect the wiring connector **(see illustration)**, then release the securing clips at the rear of the switch surround and withdraw the switch from the rear of the trim panel.

13 Refitting is a reversal of removal.

4.16a Release the securing clips...

4.16b ...and remove the radio/CD cover plate

Hazard warning, heated rear window, heated front seats and ESP switches

Note: *Disconnect the battery negative lead (refer to* Disconnecting the battery *in the Reference section at the end of this manual) before removing this switch, and reconnect the lead after refitting.*

14 Remove the radio/CD/player from the facia, as described in Section 20.

15 Remove the trim panel from around the heater control unit, as described in Chapter 3 Section 9. **Note:** *The switches can be removed from inside the radio/CD aperture without this trim panel being removed.*

16 Release the securing clips at each side, and remove the radio/CD player cover plate from the facia **(see illustrations)**.

17 Unclip the plastic trim panel from above the radio/CD aperture **(see illustration)**.

18 Reaching through the radio/CD aperture, pull down the switch securing plate from the lower part of the switch assembly **(see illustrations)**.

19 Press the relevant switch down through the facia and withdraw it out from the radio/

4.17 Withdraw the trim panel

4.18a Pull down the switch securing plate

4.18b Securing plate (arrowed) – viewed with facia centre removed

CD aperture, disconnect the wiring connector **(see illustrations)**.

20 On refitting, first reconnect the switch wiring plug, and push the switch firmly into position. Make sure the switch securing plate is pressed firmly upwards and back in its original position. The rest of the procedure is the reversal of removal.

Electric window switches

21 The electric window switch is covered when covering the window regulator assembly, refer to Chapter 11 Section 18.

Electric mirror switch

22 The electric mirror switch is covered when covering the mirror assembly, refer to Chapter 11 Section 19.

Air conditioning switches

23 The switches are integral with the heater control panel, and cannot be removed separately. Refer to Chapter 3 Section 9 for details of heater control panel removal and refitting.

Heater blower motor switch

24 The switch is integral with the heater control panel, and cannot be removed separately. Refer to Chapter 3 Section 9 for details of heater control panel removal and refitting.

Handbrake 'on' warning switch

25 The handbrake switch is covered when covering the handbrake lever assembly, refer to Chapter 9 Section 16.

Brake light switch

26 The brake switch is covered in Chapter 9 Section 17.

Reversing light switch

27 The reversing light switch is covered in Chapter 7A Section 5.

Courtesy light switches

28 The courtesy light switch is integrated into the door lock mechanism, and cannot be renewed independently. If the courtesy light switch is faulty, renew the door lock mechanism as described in Chapter 11 Section 12.

Luggage area light switch

29 The luggage compartment light switch is integrated into the tailgate/boot lid lock mechanism, and cannot be renewed independently. If the luggage compartment light switch is faulty, renew the tailgate/boot lid lock mechanism as described in Chapter 11 Section 16.

Glovebox light switch

30 The switch is connected to the rear hinge section of the glovebox, refer to Chapter 11 Section 26.

Fuel filler flap release switch

31 Carefully prise the switch from the housing, and disconnect the wiring plug.

32 The fuel filler flap has a cable operated release, if the electrics are not operating. Open the trim cover in the right-hand side of the luggage compartment and pull cable **(see illustrations)**.

Switches at the front of centre console

Note: *Depending on model, there can be a number of different switches fitted to the centre console.*

Note: *Switch off the ignition and all electrical consumers before commencing work.*

33 Open the compartment at the front of the centre console and unclip the switch panel, then disconnect the wiring connectors and remove **(see illustration)**.

34 Release the securing clips at the rear of the switch panel, and then withdraw the relevant switch from the switch panel.

35 Refitting is a reversal of removal.

Switches in the centre console

Note: *Depending on model, there can be a number of different switches fitted to the centre console (eg. Interior locking switch, function selection switch, convertible windbreak switch and convertible actuation switch).*

Note: *Switch off the ignition and all electrical consumers before commencing work.*

36 Unclip the trim panel from the rear of the centre, on models with cup holder, remove the rubber mats, undo the retaining screws and remove the cup holder and trim **(see illustration)**.

4.19a Press the switch out of the facia...

4.19b ...and disconnect the wiring connector

4.32a Open the flap...

4.32b ...and pull the cable

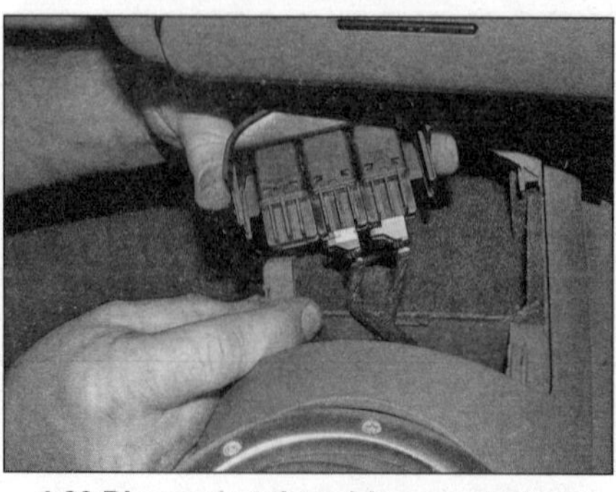

4.33 Disconnect the wiring connectors

4.36 Remove the trim panel

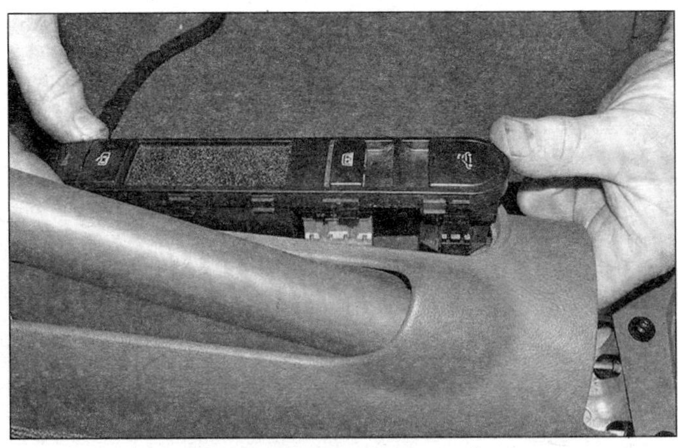
4.37a Unclip the switch panel...

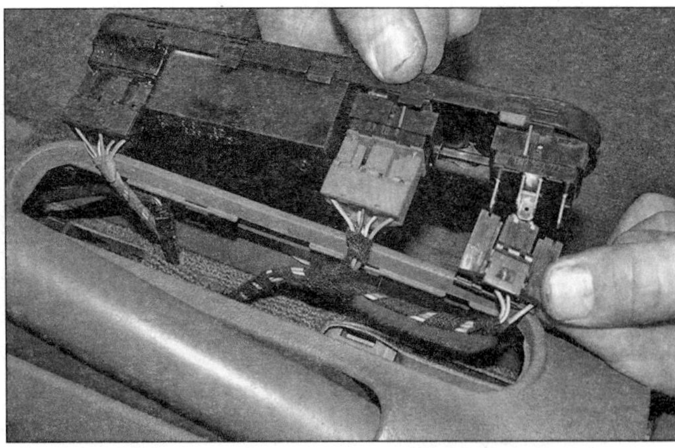
4.37b ...and disconnect the wiring connections

37 Reaching inside the rear of the console, push the switch panel upwards and out from the centre console **(see illustration)**. Disconnect the wiring connectors and remove the switch panel from the console **(see illustration)**.

38 Release the securing clips at the rear of the switch panel, and then withdraw the relevant switch from the switch panel.

39 Refitting is a reversal of removal.

5 Bulbs (exterior lights) - renewal

General

Note: *The illustrations in this section show the headlight unit removed from the vehicle for clarity.*

1 Whenever a bulb is renewed, note the following points:

a) Switch off the ignition and all electrical consumers before commencing work. On models with gas discharge headlights fitted, disconnect the earth cable from the battery (refer to Disconnecting the battery in the Reference section at the end of this manual)

b) Remember that if the light has just been in use the bulb may be extremely hot.

c) Always check the bulb contacts and holder, ensuring that there is clean metal-to-metal contact between the bulb and its live(s) and earth. Clean off any corrosion or dirt before fitting a new bulb.

d) Wherever bayonet-type bulbs are fitted ensure that the live contact(s) bear firmly against the bulb contact.

e) Always ensure that the new bulb is of the correct rating and that it is completely clean before fitting it.

f) When working on the headlight bulbs, depending on which headlight is being worked on, release the fasteners and remove the trim panel from over the battery for the left-hand headlight or the trim panel from over the coolant reservoir for the right-hand headlight unit.

Headlight main beam

2 Working at the rear of the headlight unit, release the securing clip, and remove the plastic cover **(see illustration)**.

3 Release the retaining clip and withdraw the bulb holder from the light unit **(see illustrations)**.

4 Pull the headlight bulb from the bulbholder **(see illustration)**.

5 When handling the new bulb, use a tissue or clean cloth to avoid touching the glass with the fingers; moisture and grease from the skin can cause blackening and rapid failure of this type of bulb. If the glass is accidentally touched, wipe it clean using methylated spirit.

6 Install the new bulb, then refit the bulbholder into the rear of the light unit and secure it in position with the retaining clip**(see illustration)**.

5.2 Remove the plastic cover

5.3a Release the retaining clip...

5.3b ...and withdraw the bulb holder

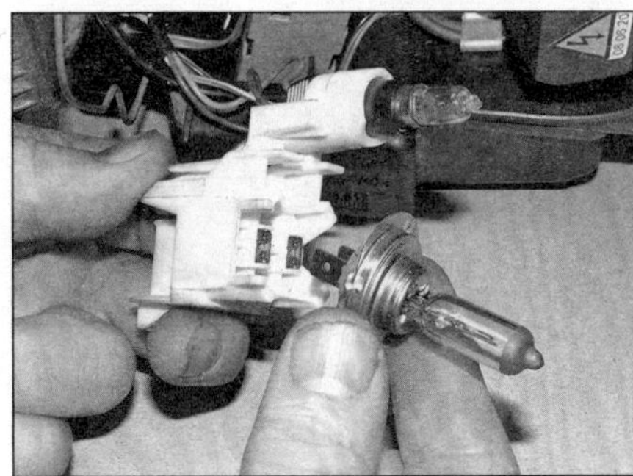
5.4 ... and remove the bulb

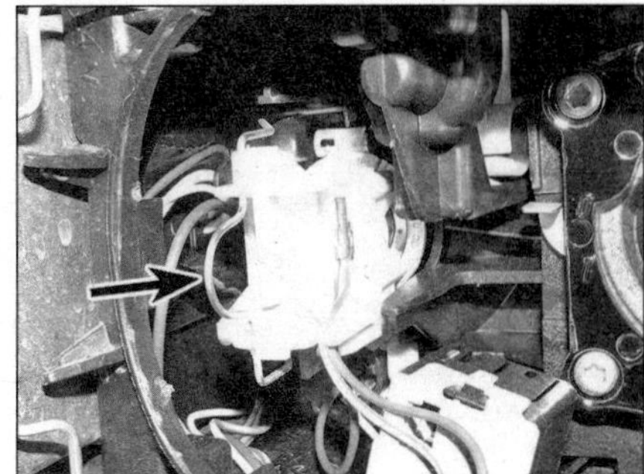
5.6 Make sure the clip (arrowed) is secure

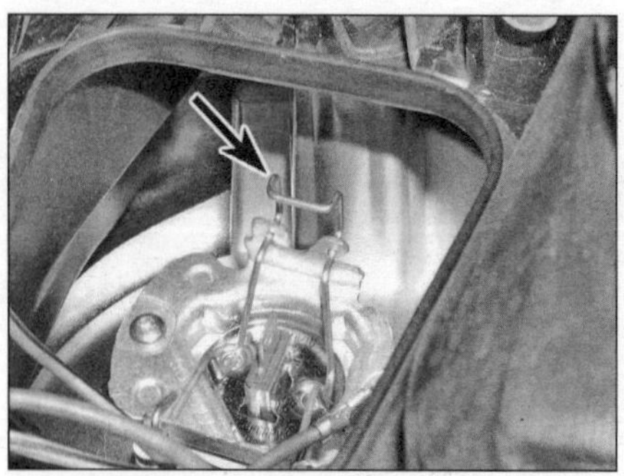
5.9a Unhook the retaining clip (arrowed)...

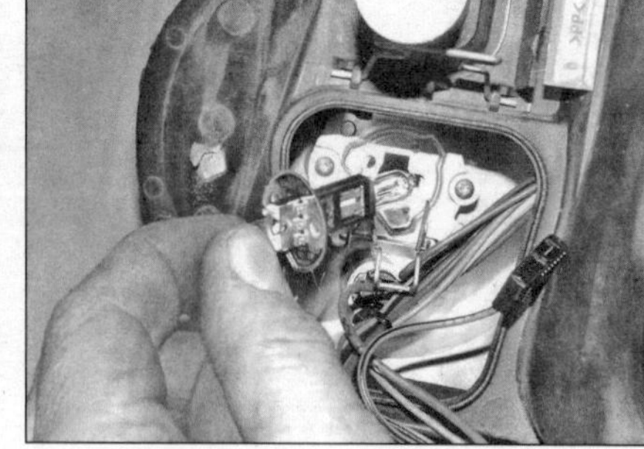
5.9b ... and remove the bulb

7 Refit the headlight cover, making sure that it is clipped into position correctly.

Headlight dip beam

Models with halogen headlights

8 Working at the rear of the headlight unit, release the securing clip, and remove the plastic cover **(see illustration 5.2)**.

9 Disconnect the wiring connector from the rear of the bulb. Release the ends of the bulb retaining clip from the light unit, and then withdraw the bulb **(see illustrations)**.

10 When handling the new bulb, use a tissue or clean cloth to avoid touching the glass with the fingers; moisture and grease from the skin can cause blackening and rapid failure of this type of bulb. If the glass is accidentally touched, wipe it clean using methylated spirit.

11 Install the new bulb, ensuring that its locating tabs are correctly located in the light cut-outs, and secure it in position with the retaining clip.

12 Reconnect the wiring connector and refit the headlight cover, making sure that it is clipped into position correctly.

Gas discharge headlights

Caution: Before attempting to remove the dipped beam bulb, it is absolutely necessary to disconnect the battery negative lead (refer to ' Disconnecting the battery 13 Section 6 ' in the Reference section at the rear of this manual), and then turn the relevant beam on and off to dissipate any residual voltage. It is also strongly recommended that safety goggles/glasses are worn prior to handling gas discharge bulbs, as the interior of the bulb is pressurised to in excess of 10 bar.

13 Working at the rear of the headlight unit, release the securing clip, and remove the plastic cover **(see illustration 5.2)**.

14 Release the bulb connector by turning it 90° anti-clockwise **(see illustration)**.

15 Turn the bulb retaining ring anti-clockwise and remove it **(see illustration)**.

16 Carefully pull the bulb from the reflector **(see illustration)**.

17 Install the new bulb, ensuring that its cut-out is at the top, and it locates with the locating tab in the light unit **(see illustration)**, then secure it in position with the retaining ring. When handling the new bulb, use a tissue or clean cloth to avoid touching the glass with the fingers; moisture and grease from the skin can cause blackening and rapid failure of this type of bulb. If the glass is accidentally touched, wipe it clean using methylated spirit.

18 Reconnect the wiring connector and refit the headlight cover, making sure that it is clipped into position correctly.

Caution: After refitting a gas discharge headlamp, the basic setting of the Automatic Range Control system should be checked. Because of the requirement for specialised equipment, this can only be carried out by an Audi dealer or suitably-equipped specialist.

Front sidelight

19 The front side light bulb is fitted into the same bulb holder as the headlight main beam bulb. Working at the rear of the headlight unit, release the securing clip, and remove the plastic cover **(see illustration 5.2)**.

20 Release the retaining clip and withdraw the bulb holder from the light unit **(see illustrations 5.3a and 5.3b)**.

21 The bulb is a bayonet-fit in the bulbholder – push the bulb into the holder and twist anti-clockwise to remove **(see illustration)**.

22 Refitting is a reversal of removal, making sure that the cover is clipped into position correctly.

Front direction indicator

23 Working at the rear of the headlight unit, release the securing clip, and disconnect the

5.14 Disconnect the wiring connector...

5.15 ...remove the retaining ring...

5.16 ...and withdraw the bulb

5.17 Align the bulb with the locating tab (arrowed)

5.21 Removing the sidelight bulb

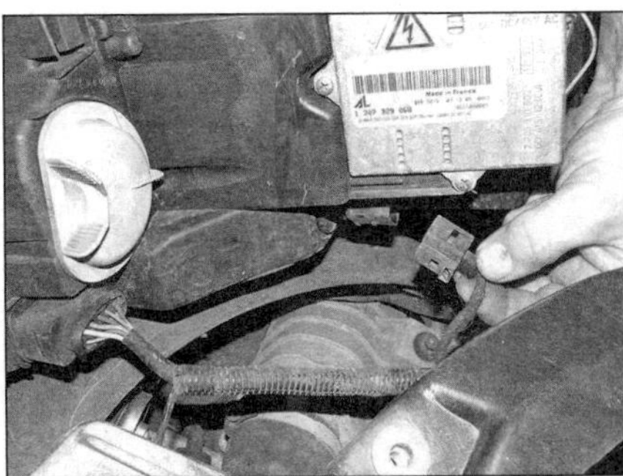
5.23 Disconnect the wiring connector

5.24 Remove the bulb holder...

5.25 ...and the bulb

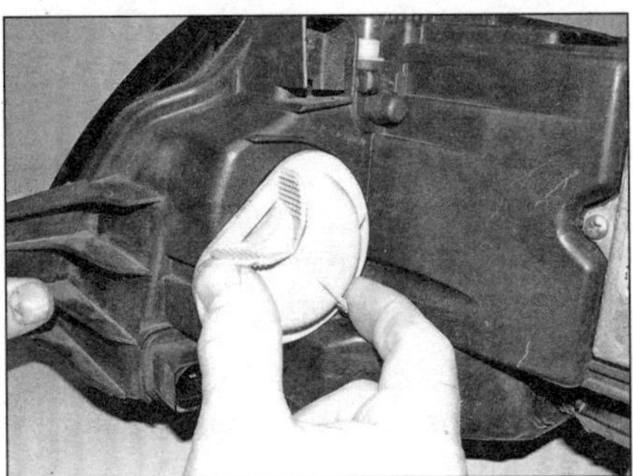
5.27a Turn the cover (clockwise on right-hand light unit)...

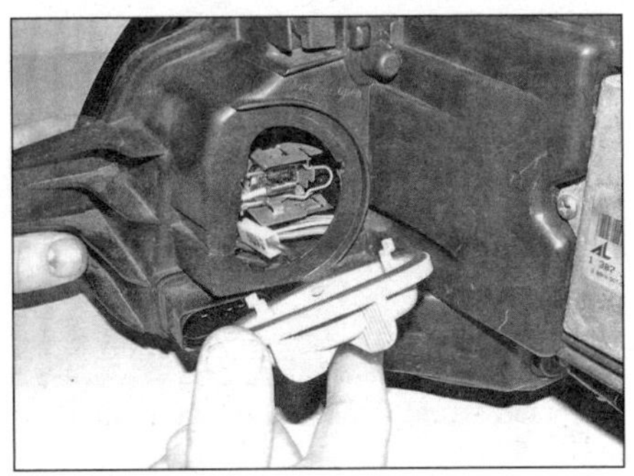
5.27b ...and remove the cover

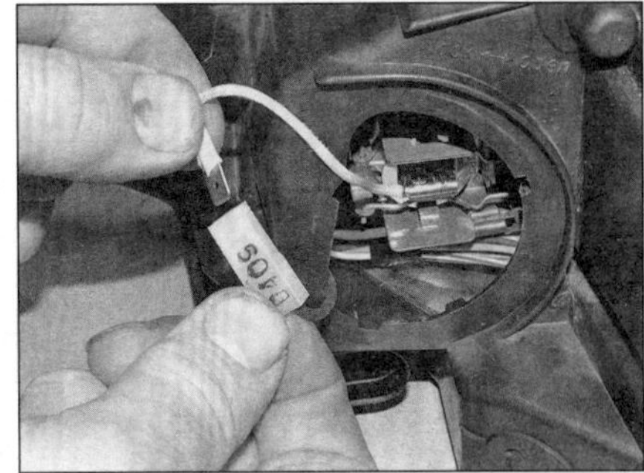
5.28 Disconnect the wiring connector

wiring connector from the lower part of the headlight unit **(see illustration)**.

24 Turn the bulbholder anti-clockwise, and withdraw it from the rear of the light unit **(see illustration)**.

25 The bulb is a bayonet-fit in the bulbholder – push the bulb into the holder and twist anti-clockwise to remove **(see illustration)**.

26 Fit the new bulb using a reversal of the removal procedure.

Front foglight

Note: *When working on the left-hand front fog light, it will be necessary to remove the battery to access the bulb removal.*

27 Working at the rear of the headlight unit, turn the plastic cover and remove it from the headlight unit **(see illustrations)**. **Note:** *On left-hand headlight units turn the cover anti-clockwise to remove and on right-hand headlight units turn it clockwise to remove.*

28 Disconnect the wire leading to the foglight bulb from the connector **(see illustration)**.

29 Unhook and release the ends of the bulb retaining clip and release it from the light unit, then withdraw the bulb **(see illustrations)**.

30 When handling the new bulb, use a tissue or clean cloth to avoid touching the glass with the fingers; moisture and grease from the skin can cause blackening and rapid failure of this type of bulb. If the glass is accidentally touched, wipe it clean using methylated spirit.

31 Install the new bulb, ensuring that its locating tabs are correctly located in the light cut-outs, and secure it in position with the retaining clip **(see illustration)**.

32 Reconnect the wiring and refit the headlight cover, making sure that it is secured into position correctly. **Note:** *On left-hand headlight units turn the cover clockwise to refit and on right-hand headlight units turn it anti-clockwise to refit.*

Direction indicator side repeater

33 Great care must be taken when removing the direction indicator side repeater, as there is a risk of damaging the vehicle paintwork.

34 Carefully push the repeater towards

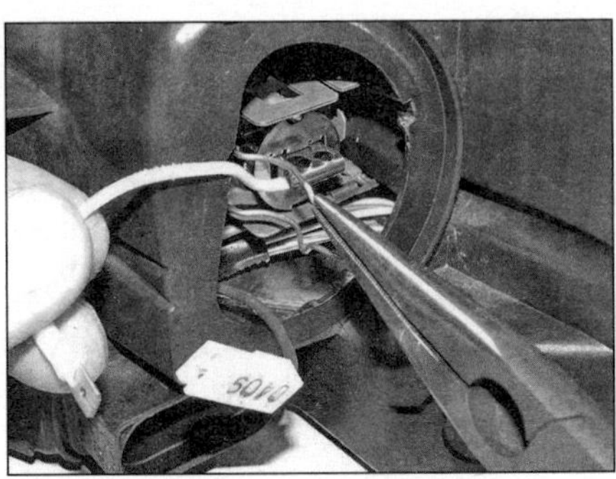
5.29a Unhook the retaining clip ...

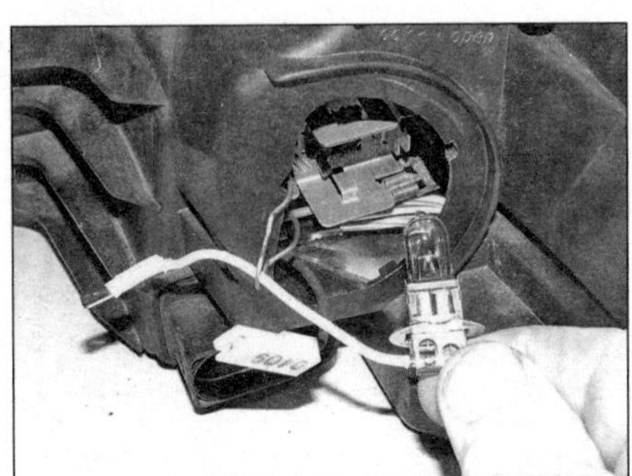
5.29b ... and withdraw the bulb

5.31 Make sure the clip (arrowed) is secure

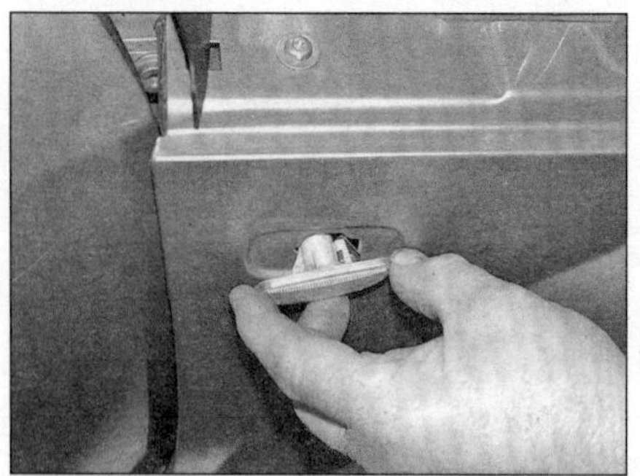
5.34 Ease the side repeater from the wing

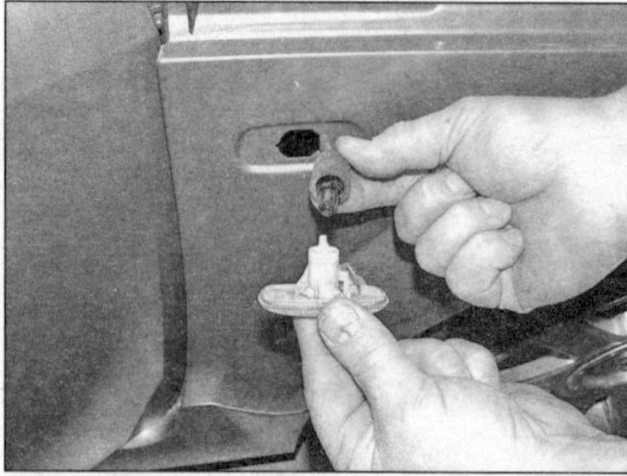
5.35a Pull the bulbholder from the light...

5.35b ...and pull out the wedge-type bulb

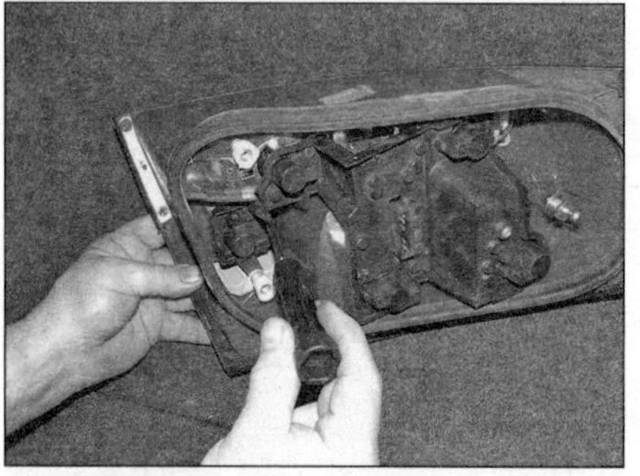
5.38a Undo the retaining screw...

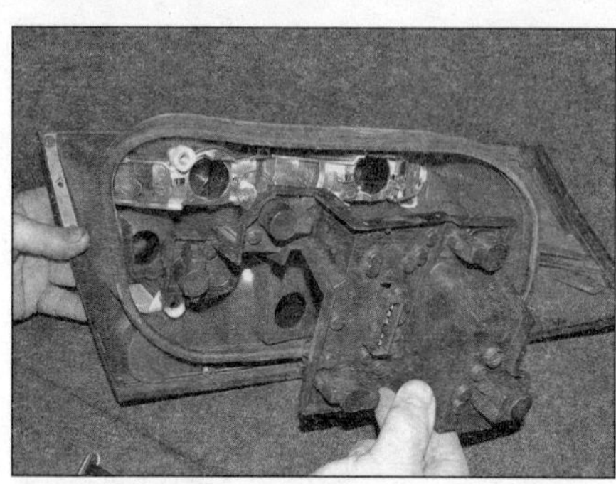
5.38b ...and remove the bulb holder

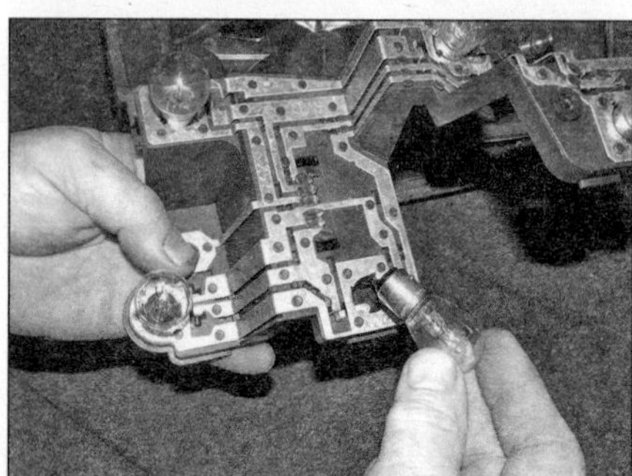
5.39 The bulbs are a bayonet fit

the front of the vehicle, in the direction of the spring clip. Once the spring clip is compressed, it should be possible to ease the rear end of the repeater out of the aperture, and manoeuvre the assembly from the wing **(see illustration)**.

35 Pull the rubber bulbholder from the repeater, and then pull the push-fit bulb from the holder **(see illustrations)**.

36 Refitting is a reversal of removal.

Rear light cluster

37 Remove the rear light unit, as described in Section 7.

38 Using the screwdriver from the tool kit, undo the retaining screw and remove the bulbholder from the light unit **(see illustrations)**.

39 The bulbs are a bayonet-fit in the bulbholder – push the bulb into the holder and twist anti-clockwise **(see illustration)**.

40 Fit the new bulb using a reversal of the removal procedure.

High level brake light

Roadster 'convertible' models

41 Unclip the colour coded trim cover from the high level brake light unit **(see illustration)**.

42 Undo the two retaining screws and remove the light unit from the rear panel **(see illustrations)**.

43 Release the wiring rubber grommet and withdraw the wiring and disconnect the connector **(see illustrations)**. It will be necessary to open the boot lid and remove the

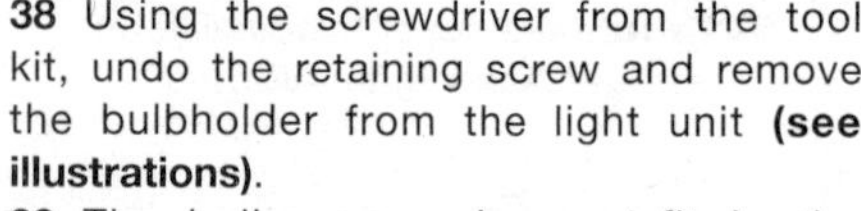

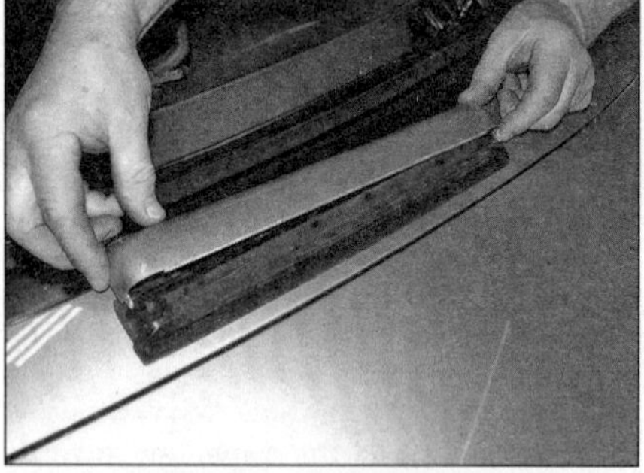
5.41 Unclip the trim cover

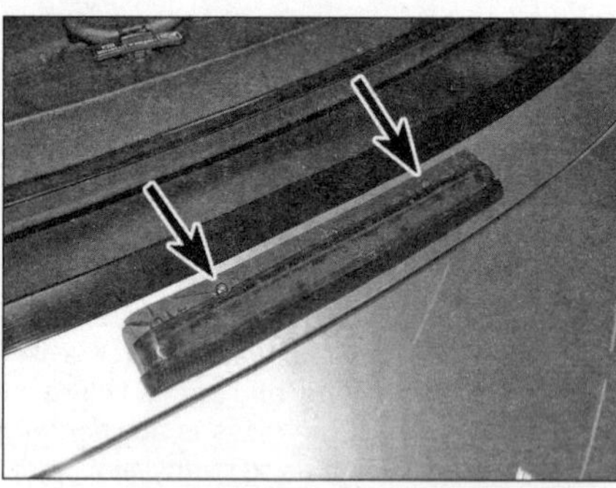
5.42a Undo the retaining screws (arrowed)...

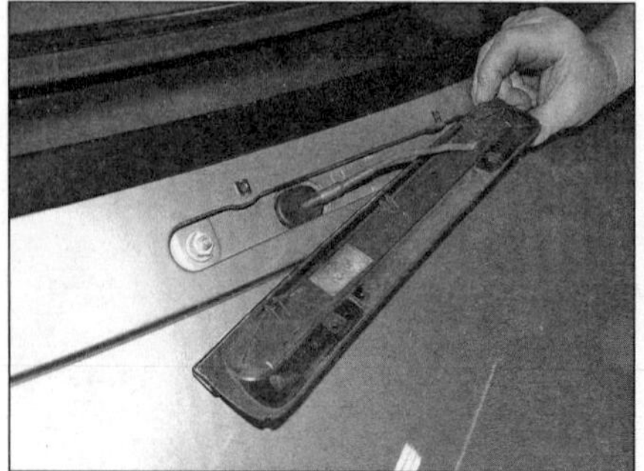
5.42b ...and remove the light unit

5.43a Release the grommet from the body panel

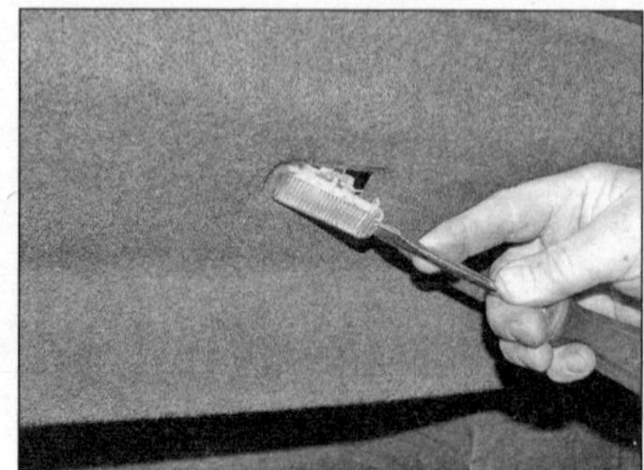
5.43b Disconnect the wiring from the light unit

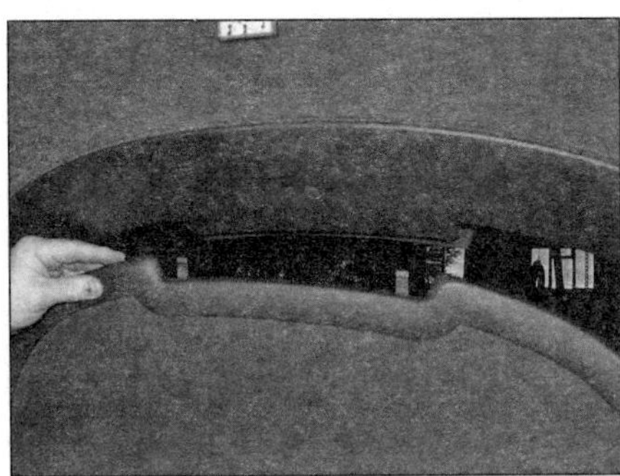

5.46 Remove the shelf panel

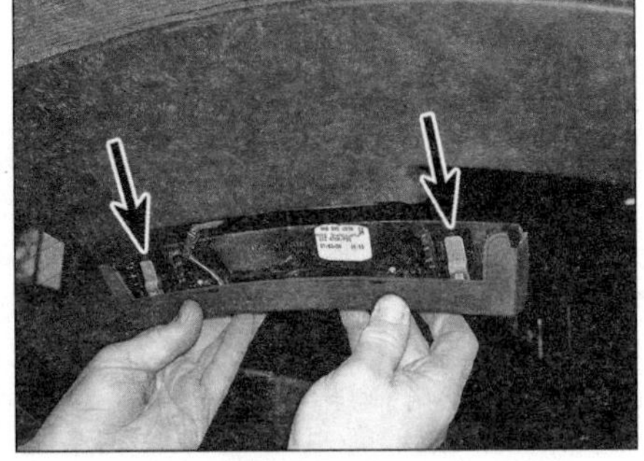

5.47 Pull down to release the securing clips (arrowed)

5.51a Push the light unit outwards...

luggage compartment light unit and disconnect the wiring connector, so as to remove the wiring for the high level brake light.

44 As the LED's are soldered in position and covered with a plastic strip, it is not possible to renew individual LED's. The complete light unit must be renewed.

45 Refitting is a reversal of removal.

Coupe models

46 Open the tailgate and detach the shelf panel from inside the tailgate **(see illustration)**.

47 Pull the light unit downwards to unclip it from the tailgate **(see illustration)**, then disconnect the wiring connector.

48 Release the retaining clips and separate the bulb holder from the plastic trim cover.

49 As the LED's are soldered in position and covered with a plastic strip, it is not possible to renew individual LED's. The complete light unit must be renewed.

50 Refitting is a reversal of removal.

Rear number plate light

51 Carefully push the light unit towards the outside of the vehicle, in the direction of the spring clip. Once the spring clip is compressed, it should be possible to ease the other end of the light unit out of the aperture, and manoeuvre the assembly from the boot lid/tailgate **(see illustrations)**. **Note:** *The plastic spring clip on the outside of the light unit, is part of the light unit. Take care not to brake the plastic clip, otherwise a new light unit will be required.*

5.51b ...against the spring clip (arrowed)

5.52 Remove the bulb

52 The bulb is a festoon type bulb and can be unclipped from the connectors inside the light unit **(see illustration)**.

53 Fit the new bulb and light unit, using a reversal of the removal procedure.

6 Bulbs (interior lights) – renewal

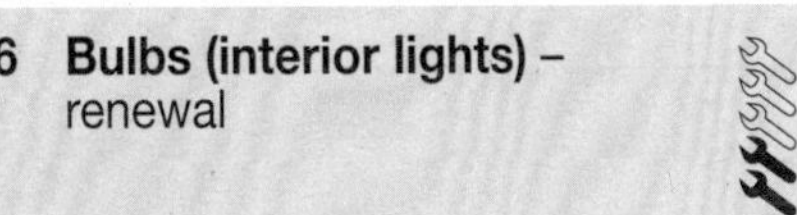

General

1 Whenever a bulb is renewed, note the following points:

a) *Switch off the ignition and all electrical consumers before commencing work.*

b) *Remember that if the light has just been in use the bulb may be extremely hot.*

c) *Always check the bulb contacts and holder, ensuring that there is clean metal-to-metal contact between the bulb and its live(s) and earth. Clean off any corrosion or dirt before fitting a new bulb.*

d) *Wherever bayonet-type bulbs are fitted ensure that the live contact(s) bear firmly against the bulb contact.*

e) *Always ensure that the new bulb is of the correct rating and that it is completely clean before fitting it.*

Front courtesy/reading light

Coupe models

2 Carefully prise the lens from the light unit, using a small flat-bladed screwdriver **(see illustration)**

3 The courtesy light bulb is a festoon type bulb and can be pulled from the spring contacts. The reading lamp bulbs are a wedge type and can be pulled out from there fitting **(see illustration)**.

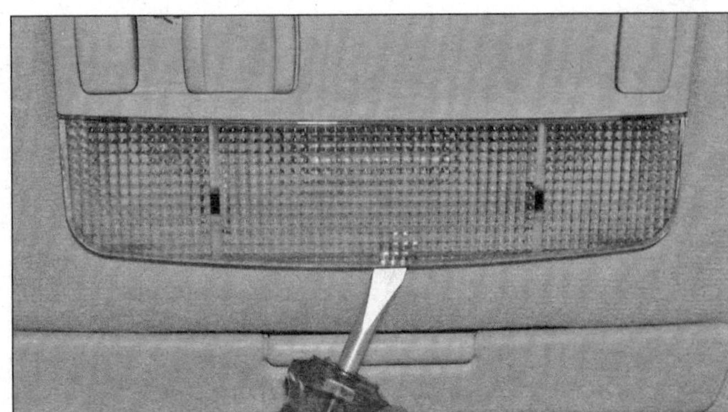

6.2 Carefully prise the lens from the unit

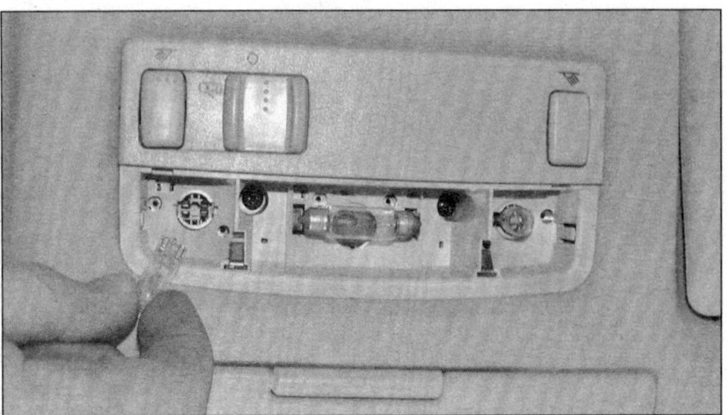

6.3 The reading light bulb is a wedge type

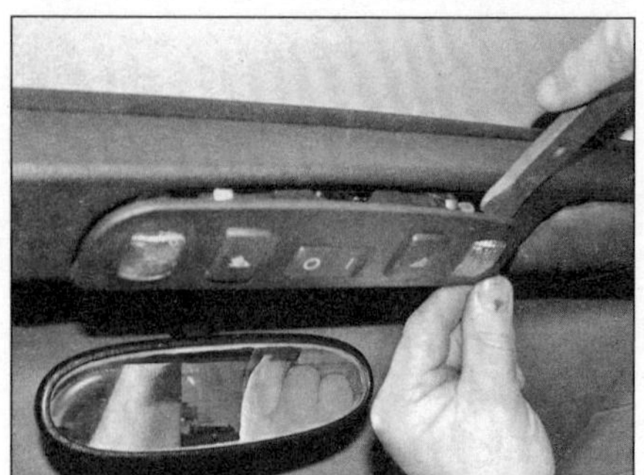

6.5a Lever the light unit out...

6.5b ...and disconnect the wiring connector

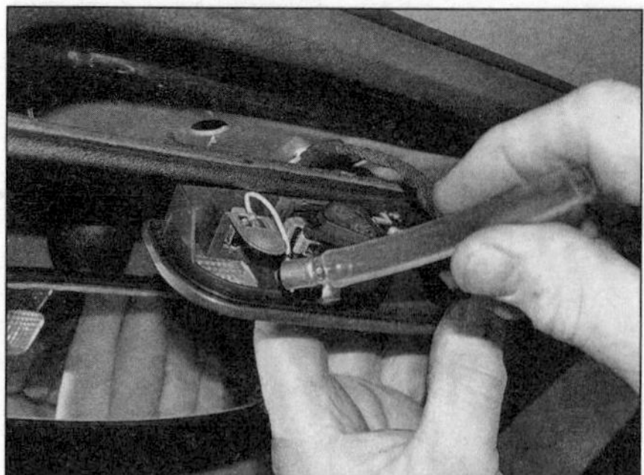

6.6 Using a piece of tube, to remove the bulb

4 Fit the new bulb using a reversal of the removal procedure.

Roadster 'convertible' models

5 Carefully prise the light assembly from the front upper crossmember and disconnect the wiring connector **(see illustrations)**.

6 The reading lamp bulbs are a bayonet type and can be pressed inwards slightly and turned anti-clockwise to remove them from there fitting **(see illustration)**.

7 Fit the new bulb using a reversal of the removal procedure.

Front vanity mirror light – Coupe models

8 Hinge the passenger sun visor downwards and carefully prise the light unit from the headlining.

9 Disconnect the wiring connector and then unclip the plastic cover on the back of the light unit.

10 The bulb is of a wedge type and can be pulled out from the contacts inside the light unit.

11 Fit the new bulb using a reversal of the removal procedure.

Luggage compartment light

12 Carefully prise the light unit from its location in the luggage compartment. The bulb is of a wedge type and is a push-fit in the spring contacts **(see illustrations)**.

13 Fit the new bulb using a reversal of the removal procedure.

Glovebox illumination light

14 Open the glovebox and prise the light unit from its location and disconnect the wiring connector **(see illustrations)**.

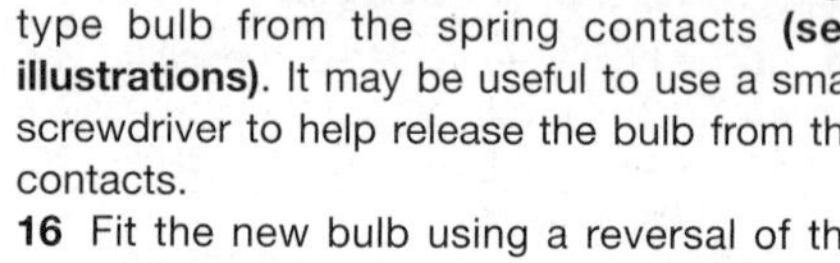

15 Unclip the plastic cover on the back of the light unit and then. remove the wedge type bulb from the spring contacts **(see illustrations)**. It may be useful to use a small screwdriver to help release the bulb from the contacts.

16 Fit the new bulb using a reversal of the removal procedure.

Instrument panel illumination/ warning lights

17 The instrument panel illumination/warning lights are non-renewable LEDs. Refer to Section 10 for the removal and refitting of the instrument panel.

Heater/ventilation control panel illumination

18 The heater/ventilation control panel is illuminated by LEDs built into the panel. Refer

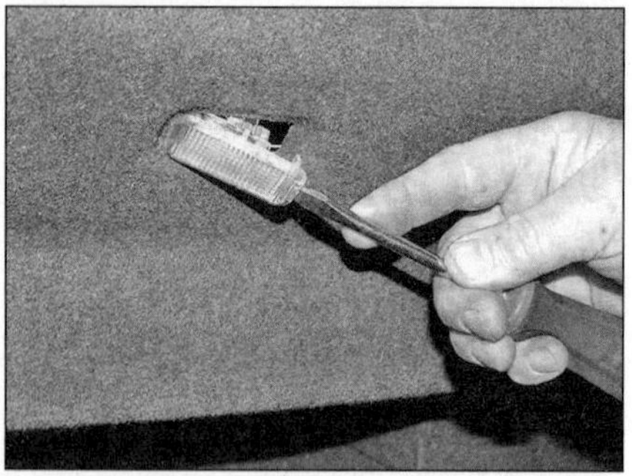

6.12a Lever the light from the trim...

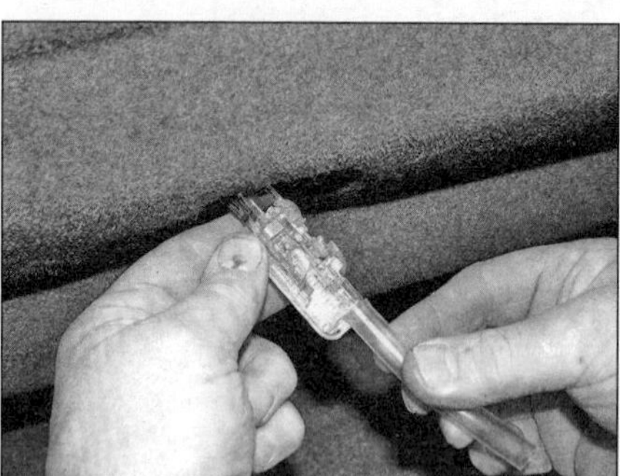

6.12b ...and remove the bulb with a piece of plastic tube

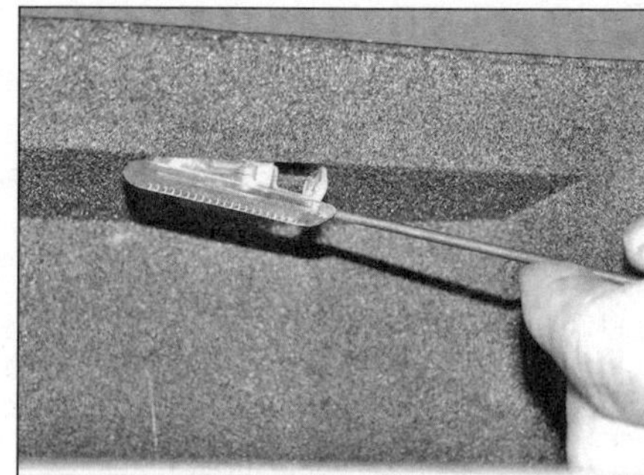

6.14a Prise out the glovebox light...

6.14b ...and disconnect the wiring plug

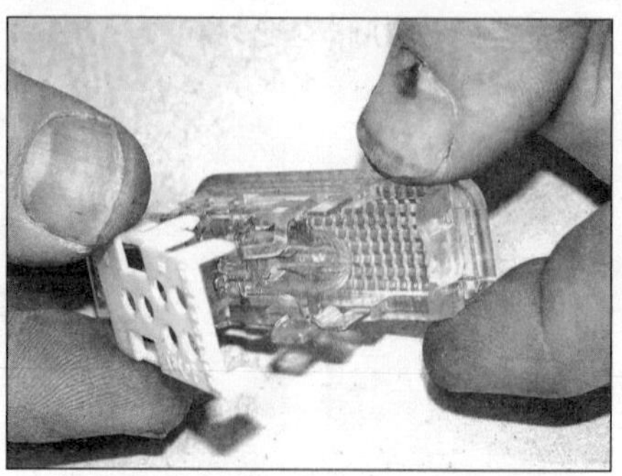

6.15a Unclip the plastic cover...

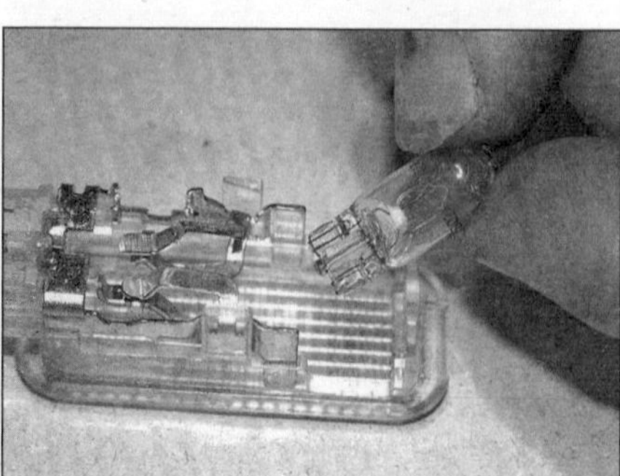

6.15b ...and remove the bulb

7.2a Unscrewing the headlight upper screws (arrowed)...

7.2b ...and inner retaining screw (arrowed)...

7.2c ...then release the locating peg (arrowed)

to Chapter 3 Section 9 for the removal and refitting of the control panel.

Switch illumination

19 The switch illumination bulbs are integral with the switches. If a bulb fails, the complete switch must be renewed.

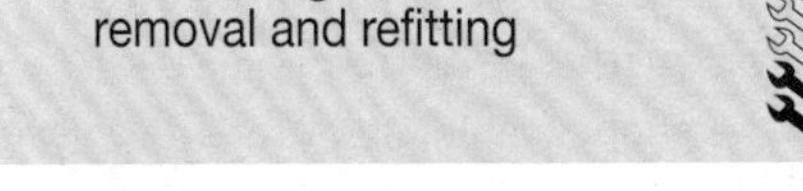
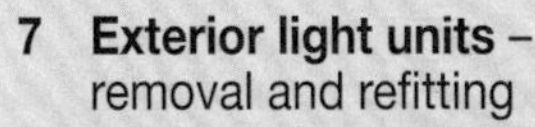

7 Exterior light units – removal and refitting

Headlight

1 Remove the front bumper cover, as described in Chapter 11 Section 6.

2 Undo the three retaining screws, and move the headlight unit towards the centre of the vehicle slightly, to release the locating peg on the outside of the headlight unit **(see illustrations)**.

3 Withdraw the light unit and disconnect the indicator wiring connector and the headlight multi-pin connector **(see illustrations)**.

4 Remove the headlight unit from the vehicle.

5 Refitting is a reversal of removal, but on completion, have the headlight alignment checked at the earliest opportunity. To align the headlight with the bumper, once the bumper is fitted, insert a screwdriver through the front of the grille panel, to slacken the inner retaining screw. Slacken the upper screws, align the headlight with the bumper and then tighten all three retaining screws.

Gas discharge light bulb control unit

6 The gas discharge control unit is fitted to the rear of the headlight unit **(see illustration)**. When removing the control unit from the left-hand headlight, the battery and tray will need to be removed as described in Chapter 5A Section 3.

7 Undo the three securing screws and remove the control unit from the rear of the headlight unit **(see illustrations)**.

8 Refitting is a reversal of removal.

Direction indicator side repeater

9 The procedure is described as part of the bulb renewal procedure in Section 5.

Rear light cluster

10 Working inside the luggage compartment, fold back the access panel to the rear of the light unit **(see illustration)**.

11 Reach inside the access panel and remove the two knurled securing bolts (white

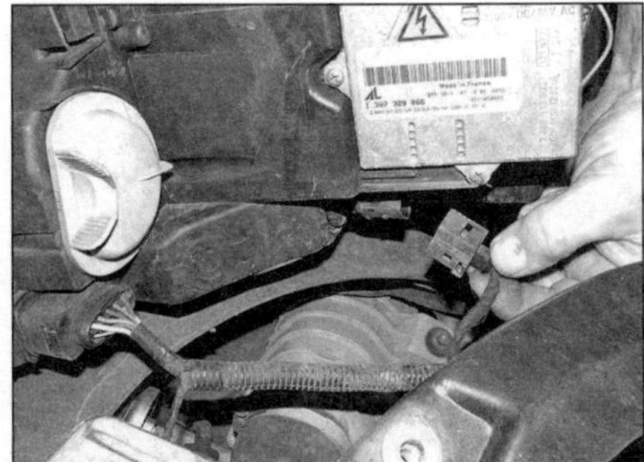

7.3a Disconnecting the indicator wiring connector...

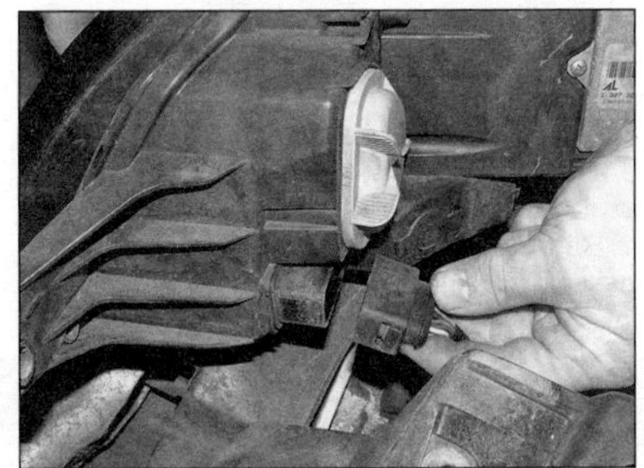

7.3b ...and the headlight multi-pin connector

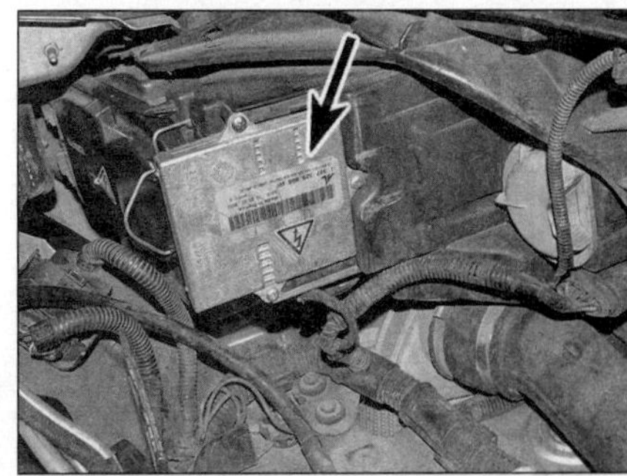

7.6 Gas discharge control unit (arrowed)

7.7a Undo the three retaining screws (arrowed)...

7.7b ...and remove the control unit

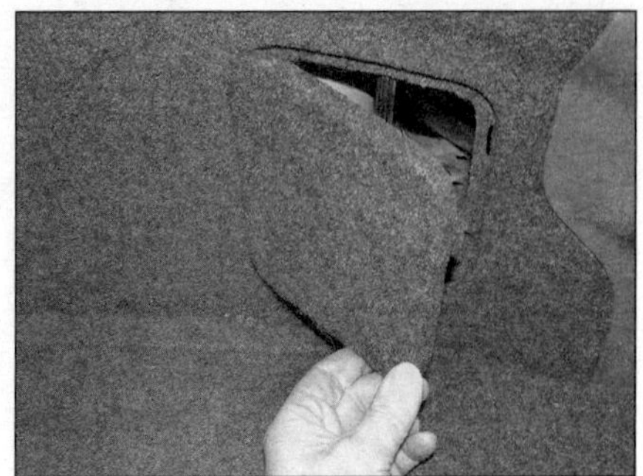

7.10 Open the access panel

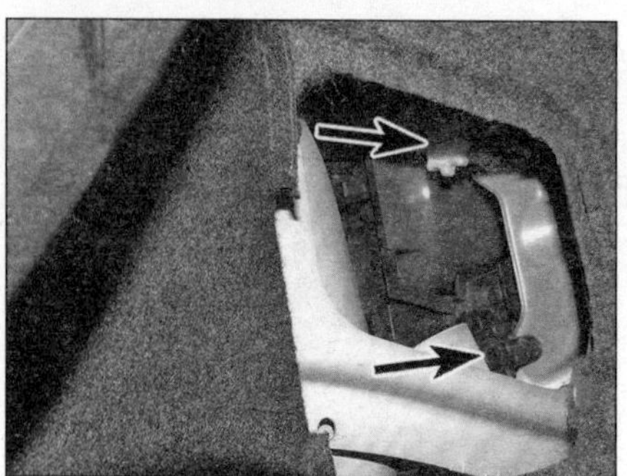
7.11a Remove the securing bolts (arrowed)...

7.11b ...white at the top and black at the bottom

7.12a Release the light from the locating ball joint (arrowed)

7.12b Disconnect the wiring connector

upper bolt and black lower bolt) from the rear of the light unit **(see illustrations)**.

12 Withdraw the light unit from the location holes in the wing panel and disconnect the wiring connector **(see illustrations)**.

13 Refitting is a reversal of removal, making sure the locating ball joint is aligned correctly.

High level brake light

14 The procedure is described as part of the bulb renewal procedure in Section 5.

Rear number plate light

15 The procedure is described as part of the rear number plate light bulb renewal pro-cedure in Section 5.

8 Headlight beam adjustment components – removal and refitting

Headlight adjustment switch

1 The switch is integral with the headlight switch in the lower facia panel.

2 Removal and refitting of the switch assembly is covered in Section 4.

Headlight adjustment motor

3 The headlight adjustment motor is integral with the headlight unit and at the time of writing there was no information on the removal of the adjuster motor. See your local Audi dealer to see what parts are available.

Automatic range control ECU

Note: *Although it is possible to remove and refit the ECU, the new unit may need to be 'coded' before it will function correctly. This task can only be carried out by an Audi dealer or suitably-equipped specialist.*

4 The ECU is located on the floor panel at the rear of the vehicle. On Coupe models, it is under the left-hand side of the rear seat cushion. On Roadster 'convertible' models, it is behind the rear centre speaker, behind the seats **(see illustrations)**. Remove the rear seat cushion and trim panels, as described in Chapter 11.

5 Undo the fasteners and remove the ECU from the floor panel, then disconnect the wiring connector.

6 Refitting is a reversal of removal.

Vehicle level sender

7 Where applicable, there are two level senders fitted, one to the left-hand front suspension and one to the left-hand rear suspension, refer to Chapter 10 Section 17.

9 Headlight beam alignment – general information

1 Accurate adjustment of the headlight beam is only possible using optical beam setting equipment and this work should therefore be carried out by an Audi dealer or suitably-equipped workshop.

2 For reference, the headlights can be

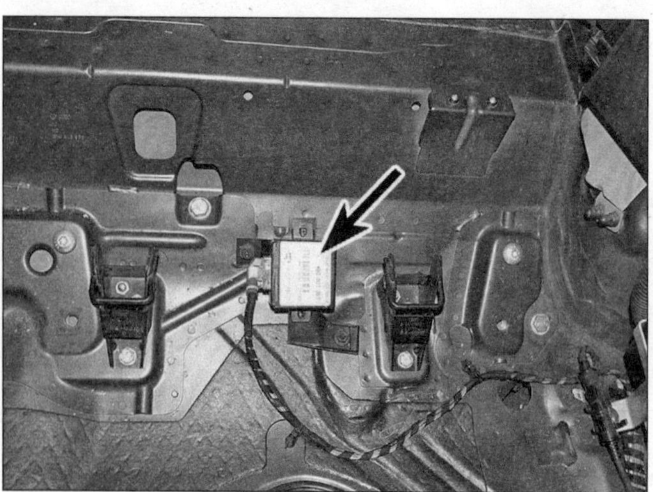
8.4a Location of ECU on Coupe models

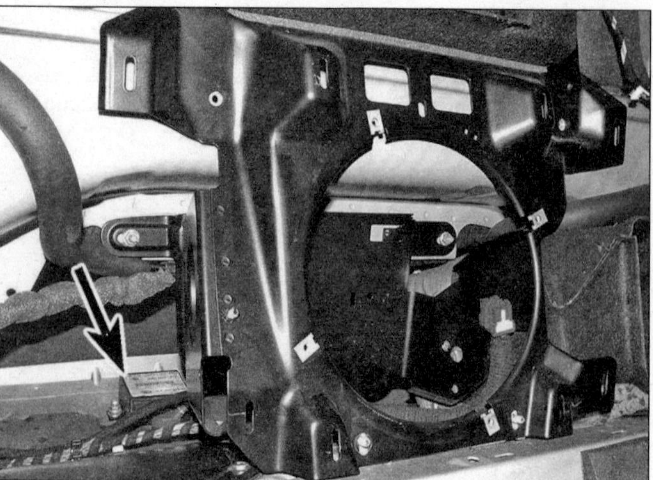
8.4b Location of ECU on Roadster models

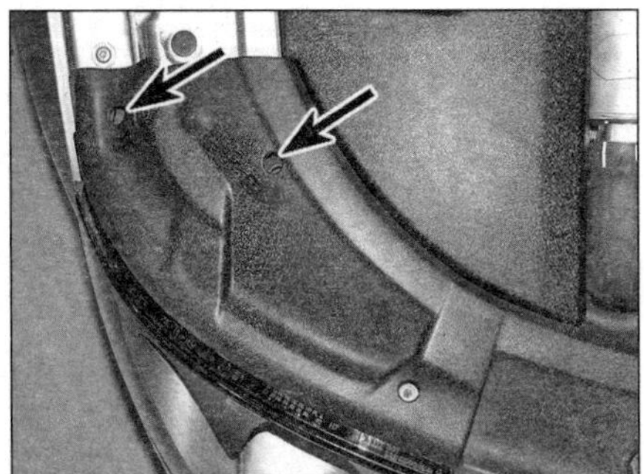

9.2 Headlamp adjustment screws (arrowed)

9.3a Vertical position – Up and Down

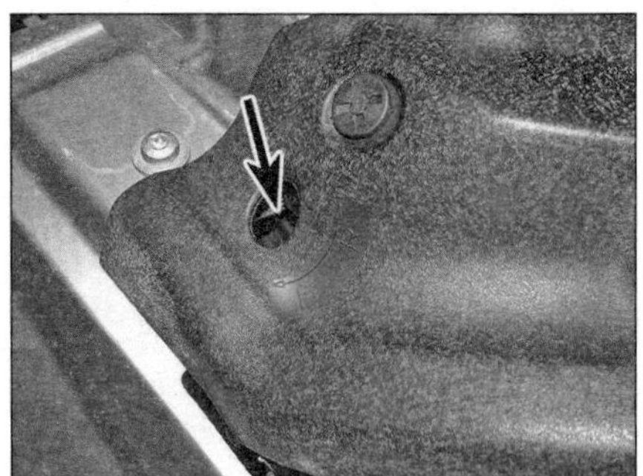

9.3b Horizontal aim – Left and Right

adjusted using the adjuster assemblies fitted to the top of each light unit **(see illustration)**.

3 The inner adjuster alters the vertical position (Up and Down) of the beam, whilst the outer adjuster alters the horizontal aim (Left and Right) of the beam **(see illustrations)**.

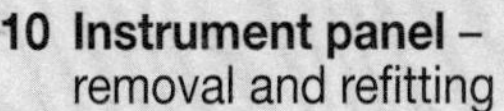

10 Instrument panel – removal and refitting

Removal

1 Disconnect the battery negative lead. **Note:** *Before disconnecting the battery, refer to* Disconnecting the battery *in the Reference section at the rear of this manual.*

2 Release the steering wheel adjustment lock under the steering column, then pull the steering wheel out as far as possible, and set it in the lowest position. **Note:** *In the following illustrations there is no steering wheel or switches fitted, this is only done for clarity and they do not need to be removed.*

3 Remove the drivers side lower facia trim panel as described in Chapter 11 Section 28.

4 Remove the two instrument panel retaining screws, then lift the panel out at the bottom, releasing the two retaining clips at the upper edge. Withdraw the panel from the facia, then release the securing clips and disconnect the wiring plug connectors on the rear of the unit **(see illustrations)**.

5 Withdraw the instrument panel from the facia.

Refitting

6 Refitting is a reversal of removal, making sure that the wiring plugs are securely reconnected.

10.4a Undo the screws (arrowed)...

10.4b ...pull panel out from the bottom...

10.4c ...to release the upper securing clips (arrowed)

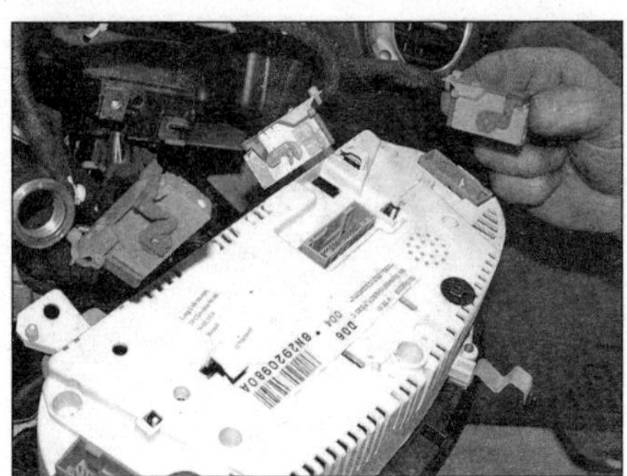

10.4d ... and then disconnect the wiring plugs

11 Instrument panel components – removal and refitting

1 It is not possible to dismantle the instrument panel. If any of the gauges are faulty, the complete instrument panel must be renewed.

12 Service interval indicator – general information and resetting

1 All Audi models are equipped with a service interval indicator. After all necessary maintenance work has been completed the service interval display must be reset. If more than one service schedule is carried out, note that the relevant display intervals must be reset individually.

2 The display is reset using the buttons on the right-hand side of the instrument panel (below the speedometer) and the clock setting button on the left-hand side of the panel (below the clock/tachometer). Resetting is described in Chapter 1 Section 10.

13 Clock – removal and refitting

1 The clock is integral with the instrument panel, and cannot be removed separately. The instrument panel is a sealed unit, and if the clock, or any other components, are faulty, the complete instrument panel must be renewed. Refer to Section 10 to remove it.

14 Cigarette lighter – removal and refitting

Removal

1 Disconnect the battery negative lead. **Note:** *Before disconnecting the battery, refer to* Disconnecting the battery *in the Reference section at the rear of this manual.*

14.2 Undo the retaining screw

14.3a Remove the ashtray...

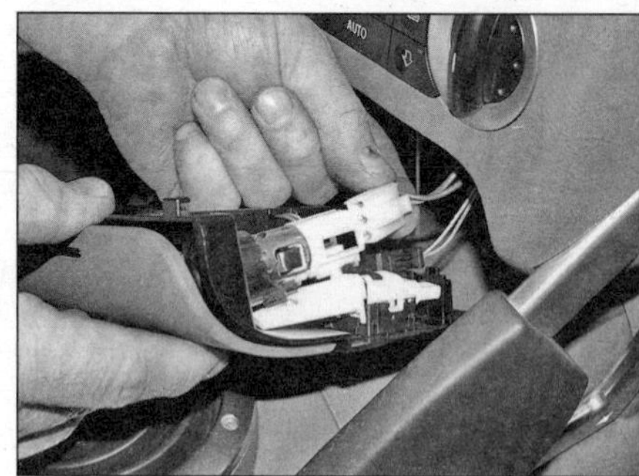
14.3b ...and disconnect the wiring connectors

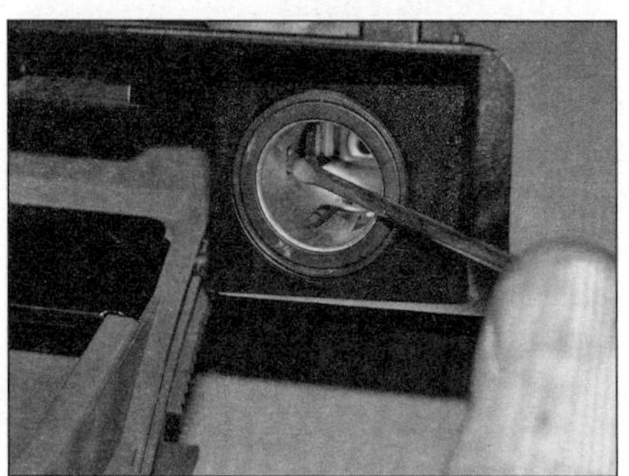
14.4a Release the retaining clips...

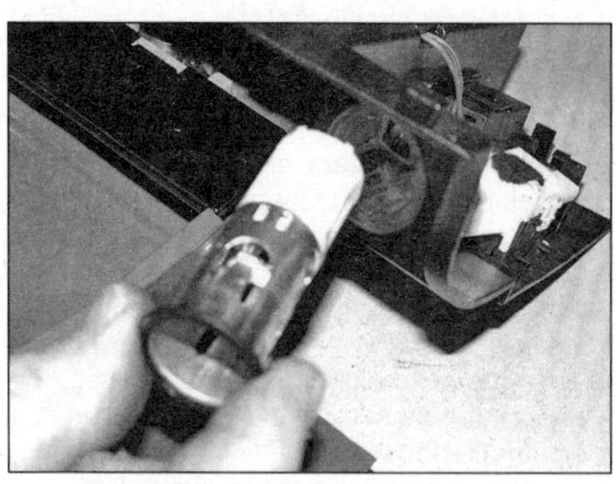
14.4b ...push out the centre element...

14.4c ...then remove the outer coloured plastic collar

2 Open the ashtray and undo the retaining screw inside the upper edge **(see illustration)**.

3 Withdraw the ashtray/cigarette lighter assembly out from the facia and disconnect the wiring connectors **(see illustrations)**.

4 Release the plastic outer retaining clips, then push the metal centre element out of the ashtray, the outer coloured plastic collar can then be removed **(see illustrations)**.

5 The wiring and bulbs for the ashtray/lighter assembly come as one piece and are removed as one unit **(see illustration)**.

Refitting

6 Refitting is a reversal of removal.

15 Horn – removal and refitting

Removal

1 Disconnect the battery negative lead. **Note:** *Before disconnecting the battery, refer to* Disconnecting the battery *in the Reference section at the rear of this manual.*

2 Release the fasteners and remove the engine undershields, and also the inner side trims from under the wheel arch, depending on which side is being worked on. There are two horns fitted, one at each side of the lower part of the radiator housing.

3 Disconnect the horn wiring plug, then unscrew the securing bolt, and withdraw the horn from its mounting bracket **(see illustrations)**.

Refitting

4 Refitting is a reversal of removal.

16 Speedometer sensor – general information

1 All models are fitted with an electronic speedometer sensor. This device measures the rotational speed of the transmission final drive and converts the information into an electronic signal, which is then sent to the

14.5 Wiring and bulbs clipped into position on housing

15.3a Location of horn (arrowed) – Left-hand side

15.3b Location of horn (arrowed) – Right-hand side

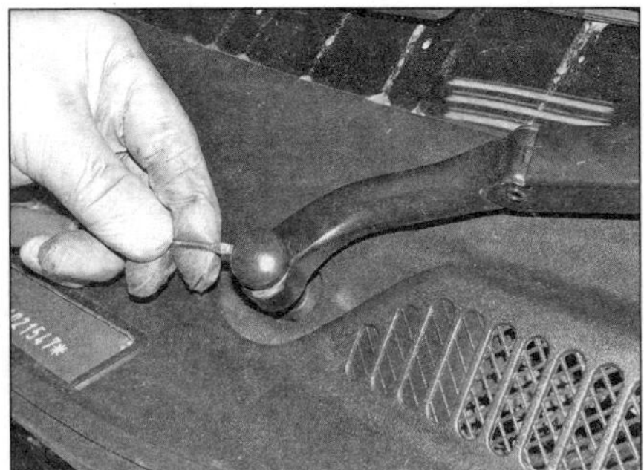

17.3 Remove the cap and slacken the nut

17.4 Using a puller to release the wiper arm from the spindle

18.2 Remove the rubber sealing strip

speedometer module in the instrument panel. On certain models, the signal is also used as an input by the engine management system ECU, and the trip computer.

2 Refer to Chapter 7A Section 6 for details of the removal procedure.

17 Wiper arm – removal and refitting

Removal

1 Operate the wiper motor, then switch off so that the wiper arms return to the at-rest position.

2 Stick a piece of masking tape to the glass along the edge of the wiper blade to use as an alignment aid on refitting.

3 Prise off the wiper arm spindle nut cover, then slacken but do not completely remove the spindle nut. Lift the blade off the glass and pull the wiper arm until it releases from the spindle **(see illustration)**.

4 With the wiper arm released, remove the spindle nut and then remove the wiper arm from the spindle. If the wiper arm is a tight fit on the spindle, then a small puller can be used to release the wiper arm **(see illustration)**. **Note:** *If both wiper arms are to be removed at the same time, mark them for identification; the arms are not interchangeable.*

Refitting

5 Ensure that the wiper arm and spindle splines are clean and dry, then refit the arm to the spindle, aligning the wiper blade with the tape fitted on removal. Refit the spindle nut, tightening it securely, and clip the nut cover back in position.

18 Windscreen wiper motor and linkage – removal and refitting

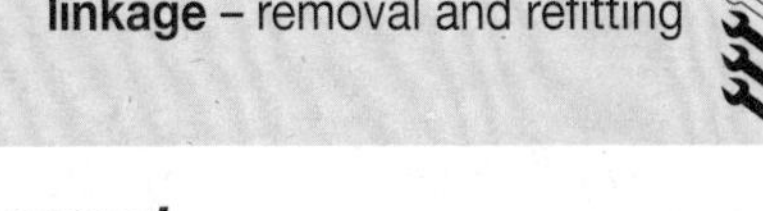

Removal

1 Remove the wiper arms as described in Section 17.

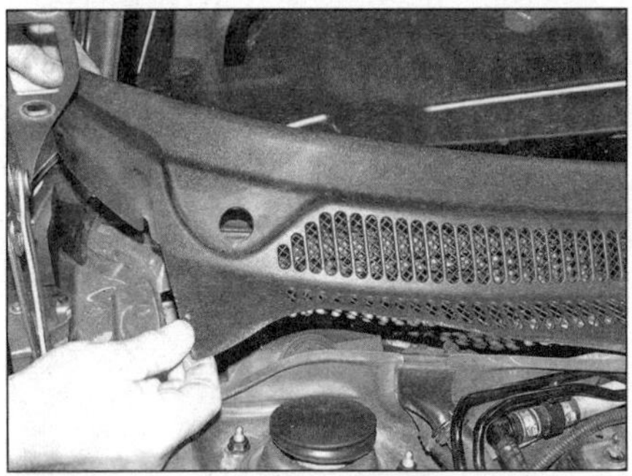

18.3 Remove the windscreen cowling

2 Remove the rubber sealing strip from along the top of the bulkhead **(see illustration)**.

3 The windscreen cowling can then be unclipped from the base of the windscreen and moved to one side **(see illustration)**.

4 To remove the windscreen cowling completely from the vehicle, it will be necessary to disconnect the washer hose and wiring connectors for the heated washer jets **(see illustrations)**.

Caution: Do not use a screwdriver to lever between the cowling and windscreen as this is likely to result in the windscreen cracking.

5 Where fitted, remove the plastic covers from over the wiper spindles **(see illustration)**.

6 Undo the three securing bolts, then carefully

18.4a Disconnect the washer hose...

18.4b ...and wiring connectors

18.5 Remove the wiper spindle plastic covers

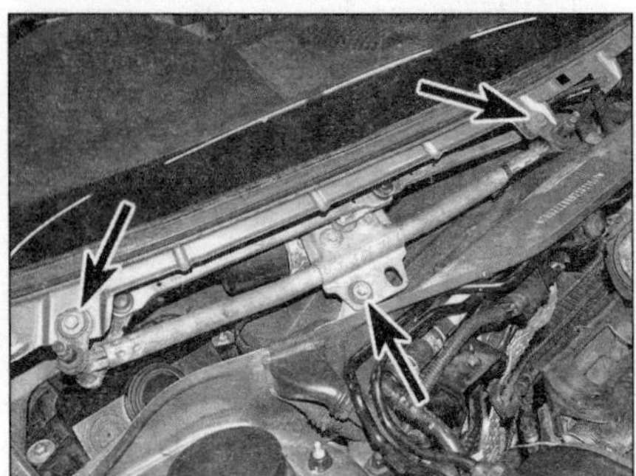
18.6a Remove the three mounting bolts (arrowed)...

18.6b ...then manoeuvre the motor/linkage from the scuttle...

18.6c ...and disconnect the wiring connector

18.8 Crank arm parallel with frame when refitted

manoeuvre the windscreen wiper motor and linkage out from the scuttle, taking care not to damage the paintwork. Disconnect the wiring plug from the motor **(see illustrations)**.

7 Inspect the rubber mountings for signs of damage or deterioration, and renew if necessary.

8 To remove the motor from the linkage, proceed as follows.

a) First prise off the two wiper linkage arms (from the right and left-hand wiper spindles), to the ball joint on the wiper motor crank arm.

b) Check the position of the crank arm on the wiper motor spindle. When the crank arm is refitted on the motor spindle, it should be parallel with the frame of the wiper linkage ***(see illustration)****.*

c) Unscrew the nut securing the crank arm to the motor spindle, and remove the crank arm.

d) Unscrew the three bolts securing the motor to the mounting plate, then withdraw the motor.

Refitting

9 Refitting is a reversal of removal, bearing in mind the following points.

a) If the wiper motor has been separated from the linkage, ensure that the crank arm is aligned to the wiper linkage **(see illustration 18.8)**.

b) Ensure that the mounting rubbers and spacers are fitted to the wiper linkage assembly.

c) Clean-out and lubricate the windscreen cowling mounting slots with a silicone-based spray lubricant to ease installation. Do not strike the cowling to seat it in position as this could result in the windscreen cracking.

d) Refit the wiper arms as described in Section 17.

19 Washer system components – removal and refitting

Washer fluid reservoir

Removal

1 Switch off the ignition and all electrical consumers.

2 Apply the handbrake, then jack up the front of the vehicle and support it on axle stands (see *Jacking and vehicle support*). Remove the left-hand front roadwheel and remove the inner liner from the rear of the wheel arch.

3 Open the plastic cap from the top of the washer reservoir, then release the plastic ring from around the neck of the reservoir and remove the cap completely **(see illustration)**.

4 Working up inside the rear of the wheel arch, undo the two reservoir retaining bolts **(see illustration)**.

5 Place a container below the washer reservoir, to catch any washer fluid still inside, and then disconnect the headlight washer hose from the pump fitted to the lower part of the washer reservoir **(see illustration)**.

6 Disconnect the wiring connector from the headlight washer pump, at the lower part of the washer reservoir **(see illustration)**.

7 Unclip the windscreen washer hose from the side of the reservoir and disconnect it from the washer pump. Disconnect the wiring connectors from the windscreen washer pump and washer fluid level sensor **(see illustration)**.

8 The reservoir can then be removed from under the wheel arch, complete with washer pumps.

Refitting

9 Refitting is a reversal of removal, making sure that the locating peg on the top of the reservoir

19.3 Remove the plastic cap

19.4 Reservoir mounting bolts (arrowed)

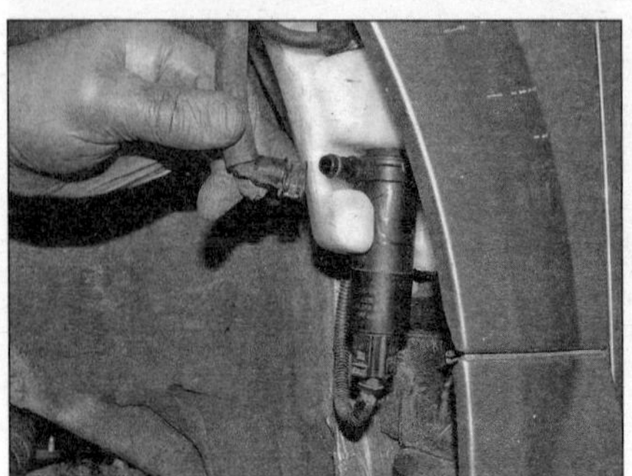
19.5 Disconnect the headlight washer hose

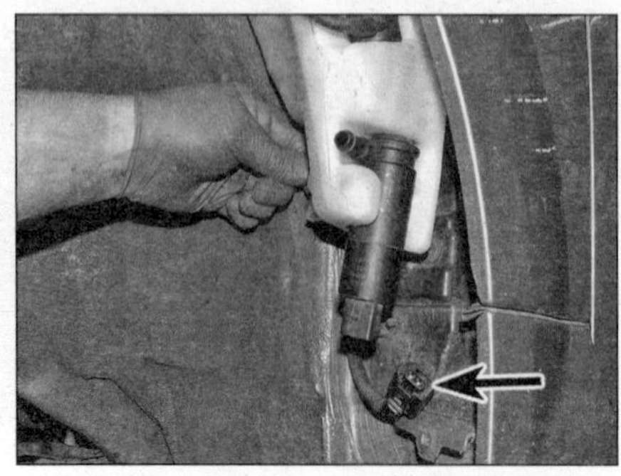
19.6 Disconnect the wiring connector

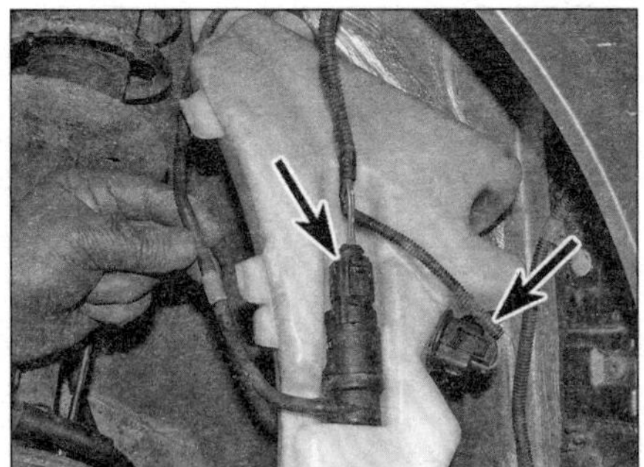

19.7 Disconnect the washer hose and the wiring connectors (arrowed)

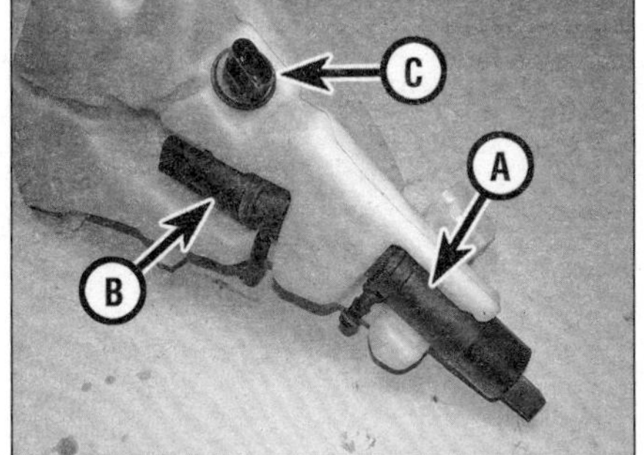

19.12b Washer reservoir pumps and level sender

(A) Headlight washer pump
(B) Windscreen washer pump
(C) Washer fluid level sensor

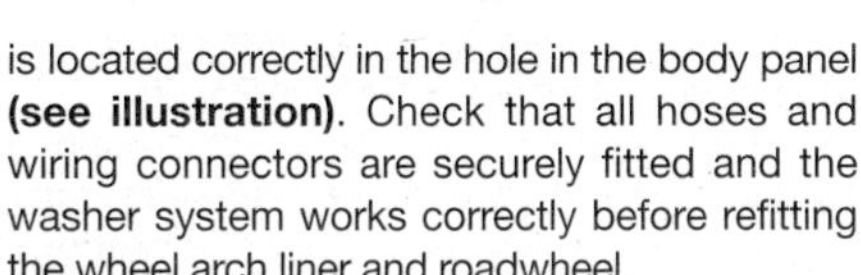

is located correctly in the hole in the body panel **(see illustration)**. Check that all hoses and wiring connectors are securely fitted and the washer system works correctly before refitting the wheel arch liner and roadwheel.

Washer fluid pumps and level sensor

Removal

10 Switch off the ignition and all electrical consumers.

11 Remove the washer fluid reservoir as described previously in this Section.

12 Carefully pull the pump from its grommet in the reservoir **(see illustrations)**. If not already done, disconnect the washer fluid hose(s) and the wiring plug from the pump.

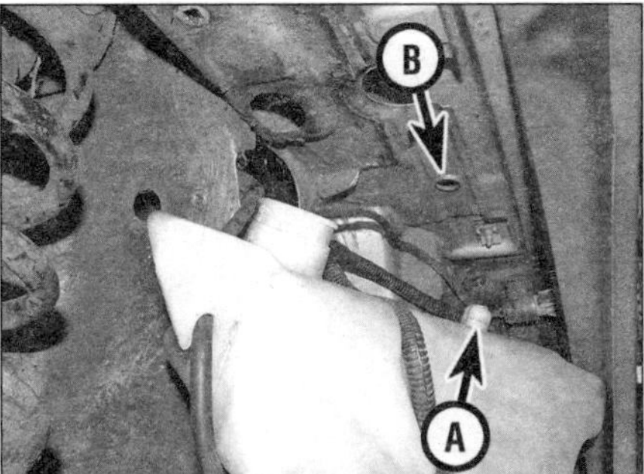

19.9 Align the locating peg (A) with the hole in the body (B)

19.15 Unclip the washer jet from the cowling

Refitting

13 Refitting is a reversal of removal, but take care not to push the pump grommet into the reservoir. Use a little soapy water to ease the pump into the grommet.

Windscreen washer jets

Removal

14 Open the bonnet, and remove the windscreen lower cowling as described in Section 18.

15 Unclip the washer jet from the top of the windscreen cowling, and then withdraw the jet with the wiring and washer hose **(see illustration)**. Unclip the wiring and washer hose from along the length of the windscreen lower cowling.

Refitting

16 Refitting is a reversal of removal. Note

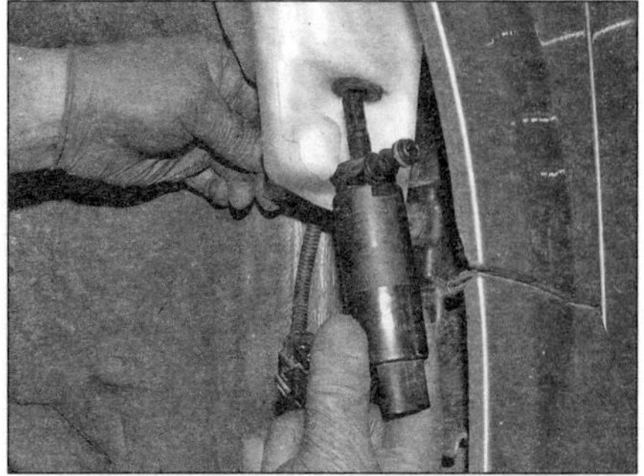

19.12a Pull the headlight washer pump from the grommet

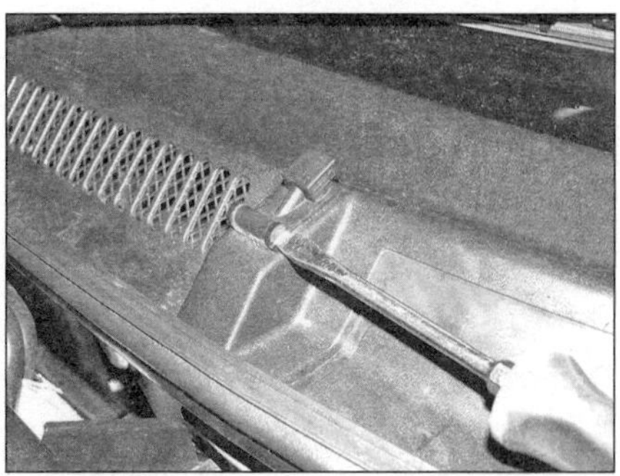

19.16 Turn the eccentric to adjust the jet

that the aim of the jet can be adjusted using a screwdriver and turning the eccentric shaft at the base of the washer jet **(see illustration)**. **Note:** *The aim of the washer jet should be just above the centre line of the windscreen once adjusted.*

Headlight washer jets

Removal

17 Remove the front bumper, as described in Chapter 11 Section 6.

18 Undo the five retaining screws and remove the headlight washer jet assembly from the rear of the bumper **(see illustrations)**.

19 Release the retaining clip and disconnect the hose from the base of the washer jet assembly **(see illustration)**.

Refitting

20 Refitting is a reversal of removal.

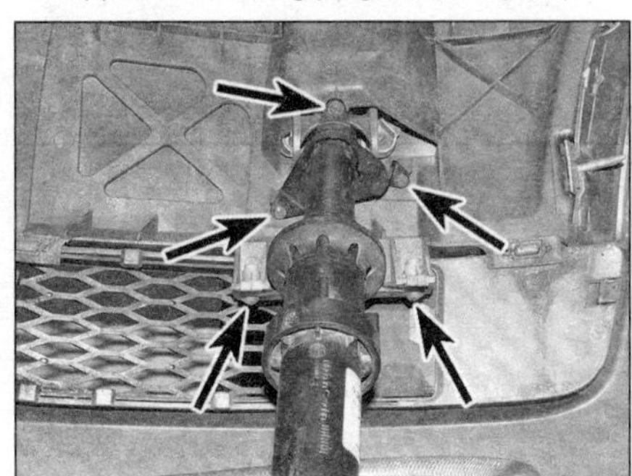

19.18a Undo the retaining screws (arrowed)...

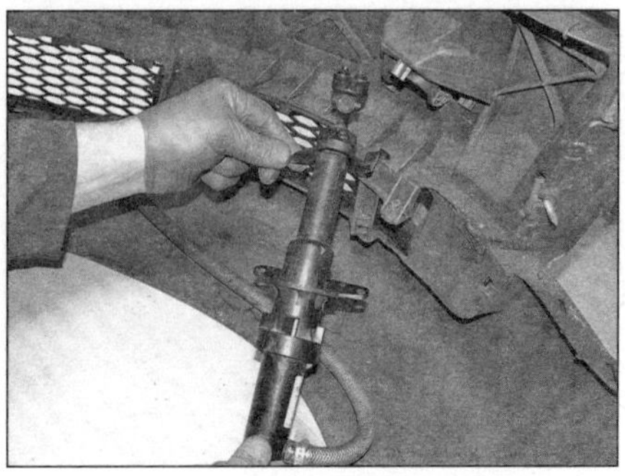

19.18b ...and remove the washer jet assembly

19.19 Washer hose fitted to base of assembly

20.3a Withdraw the radio/CD player...

20.3b ...disconnect the aerial lead...

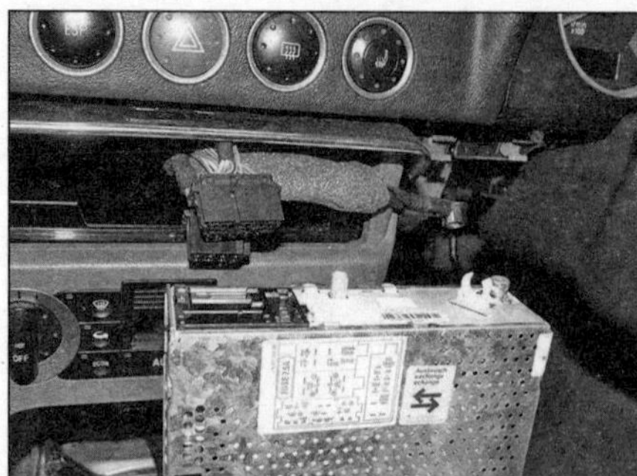
20.3c ...and wiring block connectors

20 Radio/CD player/changer – removal and refitting

Note: *This Section only applies to standard-fit audio equipment.*

Radio/CD player

Removal

1 The radio is fitted with special mounting clips, requiring the use of special removal tools, which should be supplied with the vehicle, or may be obtained from an in-car entertainment specialist.

2 Switch off the ignition and all electrical consumers.

3 Insert the tools into the slots on the lower edge of the unit and push them until they snap into place. The radio/CD player can then be pulled out of the facia using the tools, and the wiring connectors and aerial disconnected **(see illustrations)**.

Refitting

4 Refitting is a reversal of removal, reconnect the wiring connectors and aerial lead then push the unit into the facia until the retaining lugs snap into place.

CD changer

Roadster 'convertible' models

5 Switch off the ignition and all electrical consumers, then remove the CD changer.

20.7 Location of CD changer (arrowed) – Rear trim panels removed

6 Remove the trim panels at the rear of the passenger seat, with reference to Chapter 11 Section 26.

7 The CD changer (where fitted) is located behind the passenger seat inside the small compartment in the rear trim panel **(see illustration)**. The changer is fitted into a mounting bracket and has a bolt at each side to hold it in place. Undo the two retaining bolts and withdraw the changer from the mounting bracket and disconnect the wiring connector as it is removed.

8 Refitting is a reversal of removal, reconnect the wiring then push the unit into the mounting bracket and tighten the retaining bolts.

Coupe models

9 Switch off the ignition and all electrical consumers, then remove the CD changer.

20.11 Location of CD changer (arrowed) – Side trim panel removed

10 Remove the left-hand side trim panel, with reference to Chapter 11 Section 25, 26.

11 The CD changer (where fitted) is located to the left-hand side of the rear passenger seat in the side trim panel **(see illustration)**. The changer is fitted into a mounting bracket and has a screw at the front to hold it in place. Disconnect the wiring connector and undo the retaining screw, then withdraw the changer from the mounting bracket.

12 Refitting is a reversal of removal, push the unit into the mounting bracket and tighten the retaining screw, then reconnect the wiring connector.

21 Loudspeakers – removal and refitting

Front door-mounted mid-range/ bass

1 Switch off the ignition and all electrical consumers.

2 Remove the door inner trim panel, as described in Chapter 11 Section 11.

3 Undo the three retaining nuts and remove the plastic ring from the rear of the speaker, and then pull back the insulation sheet **(see illustrations)**.

4 Undo the retaining nuts, disconnect the wiring connector **(see illustration)**, and then

21.3a Remove the plastic retaining ring...

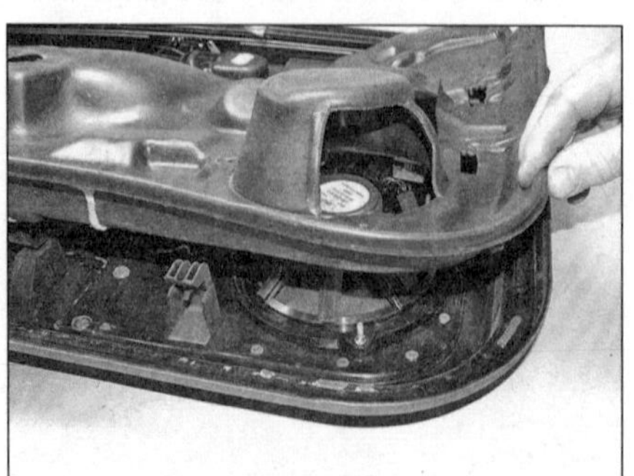
21.3b ...and then pull back the insulation

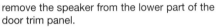

21.4 Speaker retaining nuts and wiring connector

remove the speaker from the lower part of the door trim panel.

5 Refitting is a reversal of removal.

Front door-mounted treble

6 Switch off the ignition and all electrical consumers.

7 Remove the door trim as described in Chapter 11.

8 Undo the three retaining nuts and remove the plastic ring from the rear of the speaker, and then pull back the insulation sheet **(see illustrations 21.3a and 21.3b)**.

9 Undo the retaining screws, disconnect the wiring connector **(see illustration)**, and then remove the speaker from the door trim panel.

10 Refitting is a reversal of removal.

Rear mounted bass – Roadster models

11 Switch off the ignition and all electrical consumers.

12 There are two bass speakers fitted, one to the left-hand corner and one to the right-hand corner behind the front seats. Remove the rear trim panels from behind the seats, with reference to Chapter 11 Section 26.

13 Undo the retaining screws and remove the speaker from the mounting bracket, then disconnect the wiring connector **(see illustration)**.

14 Refitting is a reversal of removal.

Rear mounted bass – Coupe models

15 Switch off the ignition and all electrical consumers.

21.9 Speaker retaining screws

21.17 Undo the speaker retaining screws

16 There are two bass speakers fitted, one to the left-hand side and one to the right-hand side of the rear seats. Remove the side trim panels, with reference to Chapter 11 Sections 25 and 26.

17 Undo the retaining screws and remove the speaker from the body panel, then disconnect the wiring connector as the speaker is removed **(see illustration)**.

18 Refitting is a reversal of removal.

Rear mounted centre – Roadster models

19 Switch off the ignition and all electrical consumers.

20 There is a centre speakers fitted, in the rear trim panel behind the front seats. Remove the rear trim panels from behind

21.13 Left-hand rear bass speaker shown

21.20 Remove the rear trim panels

the seats **(see illustration)**, with reference to Chapter 11 Section 26.

21 Undo the retaining screws and remove the speaker assembly from the mounting bracket, then disconnect the wiring connectors **(see illustrations)**.

22 Refitting is a reversal of removal.

Front mounted centre in facia

23 Depending on model there may be a speaker fitted in the top centre of the facia panel, under the left-hand air vent, behind the sunlight penetration sensor. Remove the air vent from the top of the facia with reference to Chapter 3 Section 10. With the vent removed, undo the retaining screws and remove the speaker from the facia, then disconnect the wiring connector as it is removed. Tape the end of the wiring once removed, to prevent it dropping down inside the top of the facia.

21.21a Undo the outer retaining screws...

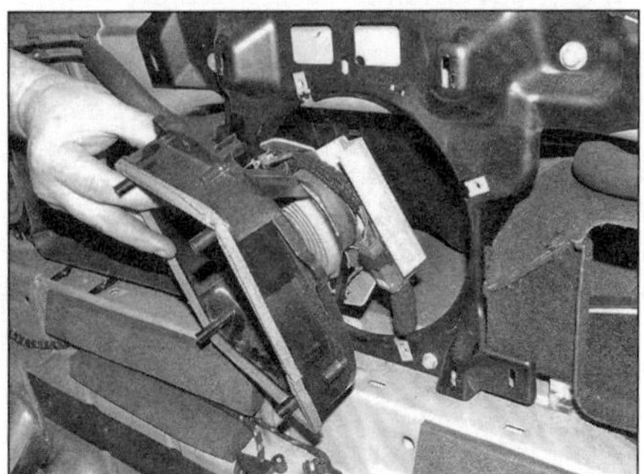
21.21b ...withdraw the speaker...

21.21c ...and disconnect the wiring connector

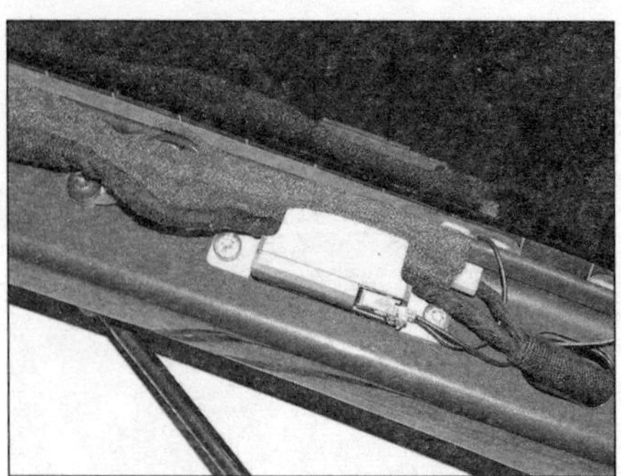

22.4 Aerial amplifier location

22 Radio aerial – removal and refitting

Roadster 'convertible' models

1 The aerial is located on the left-hand rear wing of the vehicle, first the aerial mast can be unscrewed from the base by twisting anti-clockwise.

2 If the aerial base is to be removed, open the small flap in the left-hand side trim in the luggage compartment to access the aerial wires. Unclip the plastic cover from the top of the base on the wing panel and undo the retaining nut from the top of the aerial base. The wiring can then be removed from the base of the aerial from inside the wing panel.

3 Refitting is a reversal of removal.

Coupe models

4 The aerial is part of the rear screen, and an aerial amplifier is fitted to the left-hand side of the rear screen on the inside of the tailgate **(see illustration)**.

5 Remove the tailgate inner trim panel, as described in Chapter 11 Section 14.

6 Undo the retaining screws and withdraw the amplifier away from the tailgate and disconnect the wiring connectors.

7 Refitting is a reversal of removal.

23 Anti-theft alarm system and engine immobiliser – general information

Note: *This information is applicable only to the anti-theft alarm system fitted by Audi as standard equipment.*

1 Models in the range are fitted with an anti-theft alarm system as standard equipment. The alarm has switches on all the doors (including the tailgate/boot lid), the bonnet and the ignition switch. If the tailgate/boot lid, bonnet or any of the doors are opened, or the ignition switch is switched on whilst the alarm is set, the alarm horn will sound and the hazard warning lights will flash. Some models are equipped with an internal monitoring system, which will activate the alarm system if any movement in the cabin is detected.

2 The alarm is set using the key in the driver's or passenger's front door lock, and tailgate/boot lid lock, or via the central locking remote control transmitter. The alarm system will then start to monitor its various switches approximately 30 seconds later.

3 With the alarm set, if the tailgate/boot lid is unlocked, the lock switch sensing will automatically be switched off but the door and bonnet switches will still be active. Once the tailgate/boot lid is shut and locked again, the switch sensing will be switched back on.

4 Certain models are fitted with an immobiliser system, which is activated via the ignition switch. A module incorporated in the ignition switch reads a code contained within the ignition key. The module sends a signal to the engine management electronic control unit (ECU) which allows the engine to start if the code is correct. If an incorrect ignition key is used, the engine will not start.

5 If a fault is suspected with the alarm or immobiliser systems, the vehicle should be taken to an Audi dealer for examination. They will have access to a special diagnostic tester which will quickly trace any fault present in the system.

24 Airbag system – general information and precautions

Warning: Before carrying out any operations on the airbag system, disconnect the battery negative terminal (refer to ' Disconnecting the battery 13 Section 6 ' in the Reference section at the rear of this manual). When operations are complete, make sure no one is inside the vehicle when the battery is reconnected.

- ***Note that the airbag(s) must not be subjected to temperatures in excess of 90°C (194°F). When the airbag is removed, ensure that it is stored the with the pad upwards to prevent possible inflation.***
- ***Do not allow any solvents or cleaning agents to contact the airbag assemblies. They must be cleaned using only a damp cloth.***
- ***The airbags and control unit are both sensitive to impact. If either is dropped or damaged they should be renewed.***
- ***Remove the airbag units prior to using arc-welding equipment on the vehicle.***

1 A driver's airbag, passenger's airbag and side airbags were fitted as standard to the all models. The airbag system comprises of the airbag unit (complete with gas generator) which is fitted to the steering wheel (driver's side), facia (passenger's side) and front seats, an impact sensor, the control unit and a warning light in the instrument panel.

2 The airbag system is triggered in the event of a heavy frontal or side impact above a predetermined force; depending on the point of impact. The airbag is inflated within milliseconds and forms a safety cushion between the driver and the steering wheel, the passenger and the facia, and in the case of side impact, between front seat occupants and the sides of the cabin. This prevents contact between the upper body and cabin interior, and therefore greatly reduces the risk of injury. The airbag then deflates almost immediately.

3 Every time the ignition is switched on, the airbag control unit performs a self-test. The self-test takes approximately 3 seconds and during this time the airbag warning light on the facia is illuminated. After the self-test has been completed the warning light should go out. If the warning light fails to come on, remains illuminated after the initial 3 second period or comes on at any time when the vehicle is being driven, there is a fault in the airbag system. The vehicle should then be taken to an Audi dealer for examination at the earliest possible opportunity.

25 Airbag system components – removal and refitting

Note: *Refer to the warnings in Section 24 before carrying out the following operations.*

1 Disconnect the battery negative terminal, then continue as described under the relevant heading. **Note:** *Before disconnecting the battery, refer to* Disconnecting the battery *in the Reference section at the rear of this manual.*

Driver's side airbag

Removal

2 With the battery disconnected, set the front wheels in the straight-ahead position, and release the steering lock by inserting the ignition key.

3 Adjust the steering column to its lowest position by releasing the adjustment handle, then pull out the column and lower it as far as possible. Lock the column in this position by returning the adjustment handle.

4 With the spokes in the vertical position, undo the driver's airbag Torx screw at the rear of the steering wheel hub. Then turn the steering wheel through 180° and undo the remaining airbag Torx screw **(see illustrations)**. Note the screws stay in position in the steering wheel and do not need to be completely removed.

5 Carefully withdraw the driver's airbag from the centre of the steering wheel, release the locking clip and and disconnect the wiring connector **(see illustrations)**.

Warning: Position the airbag in a safe and secure place, away from the work area.

Refitting

6 On refitting, reconnect the wiring connector and seat the airbag unit in the steering wheel, making sure that the wire does not become trapped. Tighten the airbag retaining screws, then reconnect the battery negative lead, ensuring that no-one is inside the vehicle as the lead is connected.

Passenger's side airbag

Removal

7 With reference to Chapter 11 Section 26, remove the passenger side glovebox.

8 With the battery earth lead disconnected, disconnect the wiring connector from the lower part of the airbag unit **(see illustration)**.

9 Unscrew the four Torx screws securing the airbag support bracket to the facia crossmember and the two Torx screws securing the air bag to the upper facia panel **(see illustration)**.

10 Carefully withdraw the airbag unit from under the facia **(see illustration)**.

Warning: Position the airbag in a safe and secure place, away from the work area.

Refitting

11 On refitting, manoeuvre the airbag into position, then refit and tighten the securing screws. Reconnect the wiring connector.

12 Refit the glovebox, then reconnect the battery negative lead, ensuring that no-one is inside the vehicle as the lead is connected.

Front seat side impact airbags

13 The side impact air bags are integral with the seats. As seat upholstery removal requires considerable skill and experience, if it is to be carried out without damage, it is best entrusted to an expert.

Airbag control unit

Removal

14 The control unit is located under the facia, beneath the heater matrix housing **(see illustration)**.

15 Disconnect the battery negative lead. **Note:** *Before disconnecting the battery, refer to* Disconnecting the battery *in the Reference section at the rear of this manual.*

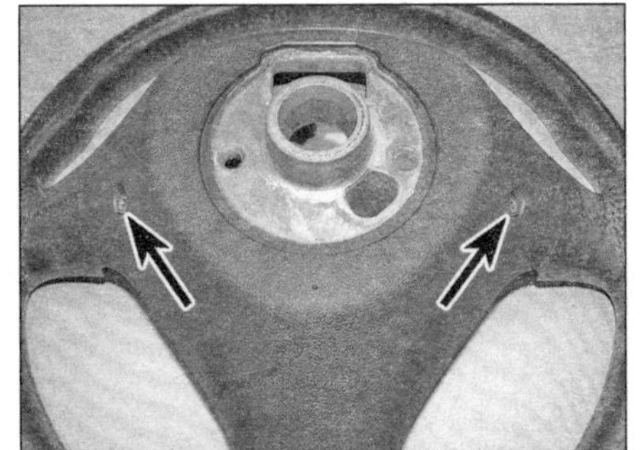

25.4a Position of screws (arrowed) in the rear of the steering wheel

25.4b Remove the Torx screw (arrowed)

25.5a Carefully withdraw from the steering wheel...

25.5b ...and release the locking clip...

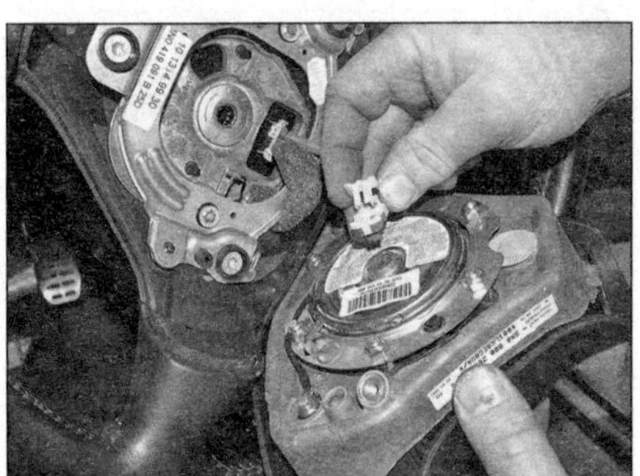

25.5c ...then disconnect from the airbag module

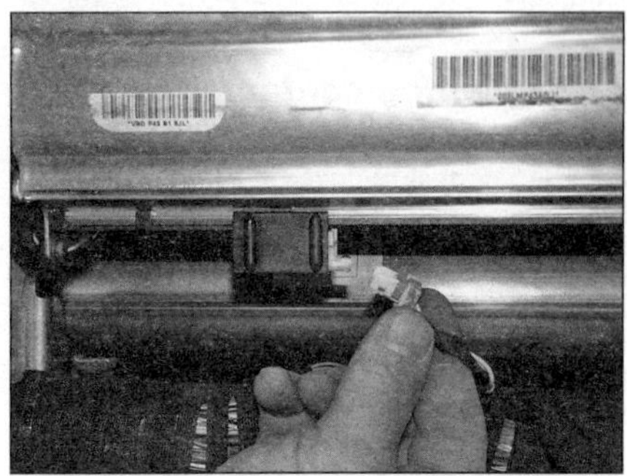

25.8 Disconnect the wiring connector

16 Undo the retaining bolts and remove the right-hand grab handle from the front of the centre console **(see illustrations)**. Retrieve the spacers at the rear of the grab handle, on the top two retaining bolts, for refitting.

17 Working in the driver's side footwell, undo

25.9 Undo the Torx screws (arrowed)

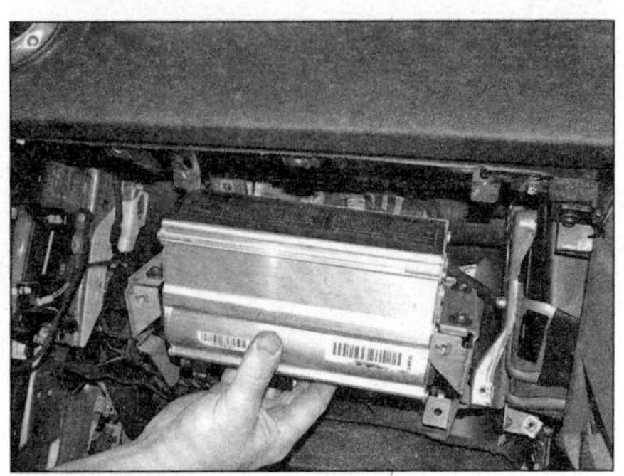

25.10 Withdraw the airbag from under the facia

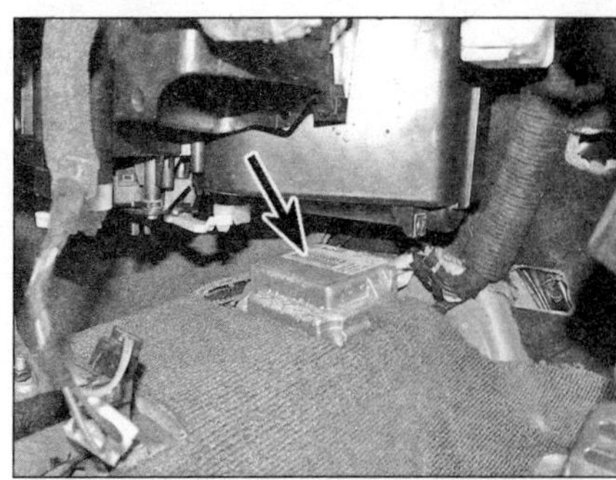

25.14 Airbag ECU location (arrowed)

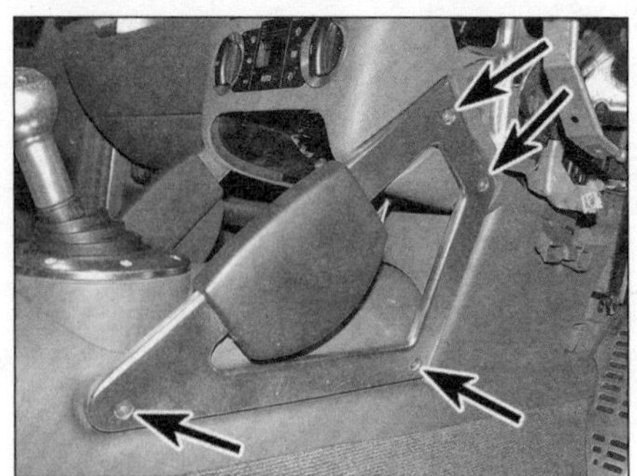
25.16a Undo the grab handle retaining bolts (arrowed)...

the plastic plug from over the front retaining screw, then remove the two retaining screws and withdraw the trim panel and footwell air vent housing from the side of the heater housing **(see illustrations)**.

18 Reach under the heater housing, move the retaining clip to the open position, and disconnect the control unit wiring plug. Unscrew the nuts securing the control unit to the floor, then withdraw the control unit out from under the heater unit.

Refitting

19 Refitting is the reverse of removal making sure the wiring connector is securely reconnected. Reconnect the battery negative lead, ensuring that no-one is inside the vehicle as the lead is connected.

Airbag wiring contact unit

20 The airbag wiring contact unit (return ring with slip ring) is removed from the top of the steering column, before removing the steering column switch assembly. Refer to Section 4, for the removal and refitting procedure.

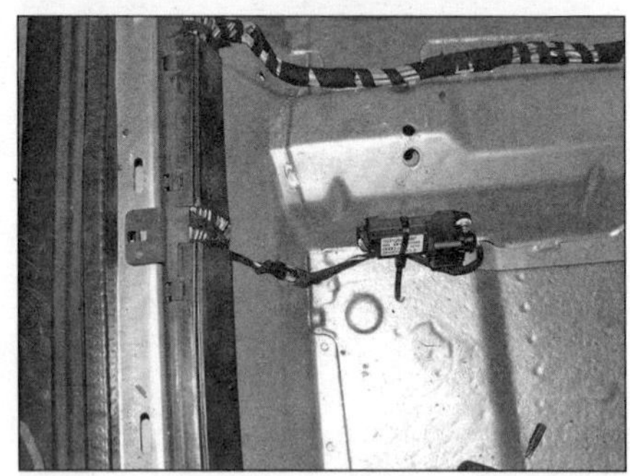
25.21a Sensor fitted on the drivers side...

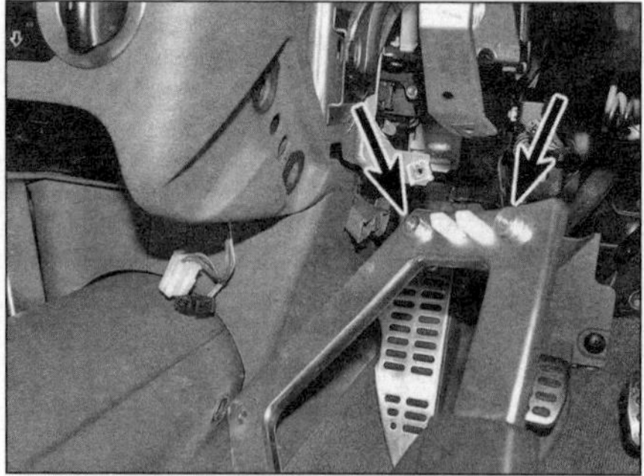
25.16b ...making sure the two spacers (arrowed) are not lost

25.17b ...withdraw the trim panel...

Lateral acceleration sensors

21 There are two lateral acceleration sensors fitted, one at each side of the vehicle. They are positioned on the floor panel under the front seats **(see illustrations)**.

22 To access the sensors, first remove the seat, as described in Chapter 11 Section 23. Then pull back the carpet from the sill trim and disconnect the wiring connector from the sensor. Undo the retaining screws and remove the sensors from the floor panel **(see illustration)**. Note.The sensors are handed and can only be fitted to the correct side of the vehicle, There is an arrow on the front of the sensor and this should be pointing to the outside of the vehicle when in position.

25.21b ...and on the passenger side

25.17a Undo the retaining screws (arrowed)...

25.17c ...and remove the air vent housing

25.22 Note the direction of the arrow on the label

FUSE BOX IN ENGINE COMPARTMENT

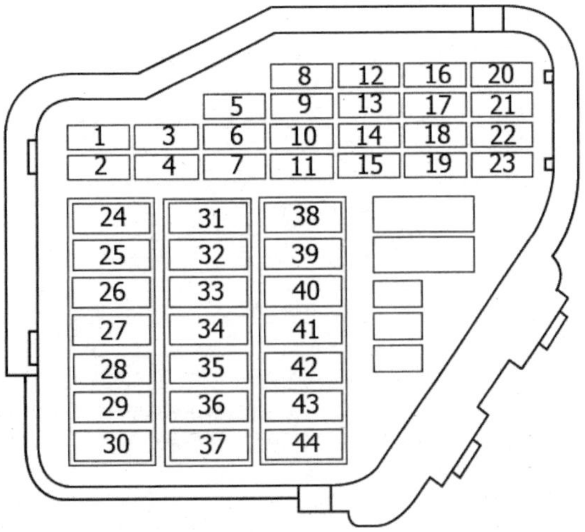

FUSE/RELAY	VALUE	DESCRIPTION
F1	10 A	Heated mirror, Heated washer
F2	10 A	Hazard warning light switch
F3	5 A	Glove box light, Fog light relay, Air Conditioning system / Climatronic operating and display unit
F4	5 A	Number plate light
F5	7.5 A	Fresh air/air recirculating flap switch, Brake pedal switch, Bulb monitoring device, front, Continued coolant circulation relay
F6	5 A	Central locking control unit
F7	10 A	Diagnosis connection, Reversing light switch, Hazard warning light switch, Speedometer sender
F8	5 A	Mobile telephone operating electronics control unit
F9	5 A	ABS control unit
F10	10 A	Up to 10.2001 Motronic control unit, Motronic current supply relay, 15 A also used / From 11.2001 S contact, Central locking control unit, Control unit in dash panel insert
F11	5 A	Control unit in dash panel insert, Oil level and oil temperature sender
F12	7.5 A	Diagnosis connection, Mobile telephone operating electronics control unit, Aerial amplifier for mobile telephone
F13	10 A	Brake light switch
F14	10 A	Central locking control unit, Door warning lamp, Interior monitor, dezactivation switch, Interior locking switch, Rear lid remote release switch
F15	5 A	Control unit in dash panel insert, Automatic gearbox control unit
F16	10 A	Radiator fan control unit
F17	-	Not used
F18	10 A	Main beam bulb, right, Fog light relay, Control unit in dash panel insert
F19	10 A	Main beam bulb, left
F20	15 A	Headlight range controls, Bulb monitoring device
F21	15 A	Bulb monitoring device
F22	5 A	Bulb monitoring device, Control unit in dash panel insert, Side light bulb, right

Fuses and relays

F23	5 A	Bulb monitoring device, Side light bulb, left, Control unit in dash panel insert
F24	20 A	Automatic intermittent wash and wipe relay, Intermittent wiper switch
F25	25 A	Air conditioning system/Climatronic operating and display unit, Heated rear window relay, Fresh air blower, Fresh air blower control unit
F26	25 A	Heated rear window switch
F27	30 A	Cabrio windbreak control unit, Cabrio windbreak switch
F28	20 A	Fuel system pressurisation pump
F29	15 A	Motronic control unit
F30	-	Not used
F31	5 A	Four-wheel drive control unit, Automatic gearbox control unit
F32	10 A	Injectors
F33	20 A	Automatic intermittent wash and wipe relay
F34	10 A	Charge pressure control solenoid valve, Inlet camshaft control valve 1, Turbocharger air recirculation valve
F35	-	Not used
F36	15 A	Front and rear fog light switch
F37	10 A	S contact, Central locking control unit, Control unit in dash panel insert 20 A also used
F38	15 A	Central locking control unit, Anti-theft alarm system horn
F39	15 A	Hazard warning light switch
F40	20 A	Dual tone horn relay
F41	15 A	Cigarette lighter
F42	20 A	Radio / Amplifier
F43	10 A	Activated charcoal filter system solenoid valve 1, Secondary air inlet valve, Air mass meter, Exhaust gas temperature sender 1
F44	15 A	Heated seats

Fuses and relays (continued)

Relay Box with 13 relays

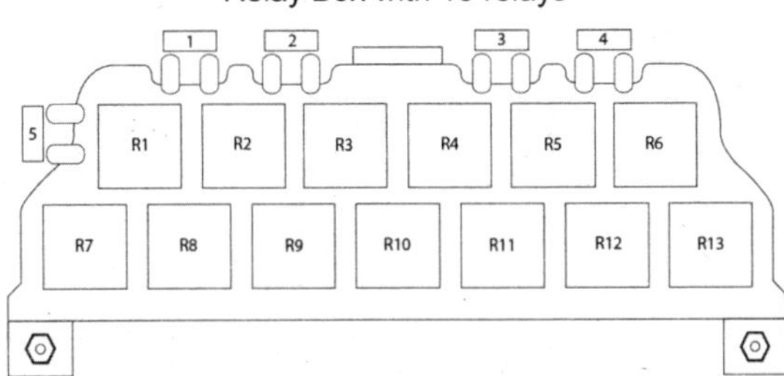

FUSE/RELAY	VALUE	DESCRIPTION
R1	-	Not used
R2	-	Bulb check control unit
R3	-	Bulb check control unit
R4	-	Fog light relay
R5	-	Starter inhibitor relay
R6	-	Not used
R7	-	Brake light suppression relay
R8	-	Not used
R9	-	Not used
R10	-	Heated rear window relay
R11	-	Starter inhibitor relay
R12	-	Cabrio windbreak control unit
R13	-	Continued coolant circulation relay / Reversing light relay
1	-	No information is available
2	-	No information is available
3	-	No information is available
4	-	No information is available
5	-	No information is available

Fuses and relays (continued)

Relays in engine compartment

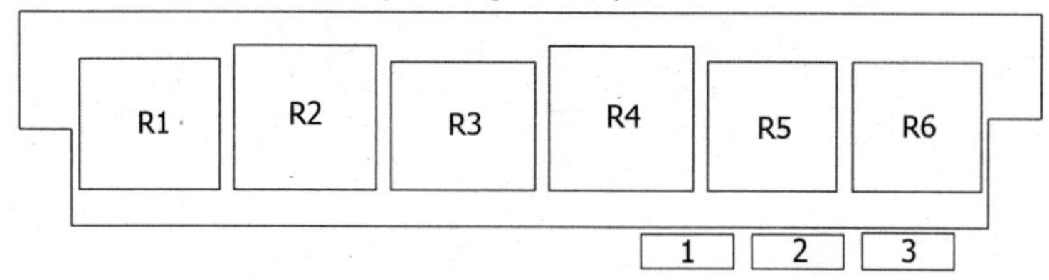

FUSE/RELAY	VALUE	DESCRIPTION
R1	-	Horn relay
R2	-	X contact relief relay
R3	-	Not used
R4	-	Fuel pump
R5	-	Wash / Wiper sysyem
R6	-	Wash / Wiper sysyem
1	-	Convertible roof actuation fuse
2	-	Hydraulic pump relay
3	-	Not used

MAIN FUSE BOX / RELAY

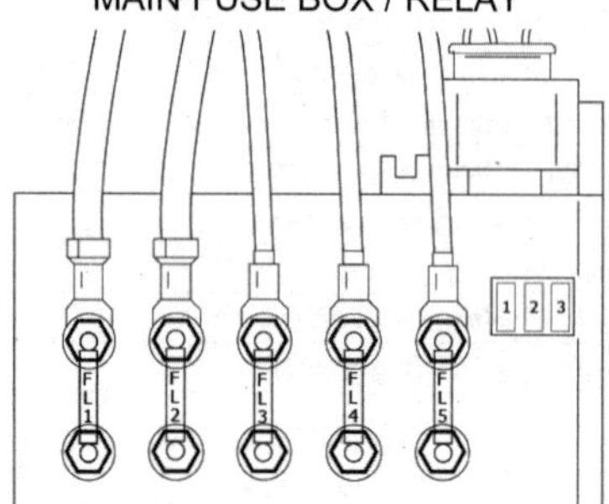

FUSE/RELAY	VALUE	DESCRIPTION
FL1	-	No information is available
FL2	-	No information is available
FL3	-	No information is available
FL4	-	No information is available
FL5	-	No information is available
1	-	No information is available
2	-	No information is available

Fuses and relays (continued)

Starting and charging

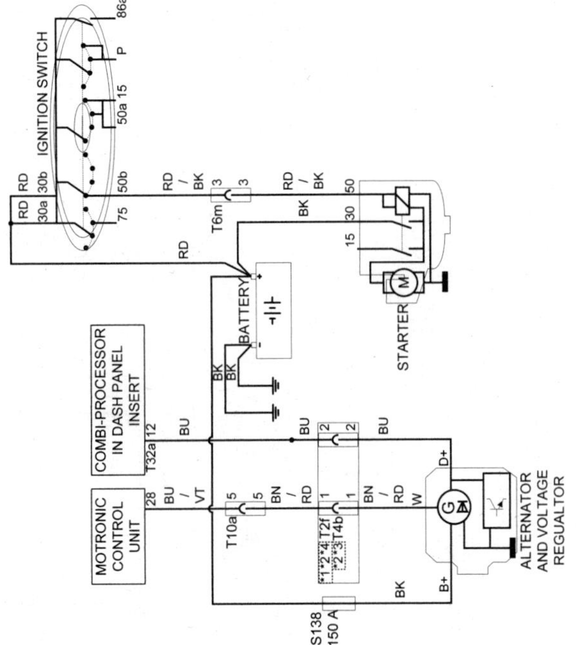

*1 Up to 2000
*2 From 2001 to 2002
*3 With air conditioning
*4 Without air conditioning
*5 Engine code: BAM

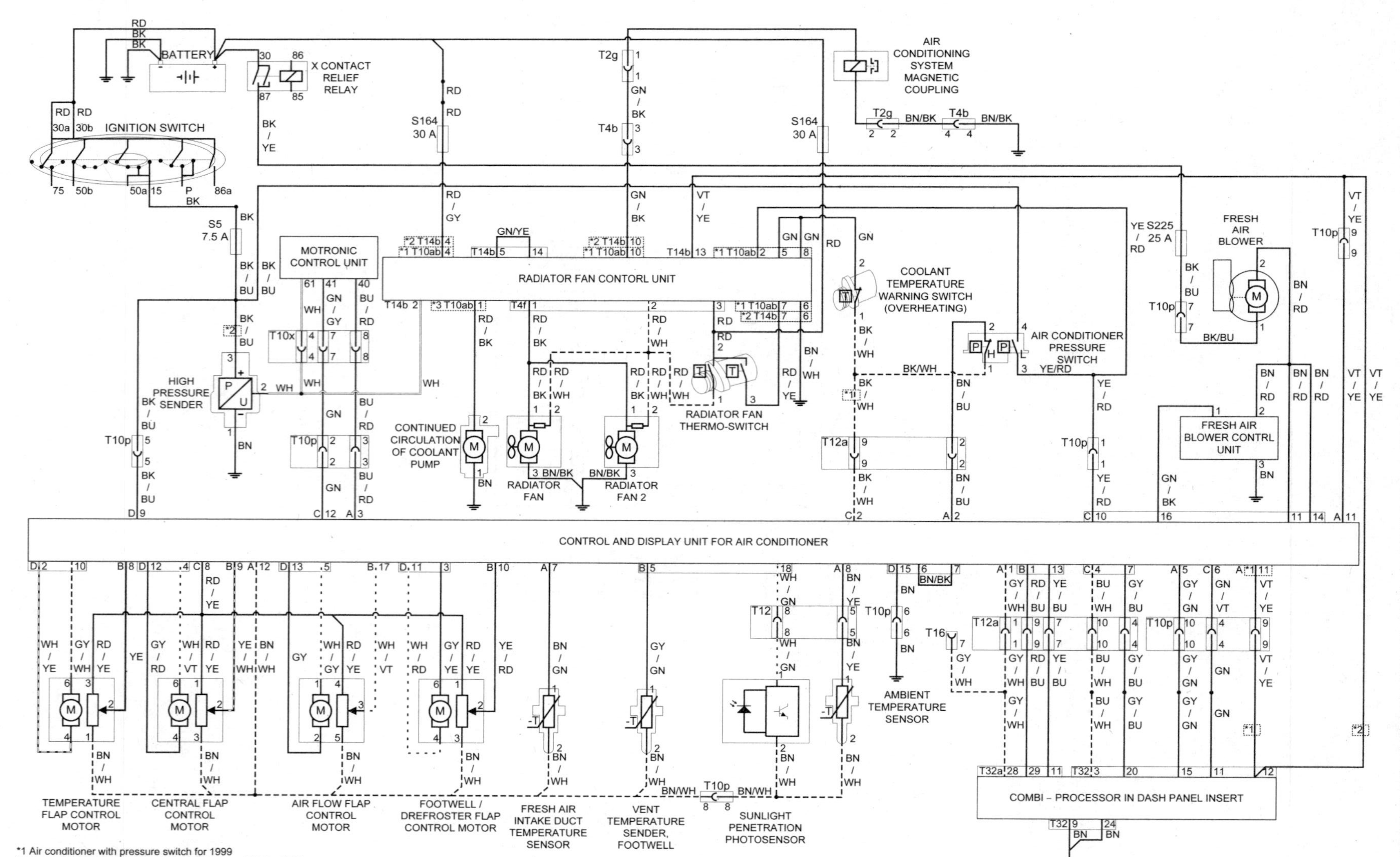

BATTERY
IGNITION SWITCH
X CONTACT RELIEF RELAY
S164 30 A
S5 7.5 A
S225 25 A
AIR CONDITIONING SYSTEM MAGNETIC COUPLING
FRESH AIR BLOWER
FRESH AIR BLOWER CONTRL UNIT
AIR CONDITIONER PRESSURE SWITCH
COOLANT TEMPERATURE WARNING SWITCH (OVERHEATING)
MOTRONIC CONTROL UNIT
RADIATOR FAN CONTORL UNIT
RADIATOR FAN THERMO-SWITCH
HIGH PRESSURE SENDER
CONTINUED CIRCULATION OF COOLANT PUMP
RADIATOR FAN
RADIATOR FAN 2
CONTROL AND DISPLAY UNIT FOR AIR CONDITIONER
AMBIENT TEMPERATURE SENSOR
COMBI – PROCESSOR IN DASH PANEL INSERT
TEMPERATURE FLAP CONTROL MOTOR
CENTRAL FLAP CONTROL MOTOR
AIR FLOW FLAP CONTROL MOTOR
FOOTWELL / DREFROSTER FLAP CONTROL MOTOR
FRESH AIR INTAKE DUCT TEMPERATURE SENSOR
VENT TEMPERATURE SENDER, FOOTWELL
SUNLIGHT PENETRATION PHOTOSENSOR
*1 Air conditioner with pressure switch for 1999
*2 Air conditioner with high pressure sender from 1999 to 2006
*3 Only models with 165 kW engine
Air conditioning and heating

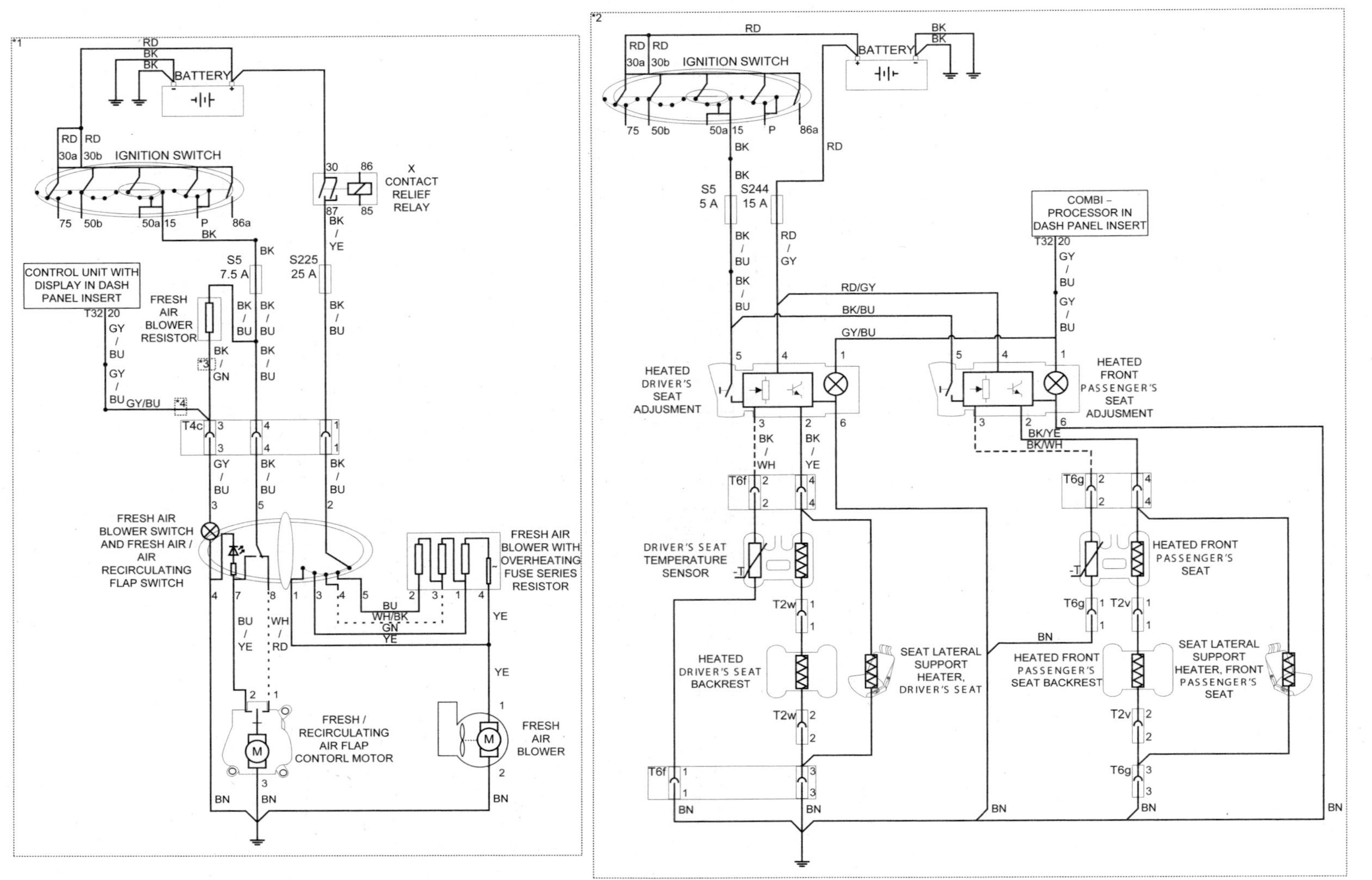

*1 Air blower
*2 Heated seats
*3 From 1999 to 2001
*4 From 2002

Seat heating and air blower

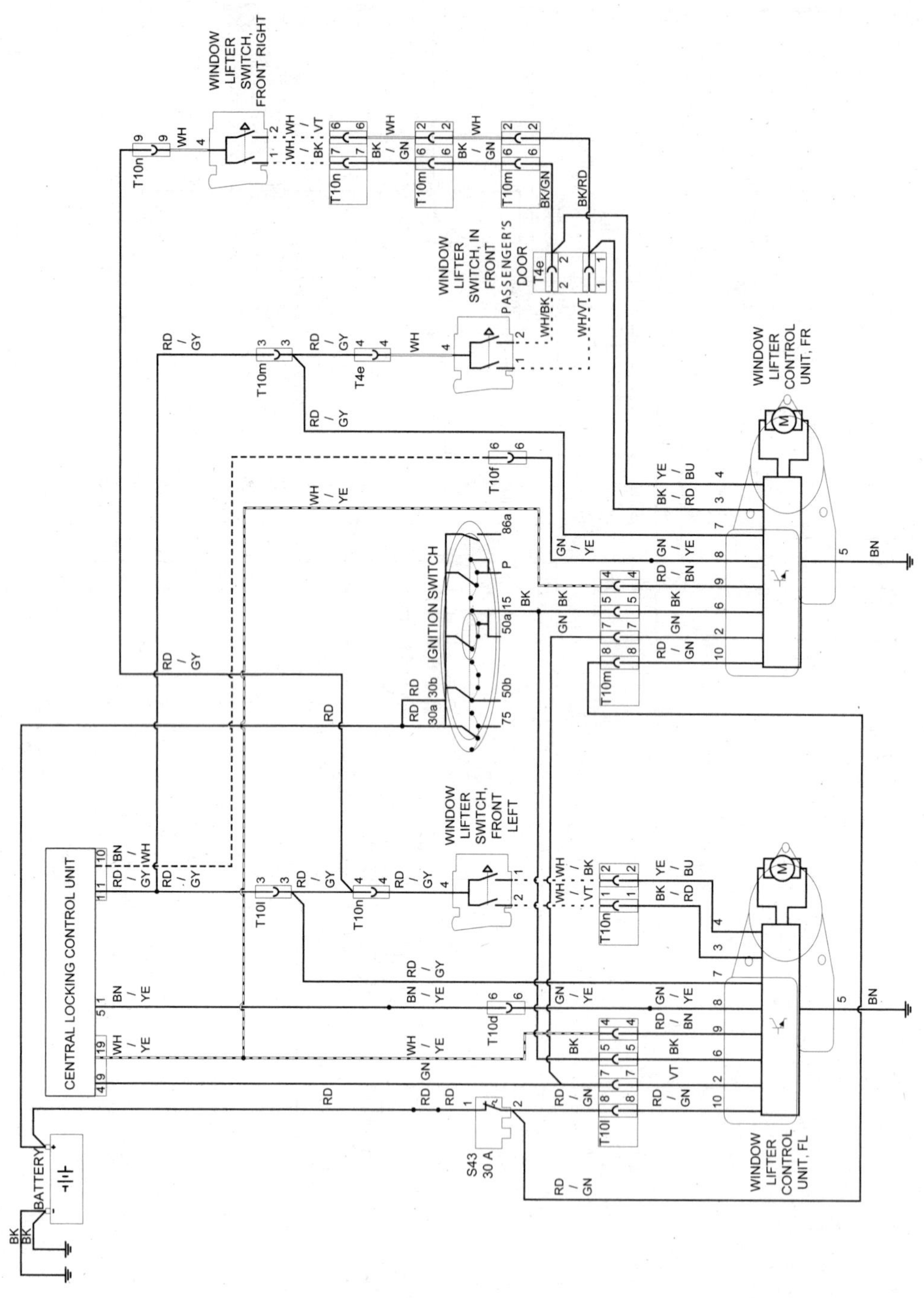

Power windows

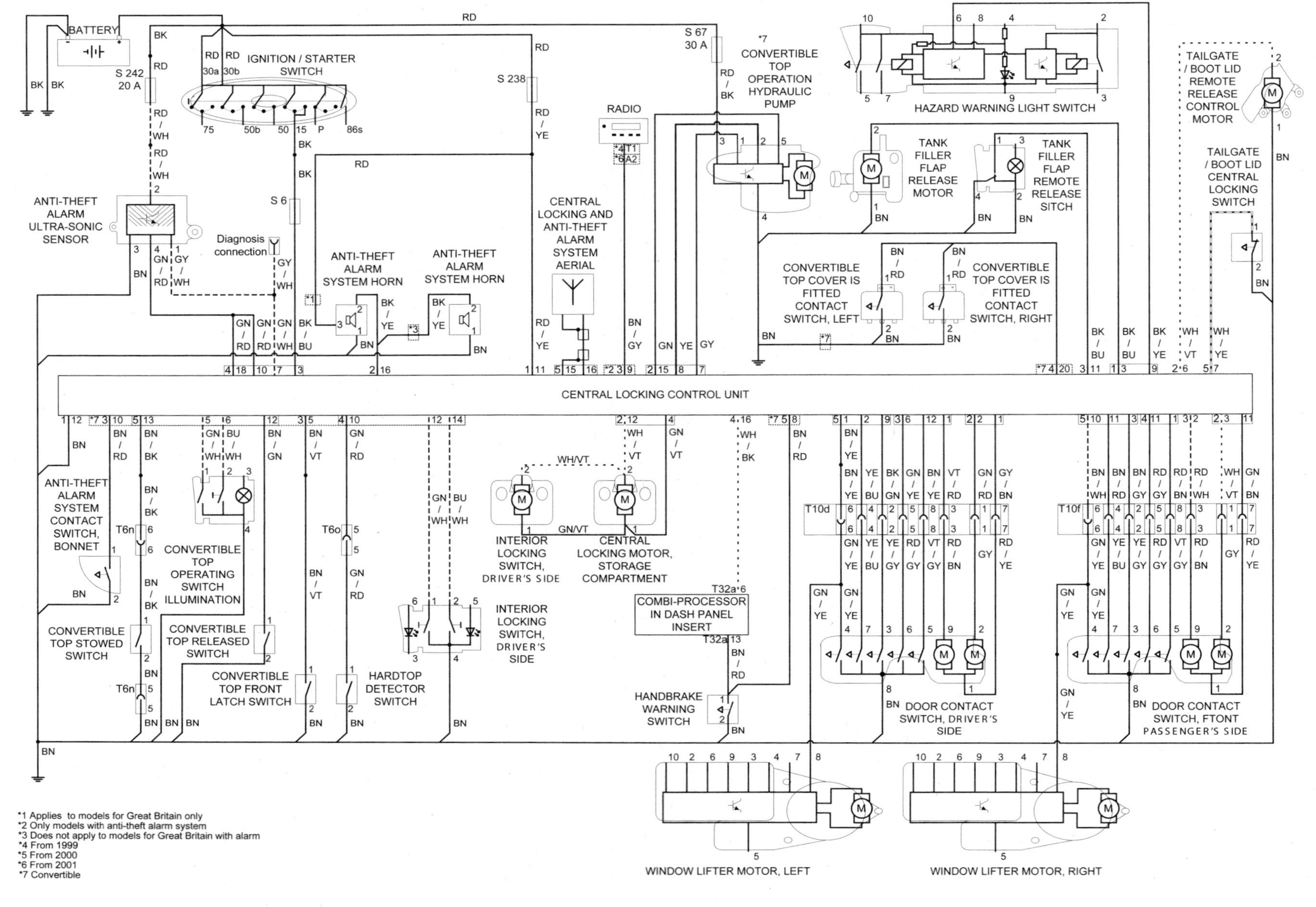

Central locking

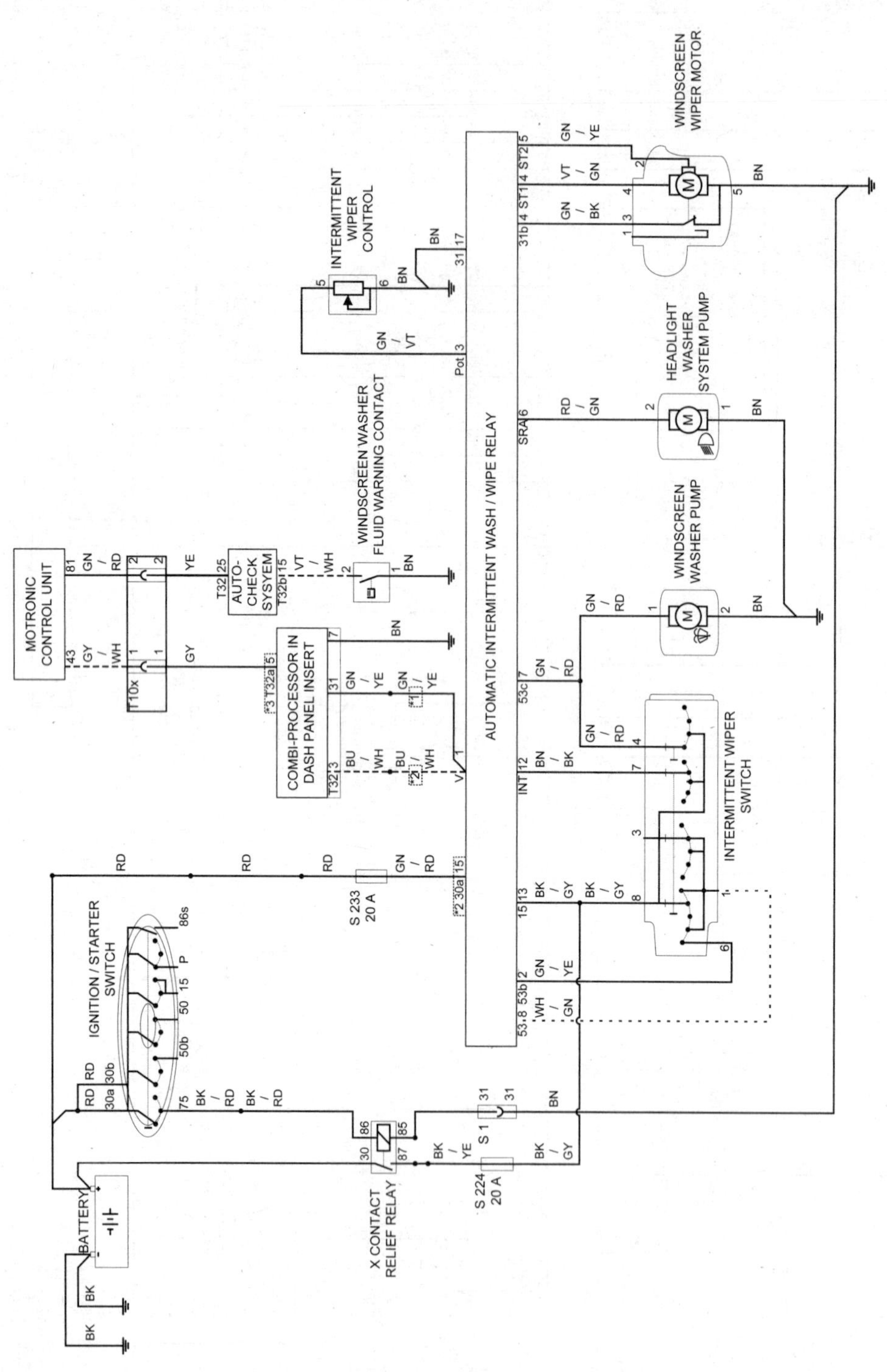

Wipers and washers

*1 From 1999 to 2000
*2 From 1999 to 2001
*3 From 2000

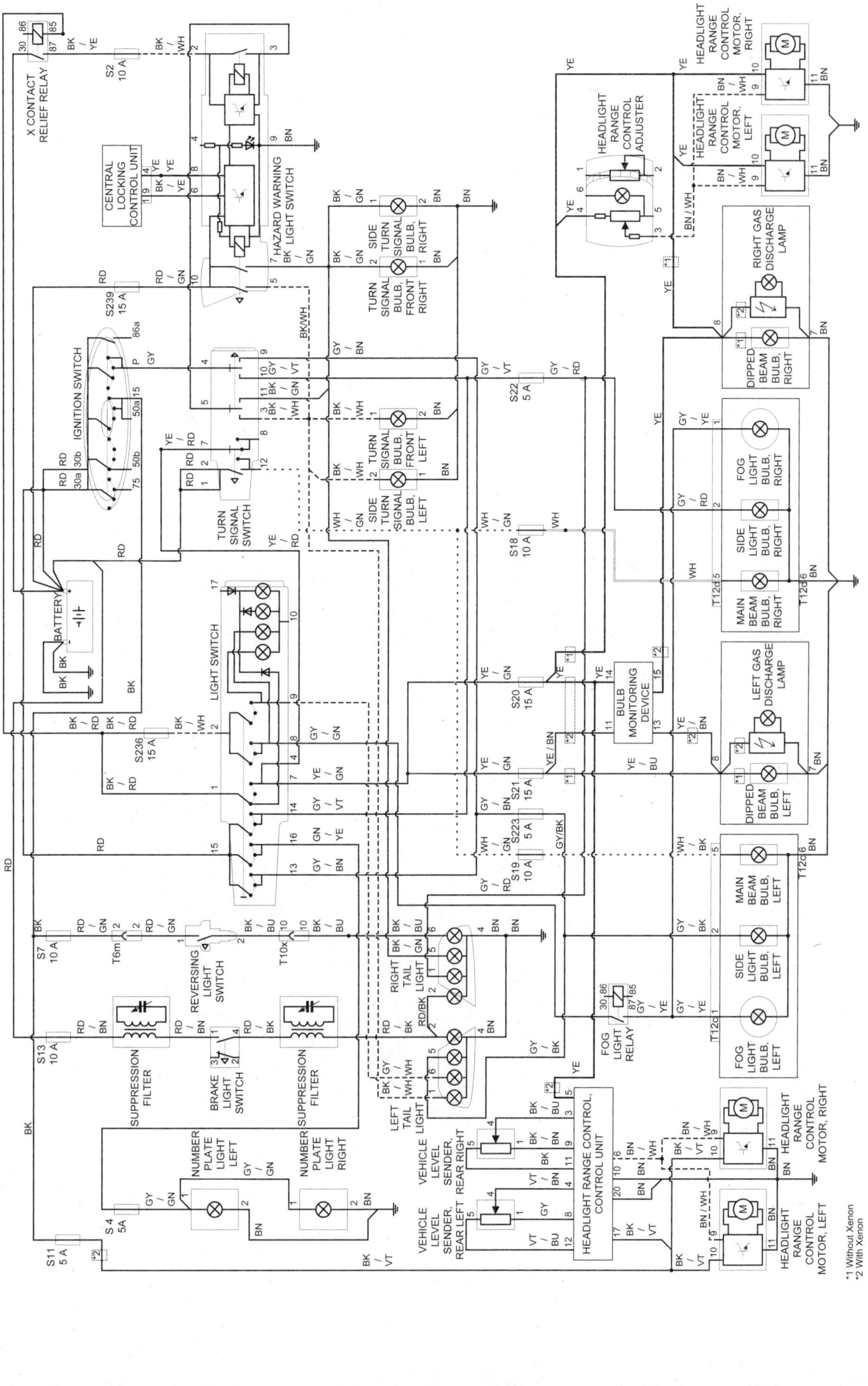

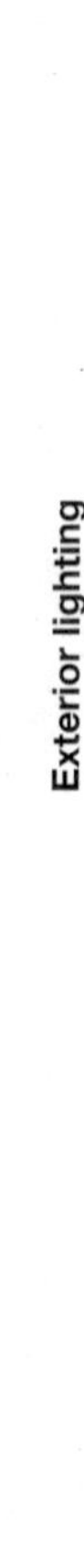

Exterior lighting

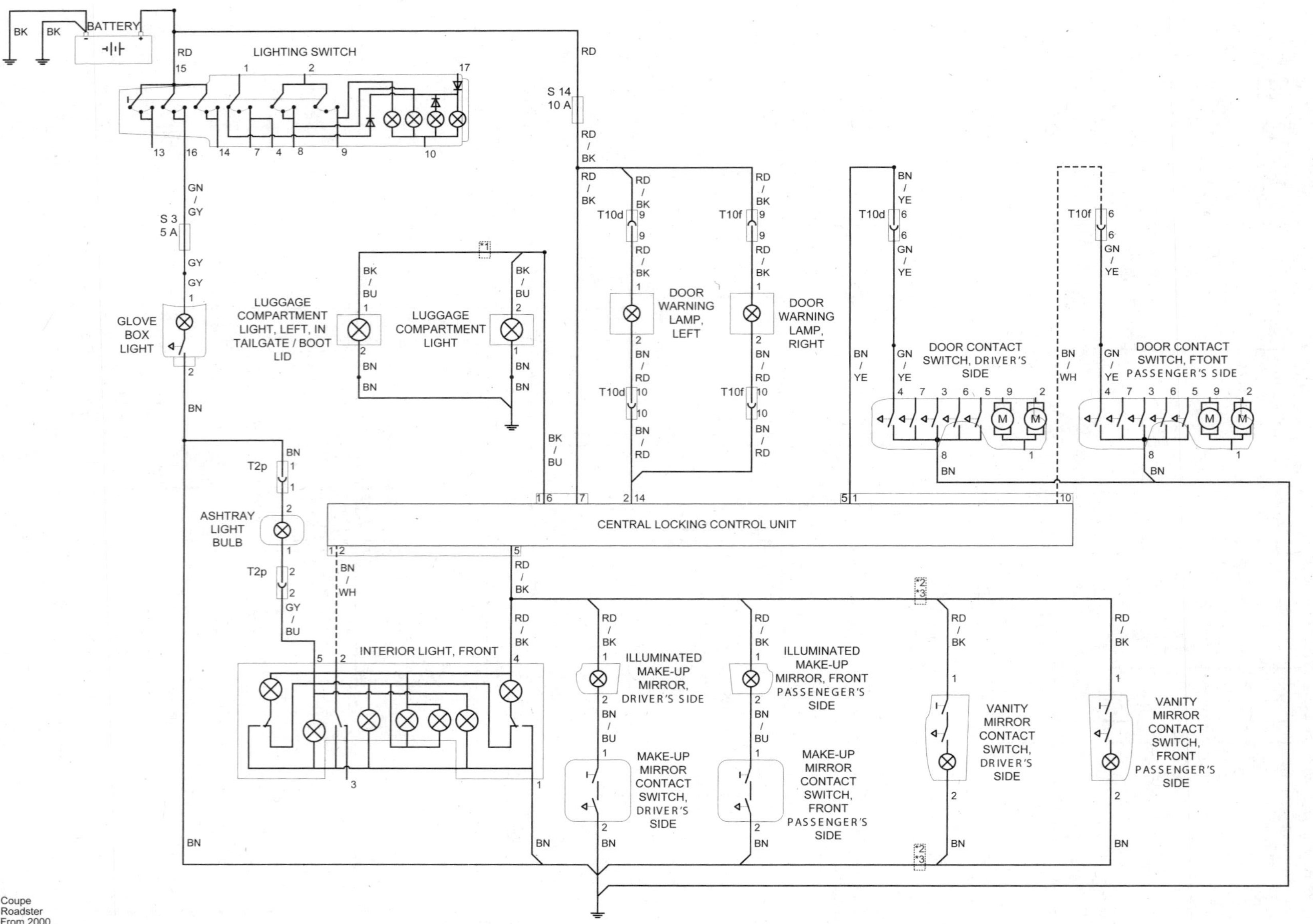

Interior lighting

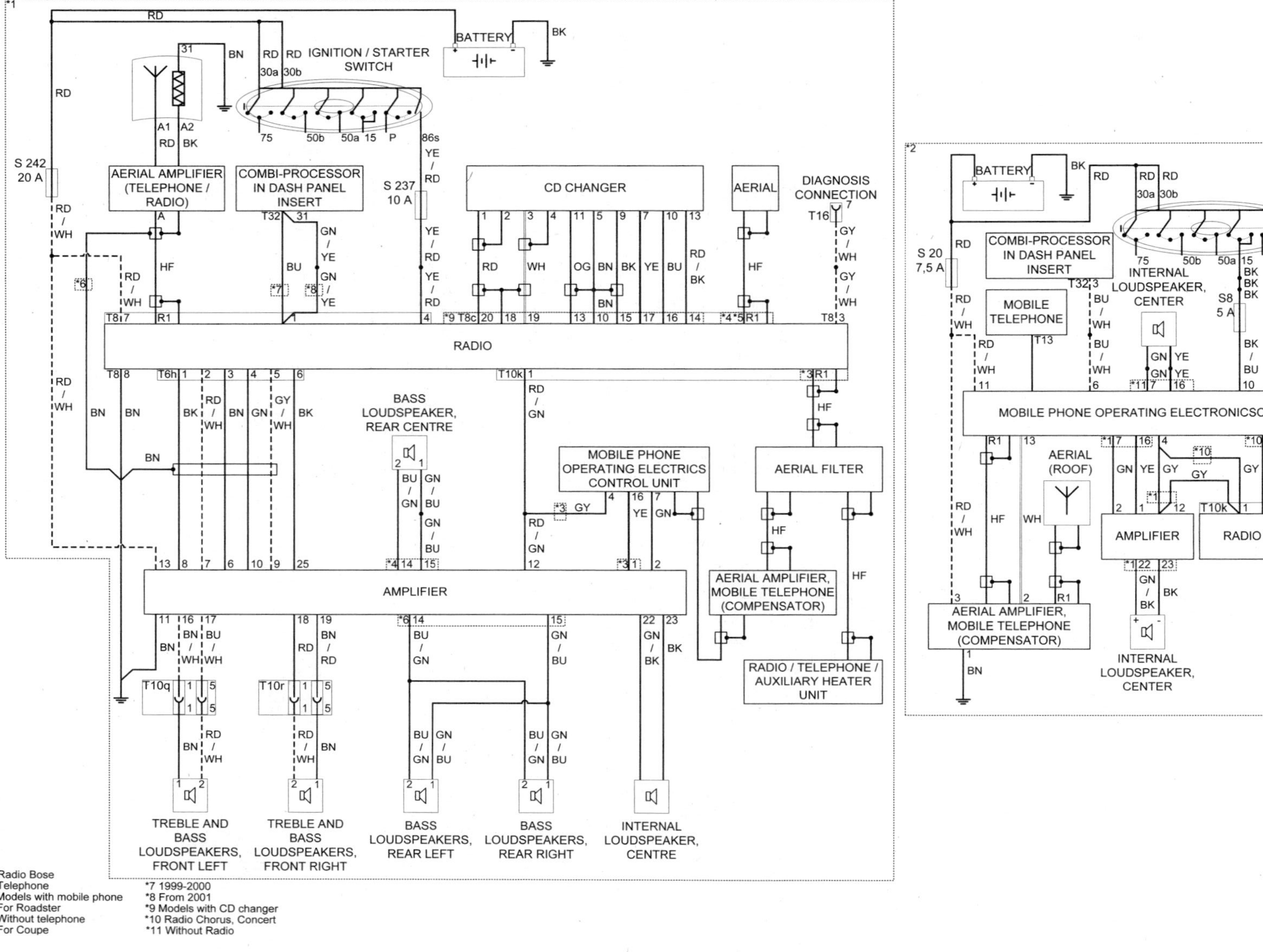

Sound system – Bose system and telephone

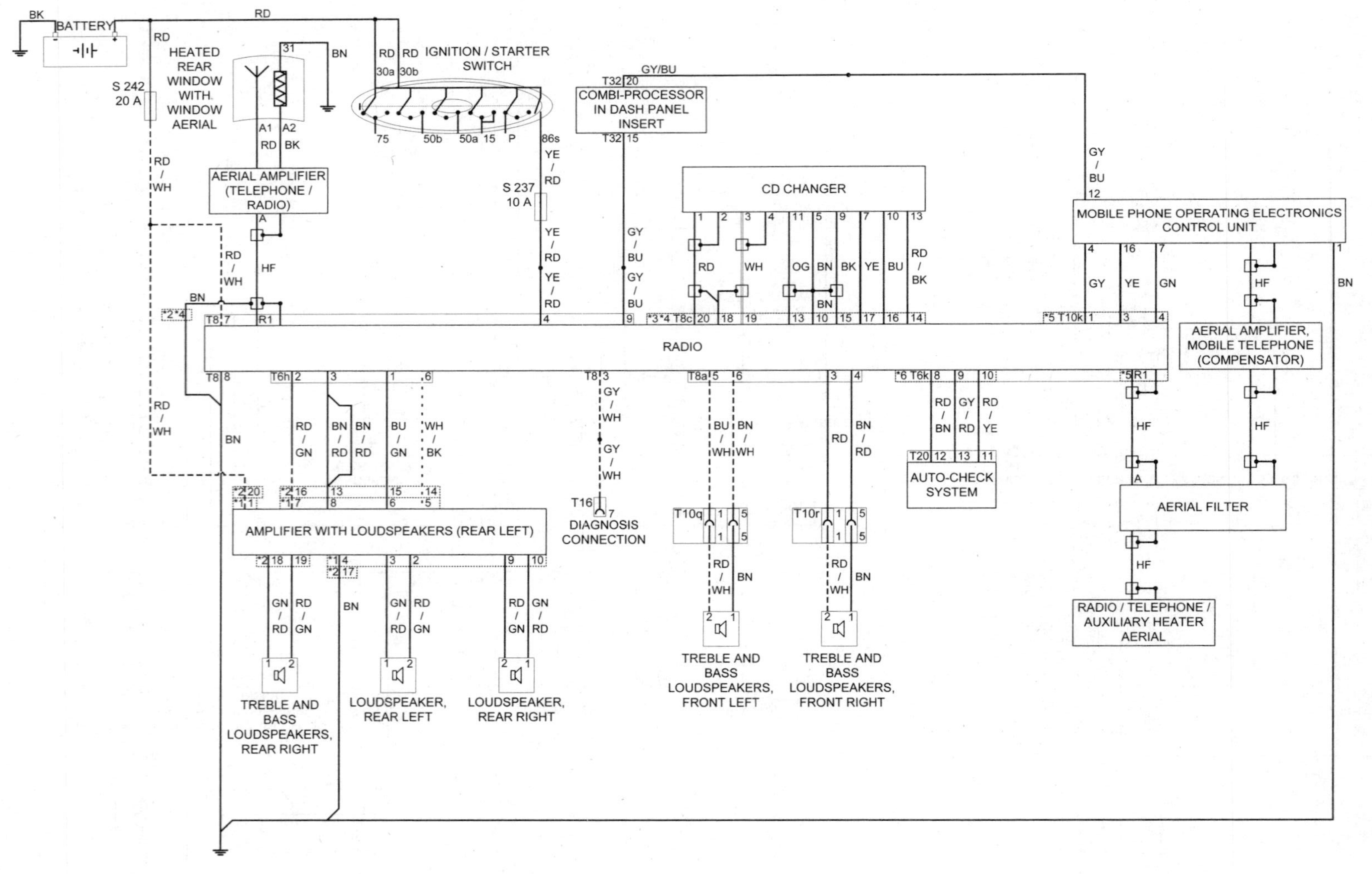

*1 Roadster
*2 Coupe
*3 Models with CD Changer
*4 From 2000
*5 Only models with mobile telephone
*6 Only models with auto-check system

Sound system – Chorus, Concert

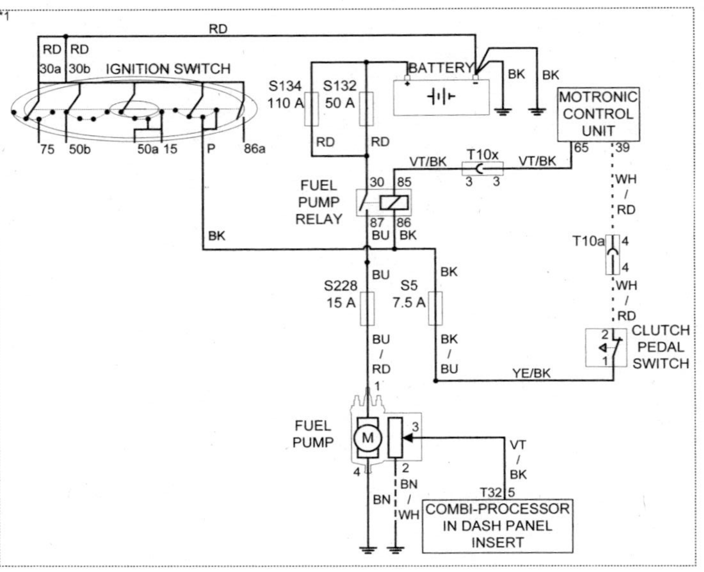

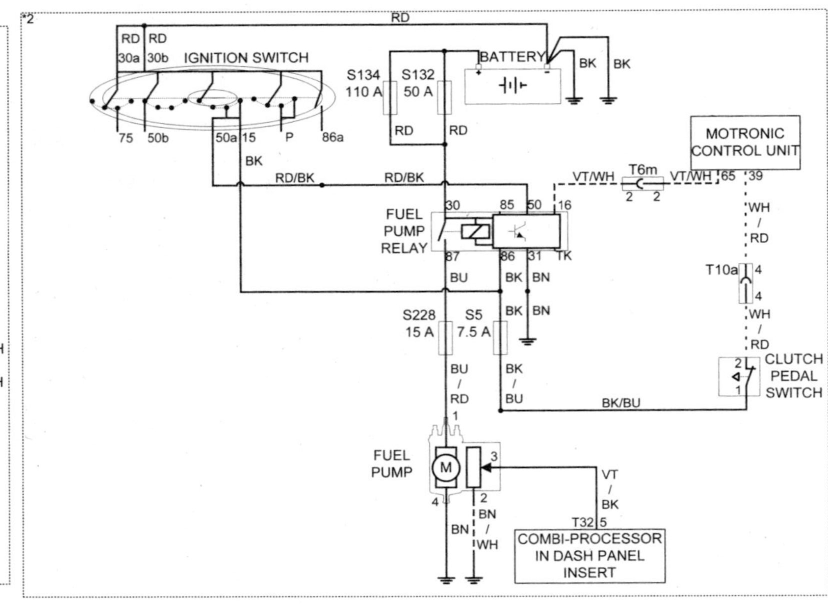

*1 From 1999 to 2001
*2 From 2001

Fuel pump

Dimensions and weights

Note: *All figures and dimensions are approximate and may vary according to model. Refer to manufacturer's data for exact figures.*

Overall length

All models	4041 mm

Overall height (unladen)

Front Wheel Drive (FWD) models	1354 mm
Four Wheel Drive (4WD) models	1351 mm

Overall width

All models (without mirrors)	1764 mm
All models (including mirrors)	1856 mm

Wheelbase

Front Wheel Drive (FWD) models	2419 mm
Four Wheel Drive (4WD) models	2427 mm

Track width

All models – Front	1525 mm
Front Wheel Drive (FWD) models – Rear	1507 mm
Four Wheel Drive (4WD) models – Rear	1503 mm

Ground clearance

All models (unladen)	120 mm

Turning circle

All models	10.5 m

Weights

Kerb weight (without driver) *

Front Wheel Drive (FWD) models	1205 kg
Four Wheel Drive (4WD) models	1395 kg

Maximum gross vehicle weight **

Front Wheel Drive (FWD) models	1575 kg
Four Wheel Drive (4WD) models	1765 kg

** Exact kerb weights depend upon model and specification – details are given in the owner's handbook, and on a sticker affixed to the top of the right-hand front wing panel.*
*** Exact maximum gross vehicle weights depend upon model and specifications – details are given in the owner's handbook, and on a sticker affixed to the top of the right-hand front wing panel.*

Maximum roof rack load

Coupe models	75 kg

Fuel economy

Although depreciation is still the biggest part of the cost of motoring for most car owners, the cost of fuel is more immediately noticeable. These pages give some tips on how to get the best fuel economy.

Working it out

Manufacturer's figures

Car manufacturers are required by law to provide fuel consumption information on all new vehicles sold. These 'official' figures are obtained by simulating various driving conditions on a rolling road or a test track. Real life conditions are different, so the fuel consumption actually achieved may not bear much resemblance to the quoted figures.

How to calculate it

Many cars now have trip computers which will display fuel consumption, both instantaneous and average. Refer to the owner's handbook for details of how to use these.

To calculate consumption yourself (and maybe to check that the trip computer is accurate), proceed as follows.

1. Fill up with fuel and note the mileage, or zero the trip recorder.
2. Drive as usual until you need to fill up again.
3. Note the amount of fuel required to refill the tank, and the mileage covered since the previous fill-up.
4. Divide the mileage by the amount of fuel used to obtain the consumption figure.

For example:

Mileage at first fill-up (a) = 27,903
Mileage at second fill-up (b) = 28,346
Mileage covered (b - a) = 443
Fuel required at second fill-up = 48.6 litres

The half-completed changeover to metric units in the UK means that we buy our fuel in litres, measure distances in miles and talk about fuel consumption in miles per gallon. There are two ways round this: the first is to convert the litres to gallons before doing the calculation (by dividing by 4.546, or see Table 1). So in the example:

48.6 litres ÷ 4.546 = 10.69 gallons
443 miles ÷ 10.69 gallons = 41.4 mpg

The second way is to calculate the consumption in miles per litre, then multiply that figure by 4.546 (or see Table 2).

So in the example, fuel consumption is:

443 miles ÷ 48.6 litres = 9.1 mpl
9.1 mpl x 4.546 = 41.4 mpg

The rest of Europe expresses fuel consumption in litres of fuel required to travel 100 km (l/100 km). For interest, the conversions are given in Table 3. In practice it doesn't matter what units you use, provided you know what your normal consumption is and can spot if it's getting better or worse.

Table 1: conversion of litres to Imperial gallons

litres	1	2	3	4	5	10	20	30	40	50	60	70
gallons	0.22	0.44	0.66	0.88	1.10	2.24	4.49	6.73	8.98	11.22	13.47	15.71

Table 2: conversion of miles per litre to miles per gallon

miles per litre	5	6	7	8	9	10	11	12	13	14
miles per gallon	23	27	32	36	41	46	50	55	59	64

Table 3: conversion of litres per 100 km to miles per gallon

litres per 100 km	4	4.5	5	5.5	6	6.5	7	8	9	10
miles per gallon	71	63	56	51	47	43	40	35	31	28

Maintenance

A well-maintained car uses less fuel and creates less pollution. In particular:

Filters

Change air and fuel filters at the specified intervals.

Oil

Use a good quality oil of the lowest viscosity specified by the vehicle manufacturer (see *Lubricants and fluids*). Check the level often and be careful not to overfill.

Spark plugs

When applicable, renew at the specified intervals.

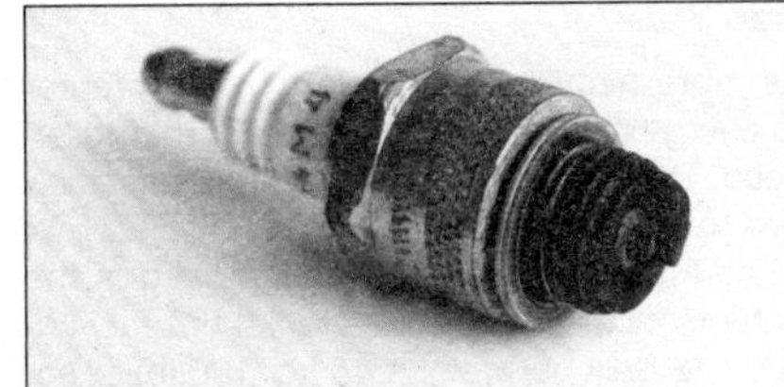

Tyres

Check tyre pressures regularly. Under-inflated tyres have an increased rolling resistance. It is generally safe to use the higher pressures specified for full load conditions even when not fully laden, but keep an eye on the centre band of tread for signs of wear due to over-inflation.

When buying new tyres, consider the 'fuel saving' models which most manufacturers include in their ranges.

Driving style

Acceleration

Acceleration uses more fuel than driving at a steady speed. The best technique with modern cars is to accelerate reasonably briskly to the desired speed, changing up through the gears as soon as possible without making the engine labour.

Air conditioning

Air conditioning absorbs quite a bit of energy from the engine – typically 3 kW (4 hp) or so. The effect on fuel consumption is at its worst in slow traffic. Switch it off when not required.

Anticipation

Drive smoothly and try to read the traffic flow so as to avoid unnecessary acceleration and braking.

Automatic transmission

When accelerating in an automatic, avoid depressing the throttle so far as to make the transmission hold onto lower gears at higher speeds. Don't use the 'Sport' setting, if applicable.

When stationary with the engine running, select 'N' or 'P'. When moving, keep your left foot away from the brake.

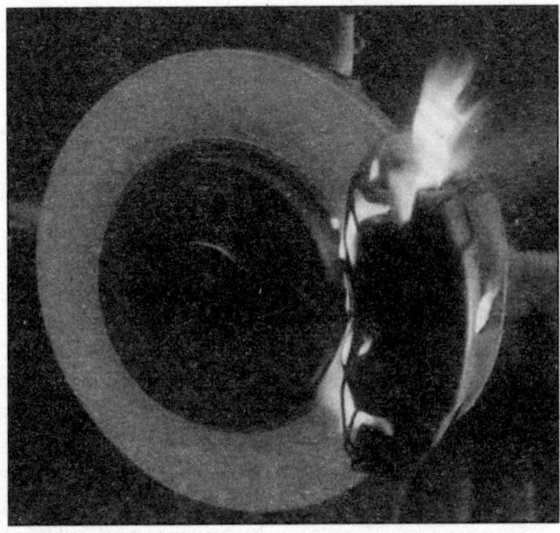

Braking

Braking converts the car's energy of motion into heat – essentially, it is wasted. Obviously some braking is always going to be necessary, but with good anticipation it is surprising how much can be avoided, especially on routes that you know well.

Carshare

Consider sharing lifts to work or to the shops. Even once a week will make a difference.

Electrical loads

Electricity is 'fuel' too; the alternator which charges the battery does so by converting some of the engine's energy of motion into electrical energy. The more electrical accessories are in use, the greater the load on the alternator. Switch off big consumers like the heated rear window when not required.

Freewheeling

Freewheeling (coasting) in neutral with the engine switched off is dangerous. The effort required to operate power-assisted brakes and steering increases when the engine is not running, with a potential lack of control in emergency situations.

In any case, modern fuel injection systems automatically cut off the engine's fuel supply on the overrun (moving and in gear, but with the accelerator pedal released).

Gadgets

Bolt-on devices claiming to save fuel have been around for nearly as long as the motor car itself. Those which worked were rapidly adopted as standard equipment by the vehicle manufacturers. Others worked only in certain situations, or saved fuel only at the expense of unacceptable effects on performance, driveability or the life of engine components.

The most effective fuel saving gadget is the driver's right foot.

Journey planning

Combine (eg) a trip to the supermarket with a visit to the recycling centre and the DIY store, rather than making separate journeys.

When possible choose a travelling time outside rush hours.

Load

The more heavily a car is laden, the greater the energy required to accelerate it to a given speed. Remove heavy items which you don't need to carry.

One load which is often overlooked is the contents of the fuel tank. A tankful of fuel (55 litres / 12 gallons) weighs 45 kg (100 lb) or so. Just half filling it may be worthwhile.

Lost?

At the risk of stating the obvious, if you're going somewhere new, have details of the route to hand. There's not much point in achieving record mpg if you also go miles out of your way.

Parking

If possible, carry out any reversing or turning manoeuvres when you arrive at a parking space so that you can drive straight out when you leave. Manoeuvering when the engine is cold uses a lot more fuel.

Driving around looking for free on-street parking may cost more in fuel than buying a car park ticket.

Premium fuel

Most major oil companies (and some supermarkets) have premium grades of fuel which are several pence a litre dearer than the standard grades. Reports vary, but the consensus seems to be that if these fuels improve economy at all, they do not do so by enough to justify their extra cost.

Roof rack

When loading a roof rack, try to produce a wedge shape with the narrow end at the front. Any cover should be securely fastened – if it flaps it's creating turbulence and absorbing energy.

Remove roof racks and boxes when not in use – they increase air resistance and can create a surprising amount of noise.

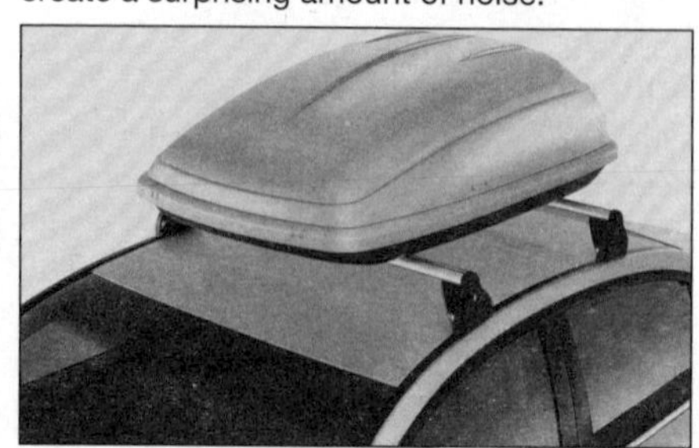

Short journeys

The engine is at its least efficient, and wear is highest, during the first few miles after a cold start. Consider walking, cycling or using public transport.

Speed

The engine is at its most efficient when running at a steady speed and load at the rpm where it develops maximum torque. (You can find this figure in the car's handbook.) For most cars this corresponds to between 55 and 65 mph in top gear.

Above the optimum cruising speed, fuel consumption starts to rise quite sharply. A car travelling at 80 mph will typically be using 30% more fuel than at 60 mph.

Supermarket fuel

It may be cheap but is it any good? In the UK all supermarket fuel must meet the relevant British Standard. The major oil companies will say that their branded fuels have better additive packages which may stop carbon and other deposits building up. A reasonable compromise might be to use one tank of branded fuel to three or four from the supermarket.

Switch off when stationary

Switch off the engine if you look like being stationary for more than 30 seconds or so. This is good for the environment as well as for your pocket. Be aware though that frequent restarts are hard on the battery and the starter motor.

Windows

Driving with the windows open increases air turbulence around the vehicle. Closing the windows promotes smooth airflow and reduced resistance. The faster you go, the more significant this is.

And finally . . .

Driving techniques associated with good fuel economy tend to involve moderate acceleration and low top speeds. Be considerate to the needs of other road users who may need to make brisker progress; even if you do not agree with them this is not an excuse to be obstructive.

Safety must always take precedence over economy, whether it is a question of accelerating hard to complete an overtaking manoeuvre, killing your speed when confronted with a potential hazard or switching the lights on when it starts to get dark.

Conversion factors

Length (distance)

Inches (in)	x 25.4	= Millimetres (mm)	x 0.0394	= Inches (in)
Feet (ft)	x 0.305	= Metres (m)	x 3.281	= Feet (ft)
Miles	x 1.609	= Kilometres (km)	x 0.621	= Miles

Volume (capacity)

Cubic inches (cu in; in^3)	x 16.387	= Cubic centimetres (cc; cm^3)	x 0.061	= Cubic inches (cu in; in^3)
Imperial pints (Imp pt)	x 0.568	= Litres (l)	x 1.76	= Imperial pints (Imp pt)
Imperial quarts (Imp qt)	x 1.137	= Litres (l)	x 0.88	= Imperial quarts (Imp qt)
Imperial quarts (Imp qt)	x 1.201	= US quarts (US qt)	x 0.833	= Imperial quarts (Imp qt)
US quarts (US qt)	x 0.946	= Litres (l)	x 1.057	= US quarts (US qt)
Imperial gallons (Imp gal)	x 4.546	= Litres (l)	x 0.22	= Imperial gallons (Imp gal)
Imperial gallons (Imp gal)	x 1.201	= US gallons (US gal)	x 0.833	= Imperial gallons (Imp gal)
US gallons (US gal)	x 3.785	= Litres (l)	x 0.264	= US gallons (US gal)

Mass (weight)

Ounces (oz)	x 28.35	= Grams (g)	x 0.035	= Ounces (oz)
Pounds (lb)	x 0.454	= Kilograms (kg)	x 2.205	= Pounds (lb)

Force

Ounces-force (ozf; oz)	x 0.278	= Newtons (N)	x 3.6	= Ounces-force (ozf; oz)
Pounds-force (lbf; lb)	x 4.448	= Newtons (N)	x 0.225	= Pounds-force (lbf; lb)
Newtons (N)	x 0.1	= Kilograms-force (kgf; kg)	x 9.81	= Newtons (N)

Pressure

Pounds-force per square inch (psi; lbf/in^2; lb/in^2)	x 0.070	= Kilograms-force per square centimetre (kgf/cm^2; kg/cm^2)	x 14.223	= Pounds-force per square inch (psi; lbf/in^2; lb/in^2)
Pounds-force per square inch (psi; lbf/in^2; lb/in^2)	x 0.068	= Atmospheres (atm)	x 14.696	= Pounds-force per square inch (psi; lbf/in^2; lb/in^2)
Pounds-force per square inch (psi; lbf/in^2; lb/in^2)	x 0.069	= Bars	x 14.5	= Pounds-force per square inch (psi; lbf/in^2; lb/in^2)
Pounds-force per square inch (psi; lbf/in^2; lb/in^2)	x 6.895	= Kilopascals (kPa)	x 0.145	= Pounds-force per square inch (psi; lbf/in^2; lb/in^2)
Kilopascals (kPa)	x 0.01	= Kilograms-force per square centimetre (kgf/cm^2; kg/cm^2)	x 98.1	= Kilopascals (kPa)
Millibar (mbar)	x 100	= Pascals (Pa)	x 0.01	= Millibar (mbar)
Millibar (mbar)	x 0.0145	= Pounds-force per square inch (psi; lbf/in^2; lb/in^2)	x 68.947	= Millibar (mbar)
Millibar (mbar)	x 0.75	= Millimetres of mercury (mmHg)	x 1.333	= Millibar (mbar)
Millibar (mbar)	x 0.401	= Inches of water (inH_2O)	x 2.491	= Millibar (mbar)
Millimetres of mercury (mmHg)	x 0.535	= Inches of water (inH_2O)	x 1.868	= Millimetres of mercury (mmHg)
Inches of water (inH_2O)	x 0.036	= Pounds-force per square inch (psi; lbf/in^2; lb/in^2)	x 27.68	= Inches of water (inH_2O)

Torque (moment of force)

Pounds-force inches (lbf in; lb in)	x 1.152	= Kilograms-force centimetre (kgf cm; kg cm)	x 0.868	= Pounds-force inches (lbf in; lb in)
Pounds-force inches (lbf in; lb in)	x 0.113	= Newton metres (Nm)	x 8.85	= Pounds-force inches (lbf in; lb in)
Pounds-force inches (lbf in; lb in)	x 0.083	= Pounds-force feet (lbf ft; lb ft)	x 12	= Pounds-force inches (lbf in; lb in)
Pounds-force feet (lbf ft; lb ft)	x 0.138	= Kilograms-force metres (kgf m; kg m)	x 7.233	= Pounds-force feet (lbf ft; lb ft)
Pounds-force feet (lbf ft; lb ft)	x 1.356	= Newton metres (Nm)	x 0.738	= Pounds-force feet (lbf ft; lb ft)
Newton metres (Nm)	x 0.102	= Kilograms-force metres (kgf m; kg m)	x 9.804	= Newton metres (Nm)

Power

Horsepower (hp)	x 745.7	= Watts (W)	x 0.0013	= Horsepower (hp)

Velocity (speed)

Miles per hour (miles/hr; mph)	x 1.609	= Kilometres per hour (km/hr; kph)	x 0.621	= Miles per hour (miles/hr; mph)

Fuel consumption*

Miles per gallon, Imperial (mpg)	x 0.354	= Kilometres per litre (km/l)	x 2.825	= Miles per gallon, Imperial (mpg)
Miles per gallon, US (mpg)	x 0.425	= Kilometres per litre (km/l)	x 2.352	= Miles per gallon, US (mpg)

Temperature

Degrees Fahrenheit = (°C x 1.8) + 32

Degrees Celsius (Degrees Centigrade; °C) = (°F - 32) x 0.56

** It is common practice to convert from miles per gallon (mpg) to litres/100 kilometres (l/100km), where mpg x l/100 km = 282*

Spare parts are available from many sources, including maker's appointed garages, accessory shops, and motor factors. To be sure of obtaining the correct parts, it will sometimes be necessary to quote the vehicle identification number. If possible, it can also be useful to take the old parts along for positive identification. Items such as starter motors and alternators may be available under a service exchange scheme – any parts returned should be clean.

Our advice regarding spare parts is as follows.

Officially appointed garages

This is the best source of parts which are peculiar to your car, and which are not otherwise generally available (eg, badges, interior trim, certain body panels, etc). It is also the only place at which you should buy parts if the vehicle is still under warranty.

Accessory shops

These are very good places to buy materials and components needed for the maintenance of your car (oil, air and fuel filters, light bulbs, drivebelts, greases, brake pads, touch-up paint, etc). Components of this nature sold by a reputable shop are usually of the same standard as those used by the car manufacturer.

Besides components, these shops also sell tools and general accessories, usually have convenient opening hours, charge lower prices, and can often be found close to home. Some accessory shops have parts counters where components needed for almost any repair job can be purchased or ordered.

Motor factors

Good factors will stock all the more important components which wear out comparatively quickly, and can sometimes supply individual components needed for the overhaul of a larger assembly (eg, brake seals and hydraulic parts, bearing shells, pistons, valves). They may also handle work such as cylinder block reboring, crankshaft regrinding, etc.

Tyre and exhaust specialists

These outlets may be independent, or members of a local or national chain. They frequently offer competitive prices when compared with a main dealer or local garage, but it will pay to obtain several quotes before making a decision. When researching prices, also ask what extras may be added – for instance fitting a new valve and balancing the wheel are both commonly charged on top of the price of a new tyre.

Other sources

Beware of parts or materials obtained from market stalls, car boot sales or similar outlets. Such items are not invariably sub-standard, but there is little chance of compensation if they do prove unsatisfactory. in the case of safety-critical components such as brake pads, there is the risk not only of financial loss, but also of an accident causing injury or death.

Second-hand components or assemblies obtained from a car breaker can be a good buy in some circumstances, but this sort of purchase is best made by the experienced DIY mechanic.

Vehicle identification numbers

1 Modifications are a continuing and unpublicised process in vehicle manufacture, quite apart from major model changes. Spare parts manuals and lists are compiled upon a numerical basis, the individual vehicle identification numbers being essential to correct identification of the component concerned.

2 When ordering spare parts, always give as much information as possible. Quote the car model, year of manufacture and registration, chassis and engine numbers as appropriate.

3 The Vehicle Identification Number plate is located in a number of places on the vehicle. It is stamped on a plate at the front left-hand corner of the windscreen, visible through a cut-out in the windscreen cowl panel. On the right-hand side of the bulkhead at the rear of the engine compartment. On a sticker affixed to the top of the right-hand front wing panel and also on a label affixed to the floor panel in the luggage compartment **(see illustrations)**.

4 The engine number is stamped onto the right-hand end of the cylinder head. A barcode identification sticker is also located on the uppe timing belt cover **(see illustrations)**.

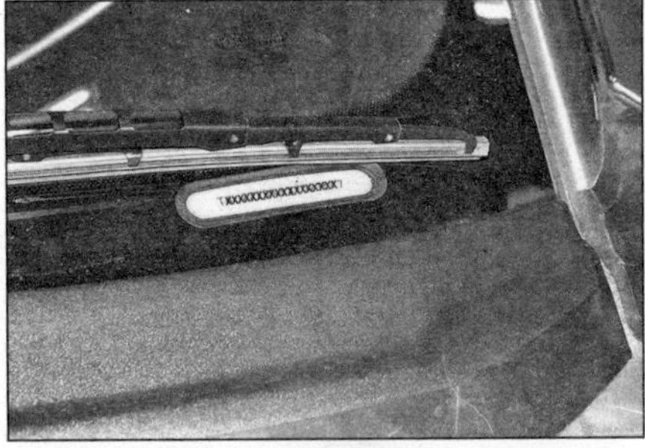

3.3a Vehicle Identification Number (VIN) located on the left-hand lower edge of the windscreen

3.3b ...on the right-hand side rear of the engine compartment...

3.3c ...on a sticker affixed to the top of the right-hand wing panel...

3.3d ...and on a label on the floor panel of the luggage compartment

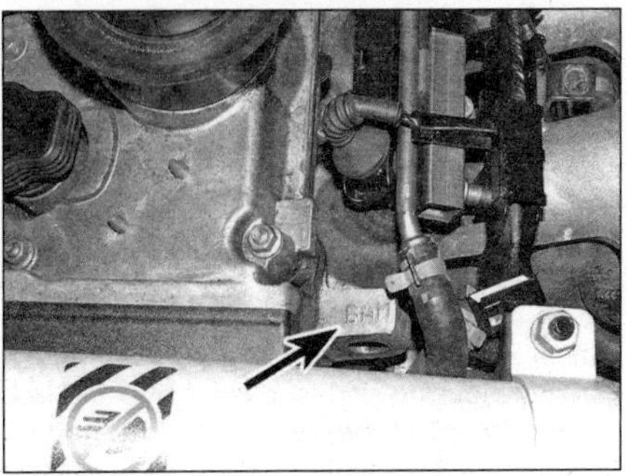

3.4a Engine code (arrowed) located on the cylinder head

3.4b Engine barcode sticker on the timing belt cover

Whenever servicing, repair or overhaul work is carried out on the car or its components, observe the following procedures and instructions. This will assist in carrying out the operation efficiently and to a professional standard of workmanship.

Joint mating faces and gaskets

When separating components at their mating faces, never insert screwdrivers or similar implements into the joint between the faces in order to prise them apart. This can cause severe damage which results in oil leaks, coolant leaks, etc upon reassembly. Separation is usually achieved by tapping along the joint with a soft-faced hammer in order to break the seal. However, note that this method may not be suitable where dowels are used for component location.

Where a gasket is used between the mating faces of two components, a new one must be fitted on reassembly; fit it dry unless otherwise stated in the repair procedure. Make sure that the mating faces are clean and dry, with all traces of old gasket removed. When cleaning a joint face, use a tool which is unlikely to score or damage the face, and remove any burrs or nicks with an oilstone or fine file.

Make sure that tapped holes are cleaned with a pipe cleaner, and keep them free of jointing compound, if this is being used, unless specifically instructed otherwise.

Ensure that all orifices, channels or pipes are clear, and blow through them, preferably using compressed air.

Oil seals

Oil seals can be removed by levering them out with a wide flat-bladed screwdriver or similar implement. Alternatively, a number of self-tapping screws may be screwed into the seal, and these used as a purchase for pliers or some similar device in order to pull the seal free.

Whenever an oil seal is removed from its working location, either individually or as part of an assembly, it should be renewed.

The very fine sealing lip of the seal is easily damaged, and will not seal if the surface it contacts is not completely clean and free from scratches, nicks or grooves. If the original sealing surface of the component cannot be restored, and the manufacturer has not made provision for slight relocation of the seal relative to the sealing surface, the component should be renewed.

Protect the lips of the seal from any surface which may damage them in the course of fitting. Use tape or a conical sleeve where possible. Where indicated, lubricate the seal lips with oil before fitting and, on dual-lipped seals, fill the space between the lips with grease.

Unless otherwise stated, oil seals must be fitted with their sealing lips toward the lubricant to be sealed.

Use a tubular drift or block of wood of the appropriate size to install the seal and, if the seal housing is shouldered, drive the seal down to the shoulder. If the seal housing is unshouldered, the seal should be fitted with its face flush with the housing top face (unless otherwise instructed).

Screw threads and fastenings

Seized nuts, bolts and screws are quite a common occurrence where corrosion has set in, and the use of penetrating oil or releasing fluid will often overcome this problem if the offending item is soaked for a while before attempting to release it. The use of an impact driver may also provide a means of releasing such stubborn fastening devices, when used in conjunction with the appropriate screwdriver bit or socket. If none of these methods works, it may be necessary to resort to the careful application of heat, or the use of a hacksaw or nut splitter device. Before resorting to extreme methods, check that you are not dealing with a left-hand thread!

Studs are usually removed by locking two nuts together on the threaded part, and then using a spanner on the lower nut to unscrew the stud. Studs or bolts which have broken off below the surface of the component in which they are mounted can sometimes be removed using a stud extractor.

Always ensure that a blind tapped hole is completely free from oil, grease, water or other fluid before installing the bolt or stud. Failure to do this could cause the housing to crack due to the hydraulic action of the bolt or stud as it is screwed in.

For some screw fastenings, notably cylinder head bolts or nuts, torque wrench settings are no longer specified for the latter stages of tightening, "angle-tightening" being called up instead. Typically, a fairly low torque wrench setting will be applied to the bolts/nuts in the correct sequence, followed by one or more stages of tightening through specified angles.

When checking or retightening a nut or bolt to a specified torque setting, slacken the nut or bolt by a quarter of a turn, and then retighten to the specified setting. However, this should not be attempted where angular tightening has been used.

Locknuts, locktabs and washers

Any fastening which will rotate against a component or housing during tightening should always have a washer between it and the relevant component or housing.

Spring or split washers should always be renewed when they are used to lock a critical component such as a big-end bearing retaining bolt or nut. Locktabs which are folded over to retain a nut or bolt should always be renewed.

Self-locking nuts can be re-used in non-critical areas, providing resistance can be felt when the locking portion passes over the bolt or stud thread. However, it should be noted that self-locking stiffnuts tend to lose their effectiveness after long periods of use, and should then be renewed as a matter of course.

Split pins must always be replaced with new ones of the correct size for the hole.

When thread-locking compound is found on the threads of a fastener which is to be re-used, it should be cleaned off with a wire brush and solvent, and fresh compound applied on reassembly.

Special tools

Some repair procedures in this manual entail the use of special tools such as a press, two or three-legged pullers, spring compressors, etc. Wherever possible, suitable readily-available alternatives to the manufacturer's special tools are described, and are shown in use. In some instances, where no alternative is possible, it has been necessary to resort to the use of a manufacturer's tool, and this has been done for reasons of safety as well as the efficient completion of the repair operation. Unless you are highly-skilled and have a thorough understanding of the procedures described, never attempt to bypass the use of any special tool when the procedure described specifies its use. Not only is there a very great risk of personal injury, but expensive damage could be caused to the components involved.

Environmental considerations

When disposing of used engine oil, brake fluid, antifreeze, etc, give due consideration to any detrimental environmental effects. Do not, for instance, pour any of the above liquids down drains into the general sewage system, or onto the ground to soak away, as this is likely to pollute your local environment. Many local council refuse tips provide a facility for waste oil disposal, as do some garages. You can find your nearest disposal point by calling the Environment Agency on 03708 506 506 or by visiting www.oilbankline.org.uk.

Note: It is illegal and anti-social to dump oil down the drain. To find the location of your local oil recycling bank, call 03708 506 506 or visit www.oilbankline.org.uk.

The jack supplied with the vehicle tool kit should only be used for changing the roadwheels – see Wheel changing at the front of this book. When carrying out any other kind of work, raise the vehicle using a hydraulic (or 'trolley') jack, and always supplement the jack with axle stands positioned under the vehicle jacking points.

When using a hydraulic jack or axle stands, always position the jack head or axle stand head under one of the relevant jacking points.

To raise the front and/or rear of the vehicle, use the jacking/support points at the front and rear ends of the door sills, indicated by the square depressions in the sill panel **(see illustration)**. Supplement the jack with axle stands positioned as close as possible to the jacking point, under a structural strengthened part of the chassis or subframe.

Do not jack the vehicle under any other part of the sill, sump, floor pan, or any of the steering or suspension components.

Warning: Never work under, around, or near a raised car, unless it is adequately supported in at least two places.

The jacking point (arrowed) on the sill

Disconnecting the battery

Caution: After reconnecting the battery, the safety function of the electric windows will not be re-instated until the windows have been reprogrammed. This could potentially cause severe pinching injuries.

1 Several of the systems require battery power to be available at all times (permanent live). This is either to ensure their continued operation (such as the clock), or to maintain electronic memory settings which would otherwise be erased. Whenever the battery is to be disconnected, first note the following points, to ensure there are no unforeseen consequences:

a) *Firstly, on any vehicle with central door locking, it is a wise precaution to remove the key from the ignition, and to keep it with you. This avoids the possibility of the key being locked inside the car, should the central locking engage when the battery is reconnected.*

b) *If a security-coded audio unit is fitted, and the unit and/or the battery is disconnected, the unit will not function until the correct security code has been entered. Therefore, if you do not know the correct security code for the radio/cassette unit, do not disconnect either of the battery terminals, or remove the radio/cassette unit from the vehicle. The code appears on a code card suplied with the car when new. Details for entering the code appear in the vehicle handbook. Should the code have been misplaced or forgotten, on production of proof of ownership, an Audi dealer or in-car entertainment specialist may be able to help.*

c) *The engine management system ECU is of the 'self-learning' type, meaning that, as it operates, it adapts to changes in operating conditions, and stores the optimum settings found (this is especially true for idle speed settings). When the battery is disconnected, these 'learned' settings are lost, and the ECU reverts to the base factory settings. When the engine is restarted, it may idle and run roughly until the ECU has 'relearned' the best settings. To further this 'learning' process, take the car for a road test of at least 15 minutes' duration, covering as many engine speeds and loads as possible, and concentrating on the 2000 to 4000 rpm range. On completion, let the engine idle for at least 10 minutes, turning the steering wheel occasionally and switching on high-current-draw equipment such as the heater fan or heated rear window. If the engine does not regain its normal performance, have the system checked for faults by an Audi dealer.*

d) *On vehicles equipped with an original equipment anti-theft alarm system, before disconnecting the battery, de-activate the alarm system, otherwise the alarm will be triggered.*

e) *After the battery has been reconnected, the electric window 'closed' positions must be reprogrammed as follows. With the windows and sunroof closed, close all the doors and lock the vehicle manually at the driver's or passenger's door. Unlock the vehicle, then lock it again while holding the key in the locked position for at least one second. The windows are now reprogrammed. Similarly, reprogram the electrically-adjustable driver's seat as follows. Open the driver's door and switch on the ignition, then move the seat cushion forwards and upwards onto the stop limit. Now move the seat backrest forwards onto its stop limit, and switch off the ignition.*

f) *When starting a petrol engine for the first time after having disconnected the battery, turn on the ignition for 30 seconds, then switch off the ignition – the engine may now be started*

2 Devices known as 'memory-savers' or 'code-savers' can be used to avoid some of the above problems. Precise details of use vary according to the device used. Typically, it is plugged into the cigarette lighter socket, and is connected by its own wiring to a spare battery; the vehicle battery is then disconnected from the electrical system, leaving the memory-saver to pass sufficient current to maintain audio unit security codes, and other memory values, and also to run permanently-live circuits such as the clock.

Warning: Some of these devices allow a considerable amount of current to pass, which can mean that many of the vehicle's systems are still operational when the main battery is disconnected. If a memory-saver is used, ensure that the circuit concerned is actually 'dead' before carrying out any work on it.

Tools and working facilities

Introduction

A selection of good tools is a fundamental requirement for anyone contemplating the maintenance and repair of a motor vehicle. For the owner who does not possess any, their purchase will prove a considerable expense, offsetting some of the savings made by doing-it-yourself. However, provided that the tools purchased meet the relevant national safety standards and are of good quality, they will last for many years and prove an extremely worthwhile investment.

To help the average owner to decide which tools are needed to carry out the various tasks detailed in this manual, we have compiled three lists of tools under the following headings: *Maintenance and minor repair*, *Repair and overhaul*, and *Special*. Newcomers to practical mechanics should start off with the *Maintenance and minor repair* tool kit, and confine themselves to the simpler jobs around the vehicle. Then, as confidence and experience grow, more difficult tasks can be undertaken, with extra tools being purchased as, and when, they are needed. In this way, a *Maintenance and minor repair* tool kit can be built up into a *Repair and overhaul* tool kit over a considerable period of time, without any major cash outlays. The experienced do-it-yourselfer will have a tool kit good enough for most repair and overhaul procedures, and will add tools from the *Special* category when it is felt that the expense is justified by the amount of use to which these tools will be put.

Maintenance and minor repair tool kit

The tools given in this list should be considered as a minimum requirement if routine maintenance, servicing and minor repair operations are to be undertaken. We recommend the purchase of combination spanners (ring one end, open-ended the other); although more expensive than open-ended ones, they do give the advantages of both types of spanner.

- ☐ *Combination spanners:*
  Metric - 8 to 19 mm inclusive
- ☐ *Adjustable spanner - 35 mm jaw (approx.)*
- ☐ *Spark plug spanner (with rubber insert) - petrol models*
- ☐ *Spark plug gap adjustment tool - petrol models*
- ☐ *Set of feeler gauges*
- ☐ *Brake bleed nipple spanner*
- ☐ *Screwdrivers:*
  Flat blade - 100 mm long x 6 mm dia
  Cross blade - 100 mm long x 6 mm dia
  Torx - various sizes (not all vehicles)
- ☐ *Combination pliers*
- ☐ *Hacksaw (junior)*
- ☐ *Tyre pump*
- ☐ *Tyre pressure gauge*
- ☐ *Oil can*
- ☐ *Oil filter removal tool (if applicable)*
- ☐ *Fine emery cloth*
- ☐ *Wire brush (small)*
- ☐ *Funnel (medium size)*
- ☐ *Sump drain plug key (not all vehicles)*

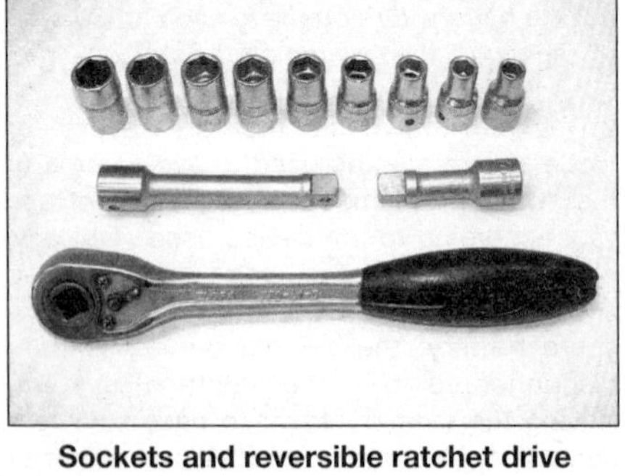

Sockets and reversible ratchet drive

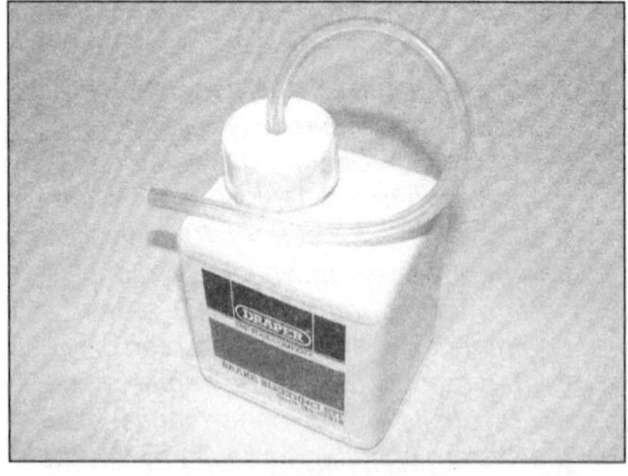

Brake bleeding kit

Repair and overhaul tool kit

These tools are virtually essential for anyone undertaking any major repairs to a motor vehicle, and are additional to those given in the *Maintenance and minor repair* list. Included in this list is a comprehensive set of sockets. Although these are expensive, they will be found invaluable as they are so versatile - particularly if various drives are included in the set. We recommend the half-inch square-drive type, as this can be used with most proprietary torque wrenches.

The tools in this list will sometimes need to be supplemented by tools from the *Special* list:

- ☐ *Sockets to cover range in previous list (including Torx sockets)*
- ☐ *Reversible ratchet drive (for use with sockets)*
- ☐ *Extension piece, 250 mm (for use with sockets)*
- ☐ *Universal joint (for use with sockets)*
- ☐ *Flexible handle or sliding T "breaker bar" (for use with sockets)*
- ☐ *Torque wrench (for use with sockets)*
- ☐ *Self-locking grips*
- ☐ *Ball pein hammer*
- ☐ *Soft-faced mallet (plastic or rubber)*
- ☐ *Screwdrivers:*
  Flat blade - long & sturdy, short (chubby), and narrow (electrician's) types
  Cross blade – long & sturdy, and short (chubby) types
- ☐ *Pliers:*
  Long-nosed
  Side cutters (electrician's)
  Circlip (internal and external)
- ☐ *Cold chisel - 25 mm*
- ☐ *Scriber*
- ☐ *Scraper*
- ☐ *Centre-punch*
- ☐ *Pin punch*
- ☐ *Hacksaw*
- ☐ *Brake hose clamp*
- ☐ *Brake/clutch bleeding kit*
- ☐ *Selection of twist drills*
- ☐ *Steel rule/straight-edge*
- ☐ *Allen keys (inc. splined/Torx type)*
- ☐ *Selection of files*
- ☐ *Wire brush*
- ☐ *Axle stands*
- ☐ *Jack (strong trolley or hydraulic type)*
- ☐ *Light with extension lead*
- ☐ *Universal electrical multi-meter*

Torx key, socket and bit

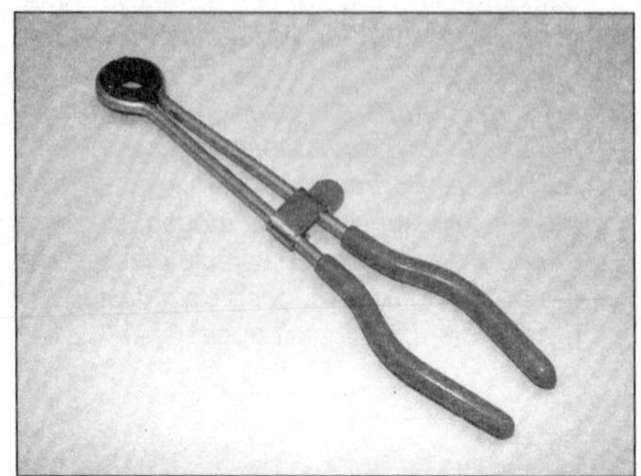

Hose clamp

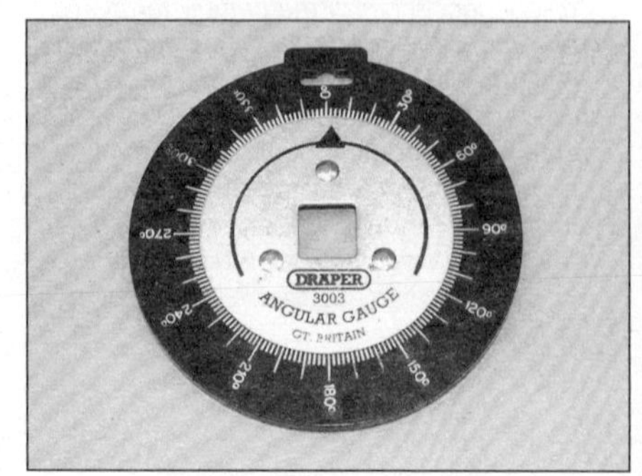

Angular-tightening gauge

Special tools

The tools in this list are those which are not used regularly, are expensive to buy, or which need to be used in accordance with their manufacturers' instructions. Unless relatively difficult mechanical jobs are undertaken frequently, it will not be economic to buy many of these tools. Where this is the case, you could consider clubbing together with friends (or joining a motorists' club) to make a joint purchase, or borrowing the tools against a deposit from a local garage or tool hire specialist.

The following list contains only those tools and instruments freely available to the public, and not those special tools produced by the vehicle manufacturer specifically for its dealer network. You will find occasional references to these manufacturers' special tools in the text of this manual. Generally, an alternative method of doing the job without the vehicle manufacturers' special tool is given. However, sometimes there is no alternative to using them. Where this is the case and the relevant tool cannot be bought or borrowed, you will have to entrust the work to a dealer.

- ☐ *Angular-tightening gauge*
- ☐ *Valve spring compressor*
- ☐ *Valve grinding tool*
- ☐ *Piston ring compressor*
- ☐ *Piston ring removal/installation tool*
- ☐ *Cylinder bore hone*
- ☐ *Balljoint separator*
- ☐ *Coil spring compressors (where applicable)*
- ☐ *Two/three-legged hub and bearing puller*
- ☐ *Impact screwdriver*
- ☐ *Micrometer and/or vernier calipers*
- ☐ *Dial gauge*
- ☐ *Tachometer*
- ☐ *Fault code reader*
- ☐ *Cylinder compression gauge*
- ☐ *Hand-operated vacuum pump and gauge*
- ☐ *Clutch plate alignment set*
- ☐ *Brake shoe steady spring cup removal tool*
- ☐ *Bush and bearing removal/installation set*
- ☐ *Stud extractors*
- ☐ *Tap and die set*
- ☐ *Lifting tackle*

Buying tools

Reputable motor accessory shops and superstores often offer excellent quality tools at discount prices, so it pays to shop around.

Remember, you don't have to buy the most expensive items on the shelf, but it is always advisable to steer clear of the very cheap tools. Beware of 'bargains' offered on market stalls, on-line or at car boot sales. There are plenty of good tools around at reasonable prices, but always aim to purchase items which meet the relevant national safety standards. If in doubt, ask the proprietor or manager of the shop for advice before making a purchase.

Care and maintenance of tools

Having purchased a reasonable tool kit, it is necessary to keep the tools in a clean and serviceable condition. After use, always wipe off any dirt, grease and metal particles using a clean, dry cloth, before putting the tools away. Never leave them lying around after they have been used. A simple tool rack on the garage or workshop wall for items such as screwdrivers and pliers is a good idea. Store all normal spanners and sockets in a metal box. Any measuring instruments, gauges, meters, etc, must be carefully stored where they cannot be damaged or become rusty.

Take a little care when tools are used. Hammer heads inevitably become marked, and screwdrivers lose the keen edge on their blades from time to time. A little timely attention with emery cloth or a file will soon restore items like this to a good finish.

Working facilities

Not to be forgotten when discussing tools is the workshop itself. If anything more than routine maintenance is to be carried out, a suitable working area becomes essential.

It is appreciated that many an owner-mechanic is forced by circumstances to remove an engine or similar item without the benefit of a garage or workshop. Having done this, any repairs should always be done under the cover of a roof.

Wherever possible, any dismantling should be done on a clean, flat workbench or table at a suitable working height.

Any workbench needs a vice; one with a jaw opening of 100 mm is suitable for most jobs. As mentioned previously, some clean dry storage space is also required for tools, as well as for any lubricants, cleaning fluids, touch-up paints etc, which become necessary.

Another item which may be required, and which has a much more general usage, is an electric drill with a chuck capacity of at least 8 mm. This, together with a good range of twist drills, is virtually essential for fitting accessories.

Last, but not least, always keep a supply of old newspapers and clean, lint-free rags available, and try to keep any working area as clean as possible.

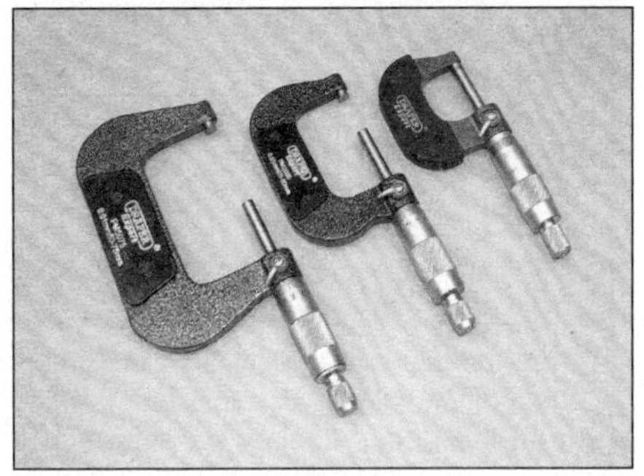

Micrometers

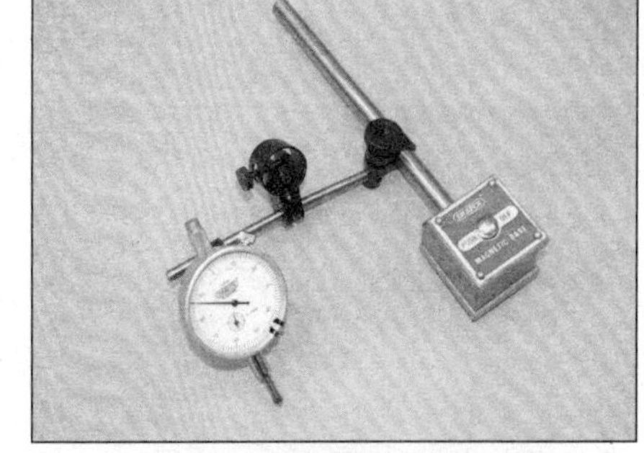

Dial test indicator ("dial gauge")

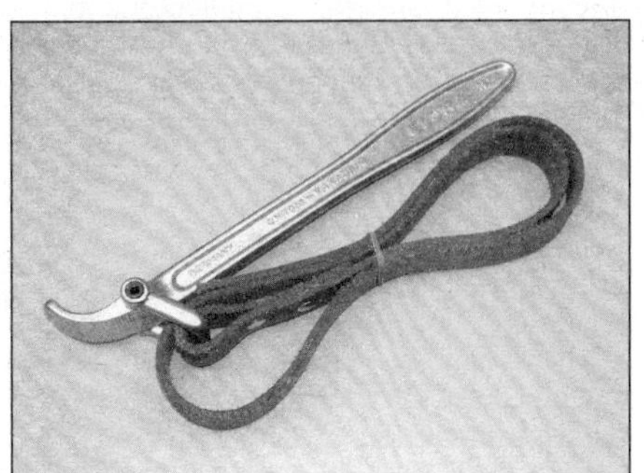

Oil filter removal tool (strap wrench type)

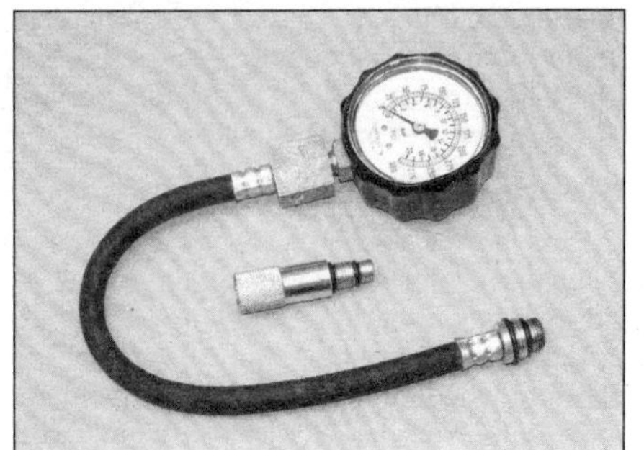

Compression tester

Bearing puller

This is a guide to getting your vehicle through the MOT test. Obviously it will not be possible to examine the vehicle to the same standard as the professional MOT tester. However, working through the following checks will enable you to identify any problem areas before submitting the vehicle for the test.

It has only been possible to summarise the test requirements here, based on the regulations in force at the time of printing. Test standards are becoming increasingly stringent, although there are some exemptions for older vehicles.

An assistant will be needed to help carry out some of these checks.

The checks have been sub-divided into four categories, as follows:

1 Checks carried out **FROM THE DRIVER'S SEAT**

2 Checks carried out **WITH THE VEHICLE ON THE GROUND**

3 Checks carried out **WITH THE VEHICLE RAISED AND THE WHEELS FREE TO TURN**

4 Checks carried out on **YOUR VEHICLE'S EXHAUST EMISSION SYSTEM**

1 Checks carried out FROM THE DRIVER'S SEAT

Handbrake (parking brake)

☐ Test the operation of the handbrake. Excessive travel (too many clicks) indicates incorrect brake or cable adjustment.

☐ Check that the handbrake cannot be released by tapping the lever sideways. Check the security of the lever mountings.

☐ If the parking brake is foot-operated, check that the pedal is secure and without excessive travel, and that the release mechanism operates correctly.

☐ Where applicable, test the operation of the electronic handbrake. The brake should engage and disengage without excessive delay. If the warning light does not extinguish when the brake is disengaged, this could indicate a fault which will need further investigation.

Footbrake

☐ Depress the brake pedal and check that it does not creep down to the floor, indicating a master cylinder fault. Release the pedal, wait a few seconds, then depress it again. If the pedal travels nearly to the floor before firm resistance is felt, brake adjustment or repair is necessary. If the pedal feels spongy, there is air in the hydraulic system which must be removed by bleeding.

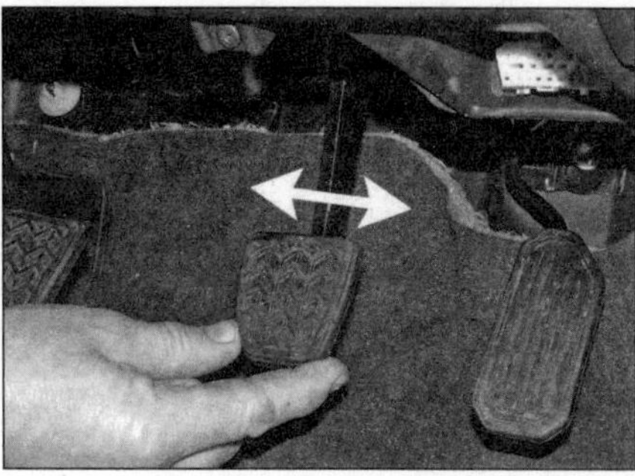

☐ Check that the brake pedal is secure and in good condition. Check also for signs of fluid leaks on the pedal, floor or carpets, which would indicate failed seals in the brake master cylinder.

☐ Check the servo unit (when applicable) by operating the brake pedal several times, then keeping the pedal depressed and starting the engine. As the engine starts, the pedal will move down slightly. If not, the vacuum hose or the servo itself may be faulty.

Steering wheel and column

☐ Examine the steering wheel for fractures or looseness of the hub, spokes or rim.

☐ Move the steering wheel from side to side and then up and down. Check that the steering wheel is not loose on the column, indicating wear or a loose retaining nut. Continue moving the steering wheel as before, but also turn it slightly from left to right.

☐ Check that the steering wheel is not loose on the column, and that there is no abnormal movement of the steering wheel, indicating wear in the column support bearings or couplings.

☐ Check that the ignition lock (where fitted) engages and disengages correctly.

☐ Steering column adjustment mechanisms (where fitted) must be able to lock the column securely in place with no play evident.

Windscreen, mirrors and sunvisor

☐ The windscreen must be free of cracks or other significant damage within the driver's field of view. (Small stone chips are acceptable.) Rear view mirrors must be secure, intact, and capable of being adjusted.

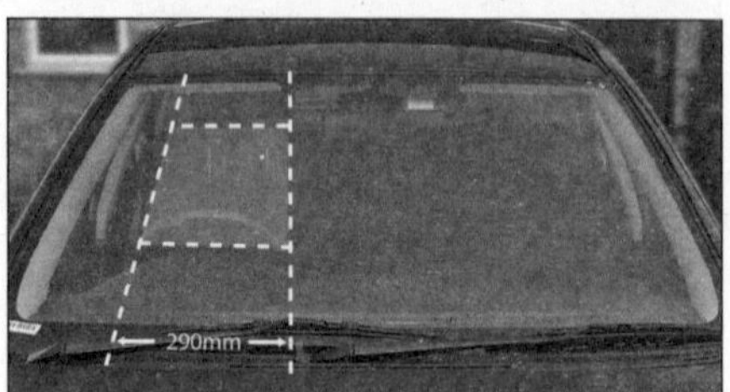

☐ The driver's sunvisor must be capable of being stored in the "up" position.

Seat belts and seats

Note: *The following checks are applicable to all seat belts, front and rear.*

☐ Examine the webbing of all the belts (including rear belts if fitted) for cuts, serious fraying or deterioration. Fasten and unfasten each belt to check the buckles. If applicable, check the retracting mechanism. Check the security of all seat belt mountings accessible from inside the vehicle, ensuring any height adjustable mountings lock securely in place.

☐ Seat belts with pre-tensioners, once activated, have a "flag" or similar showing on the seat belt stalk. This, in itself, is not a reason for test failure.

☐ The front seats themselves must be securely attached and the backrests must lock in the upright position.

Doors

☐ Both front doors must be able to be opened and closed from outside and inside, and must latch securely when closed.

Bonnet and boot/tailgate

☐ The bonnet and boot/tailgate must latch securely when closed.

2 Checks carried out WITH THE VEHICLE ON THE GROUND

Vehicle identification

☐ Number plates must be in good condition, secure and legible, with letters and numbers correctly spaced – spacing at (A) should be 33 mm and at (B) 11 mm. At the front, digits must be black on a white background and at the rear black on a yellow background. Other background designs (such as honeycomb) are not permitted.

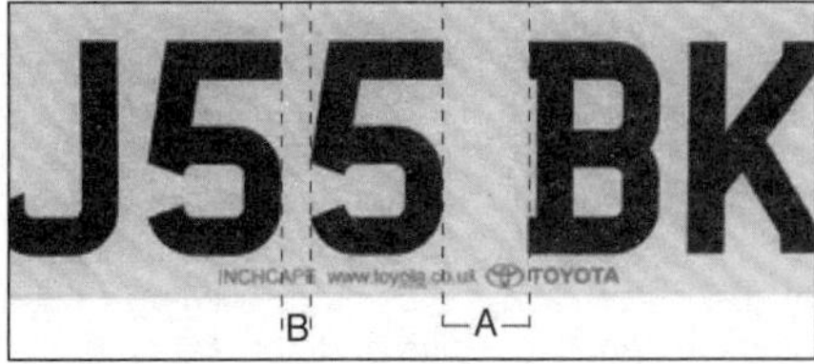

☐ The VIN plate and/or homologation plate must be permanently displayed and legible.

Electrical equipment

☐ Switch on the ignition and check the operation of the horn.

☐ Check the windscreen washers and wipers, examining the wiper blades; renew damaged or perished blades. Also check the operation of the stop-lights.

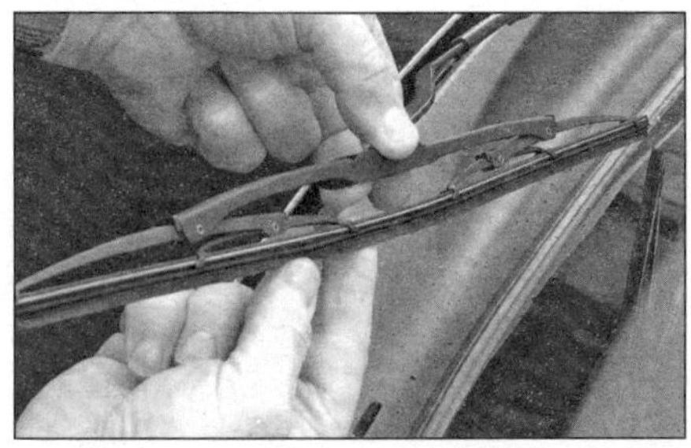

☐ Check the operation of the sidelights and number plate lights. The lenses and reflectors must be secure, clean and undamaged.

☐ Check the operation and alignment of the headlights. The headlight reflectors must not be tarnished and the lenses must be undamaged.

☐ Switch on the ignition and check the operation of the direction indicators (including the instrument panel tell-tale) and the hazard warning lights. Operation of the sidelights and stop-lights must not affect the indicators - if it does, the cause is usually a bad earth at the rear light cluster. Indicators should flash at a rate of between 60 and 120 times per minute – faster or slower than this could indicate a fault with the flasher unit or a bad earth at one of the light units.

☐ Check the operation of the rear foglight(s), including the warning light on the instrument panel or in the switch.

☐ The warning lights must illuminate in accordance with the manufacturer's design. For most vehicles, the ABS and other warning lights should illuminate when the ignition is switched on, and (if the system is operating properly) extinguish after a few seconds. Refer to the owner's handbook.

Footbrake

☐ Examine the master cylinder, brake pipes and servo unit for leaks, loose mountings, corrosion or other damage. If ABS is fitted, this unit should also be examined for signs of leaks or corrosion.

☐ The fluid reservoir must be secure and the fluid level must be between the upper (**A**) and lower (**B**) markings.

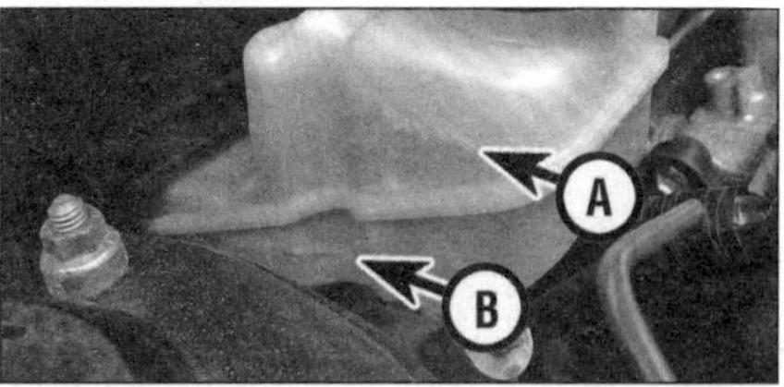

☐ Inspect both front brake flexible hoses for cracks or deterioration of the rubber. Turn the steering from lock to lock, and ensure that the hoses do not contact the wheel, tyre, or any part of the steering or suspension mechanism. With the brake pedal firmly depressed, check the hoses for bulges or leaks under pressure.

Steering and suspension

☐ Have your assistant turn the steering wheel from side to side slightly, up to the point where the steering gear just begins to transmit this movement to the roadwheels. Check for excessive free play between the steering wheel and the steering gear, indicating wear or insecurity of the steering column joints, the column-to-steering gear coupling, or the steering gear itself.

☐ Have your assistant turn the steering wheel more vigorously in each direction, so that the roadwheels just begin to turn. As this is done, examine all the steering joints, linkages, fittings and attachments. Renew any component that shows signs of wear or damage. On vehicles with power steering, check the security and condition of the steering pump, drivebelt and hoses.

☐ Check that the vehicle is standing level, and at approximately the correct ride height.

Shock absorbers

☐ Depress each corner of the vehicle in turn, then release it. The vehicle should rise and then settle in its normal position. If the vehicle continues to rise and fall, the shock absorber is defective. A shock absorber which has seized will also cause the vehicle to fail.

Exhaust system

☐ Start the engine. With your assistant holding a rag over the tailpipe, check the entire system for leaks. Repair or renew leaking sections.

3 Checks carried out WITH THE VEHICLE RAISED AND THE WHEELS FREE TO TURN

Jack up the front and rear of the vehicle, and securely support it on axle stands. Position the stands clear of the suspension assemblies. Ensure that the wheels are clear of the ground and that the steering can be turned from lock to lock.

Steering mechanism

☐ Have your assistant turn the steering from lock to lock. Check that the steering turns smoothly, and that no part of the steering mechanism, including a wheel or tyre, fouls any brake hose or pipe or any part of the body structure.

☐ Examine the steering rack rubber gaiters for damage or insecurity of the retaining clips. If power steering is fitted, check for signs of damage or leakage of the fluid hoses, pipes or connections. Also check for excessive stiffness or binding of the steering, a missing split pin or locking device, or severe corrosion of the body structure within 30 cm of any steering component attachment point.

Front and rear suspension and wheel bearings

☐ Starting at the front right-hand side, grasp the roadwheel at the 3 o'clock and 9 o'clock positions and rock gently but firmly. Check for free play or insecurity at the wheel bearings, suspension balljoints, or suspension mount-ings, pivots and attachments.

☐ Now grasp the wheel at the 12 o'clock and 6 o'clock positions and repeat the previous inspection. Spin the wheel, and check for roughness or tightness of the front wheel bearing.

☐ If excess free play is suspected at a component pivot point, this can be confirmed by using a large screwdriver or similar tool and levering between the mounting and the component attachment. This will confirm whether the wear is in the pivot bush, its retaining bolt, or in the mounting itself (the bolt holes can often become elongated).

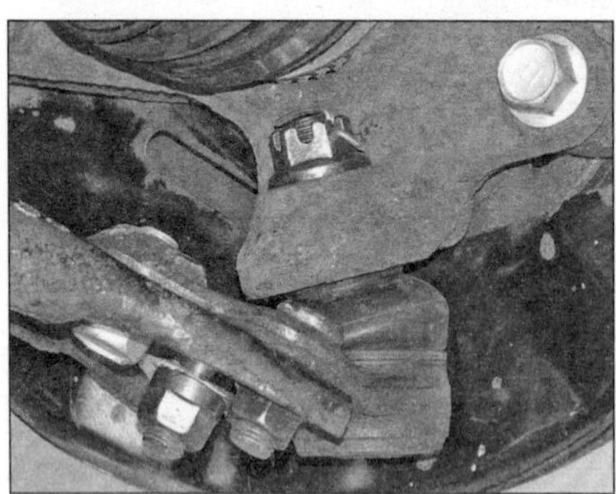

☐ Carry out all the above checks at the other front wheel, and then at both rear wheels.

Springs and shock absorbers

☐ Examine the suspension struts (when applicable) for serious fluid leakage, corrosion, or damage to the casing. Also check the security of the mounting points.

☐ If coil springs are fitted, check that the spring ends locate in their seats, and that the spring is not corroded, cracked or broken.

☐ If leaf springs are fitted, check that all leaves are intact, that the axle is securely attached to each spring, and that there is no deterioration of the spring eye mountings, bushes, and shackles.

☐ The same general checks apply to vehicles fitted with other suspension types, such as torsion bars, hydraulic displacer units, etc. Ensure that all mountings and attachments are secure, that there are no signs of excessive wear, corrosion or damage, and (on hydraulic types) that there are no fluid leaks or damaged pipes.

☐ Inspect the shock absorbers for signs of serious fluid leakage. Check for wear of the mounting bushes or attachments, or damage to the body of the unit.

Driveshafts (fwd vehicles only)

☐ Rotate each front wheel in turn and inspect the constant velocity joint gaiters for splits or damage. Also check that each driveshaft is straight and undamaged.

Braking system

☐ If possible without dismantling, check brake pad wear and disc condition. Ensure that the friction lining material has not worn excessively, (A) and that the discs are not fractured, pitted, scored or badly worn (B).

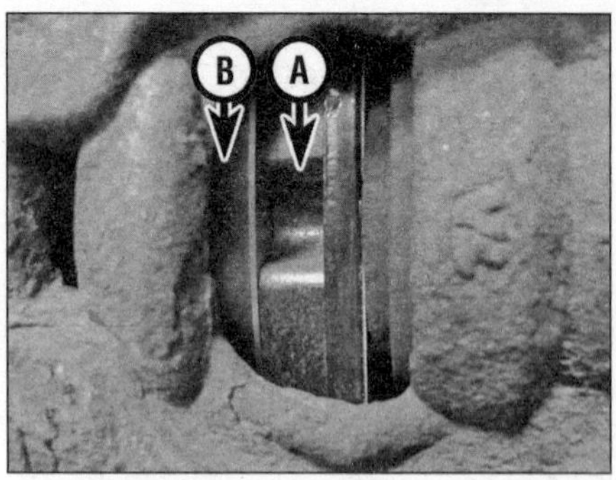

☐ Examine all the rigid brake pipes underneath the vehicle, and the flexible hose(s) at the rear. Look for corrosion, chafing or insecurity of the pipes, and for signs of bulging under pressure, chafing, splits or deterioration of the flexible hoses.

☐ Look for signs of fluid leaks at the brake calipers or on the brake backplates. Repair or renew leaking components.

☐ Slowly spin each wheel, while your assistant depresses and releases the footbrake. Ensure that each brake is operating and does not bind when the pedal is released.

☐Examine the handbrake mechanism, checking for frayed or broken cables, excessive corrosion, or wear or insecurity of the linkage. Check that the mechanism works on each relevant wheel, and releases fully, without binding.

☐It is not possible to test brake efficiency without special equipment, but a road test can be carried out later to check that the vehicle pulls up in a straight line.

Fuel and exhaust systems

☐Inspect the fuel tank (including the filler cap), fuel pipes, hoses and unions. All components must be secure and free from leaks. Locking fuel caps must lock securely and the key must be provided for the MOT test.

☐Examine the exhaust system over its entire length, checking for any damaged, broken or missing mountings, security of the retaining clamps and rust or corrosion.

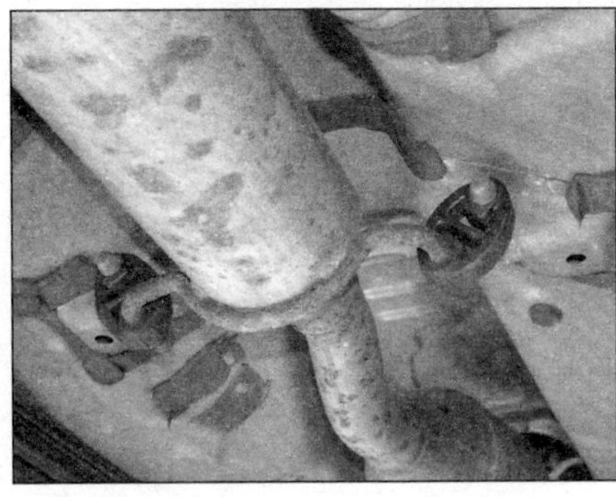

Wheels and tyres

☐Examine the sidewalls and tread area of each tyre in turn. Check for cuts, tears, lumps, bulges, separation of the tread, and exposure of the ply or cord due to wear or damage. Check that the tyre bead is correctly seated on the wheel rim, that the valve is sound and properly seated, and that the wheel is not distorted or damaged.

☐Check that the tyres are of the correct size for the vehicle, that they are of the same size and type on each axle, and that the pressures are correct.

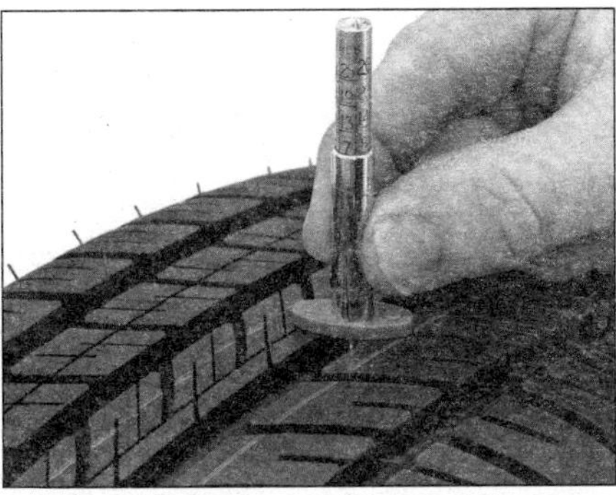

☐Check the tyre tread depth. The legal minimum at the time of writing is 1.6 mm over the central three-quarters of the tread width. Abnormal tread wear may indicate incorrect front wheel alignment or wear in steering or suspension components.

☐If the spare wheel is fitted externally or in a separate carrier beneath the vehicle, check that mountings are secure and free of excessive corrosion.

Body corrosion

☐Check the condition of the entire vehicle structure for signs of corrosion in load-bearing areas. (These include chassis box sections, side sills, cross-members, pillars, and all suspension, steering, braking system and seat belt mountings and anchorages.) Any corrosion which has seriously reduced the thickness of a load-bearing area (or is within 30 cm of safety-related components such as steering or suspension) is likely to cause the vehicle to fail. In this case professional repairs are likely to be needed.

☐Damage or corrosion which causes sharp or otherwise dangerous edges to be exposed will also cause the vehicle to fail.

Towbars

☐Check the condition of mounting points (both beneath the vehicle and within boot/hatchback areas) for signs of corrosion, ensuring that all fixings are secure and not worn or damaged. There must be no excessive play in detachable tow ball arms or quick-release mechanisms.

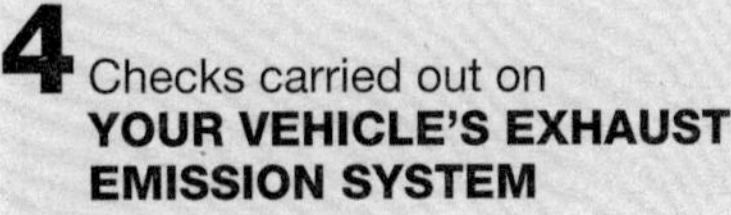

4 Checks carried out on **YOUR VEHICLE'S EXHAUST EMISSION SYSTEM**

Petrol models

☐The engine should be warmed up, and running well (ignition system in good order, air filter element clean, etc).

☐Before testing, run the engine at around 2500 rpm for 20 seconds. Let the engine drop to idle, and watch for smoke from the exhaust. If the idle speed is too high, or if dense blue or black smoke emerges for more than 5 seconds, the vehicle will fail. Typically, blue smoke signifies oil burning (engine wear); black smoke means unburnt fuel (dirty air cleaner element, or other fuel system fault).

☐An exhaust gas analyser for measuring carbon monoxide (CO) and hydrocarbons (HC) is now needed. If one cannot be hired or borrowed, have a local garage perform the check.

CO emissions (mixture)

☐The MOT tester has access to the CO limits for all vehicles. The CO level is measured at idle speed, and at 'fast idle' (2500 to 3000 rpm). The following limits are given as a general guide:

At idle speed – Less than 0.5% CO
At 'fast idle' – Less than 0.3% CO
Lambda reading – 0.97 to 1.03

☐If the CO level is too high, this may point to poor maintenance, a fuel injection system problem, faulty lambda (oxygen) sensor or catalytic converter. Try an injector cleaning treatment, and check the vehicle's ECU for fault codes.

HC emissions

☐The MOT tester has access to HC limits for all vehicles. The HC level is measured at 'fast idle' (2500 to 3000 rpm). The following limits are given as a general guide:

At 'fast idle' – Less then 200 ppm

☐Excessive HC emissions are typically caused by oil being burnt (worn engine), or by a blocked crankcase ventilation system ('breather'). If the engine oil is old and thin, an oil change may help. If the engine is running badly, check the vehicle's ECU for fault codes.

Diesel models

☐The only emission test for diesel engines is measuring exhaust smoke density, using a calibrated smoke meter. The test involves accelerating the engine at least 3 times to its maximum unloaded speed.

Note: *On engines with a timing belt, it is VITAL that the belt is in good condition before the test is carried out.*

☐With the engine warmed up, it is first purged by running at around 2500 rpm for 20 seconds. A governor check is then carried out, by slowly accelerating the engine to its maximum speed. After this, the smoke meter is connected, and the engine is accelerated quickly to maximum speed three times. If the smoke density is less than the limits given below, the vehicle will pass:

Non-turbo vehicles: 2.5m-1
Turbocharged vehicles: 3.0m-1

☐If excess smoke is produced, try fitting a new air cleaner element, or using an injector cleaning treatment. If the engine is running badly, where applicable, check the vehicle's ECU for fault codes. Also check the vehicle's EGR system, where applicable. At high mileages, the injectors may require professional attention.

Engine

- ☐ Engine fails to rotate when attempting to start
- ☐ Engine rotates, but will not start
- ☐ Engine difficult to start when cold
- ☐ Engine difficult to start when hot
- ☐ Starter motor noisy or excessively rough in engagement
- ☐ Engine starts, but stops immediately
- ☐ Engine idles erratically
- ☐ Engine misfires at idle speed
- ☐ Engine misfires throughout the driving speed range
- ☐ Engine hesitates on acceleration
- ☐ Engine stalls
- ☐ Engine lacks power
- ☐ Engine backfires
- ☐ Oil pressure warning light on with engine running
- ☐ Engine runs-on after switching off
- ☐ Engine noises

Cooling system

- ☐ Overheating
- ☐ Overcooling
- ☐ External coolant leakage
- ☐ Internal coolant leakage
- ☐ Corrosion

Fuel and exhaust systems

- ☐ Excessive fuel consumption
- ☐ Fuel leakage and/or fuel odour
- ☐ Excessive noise or fumes from exhaust system

Clutch

- ☐ Pedal travels to floor – no pressure or very little resistance
- ☐ Clutch fails to disengage (unable to select gears)
- ☐ Clutch slips (engine speed rises, with no increase in vehicle speed)
- ☐ Judder as clutch is engaged
- ☐ Noise when depressing or releasing clutch pedal

Manual transmission

- ☐ Noisy in neutral with engine running
- ☐ Noisy in one particular gear
- ☐ Difficulty engaging gears
- ☐ Jumps out of gear
- ☐ Vibration
- ☐ Lubricant leaks

Automatic transmission

- ☐ Fluid leakage
- ☐ Transmission fluid brown, or has burned smell
- ☐ General gear selection problems
- ☐ Transmission will not downshift (kickdown) at full throttle
- ☐ Engine won't start in any gear, or starts in gears other than Park or Neutral
- ☐ Transmission slips, shifts roughly, is noisy, or has no drive in forward or reverse gears

Driveshafts

- ☐ Clicking or knocking noise on turns (at slow speed on full-lock)
- ☐ Vibration when accelerating or decelerating

Braking system

- ☐ Vehicle pulls to one side under braking
- ☐ Noise (grinding or high-pitched squeal) when brakes applied
- ☐ Excessive brake pedal travel
- ☐ Brake pedal feels spongy when depressed
- ☐ Excessive brake pedal effort required to stop vehicle
- ☐ Judder felt through brake pedal or steering wheel when braking
- ☐ Brakes binding
- ☐ Rear wheels locking under normal braking

Suspension and steering

- ☐ Vehicle pulls to one side
- ☐ Wheel wobble and vibration
- ☐ Excessive pitching and/or rolling around corners, or during braking
- ☐ Wandering or general instability
- ☐ Excessively-stiff steering
- ☐ Excessive play in steering
- ☐ Lack of power assistance
- ☐ Tyre wear excessive

Electrical system

- ☐ Battery won't hold a charge for more than a few days
- ☐ Ignition/no-charge warning light stays on with engine running
- ☐ Ignition/no-charge warning light fails to come on
- ☐ Lights inoperative
- ☐ Instrument readings inaccurate or erratic
- ☐ Horn inoperative, or unsatisfactory in operation
- ☐ Windscreen/tailgate wipers failed, or unsatisfactory in operation
- ☐ Windscreen/tailgate washers failed, or unsatisfactory in operation
- ☐ Electric windows inoperative, or unsatisfactory in operation
- ☐ Central locking system inoperative, or unsatisfactory in operation

Introduction

The vehicle owner who does his or her own maintenance according to the recommended service schedules should not have to use this section of the manual very often. Modern component reliability is such that, provided those items subject to wear or deterioration are inspected or renewed at the specified intervals, sudden failure is comparatively rare. Faults do not usually just happen as a result of sudden failure, but develop over a period of time. Major mechanical failures in particular are usually preceded by characteristic symptoms over hundreds or even thousands of miles. Those components that do occasionally fail without warning are often small and easily carried in the vehicle.

With any fault-finding, the first step is to decide where to begin investigations. Sometimes this is obvious, but on other occasions, a little detective work will be necessary. The owner who makes half a dozen haphazard adjustments or component renewals may be successful in curing a fault (or its symptoms). However, will be none the wiser if the fault recurs, and ultimately may have spent more time and money than was necessary. A calm and logical approach will be found to be more satisfactory in the long run. Always take into account any warning signs or abnormalities that may have been noticed in the period preceding the fault – power loss, high or low gauge readings, unusual smells, etc – and remember that failure of components such as fuses or spark plugs may only be pointers to some underlying fault.

3 The pages which follow provide an easy-reference guide to the more common problems which may occur during the operation of the vehicle. These problems and their possible causes are grouped under headings denoting various components or systems, such as Engine, Cooling system, etc. The general Chapter which deals with the problem is also shown in brackets; refer to the relevant part of that Chapter for system-specific information. Whatever the fault, certain basic principles apply. These are as follows:

Verify the fault. This is simply a matter of being sure that you know what the symptoms are before starting work. This is particularly important if you are investigating a fault for someone else, who may not have described it very accurately.

Do not overlook the obvious. For example, if the vehicle will not start, is there petrol in the tank? (Do not take anyone else's word on this particular point, and do not trust the fuel gauge either!) If an electrical fault is indicated, look for loose or broken wires before digging out the test gear.

Cure the disease, not the symptom. Substituting a flat battery with a fully-charged one will get you off the hard shoulder, but if the underlying cause is not attended to, the new battery will go the same way. Similarly, changing oil-fouled spark plugs for a new set will get you moving again, but remember that the reason for the fouling (if it was not simply an incorrect grade of plug) will have to be established and corrected.

Do not take anything for granted. Particularly, do not forget that a new component may itself be defective (especially if it's been rattling around in the boot for months). Also do not leave components out of a fault diagnosis sequence just because they are new or recently fitted. When you do finally diagnose a difficult fault, you will probably realise that all the evidence was there from the start.

Engine

Engine fails to rotate when attempting to start

- ☐ Battery terminal connections loose or corroded (Weekly checks).
- ☐ Battery discharged or faulty (Chapter 5A).
- ☐ Broken, loose or disconnected wiring in the starting circuit (Chapter 5A).
- ☐ Defective starter motor (Chapter 5A).
- ☐ Starter pinion or flywheel/driveplate ring gear teeth loose or broken (Chapter 2A and 5A).
- ☐ Engine earth strap broken or disconnected (Chapter 5A).

Engine rotates, but will not start

- ☐ Fuel tank empty.
- ☐ Battery discharged (engine rotates slowly) (Chapter 5A).
- ☐ Battery terminal connections loose or corroded (Weekly checks).
- ☐ Worn, faulty or incorrectly-gapped spark plugs (Chapter 1).
- ☐ Engine management system fault (Chapter 4A).
- ☐ Low cylinder compressions (Chapter 2A).
- ☐ Major mechanical failure (e.g. camshaft drive) (Chapter 2A).

Engine difficult to start when cold

- ☐ Battery discharged (Chapter 5A).
- ☐ Battery terminal connections loose or corroded (Weekly checks).
- ☐ Worn, faulty or incorrectly-gapped spark plugs (Chapter 1).
- ☐ Engine management system fault (Chapter 4A).

Engine difficult to start when hot

- ☐ Engine management system fault (Chapter 4A).
- ☐ Low cylinder compressions (Chapter 2A).

Starter motor noisy or excessively rough in engagement

- ☐ Starter pinion or flywheel/driveplate ring gear teeth loose or broken (Chapters 2A and 5A).
- ☐ Starter motor mounting bolts loose or missing (Chapter 5A).
- ☐ Defective starter motor (Chapter 5A).

Engine starts, but stops immediately

- ☐ Vacuum leak at the throttle housing/inlet manifold (Chapter 4A).
- ☐ Engine management system fault (Chapter 4A).

Engine idles erratically

- ☐ Vacuum leak at the throttle housing/inlet manifold (Chapter 4A).
- ☐ Worn, faulty or incorrectly-gapped spark plugs (Chapter 1).
- ☐ Engine management system fault (Chapter 4A).
- ☐ Uneven or low cylinder compressions (Chapter 2A).
- ☐ Camshaft lobes worn (Chapter 2A).
- ☐ Timing belt incorrectly fitted (Chapter 2A).

Engine misfires at idle speed

- ☐ Worn, faulty or incorrectly-gapped spark plugs (Chapter 1).
- ☐ Vacuum leak at the throttle housing/inlet manifold (Chapter 4A).
- ☐ Engine management system fault (Chapter 4A).
- ☐ Uneven or low cylinder compressions (Chapter 2A).
- ☐ Disconnected, leaking, or perished crankcase ventilation hoses (Chapter 4B).

Engine (continued)

Engine misfires throughout the driving speed range

- ☐ Fuel filter blocked (Chapter 1).
- ☐ Fuel pump faulty (Chapter 4A).
- ☐ Fuel tank vent blocked, or fuel pipes restricted (Chapter 4A).
- ☐ Worn, faulty or incorrectly-gapped spark plugs (Chapter 1).
- ☐ Vacuum leak at the throttle housing/inlet manifold (Chapter 4A).
- ☐ Engine management system fault (Chapter 4A).
- ☐ Faulty ignition HT coils (Chapter 5B).
- ☐ Uneven or low cylinder compressions (Chapter 2A).

Engine hesitates on acceleration

- ☐ Worn, faulty or incorrectly-gapped spark plugs (Chapter 1).
- ☐ Vacuum leak at the throttle housing/inlet manifold (Chapter 4A).
- ☐ Engine management system fault (Chapter 4A).

Engine stalls

- ☐ Fuel filter blocked (Chapter 1).
- ☐ Fuel pump faulty (Chapter 4A).
- ☐ Fuel tank vent blocked, or fuel pipes restricted (Chapter 4A).
- ☐ Worn, faulty or incorrectly-gapped spark plugs (Chapter 1).
- ☐ Vacuum leak at the throttle housing/inlet manifold (Chapter 4A).
- ☐ Engine management system fault (Chapter 4A).

Engine lacks power

- ☐ Timing belt incorrectly fitted (Chapter 2A).
- ☐ Fuel filter blocked (Chapter 1).
- ☐ Fuel pump faulty (Chapter 4A).
- ☐ Uneven or low cylinder compressions (Chapter 2A).
- ☐ Worn, faulty or incorrectly-gapped spark plugs (Chapter 1).
- ☐ Vacuum leak at the throttle housing/inlet manifold (Chapter 4A).
- ☐ Engine management system fault (Chapter 4A).
- ☐ Brakes binding (Chapters 1 and 9).
- ☐ Clutch slipping (Chapter 6).

Engine backfires

- ☐ Timing belt incorrectly fitted (Chapter 2A).
- ☐ Vacuum leak at the throttle housing/inlet manifold (Chapter 4A).
- ☐ Engine management system fault (Chapter 4A).

Oil pressure warning light on with engine running

- ☐ Low oil level, or incorrect oil grade (Weekly checks).
- ☐ Faulty oil pressure warning light switch (Chapter 5A).
- ☐ Worn engine bearings and/or oil pump (Chapter 2B).
- ☐ High engine operating temperature (Chapter 3).
- ☐ Oil pressure relief valve defective (Chapter 2A).
- ☐ Oil pick-up strainer clogged (Chapter 2A).

Engine runs-on after switching off

- ☐ Excessive carbon build-up in engine (Chapter 2B).
- ☐ High engine operating temperature (Chapter 3).
- ☐ Engine management system fault (Chapter 4A).

Engine noises

Pre-ignition (pinking) or knocking during acceleration or under load

- ☐ Engine management system fault (Chapter 4A).
- ☐ Incorrect grade of spark plug (Chapter 1).
- ☐ Incorrect grade of fuel (Chapter 4A).
- ☐ Vacuum leak at the throttle housing/inlet manifold (Chapter 4A).
- ☐ Excessive carbon build-up in engine (Chapter 2B).

Whistling or wheezing noises

- ☐ Leaking inlet manifold or throttle housing gasket (Chapter 4A).
- ☐ Leaking vacuum hose (Chapters 4A and 9).
- ☐ Blowing cylinder head gasket (Chapter 2A).

Tapping or rattling noises

- ☐ Worn valve gear or camshaft (Chapter 2A).
- ☐ Ancillary component fault (coolant pump, alternator, etc) – (Chapters 3, 5A, etc).

Knocking or thumping noises

- ☐ Worn big-end bearings (regular heavy knocking, perhaps less under load) (Chapter 2B).
- ☐ Worn main bearings (rumbling and knocking, perhaps worsening under load) (Chapter 2B).
- ☐ Piston slap (most noticeable when cold) (Chapter 2B).
- ☐ Ancillary component fault (coolant pump, alternator, etc) – (Chapters 3, 5A, etc).

Cooling system

Overheating

- ☐ Insufficient coolant in system (Weekly checks).
- ☐ Thermostat faulty (stuck closed) (Chapter 3).
- ☐ Radiator core blocked, or grille restricted (Chapter 3).
- ☐ Electric cooling fan or sensor faulty (Chapter 3).
- ☐ Pressure cap faulty (Chapter 3).
- ☐ Inaccurate temperature gauge/sensor (Chapter 3).
- ☐ Airlock in cooling system (Chapter 1).
- ☐ Engine management system fault (Chapter 4A).

Overcooling

- ☐ Thermostat faulty (stuck open) (Chapter 3).
- ☐ Inaccurate temperature gauge/sensor (Chapter 3).

External coolant leakage

- ☐ Deteriorated or damaged hoses or hose clips (Chapter 1).
- ☐ Radiator core or heater matrix leaking (Chapter 3).
- ☐ Pressure cap faulty (Chapter 3).
- ☐ Coolant pump leaking (Chapter 3).
- ☐ Boiling due to overheating (Chapter 3).
- ☐ Core plug leaking (Chapter 2B).

Internal coolant leakage

- ☐ Leaking cylinder head gasket (Chapter 2A).
- ☐ Cracked cylinder head or cylinder bore (Chapter 2A).

Corrosion

- ☐ Infrequent draining and flushing (Chapter 1).
- ☐ Incorrect coolant mixture or inappropriate coolant type (Chapter 1).

Fuel and exhaust systems

Excessive fuel consumption

- ☐ Air filter element dirty or clogged (Chapter 1).
- ☐ Engine management system fault (Chapter 4A).
- ☐ Faulty injector(s) (Chapter 4A).
- ☐ Tyres under-inflated (Weekly checks).
- ☐ Brakes binding (Chapters 1 and 9).

Fuel leakage and/or fuel odour

- ☐ Damaged or corroded fuel tank, pipes or connections (Chapter 4A).

Excessive noise or fumes from exhaust system

- ☐ Leaking exhaust system or manifold joints (Chapters 1 and 4A).
- ☐ Leaking, corroded or damaged silencers or pipe (Chapters 1 and 4A).
- ☐ Broken mountings causing body or suspension contact (Chapters 1 and 4A).

Clutch

Pedal travels to floor – no pressure or very little resistance

- ☐ Air in hydraulic system/faulty master or slave cylinder (Chapter 6).
- ☐ Broken clutch release bearing or fork (Chapter 6).
- ☐ Broken diaphragm spring in clutch pressure plate (Chapter 6).

Clutch fails to disengage (unable to select gears)

- ☐ Air in hydraulic system/faulty master or slave cylinder (Chapter 6).
- ☐ Clutch disc sticking on gearbox input shaft splines (Chapter 6).
- ☐ Clutch disc sticking to flywheel or pressure plate (Chapter 6).
- ☐ Faulty pressure plate assembly (Chapter 6).
- ☐ Clutch release mechanism worn or incorrectly assembled (Chapter 6).

Clutch slips (engine speed rises, with no increase in vehicle speed)

- ☐ Faulty hydraulic release system (Chapter 6).
- ☐ Clutch disc linings excessively worn (Chapter 6).
- ☐ Clutch disc linings contaminated with oil or grease (Chapter 6).
- ☐ Faulty pressure plate or weak diaphragm spring (Chapter 6).

Judder as clutch is engaged

- ☐ Clutch disc linings contaminated with oil or grease (Chapter 6).
- ☐ Clutch disc linings excessively worn (Chapter 6).
- ☐ Faulty or distorted pressure plate or diaphragm spring (Chapter 6).
- ☐ Worn or loose engine or gearbox mountings (Chapter 2A).
- ☐ Clutch disc hub or gearbox input shaft splines worn (Chapter 6).

Noise when depressing or releasing clutch pedal

- ☐ Worn clutch release bearing (Chapter 6).
- ☐ Worn or dry clutch pedal bushes (Chapter 6).
- ☐ Faulty pressure plate assembly (Chapter 6).
- ☐ Pressure plate diaphragm spring broken (Chapter 6).
- ☐ Broken clutch disc cushioning springs (Chapter 6).

Manual transmission

Noisy in neutral with engine running

- ☐ Input shaft bearings worn (noise apparent with clutch pedal released, but not when depressed) (Chapter 7A).*
- ☐ Clutch release bearing worn (noise apparent with clutch pedal depressed, possibly less when released) (Chapter 6).

Noisy in one particular gear

- ☐ Worn, damaged or chipped gear teeth (Chapter 7A).*

Difficulty engaging gears

- ☐ Clutch fault (Chapter 6).
- ☐ Worn or damaged gear selection cables (Chapter 7A).
- ☐ Worn synchroniser units (Chapter 7A).*

Jumps out of gear

- ☐ Worn or damaged gear selection cables (Chapter 7A).
- ☐ Worn synchroniser units (Chapter 7A).*
- ☐ Worn selector forks (Chapter 7A).*

Vibration

- ☐ Lack of oil (Chapters 1 and 7A).
- ☐ Worn bearings (Chapter 7A).*

Lubricant leaks

- ☐ Leaking differential output oil seal (Chapter 7A).
- ☐ Leaking housing joint (Chapter 7A).*
- ☐ Leaking input shaft oil seal (Chapter 7A).

**Although the corrective action necessary to remedy the symptoms described is beyond the scope of the home mechanic, the above information should be helpful in isolating the cause of the condition, so that the owner can communicate clearly with a professional mechanic.*

Automatic transmission

Note: *Due to the complexity of the automatic transmission, it is difficult for the home mechanic to properly diagnose and service this unit. For problems other than the following, the vehicle should be taken to a Citroen dealer service department or suitably equipped specialist.*

Fluid leakage

- ☐ Automatic transmission fluid is usually dark in colour. Fluid leaks should not be confused with engine oil, which can easily be blown onto the transmission by airflow.
- ☐ To determine the source of a leak, first remove all built-up dirt and grime from the transmission housing and surrounding areas using a degreasing agent, or by steam-cleaning. Drive the vehicle at low speed, so airflow will not blow the leak far from its source. Raise and support the vehicle, and determine where the leak is coming from.

Transmission fluid brown, or has burned smell

- ☐ Transmission fluid level low, or fluid in need of renewal (Chapter 1 and 7B).

General gear selection problems

- ☐ Chapter 7B deals with checking and adjusting the selector cable on automatic transmissions. The following are common problems, which may be caused by a poorly adjusted cable:
  - *a) Engine starting in gears other than Park or Neutral.*
  - *b) Indicator panel showing a gear other than that being used.*
  - *c) Vehicle moves when in Park or Neutral.*
  - *d) Poor gear shift quality or erratic gear changes.*
- ☐ Refer to Chapter 7B for the selector cable adjustment procedure.

Transmission will not downshift (kickdown) at full throttle

- ☐ Low transmission fluid level (Chapter 1).
- ☐ Incorrect selector cable adjustment (Chapter 7B).

Engine won't start in any gear, or starts in gears other than Park or Neutral

- ☐ Incorrect multi-function switch adjustment (Chapter 7B).
- ☐ Incorrect selector cable adjustment (Chapter 7B).

Transmission slips, shifts roughly, is noisy, or has no drive in forward or reverse gears

- ☐ There are many probable causes for the above problems, but the home mechanic should be concerned with only one possibility – fluid level. Before taking the vehicle to a dealer or transmission specialist, check the fluid level as described in Chapter 1. Correct the fluid level as necessary, or change the fluid. If the problem persists, professional help will be necessary.

Driveshafts

Clicking or knocking noise on turns (at slow speed on full-lock)

- ☐ Lack of constant velocity joint lubricant, possibly due to damaged gaiter (Chapter 8).
- ☐ Worn outer constant velocity joint (Chapter 8).

Vibration when accelerating or decelerating

- ☐ Worn inner constant velocity joint (Chapter 8).
- ☐ Bent or distorted driveshaft (Chapter 8).
- ☐ Worn intermediate bearing (Chapter 8).

Braking system

Note: *Before assuming that a brake problem exists, make sure that the tyres are in good condition and correctly inflated, that the front wheel alignment is correct, and that the vehicle is not loaded with weight in an unequal manner. Apart from checking the condition of all pipe and hose connections, any faults occurring on the anti-lock braking system should be referred to a Citroen dealer for diagnosis.*

Vehicle pulls to one side under braking

- ☐ Worn, defective, damaged or contaminated brake pads on one side (Chapter 9).
- ☐ Seized or partially-seized front brake caliper (Chapter 9).
- ☐ A mixture of brake pad materials fitted between sides (Chapter 9).
- ☐ Brake caliper mounting bolts loose (Chapter 9).
- ☐ Worn or damaged steering or suspension components (Chapters 1 and 10).

Noise (grinding or high-pitched squeal) when brakes applied

- ☐ Brake pad material worn down to metal backing (Chapters 1 and 9).
- ☐ Excessive corrosion of brake disc. May be apparent after the vehicle has been standing for some time (Chapter 9).
- ☐ Foreign object (stone chipping, etc) trapped between brake disc and shield (Chapter 9).

Excessive brake pedal travel

- ☐ Faulty master cylinder (Chapter 9).
- ☐ Air in hydraulic system (Chapter 9).
- ☐ Faulty vacuum servo unit (Chapter 9).

Brake pedal feels spongy when depressed

- ☐ Air in hydraulic system (Chapter 9).
- ☐ Deteriorated flexible rubber brake hoses (Chapters 1 and 9).
- ☐ Master cylinder mounting nuts loose (Chapter 9).
- ☐ Faulty master cylinder (Chapter 9).

Excessive brake pedal effort required to stop vehicle

- ☐ Faulty vacuum servo unit (Chapter 9).
- ☐ Disconnected, damaged or insecure brake servo vacuum hose (Chapter 9).
- ☐ Primary or secondary hydraulic circuit failure (Chapter 9).
- ☐ Seized brake caliper (Chapter 9).
- ☐ Brake pads incorrectly fitted (Chapter 9).
- ☐ Incorrect grade of brake pads fitted (Chapter 9).
- ☐ Brake pads contaminated (Chapter 9).

Judder felt through brake pedal or steering wheel when braking

- ☐ Excessive run-out or distortion of discs (Chapters 9).
- ☐ Brake pads worn (Chapters 1 and 9).
- ☐ Brake caliper mounting bolts loose (Chapter 9).
- ☐ Wear in suspension or steering components or mountings (Chapters 1 and 10).

Brakes binding

- ☐ Seized brake caliper (Chapter 9).
- ☐ Incorrectly-adjusted handbrake mechanism (Chapter 9).
- ☐ Faulty master cylinder (Chapter 9).

Rear wheels locking under normal braking

- ☐ Rear brake pads contaminated (Chapters 1 and 9).
- ☐ ABS system fault (Chapter 9).

Suspension and steering

Note: *Before diagnosing suspension or steering faults, be sure that the trouble is not due to incorrect tyre pressures, mixtures of tyre types, or binding brakes.*

Vehicle pulls to one side

- ☐ Defective tyre (Weekly checks).
- ☐ Excessive wear in suspension or steering components (Chapters 1 and 10).
- ☐ Incorrect front wheel alignment (Chapter 10).
- ☐ Damage to steering or suspension components (Chapter 1).

Wheel wobble and vibration

- ☐ Front roadwheels out of balance (vibration felt mainly through the steering wheel) (Chapters 1 and 10).
- ☐ Rear roadwheels out of balance (vibration felt throughout the vehicle) (Chapters 1 and 10).
- ☐ Roadwheels damaged or distorted (Chapters 1 and 10).
- ☐ Faulty or damaged tyre (Weekly checks).
- ☐ Worn steering or suspension joints, bushes or components (Chapters 1 and 10).
- ☐ Wheel bolts loose (Chapters 1 and 10).

Excessive pitching and/or rolling around corners, or during braking

- ☐ Defective shock absorbers (Chapters 1 and 10).
- ☐ Broken or weak spring and/or suspension part (Chapters 1 and 10).
- ☐ Worn or damaged anti-roll bar or mountings (Chapter 10).

Wandering or general instability

- ☐ Incorrect front wheel alignment (Chapter 10).
- ☐ Worn steering or suspension joints, bushes or components (Chapters 1 and 10).
- ☐ Roadwheels out of balance (Chapters 1 and 10).
- ☐ Faulty or damaged tyre (Weekly checks).
- ☐ Wheel bolts loose (Chapters 1 and 10).
- ☐ Defective shock absorbers (Chapters 1 and 10).

Excessively-stiff steering

- ☐ Lack of power steering fluid (Chapter 10).
- ☐ Seized track rod end balljoint or suspension balljoint (Chapters 1 and 10).
- ☐ Incorrect front wheel alignment (Chapter 10).
- ☐ Steering rack or column bent or damaged (Chapter 10).
- ☐ Power steering pump fault (Chapter 10).

Excessive play in steering

- ☐ Worn steering column universal joint (Chapter 10).
- ☐ Worn steering track rod end balljoints (Chapters 1 and 10).
- ☐ Worn steering rack (Chapter 10).
- ☐ Worn steering or suspension joints, bushes or components (Chapters 1 and 10).

Lack of power assistance

- ☐ Incorrect power steering fluid level (Weekly checks).
- ☐ Restriction in power steering fluid hoses (Chapter 1).
- ☐ Faulty power steering pump (Chapter 10).
- ☐ Faulty steering rack (Chapter 10).

Tyre wear excessive

Tyre treads exhibit feathered edges

- ☐ Incorrect toe setting (Chapter 10).

Tyres worn in centre of tread

- ☐ Tyres over-inflated (Weekly checks).

Tyres worn on inside and outside edges

- ☐ Tyres under-inflated (Weekly checks).

Tyres worn on inside or outside edges

- ☐ Incorrect camber/castor angles (wear on one edge only) (Chapter 10).
- ☐ Worn steering or suspension joints, bushes or components (Chapters 1 and 10).
- ☐ Excessively-hard cornering.
- ☐ Accident damage.

Tyres worn unevenly

- ☐ Tyres/wheels out of balance (Weekly checks).
- ☐ Excessive wheel or tyre run-out (Chapter 1).
- ☐ Worn shock absorbers (Chapters 1 and 10).
- ☐ Faulty tyre (Weekly checks).

Electrical system

Note: *For problems associated with the starting system, refer to the faults listed under 'Engine' earlier in this Section.*

Battery won't hold a charge for more than a few days

- ☐ Battery defective internally (Chapter 5A).
- ☐ Battery terminal connections loose or corroded (Weekly checks).
- ☐ Auxiliary drivebelt broken, worn or incorrectly adjusted (Chapter 1).
- ☐ Alternator not charging at correct output (Chapter 5A).
- ☐ Alternator or voltage regulator faulty (Chapter 5A).
- ☐ Short-circuit causing continual battery drain (Chapters 5A and 12).

Ignition/no-charge warning light stays on with engine running

- ☐ Auxiliary drivebelt broken, worn, or incorrectly adjusted (Chapter 1).
- ☐ Internal fault in alternator or voltage regulator (Chapter 5A).
- ☐ Broken, disconnected, or loose wiring in charging circuit (Chapter 5A).

Ignition/no-charge warning light fails to come on

- ☐ Warning light bulb blown (Chapter 12).
- ☐ Broken, disconnected, or loose wiring in warning light circuit (Chapter 12).
- ☐ Alternator faulty (Chapter 5A).

Lights inoperative

- ☐ Bulb blown (Chapter 12).
- ☐ Corrosion of bulb or bulbholder contacts (Chapter 12).
- ☐ Blown fuse (Chapter 12).
- ☐ Faulty relay (Chapter 12).
- ☐ Broken, loose, or disconnected wiring (Chapter 12).
- ☐ Faulty switch (Chapter 12).

Instrument readings inaccurate or erratic

Fuel or temperature gauges give no reading

- ☐ Faulty gauge sensor unit (Chapter 3 or 4A).
- ☐ Wiring open-circuit (Chapter 12).
- ☐ Faulty gauge (Chapter 12).

Fuel or temperature gauges give continuous maximum reading

- ☐ Faulty gauge sensor unit (Chapter 3 or 4A).
- ☐ Wiring short-circuit (Chapter 12).
- ☐ Faulty gauge (Chapter 12).

Horn inoperative, or unsatisfactory in operation

Horn operates all the time

- ☐ Horn push either earthed or stuck down (Chapter 12).
- ☐ Horn cable-to-horn push earthed (Chapter 12).

Horn fails to operate

- ☐ Blown fuse (Chapter 12).
- ☐ Cable or cable connections loose, broken or disconnected (Chapter 12).
- ☐ Faulty horn (Chapter 12).

Horn emits intermittent or unsatisfactory sound

- ☐ Cable connections loose (Chapter 12).
- ☐ Horn mountings loose (Chapter 12).
- ☐ Faulty horn (Chapter 12).

Windscreen/tailgate wipers failed, or unsatisfactory in operation

Wipers fail to operate, or operate very slowly

- ☐ Wiper blades stuck to screen, or linkage seized or binding (Chapters 1 and 12).
- ☐ Blown fuse (Chapter 12).
- ☐ Cable or cable connections loose, broken or disconnected (Chapter 12).
- ☐ Faulty built-in system interface (BSI) unit (Chapter 12).
- ☐ Faulty wiper motor (Chapter 12).

Wiper blades sweep over too large or too small an area of the glass

- ☐ Wiper arms incorrectly positioned on spindles (Chapter 12).
- ☐ Excessive wear of wiper linkage (Chapter 12).
- ☐ Wiper motor or linkage mountings loose or insecure (Chapter 12).

Wiper blades fail to clean the glass effectively

- ☐ Wiper blade rubbers worn or perished (Weekly checks).
- ☐ Wiper arm tension springs broken, or arm pivots seized (Chapter 12).
- ☐ Insufficient windscreen washer additive to adequately remove road film (Weekly checks).

Windscreen/tailgate washers failed, or unsatisfactory in operation

One or more washer jets inoperative

- ☐ Blocked washer jet (Weekly checks).
- ☐ Disconnected, kinked or restricted fluid hose (Chapter 12).
- ☐ Insufficient fluid in washer reservoir (Weekly checks).

Washer pump fails to operate

- ☐ Broken or disconnected wiring or connections (Chapter 12).
- ☐ Blown fuse (Chapter 12).
- ☐ Faulty washer switch (Chapter 12).
- ☐ Faulty washer pump (Chapter 12).

Electric windows inoperative, or unsatisfactory in operation

Window glass will only move in one direction

- ☐ Faulty switch (Chapter 12).

Window glass slow to move

- ☐ Regulator seized or damaged, or in need of lubricant (Chapter 11).
- ☐ Door internal components or trim fouling regulator (Chapter 11).
- ☐ Faulty motor (Chapter 11).

Window glass fails to move

- ☐ Blown fuse (Chapter 12).
- ☐ Broken or disconnected wiring or connections (Chapter 12).
- ☐ Faulty motor (Chapter 11).
- ☐ Faulty built-in systems interface (BSI) unit (Chapter 12).

Central locking system inoperative, or unsatisfactory in operation

Complete system failure

- ☐ Blown fuse (Chapter 12).
- ☐ Broken or disconnected wiring or connections (Chapter 12).
- ☐ Faulty built-in system interface (BSI) unit (Chapter 12).

Door/tailgate locks but will not unlock, or unlocks but will not lock

- ☐ Broken or disconnected link rod(s) (Chapter 11).
- ☐ Faulty lock motor (Chapter 11).

One lock fails to operate

- ☐ Broken or disconnected wiring or connections (Chapter 12).
- ☐ Faulty lock motor (Chapter 11).
- ☐ Broken, binding or disconnected link rod(s) (Chapter 11).

Note: *References throughout this index are in the form* **"Chapter number" • "Page number"**. *So, for example, 2C•15 refers to page 15 of Chapter 2C.*

Note: *References throughout this index are in the form* **"Chapter number" • "Page number"**. *So, for example, 2C•15 refers to page 15 of Chapter 2C.*